INTRODUCTION TO US HEALTH POLICY

Introduction to US Health Policy

The Organization, Financing, and Delivery of Health Care in America

FOURTH EDITION

Donald A. Barr, MD, PhD

Department of Pediatrics

Stanford University

Stanford, California

Johns Hopkins University Press | *Baltimore*

© 2007, 2011, 2016 Johns Hopkins University Press
All rights reserved. Published 2016
Printed in the United States of America on acid-free paper
First edition published in 2002 by Benjamin Cummings, Inc., California
Johns Hopkins edition published 2007, 2011, 2016
9 8 7 6 5 4 3 2 1

Johns Hopkins University Press
2715 North Charles Street
Baltimore, Maryland 21218-4363
www.press.jhu.edu

Library of Congress Cataloging-in-Publication Data
Names: Barr, Donald A., author.
Title: Introduction to US health policy : the organization, financing, and
    delivery of health care in America / Donald A. Barr.
Other titles: Introduction to United States health policy
Description: Fourth edition. | Baltimore, Maryland : Johns Hopkins University
    Press, 2016. | Includes bibliographical references and index.
Identifiers: LCCN 2015050789| ISBN 9781421420714 (hardcover : alk. paper) |
    ISBN 1421420716 (hardcover : alk. paper) | ISBN 9781421420721 (pbk. : alk.
    paper) | ISBN 1421420724 (pbk. : alk. paper) | ISBN 9781421420738
    (electronic) | ISBN 1421420732 (electronic)
Subjects: | MESH: United States. Patient Protection and Affordable Care Act.
    | Delivery of Health Care | Health Policy | Health Care Reform | Health
    Planning | Financing, Government | Economics, Medical | United States
Classification: LCC RA393 | NLM W 84 AA1 | DDC 362.10973—dc23
    LC record available at http://lccn.loc.gov/2015050789

A catalog record for this book is available from the British Library.

*Special discounts are available for bulk purchases of this book. For more information,
please contact Special Sales at 410-516-6936 or specialsales@press.jhu.edu.*

Johns Hopkins University Press uses environmentally friendly book materials,
including recycled text paper that is composed of at least 30 percent post-consumer
waste, whenever possible.

FOR DEBRA

CONTENTS

Preface ix

1 The Affordable Care Act and the Politics of Health Care Reform 1
2 Health, Health Care, and the Market Economy 19
3 Health Care as a Reflection of Underlying Cultural Values
   and Institutions 42
4 The Health Professions and the Organization of Health Care 81
5 Health Insurance, HMOs, and the Managed Care Revolution 112
6 Medicare 150
7 Medicaid and the State Children's Health Insurance Program 196
8 The Uninsured 228
9 The Increasing Role of For-Profit Health Care 252
10 Pharmaceutical Policy and the Rising Cost of Prescription Drugs 277
11 Long-Term Care 311
12 Factors Other Than Health Insurance That Impede Access
    to Health Care 330
13 Key Policy Issues Affecting the Direction of Health Care Reform 355
14 Epilogue/Prologue to Health Care Reform in America 380

*Appendix: Summary of the Changes Contained in
   the Affordable Care Act 389*
References 399
Index 427

PREFACE

In teaching my class on American health policy, I often show the students two statements, and then ask which is correct. The first slide states:

The United States has the best medical care system in the world.

The second states:

The United States has one of the worst health care systems among the developed countries of the world.

We spend several minutes in a discussion and debate regarding which of the statements is more accurate. The irony of US health care, and a principal message of this book, is that both statements are simultaneously true. From one perspective, we have the best health care available anywhere. From another, equally valid perspective, we are close to worst among developed countries in the way we structure our health care system. Which perspective one adopts depends on the measure of quality one selects.

This seeming paradox is illustrated by the way health care is provided in the communities adjoining the office in which this book was written. Approximately five hundred yards to the north is Stanford University Medical Center, a world leader in technological sophistication in medical care. Physicians there, who are among the best in the world, are able to perform remarkable feats, such as a life-saving organ transplantation or the reattachment of a severed hand. The physician-scientists at the Lucile Packard Children's Hospital are able to save amazingly tiny, premature babies weighing less than this book. Specialist physicians in the emergency room are able to reverse heart attacks and strokes after they have already happened. Nowhere in the world is a higher level of advanced medical care available.

Approximately two miles to the east of this office is the community of East Palo Alto. The population of East Palo Alto is predominantly low income, mainly nonwhite, and largely without health insurance. Many of the people there have no regular source of medical care. When they or their children become ill, the only source of care available to them is often the emergency room at Stanford Hospital, where physicians-in-training will see and treat them between treating patients with heart attacks or major traumatic injuries. If patients from East Palo Alto need to be hospitalized, those without a life-threatening condition who have no insurance and no means of paying for care out of pocket are not allowed treatment in Stanford Hospital. Rather, they are referred to a county hospital, several miles away. East Palo Alto has a high rate of premature babies; violence is a major health problem; diseases such as diabetes and high blood pressure often go untreated; and children can go without needed checkups and immunizations.

We are simultaneously the best and one of the worst. This is the dilemma of health care in the United States.

This book is about the US health care system. It introduces the various organizations and institutions that make our system work (or not work, as the case may be). It identifies historical forces that have brought us to our current state of health care and examines the way in which the need of the American people for health care services is sometimes met and sometimes not.

As this book describes, the United States spends more on health care, both overall and per capita, than any other country in the world. Yet the health of our society, measured by indices such as infant mortality and life expectancy, and our access to care are worse than those of nearly all other industrialized countries.

Two broad forces contribute to the relatively poor state of health in the United States: (1) socioeconomic factors, such as education, poverty, and lifestyle, and (2) the quality of our health care system. It may be that socioeconomic factors have more to do with the overall health of our society than does our system of health care. This book, however, looks at only the latter—our health care system.

It has been health care, not health, that has focused national attention and stirred national discourse for the past several years. During the intense debate that led to the passage of the Patient Protection and Affordable Care Act (ACA) of 2010 and that has continued since its passage, we have had a graphic illustration of how our health care system is made up of various organizations and groups that often can't agree on how the system should be structured. This was not the first time we tried to initiate broad reform of the health care system in this country. In the 1930s, a national health care plan was considered as part of Social Security. It was seen as too far-reaching and was dropped from Social Security to assure passage. In the years following World War II, President Harry Truman proposed a national system of health insurance but was defeated by the forces of organized medicine. In the 1960s, Congress adopted major policy reforms in the financing of health care for elderly and poor people but stopped short of comprehensive national reform. In the 1970s, facing for the first time the rapidly rising cost of health care that characterized the last part of the twentieth century, Congress came close to adopting comprehensive national reform, only to back away in the wake of the Watergate scandal. Again, in the 1990s, we came very close to enacting comprehensive health care reform, only to see the Clinton reform proposals defeated and abandoned following a midterm election that shifted the center of power within Congress.

As health care costs continued to rise and more and more people were left without health insurance, the beginning of the twenty-first century required that we deal with the same problems we confronted at the end of the twentieth century. Congress came close to inaction but in the end did approve ACA and a companion reconciliation bill, the combination of which offered access to affordable health insurance to as many as 30 million Americans who previously were uninsured. ACA has not solved all the problems inherent in our system of health care, however. While access to health insurance has expanded substantially, the rise in health care costs is predicted to continue. At some point in the future, Congress will again need to deal with the continuing problems of health care in America.

How much can we as a country afford to spend on health care? Can we both constrain the growth of health care expenditures and improve access to care? Whether as a health care professional who participates in the system, as an academician who studies the system, as a business manager who must arrange health coverage for your workers, or as a patient who turns to the system for care, you, the reader of this book, will doubtless confront these questions again. It is my hope that, by reading this book, you will be in a stronger position to help find an answer to them.

Who will be the leaders in finding the answers and making the difficult choices? Physicians, health care administrators, and those responsible for the public sector will all play an important role in this process. Many physicians and other health care professionals, however, do not receive adequate training in the knowledge and skills necessary to make informed choices about health care delivery. In 1995, Drs. Ira Nash and Richard Pasternak reported their experience in interviewing applicants for one of the most competitive and prestigious fellowship training programs in the country. They found that nearly all the applicants had consistently high clinical qualifications. They then asked these young physicians, the future leaders of the medical profession, what they thought about the issue of health care reform.

> We were shocked when we barely got a response. A few residents offered some brief insight into the scope of the challenge to reform. Fewer enunciated some broad goal of reform such as universal insurance coverage. *None* had any well-formed ideas about how to actually address these challenges or realize these goals, or could even render a reasoned opinion about *somebody else's* well-formed idea. . . . How can it be that the apparent "best and brightest" of internal medicine are on the intellectual sidelines of the debate over health system reform?

If, as is now the case, we find time in medical school and residency training to teach things that most physicians will never need to know, we should find the teachers and the time to teach what nearly every physician will soon need to know to help address the health care needs of the nation. (Nash and Pasternak 1995, p. 1534)

Medical science has been expanding steadily since the beginning of the twentieth century. Initially, physicians had a fairly small core of knowledge they needed to acquire. As scientists learned about bacteria and other microorganisms, physicians needed to expand their base of knowledge to include microbiology. When X-ray technology began to expand, physicians needed also to learn the basics of radiology. In the 1960s and 1970s, as a phenomenal number of new drugs were discovered, physicians needed to learn more about pharmacology. Every time a new development has occurred in medical practice, physicians have needed to expand their base of knowledge to include the new area.

Another new area has developed, with at least as much significance for the practice of medicine as others that came before it. This development is the tremendous change we are seeing in the financing and organization of health care and the profound consequences this change will have on health care delivery. Just as physicians expanded the knowledge required for the practice of medicine in the face of technological advances, many now suggest that health care professionals of all types need to expand their knowledge to include a familiarity with the health care delivery system and the effects of alternative delivery and financing methods on the outcomes of care. Whether acquired as part of an undergraduate education or as part of the curriculum of health professions schools, an understanding of health policy will be an important part of professional knowledge in the twenty-first century.

The purpose of this book is to provide the reader with just such knowledge. Developed from a course I have taught at Stanford University for more than two decades, it describes the historical, social, political, and economic forces that have shaped our health care system and created the policy dilemmas we face. The information offered in this book has proven to be of interest to undergraduates, medical students, and practicing professionals alike, all of whom have participated in the course.

WHAT IS HEALTH POLICY?

This book introduces health policy in the United States. The growing problems that have surrounded health care over the past several decades have created the field of health policy. Forty years ago, few if any universities or professional schools had teaching or research programs in health policy. Today, nearly every major university includes active programs in health policy. Academic journals specializing in health policy are increasingly numerous and well respected. The advent of the Internet has made an extensive library of health policy data and information immediately available to all with basic computer access.

As with any new academic discipline, there is not universal agreement as to what precisely constitutes the field of health policy. Overlapping interests among those in fields such as public health, health economics, and health services research have made agreement on a precise definition of health policy sometimes difficult to attain. This book hopes to address this issue by approaching health policy as the study of the way health care is organized, financed, and delivered. It does this by drawing on theories from fields such as economics, sociology, and organizational behavior to offer a view of the broad social forces that coalesce to create the structure of our system of health care and the problems inherent to it.

In its broadest sense, health policy includes all those factors and forces that affect the health of the public. This book, however, focuses its study of health policy more on the structure of health care than on the health of a community or society.

Health policy overlaps with health economics but broadens its scope to include social and political processes affecting health care. Health policy and health services research have much in common; however, the latter tends to look more at specific clinical issues, such as the optimal way to treat coronary artery disease, whereas health policy looks at questions such as the optimal way to structure care overall.

WHO MAKES HEALTH POLICY?

The organizing, financing, and delivery of health care in the United States is affected by a broad range of forces, public as well as private, national as well as local. Congress and the federal health agencies within the executive branch have major roles in developing health policy. Federal laws such as Medicare and Medicaid that affect the financing of care have reshaped health care organization and delivery in a number of ways. Rules established by the US Department of Health and Human Services govern much of the health care that is provided in this country. As we have experienced during the ongoing debate over ACA, the congressional system of committees and subcommittees plays a continuous role in monitoring the delivery of health care throughout the country and initiating reform when necessary.

States also play a major role in the organization and financing of health care. Most laws governing professional licensure and medical practice come from the states. Financing care for the poor has become largely the responsibility of the states.

Health policy, however, includes more than just the creation of governmental policies pertaining to health care. As discussed later in this book, private businesses play a major role, both as purchasers of health insurance and as providers of health insurance, in driving recent changes in the way health care is organized, financed, and delivered. The shift to a market-based system of managed care was largely the result of the need to control costs. The effect this shift has had on the delivery of care at every level is profound.

The providers of care also play a large role in developing health policy. The American Medical Association (AMA), the private organization representing physicians, has been one of the most powerful forces behind the creation of the private practice, fee-for-service model of delivering health care that came to dominate the health care system for much of the twentieth century. Other providers, competing with the AMA, formed cooperative associations of physicians and hospitals as an alternative to fee-for-service care. These alternative, prepaid systems created the model on which the concept of the health maintenance organization (HMO) was based. They have also provided a basis for the development and expansion of accountable care organizations (ACOs).

Local communities also play a role in creating health policy. Community hospitals, community clinics, and local government health departments continue to play a major role in the organization and delivery of care at the local level.

So the creation of health policy is more than simply passing laws. It is the coalescence of forces on multiple levels, representing multiple interests and constituencies, to organize and finance a system to deliver health care to the American people.

THE STRUCTURE OF THE BOOK

The fourteen chapters of this book present the dilemma of US health care, describe its basic structure, and identify recent changes and trends in the system. For each chapter, I identify key concepts that summarize the way social, economic, and political factors have acted to shape the delivery of health care in this country, either historically or currently. By fully understanding these concepts, the reader will have a comprehensive grasp of our system of care.

Chapter 1 offers an introduction to ACA, how it was passed, what it was intended to do, and how it has fared in the years following its enactment. In noting the extreme social and political polarization that has emerged as part of the debate over ACA, I also provide a historical perspective on other attempts to pass health care reform and the polarization of opinion they engendered.

Chapter 2 offers a brief historical background about some of the important policy decisions our country has made over time to create the system we now have. It provides data about the rising cost of health care in this country and the burdens these costs place on both government and the private sector. It compares our country to other developed countries, in both the amount we spend on health care and the overall health of our population.

Chapter 3 describes how many of the institutional norms and expectations that are unique to the United States have created a health care system that is also unique. By means of comparison, it traces the history of the Canadian health care system and examines how fundamental cultural differences between US and Canadian societies are reflected in our health care systems. It looks at institutional aspects specific to the US system such as the "technologic imperative" and the approach we take to medical malpractice.

Chapter 4 looks at the professional structure of US health care. It describes the history of the medical profession, examining such issues as the number of physicians in practice and their practice specialty. It covers the history of the nursing profession and the evolving role of advanced practice nurses. Finally, it examines the structure of hospitals and other types of specialized referral centers.

Chapter 5 addresses the various ways health insurance can be structured. It provides a close look at the health maintenance organization, or HMO. It looks at the evolution of the Kaiser Permanente system, for years the nation's largest HMO. It then describes the emergence over the last several years of newer types of HMOs and various other types of managed care organizations. It moves on to a discussion of the "managed care revolution" we experienced in the 1990s and distinguishes between the concepts of managed care and managed competition.

Chapters 6 and 7 explore the two principal government health care programs: Medicare and Medicaid. Established in the 1960s, these programs had two important outcomes: (1) they simultaneously extended health insurance coverage to millions of Americans who were previously without insurance coverage, and (2) they set off the escalation in health care costs that continues to plague us today. Chapter 6 describes some of the policy questions confronting Medicare and identifies changes in the Medicare system involving HMOs and other types of managed care organizations. It looks at some of the weaknesses and problems that have developed with the system of Medicare HMOs, as well as steps Congress has taken to reform this program. Chapter 7 describes efforts by several states to restructure their Medicaid systems to both constrain costs and broaden coverage, as well as the Supreme Court's 2012 ruling that allowed states to opt out of the Medicaid expansion included as part of ACA. It also summarizes the Children's Health Insurance Program (CHIP) enacted by the federal government to reduce the number of children without health insurance.

Chapter 8 brings up the issue of the uninsured and the impact of ACA on the number of Americans without health insurance. At the time ACA was approved by Congress, 50 million Americans were without any type of health insurance coverage and, as a result, lacked access to many types of basic medical care. The majority of these uninsured were not people who are poor and unemployed but rather were mostly people in families with at least one adult who worked on a regular basis. The chapter also looks at the earlier success of two states' efforts to reduce the number of uninsured: Hawaii's employer mandate for the provision of health insurance to workers and Massachusetts's individual mandate for basic health insurance coverage.

Chapter 9 asks how the rapid shift to for-profit health care initially seen in the 1990s has affected the delivery of care. It considers the effects of the increasing prevalence of for-profit hospitals and specialized for-profit treatment centers for conditions such as heart disease and kidney disease. It then considers the extent to which physicians have allowed the profit motive to affect their professional practice.

Chapter 10 explores the world of pharmaceuticals and pharmaceutical policy. It describes recent increases in the cost of pharmaceutical products and steps taken by managed care organizations, Medicare, and state Medicaid programs to control pharmaceutical costs. It describes the 2003 expansion of Medicare to include coverage of outpatient pharmaceuticals.

Chapter 11 explores the often hidden side of US health care: our system of long-term health care. It covers a variety of long-term care options, including nursing homes and home health care. It documents the expected surge in frail elderly Americans who will soon need long-term care services, and it looks at alternative ways of providing and financing long-term care.

Chapter 12 looks at social factors other than health insurance that affect the delivery of and access to health care. It asks, What are some of the other factors that impede people's access to health care even after financial constraints have been removed? It describes how forces such as culture, ethnicity, and social class can independently affect access to care.

Chapter 13 offers a unified model of our current health care dilemma. It suggests that forces of cost, quality, and access continue to compete for preeminence in the health policy arena, and that the interjection of the for-profit motive has complicated the model and made a solution more difficult. It proposes an ethical heuristic that physicians and other health professionals can use to navigate the currents of for-profit health care. It explores the issue of health care rationing and the lessons that can be learned from the country's response to historical shortages of flu vaccine and from the Oregon Medicaid plan, one of the country's first attempts at the explicit rationing of health care services as a means to expand access. It moves on to look at ACA's approach to the issues of comparative effective analysis, cost-effectiveness analysis, and health care rationing.

In chapter 14, I suggest that, despite the substantial improvements that have resulted from the enactment of ACA, we will continue to face unanswered questions that are central to eventually finding a means of stabilizing and securing our system of health care for the long term.

At the end of each of the aforementioned chapters, I describe the specific changes contained in ACA that affect the topics discussed in the chapters. At the end of the book, I combine these descriptions into an outline of the major changes that have resulted and will result from ACA. It would not be possible to include in this outline every change contained within the ACA legislation, given its length and level of detail. Instead, I also identify a series of websites that provide a nonpartisan summary of ACA and its specific policy effects.

I hope that, at the completion of this book, the reader will have gained an appreciation of how health care in the United States in all its complexity still presents a fundamental dilemma: How much health care can we afford and who will have access to that care? I will consider the book a success if, as a result of this appreciation, the reader will be in a better position to contribute to solving this dilemma.

The Affordable Care Act and the Politics of Health Care Reform

The headlines in March 2010 just about said it all. On March 22, a *New York Times* editorial declared, "Health Care Reform, at Last." Two days later, the *New England Journal of Medicine* announced, "Historic Passage—Reform at Last" (Iglehart 2010b). President Barack Obama had signed the Patient Protection and Affordable Care Act (ACA)—the most significant reform of our health care system since the 1965 enactment of Medicare and Medicaid under President Lyndon Johnson. After what Bruce Vladeck, administrator of the Health Care Financing Administration under President Bill Clinton, characterized as "the epochal, exhausting, and contentious task of enacting comprehensive health care reform" (Vladeck 2010, p. 1955), the tumultuous process that had begun more than a year before with the release of President Obama's first federal budget proposal had finally come to a conclusion.

The passage of reform legislation over the unanimous and strident opposition of congressional Republicans was assuredly a major step in the evolution of health care in America. ACA has extended publicly funded health insurance coverage to millions of formerly uninsured adults whose income falls near or below the federal poverty level (FPL). ACA has also made affordable health insurance available to millions more Americans who are not poor, yet who previously could not afford the cost of acquiring health insurance in the private marketplace.

As it moved through Congress, the proposed health care reform legislation exposed deep divisions among politicians and within the US population over core issues of health policy. Do Americans have a right to health care? What should the role of government be in financing or regulating health care and health insurance? To what extent should we rely on the private marketplace as the source of health insurance?

How much should the government pay for health care? Perhaps even more important, how much can the government *afford to pay* for health care?

The passage of ACA did not provide definitive answers to these questions. We may
well be discussing and debating them again in the not-too-distant future. In light of the
likelihood of this ongoing discussion and debate, it is appropriate to look more closely
at the process by which Congress and the president enacted the reforms included
in ACA and then to place that reform process in the considerably broader context of
the history of health care reform efforts in the United States.

HEALTH CARE REFORM AND THE 2008 PRESIDENTIAL ELECTION

The presidential election scheduled for November 4, 2008, began in earnest with the
primary elections in January and February of that year. Before the first vote was cast,
health care reform was an important issue in the minds of most voters. A series of
public opinion polls conducted between 1994 (the year the Clinton health reform
proposals collapsed) and 2007 showed that "about 90% of Americans were fairly
consistent in agreeing that the U.S. health care system should be completely rebuilt or
required fundamental changes" (Jacobs 2008, p. 1881).

In January 2008, Robert Blendon and his colleagues published the results of a series of
opinion surveys of likely primary voters from thirty-five states with early presidential
primaries (Blendon et al. 2008b). They found widespread awareness of problems inherent to health care in the United States among both Republicans and Democrats.
While Republicans and Democrats were in general agreement on the need to enact
some type of health care reform, however, they were divided on what the reform should
look like. Among Democrats, 65 percent favored providing health insurance to "all or
nearly all of the uninsured" and were willing to accept substantially increased government spending to accomplish this goal. By contrast, 42 percent of Republicans supported extending coverage "to only some of the uninsured," with an additional 27 percent
preferring "keeping things basically as they are now" (p. 420). Before the first vote was
cast in the presidential primaries, our country was divided largely along political party
lines as to how we should address health care reform.

In November 2008, Blendon and colleagues reported a second series of opinion
polls, this time comparing those who had voted for John McCain in the primary with
those who had voted for Barack Obama (Blendon et al. 2008a). Consistent with the
earlier polls, most Obama voters wanted the government to take responsibility for
extending health insurance to the uninsured, while McCain voters were of the view
that responsibility for acquiring health insurance should rest with the individual
consumer. Obama voters favored a larger, more comprehensive reform plan, while
McCain voters favored a more limited, smaller-scale approach. Before President Obama

was to take office, a substantial polarization of views between Democrats and Republicans was already in place.

Shortly after his inauguration, President Obama released his first budget proposal. In it, he called on Congress to work collaboratively with the White House to design major reform of the health care system. It was clear, though, that Obama had learned the lesson of the failed Clinton reform proposals of 1993–94, which I describe in chapter 5. Rather than defining the specifics of the reform proposals himself, President Obama wanted Congress to take the lead in developing reform legislation.

Within a few months of Obama's budget message, Congress had begun to work on reform legislation. The process of developing the actual legislation fell to five separate congressional committees: two in the Senate and three in the House of Representatives. A consensus began to emerge that the most promising approach to expanding health insurance coverage would be through requiring all US residents to carry health insurance (individual mandate) while also requiring most US employers to offer health insurance to their employees (employer mandate). This approach mirrored reforms that had been adopted in Massachusetts a few years earlier.

It did not take long in this process for the political divide evident in preelection polls to resurface. Mandating health insurance coverage would require creating a place for individuals and employers to go to acquire coverage. As part of its mandate program, Massachusetts had created a central clearinghouse to connect insurance companies offering coverage options with individuals or employers seeking coverage. Fairly quickly, leaders of the Senate committees dealing with reform agreed to adopt a model similar to that in Massachusetts. They would establish health insurance "exchanges" through which those seeking insurance could select from among the insurance options various companies had available.

As chair of the Senate Finance Committee, Senator Max Baucus (D-Montana) initially proposed that among the insurance options available through these health insurance exchanges would be a "public option," an insurance plan analogous to Medicare, organized and administered by the federal government. Almost immediately, Senate Republicans condemned the public option approach. Senator John Cornyn (R-Texas) criticized the public option approach as "a Washington-directed unfair-competition plan" (quoted in Iglehart 2009a, p. 2386). Senator Charles Grassley (R-Iowa) argued that the Democrats' approach "would cause us to slide rapidly down the slope towards increasing government control of health care" (Grassley 2009, p. 2397).

President Obama countered these criticisms in a *New York Times* Op-Ed. He argued that the Democrats' plan "is not about putting the government in charge of your health insurance. I don't believe anyone should be in charge of your health care decisions but you and your doctor—not government, not bureaucrats, not insurance companies" (Obama 2009b). With substantial majorities in both houses of Congress, Democratic leaders pushed for a comprehensive expansion of the existing health insurance system to include most of those who were without insurance. The federal government would take principal responsibility for organizing and financing this expansion. Republicans, on the other hand, with substantial support from the health insurance industry, argued for a more limited approach. As described by Karen Ignagni, CEO of America's Health Insurance Plans (a leading industry group), Congress should instead focus on "building on the strengths of the present public-private health care system rather than replacing it" (Ignagni 2009, p. 1134).

By the fall of 2009, the debate over health care reform had hit an impasse. There was a line drawn in the congressional sand separating Democrats from Republicans. It appeared there was no room for compromise—Democrats would not accept the approach supported by Republicans, and Republicans were equally unwilling to consider seriously the Democrats' proposals. It seemed to many that, once again, health care reform might end in failure.

At this point, President Obama chose to take decisive action, addressing a joint session of Congress in front of a prime-time viewing audience. Chiding both sides of the aisle for their impasse, Obama stated, "now is the season for action." He indicated that, from that point on, he was going to assert his leadership in the effort to enact health care reform. He identified three overarching goals for the reform effort: (1) expanding health insurance coverage to those who lacked it, (2) constraining the rising cost of health care, and (3) improving the security of coverage for those with chronic illness (Obama 2009a).

With a great deal of political maneuvering, carried out in the face of substantial public confusion, each house of Congress enacted health care reform legislation: the House of Representatives on November 7 and the Senate on December 24. While each bill had many things in common, each had unique features. Some form of compromise between the two versions would need to be agreed upon. Usually this process would involve the creation of a House-Senate Conference Committee, made up of members of both houses. The compromise struck by the Conference Committee would then be taken back for final approval in each house before being forwarded to the president for his signature.

This process turned out not to be an option, though. Senator Ted Kennedy of Massachusetts, a leader of Senate Democrats and for more than four decades a leading voice in the US Senate for health care reform, died of cancer. A special election in Massachusetts to fill his seat resulted in a Republican being elected, thereby giving the Republicans the forty-one votes needed to mount and sustain a filibuster in the Senate. With unanimous Republican opposition to passage of any health reform bill approved by Democrats, there was no chance for compromise legislation coming out of a House-Senate Conference Committee to gain passage in the Senate. Nor was there any chance the Senate would simply approve the reform bill passed previously by the House. There was only one option open to the Democrats: for the House of Representatives to approve the bill passed by the Senate, even though the Senate bill had several provisions to which House Democrats were opposed. Following House passage of the Senate bill, however, the House and Senate could then agree on a series of modifications to the bill under a special provision referred to as "reconciliation."

Not being a scholar of the intricacies of the legislative process, I will leave it to others to describe in more detail the history, purpose, and intended use of the reconciliation process in Congress (Herszenhorn 2010; Iglehart 2010a). As I understand it, the reconciliation process was established by Congress in 1974 as a simplified means of changing federal programs or policies to align them more closely with previously established budget policy. If legislation is passed that is inconsistent with the budget guidelines set by Congress, or, similarly, if an existing program is inconsistent with those guidelines, Congress can change the programs or policies to align them with the budget. Making these changes under the reconciliation process requires a simple majority vote in both houses of Congress—and therefore is not subject to a filibuster in the Senate.

Congress had previously used the budget reconciliation process at various times and for various purposes. One of the best known instances of reconciliation is the Consolidated Omnibus Budget Reconciliation Act, passed by Congress in 1986 and best known by its acronym, COBRA. COBRA gives employees who have lost their jobs the right to continue their previous group health coverage for a period of time. People frequently talk of their "COBRA benefits."

Sensing a potential procedural impasse, on February 25 President Obama convened an urgent summit meeting of leading Democrats and Republicans to discuss, and in front of a national television audience to debate, competing perspectives on health care reform. The political impasse that preceded Obama's summit was still there after it was over. All Republicans in Congress remained opposed to the bills that had been passed by the House and the Senate. President Obama and Democratic leaders had no choice but to invoke the budget reconciliation process. In an all-day session on Sunday, March 21, the House approved the health reform bill previously passed in December by the Senate, and on March 23 President Obama signed it into law. Then, on March 25, both the House and the Senate passed, by simple majority vote, the reconciliation bill that made a series of changes to the original bill that bridged the divisions between the original House and Senate bills. In essence, the reconciliation process replicated what the House-Senate Conference Committee process is intended to do: to find a middle ground between similar bills passed in the House and the Senate, and then to gain final approval of both houses of the compromise bill.

As Congress completed passage of ACA, the rhetoric on both sides made clear the continued deep divisions between Democrats and Republicans over how health care in the United States should be organized and financed, and the role government should play in the health care system. On the day he signed ACA, President Obama hailed the historic step that had been taken: "Today, after almost a century of trying . . . health insurance reform becomes law in the United States of America. . . . We have now just enshrined the core principle that everybody should have some basic security when it comes to their health care" (Obama 2010).

Republicans were not so sanguine. Representative Marsha Blackburn (R-Tennessee), following the House vote in favor of the ACA legislation, remarked, "Freedom dies a little bit today." Carl Hulse, reporting on the House's approval of ACA, stated that "Republicans were outraged, characterizing the legislation as a major step toward socialism and an aggressive government takeover of the health care system" (2010, p. A17). These comments echoed those made a few months earlier by Representative Michele Bachmann (R-Minnesota), that Democrats were pushing for "socialized medicine" and a "government takeover" of the American health care system (quoted in Herszenhorn 2009).

This continued polarization over what ACA represented for the United States—a new "core principle" assuring access to health care, or a "government takeover" and a step closer to "socialized medicine"—remained in the wake of the year-long health care reform process. It would be easy to point to President Obama and the political parties in Congress as the source of this polarization. It is fundamental to our understanding of US health care reform, however, to consider, again, what President Obama said when he signed the ACA: "Today, after almost a century of trying . . . health insurance reform becomes law in the United States of America."

The health care reform process did not begin with the inauguration of President Obama. Nor did it begin with the presidential campaign leading up to his election. The United States had been arguing over health care reform for nearly a century before President Obama was elected. A review of the repeated efforts over that century for or against reform reveals a striking similarity between what was proposed in 2009–10 and what had been proposed previously, as well as a striking similarity between the rhetoric of health care reform in the past and the rhetoric of 2009–10.

A CENTURY OF TRYING TO ACHIEVE HEALTH CARE REFORM IN THE UNITED STATES

Theodore Roosevelt first attempted to reform US health care during his presidential campaign in 1912. As part of the Progressive Party's platform, Roosevelt proposed a system of national health insurance, modeled after the German system, to be administered by a new National Health Department. Those supporting national health insurance viewed health care as a right of all members of our society, analogous to the recently recognized right to a publicly financed education for children. Teddy Roosevelt lost the 1912 presidential election to Woodrow Wilson, however, and health care reform had to wait for another day.

In 1927, a group of physicians, public health professionals, and others concerned with national health care issues came together to form the Committee on the Costs of Medical Care (CCMC) (Ross 2002). CCMC was an independent group and was supported by a number of foundations. Committee members set in motion a five-year project to study and report on the economics and organization of health care in America. On March 10, 1931, the *New York Times* carried an article titled "Family Health Bill Put at $250 a Year" in which the CCMC was cited, stating that "the average family of five in an American city" spent $250 per year on medical care, a figure that raised serious concerns about the rising costs of medical care in a time of economic hardship. The committee's majority report, issued in 1932, recommended shifting the delivery of most medical care to a model that emphasized organized medical groups and prepayment of health costs through either insurance premiums or taxation. The American Medical Association (AMA), however, was stridently opposed to this approach, labeling such prepaid medical groups "medical soviets" and suggesting that "such plans will mean the destruction of private practice. . . . They are, in a word, 'unethical'" (American Medical Association 1932, p. 1950). The AMA's House of Delegates unanimously approved a motion to oppose the majority report of the CCMC, and to mount "an intensive campaign . . . among the medical profession and the public" to prevent adoption of the CCMC's recommendations. A follow-up report to the House of Delegates reported that "all the facilities of the American Medical Association have been used to oppose this trend and the propaganda in support of it" (American Medical Association 1934b, p. 2200). The AMA prevailed in its efforts to block the recommendations of the CCMC's report, and the report was shelved.

Franklin Roosevelt took up the issue of health care reform in 1934 as part of his initial proposals for old age security and unemployment insurance for workers. In response to Roosevelt's early proposals to include national health insurance as part of Social Security, the AMA House of Delegates passed a resolution reiterating its position that "all features of medical service in any method of medical practice should be under the control of the medical profession. No other body or individual is legally or educationally equipped to exercise such control" (American Medical Association 1934b, p. 2200). When it appeared as though health insurance might be added to the pending legislation for creation of the Social Security system, the AMA House of Delegates met in special session to reiterate its "opposition to all forms of state medicine" and to "reaffirm its opposition to all forms of compulsory sickness insurance" (American Medical Association 1935, pp. 750–51). Once again, AMA opposition to government involvement in health care was effective, and when Roosevelt signed the Social Security Act in 1935, health insurance was not part of it.

Roosevelt continued to support the creation of a system of national health insurance and appointed an "Interdepartmental Committee to Coordinate Health and Welfare Activities," charging it with studying the issue of extending Social Security benefits to include health care. At a national conference held in July 1938, the committee proposed a series of changes to US health care, including "a ten year program providing for the expansion of the nation's hospital facilities" and "a comprehensive program designed to increase and improve medical services for the entire population" (Interdepartmental Committee to Coordinate Health and Welfare Activities 1938, p. 433).

One month later, the AMA convened an emergency meeting of its House of Delegates to respond to the government's "campaign for some radical changes in medical practice" (American Medical Association 1938, p. 1192). The speaker of the House of Delegates reminded the delegates that the AMA had consistently "opposed legislation which would have the effect of vesting in some governmental agency power to enforce its decrees on patients and doctors" (p. 1192). The AMA president then addressed the delegates, stating that "the Association has constantly opposed the adoption of any form of state medicine by any definition of that term" (p. 1194).

It is interesting to note that at this special session, the leaders of the National Medical Association (NMA)—the national association of black physicians, most of whom were prevented from joining the AMA because of their race—were (after majority vote of the AMA delegates) invited to address the meeting. The past president of the NMA voiced his support for the position of the AMA, arguing that "if we have socialized medicine in America, I am very sure, as you must be sure, that the standards of medical practice will degenerate . . . and the patients again will suffer as they have suffered in Europe" (American Medical Association 1938, p. 1211).

Once again, fears that "governmental agency power" over the financing of health care would lead to "state medicine" and "socialized Medicine" were sufficient to derail Roosevelt's efforts. Health care reform would have to wait another decade before it was back on the table.

In January 1948, President Harry Truman asked Oscar Ewing, one of his senior administrators, to prepare a report on the status of health care in the United States. Released in September of that year, the Ewing Report outlined a series of steps the federal government should take to make health care more available. As Roosevelt's Interdepartmental Committee did in 1938, this report recommended extensive new hospital construction and a compulsory "system of Government prepayment health insurance" (Furman 1948) that over a period of three years would provide universal insurance for both hospital care and physician care, as well as coverage of certain prescription medicines.

The response of the AMA to the Ewing proposals is interesting. The AMA first went through a formal procedure to adopt the following definition: "*Socialized medicine*— Socialized medicine is a system of medical administration by which the government promises or attempts to provide for the medical needs of the entire population or a large part thereof" (American Medical Association 1948, p. 685). A few weeks later, Morris Fishbein, the longtime editor of the *Journal of the American Medical Association*, published a special editorial in which he warned physicians that the profession of medicine was "at a point of decision which may well determine the nature and the freedom of medical practice for many years in the future" (Fishbein 1948, p. 1254). Responding to politicians who denied that President Truman's proposals for national health insurance constituted "socialized medicine," Dr. Fishbein argued that "nations that embark on such programs move inevitably into a socialized state in which . . . practically all public services become nationalized, private responsibility and ownership disappear, individual initiative is destroyed and the result is a socialized state" (p. 1256).

In 1948, the AMA hired a political consulting firm from California that had successfully defeated California governor Earl Warren's 1945 proposal for a statewide health insurance plan. With a budget of more than $1 million, funded largely by an assessment of $25 on every AMA member, the firm developed a national strategy with two principal goals, as cited by Lepore (2012): "1. The *immediate objective* is the defeat of the compulsory health insurance program pending in Congress. 2. The *long-term* objective is to put a permanent stop to the agitation for socialized medicine in this country" (p. 57). As reported by the *New York Times*, the AMA fought Truman's proposals "with all the vigor and manpower it [could] assemble" (Phillips 1949), with the result that, once again, the efforts at health care reform went down to defeat in Congress.

It would be seventeen years before Congress would take up health care reform again, this time under the leadership of President Johnson. With large majorities in both houses of Congress following the 1964 election, Johnson moved quickly to enact Medicare (health care for the elderly) and Medicaid (health care for the poor) as amendments to the Social Security system. Headlines in the *New York Times* announced, "A.M.A. Opens Bid to Kill Medicare" (Wehrwein 1965). Testifying before the Senate Finance Committee, Dr. Donovan Ward, president of the AMA, warned senators, "This may be your last chance to weigh the consequences of taking the first step toward establishment of socialized medicine in the United States" (American Medical Association 1965, p. 16).

In 1965, Congress was not swayed by claims that government financing of health care for the elderly and the poor constituted a government takeover of the health care system. It was swayed even less by claims that the proposed Medicare and Medicaid programs would be "the first step toward establishment of socialized medicine in the

United States." By substantial margins, both houses of Congress passed the Social Security Act of 1965, establishing the Medicare and Medicaid programs. President Johnson flew to the Missouri home of Harry Truman to sign the legislation in the presence of the former president.

Of course, providing government payment for health care for the elderly and the poor was only a partial fulfillment of earlier proposals for universal health insurance. As monumental an accomplishment as it represented, the passage of Medicare and Medicaid left substantial segments of the American population without the means to pay for health insurance. As we will see in later chapters, the aggregate cost of health care began to rise sharply in the years following the enactment of Medicare and Medicaid. By 1970, both President Richard Nixon and Senator Ted Kennedy were calling for expanded health insurance coverage to help individuals and families offset the rising costs of care. Nixon's plan called for private financing through what we today would call an employer mandate. Kennedy's plan called for direct government financing of care. Neither plan gained approval, and any further steps toward health care reform were lost in the wake of the Watergate scandal and President Nixon's resulting resignation.

Health care reform was again on the table in the early years of President Clinton's administration, as I discuss in chapter 5. An effective national ad campaign by the health insurance industry, warning of a new, massive federal bureaucracy taking over American health care, coupled with a shift of congressional control from Democrat to Republican majorities, led to the defeat of the Clinton reform proposals. As many had warned, in the years following the defeat of the Clinton proposals health care costs continued their steep rise, and growing numbers of Americans became or remained uninsured against the cost of illness or injury—the situation confronting the candidates in the 2008 presidential election.

PLACING THE OBAMA REFORMS IN THE HISTORICAL CONTEXT OF PREVIOUS REFORM EFFORTS

During the intensity of the yearlong debate over President Obama's proposals for health care reform, it was often difficult to gain a clear sense of what the core issues were. The heated rhetoric from all sides led to widespread confusion as to what the proposed reforms would or would not accomplish. A national poll (Kaiser Family Foundation 2010) taken two weeks after President Obama signed ACA showed that 55 percent of respondents were confused about what was in the new law. Support for the law fell largely along party lines, with 79 percent of Republicans having an unfavorable view of the law and 77 percent of Democrats having a favorable view.

Which view was correct? Would the law assure most Americans access to needed health care, as many people seemed to believe? Or would it mean the potential destruction of our health care system through a government takeover, as many others appeared to believe?

Taking a step back from this debate, it is informative to compare ACA and the political response to it with various proposals for health care reform made over the last century. As illustrated in table 1.1, there is a remarkable similarity between what ACA was intended to accomplish and what earlier proposals hoped to accomplish, and an equally striking similarity between the rhetorical opposition to ACA and the rhetoric in opposition to those earlier proposals.

In 1931, when the Committee on the Cost of Medical Care recommended programs to bring health care "within reach of persons of average means," the opposition predicted that the programs would "mean the destruction of private practice." When Franklin Roosevelt proposed "to increase and improve medical services for the entire population," the AMA labeled his proposals "socialized medicine" and predicted that, if Roosevelt's plan were implemented, "standards of medical practice will degenerate . . . and patients will suffer." Truman's proposal for "universal access to hospital and physician care" was predicted to lead to "a socialized state in which . . . practically all public services become nationalized." Johnson's proposal for Medicare and Medicaid would, the AMA predicted, "be the first step toward establishment of socialized medicine in the United States." President Obama's proposals were characterized by many Republicans as "a major step toward socialism and an aggressive government takeover of the health care system."

The history of health care reform in the United States is the history of our deep-seated divisions over core principles of health care delivery and of the role of government in the provision of health care. Is a basic level of health care a right of all Americans? If so, should the government enact and enforce the mechanism to ensure that right? Alternatively, is it inappropriate for government to interfere in the private provision of health services? Our society has struggled with these issues for a century. The kerfuffle surrounding the passage of ACA has simply been the latest episode in our attempts as a society to address these divisions.

Despite the confusion surrounding it, it is clear that ACA is bringing major change to our health care system. Among other things, it has:

- Extended Medicaid coverage to more than 10 million people living in or near poverty who previously were ineligible for coverage
- Provided health insurance to an additional 11 million formerly uninsured people with low to moderate incomes through a combination of regulated insurance exchanges and tax subsidies for the cost of insurance
- Made a series of changes to regulations affecting companies that provide health insurance with the intent of making that insurance more affordable

TABLE 1.1. A history of arguments for and against health care reform

Year/president	Argument in favor	Argument opposed
1931 / Herbert Hoover	Modern medicine can be brought within reach of persons of average means. —Committee on the Cost of Medical Care	Medical soviets . . . such plans will mean the destruction of private practice. —American Medical Association
1934–38 / Franklin Roosevelt	A comprehensive program designed to increase and improve medical services for the entire population. —Committee to Coordinate Health and Welfare Activities	Opposition to all forms of state medicine. —American Medical Association If we have socialized medicine in America . . . standards of medical practice will degenerate . . . and patients will suffer. —National Medical Association
1948 / Harry Truman	A system of Government prepayment health insurance to provide universal access to hospital and physician care. —Ewing Report	Nations that embark on such programs move inevitably into a socialized state in which . . . practically all public services become nationalized. —American Medical Association
1965 / Lyndon Johnson	To improve health care for the American people, [I propose] hospital insurance for the aged under social security. —President Johnson, 1965 budget message to Congress	The President's proposal would be the first step toward establishment of socialized medicine in the United States. —American Medical Association
1993 / Bill Clinton	We must make this our most urgent priority: giving every American health security, health care that can never be taken away. —President Clinton, special address to Congress, September 1993	New government bureaucracies will cap how much the country can spend on all health care. —"Harry and Louise" TV ads, sponsored by the Health Insurance Association of America
2010 / Barack Obama	We have now just enshrined the core principle that everybody should have some basic security when it comes to their health care. —President Obama, on signing the health reform law	A major step toward socialism and an aggressive government takeover of the health care system. —Congressional Republicans

- Made a series of changes in the Medicare program to reduce costs and improve benefits
- Created a series of new sources of tax revenues to support these programs

When Congress passed Medicare and Medicaid in 1965, our health care system was changed fundamentally. Yet those changes stopped short of solving many of the policy issues at the heart of our health care system. Nor did the passage of Medicare and Medicaid resolve our national ambivalence over what the role of government should be in our health care system.

When Congress passed ACA in 2010, our health care system was again changed fundamentally. Yet Congress again left unaddressed many continuing core questions. In future years, in future presidential elections, and in future Congresses, we will undoubtedly again be talking about health care reform. Rather than debating how to extend coverage to the uninsured, we likely will be debating what parts of ACA need to be changed and how to rein in the continuously rising cost of health care. When we have these discussions, the appropriate role of government will again be a topic of sharp debate.

Rather than trying to describe in one place what the ACA does and does not do, I instead address the changes contained in the 1,000-plus-page ACA legislation sequentially as we go through this book. In the following chapters, I address issues of the cost, quality, and availability of health care; the cultural factors unique to the United States that surround health care; the professional organization of health care; the various private and public mechanisms for financing health care; and specific health care issues such as pharmaceutical policy and long-term care. In each chapter, I describe how these aspects of health care have evolved to what they are now. I then address specifically how the new policies enacted by ACA will affect or change the topic under discussion. At the end of the book, I address what ACA has left undone—the problems in the organization, financing, and delivery of American health care that have yet to be resolved. Finally, as an appendix to the book, I provide a comprehensive listing of the various components contained in ACA.

LEGAL CHALLENGES TO THE AFFORDABLE CARE ACT AND THEIR OUTCOMES

It did not take long following the enactment of ACA for those who opposed its passage to file legal challenges against it. On March 23, 2010, the same day President Obama signed ACA, the state of Florida filed a lawsuit in federal court challenging two core aspects of the act: the "individual mandate" that all Americans either enroll in health insurance or pay a penalty to the federal government (described in chapter 5) and the mandatory expansion of state Medicaid programs to include all citizens and certain permanent residents with incomes below 138 percent of the FPL (described in chapter 7). In fairly rapid succession, twenty-five other states joined Florida in challenging the constitutionality of ACA (Kaiser Family Foundation 2012). A separate lawsuit was filed by a group of private business interests. Eventually, the Supreme Court heard both suits in a case known as *National Federation of Independent Business v. Sebelius* (132 S. Ct. 2566 [2012]).

As described in chapter 5, ACA includes a provision known commonly as the individual mandate that requires most people in the United States to maintain a minimum level of health insurance coverage for themselves and their dependents. While some individuals and families are exempted from this requirement due to their low income, those who fail to maintain this coverage will be required to pay a penalty to the federal government. The penalty will be collected as part of the individual's yearly income tax return. The plaintiffs argued that individual choices in matters of health insurance were not part of interstate commerce and therefore were not covered under Article 1 Section 8 of the US Constitution, which grants the federal government authority "to regulate commerce . . . among the several states."

The second issue raised in the lawsuits challenged the authority of the federal government to withhold preexisting Medicaid funding to states that decided not to expand Medicaid. Previously, only certain categories of poor people (children and their parents, elderly, blind, and disabled) were eligible for Medicaid coverage, with the federal government reimbursing states 50–75 percent of the cost of the program, depending on state income levels. ACA expanded coverage to all poor people, redefining "poor" as having incomes less than 138 percent of the FPL. Those states refusing this expansion of coverage would, as a consequence, lose not only the added federal support for those newly eligible but all federal funding for the program as well, both for the newly eligible and for those previously eligible. The states argued that the withholding of funds granted under the preexisting program was overly coercive and violated the federal government's constitutional authority.

The Supreme Court heard arguments from both the state suits and the private suit, issuing its ruling in June 2012. The outcome was a split decision. The Court upheld the individual mandate but removed the federal government's authority to withhold preexisting Medicaid funding from states electing not to adopt the new eligibility levels. Interestingly, the Court agreed that the interstate commerce clause of Article 1, Section 8, did not apply to the decision to purchase health insurance, as individual decisions of this type are not part of interstate commerce. However, while the federal government may not force someone to acquire health insurance, it can levy an extra tax on those who elect not to obtain coverage. Even though ACA legislation identified the required payment as a "penalty," it was included under the federal government's authority under Article 1, Section 8, to "lay and collect taxes."

In ruling on the Medicaid expansion, the Court determined that ACA did not simply expand Medicaid; rather, it fundamentally changed the program. As described by Chief Justice Roberts in his majority opinion, "It is no longer a program to care for the neediest among us, but rather an element of a comprehensive national plan to provide universal health insurance coverage" (US Supreme Court 2012, p. 53). Individual states were free to expand Medicaid eligibility or not to do so, with no loss of preexisting federal funding for the program.

The Medicaid ruling was somewhat of a surprise for many. As described by Mariner et al. (2012), "The Court had never before found a federal spending program to be coercive, and most scholars believed coercion to be an illusory standard that the Court would not apply" (p. 1157). By the end of 2015, this state-based discretion had resulted in thirty-one states (including the District of Columbia) electing to expand Medicaid eligibility, nineteen states electing not to expand coverage, and one state involved in discussions with the federal government about possible expansion (Kaiser Family Foundation 2015d).

To many observers, it appeared that the Supreme Court's 2012 decision in *National Federation of Independent Business v. Sebelius* had put to rest the issue of the constitutionality of ACA. Within weeks of that decision, however, another legal challenge arose with potentially devastating impact on coverage offered under ACA. The issue addressed in this legal challenge was not the constitutionality of ACA but rather the meaning of four words contained in the roughly one-thousand-page legislation: "established by the State."

As described in more detail in chapter 5, one of the central outcomes of ACA was the creation of publically available, online exchanges for individuals and small businesses to shop for health insurance coverage. Given that the individual mandate had been upheld as constitutional by the Supreme Court, people needed an easy place to go to acquire the mandated insurance coverage. In order to facilitate that acquisition, ACA provides federal subsidies to help pay the premiums for coverage, so long as the coverage was acquired through the new exchange. In a manner very similar to what had been proposed under the Clinton reform proposals, a separate health insurance exchange would be established for each state. As stated in Section 1311 of ACA, "Each State shall, not later than January 1, 2014, establish an American Health Benefit Exchange (referred to in this title as an "Exchange") for the State."

As part of the intense negotiations between the White House and several different congressional committees that resulted in passage of ACA, Congress decided that no state would be required to establish an exchange. For any state electing not to establish its own exchange, Section 1321 of ACA states that "the Secretary [of Health and Human Services] shall . . . establish and operate such Exchange within the State." States have the option of operating their own exchange or letting the federal government establish it on their behalf. As of the 2014 enrollment period, sixteen states had opted to establish their own exchange, while thirty-four states relied on HealthCare .gov, the federal exchange created in response to the act. Within these thirty-four states, approximately 6.4 million people were benefitting from the tax credits provided by Section 1401 of ACA (Kaiser Family Foundation 2015c). That section states that those with incomes less than 400 percent of the FPL will qualify for a "premium assistance credit" if they enroll in a qualifying health plan "through an Exchange established by the State under 1311."

In July 2012, only weeks after the Supreme Court issued its ruing in *National Federation of Independent Business v. Sebelius*, two different federal courts of appeal issued conflicting rulings on the same question: Does the wording of Section 1401 only allow premium assistance credits to go to those who enrolled in one of the sixteen exchanges that were literally "established by the State"? Alternatively, does enrollment through the federal HealthCare.gov exchange also qualify for premium assistance credits? In separate suits, the appeals court in the District of Columbia ruled that the credits were unavailable to those enrolled through HealthCare.gov, while the court in Richmond, Virginia, ruled that the credits were available both to those enrolled in individual state exchanges and in the federal exchange. To settle this issue, the Supreme Court agreed to decide this issue in a case known as *King v. Burwell*.

On June 25, 2015, the Court released its decision. As summarized by Hall (2015) in an article titled "*King v. Burwell*—ACA Armageddon Averted," "the ACA's tax subsidies for insurance premiums are available both in states with their own insurance exchanges and those relying on a federal exchange. . . . The Court emphasized that Congress obviously did not intend such destructive consequences, so it must have meant for premium subsidies to be available in all states" (p. 498). In the closing paragraph of the Court's decision, Chief Justice Roberts concluded that "Congress passed the Affordable Care Act to improve health insurance markets, not to destroy them." The 6.4 million people receiving subsidies through HealthCare.gov will continue to be eligible for those subsidies. What many had suggested would have meant the end of ACA was averted.

There was a third legal challenge to ACA that was also decided by the Supreme Court. This case, known as *Burwell v. Hobby Lobby Stores*, addressed the issue of religious exemption to the ACA requirement that larger employers offer affordable health insurance to all their full-time employees or pay a financial penalty to the federal government. As described by Gostin (2014), in accepting the case for review, "the Court thus entered a political quagmire at the intersection of religious freedom, women's health, and corporate personhood" (p. 785).

Section 2713 of ACA mandates that the insurance provided by the employer cover, without copayment or deductible, preventive health services identified as effective by the US Preventive Services Task force, as well as, "with respect to women, such additional preventive care and screenings . . . as provided for in comprehensive guidelines supported by the Health Resources and Services Administration for purposes of this paragraph." The Health Resources and Services Administration charged the Institute of Medicine (IOM) of the National Academy of Sciences to study this concern and issue guidelines for preventive services for women that must be covered under ACA.

The IOM issued its report in 2011 (IOM 2011a), which included the guideline that covered services include "a fuller range of contraceptive education, counseling, methods, and services so that women can better avoid unwanted pregnancies and space their pregnancies to promote optimal birth outcomes."

The final regulations issued by the federal government specifying the contraceptive services to be covered under ACA included the caveat that "group health plans established or maintained by certain religious employers (and group health insurance coverage provided in connection with such plans) are exempt from the otherwise applicable requirement to cover certain contraceptive services" (Federal Register 2013, p. 39870). This exemption for religious employers such as churches or religious schools is consistent with long-standing federal policy of avoiding policies that substantially burden a person's exercise of religion (Religious Freedom Restoration Act of 1993). ACA has provided other mechanisms for women who work for these types of religious institutions to obtain coverage for contraceptive services, without requiring the institution itself to provide the coverage.

Few would argue that a church or religious school should not qualify for the exemption to offering contraceptive coverage. Would a large, national, for-profit corporation that owns and operates hundreds of retail stores also qualify as a "religious employer" if its principal owner has a religious objection to certain forms of contraception for women? Hobby Lobby is just such a corporation. As described on its Facebook page, "Hobby Lobby is an industry leading retailer offering more than 70,000 arts, crafts, hobbies, home décor, holiday, and seasonal products." As described by Annas et al. (2014), "The owners of Hobby Lobby . . . objected to the inclusion of four of the FDA-approved contraceptives (two types of intrauterine devices [IUDs] and the emergency contraceptives Plan B and Ella) because they believed that these devices or drugs could induce abortion" (p. 862). Is a corporation a "person" for the purposes of exercising freedom of religion?

In its opinion, the Supreme Court cited previous acts of Congress, stating that, "the wor[d] 'person' . . . include[s] corporations, companies, associations, firms, partnerships, societies, and joint stock companies, as well as individuals" (p. 19). Accordingly, both for-profit as well as nonprofit organizations may claim the religious exemption provided by ACA for the coverage of contraception for women. As described previously, female employees of these organizations will still benefit from contraceptive coverage. Technically, however, their employer will not provide that coverage.

THE AFFORDABLE CARE ACT: ON THE CUSP?

The Oxford English Dictionary defines a *cusp* as "a point at which two branches of a curve meet and stop, with a common tangent." Since its passage in 2010, ACA has been on a steady upward curve of expanding health insurance coverage to millions of previously uninsured Americans. While the Supreme Court decisions described previously have added some interesting wrinkles to that curve, the curve has remained nonetheless on a continuous upward trajectory.

There continue to be many, however, who want to shift that curve to a downward trajectory. The *New York Times* (2015) reported that between January 2011 and March 2015, the US House of Representatives voted to repeal or defund ACA more than fifty times. While none of these votes were subsequently passed by the Senate, this pattern nonetheless bespeaks continued and strident opposition to ACA on the part of many Republicans and other political conservatives. Who will be president in 2017? Who will control Congress? Will state legislatures that have avoided Medicaid expansion continue to do so? As the American political landscape evolves over the next several years, answers to these and other related questions will play out, and the shape of the curve of health care reform will become more apparent.

Health, Health Care, and
the Market Economy

WHOSE RIGHT? (WHO'S RIGHT?)

After signing the Affordable Care Act (ACA) into law in March 2010, President Barack Obama declared that, in passing the act, "we have now just enshrined the core principle that everybody should have some basic security when it comes to their health care" (Obama 2010). As seen by President Obama (and by many of his supporters), Americans have a right to a basic level of health care, and ACA was the acknowledgment of that right.

Others, however, hold a very different view of the core principles of American health policy. In an opinion piece published in August 2009 in the *Wall Street Journal*, John Mackey, the cofounder and CEO of Whole Foods Markets, wrote, "How can we say that all people have more of an intrinsic right to health care than they have to food or shelter? Health care is a service that we all need, but just like food and shelter it is best provided through voluntary and mutually beneficial market exchanges. . . . This 'right' has never existed in America" (Mackey 2009).

This debate over who in America has a right to health care and what level of care that right entails has been going on for nearly a century. In 1918, Dr. John Bowman, at the time director of the Board of Regents of the American College of Surgeons, wrote that "as a people we are accustomed to hospital service; we look upon that service no longer as a luxury which we may buy, but rather as an inherent right. The humblest patient is entitled to the best of medical service. In the last twenty years especially this idea has taken hold of us. We regard the right to health today much as we regard the right to life" (Bowman 1918, p. 1). Made by the leader of one of the most prestigious groups of physicians in the United States, this statement bespeaks a commitment on the part of the medical profession and the country to approach health care as a basic right for all individuals. This was the position President Obama was supporting in asserting that all Americans have a right to some "basic security when it comes to their health care."

Those opposed to President Obama's position would instead agree with the comments of Dr. R. M. Sade, published in the *New England Journal of Medicine*, one of the most prestigious medical journals in the country: "Medical care is neither a right nor a privilege: it is a service that is provided by doctors and others to people who wish to purchase it" (Sade 1971, p. 1289). In Dr. Sade's approach, medical care is no different from any other type of commodity that is bought and sold in the open market. If you want new sneakers, you buy a pair from the shoe store. If you do not have enough money to pay for the sneakers, then you are out of luck—you do not have a right to sneakers. Neither do you have a right to medical care, suggests Dr. Sade. If you do not have enough money to pay for care, then you are out of luck.

While Dr. Bowman's remarks from 1918 offer for many a laudable perspective on the issue of who by rights should have access to health care, they do not accurately describe the direction health care in America actually took in the decades following 1918. Ironically, the United States Supreme Court has identified one group of Americans who have a constitutional right to an adequate level of health care: those who are incarcerated in America's prisons (Ruger et al. 2015). In addition, in 1986 Congress passed the Emergency Medical Treatment and Active Labor Act (EMTALA), assuring that all people coming to a hospital emergency room would be assured an initial assessment, without consideration of ability to pay, to determine if they were experiencing a life-threatening condition, severe pain, or active labor. Beyond these exceptions, for much of the twentieth century, the structure of our health care system was more consistent with Dr. Sade's perspective and with that of John Mackey of Whole Foods. Americans had no right to health care.

THE UNIQUE HISTORY OF HEALTH CARE IN THE UNITED STATES

When Dr. Bowman published his statement in 1918, the future direction and shape of the US health care system was still in a formative state. By the time Dr. Sade published his remarks in 1971, the shape of our system had largely been decided through a series of political and economic choices. The history of US health care during this period largely reflects the comments of Dr. Sade. With a few notable exceptions, which I address in subsequent chapters, before President Obama signed ACA, Americans did not have a right to medical care.

In 1948, as part of the founding of the United Nations, the UN General Assembly adopted a Universal Declaration of Human Rights, with "recognition of the inherent dignity and of the equal and inalienable rights of all members of the human family." Article 25 of the declaration states: "Everyone has the right to a standard of living adequate for the health and well-being of himself and of his family, including food, clothing, housing and medical care."

The United States, despite its role in founding the United Nations, did not adhere fully to the declaration, instead choosing a market approach to medical care. In approaching medical care as a market commodity that can be bought or sold, rather than as a social good that should be made available to all people, the United States adopted a policy position that was unique among developed countries. In the words of economist Uwe Reinhardt, "Americans . . . decided to treat health care as essentially a private consumer good of which the poor might be guaranteed a basic package, but which is otherwise to be distributed more and more on the basis of ability to pay" (Reinhardt and Relman 1986, p. 23).

The United States was alone among industrialized nations in approaching health care in this market-oriented way. By the end of the twentieth century, all other developed countries had adopted national health plans that assured citizens access to basic medical care. These plans ranged from fully socialized systems such as that in Great Britain to systems such as Canada's, in which most physicians are in private medical practice.*

The decision to approach medical care as a market commodity rather than a right was closely linked to a second national policy decision that was to have equally profound effects on the way health care would evolve in the United States. This was the decision made in the early part of the twentieth century to vest in the medical profession substantial authority over the organization and financing as well as the practice of medical care. At the beginning of the twentieth century, the US medical profession was a complex array of practitioners from diverse educational backgrounds with a variety of knowledge and skills. There were no standards, either legal or ethical, to maintain a consistent level of quality in the way physicians practiced medicine.

In response to what was perceived as a national crisis, a prestigious commission was asked to conduct a national study of the issue of medical education and to make recommendations about a thorough restructuring of medical education, and as a

*Until 1994, there was a second developed country that continued to approach medical care as a market commodity. In that country, those citizens without the ability to pay for it had little, if any, access to care. As a result of a major restructuring of the country's government in 1994, the country adopted the policy of health care for all as a basic right, leaving the United States alone in treating it as a market good. That other country is South Africa.

result, medical practice. In 1910, the commission published its recommendations in its report *Medical Education in the United States and Canada*, often referred to as the Flexner Report. Based on the views expounded in this report, state and local governments increasingly relied on the American Medical Association (AMA) (the principal professional association of physicians) and on the AMA's affiliated state and local medical associations to guide the restructuring of medical practice. (For a more comprehensive discussion of this period in the history of US medicine, see Paul Starr's Pulitzer Prize–winning book, *The Social Transformation of American Medicine*.)

The rise in the sovereignty of the US medical profession was based on a somewhat idealized view of physicians. Consistent with the increasing legitimacy of science and technology common during that time, physicians were typically seen as altruistic agents who possessed valuable scientific knowledge and technical skills (Parsons 1951, 1975). Their role as social agents was guided by a code of medical ethics that placed the utmost importance on acting at all times in the best interest of the patient. They could be trusted to make decisions on behalf of the patient in a paternalistic manner, acting always as a disinterested agent on the patient's behalf. This view of the medical profession led state and local governments to vest considerable authority in physicians and their professional organizations over medical education and the practice of medicine.

In 1938, Dr. Irvin Abell, then president of the AMA, spoke to a special meeting of the AMA's House of Delegates, reminding physicians of this professional responsibility. "The medical profession by principle and tradition is committed to the idea that the prime object, the standard of value and the social reason for its existence are all one thing—the service it can render to humanity" (Abell 1938, p. 1192). Part of this obligation of service, Dr. Abell explained to the assembled physicians, was "the fundamental tenet of the American Medical Association that the poverty of a patient should demand the gratuitous service of a physician." Beyond this obligation to treat the poor without charge, however, Dr. Abell stated the AMA's position that "the individual physician has a right to determine the conditions of his service" (p. 1193).

While this view of physicians as agents of reason, worthy of our trust to act autonomously on behalf of patients, exerted substantial influence over governmental policy toward medical care, a historical examination of the ways in which physicians' professional organizations actually exerted the authority delegated to them offers a very different picture (Freidson 1970). While physicians were granted this authority because of their specialized knowledge and skills, they often used this power to further their own ends. In this view of physicians as agents of power, the medical profession is seen as using its control over knowledge to limit entry into the profession and to maintain political sovereignty over the system of medical care. The power of the medical profession has been used to support and protect the role of the individual physician as self-interested entrepreneur. Those interests were best served by establishing and maintaining the policy principle that medical care was, as described by Dr. Sade (1971), "a service that is provided by doctors and others to people who wish to purchase it" (p. 1289) under "conditions of . . . service" determined solely by the physician, as Dr. Abell described (Abell 1938, p. 1193).

By creating and maintaining a system that approached medical care as a market commodity, physicians were able to establish their right to charge a separate fee for each service they provided, and to base that fee on whatever the market would bear. In 1934, the AMA established the explicit policy that once the fee for the medical service was set, "the immediate cost should be borne by the patient if able to pay at the time of service" (American Medical Association 1934a, p. 2200). Except for the poor, patients were purchasing medical care from their physician as a market commodity and, as is typical of market exchanges, were expected to pay for it at the time the service was rendered. Thus the name applied to the system of medical care that predominated throughout much of the twentieth century: fee-for-service.

In making medical decisions in a fee-for-service system, physicians were simultaneously looking out for the needs of the patient and for their own financial interests. As medical science and medical technology evolved and expanded, more care came to be perceived as better care. More care also generated higher fees. Both the perceived quality of care and the physician's income went up as the physician did more for the patient. This system of dual loyalties, while seemingly good for patients, can also place the physician in the role of an imperfect agent when making or recommending treatment decisions on the patient's behalf (Freidson 1970). In deciding whether a patient does or does not need additional care, the financial incentive might push the physician to provide care that otherwise might not be seen as medically necessary.

These alternative views of the medical profession, as agents of reason or as agents of power, are described in table 2.1. As we proceed in our examination of health care in the United States, we will find that neither view offers a fully accurate description of the US medical profession. Physicians act neither as agents of pure reason nor as agents of pure power. Medicine in this country has instead evolved as a blending of the two models.

> **CONCEPT 2.1**
>
> Two policies established early in the twentieth century had major effects on our system of care and contributed to our current problems:
>
> 1. Approaching medical care as a market commodity
> 2. Granting sovereignty to the medical profession over the organization and financing of medical care

For much of the twentieth century, our health care system and the medical profession's authority over it were stable and noncontroversial. Only in the past few decades, as the rising cost of health care and the growing number of uninsured Americans increasingly commanded public attention, has there been a full examination of

TABLE 2.1. Two ways to look at the medical profession in the United States

Physicians as agents of reason (see Parsons 1951, 1975)	Physicians as agents of power (see Freidson 1970)

Authority of physicians based on:
    Specialized knowledge
    Technical skills
    Professional ethics
	Authority of physicians based on:
	    Control of knowledge
	    Limited entry into profession
	    Sovereignty over system

Physicians are seen as altruistic healers	Physicians act as self-interested entrepreneurs
Physicians adopt a paternalistic approach to patients	Physicians face conflicting loyalties in their dealings with patients
Physicians act as unbiased agents for their patients	Physicians act as imperfect agents for their patients

the effects of approaching medical care as a market commodity and sanctioning the use of medical knowledge as a source of political and economic power. Nonetheless, these two policies have had profound impacts on the development of our health care system and have differentiated our system from those of other industrialized countries.

THE COST OF CARE—NOW AND IN THE FUTURE

In 1970, people in the United States spent a total of $73 billion, or an average of $341 per person per year, on all types of health care combined. The total national expenditure on health care in 1970 represented 7.1 percent of the gross domestic product (GDP). At that time, people talked about a national health care expenditure of 7 percent of GDP as representing a "crisis" that needed to be addressed urgently.

In 2010, the year ACA was enacted, the United States spent $2.6 trillion on health care, or about $8,400 per person (Hartman et al. 2015). This level of expenditure represented 17.4 percent of GDP, more than twice the amount of GDP apportioned to health care in 1970. The rate of increase in health care costs had slowed somewhat in 2009 following the 2008 recession, rising only 3.8 percent, the lowest rate of growth in health care costs since we began keeping track of costs in 1960 (Mitka 2010). The year 2010 represented an increase of 3.9 percent. Without taking into account the potential effects of ACA, federal analysts had also predicted continued future growth in national health care expenditures, with health care expected to consume 19.3 percent of GDP by 2019 (Truffer et al. 2010).

Economist Victor Fuchs has pointed out that, over the years, health care costs have risen an average of 2.8 percentage points faster than GDP. If this gap continues, Fuchs suggested, the percentage of GDP going to pay for health care can be expected to double every twenty-six years (Fuchs 2010). Fuchs argued that there are "distinctive institutional features of health care and their consequences" that "distinguish health care from other goods and services" (p. 1859). Fuchs suggested that market competition alone cannot change this long-term pattern. Instead, we will need to rely on a combination of "government regulation and self-regulation [of the medical profession] through professional ethics" (p. 1860).

Where does all this money for health care come from and where does it go? Figures 2.1 and 2.2 show the sources of the money that pays for health care and the principal categories of national health care expenditures. To gain a better sense of what these data mean, we can compare our country to other developed countries. The Organisation for Economic Co-operation and Development (OECD) compiles economic and other statistics from thirty-four of the world's leading developed countries. Table 2.2 shows national expenditures on health care for a selection of OECD countries. In 2013, the United States reported to the OECD that it spent 16.4 percent of GDP on health care. This was by far the highest expenditure in the world. The closest countries to the United States were Switzerland, with an expenditure of 11.1 percent, and both Germany and Sweden, with total expenditures of 11.0 percent.

Every year, the US government publishes predictions of where health care costs will go in the future. If current government projections through 2019 are accurate, by that time nearly $1 of every $5 in the entire national economy will be spent on health care. The difference between the share of our economy going to health care and what other developed countries spend will be even larger than it is today. This investment in health care will be at the expense of other sectors of the economy, such as education and national infrastructure. We will have less money available for schools, for roads and other forms of transportation, and for investing in the capital and technology necessary for continued expansion of the economy.

Beyond the effects on the US economy in general, health care expenditures in the range of 20 percent of GDP will have severe consequences for government as well. Recall from figure 2.1 that in 2013, governments at all levels—federal, state, and local—were

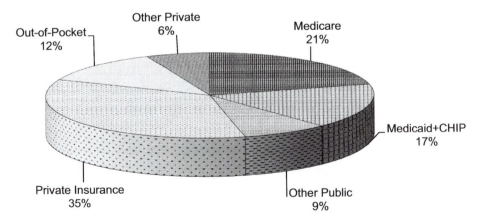

FIGURE 2.1. Health care expenditures in the United States, 2013: Where the money came from. *Source:* Data from US Centers for Medicare and Medicaid Services.

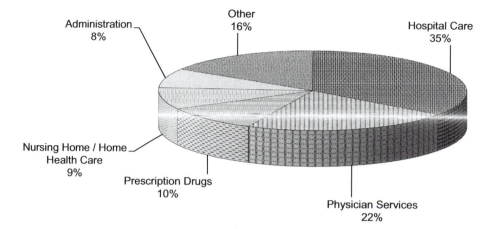

FIGURE 2.2. Health care expenditures in the United States, 2013: Where the money went. *Source:* Data from US Centers for Medicare and Medicaid Services.

TABLE 2.2. National health care expenses as a percentage of GDP for selected countries, 2013

Country	Percentage of GDP
Canada	10.2
France	10.9
Germany	11.0
Greece	9.2
Japan	10.2
Sweden	11.0
Switzerland	11.1
United Kingdom	8.5
United States	16.4

Source: Data from OECD.

responsible for a combined 47 percent of all health care expenditures (Medicare, Medicaid, and other public expenditures). Following the enactment of ACA, government expenditures will rise to more than half of all health expenditures. New sources of revenue included in ACA will offset part of this increase. Governments rely on taxation to obtain revenue. Unless tax rates change, tax revenues generally rise at the same rate as GDP. As described previously, however, historically the cost of care has risen more rapidly than GDP—especially during times of recession, when health care costs have continued to rise even in the face of a shrinking economy.

Consider the effect on governments of health care expenditures continuing to rise faster than GDP, and therefore faster than tax revenues. More than half of future increases in health care costs that are over and above the rise in GDP will have to come from government sources. *For every dollar that health care costs go up faster than GDP, government sources will pay more than half.* This is an important concept to understand.

How will government come up with the money to pay for this rise, given that *tax revenues increase only as fast as GDP increases?* There will be two options:

1. increase tax rates to cover the increased cost of care or
2. borrow the needed money, thus adding to government debt.

Neither option is palatable to politicians or the American public. Either would have a severe, long-term, destabilizing effect on the US economy. Chernew and colleagues have written about "The Specter of Financial Armageddon" if nothing is done to change this pattern (Chernew et al. 2010). Governments will face a serious dilemma if a solution is not found to the rising cost of health care.

This dilemma will be especially difficult for state and local governments, which typically are forbidden by law from engaging in deficit spending. To maintain health care expenditures at this level, growing faster than GDP growth and thus faster than the growth in state and local tax revenues, state and local governments have to either raise taxes or divert funds away from other programs such as education. This is why many states, facing an increasing crisis in their attempts to keep up with health care spending, are instead considering reducing the amount of care they pay for. Because those who receive the care paid for by state and local governments are typically the least well-off members of our society, this means that any cuts in state and local spending on health care will be felt disproportionately by those who can least afford to pay for care on their own.

> **CONCEPT 2.2**
>
> If the rising cost of health care as a percentage of GDP is not slowed, there will be substantial effects on our economy.
>
> - Investment in other sectors of the economy will shrink.
> - The federal government will have to either raise taxes or go increasingly into debt.
> - State and local governments will face increasing budgetary strain; many will reduce health benefits to their least well-off residents.

What's Causing the Rising Cost of Health Care?

To fully appreciate the implications of the rising cost of health care in this country, we need to have a better grasp of its causes. Simple inflation is, of course, one reason— both prices in general and medical prices in particular tend to rise with time. Typically, the price of medical care will rise faster than prices in general, contributing to the rising share of GDP devoted to care. Even when one adjusts for price inflation, however, the cost of health care measured in constant dollars continues to go up at a rapid rate.

Three general forces contribute to this increase in the cost of care:

1. The US population increases over time.
2. The number of people receiving treatment for a specific illness may go up for reasons not associated with increases in the population. (This is referred to as the "treated prevalence.") Either the illness is becoming more common or more people with the condition may seek treatment (e.g., mental illness).

3. The cost of treating a specific illness may go up independently of the number of people who have that illness. This will typically be due to new, more advanced (and more high-tech) treatments becoming available, replacing older, less expensive (and more low-tech) treatments.

A study published by researchers at Emory University differentiated between these three causes of rising costs in health care (Thorpe et al. 2004). They looked at the increase in the cost of care for the noninstitutionalized US population between 1987 and 2000. Controlling for inflation, health care costs increased about 3 percent per year during this period. As a proportion of GDP, health care rose from 10.5 percent to 13.3 percent during this period.

The researchers found that ten specific illnesses accounted for nearly half of this rise in the cost of care; five of these conditions accounted for more than 30 percent of the rise. The same five conditions that accounted for the highest expenditures in 2002—heart condition, trauma, cancer, mental disorders, and asthma—were also the most costly conditions in 2012 (Soni 2015).

Thorpe and colleagues then estimated how much of the rise in the cost of care attributable to these five conditions could be assigned to each of the three possible forces described previously. They found that increases in the cost of treating a specific disease, caused by the increased costs of newer, more high-tech treatments, were the largest source of the rising cost of care. Looking at spending for the period 1980–2006, Starr and colleagues (2014) came to a similar conclusion, finding that "rising costs of treatment accounted for 70 percent of growth in real average health care spending from 1980 to 2006" (p. 823). Moses and colleagues (2013) undertook a related analysis of factors contributing to the rise in health care costs between 2000 and 2011 and similarly concluded: "Since 2000, price . . . , not demand for services or aging of the population, produced 91% of cost increases" (p. 1947).

Growing Concerns about the Quality of Health Care in the United States

Beyond the rising cost of health care in the United States, it is also important to consider the quality of that care. To what extent can we be assured that the increasing amounts we spend on our system of health care provide us with care that is of the highest available quality? This question pertains both to the care provided by physicians and other health professionals, and to the care provided by hospitals and other health care institutions.

The Quality of Care Provided by Physicians

Dr. John Wennberg, of Dartmouth Medical School, first started looking in the 1970s at differences in the way physicians treat specific diseases. He found that, for a variety of conditions, there were consistent differences across geographic regions in the rates at which certain surgical procedures and other treatments were applied. Physicians in community A, for example, might use a surgical approach to prostate cancer at a certain rate, while physicians in community B might use that procedure at a substantially lower rate, relying instead on nonsurgical treatments. Wennberg and his colleagues consistently found these differences in regional patterns, referred to as "small area variations," for a wide variety of medical conditions.

Which community of physicians uses the higher-quality approach to treatment—community A or community B? That depends on whom you ask. Physicians from community A might respond that they are being appropriately aggressive in using a surgical approach, while their colleagues in community B are being too cautious. Physicians from community B, of course, might respond in the opposite way. They are using surgery appropriately, while their community A colleagues are being too cavalier in using surgery. A principal benefit of the decades of research done by Dr. Wennberg, culminating in the publication in 1998 of the *Dartmouth Atlas of Health Care*, has been the need for physicians to confront this quality conundrum.

The answer as to which community of physicians—A or B—is using a higher-quality approach to treating their patients can be determined only by using scientific evidence from well-designed studies comparing alternative approaches to care. There is a growing consensus both among physicians and among health policy analysts that "evidence-based medicine"—that is, medical care determined by scientific research to provide optimal outcomes—should be the standard by which the quality of physician care is judged. Scientific research of this type has an especially important role to play when there are multiple alternatives available for treating a specific condition. Research that compares outcomes of alternative treatments is often referred to as "comparative effectiveness research" (CER). As discussed in chapter 3, ACA includes major new programmatic efforts and funding to expand CER.

The Quality of Care Provided by Hospitals

The Institute of Medicine (IOM) of the National Academy of Sciences saw a need to study the issue of quality in the care provided to patients in hospitals and other large health care institutions. In the 1990s, it convened a Committee on Quality of Health Care in America. This committee of national experts, drawn from industry, health care organizations, professional organizations, and universities, studied the issue of quality and delivered its report in 1999 (Kohn et al. 1999). The report, titled *To Err Is Human: Building a Safer Health System*, came to some disturbing conclusions about the quality of the care provided in US hospitals: "At least 44,000 people, and perhaps as many as 98,000 people, die in hospitals each year as a result of medical errors that could have been prevented. . . . Preventable medical errors in hospitals exceed attributable deaths to such feared threats as motor-vehicle wrecks, breast cancer, and AIDS" (p. 1).

The IOM report concluded that the problems with medical mistakes are not principally due to individual human error but rather "are caused by faulty systems, processes, and conditions that lead people to make mistakes or fail to prevent them" (p. 2). It recommended two principal mechanisms to improve hospital safety:

1. Creating a "nationwide public mandatory reporting system," as well as additional voluntary reporting systems
2. Relying on existing oversight organizations to focus added scrutiny on the issue of health care quality

Both mechanisms have been initiated, with some preliminary but positive results.

Hibbard, Stockard, and Tusler (2005) reported on a study done in Wisconsin comparing the change in quality over a two-year period for three groups of hospitals: (1) those who received an independent report on the quality of their care with that report made public, (2) those who received an independent report on the quality of their care with that report kept confidential, and (3) those who received no report on the quality of their care. The quality in hospitals confronting public disclosure of their report increased significantly more than in hospitals receiving a confidential report. The lowest improvement in quality was in those hospitals receiving no report. This and other studies (e.g., Jha et al. 2005b) suggest that a system of publicly distributed "report cards" may encourage hospitals to take steps internally to improve the quality of the care they provide.

CONCEPT 2.3

Despite spending increasing amounts on health care in the United States, substantial problems remain in the quality of our care. Efforts to improve quality focus on evidence-based medicine, rewarding high-quality care, and monitoring the quality of care through "report cards" and accreditation standards.

The Joint Commission on Accreditation of Healthcare Organizations (JCAHO) is the principal body nationally that monitors hospital performance directly and sets standards for hospital accreditation. In 2002, JCAHO implemented a new program of quality improvement based on standardized performance measures. Williams et al. (2005) reported that these new standards were associated with significant improvement in the quality of care for diseases such as heart disease and pneumonia.

Following the publication in 1999 of *To Err Is Human*, Congress directed the Agency for Health Care Research and Quality (AHRQ) to study the issue of health care quality and to issue an annual report of its findings. The National Healthcare Quality Report for 2014 identified a "national quality strategy" that prioritized six areas for continued improvement: patient safety, person-centered care, care coordination, effective treatment, healthy living, and care affordability (Agency for Health

Care Research and Quality 2014). AHRQ will continue to monitor the issue of health care quality and will issue reports on a regular basis regarding our progress toward meeting established quality goals.

THE GROWING NUMBER OF UNINSURED AMERICANS

The two aspects of the US health care system discussed earlier that make us unique in the developed world—approaching health care as a market commodity and the amount of GDP spent on health care—have led to a third characteristic of our system that is also unique: the large segments of our population living without health insurance. Health care has become so expensive that fewer and fewer people can afford basic health insurance. In 2010, 50 million people in this country were without health insurance. Despite two national programs to provide health insurance to children from low-income families, this number included more than 7.3 million children (data from US Census Bureau website). For those under the age of 65, more than one person in six was unable to afford insurance. California had one in five residents without health insurance; Texas had one in four residents without insurance. In families earning less than 200 percent of the federal poverty level (FPL), 32.2 percent of people were uninsured, even after taking into account government-financed insurance through the Medicaid program for poor families. In families earning between 200 percent and 400 percent of the FPL, 14.8 percent of people were uninsured.

During much of the twentieth century, little attention was paid to the issue of the uninsured. Most physicians would take care of some poor and uninsured patients for free. Physicians would often include a number of these "charity cases" in their practice, in a manner similar to lawyers taking certain cases "pro bono." As described previously, the ethics of the medical profession expected physicians to provide this type of care. With the rising cost of medical care, and with the advent in the 1960s of government programs to pay for care for the poor and the elderly, the "charity patient" tradition has largely been abandoned by US physicians.

Who are the uninsured? It is easy to think of them as chronically poor people who do not work and who rely on government welfare for their existence. This picture could not be further from the truth. Unemployed or homeless individuals make up only a small part of the uninsured. Seventy-seven percent of adults between 18 and 64 without health insurance in 2010 were in a family in which at least one adult worked either part time or full time during the year. They are the workers in low-wage jobs, often in small companies that do not offer health insurance to their workers.

A full-time worker can be uninsured for one of three reasons (Kaiser Family Foundation 2009):

1. The person works for a company that does not offer health insurance to any of its workers. (In 2009, only 60% of firms offered health insurance benefits to their workers.)

2. The company offers health insurance, at least to some workers, but the worker is not eligible for the company-sponsored plan. (In 2009, 19% of workers in companies that offered health insurance benefits were ineligible for those benefits.)

3. The company does offer health insurance and the employee is eligible; however, the worker chooses not to sign up for the plan, due to the share of the plan cost he or she must pay. (In 2009, 19% of workers eligible for health insurance benefits chose not to enroll in those benefits.)

For each of these categories, the lower the worker's wage, the more likely he or she is to be affected.

A factor that contributes to this disproportionate lack of insurance among lower-wage workers is the size of the firm employing the worker. The smaller the firm, the less likely it is to offer health insurance to its workers. Before ACA, 46 percent of firms with fewer than ten employees offered health insurance to their workers, while 98 percent of firms with more than two hundred workers did so. Accordingly, 31 percent of workers in firms with fewer than twenty-five workers were uninsured, while 10 percent of workers in firms with more than 500 workers were uninsured.

If one thinks of the jobs that involve low-wage workers and small firms, it should be clear that the service sector is a principal source of uninsured workers. Restaurants, small businesses, contractors, and similar types of firms often fail to provide health insurance for their workers. These types of firms play a crucial role in our economy, yet they have been hit especially hard by the rising cost of health care. Chapter 5 looks at the historical roots of our employment-based system of health insurance. We will see that the adoption of a system that relies on employers to bear most of the cost of health insurance was never fully thought out.

THE HEALTH OF OUR SOCIETY: WHAT DO WE GET FOR OUR MONEY?

The United States pays more for health insurance than any other country, both per capita and as a percentage of GDP. What do we get for all the money we spend? One would hope that paying for so much health care would make our society one of the healthiest in the world, yet nothing could be further from the truth. In comparing ourselves to other developed countries, we lag far behind in most of the broad indices that measure the overall state of a society's health.

Infant mortality is one of the most common indicators used to gauge the health of a nation. Infant mortality measures how many of 1,000 babies born alive will die

TABLE 2.3. Infant mortality (infant deaths per 1,000 live births) for selected countries, 2013

Country	Percentage of GDP spent on health care	Infant mortality
Canada*	10.2	4.8
France	10.9	3.6
Germany	11.0	3.3
Greece	9.2	3.7
Japan	10.2	2.1
Sweden	11.0	2.7
Switzerland	11.1	3.9
United Kingdom	8.5	3.8
United States**	16.4	6.0

Source: Data from OECD.
*Data from 2011; **Data from 2012.

before their first birthday. Infant mortality for selected OECD countries is shown in table 2.3, along with the percentage of GDP each country spends on health care. In 2013, the United States reported an infant mortality rate of 6.0 deaths per 1,000 live births. This placed us in thirty-first position among the thirty-four OECD countries, worse off than countries such as Hungary, Poland, and the Slovak Republic. Only Mexico, Chile, and Turkey reported worse infant mortality than the United States.

It should be apparent that there is little relation between how much a country spends on health care and the health of that society, as measured by infant mortality. Even though the United States spends nearly twice as much as Japan on health care, babies in the United States still die at nearly three times the rate of babies in Japan.

Another common health index is life expectancy. Life expectancy can be measured in two ways:

1. Life expectancy at birth
2. Age-adjusted life expectancy (How long, on average, can a person who is a certain age today expect to live?)

Life expectancy, like infant mortality, is often used to measure the health of a society. It is usually reported separately for men and women, because biological differences between the sexes historically give women an advantage over men in longevity. How does the United States compare to other developed countries in this statistic? The answer is shown in table 2.4.

In 2013, male babies born in the United States could expect to live, on average, 76.4 years, while females born the same year could expect to live 81.2 years. Of the thirty-four OECD countries, the United States ranked twenty-sixth for male life expectancy and thirtieth for female life expectancy.

TABLE 2.4. Life expectancy at birth, in years, for selected countries, 2013

Country	Male	Female
Canada*	79.3	83.6
France	79.0	85.6
Germany	78.6	83.2
Greece	78.7	84.0
Japan	80.2	86.6
Sweden	80.2	83.8
Switzerland	80.7	85.0
United Kingdom	79.2	82.9
United States	76.4	81.2

Source: Data from OECD.
*Data are for 2011.

TABLE 2.5. Life expectancy for men and women at ages 40, 65, and 80 for selected countries, 2013

Country	Men at age 40	Women at age 40	Men at age 65	Women at age 65	Men at age 80	Women at age 80
Canada*	40.9	44.6	18.8	21.7	8.9	10.6
France	40.4	46.4	19.3	23.6	9.2	11.6
Germany	39.7	43.9	18.2	21.1	8.5	9.5
Greece	40.0	44.8	18.7	21.6	8.9	9.7
Japan	41.3	47.3	19.1	24.0	8.6	11.5
Sweden	41.3	44.5	18.8	21.3	8.2	9.7
Switzerland	41.8	45.7	19.4	22.4	8.6	10.4
United Kingdom	40.5	43.8	18.6	20.9	8.5	9.7
United States	38.7	42.6	17.9	20.5	8.3	9.7

Source: Data from OECD.
Notes: For a person who has attained the specified age, the table shows how many more years that person can be expected to live.
*Data are for 2011.

In addition to measuring life expectancy at birth, additional information about the health of a society can be obtained by looking at age-specific life expectancy: for adults who have attained a certain age, how many additional years can they expect to live on average? Table 2.5 compares the United States with the other developed countries shown in tables 2.3 and 2.4. Using data from the OECD for 2013, it compares additional life expectancy in these nine countries for those who have reached age 40, age 65, and age 80.

The United States is ninth of these nine countries in life expectancy at birth. We also have the lowest additional life expectancy for both men and women at age 40 and at age 65, respectively. The United States has risen to eighth place for both men and women at age 80.

It appears that a principal health benefit our society enjoys as a result of our heavy investment in health care, at least in terms of additional life expectancy, only starts to show up for our 80-year-olds. This is understandable, because the common causes of death for people in this age group—heart disease, cancer, and strokes—are often amenable to high-tech treatment. Because the United States has more health care technology available than any other country, it stands to reason that our oldest citizens should fare relatively well. At ages younger than 80, however, there seems to be little relationship between the amount we spend on health care and the health of our population. (The reader should note that for all ages, and for both men and women, life expectancy is better in Canada than it is in the United States. This fact will be of particular relevance when we compare the US and Canadian systems of health care in the next chapter.)

As we have seen so far, it is difficult to compare the quality of national health systems when different measures of quality give such disparate rankings. To reconcile some of these differences, the World Health Organization (WHO) combined eight different measures to create a single measure of the overall quality of a nation's health system. Using this combined measure, the United States ranked thirty-seventh in the world (World Health Organization 2000). In a comprehensive review of studies comparing US health care with that of other developed countries, Docteur and Berenson (2009) concluded, "on the basis of this review it is safe to say that the U.S. is not preeminent in quality."

In 2013, the National Research Council and the Institute of Medicine issued a report commissioned by the National Institutes of Health that explored the reasons behind our country's consistent pattern of lower health status than other developed countries. Titled *US Health in International Perspective: Shorter Lives, Poorer Health*, the report summarized its findings. "No single factor can fully explain the U.S. health disadvantage. . . . More likely, the U.S. health disadvantage has multiple causes and involves some combination of inadequate health care, unhealthy behaviors, adverse economic and social conditions, and environmental factors, as well as public policies and social values that shape those conditions" (National Research Council and Institute of Medicine 2013, p. 3).

> **CONCEPT 2.4**
>
> The United States spends more on health care than any other country in the world. Despite this high level of expenditure, we have one of the lowest levels of overall health of any developed country.

WHAT DETERMINES THE OVERALL HEALTH OF A SOCIETY?

It should by now be clear that, at the level of the society, health and health care are not the same thing. Using the aforementioned indicators, we find little if any correlation between the amount spent on the health care system and the health of a society. As the country spending by far the most, the United States still has health indices close to the worst.

Rather than the amount of money spent on health care, other factors largely determine the overall health of a society. Principal among these factors is overall standard of living, typically measured by per capita income and the average level of education in a society. Victor Fuchs, one of the founders of the study of health economics, has repeatedly emphasized this relationship: "The basic finding is the following: when the state of medical science and other health-determining variables are held constant, the marginal contribution of medical care to health is very small in modern nations. . . . For most of man's history, [per capita] income has been the primary determinant of health and life expectancy—the major explanation for differences in health among nations and among groups within a nation" (1986, pp. 274–76).

An excellent example of the ways in which social class and standard of living affect health independently from health care is seen in Great Britain. The Whitehall study looked at the health of people working in the British Civil Service (Marmot and Theorell 1988). Because Britain has had universal health coverage and a nationalized health system since World War II, all members of the Civil Service have access to basically the same level of health care. Thus, differences in health care cannot explain differences in health.

The study found a clear correlation between occupational category (and therefore education) and health. There was a threefold difference in mortality between the highest and the lowest ranks of the Civil Service. Even at the upper ranks, the higher on the scale a worker was, the lower the mortality he or she faced. This was true even though all subjects of the study

- worked in office jobs,
- were regularly employed,
- came from a relatively uniform ethnic background, and
- lived and worked in greater London.

These data should not be taken to mean that, in the face of the growing cost of health care in this country, there has been no improvement in overall health. Quite the contrary, data from more than fifty years show dramatic increases in health. In 1960, when the United States spent 5.2 percent of GDP on health care, infant mortality was at the level of 26 deaths per 1,000 live births; now it is 6. Male life expectancy was 66.6 years in 1960, compared to 76.4 years now. Female life expectancy went from 73.1 to 81.2 years. It is simply that, despite these improvements in overall health, the United States still lags far behind other developed countries.

There is substantial suggestion that improvements in the level of health in this country may be due more to

CONCEPT 2.5

Among developed countries, there is little correlation between the amount a country spends on health care and the overall level of health of that country. The health of a society has more to do with the level of education and income than it does with health care.

lifestyle changes than to improvements in health care. Studies from 1991 (Burke et al.) and from 2010 (Wijeysundera et al.) confirmed that the substantial decline in the death rate from heart disease was related as much to improved diet, exercise, and other lifestyle factors as it was to improvements in drugs or surgical treatments.

Victor Fuchs provides an example of the importance of lifestyle issues in his book *Who Shall Live?* (1983). He cited data for Nevada and Utah, two states with roughly comparable populations in terms of ethnic background, socioeconomic status, education, climate, and availability of medical care. In the 1960s, infant mortality in Nevada was 40 percent higher than in Utah, while life expectancy in Nevada was 40 to 50 percent lower than in Utah. If income, education, and medical care cannot explain these differences, what can?

Cigarette and alcohol consumption was markedly lower in Utah, due largely to the influence of the Mormon Church. Correspondingly, death rates from lung cancer and cirrhosis of the liver were two to three times higher in Nevada than in Utah. Lifestyle factors in Nevada and Utah, rather than medical care, seem to have explained the different levels of health in the two states.

In 2002, McGinnis and colleagues reviewed a range of demographic and health research on the principal determinants of population health in the United States. Their conclusion was clear: "Behavior patterns represent the single most prominent domain of influence over health prospects in the United States" (p. 82). Building on McGinnis's data, Schroeder (2007) estimated that, of the many deaths that occur prematurely in the United States, 40 percent are directly attributable to behavioral patterns, chief among them smoking, obesity and inactivity, and alcohol use. As Schroeder described, "The single greatest opportunity to improve health and reduce premature deaths lies in personal behavior" (p. 1222).

In 2014, Victor Fuchs reiterated his earlier conclusions from his 1983 study: "Among developed countries, there is no positive association between health care expenditures and life expectancy. . . . Epidemiologists have identified a dozen or more socioeconomic and behavioral differences between the United States and other high-income countries that are probably adverse to health" (Fuchs 2014, p. 2095).

It appears that further increasing expenditures for health care cannot be expected to result in substantial improvements in the overall health of American society. Nonetheless, there has been a strong social movement to provide increased access for the uninsured. Providing health insurance to the one-sixth of our society that is uninsured will of course add to the overall cost of health care.

There has also been an equally forceful movement to restrain the cost of medical care. Thus, for years we have faced two powerful, opposing forces: the need to expand access to health care and the need to restrain costs of care.

SUMMARY

For several decades, the United States has faced three major policy challenges in the area of health care:

1. The rapidly rising cost of providing care has resulted in an increasing share of our national economy going to support our health care system. We spend more of our GDP on health care than any other country in the world, even though we trail most developed countries in measures of population health such as infant mortality and life expectancy.
2. Researchers have raised serious and continuing questions about the quality of the care provided by our doctors and our hospitals.
3. We have been confronted by a rising number of Americans with no health insurance and, as a result, seriously impaired access to care.

The roots of our three-part dilemma are more than one hundred years old. Early in the twentieth century, our society elected to approach health care as a market commodity, available to those with the resources to pay for it. Physicians, working through their professional organizations to influence political and legal aspects of health care delivery, were able to attain a position of substantial power. They used that power for much of the twentieth century to ensure that health care remained a market good, with government playing a relatively minor role. At the beginning of the twenty-first century, we confronted the policy consequences—cost, quality, and access—that evolved as a result of those earlier policy choices. ACA, signed into law in March 2010, was an important step in addressing these policy issues.

HOW THE AFFORDABLE CARE ACT ADDRESSES THE ISSUES OF HEALTH CARE COST, QUALITY, AND ACCESS

In an Op-Ed published in August 2009, President Obama laid out four broad policy goals for health reform: (1) expanding the availability of health insurance to those who are uninsured, (2) controlling the cost of health care, (3) making Medicare more efficient in order to reduce costs, and (4) providing consumer protections against discrimination by health insurance companies based on a preexisting illness or condition. In his targeting the issues of health care costs and access to insurance, Obama was addressing two of the three principal policy issues facing US health care. In his Op-Ed remarks, he also addressed the issue of quality by promising the American people that "we will make sure that no insurance company or government bureaucrat gets between you and the care you need" (Obama 2009b).

Once it was signed into law, ACA, in combination with the accompanying reconciliation act, has begun to carry out President Obama's goals. Starting in 2014, health insurance became available to millions of people who previously were uninsured. This expansion of coverage took place through a combination of reform of the private market for health insurance and a major expansion of the existing federal-state Medicaid program. I describe these changes in more detail in chapters 5 and 7.

Coverage under these new policies established by ACA became effective in January 2014. After a tumultuous start to the online enrollment resources that first became available in October 2013, enrollment in the newly established state and federal health benefit exchanges (HBE) showed steady growth. The Congressional Budget Office (CBO) reported that 11 million people enrolled in health insurance coverage through the HBEs between January 2014 and March 2015. An additional 10 million people gained coverage through state Medicaid programs (Congressional Budget Office 2015).

As shown in figure 2.3, the US Centers for Disease Control and Prevention (2015a) reported that the United States saw substantial decreases in the number of people who were without health insurance between 2010 and March 2015. Overall, the uninsured rate dropped from 16.0 percent to 9.2 percent. The uninsured rate among children dropped from 7.8 percent to 4.6 percent; among adults younger than 65, it dropped from 22.3 percent to 13.0 percent. The largest drop was among young adults, aged 19–25, among whom the uninsured rate dropped from 33.9 percent to 16.6 percent. As discussed in chapter 5, ACA included a number of provisions targeting this young adult group, with many of these provisions taking effect in 2010, immediately on passage of ACA.

ACA addresses the issue of cost containment in two main ways: changes to the Medicare program (discussed in chapter 6) and new sources of tax revenues (described in chapter 5). While there seems to be broad consensus that ACA will meet the goal of reducing federal health care expenditures, there is less agreement as to whether ACA will be able to meet the long-term goal of constraining overall health care costs in the United States. A report issued in September 2010 by the chief actuary for the federal Center for Medicare and Medicaid Services predicted that, as a consequence of ACA, national health expenditures for the period 2010–19 would increase more than if ACA had not been passed, with expenditures rising to 19.6 percent of GDP by 2019, rather than the previously predicted amount of 19.3 percent (Sisko et al. 2010).

Enactment of ACA came shortly after the recession experienced in the United States in 2007–09—and the relatively slow economic growth that followed it. By 2011, federal analysts were reporting that not only was the overall economy growing slowly, but national health care costs were also growing substantially more slowly than in the past. "Growth in national health spending closely tracked growth in nominal gross domestic product (GDP) in 2010 and 2011, and health spending as a share of GDP

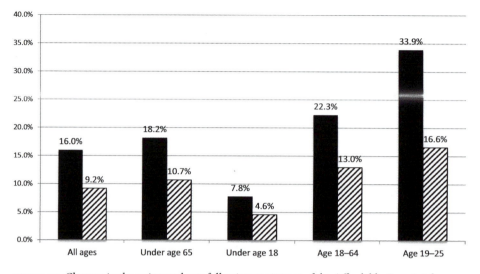

2010 **2015**

FIGURE 2.3. Changes in the uninsured rate following enactment of the Affordable Care Act, by age. *Source:* US Centers for Disease Control and prevention (2015).

remained stable from 2009 through 2011" (Hartman et al. 2013, p. 87). This slowdown in growth continued through 2013, with health care remaining at 17.4 percent of GDP from 2009 through 2013 (Hartman et al. 2015).

This slowdown in spending was also seen in overall Medicare spending, with per beneficiary spending, originally projected to grow 5.9 percent annually between 2009 and 2013, instead growing an average of 1.5 percent per year. Overall Medicare spending, originally projected to grow during this period at a rate of 8.4 percent per year, instead grew 3.4 percent per year (US Department of Health and Human Services 2015b).

This slowdown in the rate of growth of health care spending is not expected to continue, however. Federal analysts have now projected that the share of GDP going to health care will have begun to rise again in 2014 and will continue to rise over the following decade, reaching a projected 19.6 percent of GDP in 2024, rather than in 2019 as originally predicted (Keehan et al. 2015). Blumenthal and colleagues (2013) have suggested that rather than being a "Giant Slain," the growth in national health care costs remain a "Sleeping Giant." They analyzed the pattern of changes in health care costs from 1961 through 2013 and reported the following: "A central finding of our analysis is that, regardless of what happens to cost trends, current spending is far higher than needed, and it demands continued efforts at cost control. . . . The major factor in cost growth during the past 50 years has been the development and diffusion of new medical technology . . . but evidence of waste is equally impressive" (pp. 2551–53).

ACA addresses the issue of maintaining the quality of health care in a number of ways. It expands primary care services through a restructuring of the way primary care is delivered, described in chapter 4. It also expands programs for comparative effectiveness research (CER) to bring a major new focus to the issue of comparing the clinical outcomes of alternative ways of approaching the diagnosis and treatment of illness. CER, if successful, has the potential to shift the definition of "quality" in medical care from one that focuses on whether a treatment is newer or more high-tech to one that focuses on how well the treatment actually works in the context of its comparative costs. In chapter 13, I describe CER and the related issue of whether balancing costs with clinical outcomes constitutes health care "rationing." ACA also includes a range of new programs that focus on monitoring the quality of care provided by doctors, hospitals, and other providers, and linking future payments for care to these quality metrics. I discuss these new programs in chapter 6.

Since the passage of ACA in 2010, public opinion about it has fluctuated, reflecting the often caustic tone of the debate within Congress and between the major political parties about the value of and the eventual fate of ACA. The Kaiser Family Foundation has tracked public opinion about ACA since its passage (DiJulio et al. 2015). In July 2010, 50 percent of respondents reported a favorable opinion of ACA, while 35 percent reported an unfavorable opinion about it. In July 2014, following the multiple technical problems encountered during the initial online enrollment period for ACA-subsidized coverage, the share of respondents voicing a favorable opinion had fallen to 37 percent, with 53 percent reporting an unfavorable opinion. The second enrollment period went much more smoothly, and by August 2015, 44 percent of respondents reported a favorable opinion, with 41 percent reporting an unfavorable opinion.

Perhaps not surprisingly, opinions continue to differ substantially based on which political party a respondent reports an affiliation. In August 2015, 74 percent of Republicans reported that they favored either scaling back ACA or eliminating it completely, while 79 percent of Democrats favored either implementing the law as originally passed or expanding it further to increase its coverage. The elections of November 2016 may have a profound impact on ACA, and on health care in America, depending on which political party demonstrates more electoral support.

3

Health Care as a Reflection of Underlying Cultural Values and Institutions

THE CULTURAL BASIS OF HEALTH CARE: COMPARING THE UNITED STATES AND CANADA

In 1932, Walton H. Hamilton wrote that "the organization of medicine is not a thing apart which can be subjected to study in isolation. It is an aspect of culture, whose arrangements are inseparable from the general organization of society" (Hamilton 1932, p. 190). Hamilton was responding to the Report of the Committee on the Costs of Medical Care, described in chapter 1. This statement, made more than eighty years ago, still rings true in our examination of health care in the United States in the twenty-first century. To understand a nation's health care system, we must first understand the social and cultural norms and values around which that nation is organized.

To appreciate fully how the health care system in the United States reflects our unique American value system, we will first look to our neighbors to the north. Using Canada and its health care system as a mirror, we will see how differences in the organization of health care in our two countries reflect differences in the basic institutions around which our systems are organized.

It is important to recall that the American Revolution involved fourteen colonies, not just the thirteen that eventually became the United States. In some of the earliest fighting of the war, revolutionary armies captured Montreal and laid siege to Quebec. This revolutionary activity was short-lived, however, and what is now Canada remained under British rule. For many in the "fourteenth" colony of Canada, life after the Revolution seemed more attractive south of the border in the newly independent colonies. Many of those in Canada who supported the Revolution migrated south. Similarly, loyalists living in the successful, now-independent thirteen colonies thought life would be better either north of the border in Canada or back in England. Thus, in the aftermath of the American Revolution, there was a cultural migration, with those supporting the British Crown moving north and those in Canada supporting "life, liberty, and the pursuit of happiness" moving south.

Lipset (1990) summarized the fundamental similarities and differences between US and Canadian societies. Speaking of the cultural differences that arose from the time of the American Revolution, he reminds us that "the very organizing principles that frame these nations, the central cores around which institutions and events were to accommodate, were different. One was Whig and classically liberal or libertarian—doctrines that emphasize distrust of the state, egalitarianism, and populism. . . . The other was Tory and conservative in the British and European sense— accepting of the need for a strong state, for respect for authority, for deference" (p. 2).

In the United States, schoolchildren study the Declaration of Independence and learn that our society continues to be organized around the principles of "life, liberty, and the pursuit of happiness." Canadian children also learn about the founding principles of their country. In the British North America Act, the act that created the Dominion of Canada, they find that the role of the Canadian government is to assure "peace, order, and good government." Lipset (1990) described the fundamental differences between these two founding documents: "The Canadian Charter of Rights and Freedoms is not the American Bill of Rights. It preserves the principle of parliamentary supremacy and places less emphasis on individual, as distinct from group, rights than does the American document" (p. 3).

Since the American Revolution, the United States has been a country that puts primacy on the rights of individuals. Social justice is most often defined in terms of the individual. In the United States, conflicts between individual needs and group needs tend to be resolved in favor of the individual. Canada, on the other hand, has a strong social democratic tradition, a tradition of redistribution so as to maximize the common good. Canadians have come to accept and expect social policies that embody this individual-group relationship. In Canada, conflicts between individual rights and group rights tend to be resolved in favor of the common good. Table 3.1 summarizes these differences between US and Canadian societies. To see how these

TABLE 3.1. Cultural differences between the United States and Canada

United States	Canada
Distrust of central government	Accept the need for strong central government
"Life, liberty, and the pursuit of happiness"	"Peace, order, and good government"
Justice often defined in terms of what is good for the individual	Justice often defined to maximize the common good

cultural differences are reflected in our health care systems, we first examine the history of Canadian health care, followed by a parallel examination of the history of US health care.

THE HISTORY OF MEDICAL CARE IN CANADA

The British North America Act of 1867 created the Dominion of Canada. In it, responsibility for managing the delivery of health care was explicitly vested in the provinces rather than the central government. This separation of powers for health care issues remains in place today.

Canada took a serious look at establishing a national system of health care following World War I. At that time, several provinces granted statutory authority for municipalities to become directly involved in the provision of medical care. During the period of the Depression, these "municipal doctor" plans, in which local governments hired physicians to provide care to area residents, became an increasingly important source of medical care. This was especially true in the rural, agricultural provinces (Meilicke and Storch 1980).

In 1943, the report of a governmental Economic Advisory Committee recommended that a national program of medical insurance be established. It was to have been part of a larger social insurance program also covering unemployment insurance and old age security. Despite the support of both the Canadian Medical Association and the Canadian Hospital Council, the program did not become law, the result principally of the failure to achieve a financing mechanism that adequately preserved perceptions of provincial autonomy.

As a largely rural province with a widely scattered population especially hard hit by the Depression, Saskatchewan faced a particularly pressing need for governmental support of medical care. In 1944, Saskatchewan elected a populist government by giving a large legislative majority to the Cooperative Commonwealth Federation (CCF). In the face of the earlier defeat of the proposed national health care program, one of the first priorities for the CCF in Saskatchewan was to bring provincial government support to the financing of hospital care. The Saskatchewan Hospital Services Plan was passed in 1946, establishing a universal, compulsory hospital care insurance system. The program did not cover physicians' fees.

Despite increased rates of hospital use and costs in excess of initial estimates, the Saskatchewan plan maintained popular support. By 1950, three other provinces had established similar hospital insurance programs. It was only a matter of time before the others would follow. In 1957, the federal government of Canada adopted the Hospital Insurance and Diagnostic Services Act, establishing a national program of universal, compulsory hospital insurance, based on the Saskatchewan model. The program established three important principles:

1. Shared financing between the federal and the provincial governments that partially compensated for economic inequities between provinces
2. Provincial administration of the plan
3. Federally established minimum standards of participation

Saskatchewan, having previously financed hospital care solely from provincial funds, again took action that was to have national impact. The sudden addition of federal hospital funds enabled the CCF government to extend their medical insurance program to include physician care. In 1962, the province established the Saskatchewan Medical Care Insurance Plan, creating a universal, compulsory medical care system, with the provincial government maintaining a monopsony over the purchase of all medical care. (While a monopoly is an economic system with only one provider of a good, a monopsony is a system with a single payer for a good.) The plan was financed by a compulsory enrollment premium for all provincial residents. It maintained the fee-for-service method of paying physicians but established the principle that physicians must accept payment from the plan as payment in full (i.e., the physician was not allowed to bill the patient for any additional amount).

> **CONCEPT 3.1**
>
> A monopsony is an economic system that has a single payer for a set of goods or services. The Canadian health care system is an example of a government monopsony in health care, sometimes called a "single-payer" system.

The concept of government monopsony was stridently opposed by the Canadian Medical Association, its Saskatchewan division, and the American Medical Association (AMA) south of the border. (The role of the AMA in actively opposing national health insurance in Canada is seldom fully appreciated.) Nonetheless, the Saskatchewan plan was enacted despite the objections of the medical profession.

On July 1, 1962, physicians in the Saskatchewan Medical Association went on strike, refusing to participate in the plan. Leaders of the association contended that "the preservation of the basic freedoms and democratic rights of the individual is necessary to insure medical services to the people of Saskatchewan" (Taylor 1987, p. 278). Saskatchewan physicians were seen as the shock troops of the medical profession, fighting the battle against governmentally imposed medical insurance on behalf of the entire Canadian medical profession. They received strong support from the AMA in the United States, which was adamantly opposed to the plan. The AMA attempted to convey a sense of crisis to the physicians and public in Saskatchewan.

While there was some support for the strike within Saskatchewan, it received little backing from the rest of Canada. To many people, the striking physicians were seen not as altruistic professionals but as lawbreakers. By July 23, a little more than three weeks after the strike had begun, the medical profession and the government reached a compromise, and the strike was called off. The Saskatchewan Agreement created a role for private insurance companies as fiscal intermediaries, allowing physicians to bill an insurance company for their services with the insurance company being reimbursed by the government. In return, physicians agreed to accept plan payment as payment in full. In addition, the Saskatchewan government promised not to establish a salaried government medical service.

In 1964, the Royal Commission on Health Services, established by the federal government to study the issue of national health insurance, recommended that Canada set up a national program of medical care similar to Saskatchewan's. The commission's goal was to make care "available to all our residents without hindrance of any kind" (Royal Commission on Health Services 1964, p. 10). It proposed federal financial assistance for provincially administered programs. Initial response to the report was mixed. Several provinces opposed further extension of government authority over health care, supporting instead a market-based program of insurance subsidies for low-income individuals and families, as had been proposed by the Canadian Medical Association.

The Liberal Party in Canada had first made a commitment to a program of national health insurance as early as 1919. In 1965, the Liberals came to power on a widely supported platform that included establishing a national system of medical care. Under the leadership of Lester Pearson, the party pushed for such a program. In contrast to the legislative system in the United States, in a parliamentary government such as Canada's the prime minister is able to exert considerable influence over the legislative process. Pearson pursued and, despite the opposition of several provinces, in December 1966 achieved passage of the national Medicare program. Provincial participation was to be voluntary; participation, if adopted by the provinces, would result in federal payment of approximately one-half of the cost of the program. For a provincial program to qualify, it had to be comprehensive, universal, publicly administered, and portable across provinces. (A fifth principle of accessibility was added later.)

The Canadian Medicare program went into effect in 1968. The lure of a 50 percent federal cost subsidy proved to be powerful. By 1971, all ten provinces had qualifying programs, creating on a national scale the same government monopsony over the purchase of medical care that had been established in Saskatchewan. Over a period of three years, and with widespread popular support, the private market for medical insurance in Canada was effectively eliminated.

The Canadian Medicare program did not adopt a specific model for the organization or delivery of care. It was solely a financing mechanism, leaving the delivery of care to physicians and the provinces. The federal government simply agreed to reimburse 50 percent of the cost of care to any province that created a plan meeting the guiding principles. In this regard, despite some who characterize the system incorrectly, Canada does not have a system of socialized medicine. Socialized medicine involves direct government involvement in the actual provision of care through policies such as the ownership of hospitals or the employment of physicians. Hospitals in Canada are mostly privately owned. Most physicians in Canada are private, independent practitioners.

When Canadian Medicare was passed by Parliament, physicians in the province of Quebec went on strike in opposition to the plan. In Quebec, there were two separate provincial medical associations: one for general practitioners and one for specialists. The association of specialists wanted their members to be able to opt out of the plan on a case-by-case basis, billing patients directly and allowing patients to seek reimbursement from Medicare. (Those familiar with the Medicare program in the United States, discussed in chapter 6, will note that the payment mechanism sought by the specialists in Quebec was precisely the mechanism adopted by the US program only a few years earlier. The influence of the AMA on Canadian physicians' opposition to Canadian Medicare is clear.)

The specialists in Quebec voted to strike rather than participate in Medicare. In early October 1970, they held a large rally in opposition to the plan. The leaders of the specialists spoke at that rally and criticized Medicare as a "threat to liberty, freedom, and quality of care" (Taylor 1987, p. 404). The executive vice president of the AMA traveled north to speak at this rally. He supported the strike and assured any specialists who chose to do so that they could move south and establish their practices in the United States. (One should note that the cultural values espoused by the physician leaders of the Quebec strike—"liberty, freedom, and quality of care"—are more consistent with the organizing principles of US society than with the organizing principles of Canadian society. See Lipset's aforementioned comments.)

René Lévesque, at that time leader of Le Parti Québécois and later premier of Quebec, publicly criticized the physicians' strike. In doing so, he stated the following principle of Canadian society: "Organized medicine derives its power from the state, and the fact that the state has granted it a monopoly on such an indispensable service involves the responsibility to make that service available" (quoted in Taylor 1987, p. 404).

Despite government opposition, the specialists did go on strike on October 8. They refused to provide any care except for emergency cases. The Canadian press voiced a common criticism of the striking physicians, characterizing them as "operating in a social vacuum" (Taylor 1987, p. 408). Pierre Trudeau, then the prime minister of Canada, was explicit in his condemnation: "Those who would defy the law and ignore the opportunities available to them to right their wrongs, and satisfy their claims, will receive no hearing from this government. We shall ensure that the laws are respected" (quoted in Taylor 1987, p. 409).

On October 10, in an act unrelated to the Medicare controversy, Quebec's minister of labour was kidnapped and later murdered by radical separatists. Amid concerns of potential civil insurrection, the specialists called off their strike without gaining any of their demands. On November 1, Quebec Medicare began without incident, with full participation of the specialists.

Following an initial leveling of medical care costs in the period immediately following enactment of Medicare, rapid increases in the mid-1970s led to a growing concern that the costs of the program were unacceptably high, and rising. The share of Canadian gross domestic product (GDP) going to health care began to rise in ways similar to the rise seen in the United States. The federal government of Canada recognized that it needed to make future medical care costs more predictable, while the provinces wanted more direct control of financing. Accordingly, in 1977, a new arrangement was negotiated. In exchange for transferring a portion of its taxing authority to the provinces, the federal government's share of program costs was reduced from 50 percent to approximately 25 percent. In addition, future increases in the federal contribution would be limited to actual increases in GDP. Under the new formula, 100 percent of new costs exceeding the corresponding population/GDP increase would be borne by the provinces. The provinces went from being responsible for only fifty cents of every dollar spent on health care to facing responsibility for one hundred cents on the dollar for any increases in the cost of care that exceeded the growth in GDP. This limitation had a powerful effect, leading to more stringent efforts at cost control throughout Canada. For the following several years, medical care costs as a percentage of GDP were stable. As shown in figure 3.1, it was largely in this period that the gap developed between Canada and the United States in percentage of GDP going to health care.

An important modification to the original Medicare program was passed in 1984. Even though Medicare created a government monopsony on the purchase of medical care, many physicians continued the practice of "balance billing," charging patients a fee over and above the established Medicare payment. In the eyes of the Canadian government, balance billing was contrary to the principles of universality and accessibility. Led by the Ontario Medical Association, many physicians clung tenaciously to this last vestige of individual entrepreneurship. In response, the government passed the Canada Health Act in 1984. While not outlawing balance billing, it mandated that for every dollar of balance billing that occurred in a province the federal allocation to that province would correspondingly be reduced by a dollar.

The Ontario Medical Association, adamantly opposed to the act, organized a physicians' strike to protest the new restrictions. Its president contended that "today's physicians believe we have a solemn duty to preserve the professional freedom that has been handed down from generation to generation for 5000 years. It is unthinkable to us

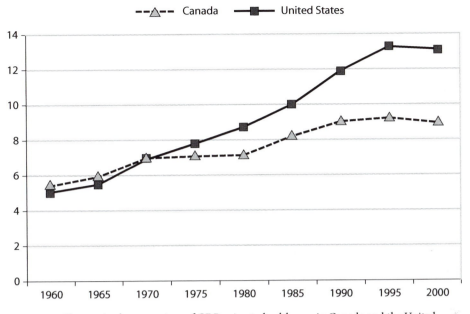

FIGURE 3.1. Changes in the percentage of GDP going to health care in Canada and the United States, 1960–2000. *Source:* Data from OECD.

that our profession's traditions, honored through the ages without the benefit of legislation, could be struck down in a modern society that has enacted a Charter of Rights and Freedoms" (quoted in Taylor 1987, p. 460).

Representatives of the Ontario government responded, "When the state grants a monopoly to an exclusive group to render an indispensable service it automatically becomes involved in whether those services are available and on what terms and conditions" (quoted in Taylor 1987, p. 460). With little support in the media, the strike was called off after twenty-eight days. As was the case in Saskatchewan twenty-two years earlier and Quebec fourteen years earlier, the Ontario physicians' strike achieved neither widespread public support nor its stated goals.

By now it should be clear that in Canada, the power of physicians and their professional associations is substantially limited, both by law and in the eyes of the public. Consistently, when physicians went on strike to protest the implementation of new health care initiatives, they were seen as violating their obligations to Canadian society. Those obligations resulted from the authority the government had granted them over the clinical practice of medicine.

The Organizing Principles of the Canadian Health Care System

From this examination of the Canadian health care system, it is possible to identify four principles around which it is organized:

1. Health care is a basic right of all Canadians.

Canada has made a social commitment to the concept that health care is a right of all citizens. Based on this right, the payment for health care is through taxes, with no direct connection between receiving care and paying for care.

2. The power of the medical profession is limited by its social obligation.

The medical profession derives its monopoly authority over the practice of medicine from the state and has a responsibility, in return, to participate in and cooperate with programs established by the government.

3. The government retains monopsony power over the payment for health care (i.e., Canada's is a "single-payer" system).

The success of the program depends on the monopsony power of the state. No other purchasers of health care (i.e., private insurance companies) are allowed.

4. There is one standard of health care for all Canadians.

All people in Canada, regardless of income or social position, receive essentially the same level of care. (There is an important exception to this principle, discussed in the following section.)

Based on these principles, Canada maintained its level of national expenditure for health care at between 9 and 10 percent of GDP for more than two decades. During this same time, US spending grew from less than 12 percent of GDP to more than 16 percent. How is it that Canada has been able to keep its expenditures so low relative to those in the United States? Most of the provinces have instituted a series of fiscal policies that ensure that rises in health care expenditures parallel rises in GDP. These policies include

- a yearly, global budget for physician fees, with fee levels negotiated between the government and physicians so as to stay within the budget;
- fixed annual budgets for all hospitals; and
- government requirements that all capital expenditures for new hospital facilities and new technology (e.g., MRI machines) be separately approved and financed.

While these fiscal policies have been successful in holding down the cost of the system, they have had an important consequence for Canadians seeking care: queuing. Queuing refers to the need for many patients to go on a waiting list before receiving certain types of tests or treatments. Once referred by their physician, people often have to wait many months before obtaining an MRI or other types of tests that rely on expensive technology. The policy

CONCEPT 3.2

The Canadian health care system is based on the following principles of social policy:

- Health care is a basic right of all Canadians.
- The power of the medical profession is limited by its social obligation.
- The government retains monopsony power over the payment for health care (i.e., Canada has a "single-payer" system).
- There is one standard of health care for all Canadians.

of holding down expenditures for these technologies has resulted in their short supply relative to demand. Similarly, patients referred for surgical procedures such as heart bypass, cataract removal, or hip replacement (all elective procedures that do not carry a major risk if delayed) may be scheduled for surgery months in the future. Generally, careful attention is paid to assure that patients in urgent need of these procedures are put in the front of the line, although budgetary problems that developed in the 1990s opened this principle to question.

Despite the spending controls that were part of their system, the cost of medical care in Canada continued to escalate throughout the 1980s. Faced with mounting economic problems at both the federal and provincial levels, many of the provincial plans began to experience severe shortages of both personnel and facilities in the mid-1990s. Newspaper and television reports documented increasing waits for services—often needed ones such as emergency room care or biopsies of possibly cancerous breast lumps. Public support for the health care system declined substantially; whereas 61 percent of the population rated the system as excellent in 1991, only 24 percent rated it as excellent in 1999 (Iglehart 2000).

The principle behind queuing for care in Canada is that in allocating scarce health care resources, those resources will go first to those in the greatest need, measured in terms of the risk to their life or health. Those with lesser need must simply wait their turn. Here is where the Canadian system of providing one level of care for all people breaks down somewhat. Nearly 90 percent of all Canadians live within one hundred miles of the US border. For those waiting in the queue for an elective test or procedure, the option is always there of simply traveling to the United States (where health care is available as a market commodity) and paying cash to obtain the test or procedure. Given the expense involved, this option is realistically available to only the wealthiest Canadians. Thus, to a certain extent, Canada operates a two-tiered system. One tier is available to every Canadian, although it frequently results in queuing for expensive tests and procedures. The second tier is available without queuing to those few who can afford to travel to the United States and pay out of pocket. A study of the extent to which wealthy Canadians seek medical care in the United States, however, determined that "the numbers found are so small as to be barely detectible" (Katz et al. 2002, p. 20).

The rising level of concern over queuing, shortages of facilities, and inadequate care led the Canadian government to undertake an exhaustive review of their system of health care. In 2001, the federal government established the Commission on the Future of Health Care in Canada. It gave the commission the charge "to recommend policies and measures . . . to ensure over the long term the sustainability of a universally accessible, publicly funded health system, that offers quality services to Canadians and strikes an appropriate balance between investments in prevention and health maintenance and those directed to care and treatment" (Romanow 2002, p. iii). While the commission was asked to make serious recommendations about reforming the Canadian system of care, it was clear from the outset that Canada intended to maintain a "universally accessible, publicly funded" system, and that the central principle of the system was to remain a balancing of the costs and benefits of care.

Led by Commissioner Roy Romanow, the commission held extensive meetings with health policy experts, medical care providers, and ordinary Canadians. In November 2002, it published its report, which included a series of recommendations that fell into two general categories.

1. The Canadian system was underfunded, leading to shortages and waits that were not consistent with the level of quality Canadians deserve in their health care. To remedy the situation, the federal government should work with the provincial governments to invest additional public resources in health care, and to monitor over time that the health care system is adequately funded.

2. Canadians did not want to change the core structure or values of their system of health care. In the words of Commissioner Romanow, "Canadians have been clear that they still strongly support the core values on which our health care system is premised—equity, fairness and solidarity. These values are tied to their understanding of citizenship. Canadians consider equal and timely access to medically necessary health care services on the basis of need as a right of citizenship, not a privilege of status or wealth" (Romanow 2002, p. xvi).

Thus, while Canadians want the assurance that funds will be adequate to pay for needed care in a timely manner, they want to maintain the concept of equal care for all within fiscal limits established through open and public discussion.

While the Romanow Report, as it has come to be called, addressed most criticisms of the Canadian system, some Canadians remain opposed to certain aspects of that system. One of the issues that remain contentious is the relatively low level of payment for physician services. Recall that, as part of the financing mechanism in most of the provincial systems in Canada, a yearly budget is adopted to cover all physician services. Based on that budget, a provincial fee schedule is established by which physicians are paid for the services they provide. (Recall that all payment comes from the Provincial Health Plan.)

As has also been the case historically in the United States, a fee-for-service system of paying physicians tends to make constraining aggregate costs for physician care difficult. Under a fee-for-service system, in which the physician is able to charge separately for each service provided, there is a clear economic incentive for the physician to provide more care. When one aggregates this incentive across all physicians, it makes it difficult to stay within a global budget intended to cover all physician services. The solution established by most provinces in Canada has been to establish a global budget for all physician services within the province, and then to monitor the extent to which physicians in aggregate stay within that budget.

For several years, provinces found that the aggregate charges of their physicians exceeded the budget established for physician care. The policy response was to reduce the fee schedule for the following year, so as to stay within the established budget. The problem with this model is in what one might consider a natural response to reductions in the payment for a given service. If a physician does not want to sustain a reduction of income, she or he will need to increase the number of services provided—either seeing more patients or providing more extensive services to each patient. While, at the level of the individual physician, this response to reduced fees might seem reasonable, if one aggregates this change in practice across all physicians, there is again a problem at the provincial level. Despite the reduction in fees enacted to account for the budget excess in the previous year, the increased level of services will again cause the province to go over budget for physicians' care.

This response of the medical profession as a whole—to react to reduced fees by providing more care—has come to be called "churning." For several years running, a reduction in physicians' fees was followed by churning among physicians, leading inevitably to further reductions in fees. As we will see later in this chapter, patients in Canada have about 40 percent more visits to the doctor per year than patients in the United States, while doctors in the United States charge more than twice as much for the care they provide. The result is that physicians' incomes in Canada tend to be substantially lower than those in the United States. In 2005, physicians in the United States earned at least one-third more than physicians in Canada (Duffin 2011).

While Canada has been dealing with the issue of physician churning in response to reduced fees, only in the past several years have physicians in the United States faced the issue of a global budget for their fees—with precisely the same response as their Canadian colleagues. I discuss the issue of the sustainable growth rate (SGR) further in chapter 6 when we look into the problems that have confronted the US Medicare system.

Growing Pressure for a Two-Tier System in Canada

With the passage of the Canada Health Act in 1984, the Canadian federal government added a fifth core principle to their national system of health care: accessibility. As described by the act, "the intent of the accessibility criterion is to ensure that insured persons in a province or territory have reasonable access to insured hospital, medical and surgical-dental services on uniform terms and conditions, unprecluded or unimpeded, either directly or indirectly, by charges (user charges or extra-billing) or other means (e.g., discrimination on the basis of age, health status or financial circumstances)" (Health Canada 2009, p. 4).

The issue of "extra-billing" or "balance billing" had been largely settled by the failure of the 1984 physician strike in Ontario, discussed previously. A growing number of physicians, however, began to develop private clinics for services such as outpatient surgery or radiology. While the physicians in these clinics would accept payment from the provincial health plan as payment in full for their services, they would also charge the patient a "facility fee"—an extra charge for the use of the clinic facilities. A 1995 ruling by Canada's minister of health stated: "The facility fees charged by private clinics for medically necessary services are a major problem which must be dealt with firmly. . . . Such fees constitute user charges and, as such, contravene the principle of accessibility set out in the *Canada Health Act*" (Marleau 1995).

Canada's federal government left it to each province to regulate private clinics and to report to the federal government any extra charges to patients levied by private clinics for "medically necessary services" that should have been provided without charge under the provincial health plan. The federal government would then deduct that amount as a penalty from the federal reimbursement to the province under the national health plan. While some provinces simply prohibited any private clinics, others permitted private clinics under certain circumstances. For example, British Columbia, Alberta, and Ontario elected to permit private facilities under certain circumstances.

With the numbers of these private clinics expanding, the provincial governments were sometimes lax in monitoring them for compliance with the federal prohibition of extra charges to patients (Lett 2008). The federal Health Ministry's 2009 report on compliance with the Canada Health Act found that "in 2008–9, the most prominent concerns with respect to compliance under the *Canada Health Act* remained patient charges and queue jumping for medically necessary health services at private clinics" (Health Canada 2009, p. 1).

Reports in the Canadian press provided examples of both the success of these private clinics in attracting affluent patients and the consternation of the Canadian public with these clinics. A June 18, 2007, *Montreal Gazette* news story ("Munro M. Layton Accused of Hypocrisy for Visiting Private Clinic") criticized Jack Layton, leader of the New Democratic Party, for "jumping the queue" and undergoing hernia surgery at a private clinic. The same story reported that the president of the Canadian Autoworkers union had jumped the queue to get an MRI of his leg. During the H1N1 flu epidemic of 2009, public health agencies in Toronto and Vancouver were reported to have given several thousand doses of the H1N1 vaccine to private clinics that only treated patients who had paid an "annual membership fee," thus allowing those affluent patients to jump the queue to obtain their vaccines (Howlett et al. 2009).

A 2005 ruling by the Canadian Supreme Court added to Canada's ongoing national debate about the future role of private clinics in the Canadian health care system. In the face of ongoing shortages of facilities and queues for important services, a number of physicians have argued that they should be permitted to provide these services on a private basis. Allowing such practices would, of course, create a two-tier health care system: one tier for those willing to pay for private services and one tier for those unable or unwilling to pay privately and thus relying on those physicians and hospitals who participate in the provincial plan.

The province of Quebec had enacted a law prohibiting private clinics from operating. A family physician in Montreal filed a lawsuit against the provincial government, claiming that, by creating long waits for care and prohibiting people from buying care privately, the health care system in Quebec was violating both his and his patients' constitutional protections of "liberty, safety and security" (Krauss 2005). After losing in two lower courts, the physician appealed to the Supreme Court of Canada, and in 2005 the court ruled by a 4–3 margin in the physician's favor. In the province of Quebec (the court ruling applied only to Quebec), physicians are permitted to set up a private medical care system in parallel to the publicly financed provincial system—the beginnings of a two-tier system.

Reaction throughout Canada to the court ruling was vocal. One newspaper commentator wrote, "The sacred trust—or sacred cow—of public-only medicine is finished. . . . Canada will have more private health-care delivery. The only questions are when, where, and how much" (Simpson 2005). Roy Romanow, author of the Romanow Report, responded to the court decision by stating: "The evidence is overwhelming and clear: The two-tiering of health care represents a march backward in time, to when good health care depended on the size of one's wallet" (Romanow 2005). The debate over shifting the Canadian system to a two-tiered system is likely to go on for a number of years.

Most Canadians want to maintain their current system but invest more resources in that system to make care more generally available. The Canadian Medical Association commissioned a national poll of public opinion regarding the issue and found that only 15 percent of Canadians were in favor of allowing the development of private-sector alternatives to Medicare (Picard 2006). Most Canadians want to maintain Canada's single-payer system that assures the same level of care for all Canadians. They want a system that provides better access to care and enhanced quality of care, however. Canada continues to struggle with providing full access to the "medically necessary services" required under its Medicare law while also constraining the cost of its national system. It remains to be seen whether a two-tier system of care will evolve as a response to these conflicting priorities.

THE HISTORY OF MEDICAL CARE IN THE UNITED STATES

While the health care system in Canada has evolved over the period of nearly one hundred years to its current form, the system in the United States was undergoing a parallel evolution, with a very different outcome. Looking back to the period surrounding World War I, we see progressive groups in the United States proposing a system of government-financed health care. While the AMA considered the issue, its affiliated state medical associations were clear and determined in their opposition to a publicly administered system. Enjoying the new legal protections that followed the publication of the Flexner Report in 1910, the medical profession was intent on consolidating its authority over medical care. By the 1930s, that authority had been firmly established. While towns and provinces in Canada were reacting to the Great Depression through a system of municipal physicians and hospitals, the medical profession in the United States was taking steps to make the private employment of physicians illegal. Even systems of paying for physician care through lump-sum payments, rather than fee-for-service payments, was deemed unethical by the AMA. (See chapter 5 for further discussion of the implications of fee-for-service versus prepayment systems of paying for care.)

The power of the medical profession, both through the AMA and through affiliated state medical associations, was substantial. As described in chapter 1, it was clear to Franklin Roosevelt that any attempt to include medical care as part of Social Security would arouse such opposition from the medical profession that it would make passage of Social Security unlikely. Harry Truman also faced the power of the medical profession to derail his attempts at reform. Despite the fact that his proposals left largely intact the private delivery system, Truman's plan was branded as "socialized medicine" by physicians and their political allies, and it was decisively defeated.

By 1960, the power of the US medical profession had reached its peak, and the system of private, market-based, fee-for-service medicine had been firmly established. While private health insurance was becoming more widespread, the medical profession maintained substantial authority over how those private plans were structured. The principle had been firmly established that there was little role for federal or state governments in the health care system. That role was largely limited to providing care for poor patients in local city or county hospitals. Only in 1965, when Lyndon Johnson was recently elected as president with large Democrat majorities in both houses of Congress, was the federal government able to take its first steps into the medical care system through the enactment of the Medicare and Medicaid systems, discussed in chapters 6 and 7.

THE ORGANIZING PRINCIPLES OF THE US HEALTH CARE SYSTEM

The principles around which the US health care system has come to be organized stand in sharp contrast to those of the Canadian system. They reflect our society's view of the importance of the rights of the individual and of our general distrust of government programs.

1. Health care is a market commodity to be distributed according to ability to pay. Other than basic emergency services, there is no acknowledged right to health care for those under 65 years of age.
I discussed this principle in chapter 2. It reflects a decision made during the early part of the twentieth century and continues to guide the distribution of access to care.

2. For much of the twentieth century, power over the organization and delivery of health care was concentrated in the medical profession.
Both state and federal governments relied on the medical profession to establish standards of education and licensure, guide medical ethics, define financing mechanisms for care, and control the ways in which hospitals are used.

3. Government has historically had relatively little role in guiding our system of health care.
Although government's role has increased in recent years due to its growing role in paying for care, throughout most of the twentieth century there was little in the way of government policy or programs intended to establish a national system of either providing care or paying for care.

4. There is no uniform standard of care. The quality of care received often reflects the ability to pay.
Ours has evolved into a multitiered health care system, with differing levels of quality at different tiers. Differences in quality reflect both differences in the training and skills of the physician and differences in access to care.

It should by now be clear that the system of care in the United States is quite different from that in Canada, reflecting fundamental cultural and historical differences between our two countries. This conclusion reinforces one of the principal messages of this text: to understand our health care system, it is necessary to understand the institutional forces unique to the United States that shape that system.

> **CONCEPT 3.3**
>
> The US health care system is based on the following principles of social policy:
>
> • Health care is a market commodity to be distributed according to ability to pay.
> • Power over the organization and delivery of health care has historically been concentrated in the medical profession.
> • Government has historically had a relatively minimal role in guiding our system of health care.
> • There is no uniform standard of care. The quality of care received often reflects the ability to pay.

THE CULTURAL INSTITUTIONS THAT DRIVE HEALTH CARE IN THE UNITED STATES

The concept of an "institution" refers to the rules a society adopts that create its social, political, and economic structure. To appreciate more fully the way culturally derived institutions shape our lives, consider the following examples.

- When meeting someone in this country for the first time, one typically offers a handshake. There are no written rules that say we must; nevertheless, failure to do so might be considered rude.
- When eating in a restaurant while traveling away from home, we typically leave a tip. Even though we may never be at that restaurant again and may never again encounter our server (thus not having to worry about how good the service will be the next time we are here), we still feel obliged to leave a tip. To not do so would be insensitive to the server.
- People often discuss "the institution of marriage," its pros and cons, and the way it has changed. Here they are talking about both the formal laws that govern marriage and the social roles people fill when married.
- In most circles, Stanford University is seen as a well-respected academic institution. In both the written rules that govern the education it offers and the unwritten rules that govern relationships among individuals and groups, the very character of the university is created.

What links all these US institutions? What do they all have in common? To understand the answer to this question is to understand one of the key driving forces behind the problems we face in health care today.

Each aforementioned example represents rules of social interaction that most people understand and take largely for granted. Douglass North, a Nobel Prize–winning economist, described how institutions shape our social as well as our economic lives: "[Institutions] are a guide to human interaction, so that when we wish to greet friends on the street, drive an automobile, buy oranges, borrow money, form a business, bury our dead, or whatever, we know (or can learn easily) how to perform those tasks. . . . Institutions may be created, as was the United States Constitution; or they may simply evolve over time, as does the common law" (North 1986, pp. 3–4).

Institutions can be formal, as in written laws, codes of ethics, and prescribed procedures, or they can be informal, such as common courtesy and the strength of family ties. Many institutions have both formal and informal aspects. Consider, for example, the medical profession. As discussed previously, in this country the medical profession is commonly viewed as exercising authority over the use of specialized knowledge in ways that contribute to the social good. This perception arose informally over time. The widely held view of the medical profession led to the creation of laws that formalized this role, granting the profession autonomous authority over medical education, licensure, and practice.

Institutions have four defining characteristics (Scott 1987):

1. They are rules that guide behavior in certain situations.
2. The rules can be formal or informal.
3. Over time, those rules come to be taken largely for granted.
4. Disobeying the rules will invoke some sort of sanction, either formal or informal.

In one way, institutions tend to be socially efficient. They allow us to enter into situations without having to figure out from scratch what to do every time. Not all institutions turn out to be quite so efficient, however. Again quoting Douglas North: "Institutions are not necessarily or even usually created to be socially efficient; rather they, or at least the formal rules, are created to serve the interests of those with the bargaining power to devise new rules" (North 1986, p. 16).

Where do institutions come from? The process through which institutions are created has been characterized as "profoundly political and reflect[ing] the relative power of organized interests and the actors who mobilize around them" (DiMaggio 1988, p. 13). Economists, political scientists, and sociologists seem to agree that institutions often reflect—at least initially—the needs of powerful, organized interests. While institutions may reflect organized economic and political interests at their outset, however, they do not change easily or quickly, even in the face of a changing economic or political context. Once established, institutions limit the opportunity for further changes in social policy over the course of a nation's history. Institutions "may assume a life of their own, a life independent of the basic causal factors that led to their creation in the first place" (Krasner 1983, p. 357). This is not to say that institutions do not change; rather, they change gradually, reflecting only changes in economic forces and social perceptions that persist over time.

In comparing health care in the United States and Canada, we find fundamental differences in policy. I identified two key policies that differentiate health care in the United States from that of Canada and other developed countries: (1) approaching medical care as a market commodity and (2) granting sovereignty to the medical profession over the organization and financing of care. In addition, I discussed how health care in Canada is organized around improving the common good, while health care in the United States is organized around the rights of the individual. These three differences in policy represent institutional differences that have developed out of the social and political differences between the United States and Canada. In the United States, these institutions tend to push up the costs of health care, while other institutional forces (e.g., the American aversion to paying taxes) hold down the funds available to pay for health care. As a result, at the time ACA was enacted, one person in six had no health insurance coverage.

Protein Deprivation, Prime Rib, and Declining Marginal Returns

To understand more fully how institutional forces affect the cost of care, let us consider a basic principle of economics: the law of declining marginal returns. To illustrate this law, I offer the following story from personal experience.

One summer I was on a backpacking trip with my son in the Wind River wilderness in Wyoming. After seven days of hiking at high altitude, during which we survived mostly on freeze-dried food, nuts, and raisins, we came out of the wilderness and went in search of a real meal. I usually don't eat much red meat, but when we walked into the restaurant in the small town near the trailhead, the aroma of prime rib of beef hit us. Having been protein deprived during our trip, my digestive system cried out for a plate of prime rib. I gave in. Never have I enjoyed a meal quite so much as I enjoyed that prime rib. I would gladly have paid $50.00 for it. Fortunately for me, at that time it cost only $11.95.

Now, while I actually stopped at one plate, for the sake of discussion let us assume a clever waiter. Seeing how much I enjoyed the first plate, he might then have encouraged me to order a second. "After all, you enjoyed the first one so much, think how much you'll enjoy the second." So, I give in and order a second plate. I find that I derive substantially less enjoyment from the second than the first. While I would have paid $50.00 for the first plate, I wouldn't pay a penny more than $11.95 for the second.

The waiter then encourages me to order a third plate. Again I give in. While I did derive some benefit from eating the third plate, it was only a small benefit—say, $1.00 worth of benefit. The waiter starts to get very pushy and brings me a fourth plate. Not wanting to hurt his feelings, I begin to eat it, but partway through I get up, go into the rest room, and throw up everything.

This story seems on the surface a bit silly. What rational person would pay $11.95 for a plate of prime rib from which he derived only $1.00 worth of benefit? Even more, who would ever willingly pay for food that he knows will probably make him sick? And besides, what does this have to do with health care? To understand, let us create a graph describing my folly in ordering prime rib, as shown in figure 3.2.

It should be clear that, consistent with the law of declining marginal returns, for each successive meal I order, I derive less benefit than from the previous meal (measured here in enjoyment and willingness to pay). It should also be easy to see that a person who is acting rationally would never order more than two meals. He or she would stop at the point where the marginal benefit equals the marginal return—often referred to as the point of indifference. Because the marginal cost and the marginal benefit are exactly the same, a rational person could choose either to accept or not to

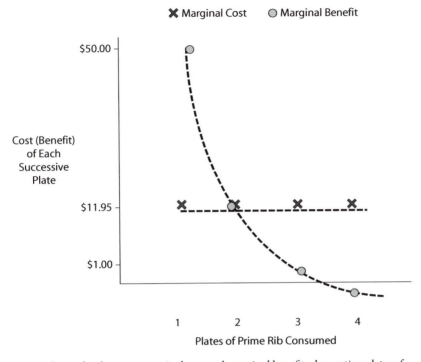

X Marginal Cost   ◯ Marginal Benefit

FIGURE 3.2. Relationship between marginal cost and marginal benefit when eating plates of prime rib.

accept one more meal. This point—the intersection of the line of marginal costs and that of marginal benefits—is one definition of economic efficiency.

Let us stay with the law of declining marginal returns but move back to health care. While the issues are quite different, the principle is the same. Figure 3.3 illustrates the effect of declining marginal returns in health care. The graph can be used to represent decisions at the level of the individual patient or at the level of the health care system overall. For the individual patient, consider the example of a college student who falls down and twists her knee while playing recreational soccer. Her knee becomes somewhat sore and swollen. Her first decision is whether to go to the doctor for an exam, or simply wait to see what happens if she rests the knee and gives it a chance to heal. If she does go to the doctor, the first decision the doctor may face after performing an examination is whether to x-ray the knee to see if it is broken. (While it is unlikely an injury of this type will break a bone, it is possible.) Assuming the physical examination performed by the doctor shows no clear evidence of a torn ligament or torn cartilage and the X-ray is negative, should the doctor obtain an MRI just to be sure he is not missing anything? In the face of a negative MRI, should the doctor perform exploratory arthroscopic surgery, just to be absolutely sure nothing is wrong?

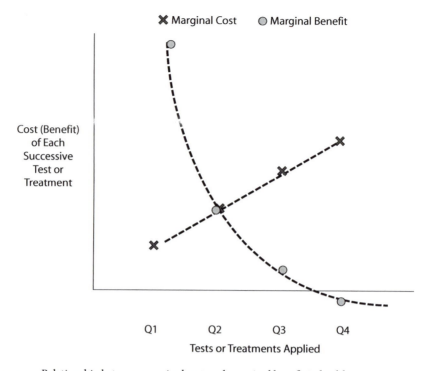

FIGURE 3.3. Relationship between marginal cost and marginal benefit in health care.

Here the physical exam represents Q1 on the graph, the X-ray represents Q2, the MRI is Q3, and arthroscopic surgery is Q4. The marginal benefit is measured as the increase in the probability the student's knee will be completely healed in six months. The one difference in this graph is that the cost of each successive test, rather than being constant, is increasing. How many tests should the patient obtain? In this example, the benefit derived from the physician's exam is more than the cost of the exam. The added benefit from the X-ray is approximately equal to its added cost. The chances of an MRI helping (given a negative exam and negative X-ray), while real and measurable, however, are less than its cost. Similarly, exploratory arthroscopic surgery not only may not help but also carries with it the chance of making the patient worse from a postoperative joint infection.

Where should a rational patient stop in obtaining tests or treatments? Where should a rational physician stop in ordering these procedures? These questions are answered differently in the United States and Canada, based on the different approaches to the trade-off between the benefit to the individual and the benefit to society. In Canada, technology such as MRI is applied sparingly, because it is felt that the added benefit to society overall does not justify the added cost of making it more widely available. In the United States, we typically expect technology to be available to us, despite its position on the marginal cost/marginal benefit curves. It is not fair to the individual, we believe, to deprive her or him of the possible benefits of the test, even though they are small compared to the cost.

As in the case of consuming prime rib, the point of intersection of the marginal cost / marginal benefit curves provides a measure of efficiency in the allocation of health care resources. In Canada, tests and procedures more closely approximate Q2 on the graph, where costs and benefits are about equal. In the United States, they typically are available all the way to Q3. (Some would say we sometimes reach Q4, providing some tests and procedures that are to the patient's detriment.) Our belief in the importance of making tests and procedures available to individuals even though the marginal costs substantially exceed the marginal benefits is uniquely American.

To illustrate, let me relate the story of a patient I took care of in my clinical practice. He was in his forties, a successful local attorney. He had twisted his knee playing sports and wanted my evaluation. After a thorough examination, I was able to determine that, in all likelihood, he had sprained a ligament in his knee without causing any permanent damage. I saw no evidence of a torn ligament or torn cartilage. Because he had simply twisted the knee and not fallen on it, the chance of a broken bone was remote. I chose not to get an X-ray, and I reassured him that he should soon have a full recovery.

"How can you be sure?" he asked. "Don't we need an MRI? Last time this happened, my doctor got the MRI right away, and even though it was negative, he went ahead and did arthroscopic surgery, *just to be sure* he hadn't missed anything. It was a good thing he did, too—during surgery he found a micro-tear in my cartilage and fixed it!"

Here was a well-educated, professional patient (an attorney, no less) whose previous doctor, in the face of a negative exam, negative X-ray, and negative MRI, had gone ahead and performed arthroscopic surgery. In doing so, he had subjected the patient to the risk of a serious joint infection with no reasonable benefit expected. I am convinced that the "micro-tear" the surgeon reported was simply a justification for having performed the surgery. I had not previously heard of "micro-tears" of the knee joint as a problem justifying surgery, but I was acutely aware that recent research reports had documented hundreds of thousands of unnecessary knee surgeries in the United States each year. Nevertheless, the patient considered my care—stopping at the exam to see if the knee healed—to be low-quality care and the care his previous surgeon had recommended to be high-quality care. To this patient, questions of marginal cost / marginal benefit had no relevance.

In Canada, it is unlikely this patient ever would have seen an MRI machine.

> **CONCEPT 3.4**
>
> In the United States, the value we as a society place on technology and technological advances encourages the development and use of high-tech medical treatments, even when the added benefit of these treatments is small compared to their cost.

The "Technological Imperative" and Its Effect on Health Care

Why is the lure of an MRI or of high-tech surgery so powerful, for both the physician and the patient? As a society, we have come to put substantial faith in new technology, and we often measure the benefit of a test or treatment not only in its actual benefit (often measured in the cost of saving an additional year of life) but also in its perceived benefit. A large part of our resistance to reducing the use of expensive, new technologies is due to what Victor Fuchs (1983, p. 60) described as "the 'technological imperative'—namely, the desire of the physician to do everything that he has been trained to do, regardless of the benefit-cost ratio." The technological imperative shapes what we define as "best medical practice." This perception, based to a large extent on the extensive use of technology so pervasive in academic medical centers, is "imprinted" on physicians during their medical school and residency training. Physicians learn to do all they feasibly can and tend to follow this institutional imperative throughout their career. Patients, in turn, tend to adopt the physician's perspective as the norm.

During the past several decades, most advances in medicine have been due to the technology we have been able to develop. New types of imaging devices such as MRI scanners, the use of fiber optics for both diagnosis and surgery, the use of lasers, and bioengineered medications all have had substantial impact on our ability to treat specific patients and specific illnesses. They have been so successful that we have come to equate technology with quality. We have a commonly held belief that the more technological a treatment is, the better it is. We also have come to believe that as patients we have not received complete treatment unless we receive the most advanced technology. Thus, physicians in the United States have a tendency to do everything that is possible, regardless of the cost/benefit ratio.

I would add to Fuchs's description a corollary institution that I refer to as the "technological benefit of the doubt." In comparing a new, high-tech approach to a problem with an older, low-tech alternative, we tend to expect the newer approach to be superior based on its use of advanced technology, even in the absence of empirical evidence to that effect. Take, for example, the prostate specific antigen (PSA) blood test, first introduced in 1987 as a screening test for prostate cancer. It was substantially more high-tech than the traditional method of screening for prostate cancer by digitally examining the prostate gland as part of a rectal examination. The PSA test was relatively expensive and was shown early on to have a high risk of false-positive results. Early data suggested that widespread use of the test "may result in poorer health outcomes and will increase costs dramatically" (Krahn et al. 1994, p. 773). Nonetheless, the test became widely accepted and used before it was approved by the US Food and Drug Administration and before data about its effectiveness became available. A poll reported in

1993 (Kolata 1993) found that 92 percent of physicians in one state used the test routinely on men over 50. By 2009, the PSA test had become a routine part of men's health care, with most men over the age of 50 getting the test despite a continuing lack of evidence that the test actually reduced prostate cancer death rates (Barry 2008).

In 2008, two large studies were published on the effect of PSA screening on death rates. One found no difference in death rates after 7 to 10 years of follow-up in men chosen randomly to be screened on a regular basis compared to men receiving their usual care (Andriole et al. 2009). Another found that after 9 years of follow-up, men screened with the PSA test had a reduction in the death rate of 0.71 deaths per 1,000 men screened (Schröder et al. 2009).

Both studies found that PSA screening identified the presence of prostate cancer more often than avoiding screening, typically leading to surgical removal of the prostate gland, a procedure that can have substantial side effects such as sexual impotence and urinary incontinence. By identifying and treating tumors in many men that would otherwise not have caused illness or death, the screening process led to substantially higher rates of these adverse outcomes, with resulting reduction in quality of life for the men affected. In the words of one commentator responding to the results of the studies, "I think that there is convincing evidence of harm. . . . The two studies together show marginal to no benefit across several years of follow-up at the cost to so many men of overdiagnosis and overtreatment" (McNaughton-Collins 2009, p. 4).

Based on the available research results, in 2012 the US Preventive Services Task Force issued a new recommendation regarding the use of PSA as a screening test for prostate cancer: "The U.S. Preventive Services Task Force recommends against prostate-specific antigen (PSA)-based screening for prostate cancer." For more than twenty years, physicians in the United States routinely used a newer, more high-tech screening test on the faith it would reduce prostate cancer deaths, absent evidence that it actually did so. When the evidence finally came in, it showed little if any benefit of the test.

Physicians and patients seem to be willing to adopt newer, more expensive technologies on the faith that they will, in the future, prove to be superior to existing alternatives. Once they have been adopted, it is extremely difficult to go back and change established patterns of behavior that prove to have little scientific or economic justification.

As another example of the technologic benefit of the doubt, let us look at the way high blood pressure has been treated in the United States over the years. For a number of years, physicians had relatively few choices for the treatment of high blood pressure. The standard treatment was to give the patient a diuretic to reduce the salt and fluid balance in the body, thereby lowering blood pressure. In clinical trials involving comparisons to patients who received only dummy placebo pills, diuretics had been proven to be effective.

Calcium-channel blockers were a category of drug that became widely used in the 1980s. They too were shown to be effective in treating high blood pressure, when compared to treatment with a placebo. Then, in the 1990s, an even newer category of drug came into use—angiotensin-converting enzyme inhibitors, commonly referred to as ACE inhibitors. As with calcium-channel blockers, these were also proven to be effective, compared to treatment with a placebo.

Which medicine should a physician prescribe for the treatment of high blood pressure? When calcium-channel blockers became widely available, they largely supplanted diuretics as a first-line treatment. After all, they were newer, so they must be better. When ACE inhibitors became available, many physicians switched to using these. Again, as an entirely new class of drug, they were considered to be better than the older alternatives. The problem, of course, is that each successive new drug category is more expensive than the older alternatives. This is especially true when the newer drug is available only in its brand-name form. (See chapter 10 on pharmaceutical policy for additional discussion of brand-name drugs, patent laws, and the cost of pharmaceutical products.) While treatment today with a diuretic pill might cost $10 to $15 per month, treatment with the newer ACE inhibitors or calcium-channel blockers can easily cost five to ten times as much.

For more than two decades, physicians relied on the newer medicines to treat high blood pressure, without clinical evidence that they were better than the older diuretics. Each category had been proven effective when compared to treatment with a placebo, but no test had compared the efficacy of the three in a head-to-head trial. Then, in 2002, a large national team of researchers reported on just such a study. In what is called a "double-blind" trial—neither the patient nor the treating physician was told what was in the pill received—they studied patients with high blood pressure who were at high risk of complications. They compared the effectiveness of the three types of drugs in a number of ways. The main outcome of the study—whether the patient had a heart attack—was no different for any of the three medicines. In other measures of outcome, however, the diuretic proved to be most effective, leading the researchers to conclude that "diuretics are superior in preventing one or more major forms of [cardiovascular disease] and are less expensive. They should be preferred for first-step antihypertensive therapy" (ALLHAT Collaborative Research Group 2002, p. 2981).

In this case, physicians for years gave the technologic benefit of the doubt to the newer drugs. Only after a well-designed scientific study finally became available, directly comparing the clinical effectiveness of the available alternatives, did they learn that giving the newer alternatives the technologic benefit of the doubt had no added benefit in clinical outcomes but led to substantial increases in cost. Despite this evidence from the 2002 study, however, by 2008, only 40 percent of patients with hypertension were receiving a diuretic medication, compared to 30 to 35 percent of patients before the study was published (Pollack 2008). Once physicians give newer, high-tech treatments the technologic benefit of the doubt, it becomes extremely difficult to change their behavior.

DIFFERING CULTURAL INSTITUTIONS AFFECT THE COST OF HEALTH CARE

We have seen that Canada spends about 10 percent of GDP on its health care system, while the United States spends more than 17 percent. It is not simply in limiting the availability of expensive care through long waiting lists, however, that Canada spends less than the United States. There are fundamental differences in the way physicians in the two countries practice medicine, with resulting differences in costs.

Victor Fuchs has done a number of studies comparing the patterns of care in comparable populations of patients in the United States and Canada (Fuchs 1993d). The results of these comparisons have a great deal to say about why health care costs so much more in this country than it does in Canada. Table 3.2 shows the pattern of care Fuchs found for physician services and hospital services. It shows the ratio of the United States to Canada in three areas: (1) expenditures on care, (2) prices of resources used in care, and (3) quantity of resources used.

Several patterns can be seen from these data. While people in the United States go to the doctor less often (28 percent less often than people in Canada) and are admitted to the hospital less often (9 percent less often than Canadians), we nonetheless spend a great deal more per patient per year (72 percent more for physicians' services and 26 percent more for hospital care). How is it that we use health care less frequently but spend a great deal more for the care? Part of the answer is the price of resources. Resources such as laboratory tests, medications, and supplies used in providing care in physicians' offices cost 30 percent more in the United States than comparable resources in Canada. The prices physicians charge for their services are nearly two-and-one-half times more than what Canadian physicians charge. Similarly, the resources used in providing hospital care cost somewhat more in the United States (4 percent more).

In addition to higher prices for resources in the United States, we find a clear pattern of using more resources per service in the United States, for both physician care (84 percent more) and hospital care (24 percent more). This means that every time we go to the doctor or the hospital, we have more tests, X-rays, medications, and treatments than Canadians with similar conditions do.

TABLE 3.2. Comparison of the use of health care resources between the United States and Canada

Services	Ratio of US to Canadian
Physician services	
Health expenditures per capita	1.72
Physicians' fees	2.39
Prices of resources used in providing service	1.30
Number of services provided per capita	0.72
Quantity of resources used per service	1.84
Hospital services	
Hospital expenses per capita	1.26
Expenses per admission	1.39
Prices of resources	1.04
Hospital admissions per capita	0.91
Quantity of resources used per admission	1.24

Source: Data from Fuchs 1993d.

Differing Approaches to the Treatment of Heart Disease in the United States and Canada

For people with heart disease, especially those with clogged blood vessels due to coronary artery disease, there is always the risk that something will cause the normal heart rhythm to malfunction. When this happens, the result is often sudden death. Anyone who has watched a television show about hospitals or emergency rooms will know that the treatment is to try to shock the person back to life using a defibrillator. Unfortunately, if a person is not in the immediate vicinity of a defibrillator and someone who knows how to use it, little can be done to prevent death due to a cardiac arrhythmia.

In the 1990s, physicians began using a new device to treat patients who might be at risk of sudden death from a cardiac arrhythmia. The device combined a small computer that can monitor the heart rhythm and determine if a life-threatening abnormality has begun and a stored electrical charge that, on command from the computer, will automatically deliver an electric shock to the heart. With advances in computer technology, these devices became small enough to implant surgically under the skin of a patient's chest.

The next question to be answered was whether these implantable cardiac defibrillators (ICDs) would be effective in saving patients' lives. In 2005, a major study appeared showing that, for patients with severe heart failure, having an ICD reduced the death rate after about four years from 29 percent of patients to 22 percent (Bardy et al. 2005). The results of this and other studies also carried with them some cautions. Some patients were found to have a difficult time with inappropriate, painful shocks being delivered by the devices, leading to a decrease in the quality of their lives. In addition, the cost of the devices was quite high—it might typically cost $50,000 to have one implanted.

Because many of the patients who might be helped by ICDs are 65 years old or older, the federal Medicare program is one of the principal payers for these devices. As we will see in chapter 6, Medicare is facing rapidly increasing costs and concerns about the long-term fiscal viability of the program. To what extent should Medicare pay for the use of ICDs? Given that fewer than one in ten patients will actually be helped by them, should Medicare pay for ICDs only for the sickest patients, leaving some low-risk patients to suffer sudden cardiac death that might have been prevented by an implantable defibrillator? Alternatively, should ICDs be made more widely available to patients with heart disease, placing the lives of patients above economic concerns about the financial impact on the Medicare program?

These were the questions the health policy experts at the federal Centers for Medicare and Medicaid Services grappled with. In early 2005, they came down on the side of preventing as many deaths as possible, substantially widening the range of patients eligible for the devices (McClellan and Tunis 2005). As a result, the aggregate cost of using ICDs was expected to rise substantially. Based on earlier research results, while a relatively small number of patients are likely to be helped by them, for most patients the use of ICDs will make no difference in the course of their disease.

Despite recent research studies, it simply is not possible to say with certainty which patients will be helped and which will not. To cover the few who will be helped, many who will not be helped will need to be treated, leading to substantially higher costs. This is the approach typically taken in the United States when a new device or treatment becomes available. It is the approach most compatible with our historic emphasis in the United States on the needs of the individual rather than on the needs of the social group.

How has Canada dealt with ICDs? In 1999, Canada convened a national Working Group on Cardiac Pacing to study the issue. This group issued a preliminary report in 2000. After the publication of further studies on the efficacy of ICDs, a national consortium of heart specialists published more detailed guidelines on the use of ICDs that recognized the usefulness of the devices and recommended a plan to make them more available to Canadians with heart disease. Recognizing that it is not possible to provide all care to all people in a health care system that must function under a fixed yearly budget, they outlined a careful approach based on the best available clinical evidence. Patients who were found by their primary care physician to be potential candidates for an ICD will be seen by two consulting specialists before a decision is made to use an ICD. They acknowledged that patient queues would develop in this process and recommended a careful monitoring program to assure that those queues do not become excessive. In addition, as is typically the case in Canada, they emphasized that the ordering of patients in the queues would be based on need—the sickest patients would always be in the front of the queue.

As a result of the more cautious approach Canada has taken compared to that of the United States, Canadian patients with heart disease receive far fewer ICDs than those in the United States. In 2003, 84 ICDs were used per 1 million people in Canada, while about 470 ICDs were used per 1 million people in the United States (*Canadian Journal of Cardiology* 2005).

A closely related issue is how doctors in the United States and Canada differ in the way they diagnose and treat patients with clogged coronary arteries that have resulted in a heart attack. Pilote et al. (2003) were able to obtain the treatment records of all patients age 65 or older who were treated for a heart attack in either the United States or the Canadian province of Quebec. For these two patient populations, they compared the increase in the use of newer, high-tech treatments for heart attacks and the death rate from heart attacks. They compared the percentage of patients with a heart attack who had a revascularization procedure (a procedure to open up the clogged blood vessels to the heart that had caused the heart attack) and the percentage of patients who died within one year of their heart attack. These data are shown in figure 3.4. It can be seen that between 1988 and 1994:

- the rate of revascularization approximately doubled in both countries,
- revascularization was used approximately three times more often in the United States than in Canada at both points in time,
- the death rate decreased for both countries by approximately the same amount, and
- the death rate was lower in Quebec than in the United States at both points in time.

It appears that, while the substantially higher rates of revascularization in the United States undoubtedly helped some of the patients treated, the marginal benefit of the extra procedures was not large enough to show up in the overall death rate from heart attacks.

Despite these data showing little long-term benefit of revascularization procedures as measured by death rates, the frequency of diagnostic tests that often lead to revascularization has been growing in the United States. One reason is that these tests are being used increasingly in patients with a low likelihood of having clogged blood vessels in the heart (Patel et al. 2010). In response to this study, Brenner suggested that "it is appropriate to ask whether current coronary imaging techniques are being used optimally" (Brenner 2010, p. 943).

This is precisely the question Ko et al. (2010) explored. They used data from the state of New York (NYS) and the Province of Ontario to compare the rates at which

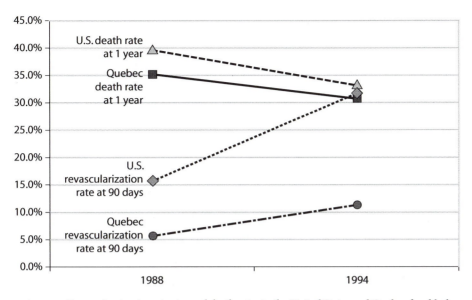

FIGURE 3.4. Comparing treatment rates and death rates in the United States and Quebec for elderly people with heart attacks, 1988 and 1994. *Source:* Data from Pilote et al. 2003.

revascularization procedures were done there. They did their analysis for two different forms of revascularization: coronary artery bypass graft (CABG), a major surgical procedure used principally in patients with multiple clogged arteries, and percutaneous coronary intervention (PCI), a less invasive and less risky procedure used principally with patients with lower expected risk of coronary artery disease (CAD). Both procedures require that cardiac catheterization, a diagnostic test typically performed by cardiologists, first be done. Ko and colleagues found that in 2006, physicians in New York and Ontario performed CABG at approximately the same rate, while physicians in New York performed both cardiac catheterization and PCI at twice the rate as physicians in Ontario. They also noted that in 2006, there were 2.9 times more interventional cardiologists in New York as compared to Ontario (on a population-adjusted basis), 1.8 times more cardiac surgeons, and 2.6 times more hospitals equipped with facilities to perform PCI.

Commenting on these findings, Ko et al. (2010) suggested that "a market-oriented approach to financing cardiac procedures provides incentives for providers to maximize the volume of procedures performed and incentives for hospitals to set up cardiac invasive facilities because cardiac procedures are profitable for hospitals. . . . It has been shown that the use of cardiac invasive procedures is highly dependent on the availability of resources, thus explaining why substantially greater numbers of additional cardiac catheterizations and subsequent PCI procedures are being performed among patients without [a heart attack] in NYS" (p. 2638).

Ko and colleagues also raised a second point of broader relevance, considering the growing focus on constraining health care costs in the United States. "One might also question whether patients in NYS with stable coronary artery disease were undergoing more unnecessary PCI procedures compared with Ontario" (2010, p. 2639). They subsequently took further steps to answer this question directly by examining data on all patients who underwent cardiac catheterization in New York and Ontario between October 2008 and September 2011 (Ko et al. 2013). They asked two fundamental questions.

1. Based on known risk factors for CAD, what was the predicted probability a patient undergoing cardiac catheterization would be found to have CAD?
2. What percentage of patients were found to have CAD, based on the outcomes of the cardiac catheterization?

Their results provided clear answers to both these questions. Of patients undergoing catheterization in New York, 19.3 percent had a greater than 50 percent probability of having CAD, while 41 percent of patients in Ontario had greater than 50 percent probability of having CAD. Consistent with these probabilities, 44.8 percent of patients in Ontario were actually found to have CAD, while 30.4 percent of patients in New York were found to have the disease. These results led the authors to conclude that "increased use of cardiac catheterization in New York relative to Ontario was primarily the result of selecting more patients at low predicted probability of obstructive CAD. . . . These findings demonstrated that a more restrictive approach in selecting patients for cardiac catheterization did not lead to substantial underdetection of patients with surgical coronary anatomy on a per capita basis" (Ko et al. 2013, pp. 167–68).

The editors of the journal *Health Affairs* suggested that there has been an "imaging boom" in US health care, with the use of CT scanners, MRI scanners, PET scanners, cardiac catheterization facilities, and other similar devices proliferating over the past several years (*Health Affairs* 2008). Hillman and Goldsmith have argued that "an unknown but substantial fraction of imaging examinations are unnecessary and do not positively contribute to patient care. . . . The evidence basis for using imaging is incomplete; much imaging practice is driven by habit or anecdote" (Hillman and Goldsmith 2010, p. 1).

In a commentary published in *JAMA*, Leff and Finucane (2008) referred to this explosion of high-tech imaging and other devices as "gizmo idolatry." They explain this concept as follows: "gizmo is used to refer to a mechanical device or procedure for which the clinical benefit in a specific clinical context is not clearly established, and gizmo idolatry refers to the general implicit conviction that a more technological approach is intrinsically better than one that is less technological unless, or perhaps even if, there is strong evidence to the contrary" (p. 1830). The explosion in the use of high-tech tests and treatments represents three common beliefs that are at the core of the US health care system: (1) that high-tech is better than low-tech, (2) that newer is better than older, and (3) that patients deserve the most advanced treatment available regardless of considerations of marginal cost / marginal benefit.

The Institutional Basis of Medical Malpractice

A final example of an institution with powerful effects on health care and its costs is our current malpractice system. Errors in medical care are dealt with under the broad category of personal injury law, often referred to as tort law. If a health care provider provides negligent care, and if a patient is injured as a result, that patient has a right to sue the provider and, if successful, to obtain economic compensation for the injury. The compensation is typically of two types:

1. compensation for the actual costs that result from the injury for things such as required medical care and lost income, referred to as "economic damages," and
2. payment to compensate the patient for the added pain and suffering that result from the injury during the patient's lifetime, referred to as "noneconomic damages."

To be protected from the possibility of having to pay these costs, nearly all physicians and hospitals purchase an insurance policy—malpractice insurance—that protects them should they be named in a malpractice suit. Malpractice suits are governed by state, rather than federal, law.

For several years after the turn of the twenty-first century, a "malpractice crisis" was seen as sweeping our country. Responding to increasing jury awards and decreasing financial returns, companies that provide physicians with malpractice insurance had been raising the rates charged for coverage by substantial amounts. Newspapers regularly reported on physicians who had chosen to leave practice rather than pay the increased cost of malpractice insurance and on the communities that found themselves without enough physicians as a result. A review of the changing world of medical malpractice in the United States concluded that "physicians revile malpractice claims as random events that visit unwarranted expense and emotional pain on competent, hardworking practitioners. . . . Within the health care industry, there is a nearly universal belief that malpractice litigation has long since surpassed sensible levels and that major tort reform is overdue" (Studdert et al. 2004b, p. 283).

As a society, we have often adopted the implicit assumption that a poor outcome from medical care implies negligence on the part of the physician. Responding to the perception that malpractice awards are based on irrational responses of lay jurors, physicians have added billions of dollars to our health care budget by ordering extra tests and procedures that add little to care but present a stronger defense in the case of a malpractice suit. This practice of "defensive medicine" offers little added benefit to patients.

Negligence in medical care occurs when a physician provides care that is not consistent with the "community standard of care"—that is, with what an expert or panel of experts would expect a reasonably competent physician to do under similar circumstances. Thus, malpractice is derived from other physicians' assessments of the quality of the care provided.

As part of a large research project, a panel of expert physicians looked at more than 30,000 hospital records in 51 different hospitals. Based on their independent review of these records, they found that hospitalized patients experienced some sort of adverse outcome from their care about 4 percent of the time. They then looked to see how many of the patients who experienced a bad outcome did so because the physician or the hospital had provided substandard care (the legal basis for a finding of negligence). They found that 28 percent of bad outcomes could be traced to negligence (Brennan et al. 1991).

The researchers then asked, of those patients who had a bad outcome and who experienced substandard care, how many filed a malpractice lawsuit? Among the patients who received negligent care, only a tiny fraction (between 1 and 2%) filed a malpractice suit in response to their care.

The panel looked at the same data in a different way. They asked, of those patients who filed malpractice suits, how many had experienced negligent care? According to this expert panel, less than 20 percent of the malpractice suits represented instances of negligent care. Thus, when negligent care occurs, the patient usually does not sue, and when a patient does sue, it more often than not does not involve negligent care. As the researchers concluded, "the civil justice system only infrequently compensates injured patients and rarely holds healthcare providers accountable for substandard care" (Localio et al. 1991, p. 250).

The panel went on to look at the eventual judgment against the physician or hospital (if any) from the malpractice suits that were filed. They found no association between the amount of money received by the patient and whether the patient had received negligent care. The only factor that was associated with the level of judgment was the level of disability of the patient. The more disabled the patient as a result of treatment, the larger was the malpractice award, independent of negligence occurring (Brennan et al. 1996).

Another series of studies looked at a small group of obstetricians who had a record of repeated malpractice suits against them. A panel of experts compared the quality of the care provided by these physicians to the quality of care provided by comparable physicians who had not been sued in the past. The panel found no difference in the quality of the care between the two groups (Entman et al. 1994).

The panel again looked at the obstetricians who had been sued and those who had not. This time they evaluated patients' satisfaction with the quality of their interpersonal interaction with these doctors. The doctors who had been sued were rated much lower on this scale of quality. From the perspective of their patients, these doctors did not communicate well, and the patients' interactions with the doctors felt more awkward (Hickson et al. 1994). It appears that the reason these obstetricians were being sued and their colleagues were not was not because the quality of their care was lower; it was because they had a weaker interpersonal relationship with their patients. An editorial that accompanied this research concluded, "The same communication skills that reduce malpractice risk lead to patient satisfaction and improved quality of care. Caring, concerned physicians who communicate well with their patients are likely to provide the best quality of care" (Levinson 1994, p. 1620).

> **CONCEPT 3.5**
>
> In the United States, the institution of medical malpractice represents a combination of the following factors:
>
> - a poor outcome for the patient,
> - a substantial level of disability as a result,
> - a poor interpersonal relationship between the patient and the physician, and,
> - only in rare circumstances, actual physician negligence.

How does malpractice in Canada differ from that in the United States? As with health care more generally, the answer lies in the differing historical and cultural traditions of the two countries. Canada's legal system is based on the British tort system. The standards by which suits are judged differ, and the rate at which lawsuits are filed is substantially lower than in the United States. Canadian physicians still have to be concerned about malpractice, but not nearly as much as their colleagues in the United States. This is because

- patients in the United States file three-and-one-half times as many malpractice suits as patients in Canada (measured as suits per one thousand population),
- plaintiffs are successful in obtaining either a judgment or a settlement at approximately the same rate in the two countries, and
- even though the average malpractice judgment or settlement is slightly higher in Canada than in the United States, the overall per capita costs of the malpractice system are approximately four times higher in the United States than in Canada (Anderson et al. 2005).

The Affordable Care Act did not include malpractice reform, other than to encourage individual states to try new approaches to addressing the issue (Bovbjerg 2010). Mello et al. (2014) summarized the principal directions state-based malpractice reform efforts are taking. A common method to reduce malpractice costs is for states to enact laws that place a cap on the "noneconomic damages" that can be awarded to a plaintiff. A study of the impact of limiting these damages to $250,000 found that, as a result, average jury awards were reduced from an average of $293,645 to $234,314—a decrease of 20 percent (Seabury et al. 2014).

A second approach many have recommended is to create what are often referred to as "safe harbors" for physicians who follow established professional guidelines for care. An example is provided by the discussion of the use of PSA tests for the possible presence of prostate cancer. What happens if a physician, adhering to the guidelines published by the US Preventive Health Services Task Force, does not order a PSA on a patient, and the patient is later found to have metastatic prostate cancer? From the patient's perspective, failure to order the test might constitute negligence on the part of the physician, subjecting him or her to a potentially large liability judgment. Under "safe harbor" policies, this physician would be immune to a finding of negligence based on his or her adherence to the national guidelines. Bovbjerg and Berenson (2012) referred to safe harbor protections as "rare trifecta—better medical quality, more cost restraint through limits on liability's influence over medicine, and a potential avenue for political compromise on malpractice reform. A win-win-win" (p. 1).

The third approach identified by Mello et al. (2014) is what they refer to as "communication and resolution" programs. If an unexpected adverse outcome were to occur, the physician and/or health care facility providing the care, with the collaboration and support of their malpractice insurance carrier, would immediately "conduct an expedited investigation, provide the patient and family with an explanation of why the harm occurred, and offer an apology and acceptance of responsibility appropriate to the circumstances" (p. 2149). Even if the investigation finds no evidence of negligence, the provider would still issue an explicit and sincere apology to the patient and family. About two-thirds of states have passed laws, often referred to as "I'm sorry" laws, encouraging these expressions of regret, and when appropriate admissions of negligence, while preventing these expressions from being admitted as evidence should a lawsuit ensue. Given that, as described earlier, poor communication between physician and patient in the context of an adverse outcome is a principal driver of malpractice suits, these innovative approaches to improving physician/patient communication in these contexts hold substantial promise for reforming the medical malpractice process. Is his editorial response to the article by Mello et al., Sage (2014) suggested that "the core commitments of a communication-and-resolution program are to explain to patients what occurred, try to put things right, improve safety for the future, and empower and support caregivers. This is simply good medicine" (p. 2104).

SUMMARY

In the United States, our fascination with technology, our orientation to the needs of the individual, our expectation that we will have expensive tests and procedures even if the added benefit is relatively small, and our propensity to sue physicians for malpractice all add up to care that is much more resource intensive and thus much more expensive than that in Canada. The marginal benefit of this extra care, measured in overall mortality rates, appears to be relatively small. The cost differences between the two countries take on even more significance, however, when we recall that, whereas all Canadians have health insurance as a right of residency, at the time ACA was enacted, more than 50 million people in the United States had no health insurance.

What about shifting the United States to a "single-payer" system of care? Some have been calling for this option for nearly three decades (Himmelstein and Woolhandler 1989). Both California and Vermont considered statewide single-payer plans in the early 1990s, only to have the Vermont legislature and California voters turn down the option. In 1994, Californians voted against a single-payer ballot initiative by a 73 percent to 23 percent margin, "largely the result of voters' attitudes against 'big government' and higher taxes" (Danelski et al. 1995, p. 1).

In May 2010, two months after passage of ACA, Vermont tried again to adopt a statewide single-payer plan. The Vermont legislature passed Act 128, committing the state to enact a new state health system based either on a single-payer approach or an alternative approach developed by a state Health Care Reform Commission. In May 2011, the legislature passed Act 48, which called for phasing out private insurance plans and, by 2017, shifting to a publicly financed, universal coverage system referred to as Green Mountain Care (Fox and Blanchet 2015). This turned out not to be feasible. Analysts determined that such a plan would require new payroll taxes of 11.5 percent for employers and up to 9.9 percent for individuals. In December 2014, Vermont's governor dropped the plan. In response, a former Massachusetts state legislator and self-avowed single-payer advocate wrote: "After years of failure, I reluctantly concluded that single payer is too heavy a political lift for a state. Though the economic case is compelling, our body politic cares about more than just economics" (McDonough 2015, p. 1585).

The US health care system has developed over time in response to our dominant cultural and political institutions. While political and cultural institutions can change over time, any new system of care will have to be consistent with those institutions.

CONCEPT 3.6

Cultural and political institutions unique to the United States have helped create a health care system that is the most expensive in the world while also excluding more people from care than any other developed country. Any attempt to reform the system to address these problems must consider the institutions that led to the problems in the first place.

PROVISIONS IN THE AFFORDABLE CARE ACT TO ADDRESS THE APPROPRIATE USE OF MEDICAL TECHNOLOGY AND OTHER HIGH-COST MEDICAL CARE

In comparing the treatment of heart disease in the United States and Canada, we find that US physicians use expensive, high-tech tests and treatments at a substantially higher rate than Canadian physicians, often with little evidence of added benefit to patients. Lee (2012) posed the question that is central to addressing the issue of potentially inappropriate use of care. "Health care costs are the pounding headache to which all of us in medicine will awaken each day for the rest of our lives. . . . How do we resolve the tension between the imperative to do all we can to help patients and the needs of societies with constrained resources?" (p. 466).

Echoing this sentiment, Rosenbaum and Lamas (2012) described the dilemma many physicians face in the context of growing efforts to constrain costs: "Many who have been in practice for decades argue that at no point, no matter the economic environment, should cost factor into physicians' decisions. . . . Yet some physicians now believe that considering cost serves not only the equitable distribution of finite services, but also the real interests of individual patients" (p. 100).

By 2015, the Affordable Care Act (ACA) had extended health insurance coverage to more than 20 million people who previously were uninsured. ACA aims to continue to expand coverage without adding to the already high cost of our health care system. With the realization that one of the principal drivers of rising health care costs is the way we have come to use newer and high-tech approaches to diagnosis and treatment, ACA creates a mechanism intended to constrain the inappropriate use of these expensive care modalities. It does so by establishing a national program of comparative effectiveness research (CER).

From our earlier discussion of the evolution of treatment alternatives for high blood pressure, we saw how, as newer medications became available, they were tested only against dummy placebo pills to measure their clinical effectiveness. For a period of several decades, medications were never tested against each other to compare their relative effectiveness. When this research was finally done, it was determined that, compared to the newer alternatives, the older diuretic medication provided the optimal clinical effectiveness. Distinct from research that asks the question "Does this treatment work?," CER asks the question "Which of these alternative treatments works best?" Patrick Conway and Carolyn Clancy, both senior officials in the US Department of Health and Human Services, explained the purpose of CER: "We defined CER as the conduct and synthesis of research comparing the benefits and harms of various interventions and strategies for preventing, diagnosing, treating, and monitoring health conditions in real-world settings. The purpose of this research is to improve health outcomes by developing and disseminating evidence-based information to patients, clinicians, and other decision makers about which interventions are most effective for which patients under specific circumstances" (Conway and Clancy 2009, p. 328). The Institute of Medicine of the National Academies of Science reports that "the purpose of CER is to assist consumers, clinicians, purchasers, and policy makers to make informed decisions that will improve health care at both the individual and population levels (Sox and Greenfield 2009, p. 203).

In order to expand the reach and impact of CER, ACA established a national Patient-Centered Outcomes Research Institute (PCORI). PCORI is structured as an independent, nonprofit organization. It has a nationally representative Board of Governors, a series of national advisory panels, and a staff of experienced researchers. With funding provided by ACA, PCORI has initiated a series of research studies that compare existing alternatives for diagnosis or treatment. The Institute of Medicine of the National Academy of Sciences has recommended a list of one hundred topics that should receive priority in being addressed by PCORI-sponsored research (Iglehart 2009c). Perhaps the most important topic on this list is a study comparing alternative models for the organization of health care delivery so as to optimize health care access and quality. Second on the list is the broad topic of identifying optimal approaches to diagnosing and treating cardiovascular diseases.

ACA is explicit in requiring that CER provide recommendations for the optimal approach to care but not create mandates as to how specific conditions should be approached. Similarly, CER results are not to be used to determine insurance coverage or payment for differing approaches to care. Thus, CER, at least as carried out under ACA, is not intended to be cost-effectiveness research, in that it will not make recommendations as to which of the available alternatives provides the optimal balancing of costs and benefits.

In our aforementioned comparisons of the Canadian and the US approach to balancing costs and benefits, we saw that Canada, under the constraint of a fixed, global budget for care, explicitly attempts to balance the cost of care and the effectiveness of care at the margins (i.e., in deciding what treatments to provide and in prioritizing patients for access to resource-intensive care). The United States, on the other hand, has stridently resisted marginal cost / marginal effectiveness considerations, seeing such an approach to care as unwarranted rationing. Weinstein and Skinner (2010) suggested that, in order to constrain the historical rise in health care costs, "at some point . . . we will have to confront the problem of cost-effectiveness at the level of the patient. The limitless pipeline of effective clinical strategies . . . offers improved outcomes, but the costs of development and production are often very high" (p. 463).

ACA leaves unanswered the question of when, if ever, it is appropriate to deny a patient care that has some small yet well-documented marginal benefit but an extremely high marginal cost. It also leaves unanswered the question of how the medical profession, for decades invested in the belief that more care is better care, will shift its institutional belief system to one that accepts health care resources as scarce, and not only supports but expects physicians and other providers to balance costs and effectiveness when making clinical recommendations for individual patients. As described by Alexander and Stafford (2009), "Despite the allure, no amount of comparative effectiveness data alone, regardless of how rigorously assembled, will suffice to fundamentally transform clinical practice. . . . The primary problem is not the absence of knowledge regarding comparative effectiveness, but the absence of the necessary mechanisms to put this knowledge to work" (p. 2490).

The Health Professions and the Organization of Health Care

The US health care system is a complex combination of public and private mechanisms for providing care and paying for care. It is financed largely through health insurance, either public or private. Patients who have traditional types of health insurance generally pay only a small portion of the cost of care out of pocket, in the range of 25 percent of physicians' charges and 10 percent of hospital costs. The rest comes from insurance. Because patients rarely see the full bill for their care, they usually are shielded from knowing what that care costs. This is in sharp contrast to other market commodities.

In addition to a wide variety of private health insurance options, there are many different types of publicly financed health insurance. These include

- Medicare—the federal program for those 65 or older and for disabled people;
- Medicaid—the combined federal-state program for poor people;
- Children's Health Insurance Program (CHIP)—a combined federal-state program for children in lower-income families who do not qualify for Medicaid;
- Veterans Affairs health system—for certain categories of military veterans;
- Defense Department health system—for those on active military duty; and
- Indian Health Service—for Native Americans both on reservations and in cities.

We end up with a wide variety of payment mechanisms for health care. Each program has its own list of what is covered and what is not and how much the patient has to pay.

Regardless of what method is used for paying for care, health care decisions are still largely made by physicians. Even though physicians account for only about 20 percent of health care expenditures, they influence between 70 and 80 percent of all expenditures. Medications are prescribed by physicians, tests are ordered by physicians, and patients are admitted to a hospital or nursing home by physicians. Thus, physicians' decisions effectively determine how much health care costs.

In 2008, there were about 741,000 physicians in this country actively involved in providing patient care—about one for every 416 people. They are not distributed equally throughout the United States, however. States vary widely in how many physicians they have, from one for every 153 people in Delaware and for every 230 people in Massachusetts, to one per 628 people in Idaho and Oklahoma (Smart 2010).

Physicians continue to earn one of the highest average incomes of any professional. In 2014, the average income of physicians ranged from about $190,000 for family physicians and general pediatricians to about $420,000 for orthopedic surgeons and $375,000 for medical specialists such as gastroenterologists and cardiologists (Peckham 2015). Being a physician in the United States, however, was not always such a rewarding profession.

THE HISTORY OF MEDICAL EDUCATION AND THE MEDICAL PROFESSION IN THE UNITED STATES

In his prize-winning novel, *Arrowsmith*, Sinclair Lewis described Doc Vickerson in the 1890s: "A fat old man and dirty and unvirtuous was the Doc; his grammar was doubtful, his vocabulary alarming, and his references to his rival, good Dr. Needham, were scandalous" (Lewis 1924, p. 5). The novel describes a doctor living in a small midwestern town and struggling with inadequate training to cope with illness for which he has little to offer. As was the case with Doc Vickerson, being a doctor in the United States before 1900 was not necessarily a great distinction. While physicians were generally honored, they did not have nearly the power nor did they earn anywhere near the amount they do today. There were several reasons for their relative lack of occupational status.

- *Lack of consistency in training*
  Medical education at that time was based largely on older physicians sharing the knowledge they had accumulated through experience. These physicians represented a wide range of theories of practice, many of them conflicting in the ways they understood the nature of health and disease. These conflicting approaches to medical practice were referred to as "sects." The largest of the sects were the homeopaths, the osteopaths, and the allopaths. (Most modern physicians are descended from the allopathic sect.) The quality of the education within these sects varied with the quality of the instructor, often with little scientific basis for the training offered. Thus, one had little idea of what any particular

physician knew and whether the chances of getting better were enhanced or impaired by seeking medical care. It was not until after the Flexner Report in 1910 that the concept of basing medical education and practice on scientific knowledge became widely accepted.

- *No licensure or certification, and thus no assurance of quality*
  Because there was no firm scientific basis for most of medical practice, there was little on which to base laws pertaining to licensure or certification. Any person with some medical training could call himself a doctor, with no public or private body overseeing the quality of medical practice.

- *Large numbers of doctors*
  In addition to the inconsistent quality of doctors, there were large numbers of doctors. Because it was relatively easy to operate a medical school (simply provide a space for senior physicians to lecture on what they knew and find enough students who were willing to pay for obtaining that knowledge), there were numerous medical schools. In the face of so many doctors representing a variety of theories of illness and treatment with little in the way of scientific basis for medical practice and no assurance of quality or consistency of care, physicians were not perceived as belonging to a high-status profession. The income they received from medical practice was accordingly much less than what is seen today.

The American Medical Association (AMA) started out as a group of young doctors who wanted to better the doctor's lot. Most of their members were drawn from the allopathic sect of practice. For about fifty years (1846–1900), the AMA had little effect in changing the nature of medical practice.

At the turn of the twentieth century, a new model of medical education was beginning to spread from Europe to the United States. It became established at places like Johns Hopkins and Harvard universities. In 1905, the AMA and the Association of American Medical Colleges (AAMC) formed the Council on Medical Education (CME) and adopted the new model of education as the national standard (Council on Medical Education 1905). The CME conducted a national study of the extent to which medical schools nationally were meeting these standards (Bevan 1907). The CME subsequently commissioned the Carnegie Foundation for the Advancement of Teaching to conduct a parallel national study, resulting in the Flexner Report (1910).

Previously, most medical schools were freestanding, without any association with universities. The new standards supported by the CME and by the Flexner Report required medical schools

- to be part of universities,
- to have at least four years of training, and
- to have the first two years of that training concentrate on basic laboratory science.

Most states adopted the recommendations contained in the Flexner Report and incorporated them into laws governing medical licensure. All new doctors, to be allowed to practice under these new licensure laws, had to graduate from a medical school that based its education on this model. The AMA and its state affiliates, representing allopathic physicians, in collaboration with the AAMC, were given responsibility for certifying which schools met the standard. With the support of newly enacted state licensure laws, the AMA was able to effectively control the number of medical schools in the United States, and therefore the number of doctors, as well as to establish the criteria for licensure.

The overall quality and consistency of medical training and practice improved substantially—as did the income of doctors, due largely to their shrinking numbers. In addition, the new medical schools provided a place for medical research. Most medical advances in the twentieth century were developed in medical schools.

The AMA also worked to establish control over the manufacture of pharmaceuticals. Only the companies that pledged to follow the AMA's code of ethics were approved and allowed to advertise in the AMA's journals (Starr 1982). Physicians were discouraged from prescribing drugs that did not meet the AMA's approval. As a result, a mutually dependent relationship developed between the drug companies and the AMA, and the drug companies came to be very powerful. They have formed their own association, the Pharmaceutical Research and Manufacturers of America (PhRMA) (formerly the Pharmaceutical Manufacturers' Association, or PMA). Over the years, the power of the PhRMA, both scientifically and politically, paralleled that of the AMA. Through its support of laws providing patent protection for new drugs and extensive marketing of new (often extremely expensive) drugs, the pharmaceutical industry has been able to maintain one of the highest profit margins of any American industry. Through their extensive program of medical research, pharmaceutical companies have provided many important advances in treatment, but they have also provided many expensive new drugs that offer relatively little marginal benefit over older, less expensive drugs. As a result, the cost of drugs has been a major contributor to the rising cost of health care. (See chapter 10 on pharmaceutical policy for a more in-depth examination of these issues.)

Building on the authority it was granted over medical school certification and medical licensure, the AMA also came to define the code of ethics that physicians must follow (Baker et al. 1999). This code of ethics covered not only issues of medical practice but also issues of medical economics. From rules governing the physician-patient relationship to methods of organizing and paying for medical practice, the AMA gained near total authority over physicians. This code of ethics was applied not just to physicians who were members of the AMA but to all physicians. As we will see in chapter 5 as part of our consideration of the origin of health maintenance organizations (HMOs), this extension of ethical standards to include the organization of medical practice led to significant splits within the profession. These splits were to have important ramifications for the efforts at health care reform in this country over the past fifty years.

Today, the AMA represents fewer than half of all physicians, but it is still the most powerful voice of the medical profession on matters of medical ethics, medical education, and the standards of medical practice. In addition, the AMA has for years been one of the biggest contributors to politicians and has one of the most powerful lobbying organizations in Washington, D.C. During much of the twentieth century, the power of the AMA was such that it was repeatedly able to block efforts in Congress to establish a system of universal health insurance.

> **CONCEPT 4.1**
>
> The American Medical Association, acting as the representative of the medical profession, was able to exert considerable power during much of the twentieth century over the organization, financing, and delivery of medical care in the United States.

RACIAL SEGREGATION AND THE MEDICAL PROFESSION

It is significant to point out that for much of its history, the AMA excluded African American physicians from membership. In addition, African American physicians were frequently blocked at the local level from joining the medical staff of predominantly white hospitals (Baker et al. 2008). As part of the unfortunate history of racial segregation in this country, we also maintained segregated systems of medical education and medical care, perpetuated for much of the twentieth century by the policies promulgated by the AMA (Smith 1999).

In the period following the Civil War, a small number of predominantly black medical schools gained substantial respect. Foremost among these were Howard University and Meharry Medical College. In the 1890s, the graduates of these schools, prevented from joining the AMA, formed a separate association—the National Medical Association (NMA)—to represent African American physicians. In the 1950s, the AMA and its affiliated state medical associations began to extend membership to African American physicians, although it was not until a period in the 1960s, following the enactment of the Civil Rights Act, that African American physicians became full members of the US medical profession. In 2008, the AMA issued a formal apology for its historic role in maintaining racial segregation (Davis 2008).

Until the 1960s, there existed in many parts of this country a system of overt segregation of white and nonwhite hospitals. Black physicians were not allowed on the medical staffs of many white hospitals and black patients were not allowed treatment. Congress then passed both landmark civil rights legislation and the laws creating the Medicare and Medicaid programs. Together, these programs extended the availability of hospital care to the poor and the elderly and, as a result, became a major source of funding for most hospitals. Those responsible for enacting Medicare and Medicaid made it clear that any hospital that continued a policy of racial segregation would be in violation of the Civil Rights Act and would be ineligible for payment under either program. Few hospitals could continue to survive without any federal funding. As a result, there was a rapid dismantling of the segregated hospital system.

The NMA continues to exist as an independent association of physicians and continues to be active in efforts to increase the number of medical students and physicians from underrepresented racial and ethnic minorities. The relatively low number of African Americans and other minorities in the US medical profession continues to be a problem. For example, while African Americans currently make up about 13 percent of the overall US population, only about 4 percent of physicians in the United States are African American (Deville et al. 2015). Between 2002 and 2012, the number of US medical school graduates from underrepresented minorities fell slightly and represent about 15 percent of all graduates (Association of American Medical Colleges 2014).

GENDER SEGREGATION AND THE MEDICAL PROFESSION

For much of the early part of the twentieth century, women were not allowed membership in the AMA. This reflected a generally held view that women were inappropriate for practice as physicians. Many medical schools refused to admit women as students, and those that did admitted only a small number. Many women physicians in this country were educated in women-only medical schools. Following the success of the women's suffrage movement in the 1920s, the AMA and the rest of the medical profession began to open its ranks to women.

When, as a medical student in the 1970s, I served as a member of the admissions committee of a nationally prestigious medical school, women applicants were given extra scrutiny to assure that their interest in establishing a family did not conflict with their interest in becoming a physician. As a result, fewer than 10 percent of medical students at that school and nationwide were women. As women in this country have attained increasing status relative to men, their numbers in the medical profession have increased accordingly. Today, slightly less than half of all medical students are women. Over time, medicine will become a profession with nearly as many women physicians as men.

NURSING IN THE UNITED STATES

Another important profession in US health care is nursing. Interestingly, the history of the nursing profession is also the history of war. Nursing was formed as a profession in the 1800s through the efforts of Florence Nightingale and others on the battlefields of the Crimean War. Following a growing public awareness of her work, schools of nursing began to be established in the United Kingdom and the United States.

Due to a shortage of nurses during World War I, a new category of subnurse was created, which eventually became the medical assistant. Today, medical assistants frequently work under the direction of registered nurses in both hospital and medical office settings. Another shortage of nursing personnel during World War II led to the creation of a third category of nurse, the licensed vocational nurse. Today, hospitals, clinics, and physicians' offices employ a combination of medical assistants, licensed vocational nurses, and registered nurses.

At the same time that the university-based medical school was spreading throughout this country, the model of the hospital-based nursing school was also expanding. Previously, nursing education had been as varied and haphazard as medical education. In 1911, a group of alumnae from these hospital-based schools formed an association and argued that only graduates of these schools should be licensed to act as nurses. This was the birth of the American Nursing Association, or ANA. The ANA has never been as powerful as the AMA. To a large extent, it has acted in the role of a collective bargaining agent in nurses' struggle with hospitals to gain the professional status and level of pay that the profession deserved. In this effort, there were often rival labor unions for nurses, with a result that the profession had difficulty becoming unified. For much of the twentieth century, the traditional training for nurses took place in hospital-based programs, typically two years in length. Beginning in the 1960s, a shift took place, with nursing education taking place increasingly at community colleges and other academic institutions rather than being based in hospitals. These "associate degree" programs typically last three years.

Many nurses argue that all nurses should have four years of education, the equivalent of a college education. Those nurses who complete a full four years of education receive a baccalaureate degree and are referred to as baccalaureate nurses. Over time, associate degree and baccalaureate programs have come to replace the traditional hospital-based diploma nursing programs. About 60 percent of recent nursing graduates received their training in associate degree programs, with about 36 percent having received a baccalaureate degree (IOM 2011b).

Many nurses have been able to upgrade their training through specialized programs to form highly skilled subgroups within the profession. For example, emergency room nurses, coronary care nurses, and neonatal care nurses have become indispensable members of the critical care team in hospitals and have considerable autonomy in the care of patients. In addition, several types of nurses have been able to obtain extra training to act as semi-independent practitioners, discussed in the following paragraphs.

A major policy issue facing the nursing profession is a projected shortage of trained nurses. The US Bureau of Labor Statistics (2015) projected that 526,800 new nurses will be needed by 2022. Several factors have contributed to a growing gap between the number of nurses working and the number of nurses needed. The first is an aging workforce, with nurses in their fifties comprising the largest age group in the workforce. Once this baby boom generation of nurses begins to retire, shortages will begin to grow rapidly.

During the economic downturn that followed the recession of 2007–08, it looked for a while as though the supply of nurses might be rebounding. Between 2005 and 2010, an estimated 386,000 full-time nurses entered the workforce, "the largest expansion over any 5-year period in our data extending back four decades" (Staiger et al. 2012, p. 1464). Based on the falling national unemployment rate experienced after 2010, many of these new nurses were expected to leave full-time employment, once again resulting in a national nursing shortage. In addition, the number of nurses who retire is expected to increase from about 20,000 per year as seen in the mid-2000s to 80,000 per year by 2025 (Auerbach et al. 2015). Despite these reductions in the nursing workforce, the US Department of Health and Human Services Health Resources and Services Administration (2014) predicted that growth in that workforce will be more than sufficient to meet national demand, with a potential surplus of as many as 340,000 registered nurses by 2025.

With a recent history of rising wages and opportunities for professional advancement, nursing has become increasingly attractive as a profession. With nearly all nursing education now taking place in colleges and universities, however, there is a shortage of nursing faculty to provide training to all those interested. As a result, many qualified applicants are turned away from nursing school or are placed on waiting lists. As described by Cleary et al. (2009, p. w636), "Today's shortage of nursing faculty is also shaped by the same demographics affecting the overall nursing shortage. The average age [in 2008] of a nursing faculty member is 53.5, and the average age of retirement is 62.5."

As fewer nurses enter the profession and more leave it, and as the shortage of trained nursing faculty grows, the problem will be felt most acutely in hospitals. In 2001, about 13 percent of hospital positions for registered nurses were unfilled; 84 percent of hospitals reported staff shortages of nurses. Between 2001 and 2007, 63 percent of the growth in nursing employment took place in hospitals (Buerhaus 2008). A problem arises as more hospital nursing positions remain vacant, in that those nurses who remain must care for a greater number of patients. As the baby boom generation ages and the demand for hospital services increases, the problem may only become more acute. One study found a vicious cycle, with nurses in hospitals with higher patient-to-nurse ratios experiencing greater rates of burnout and job dissatisfaction, making them even more likely to leave the profession. In addition, patients in hospitals with higher patient-to-nurse ratios experienced higher mortality rates than patients in hospitals with better staffing ratios (Aiken et al. 2002).

LEVELS IN THE US HEALTH CARE SYSTEM

In examining health care in the United States, we can divide our system into multiple levels:

- primary care: care provided by primary care physicians and other primary care providers,
- secondary care: care obtained from specialists and in hospitals,
- tertiary care: care obtained at regional referral centers, and
- quaternary care: care obtained at national referral centers.

We will look at each of these levels separately.

Primary Care

Primary Care Physicians

There has been a great deal of discussion among physicians, among patients, and in the media about the role of primary care physicians. In these discussions, it is important to be specific in defining "primary care." While different physician organizations have somewhat different definitions of the concept of primary care, I consider a primary care physician to be *a physician who provides continuing, comprehensive, coordinated medical care that is not differentiated by gender, disease, or organ system.* From this perspective, only those physicians who treat a comprehensive range of problems, getting to know a patient and his or her health status over time, are considered primary care physicians. Physicians with training in one of three specialties are typically considered to be primary care physicians: family medicine, general internal medicine, and general pediatrics. Geriatrics, a field in which physicians focus on providing care to older patients, is also considered a primary care field. Geriatricians are typically trained in either family medicine or general internal medicine and receive extra training in providing care to seniors.

For many, an obstetrician/gynecologist would not be considered a primary care physician because her or his practice is gender specific. Others point out that some women come to rely on their obstetrician to provide ongoing, comprehensive care for a range of problems. From this perspective, an obstetrician can be seen as a primary care physician.

A cardiologist or dermatologist would not be a primary care physician because each practice is limited to one organ system. An emergency physician, while treating

> **CONCEPT 4.2**
>
> A primary care physician is a physician who provides continuing, comprehensive, coordinated medical care that is not differentiated by gender, disease, or organ system. Typically, primary care physicians are from one of three areas of training: family practice, general internal medicine, or general pediatrics.

a comprehensive range of problems, would not be a primary care physician because he or she does not develop a continuous relationship with a patient over time.

The recent debate over health care reform has focused a great deal of attention on the need for primary care physicians. For a period of time in the 1990s, it appeared that there was a crisis in the falling number of primary care physicians. Lured by the prestige of being a specialist, fewer and fewer medical students were choosing a career in primary care. In 1982, about one-third of all medical students indicated that they planned to enter primary care. In 1992, fewer than 20 percent of medical students opted for primary care. In the mid-1990s, there was somewhat of a turnaround in this area, with one-third of graduating medical students entering primary care residencies. In 1998, that pattern was reversed, however, and every year since then fewer and fewer graduating medical students have selected residencies in a primary care specialty.

The decline has been the sharpest in family medicine (Whitcomb and Cohen 2004). Whereas in 1999 about 15 percent of graduating medical students entered residency training in family medicine, by 2009 only 7 percent of students entered family medicine training. By 2013, 6 percent of US medical school graduates in residency training were in family medicine (Brotherton and Etzel 2014).

There are a number of reasons why medical students choose to be specialists rather than primary care physicians:

- *Prestige*
  Specialists tend to deal with new technology; primary care physicians deal mainly with people. With our emphasis on technology as the basis of medical advances, physicians who use technology in their practice are frequently granted higher prestige, both by the profession and by society.
- *Money*
  It is not uncommon for some specialists to earn two to three times as much as primary care physicians. Many medical students have to rely heavily on student loans to pay the cost of their education. A number of students come out of medical school owing $150,000 to $200,000, sometimes more. Many feel they need the higher salary available to specialists to be able to pay off their loans.
- *Frustration of primary care*
  Some medical students view primary care as being boring and repetitive, dealing mostly with common problems and chronic illness for which there is no cure. As described in a report by a group of primary care physicians, the work of a primary care physician includes many responsibilities that do not involve patients directly, such as reviewing laboratory and X-ray reports, refilling prescriptions, and responding to phone calls or e-mails (Baron 2010). Under traditional payment

methods, physicians are not compensated for many of these types of duties. Specialists, on the other hand, are often perceived as dealing with challenging and interesting problems for which they might be able to offer a cure.

- *Lack of primary care role models*
  Most physicians who teach in medical schools are specialists. Medical students come in contact with few practicing primary care physicians. Students are often counseled by their teachers to stay away from primary care—not to "waste" their career.

There are also reasons, though, why primary care is an attractive career option for many students:

- *Employability*
  One factor that may be working in the favor of primary care physicians is their ability to find employment after their training. A study from the late 1990s showed that, for physicians just completing their residency, relatively few primary care physicians had difficulty finding employment, while as many as half of all physicians in certain subspecialties reported trouble finding employment (Miller et al. 1998). In 2012, for the seventh straight year, there were more job openings for family physicians than for any other specialty (American Association of Family Physicians 2013). With the growing shortage of primary care physicians relative to specialists, this employment advantage is only going to increase.

  One reason for this advantage in employment has been the increasing role of primary care physicians in managed care settings. (I discuss the origins of managed care systems in chapter 5.) In traditional medical practice, a number of specialists did not have enough patients to fill their practice, so they would spend part of their time giving specialized care and part of their time giving primary care. In the managed care setting, most specialists provide only specialty care, with the result that they need fewer specialists. As a consequence, more primary care physicians are needed in these practice settings.

- *The nontangible benefits of primary care practice*
  While it may be true that primary care physicians frequently deal with common problems and chronic illness, there is an aspect to this type of medical practice that many medical students are not aware of. In getting to know patients and their families over time and in dealing with the problems that most commonly confront patients, primary care physicians are able to develop a unique relationship with their patients. Patients tend both to trust and to admire the physician who is there for them day in and day out. It is difficult to put a dollar value on the strength of the interpersonal relationship many primary care

physicians are able to establish with their patients. This can be the most re-warding aspect of primary care practice. Those physicians who value the qual-ity of their relationship with their patients over professional prestige and in-come frequently feel at home in primary care practice, and they usually make the best primary care physicians.

An article in the *New York Times* illustrated how important an ongoing relationship of trust with a primary care physician is for many patients (Zuger 2003a). The article told the story of Robert:

> Robert is a middle-aged man with five chronic diseases and a doctor for each. He has the urologist for the prostate cancer, the rheumatologist for the arthritis, the cardiologist for the coronary artery disease, and so on. And then, like the extra candle on the cake for luck, he has yet another doctor, the one responsible for his primary care. . . . But if you ask Robert about Doctors 1 to 5 he shrugs, barely remembering their names. Ask him about No. 6 and a soft smile crosses his face. "I don't know what I would do without him," he says. "He's kept me alive all these years."

Abigail Zuger, a physician and the author of the article, goes on to conclude, "If compli-cations and mortality were all there was to medical care, that might be the end of the story—and of primary care. But anyone who has ever emerged physically intact but emotionally battered, confused, furious or appalled from an encounter with the health care system knows otherwise."

While heavy debt loads and fascination with technological approaches to care may push many medical students toward a career as a specialist, there are some clearly identified factors that draw others to a primary care career. A study of the character-istics of students at the time they first entered medical school found that "those who planned to practice in underserved communities, espoused more altruistic beliefs about health care, and ascribed greater importance to social responsibility in their choice of medicine" were significantly more likely to select a primary care career. The study also found women medical students in general to be attracted to primary care more so than men (Jeffe et al. 2010, p. 947).

Currently about 30 percent of physicians in the United States are in primary care. Many people argue that we need to increase this number to closer to 50 percent of physicians, as is the case in Canada. Others respond that if we had 50 percent of phy-sicians in primary care, there would be a shortage of specialists. Recall that Canada provides a great deal less specialized care than we do and thus needs fewer specialists. It may be that we could not keep up our current level of specialized care with 50 percent specialists. Policies adopted to influence the number of primary care physicians (and thus the number of specialists) will play an important role in determining the direction our health care system takes.

As a percentage of the medical profession, primary care has fallen steadily over time. In the period 1950–60, when there were about 145 physicians per 100,000 people, more than half of all physicians were in primary care. By 1970, there were about 160 physicians per 100,000 people, with about 37 percent of them being primary care physicians. The number of physicians rose to 278 per 100,000 in 2000 and to 293 per 100,000 in 2010. Based on the rising demand for care as a consequence of ACA and the aging of the population, the number of physicians per 100,000 population is predicted to fall to 245 by the year 2025 (Association of American Medical Colleges 2015).

In 1950, when more than half of physicians were in primary care, there were about 80 primary care physicians and about 65 specialists per 100,000 population. In 2010, with about 30 percent of physicians in primary care, there were about 88 primary care physicians and 206 specialists per 100,000 population. While the number of specialists more than tripled in these 60 years, the number of primary care physicians remained fairly constant. With fewer young physicians selecting primary care careers, however, there is growing concern as to whether there will be enough primary care physicians to provide primary care services once the expanded insurance coverage under the Affordable Care Act (ACA) becomes a reality. By 2025, the AAMC predicts there will be about 78 primary care physicians per 100,000 population. This number is expected to represent a shortage of more than 20,000 primary care physicians (US Health Resources and Services Administration 2013).

Nurse Practitioners and other Advanced Practice Nurses

An alternative to training primary care physicians is training advanced practice nurses. The most common examples are the nurse practitioner and nurse midwife. Nurse practitioners take two to three years of training beyond registered nurse training, part of it a clinical internship. They can be trained in fields such as family medicine, adult medicine, pediatrics, or obstetrics. Following their training, nurse practitioners are eligible to see and treat patients for certain specified conditions under the supervision of a physician. The physician does not have to be present to provide supervision. The physician and the nurse practitioner do not even have to be in the same office. Nurse practitioners typically work from written treatment protocols worked out with their supervising physician and refer all things beyond their capabilities to the physician. In 2014, there were 205,000 nurse practitioners in the United States, 86 percent of whom were trained in primary care (American Academy of Nurse Practitioners 2015). (Physician assistants differ from nurse practitioners in not being nurses, in having to work more directly under the supervision of a physician, and in being more limited in what they can do. In 2013, there were about 93,000 physician assistants in the United States [American Academy of Physician Assistants 2013].)

A problem for nurse practitioners historically has been that some physicians were not comfortable either supervising them or having their patients seen by them. Repeated studies (Salkever et al. 1982; US Congress, Office of Technology Assessment 1986; Maule 1994) have shown, however, that nurse practitioners can give care that is the same quality as physician care for the specific conditions they are trained for. Also, patients accept nurse practitioners quite well. In many cases, patients are more satisfied with a nurse practitioner than with a physician, due largely to the extra time and personal attention nurse practitioners are able to give. Nurse practitioners seem especially well suited for those medical conditions in which a great deal of face-to-face contact is required (e.g., well child care, arthritis, diabetes, high blood pressure).

CONCEPT 4.3

Nurse practitioners have been shown to be an effective alternative to physicians in a number of settings in terms of quality, cost, and patient satisfaction.

The question remains unanswered as to whether care provided by nurse practitioners costs less than care provided by physicians. Because nurse practitioners spend more time with patients, they see fewer patients. A study done in the 1980s by the Kaiser Permanente system of care in northern California found that overall care from nurse practitioners costs about the same as physician care, but patients liked them better than physicians in the clinic (Garfield et al. 1987).

Perhaps a more important issue than whether to train more primary care physicians or nurse practitioners is how primary care should be organized. With the spread of managed care plans, primary care is increasingly being provided by large groups of physicians. The solo physician, practicing alone in his or her own office, is rapidly becoming a thing of the past. Between 1996 and 2005, the number of physicians practicing in one- or two-physician practices declined from 40.7 percent of physicians to 32.5 percent (Liebhaber and Grossman 2007). Many people suggest that we need to look at new ways of organizing primary care practice to maintain the quality of the primary care process and to make it readily accessible to patients. This issue is especially relevant in light of the increasing load of chronic illness management that will come as the baby boom generation ages. As part of ACA, there will be substantial new emphasis on developing new models for the delivery of primary care. I discuss these at the end of this chapter.

Secondary Care

Specialist Physicians

As discussed previously, physicians are separated into two categories: primary care physicians and specialists. Specialists are those physicians who have received extra training in a specific field, and who treat only a certain type of patient. The point at which primary care physicians and specialists become identified and differentiated is during residency training. Nearly every medical student goes on after medical school to receive additional training in a residency. Residencies are usually based in a hospital and have faculty drawn from a specific field of medicine.

The concept of the "internship" no longer applies to medical training in the United States. During much of the twentieth century, medical students would initially complete a one-year, hospital-based training after medical school (the internship), and then go on to a separate residency training program. Over time, it has become the standard that the first year of training after medical school is part of residency training, often referred to as the R1 year. It is possible to obtain a license to practice medicine in many states after the R1 year, but fewer and fewer students stop at this level of training. In the past, those physicians who stopped after one year of extra training were referred to as "general practitioners." General practitioners have largely been replaced by family practitioners and other types of primary care physicians who take a full three years of residency training.

The length of residency training can vary significantly, depending on area of specialty. Emergency room specialists complete their residency training in three years, while certain types of surgeons (e.g., cardiac surgeons or neurosurgeons) can take eight or more years before completing training. Some specialties may require two separate residencies, such as an initial period of residency in general surgery followed by a separate residency in orthopedic surgery.

A number of specialists in nonsurgical fields may begin their training in the same program as primary care physicians, but then go on to take extra training in a specialized field within their discipline. For example, students wishing to become cardiologists (heart specialists) or gastroenterologists (intestinal specialists) will often take the same three-year residency in general internal medicine as primary care physicians, but will then go on to take a "fellowship" in their specialized area of interest. Similarly, a physician completing a residency in general pediatrics may then go on to a fellowship in neonatology (the care of premature babies and other newborns). A fellowship is distinguished from a residency in that it is available only to those who have completed more general training in a specific field, and it provides training in only one segment of that field. Fellowships are typically between two and four years long.

Most specialists have an income that is considerably higher than that of primary care physicians. By spending a few extra years in training, physicians can more than double their expected earning power. The higher income a specialist can expect to earn continues to play a major role in drawing students into specialty areas. In addition, many young physicians want to use the latest technology in their practice or to have the challenge of performing surgery with its attendant risks for the patient. As described earlier, a substantial majority of medical students continues to choose careers in medical specialties.

> **CONCEPT 4.4**
>
> A number of forces, including the higher level of income available, have encouraged the majority of young physicians to become specialists. Fewer than one-third of physicians become primary care physicians.

Since the changes in medical practice that accompanied the shift to managed care in this country, the way a specialist practices medicine has also changed. Previously, any patient who wanted to consult a specialist about a problem simply called the specialist's office and made an appointment. Because specialty care tends to be more expensive than primary care, some insurance companies and managed care companies have placed limits on the patients' ability to be seen by the specialist of their choice. Now many patients often must first seek care from their primary care physician, and they may have the care of a specialist covered under their medical insurance only if it is first approved by the primary care physician. In addition, certain types of specialists use expensive tests and procedures as part of their practice. In an effort to control costs, many insurance companies require these specialists to obtain approval from the insurance company before providing expensive care.

The rising number of specialists in the United States, both in absolute numbers and as a percentage of the medical profession, raises serious concerns about the effect on the rising cost of care. As in many areas of medical care, changes in the number of specialist physicians do not necessarily lead to changes in the price of specialty care. If your community had a sudden increase in the number of house painters, you could reasonably expect the cost of having your house painted to go down. With most market commodities, as the supply of a commodity (e.g., house painters) goes up, the price should come down. Despite the market approach to medical care prevalent in this country for most of the twentieth century, the number of physicians did not seem to obey the laws of supply and demand. Instead, physicians were able to avoid becoming a surplus commodity by increasing the amount of care they provided. In the case of medical care, the demand for the commodity (i.e., medical care) is determined not by the consumer but by the provider. Patients do not typically tell physicians how much and what type of care they need; physicians tell patients. Medical care in this case becomes a "market failure," in that it does not obey the classic laws of the market economy such as supply and demand (Arrow 1963).

A fundamental reality of contemporary US medical care has been demonstrated again and again: the more specialists practicing in a given community, the more specialty care will be recommended to patients and the higher the cost of care. If more surgeons move into a community (all else being equal), there will be more operations. For a variety of medical conditions and geographic locations, John Wennberg and colleagues have demonstrated tremendous variation among communities in the rate that certain types of specialized therapy are applied. Whether it is rates of prostate surgery or rates of heart surgery, Wennberg concluded that a major factor driving the different rates of these procedures is the number of physicians practicing in the community: the more physicians, the higher the rate of surgery (Wennberg and Gittelsohn 1973; Wennberg et al. 1982; Wennberg 1993).

In 2009, physician/author Atul Gawande published an article in *The New Yorker* describing his visit to McAllen, Texas. Based on Medicare data, physicians in McAllen provide some of the most expensive medical care of any community in the country—second only to Miami. The question Dr. Gawande explored in his article was why care cost so much more in McAllen than in other parts of the country. He concluded, "There's no evidence that the treatments and technologies available at McAllen are better than those found elsewhere in the country. . . . Health-care costs ultimately arise from the accumulation of individual decisions doctors make about which services and treatments to write an order for. The most expensive piece of medical equipment, as the saying goes, is a doctor's pen" (Gawande 2009). It seems that doctors in McAllen simply use their pen more often than doctors elsewhere in the country. They order more tests and do more procedures (and in doing so collect more fees from Medicare) than physicians elsewhere in the country. Yet, as described by Dr. Gawande, patients in McAllen seem no better off for all this extra treatment.

> **CONCEPT 4.5**
>
> Historically, the supply of physicians in a community has not obeyed the economic law of supply and demand. The greater the number of physicians, the greater has been the amount of care and the number of procedures. Instead of reducing the price of care, the rising number of specialist physicians has contributed to the increasing cost of care.

If doctors in McAllen order more tests on their patients than most doctors, will we also find this pattern in Miami and other areas of Florida, which have even higher Medicare costs than McAllen? Elisabeth Rosenthal, a reporter for the *New York Times*, suggested that we will. She also suggested that older patients who live in the Northeast most of the year but spend winter in Florida might want to be cautious about the tests and treatments the doctors they consult with in Florida might recommend (Rosenthal 2015). She described an elderly couple from Upstate New York who, during their winter stay in Florida, consulted with a cardiologist to be sure the 91-year-old husband's cardiac pacemaker was working properly. Much to their surprise, and despite the fact that the husband was experiencing no new symptoms, the cardiologist recommended a series of expensive tests. Confused as to what they should do, the couple contacted their New York doctor. That doctor said that none of the tests were necessary, so they canceled them. As reported by Rosenthal, this couple's experience "reflects a trend that has prompted some doctors up north to warn their older patients before they depart for Florida and other winter getaways to check in before agreeing to undergo exams and procedures" (p. A1). Given the wide variation seen nationally in the frequency with which doctors order expensive tests and procedures, one of Medicare's most pressing challenges is how to assure that patients get the care they need while avoiding the care they don't need.

International Medical Graduates and their Effect on the Medical Profession

Two policy decisions have combined to encourage young physicians completing medical school in other countries to come to the United States to live and practice medicine. The first decision was to create flexibility in immigration laws to allow hospitals in the United States that are unable to fill all their residency training slots with graduates of US medical schools to fill those slots with graduates of medical schools outside of the United States or Canada. These international medical graduates (IMGs) must first pass two standardized examinations: one documenting that they have received a medical education equivalent to that in the United States and one documenting facility in written and spoken English. Those who pass these examinations must then successfully complete an in-person assessment of their clinical skills. They are required to interact with ten standardized patients and to demonstrate their ability to take a history from a patient, conduct a physical exam, and communicate orally with the patient. Those IMGs who successfully complete these exams are allowed to apply to US hospitals for residency training. Once an IMG obtains a residency training slot, he or she is then eligible to receive a visa to enter the United States for the duration of the residency. The original intent of the immigration laws was to allow the doctor to return to the country of origin after completion of training. In recent years, however, most IMGs completing their training—typically 75 percent—have been able to obtain permanent resident status and remain in this country.

The second policy that facilitated the employment of IMGs by hospitals in the United States was the decision by the federal Medicare program to reimburse hospitals for the cost of residency training, without limits on either numbers or types of residencies. The history of this policy is an unusual one. A relatively minor policy decision in the 1960s, unrelated to the issue of international graduates or medical education, has had the unintended long-term consequence of encouraging the immigration of large numbers of international physicians.

When the Medicare program was first approved by Congress in the 1960s, the federal government used a complex formula to calculate how much to pay hospitals for treating Medicare patients. The formula allowed the hospital to obtain reimbursement for a share of the costs of running the hospital. A somewhat lengthy list was established detailing which expenses the hospital could include in calculating the federal government's share. One item that appeared on this list was the cost of any residency training programs the hospitals might have. When Medicare switched to its prospective payment system for reimbursing hospitals (discussed in the following paragraphs), hospitals that previously had included the costs of residency training in their payment formula were allowed to continue to bill Medicare for these costs *in addition* to the payment they received under prospective payment. While this policy was originally intended to allow hospitals with existing residency training programs to continue their previous level of reimbursement, it soon became apparent that newly established residency programs were also eligible for federal reimbursement. Unintentionally, the Medicare program had written a blank check to hospitals to expand residency training programs. Hospitals were quick to respond. Adding a residency program (or expanding an existing one) not only adds to the prestige of the hospital but also provides a source of inexpensive labor. In many hospitals, especially inner-city hospitals providing care to a large number of poor patients, residents provide the bulk of direct patient care.

As a result of the expansion in residency training programs, paid for by the federal government, the number of entry-level training slots has become substantially larger than the number of medical students graduating each year from US medical schools. US medical graduates tend not to choose many of the inner-city hospitals for their training, leaving numerous unfilled training slots at these hospitals. To have sufficient personnel to take care of patients, these hospitals turn to international graduates to fill the residency programs. Hospitals in cities such as New York, Chicago, and Los Angeles that once had no problem filling their residencies with US graduates now train mostly international graduates. In 2014, there were 30,397 (25.9%) IMGs out of a total of 117,427 physicians in residency training in the United States (Brotherton and Etzel 2014).

A consequence of the expansion of training that followed the federal government's decision to subsidize residency training has been increasingly rapid growth in the number of physicians in the United States. In addition, because IMGs are more likely than US graduates to become specialists rather than primary care physicians, the policy has been a major factor contributing to the growing number of specialists in the country.

> **CONCEPT 4.6**
>
> As a consequence of the decision by Medicare to pay for the residency training of physicians, the number of training positions has increased dramatically. One of every four physicians entering residency training is a graduate of a medical school outside the United States or Canada. The influx of international medical graduates has contributed to the oversupply of specialists and thus to the rising cost of care.

As a consequence of the declining interest in primary care residency training, especially in the case of family medicine, however, IMGs are increasingly filling the primary care training slots left empty by graduates of US medical schools. In addition, IMGs who train in primary care and then locate their practice in a federally designated manpower shortage area can become eligible for permanent residency status and eventually US citizenship.

Hospitals

Throughout much of history, hospitals were not places of healing; they were places to die, mostly for poor people. It was during the Napoleonic Wars that doctors first started treating all of the wounded and sick soldiers in one place. Hospitals gradually became places for the scientific study of medicine instead of places for poor people to go to die. As part of the shift to medicine as a science-based discipline seen in the early twentieth century, hospitals increasingly became important for treating ill patients in an effort to prevent death. Following the Flexner Report on medical education and the affiliation of medical schools with universities, hospitals—especially university-based hospitals—became the principal locations for medical research. Thus, the hospital as we know it is a relatively young institution.

During the Great Depression of the 1930s, patients often could not pay their hospital bills, with the result that many hospitals had a hard time staying open. Hospitals decided to group together to offer, for the first time, insurance to cover the cost of hospital care. The hope was that people who could not afford to pay a large hospital bill once they got sick could afford monthly insurance premiums to protect themselves if they ever did get sick. These hospital-sponsored insurance plans, operated on a nonprofit basis, were the origin of the nationwide Blue Cross program. Every state had its own program of Blue Cross hospital insurance. Some states added an option for insuring against the cost of physicians' services. These were the Blue Shield plans. The AMA and its local affiliates supported the establishment of the Blue Cross / Blue Shield program so long as physicians maintained control over all medical decisions within the hospital.

In much of Europe, specialist physicians typically work only in the hospital, with primary care physicians working only in the community. When a community physician has a patient who needs to be hospitalized, the patient will often be referred to the hospital-based specialist. In the United States, community physicians traditionally admitted their patients to the hospital and supervised their care while they were in the hospital. This arrangement gave community physicians in the United States substantially more authority over hospital policies and practices than their counterparts in Europe. In many areas of the country, however, a new type of physician has begun to develop—the hospitalist.

A hospitalist is a physician who, similar to specialists in Europe, treats patients only in a hospital setting. Primary care physicians, especially those in large medical groups, may refer their patients in need of hospitalization to the hospitalist, who will then manage the care of the patient while in the hospital. Upon discharge, the patient will return to the primary care physician for ongoing care. The hospitalist has reduced the workload for primary care physicians, who no longer must take the one to two hours per day required to see patients in the hospital as well as seeing patients in the office.

The initial expectation was that the growing number of hospitalists would increase the efficiency of the care process, thereby reducing costs while maintaining (or perhaps improving) the quality of hospital care (Wachter and Goldman 1996). As hospitalists have grown in popularity, a number of analysts have questioned their role, suggesting that they weaken the underlying physician-patient relationship and make coordination of care more difficult (Pham et al. 2008). A study comparing hospital care provided by hospitalists with that provided by family physicians and general internists found that patients treated by hospitalists had a slightly shorter length of stay in the hospital, without any adverse effect on clinical outcomes. The costs of care provided by hospitalists were less than that provided by internists but no different from hospital care provided by family physicians (Lindenauer et al. 2007).

Hospitals in the United States generally have a dual system of administration. The physicians who treat patients in the hospital are members of the medical staff. No physician may treat a patient in the hospital unless he or she has first been accepted to membership in the medical staff. The medical staff governs all aspects of hospital care relating to physician care, such as quality review. A nonphysician hospital administrator governs all other nonphysician aspects of hospital activities, such as the nursing, managerial/administrative, and facilities staffs. Most hospitals have an executive committee where the leaders of the medical staff and hospital administrators can jointly discuss hospital management issues.

Hospitals in the United States are more expensive both per day and per stay than hospitals in European countries and Canada. Part of the reason for this is that up until 1983, hospitals had no incentives to limit the amount of care they offered. In fact, the payment system encouraged the acquisition of new facilities and technology, even if they duplicated facilities and services readily available elsewhere in the community.

Since the 1940s, there had been a government program (the Hill-Burton program) to finance the construction of new hospitals throughout the country, many of them in rural communities. In addition, the federal Medicare program included a payment formula that reimbursed hospitals for a large part of the cost of new technology. The result was considerable expansion of the number of hospital beds and the level of hospital technology throughout the country. For most patients, hospitals simply submitted bills to insurance companies (or the federal government, in the case of Medicare) and were fully reimbursed. There was little questioning of whether the care or the cost of care was appropriate.

Because the federal government typically paid about 40 percent of hospital bills throughout the country, primarily through the Medicare and Medicaid programs, it was beginning to cost the federal government a huge amount to continue simply re-imbursing hospitals for whatever they spent taking care of patients. The federal gov-ernment came up with a series of plans to reduce that cost. The first, in the 1970s, was the system of professional standards review organizations, or PSROs. PSROs were groups of local physicians who would review the care provided to Medicare and Med-icaid patients to assure that it was appropriate. While this effort was well intentioned, it had little effect, and hospital costs continued to rise.

In an effort to reduce rapidly rising costs, the federal government established a new program. Under this program, rather than simply reimbursing a hospital for the costs of care after the fact, the Medicare program began to pay a fixed amount each time a patient was admitted to the hospital. This plan has two names: the diagnosis-related group (DRG) system and the prospective payment system (PPS); both names mean the same thing. Under the PPS, instead of paying the hospital for each indi-vidual service, the government pays hospitals a fixed amount based on how much, on average, it should cost to take care of a patient of a particular type. (The PPS currently only covers hospital costs. Physicians' charges for taking care of patients in the hospi-tal are paid under a completely different system.) The amount of payment is based on what is wrong with the patient. For example, if a patient comes to the hospital with a heart attack that does not have any complications, the government pays the hospital the calculated average cost of taking care of this patient, regardless of what the hospi-tal does to treat the patient. If the patient has a heart attack with complications, the payment is more, based again on the average cost of taking care of such a patient. The same goes for treating pneumonia, appendicitis, or cancer. For each type of ill-ness, or DRG, the government pays a fixed amount. If the hospital is able to provide care for the patient at a lower cost than what the government pays, then the hospital keeps the difference. If the hospital's care costs more than what the government pays, then the hospital has to absorb the difference.

Under the previous payment system, with few controls on what the hospital could charge, the incentive was to keep a patient in the hospital as long as possible. Clearly, the incentive under the PPS is to get patients out of the hospital as quickly as possible. This situation led to many hospitals sending patients home (or to less expensive nursing homes) before they were fully recovered. The claim was made that hospitals were dis-charging patients "quicker and sicker." To counteract this tendency and to assure that patients admitted to the hospital had a legitimate need for hospital care, the federal government replaced the PSRO system with peer-review organizations, or PROs. A PRO is a local corporation that contracts with the government to provide oversight of the quality and necessity of the hospital care provided to Medicare patients. While many PROs have considerable participation by local medical associations, they give physicians substantially less control over the review of hospital care than under the previous PSRO system.

What the PPS did was to completely reverse the financial incentives given to hospitals that provide care to Medicare patients. The result was that between 1983 and 1993, there was a substantial decrease in the average length of hospital stay. Because patients were staying in the hospital fewer days, it meant that fewer hospital beds had patients in them at any one time. Fewer patients in the hospital meant less money for the hospital. The reduction in the use of hospitals following the initiation of the PPS resulted in substantially decreased revenues for hospitals.

An additional factor placed a financial squeeze on hospitals: both the federal PPS program and many private health insurers began to encourage outpatient treatment of many conditions that formerly were treated in the hospital. In 1981, only about one of six operations was performed on an outpatient basis, with the rest performed in the hospital. By 1991, about half of all operations were performed on an outpatient basis. Operations such as gall bladder surgery and knee surgery that previously had kept the patient in the hospital for several days were now being done in outpatient "surgicenters," with the patient going home the same day. There has been tremendous growth in the number of these centers dedicated to outpatient surgery. Many patients now being treated in surgicenters as outpatients used to be treated in hospitals. Again, the result was that hospital revenues went down substantially.

The net result of these changes was a decrease in the number of patients in the hospital on any given day (i.e., a decrease in the hospital occupancy rate). For several years, a typical hospital may have had 50 percent of its beds empty on any given day. This low occupancy presented a serious problem because of hospital expenses, which break down to 54 percent for labor costs, 37 percent for nonlabor costs, and 9 percent for capital (Iglehart 1993a).

Of the labor and nonlabor costs, some are fixed and some are variable. An example of fixed costs is the need for a hospital administrator. A hospital must have an administrator no matter how many patients are in the hospital. An example of variable costs is the number of nurses working on any given day. It is possible to adjust the number of nurses working based on the number of patients in the hospital. If a hospital is only 1 percent full, almost all the costs are fixed costs. If a hospital is 100 percent full, most of the costs are variable costs. The lower the occupancy rate, the fewer patients there are to share the fixed costs. The larger the share of the fixed costs that must be paid out of each patient's bill, the more expensive the care.

Hospitals that function at low occupancy are inefficient. Hospitals that function at high occupancy are much more efficient. Having large numbers of hospitals that function at low occupancy makes for an inefficient system of health care and adds substantially to the overall cost of care.

In many cities, there were several hospitals, each with 50 percent occupancy or less, when one medium-sized hospital functioning at near capacity could have provided all the hospital care for the entire city. One of the biggest problems facing the hospital industry was what to do about the oversupply of hospital beds. Few people were willing to close local hospitals, especially in rural areas. Dealing with the problem of an oversupply of hospital beds and resultant inefficiency in hospital care was a major policy challenge.

As we will see when we discuss managed care and the growth of the for-profit sector in health care, the effects of declining hospital occupancy were felt throughout the country in a number of ways. Many hospitals incurred large financial losses and faced the possibility of closing down. Hospitals began to merge so they could operate more efficiently. Many smaller hospitals had to close down completely. Hardest hit by these changes were many of the one thousand or so small rural hospitals, which are the only health care facilities available in many parts of the country, and many of the inner-city hospitals that take care of the poorest patients, most of whom rely on public support for their medical care.

> **CONCEPT 4.7**
>
> The prospective payment system coupled with the movement to outpatient surgery led to a substantial decline in hospital occupancy rates. Lower occupancy rates mean less hospital income *and* a less efficient hospital. As a result, many hospitals faced serious financial problems in the 1990s, leading to a restructuring of the hospital sector.

An additional change in the organization and structure of medical care has begun to affect how hospital care is provided. In many areas of the country, private investors have developed specialized facilities for treating specific types of medical or surgical problems. Typical examples are specialized cardiac care hospitals, orthopedic hospitals, and surgical hospitals. These are licensed hospitals to which patients are admitted, as is the case for general hospitals. In treating only specific diseases, such as heart disease, however, the specialty hospital can focus on providing care that typically pays well, assuring the financial success of the hospital. In contrast, general hospitals provide both care that pays well, such as cardiac or orthopedic care, and care that does not pay well, such as emergency care. For the general hospital, care that pays well balances care that does not pay as well. If the specialty hospital siphons off only those cases that pay well, however, the general hospital will be left with a higher proportion of cases that do not pay as well, threatening its financial viability. This issue becomes even more complicated when the investors who operate the specialty hospital include the physicians who provide the care in the hospital. This issue will be addressed in more depth in chapter 9.

A further change that is taking place at a growing number of hospitals is the abandonment of the historical separation between hospitals and the physicians who treat their patients in those hospitals. Even though physicians determine which patients should receive hospital care, physicians have traditionally maintained their practice structure separate from and independent of the entity that owned and operated the hospital. Even in large HMOs such as the Kaiser-Permanente system, discussed in the next chapter, the physician group has remained as a separate entity from the nonprofit corporation that owns the Kaiser hospitals.

With the many changes coming to the market for health insurance and the increasing role of government payment for health care, a growing number of hospitals have opted to purchase previously independent physician practices and shift those physicians to employees of the hospital. There are two potential benefits of this type of professional merger that have often been discussed: 1) such an integrated delivery system could become more efficient and thus better positioned to respond to the spread of alternative payment systems, such as accountable care organizations (ACOs) and bundled payment systems being developed as part of ACA (discussed in chapter 6); and 2) in an increasingly competitive private insurance market, the integrated system could develop enhanced competitive advantage that would allow it to negotiate for higher prices.

Baker et al. (2014) analyzed a national dataset including more than 2 million hospitalizations of nonelderly adults for the period 2001–07, looking to see if the vertical integration of hospitals with physician practices affected either utilization rates or prices. They found that those hospitals that owned physician practices and employed physicians had both higher prices for hospital care and higher overall hospital spending.

Neprash et al. (2015) reported a similar study that analyzed data from private insurers who paid for hospital care between 2008 and 2012. They found that increased hospital/physician integration was associated with higher prices for outpatient care but not for hospital care. There was no associated change in the volume of care, with the result that the higher prices lead to higher overall spending.

Responding to this study, Reschovsky and Rich (2015) suggested that "market power is achieved not only through consolidation of hospitals into systems but also through the control over a significant share of local physicians. Vertically integrated hospitals can use this market power to increase inpatient, outpatient, and physician reimbursements" (p. 1). Even with this increased market power, these integrated systems may also be better positioned to respond to the expectation from the federal government that hospital care for Medicare beneficiaries will need increasingly to be paid for through capped payment systems such as ACOs and bundled payment. Whether increased pricing will be associated with increased efficiency in providing value-based care under ACA is an issue that warrants close scrutiny.

Tertiary Care, Quaternary Care, and the Academic Medical Center

If primary care is provided in the physician's office and secondary care is provided in either the specialist's office or the hospital, tertiary care—the third level of care—is provided in specialized regional facilities that serve the needs of many hospitals and communities. Examples of tertiary care centers are neonatal intensive care units, burn centers, and transplant surgery centers. In many cities, each hospital will have facilities for taking care of newborn babies. But when a baby is born prematurely, weighing just a fraction of what a normal baby weighs, that baby is often transferred to a hospital in the region that has developed the hugely expensive facilities and personnel necessary to provide intensive care for these neonates. Similarly, patients with severe burns will typically be transferred to a facility specializing in the treatment of burns. It is at these highly specialized, tertiary referral centers that much of the training of future physicians takes place. Numerous studies have shown that when highly technical care is provided in tertiary referral centers, with a staff that frequently treats patients with those specialized needs, the outcomes for the patient are significantly better. There appears to be a strong, direct relationship between the frequency with which a physician or facility performs a specialized medical procedure and the quality of the outcome for the patient. This growing awareness of the improved quality available at many tertiary referral centers has strengthened the role of these types of facilities in the era of managed care.

For some types of new, often-experimental procedures, a fourth level of care has developed—quaternary care. Some facilities function as national referral centers for certain diseases and procedures. Examples might be combined heart and lung transplantation or experimental cancer treatment.

> **CONCEPT 4.8**
>
> There appears to be a strong, direct relationship between the frequency with which a physician or facility performs a specialized medical procedure and the quality of the outcome for the patient.

Most tertiary care centers, and nearly all quaternary care centers, are located within hospitals affiliated with a university medical school. These academic medical centers fulfill a dual role. They provide most of the medical research that leads to new types of treatments, and they train the future physicians who will be applying those treatments. Academic medical centers play a crucial role in maintaining and advancing the quality of medical care in this country.

SUMMARY

The structure of our medical and nursing professions has evolved substantially over the past one hundred years. From a profession that limited entry to women and racial minorities, our medical profession has become one in which nearly half of all new medical students are women. While the need to expand racial and ethnic diversity persists, the explicit barriers confronting nonwhite physicians were largely removed by the 1970s.

Even as the number of primary care physicians has risen slightly over time, the number of specialists within the profession has increased substantially. Economic forces tend to pull physicians toward specialized training. The attraction of primary care is less tangible, drawn principally from the quality of the relationship that develops over time between physician and patient. Establishing and maintaining policies that result in the optimal number and distribution of physicians will remain an important policy issue for years to come.

Though not enjoying the political power of organized medicine, the nursing profession has also evolved to one with high standards of education and training. Nursing has expanded the roles and responsibilities for those nurses with advanced training in areas such as critical care. There are growing concerns, however, as to whether nursing schools will be able to train enough nurses to meet future needs for nursing services.

In light of the increased specialization within these professions, the hospital as an institution of care has also become more specialized. Many of the most technologically advanced procedures and facilities are available only at tertiary centers that serve wide geographic regions.

PROVISIONS IN THE AFFORDABLE CARE ACT TO EXPAND PRIMARY CARE DELIVERY

By 2015, ACA had expanded the availability of private health insurance to about 11 million people who previously were uninsured. Those who drafted ACA were acutely aware that expanding access to health insurance is not the same thing as expanding access to health care, especially to primary care. If there are not enough primary care physicians, those with newly acquired health insurance may have no place to go for their care. Addressing this and other issues in assuring an adequate supply of physicians nationally, in 2014 the Institute of Medicine issued a report calling for "reforming the Medicare GME payment system and building an infrastructure that can drive more strategic investment in the nation's physician workforce" (p. 4).

ACA addresses this issue in three important ways. First, it shifts the policy focus of federal funding for graduate medical education (GME), described earlier, to expanding training in primary care. It does this by shifting a portion of GME funding away from programs that train specialists and redirecting it to programs that train primary care physicians. It also provides for new types of primary care training programs that are based in community settings rather than in the traditional hospital setting. These "teaching health centers" will represent collaborations between academic training centers and nonprofit, federally certified community clinics.

A second important policy in support of primary care was the provision in ACA that provides increased payment for primary care services. Beginning in 2011 and continuing through the end of 2015, primary care physicians participating in the federal Medicare program (discussed in chapter 6) were provided a 10 percent bonus payment for treating Medicare patients. For the two-year period 2013–14, primary care physicians who treated Medicaid patients (discussed in chapter 7) also saw their payment rates, historically substantially lower than Medicare rates, raised to the same rates as those paid by Medicare, with the federal government paying the full added cost. While this enhanced payment rate was associated with improved primary care access for many Medicaid patients, it ended in 2015. Many states are hoping the federal government will reinstate funds for these enhanced payments for primary care services for both Medicare and Medicaid recipients. ACA also increased federal funding for the National Health Service Corps and other programs that provide repayment of educational loans for primary care physicians who practice in areas of the country, typically rural areas and inner cities, that have documented medical manpower shortages.

The third important policy shift ACA makes in support of expanding primary care delivery is substantially increased support for a new model of organizing primary care: the patient-centered medical home. Larson and Reid (2010) described the history of "The Patient-Centered Medical Home (PCMH) Movement." A joint statement issued by a consortium of primary care professional organizations defines the PCMH as "an approach to providing comprehensive primary care for children, youth and adults [in] a health care setting that facilitates partnerships between individual patients, and their personal physicians, and when appropriate, the patient's family" (American Academy of Family Physicians, American Academy of Pediatrics, American College of Physicians, and American Osteopathic Association 2007).

Stange et al. (2010) identified four core components of a PCMH:

1. the fundamental tenets of primary care: first contact access, comprehensiveness, integration/coordination, and relationships involving sustained partnership;
2. new ways of organizing practice;
3. development of practices' internal capabilities; and
4. related health care system and reimbursement changes (p. 601).

Rather than a traditional physician's office, the PCMH will involve a team of providers, including physicians, allied professionals such as nurse practitioners or physician's assistants, as well as support personnel with a range of professional skills. While individual patients or families may identify with one particular member of the team as their principal provider, it will be the responsibility of the team as a whole to assure quality and accessible care. This team approach will be supported by an electronic health record system that will be able to track a patient's care, enable providers access to the records of a patient's care, and facilitate ongoing quality assessments of the care provided to patients. Those practices that fully incorporate these PCMH components are eligible for recognition by the National Committee for Quality Assurance (NCQA) (NCQA 2015b). Those that receive this recognition are eligible for enhanced payment rates under ACA.

In 2009, a consortium of five private insurance companies in Colorado sponsored a pilot study of the impact of the PCMH model on care outcomes (Rosenthal et al. 2015). The study involved 15 private practice groups that provided care to nearly 100,000 patients and a comparison group of 66 comparable practices. The PCMH practices received a supplemental per-patient-per-month fee to help pay for the added expense of incorporating those changes necessary to obtain NCQA certification. After an initial three-year period, patients treated in the PCMH practices had fewer emergency room visits and few ambulatory-care-sensitive hospital admissions than comparable patients in the control practices. Presumably based on better telephone and electronic access to providers, the PCMH patients also had somewhat fewer primary care office visits. Any cost savings attained through use of the PCMH model were offset by the added costs of the supplemental payments made to establish the PCMH practices, resulting in no net change in the overall cost of care.

ACA provides targeted funding to develop, expand, and evaluate PCMH models of care in a range of geographic locations. The expectation was that by expanding the training of primary care physicians, increasing the payment for primary care services, and supporting high-quality PCMHs, ACA will expand access to quality primary care not only for those expected to obtain new health insurance coverage but for all patients throughout the country.

An initial government review of early evidence of PCMH effectiveness found that few practice organizations had been able to fully attain PCMH status (Peikes et al. 2012). A study conducted in southeastern Pennsylvania followed 32 primary care practices that had volunteered to participate in a program to transform these traditional practices into PCMHs (Friedberg et al. 2014). While all participating practices attained NCQA recognition, there was improvement in the quality of care provided on only one of eleven measures studied. In addition, there was no evidence of reduction in the cost of care provided.

By contrast, a second, parallel study was conducted in northeastern Pennsylvania between 2007 and 2012, involving 27 practice groups. This study found significant quality improvements in four quality measures, as well as lower rates of patients' visits to the emergency room for care (Friedberg et al. 2015). An added component of the northeastern study that was not part of the southeastern study was a payment of $1.50 per patient per month earmarked for provider salaries and an additional $1.50 per patient per month to support the other costs of shifting to a PCMH model. As the authors of the study suggested, "the inclusion of a substantial shared savings incentive, with shared savings bonus payments being contingent on meeting quality measure benchmarks, may have been a particularly strong motivator for practices to invest and engage more effectively in care management efforts" (p. 1366).

An editorial response to the report of the first study suggested another possible reason it had shown no improvement in care. In studying a mostly privately insured (65 percent), relatively young (average age of 44), and relatively healthy patient population, the southeastern study had not focused on the patient population most likely to benefit from the enhanced care offered under the PCMH model. Instead, the author suggested: "The next critical phase of PCMH development should focus on its strategic deployment for the care of high-utilization patients with multiple chronic comorbidities, frequently with concomitant mental illness, and often with poor social support (Schwenk 2014, p. 803).

The types of high-risk patients described by Schwenk often receive their primary care not from private providers (for reasons discussed previously) but rather from federally supported, nonprofit community clinics. High-risk patients often come from low-income and minority groups that rely on Medicaid and/or Medicare for their coverage—or who are without any health insurance. Often referred to as federally qualified health centers (FQHCs), these centers disproportionately treat patients from these high-risk groups. In 2014, of the nearly 23 million patients seen at an FQHC, 62 percent were from a racial or ethnic minority group, 71 percent had incomes below the federal poverty level (FPL), 47 percent were covered by Medicaid, and an additional 28 percent were uninsured (US Health Resources and Services Administration 2014).

FQHCs have a strong track record of providing care to these disadvantaged groups. A national study of care provided at FQHCs found that "no significant health care disparities in access to care existed among patients from different racial/ethnic and insurance groups among health centers, unlike low-income patients nationwide" (Shi et al. 2013, p. 56). A second study found that those communities with a higher density of FQHCs offering care had lower rates of preventable hospitalizations among both patients on Medicaid and uninsured patients. Based on these findings, the authors of the study concluded that "these findings suggest health centers are contributing to lowering preventable hospitalizations and supports plans to expand such health centers" (Evans et al. 2015, p. 839).

Between 2009 and 2013, largely in response to incentives included in ACA, the number of FQHCs with the capacity to act as a PCMH increased from 32 percent to 62 percent (Commonwealth Fund 2015a). The principal difficulty FQHCs have encountered in meeting PCMH standards is in coordinating care of their patients with specialists and other providers outside the FQHC. This is a well-documented and longstanding problem for FQHCs, due principally to the low reimbursement rates offered by most state Medicaid programs.

5

Health Insurance, HMOs, and the Managed Care Revolution

In looking at alternative ways to pay for health care, we must appreciate that health care does not fit well into the traditional insurance model. Insurance is based on the concept of the random hazard: houses will burn down somewhat at random; people will get into car accidents somewhat at random. It is possible to separate people into risk categories, but within a risk category, hazards are assumed to occur somewhat randomly. One can predict the average rate at which hazards will occur within a certain risk group, estimate the aggregate cost of these hazards, add on a certain percentage for profit and administrative costs, and divide the total by the number of people to be insured. This gives the insurance premium to be charged.

Two aspects of health care make this insurance model particularly inappropriate:

1. Rather than being a truly random occurrence, the need for health care is largely defined by physicians. The pattern of treatment and the associated costs of an illness or injury can vary substantially from physician to physician.
2. Health insurance is particularly subject to the problem of "moral hazard": once a person is insured, that person is more likely to define a problem as an illness and is more likely to seek care.

These factors make it difficult to predict health care expenditures for a population group. As a result, many traditional insurance companies shied away from insuring for health care. Before the 1930s, few options were available for purchasing insurance to cover the cost of medical care. Those plans that did exist usually provided services directly to members of certain employee or other work-based groups and were not available to the general public.

This all changed during the Great Depression of the 1930s. As discussed in chapter 4, the inability of many individuals and families to pay the cost of medical care led to the creation of the Blue Cross and Blue Shield programs. Both the American Medical Association (AMA) and the American Hospital Association (AHA) supported these new plans, as long as doctors maintained control over medical decisions. By 1939, the majority of states had developed insurance programs of this type.

Before World War II, these insurance plans covered a relatively small number of people. An important decision was made in the 1940s, however, that was to have far-reaching effects on health insurance and health care. During World War II, in order to prevent inflation, the federal government placed price controls on most consumer goods. This included a freeze on all wages. The government ruled, however, that any fringe benefits from work were exempt from price controls. Thus, employees and their labor unions could not bargain for increased wages, but they could bargain for better health insurance as a fringe benefit. These policies carried over into the period after World War II, leading to greater and greater emphasis on increasing fringe benefits from work as well as wages. The main fringe benefit workers sought was health insurance.

A second government decision was to have equally powerful effects. In 1954, the government ruled that fringe benefits did not count as taxable income and thus were not subject to income tax. The combination of these two policies has had profound effects on the way we pay for health care as a society and what we have come to expect from health care as individuals. Consider the following example, as illustrated in figure 5.1.

If an employer wanted to raise an employee's pay by $1, the employer would have two choices: give the $1 as additional cash wages or use the $1 to purchase additional fringe benefits. To the employer, the two options are roughly equivalent, because either can be considered a tax-deductible business expense. (The employer would have to pay certain payroll taxes on the cash contribution that are not required to be paid for the added fringe benefits.) From the perspective of the worker, however, the two options look very different. Under tax law, the added $1 of wages would be subject to a combination of federal, state, and Social Security taxes that would, for a typical middle-income worker, eat up as much as 44¢, leaving the worker with a net gain of 56¢. On the other hand, by taking the added $1 as fringe benefits such as health insurance, the worker would gain a full $1 worth of benefit, because no taxes would apply. To the worker, it is often preferable to take a wage increase as added fringe benefits rather than as cash wages. To the

---

CONCEPT 5.1

Largely as a result of two decisions by the federal government in the 1940s and 1950s, neither of which dealt specifically with health care, the United States has adopted an employment-based system of financing health care. Most people now obtain their health insurance as a nontaxable fringe benefit from work.

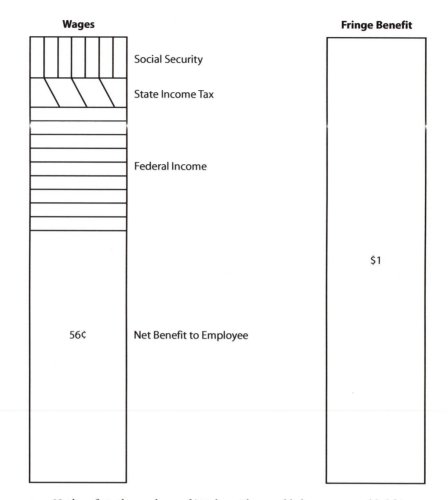

Wages   **Fringe Benefit**

Social Security

State Income Tax

Federal Income

$1

56¢   Net Benefit to Employee

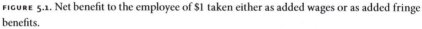

FIGURE 5.1. Net benefit to the employee of $1 taken either as added wages or as added fringe benefits.

employer, it makes less difference. Workers have thus come to expect to receive their health insurance as a fringe benefit of their employment.

In essence, this policy provides a federal tax subsidy for the purchase of health insurance as a fringe benefit. It is not a direct subsidy, but rather an indirect subsidy, in that less money comes into the federal treasury. This federal subsidy costs the treasury tens of billions of dollars in lost tax revenues every year and constitutes the third largest federal health care program after Medicare and Medicaid. The laws that created this subsidy were passed to address problems very different from health insurance, yet their cumulative effect over time has been to create a de facto national policy of employment-based health insurance. As is often the case, policy decisions at the federal level have long-range effects that were never envisioned at the time of their original passage.

A consequence of these tax policies is that people who receive health insurance as a fringe benefit tend to want more health insurance than they would if they were paying for it themselves. Consider the following example. Assume for the moment that you are a patient with a health insurance policy with a $1,000 yearly deductible (i.e., you pay the first $1,000 for medical care each year, and the insurance policy pays 100 percent of everything over $1,000). Assume also that you have a medical condition such as asthma, and you expect to incur at least $1,000 in yearly medical expenses. Finally, assume that you have more than $1,000 in a savings account.

A friendly insurance agent offers you the following option.

Option 1: The agent offers to sell you an additional health insurance policy to cover the first $1,000 of medical expenses each year. The cost of this policy is $1,200 ($1,000 to cover your expected medical costs, $100 to cover the administrative costs of the policy, and $100 to cover profit for the agent and the insurance company).

Do you want to buy the policy? Would any reasonable person in your situation choose to buy this policy?

It does not make much sense to purchase a policy to cover $1,000 in medical expenses when that policy costs $1,200. It makes more sense to politely refuse the insurance agent's offer and to pay the expenses directly, thus saving the $200 you would otherwise have to pay to cover overhead and profit for the insurance company. For people without a known medical condition, it makes even less sense to buy the additional policy.

Your employer, it turns out, has had a very good year and decides to give you a salary raise of $1,200 per year. Now consider option 2.

Option 2: The agent has heard of your good fortune and again offers to sell you the additional health insurance policy to cover the first $1,000 of medical expenses each year. The cost of the policy is again $1,200, but the agent reasons that because you have received a raise of $1,200 you will now be more interested in the policy.

As illustrated in figure 5.1, however, you pay 44 percent of any additional salary in taxes. Thus, despite your employer's generosity, you receive only $672 more per year in take-home pay after the raise ($1,200 × 56%). For the same reasons cited in option 1, it still makes no sense to buy the additional policy.

Option 3: Your employer, instead of giving you a raise in salary, offers to buy you the same supplemental health insurance policy to cover the first $1,000 in medical expenses each year. The cost of the policy to the employer is still $1,200.

Now do you want to buy the policy? What is the cost of the policy to you, in terms of income you have to forgo?

If you take the raise in pay as wages, you will receive $672 in net benefit per year. If you take the raise as added health insurance, you will receive $1,000 in benefit (the $1,000 you would otherwise have paid out of pocket for the care for your asthma). In this case, it makes sense to ask your employer to give you the raise in the form of added health insurance, even though you would never buy the same level of insurance if you were paying with your own money.

If you went out to purchase a car and you were guaranteed a government subsidy for 44 percent of the car's price, you would buy a very different car from what you would buy if you had to pay the full price yourself. The same is true of health insurance. This federal policy has led to people choosing, wanting, and expecting health insurance policies that are more comprehensive than they would select if they were paying with their own money.

Based on these federal policies, employer-provided, government-subsidized private health insurance came to be the predominant model of health insurance in this country. Until the 1980s, this employer-based health insurance provided in nearly all cases what has been referred to as indemnity insurance. The company indemnified the patient for the cost of health care. The patient sought medical care, paid for it directly to the provider, and in turn was reimbursed by the insurance company.

> **CONCEPT 5.2**
>
> The tax exclusion of health insurance obtained as a fringe benefit from work encourages employees to obtain more insurance than they would if they were paying for it themselves, often involving more comprehensive benefits and lower out-of-pocket expenditures.

Most of these employer-provided health insurance plans used what is called "experience rating" in determining how much to charge the employer for the cost of care. Premiums were set according to a combination of factors: the projected cost of providing care for employees, administrative costs and profit for the insurance company, and the carryover of any losses from the previous year. So long as insurance companies were able to predict accurately how much it would cost to provide medical care for all the employees each year, premiums paid by employers would rise at a gradual, predictable rate. If medical care costs were to rise rapidly and unpredictably, however, yearly increases in indemnity insurance premiums could be quite large, as illustrated in figure 5.2.

For a period of time in the 1980s, this was precisely the situation confronting both employers and insurers. Due largely to the explosion in medical technology, health care costs began to rise more rapidly than anyone expected. The result was that many indemnity insurance carriers found that the health care costs for which they were responsible were considerably more than they had predicted, resulting in a loss for the year. This "underwriting loss" would then be added to the premiums charged to an employer for the following year. The employer was hit with a double increase, paying both for the projected increase in the cost of care for the current year and for the underwriting loss for the previous year. Employers faced increasing costs for their employees' health insurance based on the experience of their employees during the previous year (thus the term "experience rating"). In essence, the insurance company

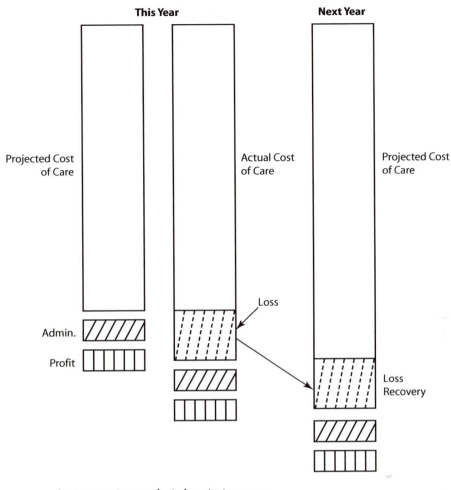

FIGURE 5.2. Setting premiums under indemnity insurance.

passed on to employers the risk involved in insuring their employees for the cost of health care.

Many of the indemnity insurance companies acted mainly as pass-through agents, taking a share of all premiums to pay overhead and profit while assuming relatively little risk. A number of large companies concluded that it would be cheaper to pay for their own employees' health care directly than to pay an insurance company to do it for them. They established self-insurance plans that lowered administrative costs, and they kept the part of the premium paid to cover insurance company profit. The money that they would have paid for health insurance premiums was put aside in a special health care fund. When employees got sick, they simply gave the bill to their employer, with no insurance intermediary. Many companies hired consulting firms to handle only the administration of the plan. At one point in the early 1990s, just before the explosion in managed care, nearly half of all employers and more than 80 percent of companies with more than five thousand employees provided health insurance through these self-insured plans. As discussed in chapter 2, however, the cost of medical care continued to rise sharply. Paying for the cost of health insurance was an increasingly large part of the cost of doing business. Insuring employees based on the indemnity model, in which most physicians and hospitals could still count on a fee for every service they performed with little oversight or constraint on the use of services, was proving to be unworkable. Thus, in 1993, when President Bill Clinton proposed a national system of care based on managed care and managed competition, many employers were initially supportive. They saw health maintenance organizations (HMOs) and other managed care plans that had developed in the previous twenty years as attractive options to traditional fee-for-service indemnity insurance.

INSURANCE PLANS, SERVICE PLANS, AND CAPITATION

Before discussing the origins of HMOs, I will first distinguish two alternative means of providing payment for health care services and define capitation as a method of paying for health care. The traditional means of paying for health care was with indemnity insurance plans under which patients sought their own source of care and were reimbursed for the cost of that care. Under these insurance plans, doctors were typically paid on a fee-for-service basis, with each separate service generating a professional fee.

> **CONCEPT 5.3**
>
> Under an *indemnity insurance plan*, patients arrange care on their own and are reimbursed for the cost of the care. Reimbursement for care is financed by insurance premiums. Under a *service plan*, patients come to an identified source of care and receive whatever service they need. Payment for these services comes from the pooling of monthly contributions.

As an alternative to fee-for-service medicine, a number of organizations in the early part of the twentieth century wanted to provide health care directly to a defined population of patients rather than reimbursing patients for the cost of care. These included organizations such as farm cooperatives, factories, and mining towns. Under these arrangements, a certain amount of money would be contributed each month, either by the workers or by their employer. This money would be pooled and would be used to hire physicians to take care of the people and to pay for hospital care for the people. Each patient covered under this type of service plan was assured the opportunity to receive necessary medical care with no fees other than the previously established monthly contribution. Physicians working under service plans were typically paid a salary rather than on a fee-for-service basis.

Both insurance plans and service plans work on a prepaid basis. The insurance plan depends on insurance premiums, paid by either the employer or the individual employee. The service plan depends on a fixed amount of money contributed (again, by either the employer or the individual employee) to a central pool of funds. The costs of providing service to patients enrolled in the plan must be drawn from this pool of funds. Thus, for the service plan, a fixed amount of money is available for care each year. Any losses incurred cannot simply be added to the costs of next year's care. Service plans use what has come to be called the "capitation" method of paying for health care.

> **CONCEPT 5.4**
>
> *Capitation* is a method of paying for health care under which a service provider receives a fixed amount of money per person (the capitation rate) and in return agrees to provide all necessary care to enrolled members. Capitation rates are usually per month or per year.

Throughout the early part of the twentieth century, as it was gaining increasing power over the practice of medicine, the AMA opposed the creation of service plans. The AMA objected to two aspects of service plans: (1) doctors being paid a salary instead of fee-for-service and (2) doctors being employed by an organization rather than being independent practitioners. Even though many patients and doctors liked these types of arrangements, the AMA declared both practices to be unethical. Any doctor who violated the ethical rules established by the AMA was barred from using local community hospitals. Because these doctors could not use a hospital, they could not take care of their patients. In the face of this opposition from the AMA, by the 1930s most of these service plans had gone out of business.

A few service plans, however, were able not only to survive but also to prosper as an alternative to the traditional fee-for-service insurance model. These included the Group Health Cooperative of Puget Sound in Seattle, the Health Insurance Plan of New York, and the Kaiser Permanente Health Care System on the West Coast. I examine the origins of Kaiser Permanente, the most successful of these service plans, to understand more about why these plans not only survived but also eventually provided the model around which the entire movement to managed care was centered.

KAISER PERMANENTE AND THE DEVELOPMENT OF HEALTH MAINTENANCE ORGANIZATIONS

In 1932, the city of Los Angeles began work on what was then a mammoth construction project: a 242-mile-long aqueduct across the Southern California desert to bring water from the Colorado River to the growing metropolis of Los Angeles. A number of industrialists collaborated on the project, among them Henry J. Kaiser. With more than five thousand workers in the field, and with on-the-job injuries all too frequent, there was a pressing need to provide medical care for workers close to the construction site.

Dr. Sidney Garfield was a young physician who had just completed training as a surgeon at Los Angeles County Hospital. With meager prospects for employment during the depth of the Depression, he saw an opportunity for an independent medical practice in the desert, close to the construction sites. He borrowed $50,000, built a small hospital, and set up a traditional fee-for-service practice in the desert. Unfortunately, he soon found the income from such a practice to be much less than he expected, and his hospital was near bankruptcy (Smillie 1991).

Dr. Garfield met with a representative of Mr. Kaiser's construction company. The construction company did not want the hospital to close, as it was the only source of care close to the construction site. The two of them worked out a plan under which the company would pay Dr. Garfield $1.50 per worker per month, and in return Dr. Garfield would provide all necessary medical care for on-the-job injuries. In addition, workers were offered the option of having an additional $1.50 taken out of their paychecks each month, in return for which they could go to Dr. Garfield for treatment of medical problems not related to their work. Mr. Kaiser enthusiastically approved, and the plan was put in place.

This capitation arrangement offered workers a service plan rather than a traditional insurance plan and turned out to be very successful. In a short time, the hospital was on firm financial ground, and Dr. Garfield was receiving a good income.

In 1938, Mr. Kaiser received the contract to build the Grand Coulee Dam on the Columbia River in eastern Washington. Because this construction project was far away from cities, many workers brought their families with them. Dr. Garfield and Mr. Kaiser agreed to establish a service plan for medical care for the workers as well as their families, based on the successful model in the California desert. For a fixed fee per person per month, paid partially by Kaiser and partially by the workers, workers and their families could receive all necessary care at the hospital and medical offices organized by Dr. Garfield. Again, the plan was successful, with Dr. Garfield hiring a number of young physicians to work for his new medical plan. The labor unions representing the construction workers were especially pleased, as previous attempts at providing medical care had been of questionable quality.

Recall, however, that the AMA had declared prepaid service plans based on capitation for workers and salaries for doctors to be unethical. An editorial published in *JAMA* in 1932 labeled these prepaid group practice plans "medical soviets" and went on to say that "such plans will mean the destruction of private practice . . . they are, in a word, 'unethical'" (American Medical Association 1932, p. 1950). Because both the Los Angeles aqueduct project and the Grand Coulee project were in rural areas, however, the AMA and their local affiliates paid little attention to them. Additionally, because Dr. Garfield operated his own hospital close to the work sites, he did not need to have the medical society's approval to use a hospital. World War II, however, was to change all of this. In Dr. Garfield's own words, "It is interesting to note that those ten years of basic development of our health plan took place in remote isolated areas of the country—areas that required us to innovate to survive, and also where we had no opposition. Nobody cared what we did. I don't think it could have ever happened in any other fashion" (Garfield 1974, p. 2).

When World War II came, Mr. Kaiser quickly began producing liberty ships at shipyards in Portland, Oregon, and Richmond, California. Much of the steel for these ships came from the Kaiser steel mill in Southern California. Again, Mr. Kaiser turned to Dr. Garfield to organize the medical care for shipyard workers and their families. This time, though, the AMA and their state affiliates opposed the plan and would not permit Dr. Garfield or his team of more than ninety doctors to use local hospitals. Despite a personal visit by Mr. Kaiser to its Chicago headquarters, the AMA would not relent. Faced with no alternative, Mr. Kaiser either built or bought a hospital in each of the three locales where the new Kaiser health plan was in operation.

After World War II, many employee groups beyond the shipyard workers wanted to join Kaiser's health plan. It provided a guarantee of all necessary care for a fixed fee per month. People liked both the price and the guaranteed availability of care. The AMA, however, continued to oppose Kaiser and other prepaid group practices. Through a series of legal actions in the 1940s and 1950s, the organized medical profession aggressively tried to put these plans out of business. Based largely on antitrust laws, the health plans were able to gain court protections, and in the late 1950s, a truce of sorts was achieved. The AMA ended its efforts to close Kaiser's health plan.

The Kaiser plan grew and flourished due largely to its success with labor unions and other large employee groups. Unfortunately, this growth and success contributed to tension between Mr. Kaiser and Dr. Garfield. Each wanted to control the growing organization. After lengthy negotiations, they agreed to maintain three separate organizations: a health plan, a hospital corporation, and a doctors' group. Kaiser would be in charge of the hospital and health plan organizations. Garfield would be in charge of the doctors' organization. Mr. Kaiser agreed that he would use only Dr. Garfield's doctors' organization for the patients covered by his health plan. Dr. Garfield agreed that his doctors would treat only patients in Kaiser's health plan. Thus, they were each dependent on the other.

The resulting Kaiser Permanente Health Plan grew and prospered throughout the 1950s and 1960s. It consistently cost less than comparable care under fee-for-service insurance. From its original three hospitals, it grew to become the largest HMO in the United States, providing care in several regions of the country. It depended on the continued cooperation and interdependence of the physicians, the hospitals, and the health plan. The health plan was set up as a nonprofit foundation, allowing it to remain tax-exempt. Likewise, the hospitals were owned and operated by a nonprofit corporation. Only the doctors operated on a for-profit basis. The structure of the Kaiser Permanente Health Plan is illustrated in figure 5.3.

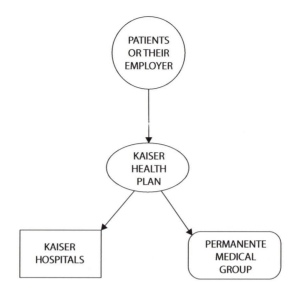

FIGURE 5.3. Structure of the Kaiser Permanente health care system.

The model represented by Kaiser Permanente and other similar plans was initially called "prepaid group practice." For a fixed monthly fee (the capitation rate) paid to the Kaiser Foundation Health Plan by either patients or their employer, the health plan would provide its members with all necessary health care. They would do this by contracting with the Kaiser Hospital Corporation for hospital care and with the Permanente Medical Group for physician care and other outpatient services.

The service plans represented by prepaid group practices such as Kaiser Permanente were consistently able to provide comprehensive care at a substantially lower cost than the insurance plans using the traditional fee-for-service method of paying for care. Repeated research studies documented this fact. Critics of these service plans, however, suggested that their lower cost of care was because they tended to attract younger, healthier patients who needed less care. If they took care of patient populations comparable to those covered by fee-for-service insurance plans, it was suggested that the service plan's cost advantage would disappear.

This issue was settled convincingly by an experiment done by the RAND Corporation in the 1980s (Manning et al. 1984). This experiment enrolled a group of 1,580 patients in Seattle and paid for their health insurance for a period of between three and five years. To be sure that patients in one type of system were not sicker on average than in the other, the experiment randomly assigned patients to receive all care either from the Group Health Cooperative of Puget Sound (a large, prepaid group practice similar in many ways to Kaiser Permanente) or from traditional fee-for-service physician offices. The results of the experiment, shown in table 5.1, demonstrated that,

TABLE 5.1. Comparison of the cost of care (per year) under prepaid group practice and fee-for-service systems

System	Total cost per patient	Hospital admissions per 1,000 patients	Office visits per patient
Prepaid group practice	$439	8.4	4.3
Fee-for-service	$609	13.8	4.2

Source: Data from Manning et al. 1984.

TABLE 5.2. Comparison of patient satisfaction with prepaid group practice (PPGP) and fee-for-service (FFS) systems

	Differences in mean satisfaction ($p < 0.05$) with	
	PPGP	FFS
Access to care	−	+
Waiting time in the office	+	−
Technical quality of care	No difference	
Interpersonal nature of care	−	+
Overall satisfaction with care	−	+

Source: Data from Davies et al. 1986.

given comparable patient populations, prepaid group practice service plans could be as much as one-third less expensive than fee-for-service insurance plans for comparable care.

The researchers also studied whether patients' health was any better in one type of plan or the other. Poor people in the prepaid group practice tended to have problems in two areas: control of blood pressure and control of glaucoma. Otherwise, the health of the two groups of patients was substantially the same (Sloss et al. 1987).

It is important to point out that the difference between prepaid group practice and fee-for service systems in this study was in the use of hospitals, and not in the use of outpatient physician services. There was no evidence that the use of primary care services and other outpatient services was different in prepaid group practices compared to fee-for-service. Patients found the experience of obtaining care from the prepaid group practices to be significantly less satisfactory than from the fee-for-service system, however (Davies et al. 1986). As shown in table 5.2, there was lower patient satisfaction in a number of aspects of the primary care process.

CONCEPT 5.5

Certain types of prepaid group practice service plans are able to provide care that is substantially less expensive than traditional fee-for-service care. Health outcomes under the two systems are approximately the same. The experience of obtaining care from a prepaid group practice, however, is often less satisfactory from the patient's perspective.

THE HEALTH MAINTENANCE ORGANIZATION ACT OF 1973 AND THE EXPANSION OF HMO MODELS

Even before the RAND health insurance experiment, a number of individuals and groups, both within government and in the private sector, had taken note of the cost savings available through prepaid group practice service plans. Several leaders of organized labor, led by Walter Reuther of the United Auto Workers Union, called for national health care reform based on expansion of the prepaid group practice model. In 1970, Senator Ted Kennedy introduced legislation to this end, setting off a national debate about health care reform. Even at that time, there remained laws in many states making prepaid group practice illegal. These laws were left over from the period when the AMA was fighting against the growth of prepaid group practice.

A number of groups introduced proposals for reform. While members of Congress were not able to agree on comprehensive reform, they did pass the Health Maintenance Organizations Act of 1973 (P.L. 93-222). Following the enactment of this law, prepaid group practices came to be known instead as health maintenance organizations, or simply HMOs. The HMO Act did five main things:

1. It removed preexisting state laws prohibiting HMOs.
2. It offered federal subsidies for the establishment of new HMOs.
3. It defined minimum standards to be certified as a "federally qualified HMO." A key element of these standards was the requirement that the HMO be organized on a nonprofit basis.
4. Where HMOs were available, it required all employers who offered health insurance to their employees also to offer an HMO as an option.
5. In a compromise with the AMA, it broadened the definition of an HMO to include a range of organizational and payment structures.

Figure 5.4 illustrates the basic structure of an HMO after enactment of the HMO Act. The HMO itself, as defined by the HMO Act, was intended to be a nonprofit corporation that contracted with employers or with individual patients to provide necessary medical care. To pay for the care, employers or individual subscribers would make a monthly capitation payment to the HMO. The HMO would then enter into contractual agreements with a range of physicians or physician groups and with a range of hospitals. Patients who join the HMO (often referred to as subscribers) are eligible to obtain care from any physician or hospital that has contracted with the HMO. If a subscriber seeks medical care from a physician or a hospital that has not contracted with the HMO, however, there would be no payment from the HMO for that care. By joining an HMO, a subscriber agrees to obtain care only from doctors and hospitals who have joined the HMO.

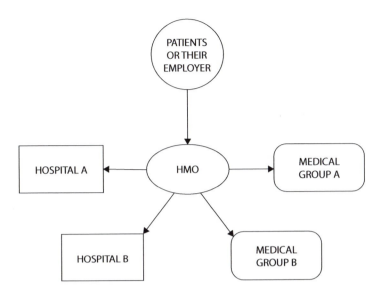

FIGURE 5.4. Model of an HMO following enactment of the HMO Act of 1973.

There are a variety of ways in which the arrangements among the HMO, the doctors, and the hospitals can be structured. Under the most common arrangement, the HMO operates a health plan that does not provide care directly. It does not own hospitals and does not hire physicians. Instead, it contracts with groups of physicians to provide care for its members and with either a chain of hospitals or a series of individual hospitals to provide hospital care for its members. The physician groups in turn are paid a "subcapitation" rate from the HMO. Through a contract with the HMO, the medical group is paid a share of the capitation rate received by the HMO, and in return, the group agrees to provide all necessary physician services for the members of the HMO who select that medical group for their care. Within each medical group, physicians can be paid by salary, by a fixed annual fee for each patient cared for, or by fee-for-service, depending on how the group is organized internally. Hospitals can be paid either a fixed amount per year or separately for each hospital admission. This type of arrangement is often referred to as a "group-model HMO."

A variation on the group-model arrangement is the independent practice association, or IPA HMO. An IPA HMO is a corporation usually formed and managed by physicians in smaller offices who are not part of large medical groups. The HMO accepts capitation payments for enrolled members and in turn contracts with individual physicians who have signed a contract with the IPA. Under the contract, the physician agrees to treat HMO patients either on a discounted fee-for-service basis or for a fixed amount per patient per year. Hospitals are paid in essentially the same manner as in a group-model HMO.

As a third option, the HMO might actually own the hospitals it uses and hire doctors as employees. This arrangement is often referred to as a "staff-model HMO." The Group Health Cooperative of Puget Sound in the state of Washington, one of the nation's oldest HMOs, was for many years structured as a staff-model HMO. In the years since passage of the HMO Act, staff-model and IPA HMOs have become much less common.

While there are similarities between the way the Kaiser Permanente system is structured, as shown in figure 5.3, and the structure illustrated in figure 5.4, there are key differences that set the two apart. Under the Kaiser system, there is only one group of doctors and only one group of hospitals. Each agrees to work only with the other. This sets up a mutual dependency in managing resources to assure success. Under the structure illustrated in figure 5.4, the medical groups contracting with the HMO may actually be competitors of the other medical groups, and the hospitals may be competitors. Additionally, the doctors have no personal stake in the success of the hospitals. While the Kaiser Permanente system has been able to maintain a culture of cooperation and collaboration among its doctors and hospitals, the same cannot be said for many of the newer types of HMOs that developed following the HMO Act.

Whatever the structure of the HMO, it operates as a service plan in that patients receive services from an established list of physicians. Patients may be responsible for a limited, partial payment for care they receive, but after having made this copayment, they have no further financial responsibility for their care. Recall that under traditional fee-for-service plans, there is no limit on how much can be spent on care each year. For all types of HMOs, a fixed amount of money is available each year, based on the capitation rate and the number of members enrolled. An HMO is obligated to provide all necessary care to all enrolled members for that amount of money and must take steps to provide care to its members while staying within its budget.

In a fee-for-service insurance system, there is no incentive to hold down costs. Costs are not minimized

- by the patient, who pays only a small amount of the bill;
- by the hospitals, which are paid for each patient regardless of how necessary the care is; or
- by physicians, whose incentive is to provide more care, because the more care they provide, the more money they get.

In an HMO, on the other hand, there is a strong incentive to hold down costs. An excessive use of services early in the year can lead to a budget shortfall later in the year, leaving inadequate funds to cover salaries and other costs.

Physicians in an HMO must be careful to provide only the care that is absolutely necessary. As we saw from the RAND health insurance experiment, the incentives in an HMO to hold down costs were associated with cost savings of more than 30 percent relative to the fee-for-service alternative. These savings were mainly in the use of the hospital and of expensive, high-tech treatments and not in the use of primary care and other outpatient services.

OTHER TYPES OF MANAGED CARE PLANS

In the period following the enactment of the HMO Act, another new type of managed care plan was developed to compete both with HMOs and with traditional fee-for-service systems. Referred to as a "preferred provider organization" (PPO), this new plan uses many of the same mechanisms to reduce utilization and costs but is more loosely structured than HMOs and does not technically qualify as an HMO.

As illustrated in figure 5.5, a PPO is usually organized by an insurance company as an alternative to traditional indemnity insurance. The insurance company contracts with physicians and hospitals that agree to give a discount to patients with this insurance. These providers, called "preferred providers," continue to be paid on a fee-for-service basis, only at a reduced rate for PPO patients. A patient with this type of insurance can go anywhere for care, but if the patient chooses a physician or a hospital not on the list of preferred providers, the patient has to pay substantially more for care. For example, the PPO might pay 100 percent of the cost of care from a preferred provider (after the patient has paid the annual deductible and makes a predefined co-payment) and only 80 percent of the cost of care from other providers. There is usually some form of control over the use of hospital treatment in PPOs, but it is not as

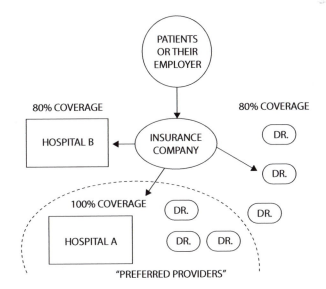

FIGURE 5.5. Preferred provider organization (PPO).

stringent as in an HMO. PPOs will typically negotiate reduced rates with a specific group of hospitals. Again, members are free to obtain care at any hospital but will have a lower level of coverage for care received from hospitals that have not signed an agreement with the PPO. It should be noted that neither the physicians in a PPO nor the hospitals have any financial stake in the success of the company.

Some companies have offered hybrid plans that include elements of both an HMO and a PPO, often referred to as point-of-service plans (POSs). Patients in a POS plan have three choices for receiving care, each with a different level of coverage.

1. If the patient receives care from physicians in the HMO, the patient pays little for care (usually on the level of a $20 to $30 copayment per visit).
2. If the patient receives care from physicians on the list of preferred providers associated with the POS, the patient pays a larger portion of the cost of care (typically 20–30% of the cost of care).
3. If the patient receives care from a physician or hospital not associated with the POS, the patient pays a substantial portion of the cost of care (typically 40–50%).

Thus, in a POS, patients have three options for obtaining care. The more patients are willing to limit their choice of physicians to those contracting with the POS, the less they have to pay. Based on this ability to choose the level of coverage, POS plans are sometimes referred to as "triple option plans."

COMPARING THE COST AND QUALITY OF NEW DELIVERY MODELS: THE MEDICAL OUTCOMES STUDY

The cost savings of HMOs documented by the RAND health insurance experiment pertained to large, centralized HMOs such as Kaiser Permanente and the Group Health Cooperative of Puget Sound. The structure of many of the newer HMOs was quite different from that of the traditional model with salaried physicians and centralized facilities. It was not known if many of the newer types of HMOs were able to achieve the same cost savings compared to fee-for-service systems. To answer this question, another large study was undertaken: the Medical Outcomes Study (Safran et al. 1994). This study involved 1,208 patients with chronic diseases and followed them for four years. The patients were enrolled in one of three types of plans: a large group-model HMO, an IPA HMO, and a traditional fee-for-service indemnity plan. The study followed two main outcomes: primary care quality and the change in patients' health status over the four years of the study. Results of the study, comparing the three alternative systems, are shown in table 5.3.

Compared to the IPA HMO and the fee-for-service option, the group HMO had a lower cost of care and better coordination among specialists and primary care physi-

TABLE 5.3. Results of the medical outcomes study comparing the quality of primary care in a group HMO, IPA HMO, and traditional fee-for-service (FFS) delivery system

	HMO	IPA	FFS
Cost of care	++	+	−
Coordination	+	−	−
Access to care	−	+	+
Comprehensiveness	−	+	+
Continuity	−	+	++
Doctor			
Interpersonal skill	NS	NS	NS
Technical skills	NS	NS	NS

Source: Data from Safran, Tarlov, and Rogers 1994.
   Notes: Results show comparative levels of quality at $p < 0.05$.
NS=no significant difference.

cians; however, it had lower ratings than either of the two alternatives for access to care, continuity of care, and comprehensiveness of care. There were no significant differences in how patients viewed either the interpersonal or the technical skills of their physicians. Overall, there were no significant differences in health outcomes for the patients studied, although low-income patients did show worse health outcomes in the group HMO.

These findings are similar to the findings of the RAND experiment: while HMOs save money, they have problems in the quality of the primary care process. These problems frequently led to lower overall levels of patient satisfaction in HMOs versus traditional fee-for-service practitioners. IPA HMOs, which rely on fee-for-service payment to physicians under an overall capitation framework, seem to fall somewhere in between group HMOs and traditional fee-for-service. In addition, these studies consistently identify worse health outcomes for low-income patients enrolled in HMOs. The causes of these lower health outcomes are not fully understood, although they may have to do with low-income patients having problems navigating the complex organizational systems inherent in many large HMOs.

THE SPREAD OF THE HMO

The development and expansion of the HMO and other types of managed care delivery systems brought a fundamental change to health care in the United States. Driven largely by concerns over rising costs, the HMO Act firmly established the role of the HMO in US health care. The federal government took a series of steps to promote the spread of HMOs, including financial incentives and regulatory support. Under the original HMO Act, to be eligible for federal support, HMOs had to meet three basic requirements:

1. The HMO had to offer a specified list of benefits to all members.
2. The HMO had to charge all members the same monthly premium, regardless of their health status (referred to as "community rating").
3. The HMO had to be structured as a nonprofit organization.

Ironically, at first the HMO Act brought the creation of new HMOs in the United States to a halt. The list of covered services required by the act was substantially more comprehensive than what was generally available in competing fee-for-service insurance plans. Both to provide the scope of benefits required by the government and to make these benefits available to everyone at the same price regardless of health status (something that competing fee-for-service plans definitely did *not* do), new HMOs would have been at a severe competitive disadvantage. As a consequence of these restrictions, no new HMOs were created in the two years following enactment of the HMO Act.

Congress acted in 1976 to loosen the requirements HMOs must meet to receive federal financial and regulatory support, and the growth in HMOs began as intended. Within a year after the amendments to the act, more than fifty new HMOs had qualified for federal support. By 1981, 10 million people were enrolled in HMOs nationwide.

As described earlier, throughout much of the twentieth century, the AMA opposed HMOs and other delivery mechanisms based on the capitation method of payment. Looking at the years following the HMO Act, we see that once HMOs were out of the box, they could never be put back. Between 1981 and 1989, enrollment in HMOs more than tripled, with more than 30 million people enrolled. Over a period of thirty years, the United States shifted from a health care system organized almost exclusively on a fee-for-service basis to one organized around HMOs, PPOs, and other forms of managed care delivery.

By the early 1990s, the accumulated evidence had demonstrated that HMOs and other types of managed care plans offered a way to reduce the cost of care without adverse effects on the health of most patients. The federal government, state governments, and employers began to look at HMOs as policy alternatives to traditional fee-for-service care. The growing popularity of these plans set the stage for the national debate on health care reform that followed the election of President Bill Clinton in 1992. At the center of this debate was a new concept: managed competition.

MANAGED COMPETITION: AN IDEA WHOSE TIME (SEEMINGLY) HAD COME

At certain times in a nation's political history, windows of opportunity open, allowing for the possibility of major social and political change. As described by Kingdon (1984), three conditions must coexist for major policy changes to take place:

1. A policy issue must rise to the top of the national agenda, with broad public awareness and support.
2. The political circumstances prevailing at the time must be amenable to significant change in policy.
3. A plan for change must be available that offers realistic solutions to the problems that are present.

In the period 1992–94, many people thought a window of opportunity had opened for major reform of our national health care system. The election of President Bill Clinton put the need for health care reform close to the top of the national policy agenda. Members of Congress appeared broadly to support the need for change. A plan was immediately available that offered a compelling theoretical model of the new form health care in the United States could take: managed competition.

In 1980, in the midst of the changes to the health care industry described previously, Professor Alain Enthoven of Stanford University published a book titled *Health Plan: The Only Practical Solution to the Soaring Cost of Medical Care.* This book proposed a national system of health care centered on the concept of groups of health care purchasers banding together to obtain health insurance from competing health insurers.

Under general economic theory, markets will function efficiently only when well-informed consumers are able to choose among competing products. Both the producer and the consumer of a good or service should approach a potential market transaction on an equal basis. A purely market approach to providing health insurance or health care, however, involves a number of inherent problems regarding this classic economic theory. (See Arrow 1963 for a more complete discussion of these issues.) Potential problems include inequality in the information available to physician and patient, the likelihood that merely having health insurance will increase the rate at which people access health care services (the "moral hazard" described earlier), and the uncertainty involved in predicting the rate at which health services will be provided in the future.

Addressing these problems, Enthoven developed a proposal to reform the market for health insurance and health care to make it more efficient. He predicted that if the market were modified through regulation to counteract the forces that create market failure, "the health care system would be transformed, gradually and voluntarily, from today's system with built-in cost-increasing incentives to a system with built-in incentives for consumer satisfaction and cost control." He proposed "a system of fair economic competition in which consumers and providers of care, making decisions in an appropriately structured private market, would do the work of reorganization" (Enthoven 1980, pp. xxi–xxii). Building on this original work, in 1989 Enthoven collaborated with Richard Kronick to propose a modification of this original plan, called the "Consumer Choice Health Plan" (Enthoven and Kronick 1989). The ideas contained in these plans form the core of proposals for national health care reform based on the concept of managed competition.

A major tenet of Enthoven's proposals for managed competition is that through a reliance on market forces the country would be able to address problems of rising costs through improved efficiency. By removing many of the constraints that had led to past market failures, managed competition would encourage the spread of health care organizations and delivery systems that are able to reduce unnecessary expenditures while also maintaining quality.

Managed competition relies on four basic principles for the organization of the health care system.

1. Rather than selecting and purchasing health insurance directly through their employer, employees from a variety of companies would join together to form a "health insurance purchasing cooperative" (HIPC).

2. These HIPCs would in turn shop among HMOs and other managed health care plans to select the best options for their members. The HIPCs would be large enough to have professional staff able to evaluate the quality of the care offered by the various plans available. Based on this quality assessment, the HIPCs would select several plans to offer to members, thus assuring a range of choice. The HIPCs would offer only plans that, in the opinion of HIPC managers, offered high quality at competitive prices.

3. All managed care plans that wanted to compete for the business of the HIPC would be required to offer a basic benefit package, covering a specified range of health care services. Historically, it has been difficult for consumers (in this case, members of the HIPC) to compare the price of competing health insurance plans, because each plan would have its own unique set of covered services. By assuring that the benefit package was the same for all plans offered, consumers could make a direct price comparison of plans.

4. HMOs and other health plans that were competing for the business of the HIPCs would be free to offer coverage options that were more comprehensive than the basic benefit package. If a consumer selected a more comprehensive (and thus more expensive) option, however, the consumer would have to pay the added cost (i.e., the difference between the plan selected and the basic plan) out of his or her own pocket. This added cost of the comprehensive plan would not be tax deductible, thus requiring the consumer to pay the full additional amount. (Recall that current tax laws encourage consumers to buy more health insurance than they would buy if they were paying for it themselves. This aspect of managed competition would require the federal government to change the tax laws.)

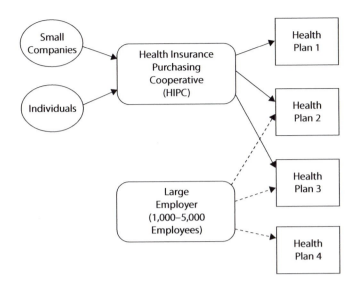

FIGURE 5.6. The structure of "managed competition."

Under managed competition, all privately purchased health insurance would be obtained through HIPCs. HIPCs would be organized on a regional basis, with one HIPC per region. The exception to this would be that employers with more than one thousand employees would be allowed to act as their own HIPC. Any type of health plan, from a staff-model HMO through a purely fee-for-service PPO, would be permitted to offer coverage through the HIPC. A health plan that did not meet the standard of quality established by the HIPC, however, would not be offered as an option to HIPC members. An exclusion of this type could mean the demise of noncompetitive plans. The theory of managed competition is illustrated in figure 5.6.

At this point, it is important to be sure that the reader understands the difference between two fundamental concepts: *managed care* and *managed competition*. *Managed care* is a means of organizing, paying for, and providing health care directly to consumers. It is paid for through a capitation arrangement, under which a particular group or organization is responsible for assuring that all necessary care is provided to a given population of patients and that the cost of that care does not exceed budgeted funds. (The budget would be equal to the capitation rate times the number of members.) The responsible group then "manages" the care process to assure that the budget is not exceeded. The responsible group may be

- an insurance company,
- a nonprofit corporation,
- a for-profit corporation, or
- physicians and hospitals in combination.

Managed competition, on the other hand, is a system for providing health care on a regional basis, in which patients choose between competing systems of managed care.

Managed care is a way of providing care directly to consumers. Managed competition is a theory of health care reform that relies on managed care as the basis of organizing, financing, and delivering health care.

Initially, critics of managed competition pointed out that the model was only a theoretical one that had never been tested. Even Enthoven and Kronick acknowledged that "the only proved method for bringing the growth in total expenditures into line with the gross national product is for government to take over most of health care financing and place it under firm global budgets." They concluded, however, that "in view of our historic preferences for limited government and decentralization," it would be more effective in the case of the United States to create a private, market-based system of managed competition that is based on "generally accepted economic theory" (Enthoven and Kronick 1989, pp. 100–101).

According to Enthoven's view of economic theory, a properly organized market would lead over time to the efficient provision of health care. Efficient in this sense refers to providing cost-effective care. As discussed in chapter 3, a common measure of economic efficiency compares the relationship between marginal benefits and marginal costs. If the marginal benefits of an activity equal or exceed the marginal costs of acquiring those added benefits, it makes economic sense to take on those added costs. If marginal benefits turn out to be less than their marginal costs, it makes little sense to make those added investments. Efficiency is achieved at that point at which marginal benefits and marginal costs are approximately equal.

> **CONCEPT 5.7**
>
> *Managed care* is a way of organizing and financing the direct delivery of care. *Managed competition* is a way of restructuring the entire health care system. It relies on managed care as the basic model for the delivery of care.

Applying this concept to health care, efficiency is achieved when, either for a specific health plan or for the system as a whole, the marginal benefits of additional care approximate the marginal costs. That is to say, the marginal resources that we apply to health care result in tangible benefits that justify the expenditure of those resources. Enthoven and Kronick predicted that, if adopted on a national scale, managed competition would lead to "a restructured market system in which the efficient prosper and the inefficient must improve or fail" (Enthoven and Kronick 1991, p. 2535). Such a state of equilibrium in the market for health care would, they argue, place reasonable limits on the cost of our health care system.

Historically, our health care system has embodied a number of political and social institutions that have resulted in substantial inefficiency in our system of care. These institutions include the tax treatment of health insurance premiums and the system of paying physicians a separate fee for each service provided regardless of the added benefits of that service. These incentives lead to patients expecting and physicians providing a great deal of expensive care with relatively little marginal benefit.

Enthoven proposed that, given the opportunity to operate without these and other perverse incentives previously embodied in tax laws and laws regulating medical practice, the market itself would tend to weed out inefficient providers of care. Whether they provide care that is of high cost or low quality, or whether they simply provide poor service to their patients, health care organizations that are not able to operate efficiently will not be able to survive in a system based on managed competition. By creating a system of competing organizations—large purchasers on the demand side and managed care organizations on the supply side—Enthoven predicted that the market would select those organizations and organizational forms that operate efficiently and in so doing would assure the provision of cost-effective, high-quality care. This belief in market efficiency forms the theoretical core of managed competition proposals. The theory behind managed competition predicts that if a properly structured market were created, "the health care system would be transformed, gradually and voluntarily, from today's system with built-in cost-increasing incentives to a system with built-in incentives for consumer satisfaction and cost control" (Enthoven 1980, p. xxii).

As we will see in the sections that follow, managed competition proved to be only partially successful in creating a more efficient health care system. The numerous social, economic, and political institutions that over time created the structure of our health care system continued to impede the ability to shift to an efficient system in the allocation of scarce health care resources. As Douglass North described (see chapter 3), and as proved to be the case with managed competition, markets alone are often unable to change broad institutional structure.

PUTTING MANAGED COMPETITION INTO ACTION: THE CLINTON HEALTH REFORM PROPOSAL

During the presidential election campaign in 1992, Bill Clinton promised that, if elected, he would move rapidly to reform the US system of health care. Shortly after assuming office, he took steps to put this plan in action. In doing so, he made a policy decision that a number of authors suggest was fundamentally flawed (Johnson and Broder 1996; Skocpol 1997). Rather than relying on the process of congressional hearings to arrive at a final plan for reform, Clinton chose to create a task force of experts within the executive branch, under the supervision of First Lady Hillary Clinton. He charged this task force with developing a comprehensive, detailed plan for national health care reform.

The plan developed by the task force and presented to Congress in 1993 had at its core Enthoven's theory of managed competition; however, the Clinton plan differed from the plan proposed by Enthoven in a number of important ways.

- The Clinton plan proposed that states establish a single, statewide, publicly financed HIPC (referred to in the Clinton Plan as a "Health Alliance"), and that all residents of the state obtain their health coverage through the HIPC. Enthoven saw HIPCs as much smaller, with one for each region within a state.
- The Clinton plan allowed employers with five thousand employees to act as their own HIPC. The Enthoven plan would have allowed employers with one thousand employees this option.
- The Clinton plan relied on a national health board to establish the benefits that must be included in the basic benefit plan. The Enthoven plan left this decision up to the HIPCs and the market.
- The Clinton plan gave the national health board the authority to regulate the rates that managed care plans could charge HIPCs for the basic benefit package. The Enthoven plan left the setting of rates up to the market and to competition among managed care providers.

Several other plans were proposed in Congress as alternatives to the Clinton plan. Many of these alternatives also relied on the theory of managed competition, only with less government authority to regulate care. It appeared that, after more than ten years of discussion and debate, the time had finally come for managed competition to be adopted as our national policy of care. Kingdon's "window of opportunity" for major national health care reform seemed to be open.

History, however, would prove otherwise. While President Clinton was taking more than a year to formulate the specifics of his plan, the political tide in the United States shifted dramatically. The Republican Party in Congress, under the leadership of Newt Gingrich, sensed that President Clinton and the Democrats had exposed their Achilles' heel—"big government." The plan offered by the Clinton administration sounded a lot like another "big government" solution to a social problem, typical of many of the failed solutions of the "War on Poverty" in the 1960s. Through a series of parliamentary procedures, the Republicans were able to stall consideration of health care reform. During this time, the health insurance industry, feeling threatened by proposals to transfer the purchasing of health insurance from them to HIPCs, ran an amazingly effective series of TV ads attacking the Clinton proposal. These "Harry and Louise" ads portrayed a typical, white, middle-class couple who was afraid that they were going to lose their health insurance to coverage provided by an immense government bureaucracy. Even though the claims of these ads were of tenuous accuracy, they hit home with American consumers. The combination of the Republican stalling tactics and the fear of government bureaucracy in health care engendered by Harry and Louise shifted the political landscape almost overnight. The political circumstances were no longer amenable to change. The three conditions identified by Kingdon no longer existed. The window of opportunity for national health care reform slammed shut. The Clinton plan was defeated, and the new Republican congressional leaders made it abundantly clear there was little if any chance for health care reform in the foreseeable future.

THE SHIFT TO MANAGED CARE: THE MARKET DOES WHAT THE GOVERNMENT WOULD NOT

Even though Congress failed to enact national health care reform, a fundamental shift took place nonetheless in the 1990s in our health care system. This shift had many, but not all, of the characteristics of managed competition proposed by Enthoven. The rapidly rising cost of care, coupled with the growing awareness of the concept of managed care engendered by the debate over the Clinton plan, led many employers to turn to managed care to control the cost of providing care to their employees. In addition, employers banded together in some parts of the country to establish private purchasing cooperatives for health care, as envisioned by the original theory of managed competition. A number of these HIPCs were quite successful for a period of several years in holding down the price of health coverage by getting the various available health plans to compete among themselves to offer the lowest price.

An example of such a private, employer-sponsored HIPC was the Pacific Business Group on Health (PBGH), established in California. PBGH involved many of the biggest employers in California. All these employers chose to offer their employees only those health insurance plans approved by PBGH, at capitation rates negotiated by PBGH. Representing hundreds of thousands of potential health plan members, PBGH was effective in negotiating low rates for health plan coverage. Few managed care providers were willing to forgo the opportunity of enrolling PBGH members. To do so would mean the potential loss of thousands of health plan members.

In contrast to the 10 to 15 percent yearly increases in health plan rates seen in the early 1990s, PBGH was able in many cases to negotiate reductions in rates from many managed care providers. For several years in a row, the cost of providing care to employees leveled out for the employers composing PBGH. Managed competition seemed to work, at least in some contexts.

Other groups had similar success in holding down the cost of care by adopting the model of managed competition. Notable among these were large, governmentally supported organizations that provided health coverage for public-sector employees such as the California Public Employees Retirement System and the Federal Employees

Health Benefits Plan. In the mid-1990s, they too experienced a dramatic leveling in the cost of providing coverage to their members.

The economics of the entire health care system in the United States changed during the 1990s. Many of the large purchasing cooperatives organized on the model of HIPCs were having substantial success. Employers and managed care plans not involved in formally structured HIPCs were able to reduce the rate at which the cost of care was increasing. Even Medicare and Medicaid began to look to managed care and managed competition as a potential solution to the rising costs of these programs.

Over the period of only a few years, our national health care system changed to one based largely on managed care. An overwhelming majority of Americans covered by health insurance today are covered under one form of managed care or another. By the year 2000—only six years after the failure of the Clinton health reform proposal—more than one thousand PPOs and more than six hundred HMOs were operating in the United States. Even though there was no national legislation mandating a shift to managed care and managed competition, the private marketplace for health insurance brought about many aspects of this model. (See Oliver 2004 for an excellent discussion of the rise of managed care.)

DID MANAGED COMPETITION AND MANAGED CARE DECREASE HEALTH CARE COSTS IN THE LONG TERM?

The economic theory behind the shift to managed competition and managed care relies on market forces to achieve a higher level of efficiency in our health care system, and in doing so, to control health care costs. A number of scholars in fields such as economics, political science, and sociology have questioned the ultimate ability of market forces alone to achieve the efficient provision of socially important goods such as health care. Their concern has been that broad social institutions inhibit the market's ability to attain efficiency.

As described in chapter 3, institutions provide the rules, both formal and informal, that govern action within a society. Douglass North was awarded the Nobel Prize in Economics for his work showing how market efficiency is constrained by the institutional context in which the market exists. North predicted that problems may arise when the set of institutional forces that drive economic markets overlaps with institutions reflecting broader social and political phenomena. This interaction of social and economic institutions may impair efficient economic activity. "If political and economic markets were efficient . . . then the choices made would always be efficient. . . .

[However], institutions . . . are always a mixed bag of those that increase and those that decrease productivity" (North 1986, p. 8).

There have been numerous instances of inefficient institutions coming to predominate in American business, even in the face of market forces. Take, for example, the standard computer keyboard, which begins with the letters QWERTY. This has been the standard keyboard configuration of typewriters and computers for decades, yet it is a relatively inefficient way to arrange the keys (David 1985). This inefficient institution has come to exist despite the effects of market forces.

Many types of institutional force inhibit the ability of markets to achieve efficiency. These countervailing forces frequently have to do with social belief systems and generally accepted rules of behavior that are not necessarily rationally or scientifically derived. These institutional constraints on market efficiency can be formalized, as in laws and regulations, or can exert their influence informally, as with social norms and professional ethics. They derive from a number of sources, both within the market itself and from the social context in which the market exists.

Chapter 3 describes the technological imperative and other institutions affecting health care in the United States. The effects of these institutions distinguish our system of health care from those in Canada and other developed countries. They also make it difficult to constrain the growth of medical technology and the inevitable increase in costs inherent in such growth. Institutions such as these all too often are not economically efficient, at least not in the way economists approach the concept. The market's ability to improve efficiency—the basis of the economic theory behind managed competition—is constrained by the institutions that surround it.

Even under a fully capitated, competitive system, it was unlikely that managed care plans would be able to overcome many of the inefficient institutions that add so much to the cost of care. To attain a meaningful, long-term stabilization in the cost of care, they must reduce the number of services they provide, especially expensive inpatient services and other types of specialized care. To do this, they must attempt to alter the behavior of the physicians practicing within their system and the expectations of patients. Public perceptions of what constitutes appropriate care, however, exist in response to the institutions that predominate in the broader social context.

There is little doubt that care provided under capitation systems costs less than comparable care under fee-for-service. The effects of capitation on the cost of care, however, may be limited. Managed care systems are able to eliminate certain types of inefficiencies within a given institutional context, but they may be powerless to change the surrounding context itself. Constraining the rapid escalation of technology, minimizing local variations in patterns of care, and coping with defensive medicine were no less a problem for successful managed care plans than they were for their fee-for-service competitors. Managed care and managed competition, while achieving

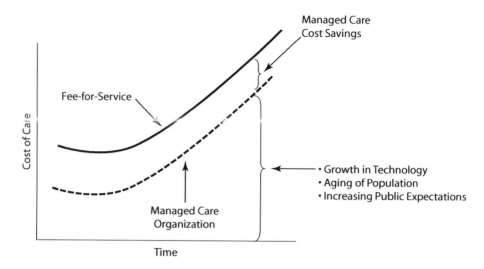

FIGURE 5.7. Managed care and the rising cost of health care.

improvements through altered financial incentives, proved not to be able to overcome the broad inertia of inefficient institutions. In the words of Victor Fuchs (1993c, p. 1679), "The market is a powerful and flexible instrument for allocating most goods and services, but it cannot create an equitable, universal system of insurance, cannot harness technologic change in medicine, and cannot cope with the potentially unlimited demand for health care by the elderly."

Figure 5.7 represents the long-term relationship between the cost of health care in the traditional fee-for-service system and in managed care organizations such as HMOs. While there is a clear cost advantage for the managed care organization, this advantage remains relatively constant over time. Both fee-for-service and managed care delivery systems must contend with broad social forces that seem inexorably to drive up the cost of care.

The theory of managed competition predicts that, by shifting from fee-for-service to a system of competing managed care organizations, it will be possible to arrest the increasing cost of care. This goal would be obtained by weeding out the inefficiencies inherent in fee-for-service.

Looking at the cost of care in the United States measured as a percentage of gross domestic product (GDP) spent on health care, we see at first that this prediction was accurate. Between 1993 and 1998, the period when managed care became the norm in the United States, health care expenditures remained relatively constant, averaging 13.6 percent of GDP.

What, though, would happen when the transition to managed care was complete? Would the cost of care remain level, as predicted by the theory of managed competition, or would the rise in the cost of care resume? Figure 5.8 illustrates this question.

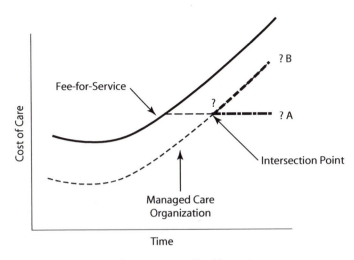

FIGURE 5.8. Can managed care stop the rising cost of health care?

The theory of managed competition predicted that the cost of care would remain level, illustrated by the line labeled A in figure 5.8. If, however, managed care organizations face the same institutional forces driving up the cost of care that affected the fee-for-service system, the cost savings of a national shift to managed care would be a one-time phenomenon. Once the cost of care bumps up against the managed care curve in figure 5.8, it would resume its yearly increase at the same rate as before. This outcome is illustrated by the line labeled B.

Figure 5.9 shows the rise in the cost of our health care system between 1987, when managed care began its spread, and 2003, by which time most health insurance plans nationally had shifted to a managed care model. It should be clear that option B was what actually occurred. During the several years in the mid-1990s when the shift took place, as we moved from the fee-for-service curve to the managed care curve, there was a flattening in the cost curve. Once the majority of the population had shifted from traditional, fee-for-service indemnity insurance to managed care alternatives, however, the cost of care measured as a percentage of GDP began to rise again at approximately the same rate as before the shift. That rise continued throughout the first decade of the new century. Our health care system shifted from the fee-for-service curve to the managed care curve without changing the slope of either curve. The economic theory behind the shift to managed care appears to have failed the test of time.

CONCEPT 5.9

The move to managed care that took place in the United States in the 1980s and 1990s appears to have realized a one-time savings in the amount we spend on health care yet failed to arrest the long-term growth in the overall cost of health care.

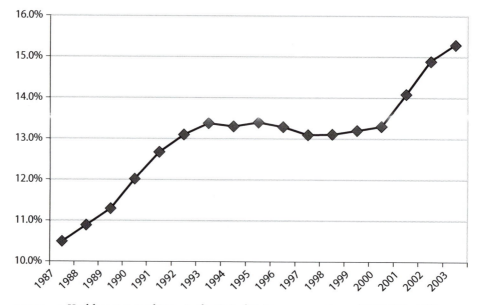

FIGURE 5.9. Health care expenditures in the United States as a percentage of GDP, 1987–2003. *Source:* Data from US Centers for Medicare and Medicaid Services.

WHY DIDN'T MANAGED COMPETITION WORK?

To work successfully, managed competition relies on employees and others who have health insurance to obtain their insurance from a HIPC. It is expected that those with health insurance will act as "informed consumers," choosing from the plans offered by the HIPC the one that provides the best value to them. One reason that managed competition did not work is that this goal—having consumers select from a variety of health plans—was available only in certain areas of the country and to certain types of employees. In 2009, only 13 percent of firms with fewer than two hundred employees offered their employees a choice of health plans; for firms with between two hundred and one thousand workers, 39 percent of firms offered their employees a choice of health plans. Only large firms—those with more than one thousand employees— were likely to give their employees a selection of plans from which to choose. As a result, 47 percent of employees receiving health insurance from their employer had only one plan available to them, while an additional 33 percent had only two plans (Kaiser Family Foundation and Health Research and Educational Trust 2009). Without a requirement that all health insurance be obtained from HIPCs and that employees be offered a choice of plans (such as was contained in the failed Clinton health plan), a fully competitive situation was never attained.

Even in places such as California, where fully functional HIPCs were established (e.g., Pacific Business Group on Health and California Public Employees Retirement

System), the reductions in the cost of health insurance were only temporary. For several years in the 1990s, these HIPCs were able to get HMOs and other managed care companies to hold down the cost of care. To do this, however, these managed care plans needed, in return, to hold down the cost of care for the patients they covered.

They did this through a combination of methods intended to reduce the use of care, and through a reduction in the amount they would pay physicians and hospitals for care. As described in chapter 9, these methods came up against what is referred to as the "managed care backlash." In the long run, the managed care companies made it clear to the HIPCs that, to provide the type of care expected by patients, they would have to raise their rates. The HIPCs had little choice but to accept the renewed reality of increasing health care costs.

Another aspect of the managed care backlash was a growing tendency for employers to offer PPOs rather than HMOs to their employees, because of the broader choice of providers and fewer restrictions on care inherent in PPOs. In those companies offering both HMO and PPO options, employees began to favor the PPO. By 2009, PPOs had taken over the largest share of the market for employer-sponsored health insurance, with 60 percent of covered workers enrolled in PPOs. By comparison, 20 percent of workers were covered by an HMO with an additional 10 percent covered by a POS plan. An additional 8 percent of workers were enrolled in a high-deductible health plan (described in the following section), with only 1 percent of employees nationally covered by traditional indemnity health insurance (Kaiser Family Foundation and Health Research and Educational Trust 2009).

The theory of managed competition ran aground on the rocks of the institutions and resulting expectations that have driven our system of care for decades. Because the fundamental institutions underlying health care were not changed, market forces alone proved powerless in altering the long-term rise in the cost of health care.

It appears that managed care as a means of controlling health care costs (the main reason our system of care turned to it in the first place) has a fundamental inconsistency. Unless the institutions and belief systems inherent in our society change regarding what constitutes high-quality care, any success managed care achieves in holding down the cost of care is at risk of being seen as a decrease in the quality of care.

INCREASING PATIENTS' SHARE OF HEALTH CARE COSTS AS A MEANS OF CONTROLLING COSTS

The RAND Health Insurance Experiment conducted in the 1970s and 1980s had two separate phases. In addition to the study described earlier that compared the cost of care under HMO and fee-for-service care, a separate phase of the study looked instead at the question of how the amount a patient has to pay out of pocket to obtain

TABLE 5.4. Results from the RAND health insurance experiment showing the effect of coinsurance on the use of services and the average annual cost of health care

Level of insurance	Doctor's office visits per year	Average annual cost of care
Free care	5.4	$401
25 percent coinsurance	4.4	$346
50 percent coinsurance	3.2	$328
95 percent coinsurance	3.7	$254

care will affect the frequency with which the patient seeks care (Brook et al. 2006). This study demonstrated an association between the amount a patient must pay for care and the frequency with which the patient will obtain care (Newhouse et al. 1981). The study looked at people who were randomly assigned to one of four different insurance plans, each with a different level of payment required from the patient:

1. The patient pays nothing out of pocket.
2. The patient pays 25 percent of the first $4,000.
3. The patient pays 50 percent of the first $2,000.
4. The patient pays 95 percent of the first $1,053.

The percentage of the cost that the patient must pay is called the "co-insurance rate." In plans 2–4, the patient had a yearly cap of $1,000 in out-of-pocket expenditures. After that amount, all additional care was 100 percent covered. Table 5.4 shows the results of this study, comparing the frequency with which the patient visited the doctor and the overall cost of care for different co-insurance rates.

It can be seen that the amount of coinsurance a patient faces will affect both the frequency with which the patient visits the doctor and the overall cost of care (including both doctor care and hospital care) for that patient. Patients with free care visited the doctor 23 percent more often than those with 25 percent coinsurance and 69 percent more than patients with 50 percent coinsurance.

These findings raise the question: Will coinsurance prevent patients from seeking out needed care? The researchers looked at the types of outpatient visits and hospitalizations the different groups made, using a panel of experts to categorize the care received (or forgone) as necessary or unnecessary. They found that those with higher coinsurance had fewer visits and hospitalizations characterized as "necessary" as well as those characterized as "unnecessary." From this study, we can conclude that when a patient is responsible for paying for part of the cost of care, he or she is less likely to use that care. This association applies to necessary care as well as to unnecessary care.

Based on the conclusion from the RAND health insurance experiment that people who are required to pay a substantial share of their initial health care costs end up using less health care, the George W. Bush administration adopted a policy of encouraging more individuals and families to shift to health insurance policies that included high deductibles, that is, that required patients to pay out-of-pocket for all health care costs up to a certain limit. In order to encourage this model of health insurance, President Bush included in the Medicare Modernization Act (MMA) of 2003 provisions that did two things: (1) a provision removing the cap on the number of Medicare beneficiaries who could establish medical savings accounts to supplement their Medicare coverage (see chapter 6) and (2) a provision that granted those not on Medicare a tax exemption for funds set aside in a special savings account, either by an employee or his or her employer, to pay the employee's out-of-pocket medical expenses. The tax exemption was conditioned on the employee also enrolling in a health insurance plan with a high deductible amount. The minimum annual deductible required to qualify for this tax exemption was $1,000 for individuals and $2,000 for families. The accounts into which these funds are paid were referred to as "health savings accounts" (HSAs), while those intended for Medicare beneficiaries were referred to as "medical savings accounts" (MSAs).

> **CONCEPT 5.10**
>
> When a patient is responsible for paying for part of the cost of care, he or she is less likely to use that care. A 25 percent coinsurance rate was associated with a 14 percent reduction in the overall cost of care. Having a 25 percent coinsurance rate was associated with a decrease in necessary care as well as a decrease in unnecessary care.

The intent of this new policy was to encourage more employees to shift out of plans that had higher coverage and lower deductibles (and thus, it was believed, contributed to the rising cost of health care) and to enroll instead in a high-deductible health plan (HDHP) associated with an HSA or other method for the employee to put aside money to pay for his or her share of care. In 2006, three years after the creation of the HDHP under MMA, 4 percent of workers who obtained their health insurance through their employment were in an HDHP. By 2010, the year ACA was passed, that number had risen to 13 percent and had reached 20 percent by 2013, the year before the new coverage options under ACA would take effect (Kaiser Family Foundation 2014).

SUMMARY

Health insurance in the United States first became widely available following World War II. Decisions made as part of wartime economic policy were to have long-range effects on our approach to providing health insurance. Today, most people covered by private health insurance obtain their insurance as a tax-free fringe benefit from their employer. As a consequence, people have come to expect a level of coverage that is substantially more generous than the coverage they might otherwise select if they were paying for it themselves. This employment-based system with its incentives for increased coverage has been a principal factor contributing to the rising cost of care.

As an alternative to the fee-for-service model of insurance that predominated throughout most of the twentieth century, Kaiser Permanente and other nonprofit groups were able to develop systems of care financed prospectively, based on monthly capitation payments. Despite initial (and often strident) opposition from the medical profession, these prepaid systems were able to offer care of comparable quality for about one-third less than traditional fee-for-service insurance.

Building on the success of these prepaid systems (now referred to as HMOs), in 1973 the federal government passed legislation encouraging their growth and expansion. In an effort to both expand coverage to the uninsured and constrain rising costs, HMOs and other forms of managed care were at the center of efforts to enact fundamental health care reform. While reform efforts in Congress were unsuccessful, the market adopted managed care as its predominant form of health insurance coverage. This shift to managed care was associated with a leveling of health care costs during the mid-1990s. By the beginning of the new century, however, it became clear that the savings associated with the shift to managed care were only short term, and workers were being asked to pay more of the cost of their care. Despite the extensive use of managed care systems, the United States once again faced steep increases in the cost of health care.

DÉJÀ VU—THE AFFORDABLE CARE ACT AND THE MARKET FOR HEALTH INSURANCE

One of the ironies of the passage of ACA is that the act resurrects one of the core elements of managed care delivery and managed competition that was first proposed by Alain Enthoven in 1980, and then was at the heart of the failed Clinton reform proposal in 1993–94. In order to expand health insurance coverage to those currently uninsured, ACA requires that every employer with more than fifty employees must either offer affordable health insurance coverage to their workers or else pay a tax to the federal government. ACA also mandates that all US citizens and permanent residents obtain health insurance coverage or pay a penalty (a "tax" by another name, as determined by the Supreme Court). If workers are unable to obtain that coverage through their employer at a price they can afford according to income standards defined in ACA, they will be guaranteed the option of obtaining coverage through a newly created entity: the Health Benefit Exchange (HBE). The HBE largely replicates the HIPC described by Enthoven and the Health Alliance that was at the heart of the Clinton reform proposal.

The HBE is an organization that is to be created by each state with the purpose of making competing health insurance plans available to those individuals and families who do not obtain coverage through their work. In states that are unable or unwilling to create an exchange by 2014, ACA authorized the federal government to establish and operate an exchange on behalf of the state.

The purpose of the HBE is to match those seeking health insurance coverage with companies offering coverage. In order to have their plans made available through the HBE, health insurance companies are required to obtain certification from the operator of the exchange. The plan will have to meet certain requirements having to do with level of benefits, and the company offering the plan will have to comply with licensure and regulatory requirements. Each exchange must arrange for at least two qualifying plans to be available, one of which must be offered by a nonprofit organization. Qualified plans will offer one of four predefined levels of benefits, referred to as bronze, silver, gold, and platinum. Other than variations in price based on the subscriber's age, family composition, tobacco use, and geographic area of residence, each plan must be available at the same price to all subscribers without regard to the subscriber's past medical history.

Beginning in October 2013, individuals who did not receive coverage through their work were eligible to contact the HBE, get information about competing plans and their comparative prices for a given level of coverage, and select a plan for themselves and their families for coverage beginning in 2014. In addition, small businesses with up to fifty employees are eligible to obtain coverage for their employees through a separate HBE set up specifically for them under the Small Business Health Options Program (SHOP). SHOP exchanges can operate under two alternative models: one in which the employer selects a single plan from the exchange and the employees can then enroll in that plan, and another in which the employer would contribute a fixed amount to the exchange and the employees can then select from among the competing plans. Employers with fifty or fewer employees, while not required to provide coverage under the employer mandate, are eligible for a 50 percent federal tax credit if they elect to offer employees coverage through the SHOP exchanges.

For individuals and families earning between 138 and 400 percent of the federal poverty level (FPL), there will be a cap on the premium paid by the subscriber, with the balance paid through a federal subsidy. The cap ranges from 2 percent of income for those earning 138 percent of the FPL to 9.5 percent of income for those earning 400 percent of the FPL. (Those earning less than 138% of the FPL will be eligible for free coverage through Medicaid [discussed in chapter 7].)

The concept behind the HBE is essentially that of the HIPC, described earlier as a central component of Enthoven's original theory of managed competition. As a HIPC was intended to do, an HBE is a publicly organized, nonprofit entity that evaluates competing health plans, and then makes qualifying plans available to individuals on a competitive basis. Individuals and small employers are able to select freely from among competing plans based on price, level of benefits, and quality. The concept of the HIPC, once portrayed by the Harry and Louise ads of 1993–94 as unreasonable bureaucratic encroachment on a family's access to health insurance, has, under another name, become one of the central components of expanded health insurance coverage through ACA.

The state HBEs were to be established as internet-based resources that consumers could access online, starting October 1, 2013. For the initial enrollment period, seventeen states and the District of Columbia elected to establish their own exchange, while thirty-three states instead left it to the federal government to operate an exchange on their behalf. In order to do this, the US Department of Health and Human Services (HHS) created HealthCare.gov and established a website by the same name (www .healthcare.gov). HHS contracted with a range of private consulting firms to do the technical work involved in creating the site. This work proved to be far more complex than initially envisioned. As a result, when the HealthCare.gov site went live on October 1, 2013, consumers who went there to compare plans encountered immense problems and delays, due mainly to the site's difficulty in communicating with the multiple public and private databases necessary to determine eligibility for enrollment or for subsidies. Several of the state-based exchanges functioned smoothly, although others encountered technical difficulties comparable to those encountered on HealthCare.gov.

While these technical glitches were largely resolved by December, HHS had to extend the open enrollment period to allow more people time to sign up. Similar technical difficulties necessitated postponing the employer mandate requirements until 2015, although the individual mandate requirements remained in place. Largely as a result of these technical problems, initial enrollment was much lower than expected. Between October 1 and December 28, only about 2.2 million people had enrolled for coverage through the HBEs: 1.2 million through the federal exchange and 1 million through the state exchanges. Fortunately, most of the technical problems had been resolved by the end of December, and total enrollment at the end of the open-enrollment period (which had been extended to March 31) reached more than 8 million: 5.4 million through the federal exchange and 2.6 million through the state exchanges (US Department of Health and Human Services 2014b).

While not all of those who enrolled followed through by initiating payment for their coverage, despite the early problems encountered, ACA had met its initial enrollment targets for the HBEs. A growing consensus emerged that ACA was, as described by economist Henry Aaron, "Here to Stay" (Aaron 2014). Aaron went on to describe what he saw as the source of these initial enrollment difficulties. "Most features of the ACA derive from one binding constraint: . . . the ACA was crafted to leave in place as much as possible of the preexisting system of health insurance . . . reform had to be built on the most complex, kludgy, and costly system on planet Earth" (pp. 2257–58).

Given the trend prior to ACA enactment of fewer employers offering health insurance coverage to their workers, Blavin et al. (2015) looked to see if either the rate at which employers offered insurance to their workers or the rate at which workers elected this coverage changed as a result of the first open-enrollment period under ACA. Using data from a representative national survey, they reported: "The key result from this analysis is that there were no significant changes in offer, take-up, and coverage rates of employer-sponsored insurance between mid-2013 and late 2014" (p. 170).

By the second enrollment period, which began on November 15, 2014, most of the technical problems had been resolved, and most consumers reported a much easier time accessing coverage and pricing information on alternative plans. Some states that had initially operated their own exchange elected to shift to the federal exchange for the second enrollment period. By the end of the enrollment period on February 15, 2015, 11.7 million people had signed up for coverage: 8.8 million from the thirty-seven states that used HealthCare.gov and 2.9 million from the remaining state exchanges (US Department of Health and Human Services 2015a). Of these, about 10.2 million had paid their required premium by March 31 (US Centers for Medicare and Medicaid Services 2015a). A national survey of those enrolled in health plans through the exchanges found that 74 percent rated their coverage as excellent or good and 59 percent indicated that, based on their share of the cost of the plan, the overall value of their plan was excellent or good (Hamel et al. 2015).

In 2014, the Congressional Budget Office estimated that in 2016, after the third ACA enrollment period, about 30 million nonelderly US residents would remain uninsured, thus making them potentially liable for the tax penalty under the individual mandate established by ACA. All but about 4 million of those people, however, will qualify for an exemption from the mandate based on their income levels or other exemptions (Congressional Budget Office 2014).

6

Medicare

In the mid-1990s, my teenage son got a summer job in a dining hall at Stanford. When he got his first paycheck, I was reminded of whose job it is to pay for government-sponsored health insurance programs such as Medicare and Medicaid. A facsimile of his pay stub from that summer, shown in figure 6.1, offers a statement of the extent to which workers and employers are currently paying for government programs in health care. Of the five categories of taxes withheld from his pay, three went, at least in part, to pay for these programs.

The federal Medicare program, which is our system of universal health insurance for everyone 65 years old or older, is paid for from both the Medicare withholding tax and the general federal withholding tax (shown on the pay stub as Fed tax). The Medicaid program (discussed in chapter 7), which is a federal-state partnership to provide medical insurance to poor and disabled people, is paid for from a combination of federal taxes and state taxes (shown as State tax).

Even though every worker contributes to paying the cost of these programs, only a minority of people in this country are covered by them. In contrast to most other countries, which have adopted universal health insurance for all their citizens, the United States has historically pursued a policy of incrementalism: establishing government-funded programs for specific populations felt to be most vulnerable. The two largest groups benefiting from this incremental approach to national health care have been elderly people and poor people. Both programs were established in 1965 after decades of debate about the proper role of government in paying for health care.

As described in chapter 1, as part of the social programs enacted under Franklin Roosevelt's New Deal, proposals for comprehensive medical insurance were consid-

Statement of Earnings and Taxes University Office of Dining Services			
Employee: xxxxx xxxxxx	**Social Security No.** 999-99-999		

Hours:		Amount	
Overtime	10.70	89.88	
Regular	78.60	440.16	
Total gross		530.04	

Gross pay:	530.04	**Taxes:**	115.19	**Net pay:**	414.85

Taxes deducted:	
FICA/OAS	32.86
Medicare	7.69
Fed tax	63.26
State tax	6.61
VDI	4.77
Total tax:	115.19

FIGURE 6.1. Sample statement of earnings and taxes.

ered but ultimately abandoned in the face of overriding opposition from the American Medical Association (AMA) and other groups within the medical profession. Following World War II, President Harry Truman again proposed a program of national health insurance, but again the opposition of the medical profession blocked the proposal. Only under the unique circumstances in the mid-1960s of a Democratic president, a strongly Democratic Congress, and a national momentum for social reform was the federal government able finally to overcome the opposition and enact the Medicare and Medicaid programs.

MEDICARE: UNIVERSAL HEALTH INSURANCE FOR ELDERLY PEOPLE

Medicare is the federal program that helps to pay for health care for elderly people in this country. All people 65 years of age or older who qualify for Social Security benefits are automatically eligible for Medicare. Rather than being a separate law, Medicare was enacted as an amendment to the existing Social Security Act. It is thus often referred to as "Title XVIII."

When Medicare was passed in 1965, only 56 percent of elderly people had hospital insurance. The costs of treating a serious illness were seen as a threat to the financial security of seniors. There was a strong national consensus that none of the elderly people in our country should face financial ruin due to illness. Medicare was the way to ensure this outcome.

As discussed in chapter 5, there are two general types of health plan: a service plan, in which all participants are provided with a given level of service, and an insurance plan, in which participants receive reimbursement for the cost of services. The

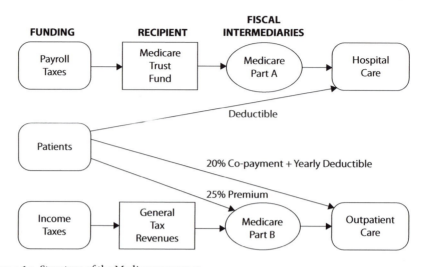

FIGURE 6.2. Structure of the Medicare program.

initial proposal was to create a service plan covering hospital care. Under this type of plan, elderly people would simply go to the hospital as needed, and the hospital would be paid directly by the government.

The AMA was opposed to the service plan concept. If Medicare was to be passed at all, they wanted to establish an insurance plan covering both hospital care and the care provided by doctors, with patients paying for care directly and being reimbursed from the government insurance program. The AMA also wanted to keep the government out of running the program; they preferred that it be run by private insurance companies.

A last-minute compromise was struck that incorporated both proposals (Ball 1995). Under the compromise, Medicare became a combined service and insurance program. The structure of the original Medicare program is illustrated in figure 6.2.

CONCEPT 6.1

As a result of a last-minute political compromise, the federal Medicare program was designed as a combined service plan (Part A) and insurance plan (Part B).

Medicare Part A

Medicare Part A is a service plan for hospital care. All eligible patients receive any necessary hospital care, paid for by the government. The patient is responsible for a deductible payment equal roughly to the cost of the first day of hospitalization. (In 2015, this amount was $1,260.) After this deductible amount, all the costs of hospitalization are paid by Medicare for up to 60 days in the hospital per illness. If the patient needs to stay longer in the hospital, the patient is responsible for $315 per day for additional days up to a maximum of 90 days per illness. If more time in the hospital is necessary, the patient must pay $630 per day up to a total of 150 days. After these 150 days in the hospital, there is no further Medicare coverage for that illness.

Part A also pays for up to twenty days in a skilled nursing facility (SNF) following hospitalization, so long as the care is necessary to continue the healing or rehabilitation process. After twenty days of care in an SNF, patients must pay $157.50 per day, with Medicare paying the balance for up to one hundred days. After one hundred days in an SNF, there is no further Medicare coverage.

For those patients who need to spend time in a nursing home simply because they cannot care for themselves but are not undergoing an active treatment program, Medicare provides no payment whatsoever. These patients are referred to as receiving "custodial care" in contrast to "skilled nursing care." The problems associated with custodial care and other types of long-term care are discussed in chapter 11.

Until 1997, Part A also paid for home health care. This is medically necessary care provided in the patient's home, involving such services as nursing care, physical therapy, or occupational therapy. These services are provided by Medicare-certified home health agencies by prescription of the treating physician. Because of the rising cost of the home health care benefit and the growing realization that it was not particularly effective in its intended purpose of keeping patients out of the hospital, in 1997 the costs of home health care were transferred to the Medicare Part B budget.

Finally, Part A pays for hospice care for terminally ill people. Enacted in the 1980s as an amendment to the original Medicare legislation, the Medicare hospice program pays for extra services during the last months of a patient's life as long as the patient is certified by a physician as terminally ill (i.e., not likely to survive more than six months) and the patient agrees to forgo aggressive treatment measures such as surgery or intensive care.

All the money to pay for Part A comes from a 1.45 percent payroll tax levied on all workers earning less than $200,000 per year and 2.35 percent for incomes over $200,000. (On the pay stub in figure 6.1, the tax labeled "Medicare" goes purely to finance Part A.) For every dollar in tax paid by employees, the employer is required to pay an additional dollar. The money from this tax is deposited into a Medicare trust fund, essentially a savings account established by the federal government to pay hospital bills when they come in.

The government does not actually pay bills submitted by hospitals. Instead, the government contracts with private companies to accept the bills from the hospitals and issue payment of these bills to the hospitals. These companies, referred to as "fiscal intermediaries," are then reimbursed from the Medicare trust fund. The creation of the fiscal intermediary was part of the compromise struck with the AMA at the time of the original passage of the Medicare legislation.

It is important to note that the money paid in payroll taxes into the Medicare trust fund is not put aside to pay for the care of current workers when they retire. Instead, it is used to pay for the care of people already retired. The financing of the Medicare program is based on the concept that current workers pay the medical care costs of current retirees. When today's workers are retired, their care will be paid for by those who are working at that time. Medical care during the retirement of the baby boom generation will therefore be financed by the substantially smaller number of people born after the baby boom.

About 90 percent of all Medicare funds come from people currently working. For the system to work, there have to be enough workers paying enough taxes to pay for the care needed by elderly people. In 2003, there were about 3.9 workers for each Medicare beneficiary. In 2014, this number had fallen to 3.2 workers per beneficiary. In 2030, as the last baby boomer turns 65, there will be only about 2.4 workers per beneficiary.

The ratio will continue to decline until there are only 2.1 workers per beneficiary by 2089 (data from Medicare Payment Advisory Commission website). If the cost of care per beneficiary remains relatively constant, the tax burden on each worker will increase by nearly 70 percent in the next thirty years. If the cost per beneficiary goes up (as it is almost certain to do), the tax burden will increase even more. This policy dilemma inherent in the current Medicare program is one of the most pressing aspects of the forces that threaten the long-term financial viability of Medicare.

CONCEPT 6.2

The Medicare program looks to today's workers to pay the costs of today's retirees. The number of active workers per beneficiary is projected to decline from 3.5 in 2009 to 2.4 in 2030.

Medicare Part B

Medicare Part B pays for doctor bills and other medical care costs that are incurred on an outpatient basis (i.e., for care provided outside the hospital). Under Part B, patients going to physicians, laboratories, X-ray offices, and other outpatient providers of care receive a bill for each service provided. As with Part A, private companies acting as fiscal intermediaries handle all paperwork and pay out all the funds. The government acts to hold the money collected, and to transfer it to the fiscal intermediaries as needed.

As an insurance plan, Part B involves an insurance premium paid by the beneficiaries. This premium is withheld from the Social Security checks of all those participating in the plan, so there is no need to bill patients for the cost of the premium. In addition, Part B is voluntary; only those seniors electing to have the premium deducted from their check are covered. (This is in contrast to Part A, which is universal for all seniors receiving Social Security.) Nearly all seniors select Part B coverage.

The original intent for Part B was to have the premiums collected from the patients cover about half the cost of the program, with the other half of the cost coming from general tax revenues. It rapidly became apparent that this 50/50 cost sharing was going to be too expensive for seniors to bear, so over time the premium was reduced substantially. Currently, the premium charged to beneficiaries for Part B coverage is set so that beneficiaries pay 25 percent of the cost. Thus, 75 cents of every dollar spent on Part B comes from general tax revenues. In 2015, the Part B premium was $104.90 per month for beneficiaries with incomes less than $85,000 for a single person or $170,000 for a married couple. For higher-income beneficiaries, the premium is increased, up to a maximum of $335.70 for individuals earning more than $214,000 or couples earning more than $428,000. Part B has two mechanisms to pay for the care seniors receive from physicians and other outpatient providers. They are referred to as the provider "accepting assignment" and "not accepting assignment." The choice is up to the provider (not the patient) and will affect the amount and the manner of payment for services. For both options, in 2015 the patient was responsible for paying a yearly deductible of $147.

> **CONCEPT 6.3**
>
> Medicare beneficiaries pay for 25 percent of the cost of Part B coverage. Thus, 75 cents of every dollar spent on Medicare Part B comes from general tax revenues.

Under the first option, illustrated in figure 6.3, the physician (or other provider) agrees to accept an amount set by Medicare as payment in full for the service provided. (See the section that describes changes in the way Medicare pays physicians for an indication of how these amounts are set.) In return for the physician's willingness to set the fee at this level, Medicare will pay the physician directly an amount equal to 80 percent of that fee. The patient then is responsible for paying the physician only the remaining 20 percent of the fee. Physicians and other providers who agree to accept assignment are referred to as "participating providers."

The fee allowed by Medicare, however, is generally much lower than the fee a physician usually charges other patients for the same service. Medicare fees typically are about two-thirds of the fees the physician usually charges. About half of all physicians have elected not to accept assignment, so they can charge Medicare patients a higher fee. In this case, illustrated in figure 6.4, the patient is responsible for paying the

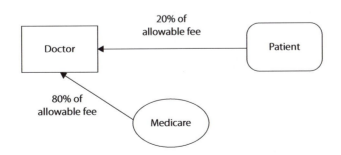

FIGURE 6.3. Medicare Part B payment: Doctor does accept assignment.

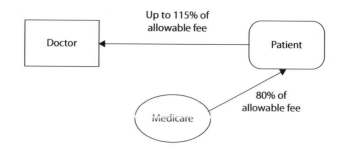

FIGURE 6.4. Medicare Part B payment: Doctor does not accept assignment.

physician directly for the full amount billed. The patient may then send a form into Medicare and be reimbursed for 80 percent of Medicare's allowable fee.

To protect Medicare beneficiaries from having to pay extremely high physicians' fees, a law was enacted that limits the amount any physician can charge a Medicare beneficiary to 115 percent of Medicare's allowable fee. Thus, if the allowable Medicare fee for a service is $100, the most a physician may charge a Medicare patient is $115.

Even with this limitation, the fees paid by Medicare patients to physicians and other providers can be quite high. The patient is responsible for 20 percent of the fee to begin with; going to a physician who does not accept assignment will add another 15 percent. Thus, even though they are covered by Part B insurance, patients can be required to pay 35 percent of all doctor bills out of pocket. (This is in addition to the $155 yearly deductible.) Considering that in 2013, 25 percent of all people on Medicare had incomes less than the federal poverty level (FPL) ($11,173 for individuals and $14,095 for couples), while an additional 25 percent had incomes between the FPL and twice the FPL (Cubanski et al. 2015), it is easy to see that out-of-pocket expenses for medical care can be a substantial burden on Medicare beneficiaries. For these families and individuals, one-third of their household income might go for health care.

MEDIGAP INSURANCE

As discussed previously, patients covered by Medicare are still responsible for paying a number of different costs. These include

- the Part A hospital deductible for each time they are in the hospital,
- the yearly Part B deductible,
- 20 percent of all charges covered by Part B, and
- the extra charges (up to 15% of allowable charges) of physicians who do not accept assignment.

To gain coverage for these items, 86 percent of Medicare beneficiaries obtain some form of supplemental medical insurance policy, often referred to as a "Medigap" policy.

As the name suggests, a Medigap policy is a medical insurance policy that pays for these gaps in Medicare coverage. There are four principal ways for beneficiaries to obtain Medigap coverage.

1. The beneficiary can purchase the policy from a private insurance company (about 15% of beneficiaries in 2010).
2. The beneficiary can obtain the policy from her or his former employer as a retirement benefit (about 30% of beneficiaries in 2010).
3. The beneficiary can receive Medigap coverage from the Medicaid program or other publicly financed programs if his or her income is below the FPL (about 19% of beneficiaries in 2010).
4. The beneficiary can join a Medicare managed care plan, described in the section on Medicare and managed care, which includes coverage for these out-of-pocket costs (about 22% of beneficiaries in 2010).

Each Medigap supplemental insurance plan will have its own set of covered benefits. Most will pay for the Part A hospital deductible, the Part B yearly deductible, and the 20 percent share of providers' bills not covered by Medicare.

> **CONCEPT 6.4**
>
> Only 14 percent of Medicare beneficiaries have coverage limited to Medicare. The other 86 percent of beneficiaries obtain a supplemental Medigap policy or other supplementary policy to cover costs not paid by Medicare.

THE EXTENSION OF MEDICARE TO DISABLED PEOPLE AND PEOPLE WITH KIDNEY FAILURE

Within a few years of the enactment of Medicare, Congress made some additions to the program that were to have significant effects on long-term policy. The first was to extend eligibility for the program to disabled people under 65. People who are determined to be permanently disabled are eligible to receive Social Security benefits before they turn 65. As part of this benefit, in 1972 they were also included in Medicare.

Another category of patient eligible for Medicare coverage before age 65 is patients with kidney failure (referred to as end-stage renal disease, or ESRD). Before the 1960s, there was no effective treatment for people who developed ESRD—those who got it usually died. During the 1960s, the technology of kidney dialysis was developed. As with most new technologies, dialysis was very expensive and was in short supply. It became apparent that this life-saving alternative was available selectively to those with either the money or the insurance coverage to pay for it. People with ESRD who could not pay for it had no access to it and were left to die. This allocation of life-saving technology according to the ability to pay was viewed as unacceptable by many in Congress. Such a policy was simply not consistent with American norms and values.

Accordingly, Congress acted to include all people with ESRD in the Medicare program, regardless of age. The costs of dialysis would be paid by the government.

The decision to include ESRD under Medicare coverage was to have long-range effects that could not have been fully envisioned in 1972. The technology of surgical kidney transplantation was improving rapidly at that time. These costs were also paid by Medicare. The technology of dialysis has improved over the years, keeping more and more people alive but also adding more and more to the cost of care for ESRD. In the era of genetic engineering, new types of treatments were developed to improve the quality of life for people with ESRD. These newer treatments often cost as much as dialysis itself. Finally, in the era of the for-profit health care provider, the guaranteed availability of Medicare financing for all ESRD-related care led to the development of a growing number of for-profit, investor-owned corporations providing kidney dialysis. A number of analysts have questioned the quality of the care provided by these for-profit dialysis centers, as well as the appropriateness of the federal government being the principal source of payment (and thus profit) for them. (See chapter 9 for further discussion of these issues.)

Perhaps not surprisingly, it is quite costly to pay for the care of patients with ESRD. For example, in 2011, Medicare spent on average $9,978 per elderly beneficiary. The figure for each beneficiary eligible for Medicare due to ESRD was $76,078 (Medicare Payment Advisory Commission 2015a).

THE RISING COST OF MEDICARE

It did not take long after the enactment of Medicare in 1965 for the cost of the program to become much larger than expected. Within a few years, the cost of the program more than doubled, from $4.2 billion in 1967 to $9.3 billion in 1973. It doubled again between 1973 and 1977. As more and more people received Medicare coverage and as the increasing availability of technology led to a rapidly rising cost of care, the cost of the program continued to balloon.

Figure 6.5 shows the yearly cost of Parts A and B of the Medicare program between 1968 and 2014. It shows the cost of Part B added to the cost of Part A to give the total cost for these two programs each year. (These figures do not include the cost of Medicare Part D, the pharmaceutical benefit, discussed in chapter 10.) It can be seen that Part B, covering physicians' services and other nonhospital care, has become an increasingly large part of overall expenditures. In 1968, the year Medicare first provided coverage, Part B expenditures were about 30 percent of the Part A + Part B total. By 1990, Part B made up 39 percent of that total; in 2014, when Medicare expenditures for Part A + Part B totaled $535 billion, it was 50 percent of the total.

By 2014, the cost of all Medicare programs combined was $613 billion. This amount is bigger than the national health budget of most other countries and represents a

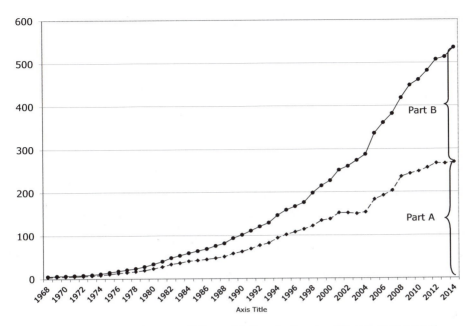

FIGURE 6.5. Medicare expenditures, in billions of dollars, for Part A and Part B, 1967–2014 (does not include Medicare + Choice). *Sources:* Data from US Centers for Medicare and Medicaid Services; Medicare Trustees Report.

20 percent increase in just five years. With more and more of the cost of Medicare coming from Part B and 75 percent of the cost of Part B coming out of general tax revenues, the rising cost of Medicare is placing an increasing burden on the federal budget. The rising cost of Part A is also placing a severe strain on the Part A trust fund.

> **CONCEPT 6.5**
>
> The costs of Medicare Part B have grown as a proportion of combined Part A and Part B expenditures, from 39 percent in 1990 to 50 percent in 2014.

The political reality of Medicare's rapidly rising costs led Congress to make a number of changes over the years to the original Medicare program in an effort to constrain those costs. The first of these changes came in 1972 with the enactment of the system of professional standards review organizations, or PSROs. These were independent review bodies, often created as an offshoot of local medical societies, charged with reviewing the appropriateness of the hospital care provided to Medicare and Medicaid patients. It was thought that groups of community physicians could advise their peers on avoiding unnecessary hospital costs and thus reduce the cost of hospitalization. While well intended, the PSROs had little effect on stemming the rise in hospital costs.

The next major step intended to reduce hospital costs was the prospective payment system (PPS), discussed in chapter 4. Enacted in 1983, the PPS reversed the incentives faced by hospitals, encouraging the rapid discharge of Medicare patients. The PPS was widely viewed as a success, with the increases in the cost of hospital care moderating substantially in the years following its enactment.

By the late 1990s, however, government reports began to indicate that the Medicare trust fund (the fund that holds the money to pay for Part A services) was spending money faster than it was bringing money in, and if nothing changed, the trust fund would go broke in 2001. These predictions started to come true. In 1997, for the first time, the trust fund spent more than it took in—by about $4 billion. As a result, Congress passed a series of changes to Medicare as part of the Balanced Budget Act of 1997, discussed in the following section. These changes led to a short-term stabilization of the Part A trust fund. The continuing rise in Medicare hospital costs and the impending retirement of the baby boom generation, however, have led the Medicare trustees to predict that the trust fund will soon start once more to spend more than it takes in from payroll taxes. Actuarial projections from the Trustees' Report from 2015 predicted that funds in the Part A trust would be exhausted in 2030 (Boards of Trustees of the Federal Hospital Insurance and Federal Supplementary Medical Insurance Trust Funds 2015).

CHANGES IN THE WAY MEDICARE PAYS PHYSICIANS

Largely as a result of the rising costs of Part B, Congress began to look closely at the fees it was paying physicians. The original schedule of acceptable fees for physician services was based on a weighted average of what other physicians in the same community charged for the same service, referred to as the usual, customary, and reasonable (UCR) charge. The original Part B payment schedule would pay physicians 80 percent of UCR. Analysts in the federal Health Care Financing Administration and Congress began to question the level of the physicians' fees. Under directions from Congress, the government commissioned a detailed study of physicians' fees and, based on the results of these studies, created the resource-based relative value scale (RBRVS).

The RBRVS created a system of measuring the resources that go into the provision of a medical service and assigning a value reflecting those resources, using a new scale based on the relative value unit (RVU). Every possible procedure was assigned a specific number of RVUs according to the resources required to perform the procedure. If one procedure involved twice as many RVUs as another, it was seen as requiring twice as many resources. Medicare simply established a standard payment rate per RVU and used this figure to calculate the eligible charge for all procedures.

The Centers for Medicare and Medicaid Services (CMS) is the federal agency that manages the Medicare program. (CMS was formerly called the Health Care Financing Administration, or HCFA.) Initially, CMS distinguished between an RVU involved in doing a procedure (e.g., surgery or repairing a broken bone) and an RVU involved in the ongoing evaluation and management of a patient (e.g., an office visit to treat high blood pressure). Physicians whose practice included procedures were paid more per RVU than those involved mainly in evaluation and management services. For a number of years, there was a debate as to whether procedural services and the services of evaluation and management should receive different levels of payment. CMS ultimately took steps to equalize payment for the two services.

> **CONCEPT 6.6**
>
> The resource-based relative value scale (RBRVS) established a simplified method for paying physicians treating Medicare patients. Instituting the scale improved the equity in the way primary care physicians and procedural specialists are paid, and it provided a mechanism for controlling overall payments to physicians.

TAKING CARE OF THE FEW: THE SKEWED NATURE OF THE MEDICARE POPULATION

Increases in life expectancy for all Americans and changes in demographic patterns have had a substantial impact on the cost of Medicare. When Medicare was established in the 1960s, approximately 9.5 percent of the country's population was 65 years or older. A man who was 65 years old at that time could expect to live an additional 13 years on average, and a woman, 17 years. By 1990, 12.3 percent of the population was 65 or older, and additional life expectancy at age 65 had increased to 15.1 years for men and 18.9 years for women. In 2010, 13.0 percent of the population was 65 or older. Current projections predict that the proportion of the population 65 or over will rise to 17 percent by 2020 and 22 percent by 2030 (Colby and Ortman 2015).

In 2010, Medicare spent an average of $10,584 per elderly beneficiary (Cubanski et al. 2015). This amount varied widely, however, depending on the health of the beneficiary. For beneficiaries enrolled in traditional, fee-for-service Medicare, the sickest 10 percent of beneficiaries had an average annual per capita cost of $61,722 and accounted for nearly 60 percent of all spending. By contrast, the healthiest 90 percent of beneficiaries that year had per capita costs of $4,897. In 2011, the median expenditure was $4,206 per beneficiary, while spending for a beneficiary at the 25th percentile was $1,478 (Mirel and Carper 2014).

> **CONCEPT 6.7**
>
> Medicare spends most of its money taking care of a very few people; the care of 10 percent of the elderly population uses 60 percent of Medicare funds.

MEDICARE AND MANAGED CARE

As discussed in chapter 5, the 1980s and 1990s were periods of rapid change in US health care. As the cost of care began to skyrocket, employers and other large purchasers of health insurance turned to health maintenance organizations (HMOs) and other types of managed care delivery systems. The number of Americans receiving their care from managed care organizations increased by several orders of magnitude.

During this time, the federal government experienced the same cost pressures as businesses. As the cost of the Medicare program began to increase rapidly, administrators in the federal government began to look to HMOs as potential solutions to the problem of rising costs. As early as 1976, Congress took steps to allow Medicare beneficiaries to enroll in HMOs as an alternative to traditional Medicare coverage. As the costs of Medicare continued to increase despite previous efforts to contain them, the federal government took several steps to reform the program. A number of these steps have been quite controversial. Not all have worked as intended.

Medicare needed a way to take advantage of the potential cost savings that appeared to be inherent in HMOs. It created a new way of paying HMOs that shifted most of the risk for cost overruns to the HMO, yet provided the HMO with an incentive to control costs. The government estimated that, on average, an HMO should be able to take care of a Medicare beneficiary for about 95 percent of what it costs to take care of beneficiaries in traditional, fee-for-service Medicare. A well-run HMO might even be able to provide care for less than 95 percent.

In 1985, Medicare created a policy under which any HMO that enrolled a Medicare beneficiary would be paid a yearly capitation fee that was equal to 95 percent of the average cost of providing care to the other beneficiaries. Because the average cost of caring for a Medicare beneficiary varies substantially across different communities and different regions of the country, the 95 percent rate was based on the average cost of care locally. The HMO was required to provide the same range of services that were available to beneficiaries under the traditional plan. If the HMO could provide care for less than 95 percent of the average local cost, however, it was free to keep the difference so long as it used the remaining funds either to expand services to beneficiaries or to reduce the out-of-pocket expenses required of them.

HMOs initially reacted favorably to the risk-contracting option. By 1987, 161 HMOs had signed risk contracts with HCFA allowing them to enroll Medicare beneficiaries. The early 1990s saw the rapid expansion of HMOs in many areas of the country. As the number of HMOs increased, the number of HMOs willing to enter risk contracts also increased. California, Florida, Pennsylvania, New York, and Texas saw increases in HMOs operating in the market and HMOs contracting with HCFA. By 1997, 307 HMOs nationwide had signed Medicare risk contracts.

Most of the HMOs enrolling Medicare patients found that the cost of providing care for their members was below the 95 percent capitation rate. Accordingly, they began to expand the types of services they provided to these members. By 1995, 48 percent of all plans offered Medicare beneficiaries supplemental coverage for prescription drugs, 86 percent provided routine eye exams, 65 percent provided hearing exams, and 33 percent provided foot care. Most of the time, these added services were at no extra charge to the beneficiary. In fact, the cost to the beneficiary was often less than traditional Medicare, even before taking into account the cost of Medigap coverage.

In traditional Medicare, beneficiaries must obtain their own Medigap policies to cover many of the items not covered by Medicare. Those who enrolled in a Medicare HMO that offered the supplemental coverage for these costs and services, however, did not need their Medigap coverage. Thus, for many beneficiaries, enrolling in a Medicare HMO resulted in substantial savings. For less money than traditional Medicare, beneficiaries in HMOs were provided with substantially increased benefits. For many, this was an option that proved hard to pass up.

> **CONCEPT 6.8**
>
> In an attempt to reduce program costs, Medicare created the option for beneficiaries to enroll in certain approved HMOs. Because most of these Medicare HMOs offered benefits not provided by traditional Medicare, they proved to be successful in enrolling large numbers of beneficiaries.

By 1997, the number of Medicare beneficiaries enrolling in HMOs had increased to more than 5 million, representing nearly 15 percent of all beneficiaries. In states like California, Arizona, and Oregon, where HMOs had gained a wide share of the overall health care market, more than one-third of Medicare beneficiaries had enrolled in HMOs.

Enrolling in an HMO did have certain drawbacks for Medicare beneficiaries, mostly with the choice of physician or hospital. Under traditional Medicare, each beneficiary is able to obtain care from any physician who has registered with Medicare. Because nearly all practicing physicians in the country are registered, traditional Medicare essentially gives beneficiaries their choice of physician anywhere in the country. Similarly, beneficiaries are able to obtain hospital care at any hospital that is certified by Medicare. Thus, if a beneficiary in California chooses to fly to the Mayo Clinic in Minnesota for consultation with a physician and to undergo surgery, traditional Medicare will provide the same coverage as if the beneficiary had obtained the care in his or her hometown. Finally, under traditional Medicare, beneficiaries are free to consult a specialist without a referral. Under many HMOs, a beneficiary must first obtain a referral from a primary care physician before consulting a specialist. Once the referral has been obtained, the beneficiary is limited to those specialists who are on the HMO's list of eligible providers. Thus, even though enrolling in an HMO held a substantial cost advantage for beneficiaries, it also meant giving up a certain amount of choice in the selection of a physician or a hospital. For those beneficiaries who already had a doctor they felt comfortable with, however, there was little disadvantage in enrolling in an HMO in which their doctor participated.

PROBLEMS IN HMO RISK CONTRACTING: FAVORABLE SELECTION AND THE AVERAGE COST OF CARE

Officials in the federal government closely followed the growth of Medicare HMO enrollment throughout the early and mid-1990s. As part of the risk contract, Medicare kept track of the care provided to beneficiaries enrolled in HMOs to determine if any cost savings realized by the HMOs were returned to beneficiaries in the form of added benefits. A pattern began to emerge: it appeared that HMOs were more attractive to younger, healthier Medicare beneficiaries. Beneficiaries with more serious medical problems seemed to be more likely to stay with traditional coverage.

Favorable selection refers to a situation that can exist when two or more competing health care plans are available to potential members. If the plans are equally attractive to all members, then the average health status of those enrolling in one plan should be approximately the same as the health status of those enrolling in the alternative plan. If one plan is more attractive to healthier members and the second plan is

> **CONCEPT 6.9**
>
> If a managed care health plan is able to enroll members who, on average, are healthier than the general population, it has benefited from *favorable selection*. If a plan finds that it has enrolled members who, on average, are sicker than the general population, it has experienced *adverse selection*.

more attractive to members who, on average, are sicker, however, there will be favorable consequences for the first plan and adverse consequences for the second. Having a higher percentage of its members being sicker means the second plan will have higher costs than the first.

In the case of Medicare, it appears that favorable selection did occur. Those selecting the HMO option were healthier, on average, than those remaining in traditional Medicare. This pattern raised serious questions about the entire financing structure of Medicare HMO enrollment.

Figure 6.6 illustrates the tremendous potential impact that favorable selection and adverse selection can have, as applied to Medicare HMOs and traditional Medicare. Using CMS data for 1997, the graph looks at the cost of providing care to beneficiaries at the 25th, 50th, 75th, and 90th percentiles of yearly cost. For each level it shows

- the average cost per beneficiary at this level,
- 95 percent of the average cost of all beneficiaries, and
- the difference between 95 percent of the average cost of care and what it actually costs to provide care to a beneficiary at this level.

The third point refers to the profit (or loss) that a Medicare HMO will realize if it enrolls a Medicare beneficiary whose cost of care is at the specified level.

Take, for example, a beneficiary at the 50th percentile of annual cost. In 1997, it cost an average of $779 to provide care for this beneficiary. Ninety-five percent of the

FIGURE 6.6. Comparing the average cost of care for Medicare beneficiaries at the 25th, 50th, 75th, and 90th percentiles of yearly costs with 95 percent of the average cost of all beneficiaries, 1997. *Source:* Data from US Centers for Medicare and Medicaid Services.

average cost of taking care of other beneficiaries was $5,584, which was the amount an HMO received from Medicare to care for the beneficiary. The HMO received $4,805 more than it actually cost to provide care for the beneficiary.

Now look at a beneficiary at the 90th percentile of annual cost. It took $14,000, on average, to provide care for this beneficiary, which was $8,416 *more* than the HMO was paid. For approximately 80 percent of beneficiaries, the annual cost of care was less than the amount paid by Medicare for HMO care. For the remaining 20 percent, the cost of care was more than the Medicare capitation rate. If an HMO could attract more of the younger, healthier beneficiaries and fewer of the older, sicker beneficiaries, it could keep its annual cost of care substantially below the amount it received from Medicare.

One additional point is worth mentioning. Recall that the 95 percent capitation rate was calculated based on what it cost to provide care to beneficiaries remaining with traditional Medicare. (Recall also that this figure was calculated regionally.) If, as appears to have been the case, those remaining with traditional Medicare were drawn disproportionately from the population of older and sicker beneficiaries, the cost of providing care for these remaining beneficiaries would be even higher than the overall average cost of providing care for all beneficiaries. This situation only magnified the potential benefit of favorable selection for those HMOs who enrolled younger, healthier beneficiaries.

Under the regulations established by Medicare, any surplus funds obtained through enrolling Medicare beneficiaries had to be returned to the beneficiaries in the form of either lower costs or higher benefits. The HMOs that benefited from the lower costs associated with healthier beneficiaries added the benefits described earlier. Even with these added benefits, it still cost many HMOs less to care for their beneficiaries than the capitation payment they received for providing care. These HMOs were able to increase their profits through enrolling Medicare beneficiaries. The end result was that the Medicare HMO program increased overall spending rather than decreasing spending, as was intended when the program was established.

Analysts within the federal government were able to build a strong case for adjusting downward the capitation rate paid to HMOs. They estimated that, as a consequence of disproportionately enrolling younger, healthier beneficiaries, HMOs were facing actual costs that were 5 percent lower than the costs initially estimated. At a time in the 1990s when there was a major national effort to reduce the overall federal budget deficit and control the rising cost of Medicare, the identification of *overpayments* to HMOs was of concern to both federal analysts and members of Congress. In response to these calculations, Congress took action that would prove to have a profound effect on the entire Medicare HMO program.

> **CONCEPT 6.10**
>
> Data gathered by the federal government demonstrated that in the 1990s most Medicare HMOs benefited from substantial favorable selection in the enrollment of beneficiaries.

THE BALANCED BUDGET ACT OF 1997 AND ITS EFFECT ON MEDICARE

The Balanced Budget Act of 1997, approved by Congress and signed by President Bill Clinton, was a complex set of changes to the financing and organization of a broad range of federal policies. Medicare was only one of the topics covered in this attempt to shift the federal government from chronically spending more on programs than it received in taxes. Years of deficit spending had led to what was then perceived as a huge federal debt. The Balanced Budget Act attempted to ensure that the federal government would balance its budget on an ongoing basis.

One of the first things the Balanced Budget Act did was change the way that Medicare paid HMOs to enroll beneficiaries. As discussed previously, for years Medicare had paid HMOs 95 percent of the average cost of caring for fee-for-service Medicare patients, adjusted for regional differences. The 95 percent payment rate was thought to be too generous, so the act cut this yearly capitation rate to approximately 90 percent of the average cost of providing care to fee-for-service Medicare beneficiaries. Medicare contended that the pattern of favorable selection that had gone on previously made the 90 percent figure more appropriate.

At the same time that Medicare was raising concerns about the financing structure of the Medicare HMO program, members of Congress were looking to reform Medicare in a number of additional ways. Leaders of the Republican Party in Congress, in a position of control of both houses for the first time since Medicare was established, wanted to shift certain portions of Medicare to reflect a more market-based approach.

To many in Congress, HMOs represented a form of health care that was overly bureaucratic and that unnecessarily limited the options open to patients. The 1990s had seen the proliferation of other managed care financing and delivery systems that were not strictly HMOs. The widely held belief in the ability of market forces to improve the efficiency of health care delivery led to the decision within the Balanced Budget Act to open Medicare to a wide variety of options that were less closely regulated by the government. The proposal was to assure Medicare beneficiaries the range of services covered by Medicare but to allow them a wide choice of market-based options beyond HMOs as an alternative. Thus the name for this new program: Medicare + Choice (renamed Medicare Advantage in 2004).

Medicare + Choice allowed Medicare beneficiaries to select from any of the following options for their Medicare coverage:

- a Medicare HMO,
- a Medicare HMO that in addition provides a point-of-service (POS) option,
- a preferred provider organization (PPO) that allows a wide range of choice of physician and hospital and pays for care on a discounted fee-for-service basis,
- a traditional fee-for-service insurance plan operated by a private insurance company, with the option of including a Medical Savings Account, or
- the traditional Medicare program.

All Medicare + Choice options would be required to provide the same level of benefits as the traditional program. Like Medicare HMOs, other Medicare + Choice plans would be required to return any cost savings to beneficiaries in the form of increased benefits or lower premiums. For the managed care plans under Medicare + Choice, the total out-of-pocket expenditures for beneficiaries could not exceed the average out-of-pocket expenses under the traditional plan. (Beneficiaries enrolling in the private, fee-for-service option under Medicare + Choice would be subject to somewhat higher out-of-pocket expenses.)

Beneficiaries would continue to have the premium for Part B withheld from their Social Security check, and Medicare would pay a yearly premium to any of the plans eligible under Medicare + Choice, based on a percentage of the average cost of care for beneficiaries in traditional Medicare. Beneficiaries would have the option of changing plans only once a year. The issue of favorable selection would be monitored by CMS, and yearly premiums or capitation rates adjusted accordingly. Congress mandated in the Balanced Budget Act that Medicare develop a method of risk-adjusting capitation payments for its managed care options. Using its extensive database about the problems each beneficiary is treated for each year, CMS worked to develop a more equitable method of paying managed care plans for providing care to Medicare beneficiaries. In this way, the cost of the Medicare + Choice options should be more comparable to the cost of providing care under traditional Medicare, even if the traditional option is subject to adverse selection based on beneficiaries' health status.

> **CONCEPT 6.11**
>
> The Balanced Budget Act of 1997 added several new alternatives for Medicare beneficiaries to obtain care, referred to collectively as "Medicare + Choice." The intent was to reduce the long-term costs of Medicare by introducing a larger role for market forces.

The concept of the medical savings account (MSA) option for Medicare beneficiaries was based on the results of the RAND health insurance experiment, discussed in chapter 5. That study showed that when patients are required to pay for a substantial portion of their care out of pocket, they will use less care. The concept of the MSA is based on the assumption that if a Medicare beneficiary is personally responsible for the first several thousand dollars of medical care costs per year, that beneficiary will use less care and the overall cost of care will be less. For those who selected it, the MSA would provide a modified, high-deductible plan based on the traditional fee-for-service payment method. However, the coverage offered by the plan would take effect only after the patient had met the required annual deductible of several thousand dollars per year. It can reasonably be expected that the cost of such private, high-deductible plans would be substantially less than the cost of providing care under traditional Medicare. Under the MSA, an amount equal to the difference between the cost of the high-deductible plan and the cost to Medicare to enroll the beneficiary in a Medicare HMO would be placed in a savings account in the beneficiary's name. For example (using figures for 1998, the year after Medicare MSAs were first approved), if the annual premium for the high-deductible plan was $3,000 and the amount available for HMO enrollment was $5,800, Medicare would deposit $2,800 into a savings account for use by the beneficiary. If the beneficiary did not use the full $2,800 during the year, the remaining balance would be rolled over to the following year. Medicare would deposit an additional $2,800 into the account for that next year.

Recall from figure 6.6 that for 75 percent of Medicare beneficiaries the cost of providing their medical care in 1997 was $3,095 or less. For the majority of these beneficiaries, there was a good chance that money would be left over in the MSA at the end of the year for several years in a row. The amount in the MSA could easily build up. So long as the beneficiary maintained at all times an amount in the MSA equal to 60 percent of the yearly deductible, the beneficiary would be allowed to withdraw additional funds and use the money for any purpose the beneficiary chose. Funds used in this manner would be subject to income tax.

The Balanced Budget Act created the option for beneficiaries to enroll in MSAs on a trial basis for four years, ending in 2002. CMS was then to evaluate the plans to see if they did provide a viable alternative to the traditional fee-for-service program and the Medicare HMO option. Few insurance companies and few Medicare beneficiaries found this option to be attractive. During the trial period, MSA enrollment was less than 20 percent of what had been hoped for. The MSA model was adopted on a much broader basis, however, as part of the Medicare Modernization Act, passed in 2003. Renamed health savings accounts (HSAs), they are now available to the general public and have been fairly widely adopted.

The Balanced Budget Act included a number of other changes in the way Medicare was financed. One of the most significant of these was the decision to shift funding for home health services provided to Medicare beneficiaries from Part A to Part B. The reader will recall that the Part A trust fund is financed through the payroll tax contributions of employers and employees. In contrast to Part B financing, which can draw on the general federal treasury if costs increase, there is no mechanism to increase funding for Part A if tax revenues are not sufficient to meet Part A expenses. The two principal categories of Part A expenses before 1997 were hospital care and home health care.

The Medicare home health care benefit had initially been designed to provide a means of getting patients who were being treated in the hospital back home as soon as possible. Medicare would pay for a range of services provided to patients in their home, including skilled nursing care, physical therapy, occupational therapy, and assistance with activities of daily living from a home health aide (see chapter 11 for a description of "activities of daily living"). Because home health care was seen as a way of getting patients out of the hospital sooner, it seemed appropriate to place the budget for home health services under the Part A trust fund.

The experience with home health care proved to be different from the predictions. Home health care was successful in its goal of improving the quality of life of home-bound, elderly individuals. Rather than providing care to recently hospitalized patients, however, the program ended up offering services mainly to patients who had not been in the hospital. Rather than being a substitute for hospital care, it turned out to provide services that were in addition to hospital care. While serving millions of elderly patients, it did not appear to cut down substantially on the cost of hospital care. Allocating the cost of home health care to the Part A trust fund appeared to be less appropriate than initially intended. In the Balanced Budget Act, the solution to this problem was quite simple: reallocate the cost of home health services that are not associated with an episode of hospital care from Part A to Part B. This switch did nothing to change the cost of home health care. It simply changed the fund from which the cost of these services would come. In doing so, it removed a major drain on the trust fund.

The need to maintain the solvency of the Part A trust fund also led Congress to reduce the amount Medicare would pay for hospital care. Recall that most hospital care is paid through the PPS. Historically, as the cost of providing hospital care rose, Medicare increased the PPS payment for that care. Based on a political decision to reduce payments to providers as a principal means of stabilizing Medicare's financing, the Balanced Budget Act mandated that Medicare reduce payments to hospitals in a variety of ways. The first was to keep payments under the PPS the same in 1998 as they were in 1997, even though the actual costs faced by hospitals had gone up. For the years 1999–2002, PPS payments would rise, but at a rate that was less than the actual increase in the cost of care.

A second step was to further reduce payments to hospitals that treat large numbers of poor patients. Medicare keeps track of the percentage of poor patients treated in every hospital. Those hospitals that treated a disproportionate number of poor patients had received extra payment over and above the usual PPS payment, on the assumption that caring for poor patients can be more expensive than caring for comparable patients who are not poor. These "disproportionate-share" hospitals were thus hit twice by the Balanced Budget Act: their payments were reduced under the standard PPS reductions and also under the specific disproportionate-share reductions. The Balanced Budget Act also reduced the amount paid to teaching hospitals for training residents and fellows, capped the number of residents who can be trained, and provided financial incentives for hospitals to decrease the number of residents in their programs.

The Best-Laid Plans: Unintended Consequences of Policy Changes in the Balanced Budget Act

The Balanced Budget Act of 1997 was intended to stabilize the financing of the Medicare program while maintaining the quality and accessibility of care to beneficiaries. As is often the case with complex policy changes, the act failed to achieve many of its intended outcomes. In some cases, the results of the policy changes were the opposite of what was intended.

Financial Hardship for Hospitals

The payment reductions to hospitals included in the Balanced Budget Act were intended primarily to stabilize the Part A trust fund. Congress had no desire to cause financial hardship for hospitals. Nevertheless, the reductions created substantial financial hardship for a number of hospitals. The reductions in Medicare payments were more than many hospitals could withstand. Hospitals in numerous cities faced either closing to prevent insolvency or selling out to larger hospital corporations. Teaching hospitals and disproportionate-share hospitals faced additional losses, leading many of them to the brink of insolvency. Perhaps hardest hit were those hospitals with the dual role of caring for the poor and training physicians. Many of these hospitals are in the inner city and are supported by local public funds. A number of hospitals in this situation had to close down, leaving many of the most vulnerable segments of the population with even greater difficulty in obtaining care. Fortunately, Congress and CMS became aware of the unintended consequences the Balanced Budget Act had on hospitals. They acted quickly to increase payments to hospitals (though not back to the level before the act) to maintain their financial stability.

Decreasing Availability and Increasing Cost for Medicare HMOs

The government had data to show that many Medicare HMOs were being paid more than was intended, due to favorable selection of enrolled beneficiaries. The reduction in capitation rate included as part of the Balanced Budget Act was intended to rectify this imbalance. The intent was that HMOs and other managed care plans made available through Medicare + Choice would at least maintain their coverage, if not expand it.

Instead, many HMOs reacted to the decrease in capitation payment by simply canceling their risk contract with Medicare, and in doing so canceling the HMO coverage of beneficiaries previously covered by their plan. HMOs have the option of canceling contracts on a county-by-county basis. Because the capitation rates were set on a county-wide basis, the rates in one county could be quite different from the rates in nearby counties. Thus, HMOs were allowed to "disenroll" covered beneficiaries in one county while maintaining coverage in others. In 1999 and 2000, the two years following enactment of the Balanced Budget Act, HMOs pulled out of more than 400 counties in 33 states, leading to the involuntary disenrollment of more than 700,000 Medicare beneficiaries. Between 1999 and 2003, 2.4 million Medicare beneficiaries were disenrolled in this way. The reason given by most HMOs for canceling their Medicare contracts was low payment rates.

In attempting to adjust the capitation rate to a more equitable level, the Balanced Budget Act led to a mass exodus of HMOs from Medicare, affecting more than 25 percent of those beneficiaries enrolled in HMOs. Some beneficiaries who lost their coverage were able to switch into other HMOs. Many did not have this option and were required to revert to traditional Medicare coverage. For those seniors with chronic medical problems who had to revert to traditional coverage, finding a private Medigap insurer to supplement Medicare coverage often proved difficult. Those seniors who were able to maintain HMO coverage faced substantial increases in premiums. In addition, they found that many of the extra benefits previously offered by HMOs were sub-

stantially reduced. Especially vulnerable to reductions in coverage were prescription drugs. Many seniors who joined HMOs principally to obtain prescription drug coverage found this coverage markedly reduced.

> **CONCEPT 6.12**
>
> The Balanced Budget Act of 1997 had a number of adverse consequences that Congress had not intended. Among these were a large-scale exodus of many HMOs from the Medicare program and severe financial hardship for many hospitals.

The exodus of HMOs from the Medicare market and the distrust this change created among Medicare beneficiaries dealt a severe blow to the concept of Medicare + Choice. Nonetheless, many still contended that private, market-based plans are a better long-term alternative than the traditional Medicare plan. As part of the Medicare Modernization Act, passed in 2003, Congress instructed CMS to increase capitation payments to private plans under Medicare + Choice (renamed by the act as "Medicare Advantage").

WHY DID MEDICARE HMOS HAVE SO LITTLE SUCCESS IN HOLDING DOWN COSTS?

The rising cost of health care seen generally in this country over the thirty years leading up to the Balanced Budget Act contributed to rising costs for Medicare as well. The federal government took a number of steps that were successful in constraining that rise. Examples of these successful policy changes include the PPS and the RBRVS method of paying physicians.

Medicare's move to managed care as an alternative to fee-for-service was substantially less successful, however. Initially, enrollment in Medicare HMOs grew rapidly. When it was discovered that Medicare HMOs were benefiting substantially from favorable selection of enrollees, however, Congress acted to reduce payments to HMOs to a more equitable level. As a cost-saving device, Medicare + Choice turned out largely to be a failure. Rather than reducing costs, it increased costs.

Why did it turn out that Medicare HMOs and other Medicare managed care plans did not save money compared to the fee-for-service alternative? Recall that the original RAND health insurance experiment carried out in the 1980s demonstrated that HMOs saved money over their fee-for-service competitors largely in the way they used the hospital. HMO patients were hospitalized less often and for shorter periods of time. Now recall that the Medicare PPS, also enacted in the 1980s, was quite successful in reducing hospital costs for Medicare beneficiaries. It appears that the PPS had achieved roughly the same savings in hospital costs for Medicare beneficiaries that HMOs had achieved for the general public. There may not have been any further savings to be realized by switching Medicare from a fee-for-service to a capitated system of payment. While HMOs in the 1980s worked as less costly alternatives to fee-for-service plans, the basis of these cost savings (reduced use of hospitals) did not exist for Medicare in the 1990s. There was little reason to believe, and little scientific data to suggest, that market-based managed care plans would be any more successful in constraining the inexorable rise in Medicare costs than the traditional plan that is based on fee-for-service payment for physicians and prospective payment for hospitals.

"MEDICARE ADVANTAGE" AS THE NEW MEDICARE MARKET OPTION

When President George W. Bush was elected in 2000, one of his principal campaign pledges had been to initiate fundamental reforms to Medicare. He was successful in this effort, securing passage of the Medicare Prescription Drug, Improvement, and Modernization Act (MMA) of 2003. The principal component of MMA was the creation of a prescription drug benefit for Medicare beneficiaries, discussed in chapter 10. A second major outcome of MMA was to replace Medicare + Choice with a new plan referred to as Medicare Advantage (MA). MA fundamentally altered the method of funding the private plans available to Medicare beneficiaries. Instead of paying the private plans 90 percent of the average cost of beneficiaries in the traditional Medicare system, MA guaranteed these plans 100 percent of that average cost. In addition, private plans were guaranteed annual increases in their payment rates. With these changes, coupled with a complex formula for calculating plan reimbursement on a county-by-county basis, it rapidly became apparent that the cost of MA plans was going to be substantially greater than that of traditional Medicare. Much of this added cost went to expanded benefits and lower premiums for those Medicare beneficiaries enrolling in them.

Not surprisingly, with this added funding and increased level of benefits, MA plans grew substantially in popularity. From a low of 5.3 million enrolled beneficiaries in 2004, the year MA first came into effect, enrollment grew to 16.8 million beneficiaries in 2010, representing 31 percent of all beneficiaries (Jacobson et al. 2015). Of those enrolled in MA in 2015, 64 percent were in an HMO, 31 percent in a PPO, and 5 percent in one of the other private plan options.

This expansion, however, came at a substantial cost to the Medicare program. In 2009, the average cost of a MA plan was 114 percent that of traditional Medicare, with some plans such as PPOs and private fee-for-service plans costing 118 percent of traditional Medicare (Medicare Payment Advisory Commission 2009). The added cost of

> **CONCEPT 6.13**
>
> The Medicare Modernization Act of 2003 provided additional funding to managed care plans enrolling Medicare beneficiaries. Care provided in these plans costs an average of 114 percent of the cost of care under the traditional Medicare system.

these plans contributed to higher Part B premiums paid by all Medicare beneficiaries and were seen as contributing to the long-term financial instability of the Medicare program. In the words of officials working with the Medicare Payment Advisory Commission, "The higher MA payment rates have financed what is essentially a Medicare benefit expansion for MA enrollees, without producing any overall savings for the Medicare program, and with increased costs borne by all beneficiaries and taxpayers" (Zarabozo and Harrison 2009, p. w66).

PAYING PHYSICIANS UNDER MEDICARE—THE SUSTAINABLE GROWTH RATE

Starting in 1992, the RBRVS system created a mechanism to constrain the rising cost of physicians' services under Part B of Medicare. By establishing a single payment rate based on the relative value unit, or RVU, Congress could act to change the payment per RVU, and in so doing adjust the entire physician payment structure under Medicare either up or down. As part of the Balanced Budget Act of 1997, Congress took just such action, creating what it called the sustainable growth rate (SGR) for physician services.

Recall from our discussion in chapter 3 the method various Canadian provinces used to control the cost of physician services. Each year, the province would set a budgeted amount to spend on all physician services in aggregate. As physicians in Canada billed largely on a fee-for-service basis, only by setting and enforcing budget caps could the provincial health plans control the cost of physicians' services. As it turned out, in many of the provinces the aggregate cost of physicians' services exceeded the budgeted amount, leading the provincial health plans to reduce the amount they paid physicians for the following year.

Faced with these reduced fees, physicians tended to see patients more frequently and to perform more services each time they saw a patient. These increased costs, triggered in response to a reduced payment rate, once again exceeded the budget for that year, leading to a further round of fee reductions. This process of serial fee reductions and utilization increases, referred to as "churning," resulted in a downward spiral in physician incomes in Canada. The spiral was finally arrested when provincial medical associations, in collaboration with government agencies, were able to alter the pattern of physicians' care.

SGR, as established by the Balanced Budget Act, adopted essentially the same approach to constraining the cost of physicians' services as that used in Canada. Rather than setting a fixed yearly budget for physician care under Part B of Medicare, it set an expenditure "target" based on current year expenditures. To establish the target, the CMS adjusted expenditures from one year to the next based on the following factors (Congressional Budget Office 2006):

1. adjustment for inflation that accounts for changes in the prices of goods and services used by physicians' practices,
2. changes in the number of people enrolled in Medicare's fee-for-service program,
3. the average annual growth rate of real gross domestic product (GDP) per capita, and
4. changes in the benefit structure of Part B that result from new legislation or regulations.

The SGR worked reasonably well in the first few years following its enactment in 1997. In 2000 and 2001, for example, physicians' fees under Part B went up 5.3 percent and 4.8 percent, respectively (Iglehart 2002). By 2002, however, physicians' charges had begun to exceed the SGR formula, and Medicare reduced physicians' fees by 4.8 percent. By 2003, charges had gone up even more, and payments were scheduled to go down an additional 4.4 percent. In testimony before Congress, Donald B. Marron, acting director of the Congressional Budget Office, reported that "considerable evidence exists that a reduction in [Medicare] payment rates leads physicians to increase the volume and intensity of the services they perform" (2006, p. 4). Physicians were treating Medicare beneficiaries more often (volume) and using more resources for each treatment (intensity). Physicians in the United States were, perhaps not surprisingly, responding to relative reductions in the fees Medicare paid as compared to their usual fees by increasing the volume and intensity of their services—that is, they were engaging in churning.

CMS, the federal agency that oversees the Medicare program, initially responded to the pattern of expenditures rising faster than the target rate by scheduling a 4.8 percent cut in the amount it paid per RVU, with an additional 4.4 percent cut scheduled for 2003. In 2003, however, Congress responded to intense lobbying on the part of physicians' professional organizations by postponing the scheduled fee reductions for a year. When the time came to reenact those reductions, aggregate physician costs had again exceeded the SGR limit, resulting in a larger mandated reduction. This happened every year until 2015 when, in the face of a scheduled 21 percent reduction in payments to physicians, Congress decided to abandon the SGR program altogether (Aaron 2015), replacing it with a new "Merit-based Incentive Payment System" (MIPS), limiting future increases in payment rates and linking them to the physician's individual performance ranking based on a composite measure of quality.

MIPS is an extension of the Physician Quality Reporting System, established in 2011, under which payments to physicians can be adjusted up or down by a small amount based on the quality of the care provided. Under this new payment system, between 2016 and 2019, physicians will receive a guaranteed increase in payment rates of 0.5 percent per year. After that, payment rates will be adjusted annually, either up or down, according to the physician's performance on the MIPS scale. Payment adjustments can be as large as 4 percent beginning in 2019, growing to as large as 9 percent by 2022. Physicians who have shifted a substantial portion of their practice to alternative payment models (APM) such as ACOs and bundled payment will be exempt from the MIPS adjustments, receiving instead a 5 percent annual increase in payment rates through 2024. As described by Oberlander and Laugesen (2015), "These changes mark a new era, in which Medicare offers powerful incentives for physicians to participate in ACOs and other innovative payment and delivery models. Indeed, the chief actuary of the Centers for Medicare and Medicaid Services (CMS) predicts that eventually all physicians participating in Medicare will be paid through such APMs" (p. 1185).

> **CONCEPT 6.14**
>
> The Balanced Budget Act of 1997 established a capped target for annual aggregate expenditures for physician care under Medicare Part B, referred to as the sustainable growth rate (SGR). For several years, the SGR formula called for substantial reductions in payments to physicians. However, Congress repeatedly postponed those reductions, finally abandoning SGR in 2015.

Steinbrook (2015) questioned whether Congress's repeal of SGR will work any better than the old SGR did: "The SGR fix, however, should not be viewed as a permanent solution to the ferment over the physician payment system. . . . The SGR formula lasted 18 years. Within the decade, its replacement is likely to be under scrutiny as well" (p. 2026). The SGR was modeled largely on the historically successful efforts in Canada to constrain the costs of physicians' services. The difference, of course, is in the political will to permit the mechanism to work. In Canada, provincial governments had the political will to enforce their budgets for physician care. In the United States, that will simply has not been there.

ADDITIONAL POINTS ABOUT THE MEDICARE PROGRAM

Two additional points should be made about the Medicare program. As discussed previously, the cost of providing medical care to elderly people has become increasingly expensive over time. The result has been that most current beneficiaries receive substantially more in benefits—in the range of five to ten times more—than they contributed to the system during their working years. Medicare is a system based on shifting financial resources from current workers to current elderly people.

The second point has to do with the administrative efficiency of the Medicare system. During the debate over national health care reform in 1993–94, opponents made much of the added federal bureaucracy that would be developed if the Clinton reform proposals were adopted. The implication was that giving the government greater responsibility in administering health care resources would lead to massive inefficiency.

The Medicare system, despite being one of the largest government programs in history, has proven to be one of the most efficient administrative systems for providing health care to a defined population of patients. A common measure of efficiency in health care is the percentage of all costs that go to administration rather than patient care. Employer-based insurance typically spends 10 to 30 percent of costs on administration and other expenses not related to patient care (e.g., corporate profit). For nonprofit HMOs such as Kaiser Permanente, this figure is in the range of 3 to 7 percent. Part A spent 1 to 2 percent of all funds on administrative costs; the figure for Part B is typically 2 to 2.5 percent. Using this measure of administrative efficiency, Medicare is the most efficient medical payment system in the country.

> **CONCEPT 6.15**
>
> The administrative structure of Medicare, managed by the federal Centers for Medicare and Medicaid Services, is the most efficient medical payment system in the country.

Before moving on to look at the changes to Medicare included in the Affordable Care Act, we should also consider Medicare's current policies of paying for graduate medical education (GME). GME refers to the training physicians receive after they graduate from medical school. It includes training offered in residency programs and specialty fellowship programs. Since 1983, the federal government has taken principal responsibility for paying the costs of GME, essentially reimbursing most of the training costs to hospitals that offer GME. The cost of GME is paid from the Part A trust fund.

It may seem odd that the program intended to pay for hospital care for seniors has taken on responsibility for paying the costs of GME. Such a perception is accurate and represents a strange and unintended twist in the history of Medicare. As described in chapter 4, Medicare was not initially intended to be the principal source of funding for GME. As a result of a political compromise enacted at the time the PPS was initiated in 1983, however, Medicare became responsible for paying most of the costs of GME.

For decades, no limits were placed on the number of GME positions that could be funded, resulting in a powerful financial incentive for hospitals to increase the size of their GME programs. It became readily apparent to hospitals that by increasing the number of GME slots, they would receive a larger subsidy from the federal government. For many hospitals, particularly inner-city hospitals that provide care to low-income patients, resident physicians provide the bulk of the care (albeit under the supervision of fully trained physicians on the hospital staff). The Medicare payments for GME provided a source of inexpensive physicians for inner-city hospitals.

The effect on the system overall was a growing surplus of GME training slots compared to the number of medical students graduating from US medical schools. It became necessary for hospitals to look to international medical graduates (IMGs) to fill their training programs, with a resulting influx of international physicians into the country. A substantial majority of IMGs trained in the United States under this program remain in the country after their training is completed.

CHANGES IN MEDICARE UNDER THE AFFORDABLE CARE ACT

Those responsible for the passage of the Affordable Care Act (ACA) knew that unless ACA addressed the growing issue of the cost of the Medicare program in the context of the entry into it of the baby boom generation, any attempt at system-wide health care reform would likely fail in the long run. Accordingly, ACA contains several major changes to Medicare.

In the years immediately following enactment of ACA, the concerns regarding rising Medicare costs were allayed somewhat—at least for the time being. In the summer of 2014, economist and *New York Times* columnist Paul Krugman reported what he referred to as *The Medicare Miracle*: "We've all seen projections of giant federal deficits over the next few decades. . . . But a funny thing has happened: Health spending has slowed sharply, and it's already well below projections made just a few years ago. The falloff has been especially pronounced in Medicare, which is spending $1,000 less per beneficiary than the Congressional Budget Office projected just four years ago" (p. A17). Dranove et al. (2015) analyzed the possible causes of this slowdown in Medicare spending and determined that only a small part of it was a consequence of the continued economic downturn that followed the recession of 2007–08. Two separate analyses found that decreases in mortality rates and rates of hospitalization among Medicare beneficiaries both contributed to the observed slowdown in Medicare spending (Mirel and Carper 2014; Krumholz et al. 2015).

On the occasion of the fiftieth anniversary of the 1965 enactment of Medicare, Blumenthal and colleagues (2015) looked carefully at the future of Medicare spending and concluded that "over the next decade, slow growth in Medicare spending per beneficiary is expected to continue, but because of substantial increases in the number of beneficiaries, the growth in total program spending will outpace that in the overall economy" (p. 671). Largely as a result of this increase in the number of beneficiaries, in 2015 the Medicare Trustees Report predicted that Medicare spending as a percent of GDP would increase from 3.5 percent in 2014 to 5.4 percent in 2035 (Medicare Boards of Trustees 2015).

Jacob (2015) reported on an interview he conducted with Donald Berwick, former administrator of the federal Centers for Medicare and Medicaid Services (CMS). In the interview, Berwick described the problem confronting not only Medicare but the country's health care system in general: "This country is on an expedition around discovery of new ways to pay for health care that will be better supportive of meeting the real needs of patient communities. We [know] the current payment system isn't working. It rewards doing more and more things whether they are of a value to patients or not, so it leads to overuse. It produces fragmentation because it doesn't support coordinated team-based care the way we need to" (p. 325).

Realizing that, unless fundamental changes are made in the ways providers are paid under Medicare, both the federal budget and the economy in general would be irreparably harmed, HHS secretary Sylvia M. Burwell (2015) announced a series of goals for shifting future Medicare spending. These included:

- by the end of 2016, increasing the quality/value of 30 percent of Medicare payments by linking them to alternative payment models, rising to 50 percent of payments by the end of 2018;
- adopting alternative payment models to include accountable care organizations (ACOs) and bundled-payment arrangements, under both of which health care providers will be held accountable for the quality and overall cost of the care they provide to Medicare patients; and
- linking 85 percent of all Medicare fee-for-service payments to established quality/value metrics by 2016, with 90 percent of these payments linked to these metrics by 2018.

Shifting to Accountable Care Organizations

As one of its central elements, ACA created a new Center for Medicare and Medicaid Innovation (CMMI) and charged it with developing new and innovative models of payment and service delivery for Medicare beneficiaries. Established in 2011, CMMI moved rapidly to carry out this task. One of the principal new models of care delivery called for in ACA was the accountable care organization (ACO).

As described by CMMI (2015a), "Accountable Care Organizations are groups of doctors, hospitals, and other health care providers who come together voluntarily to give coordinated high quality care to the Medicare patients they serve. . . . When an ACO succeeds in both delivering high-quality care and spending health care dollars more wisely, it will share in the savings it achieves for the Medicare program." Care provided under an ACO includes physician care, hospital care, and care provided by other types of facilities such as rehabilitation centers. A central element of the ACO is identifying a list of specific patients for whom the ACO will be responsible for providing care.

While ACA established ACOs largely to provide care to Medicare recipients, ACOs are not limited to treating Medicare patients. They can also contract with private insurers to provide care to their patients under similar constraints and expectations. Colla and colleagues (2014) reported on a national survey of 292 groups that either had qualified or were likely to qualify as ACOs under Medicare guidelines. In their survey, they defined ACOs as "groups of providers that are collectively held responsible for the care of a defined population of patients" (p. 964). Of the 173 organizations that responded to their survey, 66 percent had completed a contract with Medicare to provide care, and 51 percent had contracted with private insurers.

The core idea behind having Medicare or private insurers contract with ACOs is to create financial incentives for physicians and other provider organizations both to improve the quality of care their patients receive and to reduce cost growth. In order to function effectively, ACOs must establish close coordination among its various providers. This will necessarily mean that physicians and the hospitals they work with must agree to new administrative and financial arrangements to meet these goals.

Of the ACOs identified by Cola and colleagues, 51 percent were led by physician practice groups while 49 percent were led by some other type of organization. While 41 percent of the physician-led groups included hospitals in their ACO, 87 percent of the nonphysician groups involved hospitals. A second study of early ACOs also found that less than half included hospitals in their organization. Those hospitals that did participate in an ACO were more likely to be larger, nonprofit, and teaching hospitals. The authors also found that ACOs tended to treat patients who were higher income and less likely to be covered by Medicaid, disabled, or black (Epstein et al. 2014).

At this point, I am hoping that, as the reader, you are asking, "Haven't we seen this happen before? What about the managed care revolution from the 1990s?" This is the question posed by Burns and Pauly (2012) in response to the ACA's emphasis on expanding the role of ACOs: "Much of the enthusiasm stems from the following two assumptions about accountable care organizations: that better care coordination will improve quality at any given cost, and that the organizations will lower Medicare's rate of spending growth. However, the parallels with the disappointing 1990s seem quite strong to us, raising our concern that the fate of the organizations may resemble that of the earlier integrated delivery networks" (p. 2408).

Recall from the discussion in chapter 5 of the origins in the 1950s of the Kaiser Permanente Health Care system that, in the face of rapid expansion following Word War II, Henry Kaiser, as owner of the hospitals, and Sidney Garfield, as leader of the physicians, had disparate views as to who should run their new health care system. Mr. Kaiser wanted the hospitals to take the lead, while Dr. Garfield wanted the physicians to be in charge. Fortunately, they were able to come to a compromise (see figure 5.3). Mr. Kaiser would manage the hospitals and the separate entity set up to receive and distribute the income of the system, and Dr. Garfield would manage a separate organization of physicians. They also agreed, however, that the hospitals and the physicians would collaborate closely in order to provide high-quality care within the strict budget created by the capitation system of payment.

Recall also the alternative organizational structure for HMOs created by the HMO Act of 1973 (see figure 5.4). In this new model, there was little or no collaboration between the various physician groups and the various hospitals that contracted with the separate corporation at the center of the HMO. This lack of collaboration, complicated by the growing influence of the for-profit structure of many of these HMOs (as discussed in chapter 9), led to the failure of many of these organizations. As described by Burns and Pauly (2012): "Most of the organizations did not really take a systems approach that involved integrated organizational planning for everything from hiring and other personnel matters to physician culture. Instead, they bolted together various providers, . . . hoping the combinations would work" (p. 2408).

Perhaps as a response to these problems in managed care delivery experienced in the 1990s, both ACA and CMMI, the federal agency charged with developing and evaluating the ACO model of care, have taken a more cautious approach. There are no plans at this time to require ACOs to accept capitation payment. Instead, as described earlier, HHS secretary Sylvia M. Burwell has set a target of shifting 30 percent of Medicare payments to alternative payment models by 2016, rising to 50 percent by the end of 2018.

The initial alternative payment models established by CMMI have largely maintained the fee-for-service model of paying physicians and the prospective payment system of paying hospitals. They will, however, offer ACOs a financial bonus if they are able to reduce aggregate costs of caring for their Medicare patients. CMMI has established three principal payment options for ACOs to select from: the Shared Savings Program, the Pioneer ACO Model, and the ACO Investment Model (Pham et al. 2015).

1. Shared Savings Program (SSP): To qualify as a SSP, an ACO must agree to accept full responsibility for the care of at least 5,000 Medicare beneficiaries for a period of at least three years. While Medicare will continue to pay providers in the ACOs based on current payment policies (fee-for-service for physicians and PPS for hospitals). Medicare will also establish a targeted amount of cost savings to be achieved by the ACO, as well as a set of quality metrics for the ACO to maintain. Those ACOs that achieve at least partial cost savings while maintaining adequate quality will then be eligible for a share of those savings as a supplemental payment. If the ACO is also willing to risk paying a penalty if it instead goes over previous payment levels, it would then qualify for a larger share of any savings it attains. Clough et al. (2015, supplementary e-table) reported that SSP ACOs were providing care for 7.3 million Medicare beneficiaries as of April 2015. Of the 220 ACOs that had completed at least one year of SSP participation, 58 (26 percent) had earned shared savings, while only one had experienced a loss resulting in a penalty. In general, the SSP ACOs had shown improvement on most of the quality metrics being followed.

2. Pioneer ACOs: The Pioneer ACO Model was designed to be more appropriate for larger organizations that have had more experience with integrated care delivery. Pioneer ACOs need to provide care for at least 10,000 Medicare beneficiaries and are required to accept shared responsibility for both savings as well as losses that may occur. The quality metrics for Pioneer ACOs are similar to those applied to SSP ACOs. As described by Pham et al. (2014): "The Pioneer model complements and will inform refinements to the Shared Savings Program by offering payment arrangements with higher levels of risk and reward and by testing key design elements for the future of ACOs" (p. 1635).

As of April 2015, 23 Pioneer ACOs were providing care for a total of about 610,000 Medicare beneficiaries. Pioneer ACOs reduced the cost of care by an average of $35.62 per beneficiary per month during 2012, their first year of operation, and an average of $11.18 per beneficiary per month during 2013 (Nyweide et al. 2015). Reduced hospital costs accounted for the largest part of the savings, especially during 2013. In addition, in their first year of the Pioneer ACO program, Pioneer ACOs reduced their use of low-value services (as defined by national professional organizations) by about 5 percent, with those ACOs having a higher initial rate of low-value services showing the largest reduction (Schwartz et al. 2015). Patients' perceptions of their access to care and the quality of care were better in the ACOs than in traditional Medicare.

While meeting the overall goals of the program, these savings were relatively small in terms of the percentage of overall expenditures. The savings represented a 4 percent reduction in 2012 and a 1.5 percent reduction in 2013. Responding to these results, Casalino (2015) suggested that "this amount may seem small, but if this rate of savings could be sustained, and achieved throughout a large part of the US health care system, it would be more than enough to 'bend the cost curve' so that health care expenditures do not continue to increase as a percentage of the gross domestic product and the federal budget" (p. 2126). Casalino also noted, however, that thirteen organizations that initially signed up to be Pioneer ACOs had instead dropped out of the program.

Responding to the initial results of the Pioneer ACO experience, former CMS administrator Mark McClellan (2015) found that the Pioneer ACO program represented only a "limited shift away from FFS payments." McClellan went on to suggest that "payment reform has a long way to go" and called for continued research in alternative payment models (p. 2129).

3. Investment Model ACOs: CMMI has acknowledged that neither SSP nor Pioneer ACOs are suitable for many rural or otherwise underserved areas. As described on the CMMI website (2015a), "The ACO Investment Model was developed in response to stakeholder concerns and available research suggesting that some

providers lack adequate access to the capital needed to invest in infrastructure necessary to successfully implement population care management." Accordingly, beginning in 2015, CMMI offered grant funding to organizations that provide care in these areas to initiate ACOs under the SSP Model. This funding will include three types of payment to cover the costs of establishing an ACO: an initial fixed payment, an additional fixed payment based on the number of Medicare beneficiaries to be served, and a monthly payment in addition to usual payment for care based on the number of beneficiaries covered. It is hoped that these incentives will bring the ACO model of care and the potential benefits that go with it to these underserved communities.

CMMI has also proposed developing other specialized types of ACOs, such as ACOs to provide comprehensive care to patients with kidney failure and requiring either ongoing dialysis treatment or access to kidney transplantation. It has also described what it refers to as a "next generation" model of ACO for larger integrated health systems that have elected not to participate in the initial ACO demonstration projects.

All of these various approaches to ACOs have one potential problem in common: How do you define which patients the ACOs are responsible for? Recall that under Medicare Advantage (MA) plans, beneficiaries sign up voluntarily and in doing so agree to obtain care only from those providers affiliated with their plan. ACOs are separate and distinct from these MA plans. Medicare beneficiaries remain free to seek care from any provider participating in Medicare, whether or not that provider is affiliated with an ACO. If a patient obtains care from a range of providers during the year, which provider(s) are responsible for that patient's care under the ACO model? Lewis et al. (2013) studied the issue and recommended that optimal results will come by waiting until the year is over, and then assigning beneficiaries to an ACO retrospectively based on the care obtained during that year. CMMI has taken the approach of assigning beneficiaries to ACOs based principally on the primary care physician they use most during the year (Pham et al. 2015).

Based on their review of recent ACO performance, Shortell and colleagues (2015) identified a series of issues they see as central to the success of ACOs in the future. These include:

1. Patient enrollment: ACOs need to be sure they have enrolled a sufficiently large number of patients in order to be able to make the investments necessary to control costs while maintaining quality.

2. Management systems: ACO leaders will need to establish evidence-based systems for managing the care of their most complex (and therefore most costly) patients.

3. Electronic health record (EHR) systems: For both providers who manage the care of patients and for the patients themselves, high-quality EHR systems will be essential.

4. Establishing metrics of cost and quality: It will be essential for providers, Medicare, and private payers to agree on a common set of these metrics so providers can monitor their progress in attaining these metrics.

5. Developing new care alliances: Beyond the usual collaboration between physicians and hospitals, successful ACOs will also need to establish collaborative associations with other care providers, in particular post-acute care providers such as rehabilitation centers and home health agencies, as well as behavioral health providers.

6. Involving patients and their families actively in the care process.

Even if all of these issues are successfully addressed by ACOs, Shortell and colleagues raise another central issue: Will they actually work? "Less than half of leaders of either physician-led or other-led ACOs believe that such contracts have great potential to reduce cost growth. In the final analysis, it is important to recognize that while ACOs are not unicorns and appear to be having an impact, they are not a panacea for what ails the US health care delivery system" (p. 661).

Noting that "many of the historical roots of ACOs go back to the Kaiser Permanente system," Scheffler (2015) underscored a key element in the potential success of ACOs. "One of the system's key elements is the payment model, which rewards providers for keeping people well and aligns the interests of all parties involved, thus creating incentives for coordinating care across the continuum" (p. 638). Scheffler concurs with the aforementioned comments of Shortell et al. and suggests that the success of ACOs will depend to a large extent on being able to develop tools to assess the quality as well as the cost of care they provide.

Paying Hospitals for Value Rather than Volume

Responding to the comments of HHS secretary Sylvia M. Burwell cited previously about shifting Medicare to a value-based payment system, Cassel and Kronick (2015) argued that "paying for value will not work unless it can be measured. . . . What links all of this recent information is the need for timely, accurate, reliable, meaningful metrics of health care quality" (p. 875). As part of this new emphasis on value established by ACA, CMS has created a three-pronged "Pay for Performance" (PFP) program to shift the way it pays hospitals for providing care to Medicare beneficiaries (Kahn et al. 2015). Beginning in 2013, CMS began to adjust the amount they pay a hospital annually based on two metrics: the quality of the care received in the hospital (value-based purchasing) and the frequency with which Medicare patients treated in the hospital are subsequently readmitted to the hospital within thirty days of discharge (Readmission Reduction).

Under the value-based purchasing (VBP) program, the quality of the care provided while patients were in the hospital is measured in several different areas: infection rates and other measures of patient safety, mortality rates while hospitalized, patients' experience of the care process, and the overall quality of the care process based on established criteria. The care provided by the hospital using a combination of these measures is then compared to a standard set by CMS and to the hospital's previous performance on these indices. Hospitals showing high value, based on improvement from previous performance as well as performance relative to the standard set by CMS, will receive a bonus payment, while those hospitals who perform poorly can be penalized. By 2017, up to 2 percent of overall hospital payments may be redistributed by CMS in this manner, with the sum of the bonuses equaling the sum of the penalties so as to keep the program budget-neutral.

Under the hospital readmission reduction program (HRRP), hospitals will be closely monitored to determine the percentage of readmissions that were potentially preventable had the original care been of a higher quality. HRRP focuses on several specific conditions, such as heart failure, heart attack, pneumonia, and major joint surgery, for which past research has established a high rate of potentially preventable readmission. By 2017, as much as 3 percent of the hospital's Medicare revenue could be at risk if it has a higher rate of readmission than the standard set by CMS. As bonuses for lower readmission rates are not included in this program, the end result of any penalties assessed will not be budget-neutral.

CMS has initiated a third program, the hospital-acquired condition reduction program (HAC). Under this program, the rates of potentially preventable, hospital-acquired conditions are measured. These include conditions such as hospital-acquired infections and injuries sustained as a result of falls while in the hospital. While these measures were included in VBP prior to 2015, they formed their own quality measure beginning in 2015. Hospitals that show an unusually high rate of these preventable complications are subject to an additional penalty of up to 1 percent of revenue, over and above VBP and HRR payment adjustments.

While the initial level of penalties and bonuses under VBP and HRRP were somewhat lower than those for 2017, Kahn et al. reported that in fiscal year 2015, CMS had redistributed about $126 million in payment under VBP, with 55 percent of hospitals receiving a bonus averaging 0.4 percent of revenues and 45 percent assessed a penalty averaging 0.2 percent. Under HRRP, aggregate penalties totaled $424 million, with 76 percent of hospitals assessed a penalty averaging 0.5 percent of revenues.

By 2017, up to 6 percent of a hospital's Medicare revenues could be at risk based on poor performance on these three quality measures. These programs are based on the assumption that hospitals have the capacity to improve the quality of the care they provide as measured by these programs. A number of policy researchers have voiced concerns about these approaches to improving the value of care. Many of these concerns focus on the role of patients' demographic characteristics as possible causal factors of the disparate outcomes seen within certain types of hospitals.

Gilman et al. (2015) evaluated data for 2011 under VBP and found that hospitals identified as "safety-net" hospitals—defined in their study as the top 25 percent of hospitals providing care to uninsured and Medicaid patients—were significantly more likely to be penalized under VBP. While 51 percent of non-safety-net hospitals were penalized under VBP, 61 percent of safety-net hospitals were penalized. These disproportionate penalties were due to lower scores of safety-net hospitals on the process of care and patient experience measures of quality, with no significant difference in mortality rates between the two groups of hospitals. Gilman and colleagues question the potential validity of using ratings of patient experiences between fundamentally different patient populations. "Using metrics of patient experience, although potentially valuable, could also be regarded as problematic because they represent subjective attitudes that may vary according to patient demographics and may not always reflect the quality of care that the patient receives" (p. 404).

Similar concerns apply to HRRP. Herrin et al. (2015) compared thirty-day readmission rates among more than four thousand hospitals nationally for the period 2007–10 (before HRRP was in effect). They found that 58 percent of the variation among hospitals in rates of readmission was associated with the county in which the hospital was located. Henke and colleagues raised a second issue about HRRP: whether patients who are readmitted are admitted to the same hospital from which they were originally discharged. For certain conditions, Medicaid patients and uninsured patients were less likely to be readmitted to the hospital in which they were originally treated.

In addition to community characteristics, patient demographic characteristics have also been shown to be associated with rates of hospital readmission. In a study of readmissions occurring during 2010 in a large teaching hospital in Detroit, Hu et al. (2014) found that patient race, gender, and age were strongly associated with the risk of readmission. After controlling for these individual characteristics, patients living in neighborhoods with high rates of poverty or low levels of education had a readmission rate that was 24 percent greater than those living in higher-income and more highly educated neighborhoods. The authors suggest that these results "raise the question of whether CMS's readmission measures and associated financial penalties should be adjusted for the effects of factors beyond hospital influence at the individual or neighborhood level, such as poverty and lack of social support" (p. 778).

Under HRRP, CMS does adjust for patient age, gender, discharge diagnosis, and recent medical history in setting target rates by which hospitals are assessed. Consistent with the concerns raised by Hu et al., Barnett and colleagues (2015) questioned whether CMS's adjustments are sufficient to capture the role of patient characteristics as distinct from hospital care processes in affecting the risk of readmission. "This limited adjustment has raised concerns that hospitals may be penalized because they disproportionately serve patients with clinical and social characteristics that predispose them to hospitalization or rehospitalization" (p. E2). To address this issue, the authors studied more than eight thousand Medicare patients hospitalized between 2009 and 2012. In addition to the variables used by CMS in their adjustments under HRRP, Barnett also took into account additional demographic characteristics such as patient race, educational attainment, marital status, and disability level. Comparing hospitals in the highest quintile of readmissions with those in the lowest quintile, they found that adjusting for these additional patient characteristics accounted for about half of the difference in readmission rates between these hospital quintiles, leading the authors to conclude that "the higher prevalence of clinical and social predictors of readmission among patients admitted to hospitals with higher readmission rates is likely driven by factors largely outside of a hospital's influence" (p. E8).

In a commentary in response to the study by Barnett et al., van Walraven (2015) offered an important perspective: "Most people would think that early unplanned readmissions must reflect, in some way, a deficit of care during the index hospitalization. . . . However, a closer examination of early unplanned hospital readmissions reveals some deficiencies that undermine its utility as a health quality indicator" (p. E1).

Responding to a study showing that safety-net hospitals were significantly more likely than non-safety-net hospitals to be penalized under HRRP (Jha 2015), US senators Joseph Manchin (D-West Virginia) and Roger Wicker (R-Mississippi) collaborated with Andrew Boozary of the Harvard School of Public Health to publish a paper suggesting that "hospitals should not be penalized simply because of the demographic characteristics of their patients. . . . Targeting hospitals for penalties, even if indirectly, simply because those hospitals care for more poor patients is not good policy" (Boozary et al. 2015, p. 347).

Rajaram et al. (2015) raised similar questions about CMS's more recent HAC program. Using data from the first year of HAC, they found that hospitals that were teaching hospitals, that provided care to a more complex mix of patients clinically, and that were safety-net hospitals were more likely to be penalized under HAC.

Paying Physicians for Value in an Effort to Reduce Hospital Admissions

In addition to the programs described previously to improve hospital care, CMS and CMMI have also developed programs to reduce the rate of preventable hospitalizations among Medicare beneficiaries and improve the overall quality of care through improved community-based primary care. One of the first of these is the Comprehensive

Primary Care (CPC) initiative (Meltzer and Ruhnke 2014). Beginning in 2012, CPC has invested in projects to improve the quality and outcome of primary care by strengthening five core aspects of the care process: risk-stratified care management, access and continuity, planned care for chronic conditions and preventive care, patient and caregiver engagement, and coordination of care (CMMI 2015d).

In the first year of CPC, CMMI selected 502 primary care practices from around the country. They also secured the participation of thirty-one private payers who cover non-Medicare patients. Together with the private payers, CMMI paid each participating practice a supplemental, per-patient-per-month fee, which the practice was to use to improve the care process in the five areas just mentioned. The supplemental fees averaged about $70,000 per physician per year, with CMI paying 64 percent of these fees and the private payers responsible for 36 percent. In addition to these supplemental fees, CPC provided each practice group with regular feedback on the cost and patterns of use of care by enrolled patients, as well as technical assistance in developing improved systems of care.

A major focus of CPC has been to identify those patients within the primary care practices who were at the highest risk of hospitalization due to chronic illness and to provide these patients with intensive case management to reduce the need for hospital care. A report done for CMMI on the first-year outcomes of CPC found that this goal had been met to a substantial extent, and that "the initiative has generated enough savings in Medicare Part A and B health care expenditures to nearly cover the CPC care management fees paid by CMS" (Taylor et al. 2015, p. xx). Thus by investing additional funds in primary care delivery, CPC may be able, over time, to reduce preventable hospitalizations while improving outcomes for the most at-risk patients.

Bundled Payment as an Alternative to Traditional Payment

In her remarks cited previously, HHS Secretary Burwell set the goal of shifting 50 percent of payments to alternative forms of payment by the end of 2018. In addition to ACOs, Secretary Burwell also cited bundled payment (BP) as a second alternative payment system. In contrast to a capitated payment system, as described in chapter 5, under which a provider receives a fixed payment to cover care provided to a patient during a fixed time period, BP involves a fixed payment only for a specific episode of care. Based on the problem that initiated the need for care, the episode covered typically will be between 30 and 90 days.

It has been known for some time that, under traditional payment systems, the cost of care provided to Medicare patients for the same problems can vary substantially. Miller et al. (2011) evaluated the cost of care provided to Medicare patients covered under the traditional Part A / Part B payment systems between 2005 and 2007. Each patient had undergone one of a defined set of surgical procedures requiring hospitalization. They measured the total costs paid by Medicare between admission to the hospital and thirty days following hospital discharge. These costs included payments to the hospital, payments to physicians and other providers, and payments for post-acute care, such as skilled nursing care. After controlling for geographic differences and differences in the severity of illness, Miller and colleagues found that care provided at hospitals in the highest payment quintile had aggregate payments that were between 10 percent and 40 percent higher than hospitals in the lowest payment quintile—for providing the same type of care. Based on their analysis, the authors concluded: "The causes for this unexplained variation are undoubtedly complex. Broadly speaking, it appears to be driven by differences in the use of potentially discretionary physician services and—to a larger extent—in postdischarge care" (p. 2110).

These findings are consistent with the findings of an analysis by Feder (2013) that "variation in spending on post-hospital services . . . explains a full 40% of the overall geographic variation in Medicare spending per beneficiary" (p. 401). Feder based this conclusion on a report from the Institute of Medicine on the causes of geographic variation in Medicare spending. That report found that "most of the variation among geographic areas is attributable to variation in the use of post–acute care and inpatient services" (Newhouse and Garber 2013, p. 1468). Also responding to the IOM report, Mechanic (2014) suggested that shifting to a bundled payment system, under which all providers are offered the same payment for providing the same type of care, could go a long way toward reducing this variation.

Responding to the need to reduce unnecessary variation in Medicare costs, CMMI created the Bundled Payments for Care Improvement (BPCI) initiative (Center for Medicare and Medicaid Innovation 2015b). Beginning in 2013, BPCI offered hospitals the opportunity to participate in three-year pilot programs involving different forms of bundled payment. Both forms start with the initiation of an episode of care involving one of a list of conditions requiring hospitalization. Examples of these conditions include treatment of a heart attack or of pneumonia and surgical knee or hip joint replacement. One form of bundled payment continues to pay providers under the traditional payment system but then adjusts the aggregate payment at the end of the episode either by providing a supplemental payment if the aggregate costs are less than the targeted bundle amount or penalizing the providers if the aggregate amount exceeds the bundled target. A second form of payment pays the provider the bundled payment prospectively at the initiation of the episode, allowing the provider to allocate the payment among the various providers involved. In both cases, providers included in the bundled payment approach include the hospital, the participating physicians involved in the care, and any post–acute care providers, such as skilled nursing facilities and home health agencies.

Dummit et al. (2015) provided an evaluation of the early experience with these alternative payment models under BPCI. By the second year of the program, 107 hospitals were participating in the retrospective payment adjustment model, while only 20 hospitals had agreed to participate in the prospective payment model. The report was only able to provide preliminary data on the success of the programs, but that limited data showed evidence of potential reductions in the cost of care, especially in the post–acute care process.

Tsai et al. (2015) compared the characteristics of the hospitals participating in BCPI with those not participating. They found that participating hospitals "are mostly large, nonprofit, teaching hospitals in the Northeast, and they have selectively enrolled in the bundled payment initiative covering patient conditions with high clinical volumes" (p. 371). They also found that, consistent with the findings discussed earlier, spending on post-acute care accounted for the largest variation among participating providers in the aggregate costs of care.

The concept behind bundled payment is that all those involved in the care process, including physicians as well as hospitals and post–acute care providers, will share in the payment received. Nevertheless, a problem has been identified in the way bundled payments have been applied under BCPI. Only physicians who have agreed to participate in bundled payment receive payment from it. While this typically will include the surgeon or other specialist who initiates the care process, patients are still free to receive subsequent care from any registered Medicare physician. Mulcahy et al. (2015) reported on findings of the Office of the Inspector General of the Department of Health and Human Services that surgeons involved in bundled payment may have been providing fewer postoperative visits than expected, while other physicians not involved in bundled payment were providing much of the postoperative care. Medicare was paying for that care twice: once through the bundled payment and again through fee-for-service payments to physicians not involved in the bundled payment. In response, CMS announced in November 2014 that they would move to exclude physicians' services from bundled payments until they could include all providers in the bundled payment process, including physicians who have not enrolled in the program.

In July 2015, CMMI announced proposed new rules intended to address this problem in what they refer to as the Comprehensive Care for Joint Replacement (CCJR) model (CMMI 2015c). The new program would cover only major joint surgery of the knee or hip and would be applied on a trial basis in certain regions of the country. Within those regions, all hospitals would be required to participate, and all payments to physicians would be included in retrospectively adjusting those payments according to how those aggregate costs compared to the bundled payment target. These payment incentives would make it all the more important for providers to collaborate closely to optimize both the quality of care and the cost of care.

Changes to Medicare Advantage

As discussed previously, the Medicare Modernization Act of 2003 (MMA) increased payment rates to Medicare Advantage (MA) plans so as to attract additional managed care plans into the program. As a consequence, MA plans were paid an average of 114 percent of what it cost Medicare to provide care under its traditional payment systems. Acknowledging that there was little continuing support for providing a tax-financed subsidy to private health plans, ACA revised the formula under which these plans are paid. Beginning in 2010, the rates paid to plans participating in MA were gradually reduced, from an average of 110 percent of traditional Medicare spending in 2011 to 106 percent in 2014. By 2017, payments to MA plans will be essentially the same as traditional Medicare spending, although payment rates will vary based on geography and local Medicare costs (Kaiser Family Foundation 2015b). Payments are also risk-adjusted based on an enrollee's current and previous health status, so as to avoid favorable selection among MA enrollees (McWilliams et al. 2012). ACA also sets explicit quality targets for the care provided by plans under MA, based on the plan's scores on a series of national quality metrics. Under the new Five-Star Quality Rating System, each plan is assigned between one and five stars, with one star considered "poor" quality, three stars considered "average" quality, and five stars considered "excellent" quality. Those plans receiving four or five stars receive a bonus payment in addition to their regular capitation payment. In 2013, 37 percent of MA plans were rated as four or five stars; by 2015, 61 percent of plans had earned four or five stars and the associated bonus payment (Jacobson et al. 2015). Reid and colleagues (2013) found that both first-time enrollees in MA plans as well as previous enrollees who switched plans were more likely to select plans with higher star quality ratings.

Changes to Medicare Part D—The Prescription Drug Benefit

ACA makes changes to its prescription drug benefit, described in more detail in chapter 10.

Improved Coverage of Preventive Health Services

ACA changes the coverage for certain types of health services that have been recommended by the US Preventive Services Task Force. Examples of these services are mammography screening for breast cancer in women and screening for colorectal cancer. Beginning in 2011, Medicare beneficiaries have had no copayment or deductible charged for these services. In addition, beneficiaries may receive a yearly general preventive examination and consultation without charge.

Revenue Enhancements and Payment Reductions

In order to increase federal revenues to help pay for Medicare, ACA has made changes intended both to increase revenues and to reduce expenditures. The federal Medicare payroll tax has been increased from 1.45 percent to 2.35 percent for high-income taxpayers. ACA has also increased the Medicare Part B premiums for high-income beneficiaries. Perhaps the most significant payment reduction resulting from ACA is a change in the way yearly updates in payment rates to providers will be calculated. ACA assumes that, over time, institutional providers of services under Medicare will be able to improve their efficiency and productivity, and thus their cost of providing service. Based on these assumed efficiency enhancements, Medicare's increases in payment to these providers will be about 1.1 percent less each year than they would have been without the expected changes in provider efficiency.

Creation of a New National Advisory Board

In full recognition that the changes included in ACA did not guarantee that Medicare costs would not continue to rise to unsustainable levels, ACA established a new mechanism for addressing the issue of Medicare costs over time. ACA created the Independent Payment Advisory Board (IPAB), made up of fifteen members appointed by the president and confirmed by the Senate. IPAB's explicit responsibility is to monitor the rate at which Medicare's per-beneficiary spending increases over time.

ACA sets a target rate of growth for Medicare spending, tied initially to the growth in the consumer price index (a general measure of overall price inflation) and subsequently to the overall growth in GDP. Beginning in 2014, if it turns out that projected per-beneficiary spending will exceed the target amount, IPAB is charged with the responsibility of coming up with a plan to reduce Medicare spending to meet the target amount. The secretary of Health and Human Services must then carry out the IPAB's plan to control spending, unless Congress overrides the plan with one of its own.

In creating the IPAB, ACA has done two important things:

1. It has created under law a strict limit on spending growth under Medicare.
2. It has ceded authority to an independent body to enforce the limit.

In granting IPAB responsibility for enforcing the limits on Medicare spending growth, however, Congress has tied one of IPAB's hands behind its back. Section 3403.d.2.A.ii of ACA specifically states that any proposal from IPAB "shall not include any recommendation to ration health care, raise revenues [i.e., taxes] or Medicare beneficiary premiums . . . or increase Medicare beneficiary cost sharing (including deductibles, coinsurance, and copayments), or otherwise restrict benefits or modify eligibility criteria."

As discussed in chapter 13, the concept of "rationing" health care in the United States has come to have unusually negative connotations. For many, it is simply un-American even to consider rationing something as important as health care. Although ACA does not define what is meant by "rationing" care, IPAB can be expected to avoid recommendations that might be construed by the public or by Congress as "rationing." This means that cost-control mechanisms that weigh the costs versus the effectiveness of the services to be paid for by Medicare will be difficult, if not impossible, for IPAB to invoke. If IPAB is also prohibited from raising taxes or premiums, increasing cost sharing, or restricting benefits, it may be as difficult for IPAB to control the incessant rise in the cost of the Medicare program.

However, these concerns have become moot for the time being, in light of the following:

- Republicans in the Senate have vowed to block the creation of IPAB, threatening to filibuster any presidential appointments to the panel;
- the House of Representatives has voted to repeal that portion of ACA that established IPAB;
- as of 2015, President Obama has elected to avoid this potential quagmire by not appointing any of the members of IPAB; and
- since its first evaluation in 2013 and every year thereafter, largely as a result of the unexpected slowdown in Medicare spending that followed the recession, the Chief Actuary of CMS, the office charged with determining whether future Medicare spending will exceed the target set by ACA, has found that projected Medicare spending would be well below that target.

In its 2015 report, the Chief Actuary of CMS found that between 2013 and 2017, the average growth in Medicare per capita spending would be 1.70 percent, as compared to the targeted limit of 2.48 percent. The fate of IPAB may be on hold for awhile.

SUMMARY

In 1965, after decades of debate—and resistance from the medical profession—Congress enacted Medicare, providing tax-financed, universal health insurance for Americans age 65 or older. Following Medicare's initial success and popularity, Congress extended its coverage to include those with permanent disability and those with end-stage kidney disease.

As a result of a political compromise at the time of its initial passage, Medicare was divided into two parts, each part using a different method of financing and payment to providers. Medicare Part A pays for hospital care and is financed principally from payroll taxes. Medicare Part B pays for physician care and other types of outpatient care and is financed jointly from general income taxes (75%) and premiums paid by beneficiaries (25%).

Shortly after its enactment, it became clear that the system would cost substantially more than initial projections. Congress has made repeated efforts to constrain Medicare costs, including fundamental changes to the way it pays hospitals and physicians. While costs have been constrained somewhat as a result of these changes, Medicare nonetheless faces steep and continuing cost increases. Especially as the baby boom generation has become eligible for Medicare, the long-term financial viability of the program is being questioned.

A principal factor contributing to the increase in Medicare costs is the highly skewed nature of Medicare expenditures, with most Medicare funds going to pay for a small segment of the covered population. Providing care to the sickest 10 percent of covered seniors accounts for nearly 60 percent of all expenditures. Another problem has been the wide geographic variation in the rates at which physicians perform certain procedures, and in the average per-capita cost of caring for Medicare beneficiaries.

One way the federal government has attempted to address these issues has been to encourage seniors to enroll in HMOs and other forms of managed care through the MA program. Experience has shown, however, that managed care alone has not been able to change the rising cost trajectory of the Medicare program.

ACA has made a number of central changes in the way Medicare will pay for care in the future. For both hospitals and physicians, Medicare is taking steps to move away from paying principally for the volume of the care provided, to a system that focuses instead on "paying for value" in the care provided to Medicare beneficiaries. CMMI, charged by ACA with finding new ways to attain this goal, has initiated a series of pilot programs to attain it. The HHS secretary has established the explicit target of, by 2018, shifting 90 percent of fee-for-service payments to physicians and other providers to a value-based system, as well as 50 percent of all payments to alternative payment methods such as ACOs and bundled payment for care.

The changes made to Medicare under ACA have created the potential, but not the assurance, of constraining future increases in the cost of the program. In their 2015 report, the Medicare Boards of Trustees (2015) predicted that Medicare spending, which represented 3.5 percent of GDP in 2014, will increase to 5.4 percent of GDP by 2035, with even greater increases predicted for the future. By 2035, about half of all Medicare expenses will need to be paid from general tax revenues, with potentially serious implications for future federal deficits. With IPAB, the mechanism within ACA intended to control future Medicare spending, largely moribund, it will be up to future presidents and future members of Congress to address this issue.

7

Medicaid and the State Children's Health Insurance Program

In 1965, the US Congress made sweeping changes to the way health care was financed and provided. Medicare, the program to provide health care to elderly people, was discussed in the previous chapter. At the same time, Congress also enacted Medicaid, a program to provide health care to poor people. Like Medicare, Medicaid was created as an amendment to the existing Social Security Act, and thus is often referred to as "Title XIX."

Unlike Medicare, which covers all elderly people in the country who qualify for Social Security, as originally enacted Medicaid was not intended as a program for all people who fall below the federal poverty level (FPL). It covered care only for certain subgroups of poor people. Also in contrast to Medicare, Medicaid was originally structured purely on an insurance model, with no direct service component. Finally, while Medicare is financed and administered purely by the federal government, Medicaid is administered by the states, with the federal government reimbursing each state for a portion of program costs.

As with Medicare, the design and structure of the Medicaid program reflects historical and political factors that existed at the time of its passage. Before 1965, a federal program (the Kerr-Mills program) distributed federal funds to each of the states to assist in paying for medical care for elderly poor people. This program had four principal characteristics:

1. It had a combination of federal and state funding.
2. It was administered by the states under broad federal guidelines.
3. Eligibility for the program was tied to eligibility for cash welfare grants.

4. As long as the basic benefits required by the federal government were provided, each state was free to set its own level of additional benefits.

When Congress enacted Medicaid, rather than going through the process of designing a new program, it simply replicated the characteristics of the Kerr-Mills program. These principles continue to define the structure of Medicaid today, with the exception of linking eligibility to the receipt of welfare support.

Under Medicaid, each state designs its own program for paying for medical care for poor and low-income people, using existing hospitals and physicians and initially paying for care on a fee-for-service basis. Relying on the existing system was initially seen as a way to bring poor people into the "mainstream" of US medical care. As discussed in a later section, the rising costs of the program have made this goal very difficult to achieve.

Medicaid was established as a voluntary program for the states, with each state free to choose whether to participate. As a strong incentive, the federal government agreed to reimburse each participating state for a large part of the program's cost. The share of the program that the federal government pays depends on the economic condition of the state. States with lower per capita incomes have a higher share of the program costs paid by the federal government, while states with higher per capita incomes are reimbursed a lower percentage of program costs.

In 2015, the federal government reimbursed higher-income states, such as New York, Connecticut, and California, for 50 percent of expenditures. By contrast, the federal share of the Medicaid program was 71 percent in West Virginia and 74 percent in Mississippi. In 2014, the federal government paid 57 percent of the overall $476 billion cost of the Medicaid program.

> **CONCEPT 7.1**
>
> Medicaid as originally designed differed from Medicare in three important ways:
>
> 1. Rather than being universally available to all poor people, it covers only certain subgroups.
> 2. Rather than combining a service plan and an insurance plan, it originally was strictly an insurance plan.
> 3. Rather than being administered by the federal government, it is administered by the states under broad federal guidelines.

As shown in figure 7.1, funding for the Medicaid program, whether state or federal, comes straight out of general tax revenues. Thus, on the pay stub shown at the beginning of chapter 6, the employee is helping to pay for the program both through federal withholding tax and state withholding tax. As with Part B of Medicare, this reliance on general tax revenues means that at times of rapidly rising health care costs or of shrinking tax revenues a severe strain can be placed on both federal and state budgets. During times of recession, with more people out of work and thus qualifying for Medicaid coverage at the same time that tax revenues drop off sharply, the strain Medicaid places on both federal and state budgets can be a substantial problem for lawmakers.

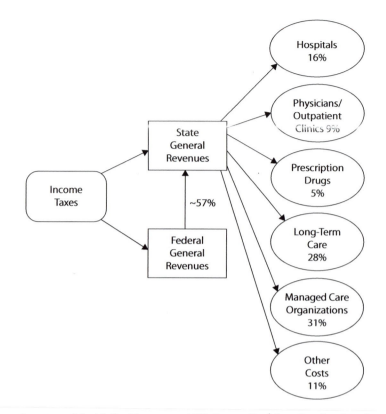

FIGURE 7.1. Structure of the Medicaid program, 2013. *Source:* Data from Paradise (2015).

SERVICE PROVIDED UNDER THE MEDICAID PROGRAM

For a state Medicaid program to be eligible for reimbursement from the federal government, it must provide certain basic services to all beneficiaries. These basic services include

- hospital care (inpatient and outpatient),
- nursing home care,
- physician services,
- laboratory and X-ray services,
- immunizations and other preventive medicine services for children,
- family planning services,
- services provided at federally qualified community health centers, and
- nurse midwife and nurse practitioner services.

States also have the option of providing certain additional services for which they receive federal matching funds. These additional services include

- prescription drugs,
- institutional care for individuals with mental retardation,
- home- and community-based care for the frail elderly,
- personal care and other community-based services for individuals with disabilities, and
- dental care and vision care.

Since 1977 and the passage of a federal law referred to as the Hyde Amendment, no federal funds may be spent to provide abortion services except for cases of rape, incest, or when the mother's life is in danger. This restriction also applies to the Medicaid program, although states are permitted to provide abortion services that are "medically necessary" to Medicaid recipients, as long as they do so using only state funds. Seventeen states provide abortion services under their Medicaid plans.

Figure 7.1 shows how the money in the Medicaid program was spent in 2013. About 31 percent of Medicaid funds were paid to managed care organizations, reflecting the increased role of Medicaid managed care, described in a later section. About 16 percent paid for acute hospital care, with an additional 9 percent going to physicians and outpatient clinics. An important thing to note is that 28 percent of all Medicaid funds go to pay for long-term care.

ELIGIBILITY FOR MEDICAID

Before the enactment of ACA, to be eligible for Medicaid, an individual must be within one of the following three groups:

1. Members of low-income families with children

Historically, Medicaid eligibility for this group was tied to eligibility for cash welfare grants under the Aid to Families with Dependent Children program. The changes included in the welfare reform that was enacted in 1996, however, broke this link. Currently, all children in families with incomes that fall below the FPL are eligible to receive Medicaid coverage. In addition, children under the age of 6 who are in families that earn up to 133 percent of the FPL are eligible for Medicaid. The parents of low-income children are eligible only if the family income is extremely low, typically 40 to 50 percent of the FPL. Pregnant women in families that earn up to 133 percent of the FPL, however, are eligible for Medicaid coverage for medical care during pregnancy and immediately after giving birth. In 2013, the year before the expansion of eligibility included in ACA took effect, Medicaid covered 55 million people, including 28 million low-income children and 13 million low-income adults.

2. Elderly people who meet certain income requirements

People over 65 whose income is below a level established by the federal government (typically about 65–70% of the poverty level) qualify for supplemental cash payments under the Supplemental Security Income (SSI) program. People eligible for SSI are also eligible for Medicaid. Some elderly people have incomes that are higher than the allowable Medicaid limit, but they face larger medical expenses than they can pay. Before these people become eligible for Medicaid, they must first use most of their personal savings to pay for their medical care. After they "spend down" their savings to a certain level (usually a few thousand dollars), they then become eligible for Medicaid. Most people eligible for Medicaid in this manner are confined to a nursing home. In 2010, more than 10 million people covered by Medicare were also enrolled in Medicaid.

As discussed in chapter 11, Medicare provides little in the way of coverage for nursing home care. Nonetheless, a growing number of elderly people are facing the prospect of nursing home care without the means to pay for it. They turn to the Medicaid program as the payer of last resort to pay for their care.

3. Disabled people

People under the age of 65 with long-term disabilities qualify for Medicaid in the same manner as elderly people. Nonelderly, disabled people who receive cash payments from SSI are also eligible for Medicaid. In addition, disabled people not covered by SSI but incurring large medical expenses are eligible for Medicaid after they meet the "spend down" requirements. As with elderly people, many of these individuals are confined to hospitals, nursing homes, or other institutional care facilities on a long-term basis.

All Medicaid beneficiaries must meet certain other general requirements, including in most cases being a US citizen. Certain legal immigrants are eligible, depending on their date of entry into the country. Those immigrants who enter the country illegally are ineligible for Medicaid, except for emergency care. In certain cases, a woman who has entered the country illegally will have a baby at a hospital in the United States. The baby will automatically be a US citizen and thus will be eligible for Medicaid (assuming the family meets the income requirements), while the mother will remain ineligible.

For a state to qualify for federal reimbursement, all members of these three groups within the state must be eligible for Medicaid. In addition, states have the option of covering other groups and receiving federal reimbursement. The additional groups include

- pregnant women and infants under the age of 1 whose family earns up to 185 percent of the FPL;
- elderly, blind, or disabled people who are not eligible for SSI payments but still have an income below the FPL; and
- children up to the age of 21 in certain low-income families.

Finally, each state has the option of covering individuals who are not in one of the aforementioned groups but whose income falls below a level set by the state. These people are the "medically needy," and most of them are low-income single adults or families without children. Because each state establishes its own cut-off level for eligibility, and because general economic conditions vary substantially from state to state, there is a wide range of eligibility levels among the states. Few states cover all poor people.

In 2011, Medicaid spent an average of $5,790 per beneficiary. Because the states administer the program and can offer a wide range of options in eligibility and coverage, the average level of Medicaid spending per eligible beneficiary varies widely among states. In 2011, spending per beneficiary ranged from $3,728 in Nevada and $3,992 in Georgia to $8,901 in New York and $9,201 in Rhode Island (Kaiser Family Foundation State Health Facts).

Poor people who are eligible for care in one state will often be ineligible in another. Treatments covered in one state may not be covered in another. The wide latitude left to states in creating their Medicaid programs and the resulting wide range of eligibility and coverage among the

> **CONCEPT 7.2**
>
> Under the Medicaid program, eligibility for benefits, the level of benefits, and the average cost of care vary widely among states.

states created a system of medical care for poor people that was distinctly different from our system of care for elderly people. Medicare is essentially government-sponsored, taxpayer-supported, universal care for elderly people. Until the changes included in ACA, Medicaid was a program intended to cover certain segments of the low-income population while leaving other segments without the means to pay for medical care. As John Iglehart (1993b) stated, "The nature of the Medicaid program underscores the ambivalence of a society that has never decided which of its citizens deserves access to publicly financed medical care or whether the problem of poverty should be addressed primarily at the national, state, or local level. . . . This situation constitutes what has been characterized as 'the greatest inequity of the American health care system . . . not between the non poor and the poor, but between the insured poor and the uninsured poor'" (p. 896).

THE RISING COST OF THE MEDICAID PROGRAM

Between 1975 and 1989, the cost of the Medicaid program increased by an average of 11.9 percent per year before adjusting for inflation. Reflecting both the rising cost of care nationwide and the increasing eligibility for program coverage, in 1989 program costs began to explode. Between 1989 and 1993, the yearly increase in overall Medicaid costs averaged 21.2 percent. As a result of these increases, both the federal government (which was already facing huge budget deficits as a result of changes in the tax laws enacted in the 1980s) and state governments (many of which were prevented by their state constitutions from engaging in deficit spending) were facing financial crises.

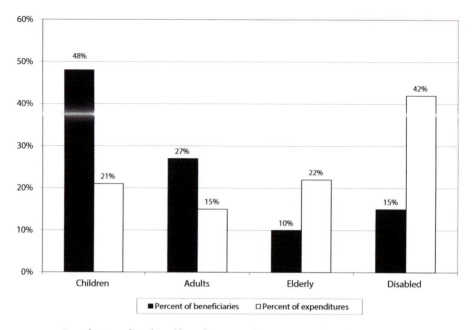

FIGURE 7.2. Distribution of Medicaid beneficiaries and costs among eligibility groups, 2011.
Source: Data from Paradise (2015).

If nothing was done to change the program, Medicaid threatened to bankrupt many of the states and the federal government. As discussed in the following section, the federal government responded by initiating a number of changes on a state-by-state basis. Medicaid rapidly began to change from a purely fee-for-service payment system to a capitation system, shifting much of the financial risk of providing care to poor people from governments to health maintenance organizations (HMOs) and other types of managed care insurers and providers.

A common misperception at that time was that, because Medicaid is primarily a program for low-income families and children, the rapid increase in program costs was due to increases in the number of poor people and to problems with fraud and abuse within the system. This picture is not at all accurate and constituted one of the major public misperceptions regarding our health care system.

CONCEPT 7.3

Sixty-four percent of Medicaid costs go to provide care for 25 percent of beneficiaries: low-income elderly and disabled people, many of whom are in nursing homes. Low-income families and children account for 36 percent of Medicaid costs.

It is true that low-income children and nonelderly, nondisabled adults make up 75 percent of Medicaid beneficiaries. As shown in figure 7.2, however, these children and adults account for only 36 percent of overall Medicaid spending. The bulk of Medicaid expenditures (64% in 2011) pay for care for low-income elderly and disabled individuals (Paradise 2015).

TABLE 7.1. Medicaid expenditures per
beneficiary, by type of beneficiary, 2011

Beneficiary	Expenditure
Elderly	$17,522
Disabled	$18,518
Adults	$4,141
Children	$2,492

Source: Data from Kaiser Family Foundation.

If one looks at the average cost of providing care for beneficiaries in each class of eligibility, shown in table 7.1, it is easy to see how this situation arises. In 2011, average expenditures per beneficiary per year ranged from $2,463 for a child to $13,249 for an elderly beneficiary and $16,643 for a disabled individual. Medicaid has become our society's safety net to assure that no elderly or disabled individual who needs medical care or care in a nursing home or other long-term care institution will be left without care due to their inability to pay. The vast majority of Medicaid expenditures go to support that commitment.

There is also a common misperception that Medicaid beneficiaries abuse the medical care system and overuse medical services. Critics frequently cite data about the high rate at which Medicaid patients use hospital emergency rooms to obtain routine medical care. It is very expensive to take care of common, nonemergency conditions in the emergency room. In many areas, Medicaid beneficiaries may be more likely than the general public to use the emergency room rather than doctors' offices for the treatment of relatively minor ailments. A study by Tang and colleagues (2010) confirmed this finding. Using a nationally representative database, the authors found that between 1997 and 2007, the rate of emergency room visits for "ambulatory care-sensitive conditions" (i.e., those more appropriate for treatment in a physician's office than in the emergency room) went up at a substantially higher rate for adults on Medicaid than for adults with other types of insurance. The authors attributed this increased utilization of the emergency room to the increase in the number of people on Medicaid, coupled with "limited access to primary care services for Medicaid enrollees" (p. 669). Consistent with previous studies, the reason Medicaid patients visit the emergency room more often than insured patients does not appear to be abusive behavior on the part of Medicaid patients but rather the poor availability of primary care services for many patients on Medicaid.

Soon after Medicaid's creation in 1965, most states began to restrict the amount they would pay physicians for treating Medicaid patients. As Medicaid costs skyrocketed in the 1980s and 1990s, states cut back even farther on what they were willing to pay. As a result, physicians in many areas of the country receive only 30 to 40 percent

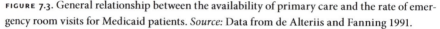

FIGURE 7.3. General relationship between the availability of primary care and the rate of emergency room visits for Medicaid patients. *Source:* Data from de Alteriis and Fanning 1991.

of their usual charge for taking care of a Medicaid patient. As a result of these payment policies, in 2013 only 69 percent of physicians nationally were willing to accept new patients on Medicaid (Hing et al. 2015).

This poor availability of physicians is largely responsible for the general relationship, illustrated in figure 7.3, between the availability of primary care services in a community and the rate at which Medicaid patients in that community visit the emergency room. The more office-based or clinic-based primary care services are available to Medicaid patients, the less those patients visit the emergency room. Friedman et al. (2015) suggested that reducing emergency room use among Medicaid patients "will depend on access to providers who are willing to take Medicaid patients. Among other things, this approach will require the establishment of new access points for Medicaid beneficiaries through the growth of community health centers" (p. 2384). A principal goal of ACA is to make primary care more available to Medicaid recipients through the expansion of federally qualified health centers.

THE MOVE TO MANAGED CARE

In the face of rapidly rising costs, both state and federal governments began to look for ways to limit the budgetary drain of Medicaid. By the early 1990s, HMOs and the other types of managed care plans discussed in chapter 5 became increasingly common in many areas of the country. It was apparent to federal and state officials that delivery systems based on the capitation method of payment had the potential of realizing cost savings for Medicaid. With the support of the federal government, many states established programs to try to enroll as many Medicaid beneficiaries as possible in HMOs. (In most states, elderly or disabled Medicaid beneficiaries were not included in the shift to HMOs.) In doing so, the state would pay a fixed premium per patient per year, and it would be up to the HMO to constrain costs.

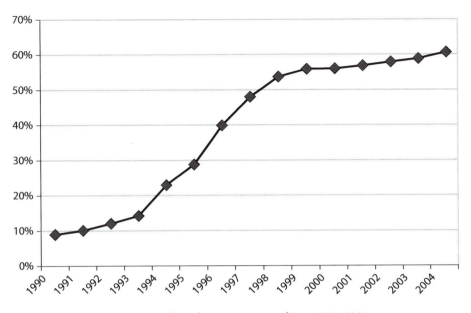

FIGURE 7.4. Percentage of Medicaid beneficiaries in managed care, 1990–2004.
Source: Data from Kaiser Family Foundation.

Figure 7.4 shows Medicaid's rapid movement beginning in 1993 from a system based predominantly on fee-for-service payment to physicians and hospitals to one that relied extensively on managed care plans for providing care. By 2014, between 50 and 75 percent of Medicaid beneficiaries, depending on the state in which they lived, were enrolled in a managed care plan.

Adopting a managed care approach for the majority of Medicaid beneficiaries, however, has had another policy effect that is perhaps even more important than the question of cost effectiveness of alternative delivery models. A capitated system of managed care allows a state government to limit its fiscal liability for Medicaid by setting a fixed yearly payment for the care of each beneficiary. Once that payment has been made, the risk for cost overruns shifts from the state to the managed care provider. Thus, managed care has become one means for states to limit the cost of their Medicaid program, irrespective of whether managed care is more cost effective.

> **CONCEPT 7.4**
>
> Over the period 1991–99, Medicaid shifted from a predominantly fee-for-service system to a system based predominantly on capitation and the use of health maintenance organizations (HMOs).

THE CREATION OF MEDICAID WAIVERS

For states to move their Medicaid beneficiaries from the fee-for-service system into HMOs and other managed care plans, a mechanism had to be developed to relax some of the federal guidelines that states must meet to qualify for federal reimbursement.

The original guidelines required states to provide all necessary services in the categories described earlier. As discussed in chapter 5, HMOs and other managed care plans save money by putting certain constraints on the use of hospitals and other expensive technologies. To reconcile the guidelines with the need to shift patients into HMOs, Congress amended the Social Security Act to allow the Secretary of the Department of Health and Human Services to waive certain guidelines on a state-by-state basis. States could apply for a "Section 1115 waiver" or a closely related "Section 1915 waiver" to create capitated systems of care for certain Medicaid beneficiaries. These waivers are typically granted for periods of five years at a time and are renewable for additional periods of five years.

States applying for these waivers in order to shift their Medicaid programs to a managed care system took different approaches. Tennessee, for example, applied to the federal government for a Section 1115 waiver to allow them to make the shift from fee-for-service to managed care essentially overnight. On December 31, 1993, nearly all state Medicaid beneficiaries were in the traditional fee-for-service system. On January 1, 1994, the new "Tenncare" program started, and virtually all Medicaid patients became members of a managed care plan. The rapidity of the shift to managed care created an initial period of confusion and frustration for many patients and providers. Over time, the initial confusion subsided, and Tenncare achieved many of its objectives. In 1994, its first year of operation, Tenncare extended eligibility to 350,000 people in addition to the 770,000 people previously enrolled in Medicaid. Over time, though, the program turned out to be far more costly than expected, and Tennessee had to amend the waiver in order to reduce covered benefits and add premiums and copayments for some adults.

By comparison, California began to create managed care plans for its Medicaid patients on a county-by-county basis. Each participating county had substantial flexibility in designing its plan. By early 1999, 2.3 million Medicaid beneficiaries, or 46 percent of the total enrollment, had been enrolled in managed care plans statewide. California experienced a series of budgetary crises resulting in reductions in payment rates to these managed care plans. By the time ACA was enacted in 2010, 60 percent of those covered by Medicaid in California and 100 percent of those covered in Tennessee were enrolled in managed care plans.

By 2004, all fifty states either had been granted or had applied for a Section 1115 waiver or a Section 1915 waiver, accounting for the increase in managed care enrollment shown in figure 7.4. Some of these waiver programs worked quite well, while others had serious problems. Some were quite controversial. Some waivers permitted states to restrict benefits and place new financial obligations on beneficiaries (Mann and Artiga 2006). States such as West Virginia, Idaho, and Kentucky were granted a waiver that permitted them to establish different "tiers" of benefits. The tier a beneficiary is eligible to receive will depend on his or her prior health status, as well as his or her adherence to medical treatment plans. Those who do not follow recommended treatment may be dropped to a lower tier, thus losing some benefits, until they have demonstrated that they are able and willing to follow recommended treatments. West Virginia's plan relies heavily on reducing benefits in response to unhealthy behaviors.

Not surprisingly, attempts such as these to lower Medicaid costs by reducing benefits have met with substantial criticism. These issues bring up again the recurring question first mentioned in chapter 2: how much health care should every American be able to expect as a right of citizenship or residency?

While some states have used Medicaid waivers to reduce benefits, others have used waivers to expand benefits—though not always with full success. Typically, efforts to expand benefits rely heavily on providing care through managed care organizations. In the following section, I look at the programs Oregon has enacted using federal waivers in its effort to expand coverage to its low-income residents.

OREGON: EXPLICIT RATIONING OF MEDICAID HEALTH CARE

In the late 1980s, Oregon was facing the same high Medicaid costs that other states were confronting. The cost of the Medicaid program had put such a strain on the state budget that Oregon was able to pay for care for only a fraction of its poor adult population. Previously, while covering all children below the FPL, Medicaid had been available only to adults younger than 65 with an income that was less than about 60 percent of the FPL, leaving those with incomes between 60 and 100 percent of the FPL without any coverage at all. Oregon wanted to find a way to provide care for all adults below the FPL, and to extend coverage to pregnant women and children with family income up to 133 percent of the FPL. They wanted to do this, however, without increasing the overall amount they spent on Medicaid.

To accomplish these seemingly irreconcilable goals, the Oregon legislature, under the leadership of one of its members who was also a physician, created an entirely new way of allocating Medicaid resources. This new program was referred to as the Oregon Health Plan (OHP). Under OHP, a broadly representative commission called the Oregon Health Services Commission undertook a lengthy process of studying all the services previously covered by Medicaid and dividing them into 712 treatment categories. The commission then ranked these treatments based on factors such as medical effectiveness, ability to avert death or disability, prevention of future costs, and public health risk. Treatments that ranked highest on these criteria (e.g., treatment of severe head injuries or insulin-dependent diabetes) were given a low number, and those that ranked lowest (e.g., treatment of viral colds and simple strains of the muscles of the back) were given a high number. The commission spent three years

FIGURE 7.5. Medicaid coverage in Oregon before the Oregon Health Plan.

establishing this list. They had many public meetings and discussions about the plan, and they modified earlier versions of the plan based on this input.

Figure 7.5 illustrates the situation that existed before the OHP was established. The horizontal axis shows seven hundred treatment categories (for simplicity), ranked from most important (low numbers) to least important (high numbers). The vertical axis shows the poor adult population of Oregon, ranked according to the percentage of the FPL represented by their family income. It can be seen that, before the OHP, there was a sharp divide at about 60 percent of the FPL, with those below the line receiving full Medicaid coverage for all seven hundred treatment categories and those above the line receiving no coverage at all.

In establishing the OHP, the Oregon legislature decided to remove some of the least effective treatments from coverage (the high numbers). It used the money saved by limiting care in this way to provide coverage for the most effective treatments for everyone below the FPL and for pregnant women and children up to 133 percent of the FPL. These changes are represented in figure 7.6.

As shown in figure 7.6, the OHP initially provided coverage for only 565 of the 700 available treatments, but it provided this limited coverage to all those below the FPL. To reallocate its Medicaid funds in this way, Oregon first had to get a Section 1115 waiver from the federal government. This waiver application was quite controversial. After several years of discussion and debate, however, the federal government approved the waiver, and in 1994 the OHP took effect. Initially, it was largely successful in achieving its goal of increased coverage. In its first year of operation it extended

FIGURE 7.6. Medicaid coverage under the Oregon Health Plan.

coverage to approximately 100,000 new poor people in addition to the 188,000 originally covered.

While the plan has had a number of problems along the way, for several years it was
able to offer coverage to those in Oregon whose income was below the FPL. The initial
success of the OHP depended on broad public acceptance of the policy of limiting
care to some so that others may be covered. Accusations of unethical health care rationing were leveled at the plan. This aspect of the plan and its implication for overall
US health care policy are discussed in chapter 13.

One of the ways the OHP saved money was to enroll as many of its members as possible in HMOs or other managed care plans and to pay for their care under capitated
risk contracts. It was quite successful in this effort, and by 1997 nearly 90 percent of
beneficiaries were covered by a managed care plan.

Despite its initial success in expanding the number of beneficiaries by limiting treatment coverage and relying on managed care plans, Oregon continued to have fiscal
problems at the state level. Once again, the costs of Medicaid were seen as a major contributor. To reduce the cost of its Medicaid program, Oregon went back to the federal
government with a request for a new waiver. While expanding eligibility somewhat
for children and pregnant women, the new waiver also included a number of steps
intended to reduce enrollment and costs. These steps included

- reductions in covered benefits,
- premiums and copayments for some adult beneficiaries, and
- explicit caps on enrollment.

These new policies were initiated in 2003 and in one year resulted in a reduction in adult enrollment of about 50,000 beneficiaries—half of those who had gained coverage under the original OHP expansion. In 2004, Oregon shut down its program of expanded Medicaid coverage. Many of the beneficiaries losing coverage had chronic medical conditions; 72 percent of them ended up back in the ranks of the uninsured (Mann and Artiga 2004). While OHP had achieved many of its initial goals of expanding coverage to poor people, it was not successful in substantially slowing the continuing rise in health care costs related to Medicaid in Oregon.

By 2008, the state government in Oregon elected to reopen its expansion of eligibility, but on a much more limited basis. With federal approval, it used a lottery system to offer Medicaid coverage to ten thousand eligible individuals out of the ninety thousand who had applied. In what is referred to as the Oregon Health Insurance Experiment (OHIE), state officials took advantage of this random selection process to compare patterns of health care utilization between those selected for coverage (the treatment group) and a comparable population of applicants not offered coverage (Allen et al. 2010).

During the first year of coverage, researchers found that "the treatment group had substantively and statistically significantly higher health care utilization (including primary and preventive care as well as hospitalizations), lower out-of-pocket medical expenditures and medical debt (including fewer bills sent to collection), and better self-reported physical and mental health than the control group" (Finkelstein et al. 2012, p. 1057). One notable aspect of the pattern of increased utilization after enrollment was a significant increase in the number of emergency room visits for those newly enrolled in Medicaid. In a comparison of the frequency of emergency room visits during the first 18 months of the program, Taubman et al. (2014) found that the frequency of emergency room use among those newly enrolled increased by 41 percent as compared to those who were not selected for enrollment. Nearly all the extra ER visits were for what the authors referred to as "primary care treatable" problems, suggesting that lack of access to a primary care physician may have been a factor in the observed increase.

Further analysis after the second year of the program "showed that Medicaid coverage generated no significant improvements in measured physical health outcomes in the first 2 years, but it did increase use of health care services, raise rates of diabetes detection and management, lower rates of depression, and reduce financial strain" (Baicker et al. 2013, p. 1713). Responding to these findings, Mennig et al. (2015) used cost-effectiveness analysis to address the question of "whether Medicaid is worth the cost." The authors reported that they "found that Medicaid is a good value, with a cost of just $62,000 per quality-adjusted life-years gained" (p. 866). A secondary benefit of the program was that the uninsured children of those adults offered enrollment (who previously were eligible for coverage but not signed up) were more likely also to become enrolled in Medicaid. DeVoe et al. (2015) reported that these children had more than double the odds of gaining Medicaid coverage than eligible children whose parents did not themselves enroll.

WHY WASN'T THE SHIFT TO MANAGED CARE MORE SUCCESSFUL IN HOLDING DOWN MEDICAID COSTS?

By 2008, 71 percent of all Medicaid beneficiaries nationwide had been enrolled in managed care plans. Nonetheless, states continue to experience severe difficulties in financing program costs. Why wasn't this shift to capitated systems of care more successful? There are two principal answers to this question: (1) the effect of shifting to managed care and (2) the dual nature of Medicaid.

Recall from chapter 6 that a principal reason why managed care was not successful in reducing Medicare costs was the previous reductions in the use of hospitals that had resulted from the prospective payment system (PPS) of paying for hospital care. While state Medicaid programs continued to pay for hospital care largely on a fee-for-service basis before the shift to managed care, in many states there had been previous efforts to control hospital costs in other ways. Nevertheless, there were continuing inefficiencies in the use of hospitals. A comprehensive national study of the change in Medicaid costs between 1987 and 1997 was able to identify reductions in hospital use and costs as a result of the shift to managed care, although those reductions were modest (Kirby et al. 2003).

It is also important to recall from chapter 5 the overall lesson of the effect of shifting from a predominantly fee-for-service system to a system based on managed care. During the period of transition, cost savings will be realized. These are, however, one-time savings—managed care plans face the same pressure as fee-for-service plans in terms of newer and more costly forms of treatment.

During the mid-1990s, as the shift to Medicaid managed care was taking place, the yearly increases in the national cost of Medicaid had moderated substantially and were in the range of 3 to 5 percent. Between 2000 and 2003, however, costs again began going up an average of more than 10 percent annually. Therefore, there does appear to have been a modest reduction in the rate at which Medicaid costs increased, but the reduction was due to one-time savings. The cost of the Medicaid program seems to have resumed its steep upward trajectory.

Recall also from the previous discussion that 64 percent of all Medicaid costs go to provide care for 25 percent of beneficiaries: low-income elderly and disabled people, many of whom are in nursing homes. Caring for elderly

> **CONCEPT 7.5**
>
> The shift to Medicaid managed care involved mainly children and nonelderly adults and realized modest, one-time cost savings. With most expenditures going to care for elderly and disabled people, Medicaid costs will continue to place a severe strain on state and federal budgets for years to come. Attempts to reduce Medicaid costs through program reductions will disproportionately affect children and nonelderly adults.

and disabled individuals accounts for by far the largest share of Medicaid costs. Of the more than 25 million Medicaid beneficiaries enrolled in managed care plans in 2004, however, less than 10 percent were elderly or disabled. Nearly all the initial movement to managed care was among children and nonelderly, nondisabled adults. Children and nonelderly adults, however, account for about one-third of Medicaid spending. While the main driver of rising Medicaid costs is caring for elderly and disabled people, the major impact of cuts in Medicaid benefits and eligibility has been on children and nonelderly adults. Despite a significant shift to managed care, the Medicaid system has continued to place a major strain on both state budgets and the federal budget.

S-CHIP TO REDUCE THE NUMBER OF UNINSURED CHILDREN

As part of the national debate that arose surrounding the Clinton health reform proposals of 1993–94, the number of uninsured children became a major national concern. Few had been aware that, at that time, nearly 10 million children were without health insurance and, as a result, without access to basic medical care. A strong national consensus developed around this issue. Republicans and Democrats alike felt that even if as a country we could not find an overall solution to the problem of the uninsured, we could at least find a way to extend basic coverage to children. Children, after all, are the least expensive age group to insure and can benefit the most from basic services such as immunizations and preventive care.

In 1997, a bipartisan coalition developed in Congress around this issue, and in August of that year, Congress enacted the State Children's Health Insurance Program (P.L. 105-33), originally referred to as S-CHIP, as Title XXI of the Social Security Act. Under S-CHIP, a federal-state partnership was established with the goal of significantly reducing the number of uninsured children. The target population was uninsured children in families that were not previously eligible for Medicaid and that earned less than 200 percent of the FPL.

Each state was given a financial incentive to create a new, statewide program for extending health insurance coverage to uninsured children. The states were given the option of three ways in which to do this. States could

1. expand the existing Medicaid program to include more children,
2. establish a program separate and distinct from Medicaid to extend coverage to those children not eligible for Medicaid, or
3. use a combination of both Medicaid expansion and new program creation.

S-CHIP was financed in a manner very similar to Medicaid. Each state that established a program would have its costs partially reimbursed by the federal government, only at a rate considerably higher than the Medicaid rate. Compared to an average Medicaid matching rate of 57 percent, the matching rate for S-CHIP averaged about 70 percent.

S-CHIP appropriated between $3 billion and $5 billion per year for ten years, with the explicit goal of cutting in half the number of uninsured children nationwide. States would design a program and apply to the federal government to have the majority of the costs of the program paid by federal funds. The first S-CHIP funds became available to the states on October 1, 1997. Once allocated funds, a state had three years in which to spend the funds to provide health insurance for eligible children. After the three-year period, any funds not used for this purpose had to be returned to the federal government.

States responded enthusiastically to S-CHIP. Of the fifty-six states and territories eligible to participate, fifty-one had established plans by April 1999. The four states with the largest number of uninsured children—California, Florida, New York, and Texas—were allocated nearly half of the available funding. States were almost evenly divided between those that used expansion of Medicaid and those that created a new program, either stand-alone or in combination with Medicaid.

The first two years of S-CHIP showed considerable success in meeting its stated goal of cutting the number of uninsured children in half. In December 1998, a year after the program was enacted, 833,303 children were covered. By December 1999, 2 million previously uninsured children had obtained coverage.

S-CHIP began to run into trouble, however, in several states. Reports from state governments as well as children's advocacy groups began to suggest that the enrollment of eligible children was lagging far behind projections in a number of areas. Some states were reluctant to invest state funds in the program, often leading to delays of up to a year in the opening of enrollment. Other states established such complex application procedures that many eligible families simply failed to apply. Other states failed to establish adequate outreach programs and were unable to find the eligible children they had hoped to enroll.

The three-year period in which states were required to spend their initial allocation of funds ended on September 30, 2000, and remaining funds had to be returned to the federal government. Nearly half of the previously allocated money—$1.9 billion of $4.2 billion—remained unspent by the states on September 30 (Pear 2000). California had to return $590 million, or 69 percent of its original allocation. Texas had to return $446 million. New Mexico, with 30,000 uninsured children, could enroll only 1,000 of them in its S-CHIP program and had to return 92 percent of its original allotment. Only ten states were able to spend the full amount given to them by the federal government to enroll uninsured children in S-CHIP. Of these, New York was perhaps the most successful, with 550,000 new children enrolled, one-fourth of the national total.

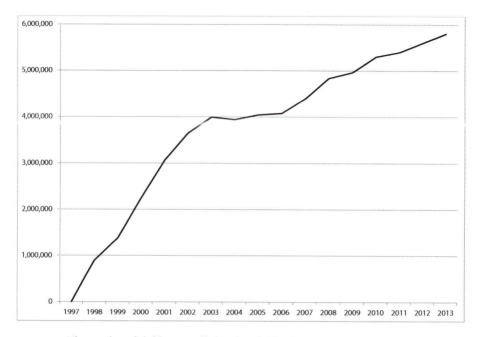

FIGURE 7.7. The number of children enrolled in the Children's Health Insurance Program (CHIP), 1997–2013. *Source:* Data from Kaiser Commission on Medicaid and the Uninsured.

Unfortunately, New York's success in enrolling children was soon cast in another light. Shortly after the federal government reported the failure of the S-CHIP program to meet its initial enrollment goals despite the success of New York's program, newspapers reported that as many as half of the children enrolled in New York may not have been eligible for S-CHIP (Steinhauer 2000). Federal law requires that uninsured children who are eligible for Medicaid be enrolled in their existing state Medicaid program and not in S-CHIP. The states pay a larger share of the cost of Medicaid, and Congress did not want them to shift Medicaid-eligible children into S-CHIP to gain a higher level of federal subsidy. It appears that this is precisely what New York did. As a result, New York was also required to return part of the funding it had received.

Figure 7.7 shows the number of children covered under S-CHIP from its inception in 1997 through 2013. Despite problems in some states, the number of children covered increased substantially during the first four years of the program. From 2003 through 2006, however, enrollment was mostly flat. In 2007, enrollment began to rise again, and by the end of 2013 there were 5.8 million children enrolled (Smith et al. 2014).

Not all of the children covered under S-CHIP had been uninsured before gaining coverage. Some of the children covered under S-CHIP in 2013 were previously covered under their parents' employment-based health insurance. The children lost private coverage either because the parents lost their health insurance at work or, in a process sometimes referred to as "crowd-out," because the parents chose to drop the children from their own insurance plan due to the increasing share of the coverage cost paid by employees. One study suggested that 38 percent of the enrollment in S-CHIP during its early years was for children who were previously covered under their parents' private health insurance (Cunningham et al. 2002).

By 2007, when S-CHIP's initial ten-year program authorization was set to expire, S-CHIP had covered several million children who previously were uninsured and a number of other children who had lost private coverage. It had not come close to achieving its initial goal of reducing the number of uninsured children by half, however. Furthermore, of the nearly 8 million children who remained uninsured at that time, about two-thirds were eligible either for Medicaid or for S-CHIP but were not enrolled, due to either state caps on enrollment or barriers encountered in the enrollment process (Kaiser Family Foundation 2009).

Congress acted in the summer of 2007 to extend S-CHIP for an additional five years and to permit states to expand eligibility to children in families with incomes above 200 percent of the FPL (the original income limit when S-CHIP was first enacted). The legislation approved by both the House and the Senate would also have nearly doubled the funding available to S-CHIP. President George W. Bush, however, saw such an expansion as an unwarranted extension of the role of government in the health care system. Accordingly, he vetoed the legislation, and his veto was upheld in Congress. In his veto message, President Bush argued that there was a "philosophical divide over the best approach to health care" and that "Democratic leaders in Congress want to put more power in the hands of government by expanding federal health care programs. Their S-CHIP is an incremental step towards the goal of government-run health care for every American" (quoted in Iglehart 2007, p. 2105). After a series of stop-gap funding extensions, in January 2008 Congress passed and President Bush signed a bill extending S-CHIP funding through March 31, 2009, without a significant expansion of either coverage or funding.

When President Barack Obama entered office in January 2009, one of the first things he asked Congress to do was to reauthorize and expand S-CHIP. Congress acted quickly. About two weeks after entering office, President Obama signed into law the Children's Health Insurance Program Reauthorization Act (CHIRPA) of 2009. The act extended S-CHIP for an additional five years, expanded eligibility to children in families up to 300 percent of the FPL, and more than doubled the funding available for the program (Iglehart 2009b). It also changed the name of the program simply to the Children's Health Insurance Program—thus its common acronym of "CHIP."

In February 2010, on the one-year anniversary of the CHIRPA, Health and Human Services secretary Kathleen Sebelius issued the following challenge:

I am asking leaders from government and the private sector to step up their efforts to cover more children. We know there are about five million uninsured children in the U.S. who are currently eligible for Medicaid or CHIP coverage, but who are not enrolled. *The Secretary's Challenge: Connecting Kids to Coverage* is a five-year campaign that will challenge federal officials, states, governors, mayors, community organizations, faith leaders, and concerned individuals to build on our success and take the next step by finding and enrolling those five million children in Medicaid and CHIP.

Congress's goal was to add an additional 4 million children to the program by 2013.

The CHIPRA extended funding for CHIP through 2014, leaving it once again up to Congress to decide on the fate of the program. As part of its reform of the Medicare Sustainable Growth Rate payment formula, in April 2015 Congress extended funding for CHIP for two additional years as part of the Medicare Access and CHIP Reauthorization Act (MACRA). There appears to be bipartisan support for CHIP, yet, as described by Oberlander and Jones (2015), "the short 2-year extension of CHIP is itself a sign of problems. . . . CHIP's 2015 journey through Congress was quick and relatively easy, but its long-term prospects remain uncertain" (p. 1981).

> **CONCEPT 7.6**
>
> The Children's Health Insurance Program (CHIP) has enrolled nearly 6 million children. Despite this success, nearly 5 million children remained uninsured in 2014, more than 60 percent of whom were eligible for either Medicaid or CHIP but were not enrolled.

As with Medicare, Medicaid continues to experience rapidly increasing costs. With states responsible for roughly 40 percent of the program's costs, many states continue to have substantial difficulty in continuing to fund the program. States have made repeated efforts to reduce their Medicaid expenditures by shifting beneficiaries to managed care while also reducing eligibility and benefits. During times of recession, these problems become more acute.

The experience over the past several decades, with repeated reductions in payment to providers and level of benefits in response to cyclical downturns in the economy, has underscored a potential weakness of the Medicaid and CHIP programs. Especially with the expansion of Medicaid coverage under ACA, described in the following section, the ability of Medicaid to meet its expected role of assuring access to health care for the nation's poor will come under increasing scrutiny.

THE AFFORDABLE CARE ACT AND ITS IMPACT ON MEDICAID AND CHIP

Among the policy changes resulting from the Affordable Care Act (ACA), one of the most profound is in the Medicaid program. As described previously, Medicaid was initially designed as a program to provide health insurance only to some groups of those living in poverty. In contrast to Medicare, which provides insurance to all those age 65 or over who qualify for Social Security benefits, Medicaid has traditionally provided coverage only to poor families with children, the elderly poor, and the disabled poor. In most states, childless adults who were neither elderly nor disabled were not eligible for Medicaid benefits.

ACA fundamentally changed the structure of Medicaid by making benefits available to *all* people who are poor, regardless of health status or family status. In addition, under ACA Medicaid will provide coverage to all those with incomes below 138 percent of the FPL, rather than the previous level of 100 percent. In essence, ACA made Medicaid analogous to Medicare, in that it will provide the same level of benefits to all those in poverty.

In light of the financial burden states have faced in paying their matching share of the cost of Medicaid, ACA defined a new level of federal support for those who are newly eligible for Medicaid benefits under ACA. Beginning in 2014, the federal government would pay 100 percent of the cost of the care provided to newly eligible Medicaid enrollees. Over a period of six years, the federal reimbursement rate for these enrollees will gradually drop to 90 percent, with the states ultimately responsible for 10 percent of the cost of their care. For those who were already eligible for Medicaid at the time ACA was enacted, the federal government has maintained the previous reimbursement rate. Thus, states will receive a substantially higher federal reimbursement rate for those who become newly eligible for Medicaid than they will receive for the traditional Medicaid coverage groups.

Of course, this higher level of reimbursement is only available to those states that have elected to expand eligibility for Medicaid benefits under ACA. As described in chapter 1, the Supreme Court decision in *National Federation of Independent Business v. Sebelius* left it up to each state to decide whether to expand their program, with continued eligibility for their previous Medicaid program unaffected by that decision.

From its inception in 1965, state participation in Medicaid has been voluntary. It was only in 1982—seventeen years after its original enactment—that all fifty states had elected to participate. State participation continues to be voluntary. Any state that does participate must continue to meet the coverage standards established by the federal government.

As originally written, ACA did not offer states the option of opting out of the new expansion while maintaining its previous program of eligibility and funding. The state either had to accept the new expansion of eligibility (and the much lower state share of costs that goes along with it) or drop out of the Medicaid program altogether. Given that few, if any, states could afford the cost of continuing to provide coverage to the poor without federal cost sharing, ACA gave states little real choice as to whether to participate in the new Medicaid expansion.

It was this requirement to join in the expansion or lose all Medicaid funding that the Supreme Court found to be overly coercive.

> The threatened loss of over 10 percent of a State's overall budget is economic dragooning that leaves the States with no real option but to acquiesce in the Medicaid expansion. . . . A State could hardly anticipate that Congress's reservation of the right to 'alter' or 'amend' the Medicaid program included the power to transform it so dramatically. The Medicaid expansion thus violates the Constitution by threatening States with the loss of their existing Medicaid funding if they decline to comply with the expansion (2012, p. 5).

This decision does not alter the terms of the Medicaid expansion called for in ACA, other than to make it voluntary for states to participate. This finding had the support of seven of the Court's justices, with only Justices Ginsburg and Sotomayor dissenting, arguing that the removal of all funding for nonparticipating states is permissible under the Constitution.

Following the release of the Court's ruling, the governors of several states announced publically that their states would not participate in the expansion of eligibility, despite the enhanced federal cost sharing. By January 2014, the date when Medicaid expansion became effective, twenty-six states and the District of Columbia had elected to expand Medicaid. Three of these states—Arkansas, Iowa, and Michigan—had been granted Section 1115 waivers to alter the manner in which they accomplished this expansion. Twenty-four states had elected not to expand their Medicaid programs. As discussed in the following section, in 2015, several of these states changed their mind, opting instead for expansion (Medicaid.gov 2015).

It is important to appreciate that many low-income, uninsured individuals within states that elected not to participate in the Medicaid expansion are still eligible to acquire insurance through the state's health benefit exchange. However, as ACA is currently written, only those individuals with incomes at or above 100 percent of the FPL will qualify for the federal premium subsidy. As specified in ACA, *those with incomes below 100 percent of the FPL do not qualify for the premium subsidy.* As many as two-thirds of individuals potentially eligible for Medicaid under the ACA expansion will have incomes below 100 percent of the FPL, and thus will be ineligible for federal subsidies in states electing not to participate in the expansion of eligibility. This situation has the potential of creating an additional level of political discord within these states regarding future participation.

An additional change included in ACA that will have substantial impact on states electing not to expand Medicaid affects the supplemental funding the federal government provides to hospitals that provide a disproportionate share of uncompensated care to those who are uninsured. Beginning in 2016, ACA calls for substantial reductions in these "disproportionate share hospital" (DSH) payments, on the assumption that many if not most of previously uninsured patients will qualify for Medicaid. The hospitals involved were expected to have substantially increased revenues from Medicaid for the care of these patients, thus justifying substantial reductions in DSH payments. Even if a state elects not to participate in the Medicaid expansion, these reductions in DSH payments will still take place. Accordingly, hospitals within these states may face little reduction in the demand for uncompensated care yet will receive substantially less federal support for providing that care.

In a report from the Office of the Assistant Secretary for Planning and Evaluation of the Department of Health and Human Services, DeLeire et al. (2014) estimated that under ACA, Medicaid DSH payments, which totaled $11.4 billion in 2012, will be reduced by $1.2 billion in 2016 and by a total of $17.6 billion by 2020. The separate DSH payments made by Medicare will also be reduced by a total of $22.1 billion by 2019, representing a reduction of 75 percent. Looking at changes in the numbers of uninsured patients receiving care from hospitals in the first several months of the ACA expansion of coverage, the authors found that "hospitals in Medicaid expansion states have seen substantial declines in their admission volumes of uninsured patients, declines in their volumes of uninsured patients visiting the ED, and increases in admissions that are covered by Medicaid. Hospitals in non-expansion states, by contrast, report relatively little change in these volumes" (p. 16).

Looking at the impact of these combined DSH reductions on states that elected not to expand Medicaid in 2014, Dorn et al. (2014) estimated that hospitals in these states would collectively lose $167.8 billion in federal funding over a ten-year period. In an analysis of which types of hospitals will be affected most by these cuts in funding, Cole et al. (2014) found that of the 529 hospitals nationally that will be most affected by the reductions in DSH payments, 43 percent were already in weak financial condition. Based on this concern, the authors argued that "policy makers should recognize that many hospitals that will be affected by cuts in Medicaid DSH payments are already financially weak, and that decreases in revenue may affect their ability to provide vulnerable populations with access to care" (p. 2030).

Beyond the loss of DSH funding for the hospitals within states electing not to expand Medicaid, the states will also be forgoing a combined total of $423.6 billion in federal funding that otherwise would have come to the states to support their Medicaid expansion. If instead these states were to decide to expand Medicaid, the combined cost to these states for their share of participating in the Medicaid expansion over this 10-year period would be $31.6 billion. States electing to expand Medicaid will receive substantially more in additional federal support than they will spend for their share of the costs of expansion. As described by Dorn et al. (2014), in states choosing to expand Medicaid, "for every $1 a state invests in Medicaid expansion, $13.41 in federal funds will flow into the state" (p. 1).

Which States Chose to Expand Medicaid and Which States Chose Not to Expand?

As described previously, when the expansion of Medicaid eligibility under ACA took effect in January 2014, 24 states elected not to expand eligibility. A number of those original nonexpansion states began to reevaluate their decision after data about the fiscal impact on the state and its hospitals became apparent. Several of these states have proposed Section 1115 waivers to allow them to offer expanded Medicaid coverage, but in a model that is specific to the state. Indiana and Alaska adopted expanded coverage in 2015 under an approved waiver, with Montana awaiting approval and Utah engaged in discussions with CMS about a possible expansion waiver (Kaiser Family Foundation 2015d). It is interesting to note that Pennsylvania initially expanded Medicaid under an 1115 waiver as of January 1, 2015, but following the election of a new Democratic governor dropped the waiver and began to shift to full expansion (Kaiser Family Foundation 2015a).

The US Census Bureau has reported changes in the percentage of the population of each state that was uninsured between 2013 and 2014 (the first year of expanded Medicaid eligibility). Figure 7.8 shows the changes in the uninsured rate experienced by the ten states with the highest percentage of their population uninsured in 2013. Three of these ten states—California, Nevada, and New Mexico—elected to expand Medicaid eligibility beginning in January 2014. It can be seen that these states had the largest decline in their uninsured rates between 2013 and 2014. Of the states with the highest uninsured rates in 2014—Texas, Alaska, and Florida—Alaska chose to adopt expansion in 2015 under a waiver and as a consequence saw a greater than 10 percent increase in its Medicaid enrollment between April 2014 and January 2015. Texas and Florida continued without expansion in 2015 and continue to have some of the highest uninsured rates in the country.

As of September 2015, nineteen states had not adopted expansion and were not pursuing waivers for possible expansion, although this number may change over time. We should recall that in 1967, the first year that the original Medicaid program was available to states, only twenty-six states had joined the program. It took until 1970—five years after initial enactment—for all the states but two to choose to adopt Medicaid. It wasn't until 1982, when Arizona elected to join, that all fifty states were participating (Oberg and Polich 1988).

In order for an 1115 expansion waiver to be approved, the state must propose an alternate approach to providing coverage equivalent to the previous Medicaid cover-

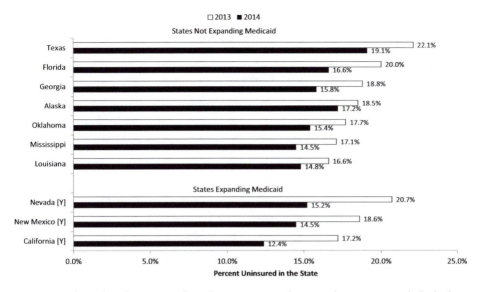

FIGURE 7.8. Changes in the uninsured rate between 2013 and 2014 in the ten states with the highest percentage of their population uninsured in 2013. *Source:* Smith and Medalia (2015).

age, with no net increase in federal expenditures. One of the most common changes states have made under waiver approval has been to charge newly eligible beneficiaries monthly premiums for enrollment. These are typically between $5 per month and $25 per month, depending on income, with those at the lowest income levels (less than 50% of the FPL) exempted. Some states require that these payments be placed into a health savings account, which is then used to pay copayments charged when the beneficiary accesses care. In some states, failure to pay the premium can lead either to a reduced level of benefits or a temporary suspension of eligibility. Several of the states adopting waivers also include incentives linked to healthy behaviors to reduce premiums or other forms of cost sharing.

Two state waiver plans are worth noting because of the different approach they have taken. Arkansas elected to use the new Medicaid funds to purchase qualified health plan (QHP) coverage for newly covered beneficiaries through the state's health benefits exchange, with some supplementary benefits not covered in the QHP covered instead through the state's traditional Medicaid program. Newly eligible beneficiaries who are found to be "medically frail" and thus likely to need long-term care services, typically not covered by marketplace QHPs in the state exchange, were exempted from the plan and instead enrolled in the preexisting fee-for-service Medicaid plan. Arkansas also established health savings accounts for covered beneficiaries to make monthly payments ranging from $5 to $25, depending on income, to cover required copayments.

This approach to expansion proved to be quite successful. Between 2013 and 2014, the state uninsured rate dropped from 16.0 percent to 11.8 percent (Smith and Medalia 2015), while the uninsured rate among nonelderly adults between the ages of 19 and 64 fell from 27.5 percent to 15.6 percent—the second largest percentage decline among this population nationally (Guyer et al. 2015).

Michigan was also granted an 1115 waiver to expand its Medicaid coverage effective January 2014. Using existing Medicaid managed care plans, the state extended enrollment eligibility under the waiver to all adults in Michigan with incomes up to 138 percent of the FPL. Those with incomes between 100 percent and 138 percent of the FPL were required to make monthly contributions into a health savings account, which would be used to make copayments for accessed care. Premiums and copayments combined were limited to a maximum of 5 percent of income. Those newly covered by this plan would not, however, lose eligibility if they failed to make either the monthly contributions or the copayments. In addition, those covered by the plan could reduce the cap on their cost sharing if they adhered to a specified list of healthy behaviors, including establishing a regular relationship with a primary care physician. Initial projections suggested that 322,000 low-income, nonelderly adults would enroll in this new plan, labeled Healthy Michigan. This level of new enrollment was achieved in the first 100 days of the plan, with a total of 328,000 new enrollees by July 2014 (Ayanian et al. 2014). Between 2013 and 2014, the uninsured rate in Michigan fell from 11.0 percent to 8.5 percent (Smith and Medalia 2015).

Section 1115 waivers granted to states that had political reservations about full Medicaid expansion under ACA have proved to be quite successful. Through their expansion plans, these states have been largely able to offset scheduled reductions in DSH payments while expanding coverage to large numbers of beneficiaries without placing undue strain on state budgets. These outcomes would suggest that additional nonexpansion states may, over time, reassess their initial decision and consider expanding under 1115 waiver authority that allows the states a level of autonomy in how they approach this expansion. This perspective is supported by Sparer (2015), who, in reviewing the fifty-year history of the Medicaid program and the many changes it has gone through, concluded that "over the next five years, most if not all of the remaining twenty-one states will sign on to the ACA expansion. The lure of federal funding combined with strong interest-group support from providers, insurers, consumer advocates, and business leaders will be too difficult to resist" (p. 1088).

The Impact of ACA on Medicaid Enrollment

The federal Centers for Medicare and Medicaid Services reported that total combined enrollment in Medicaid and CHIP increased from 58.9 million in September 2013 (when open enrollment under ACA began) to 71.7 million in May 2015—an increase of 12.8 million new enrollees. Not all of these new enrollees were covered under the expanded eligibility established by ACA. A substantial number of them were eligible under the preexisting Medicaid standards but had not enrolled. Sometimes referred to as the "woodwork" effect of ACA, the publicity surrounding ACA and the greatly facilitated, usually online application processes established by ACA helped those previously eligible to come "out of the woodwork" and enroll for coverage. In an analysis of early enrollment in states initially electing not to expand Medicaid, Galewitz (2013) reported that "in the first month of open enrollment, about 91,000 people in those non-expanding states who would have qualified for Medicaid before but had not signed up, came to the federal online marketplace and were deemed eligible for the program." Also, as described earlier, the Oregon Medicaid expansion experiment found that many previously eligible children were enrolled in Medicaid or CHIP only when the parents themselves gained new eligibility for coverage (DeVoe et al. 2015).

While ACA has been successful in extending Medicaid coverage to more than 12 million new beneficiaries, a fundamental problem remains in assuring that those newly enrolled will have access to care, especially to primary care. As described previously by Hing et al. (2015), only 68.9 percent of office-based physicians nationally indicated that they were willing to accept new patients covered by Medicaid. States with some of the largest Medicaid enrollments also have payment rates substantially lower than most states, with the result that even fewer physicians are willing to accept new Medicaid patients. As reported by Bindman (2015), physician payment rates in California, Florida, and New York were some of the lowest in the country, paying between 54 and 57 percent of what Medicare pays, as compared to the national average of 69 percent of the Medicare rate. ACA provided short-term federal support to increase payment rates to primary care physicians seeing Medicaid patients to levels equivalent to Medicare rates. While they were in effect, these increased payment rates were shown to be associated with improved availability of appointments with primary care providers, with the largest increases found in those states with the greatest relative increase in fees (Polsky et al. 2015). However, this additional federal support was provided only for the two-year period 2013–14, after which most states reverted to their previous payment rates (*Health Affairs* 2015).

The issue of reduced access to primary care in association with low Medicaid payment rates is not a new one. In 1965, the same year Congress created Medicaid, Congress also established a national network of nonprofit community health centers as part of the Office of Economic Opportunity. Now commonly referred to as federally qualified health centers (FQHC), the community-based facilities provide principally primary care services and are assured an enhanced reimbursement rate from the federal government sufficient to cover the full cost of providing care to low-income patients. In 2013, FQHCs provided care to 21.7 million people, of whom 41 percent were covered by Medicaid and 35 percent were uninsured (Shin et al. 2015).

ACA established $11.5 billion in new funding both to expand existing FQHCs and to establish new FQHCs. As described in chapter 4, ACA also invests substantial new funding in expanding the patient-centered medical home (PCMH) as a new model of primary care delivery. By 2012, a growing number of Medicaid patients reported receiving primary care with at least some attributes of the PCMH model (Cunningham 2015).

In 2015, 40 percent of physicians working in community health centers indicated that they had seen an increase in the total number of patients they were seeing, with 70 percent reporting an increase in the number of formerly uninsured patients who had acquired health insurance (Commonwealth Fund 2015b). Fifty-eight percent of physicians working in community clinics indicated that their ability to provide high-quality care to all their patients had not changed following the expansion of Medicaid under ACA, with an additional 18 percent indicating that their ability to provide this care had actually improved (Altman and Blumenthal 2015).

FQHCs and other types of community health centers will continue to play a central role in providing high-quality primary care to patients on Medicaid, as well as patients who remain uninsured. The question as to the optimal means of providing financial support for these centers remains open and will be the subject of close scrutiny under the policies and programs enacted by ACA. As summarized by Shin et al. (2015): "What is needed at this critical juncture in the evolution of US health care is a more deliberate coming together of Medicaid and community health centers, through a purposeful collaboration that builds on the valuable lessons that both programs have learned and can thus achieve what neither can accomplish alone: better and more accessible health care that rests on financing strategies designed to promote quality and efficiency" (p. 1103).

SUMMARY: A HALF-CENTURY OF MEDICAID, AND WHERE MEDICAID WILL BE GOING

Medicaid was first enacted in 1965 as part of Congress's overall support for President Lyndon Johnson's "War on Poverty." Largely under the guidance of Rep. Wilbur Mills (D-AR), chair of the House Ways and Means Committee, the program was modeled on the Kerr-Mills Act of 1960, a previous program Mills had coauthored to provide federal support to states to help pay for health care for low-income, elderly adults. At the time, the federal Medicare program received a great deal more attention than Medicaid. As described by Iglehart and Sommers (2015), "Over its 50-year history, the federal–state Medicaid program has evolved from a neglected stepchild of Medicare to the nation's largest health care program, providing coverage to tens of millions of persons and families of limited means" (p. 2152). Eligibility was initially linked to receipt of cash welfare payments. While this link was removed in 1996, the policy of targeting families with young children for eligibility remained. Medicaid excluded from coverage nonelderly, nondisabled adults without young children.

By 2010, Medicaid had grown to make up more than half of all federal funding to states. Medicaid funding by states for their share of the program grew to be one of the largest segments of state budgets, typically less only than state spending on education. The growing burden on state budgets led many states to reduce its payments to providers substantially, often resulting in reduced access to care for those covered by Medicaid.

While the number of individuals covered under Medicaid has grown consistently, it has not principally been the number of beneficiaries that has placed the strain on state budgets. Rather, it has been the highly skewed patterns of spending under Medicaid. As reported by the US General Accounting Office (2014), in 2009, 5 percent of Medicaid beneficiaries accounted for 45 percent of all Medicaid costs. A small group of dual-eligible beneficiaries (those covered both by Medicare and by Medicaid), many of whom were in nursing homes or other types of long-term care programs, accounted for 0.7 percent of all beneficiaries but 13.3 percent of all costs. A small group of high-expenditure, Medicaid-only beneficiaries, making up 4.3 percent of beneficiaries, accounted for 31.6 percent of all costs. In most cases, however, these beneficiaries were excluded from enrollment in Medicaid managed care organizations and were less affected by low rates of payments to providers.

Nonelderly, nondisabled Medicaid beneficiaries accounted for only 36 percent of all costs, yet it has been these beneficiaries who have been the focus of most state changes to Medicaid coverage and payment policies. Responding to the growing problem of limited access to providers in association with reduced payment rates, most states began to shift their nonelderly, nondisabled Medicaid populations into managed care plans, in which the state paid a fixed, per capita payment to the plan, and the plan took responsibility for providing care. As described by Hurley and Somers (2003), states that began to adopt a managed care approach to their Medicaid program "discovered that by embracing managed care, they gained contractually guaranteed access to health plans or primary care physicians" (p. 79) and that "managed care, with its focus on cost-conscious consumption and provision of services, seemed to make for an especially good match for Medicaid" (p. 77). Many of these managed care plans were created by state and local governments intently to provide care under the constraints of capped budgets.

Most of those enrolled in these plans were relatively low-cost beneficiaries, leading to the problem identified by Iglehart and Sommers (2015): "Although about two thirds of Medicaid beneficiaries were receiving services through managed-care plans by 2010, less than 30% of Medicaid dollars flowed to such plans because their enroll-ees were typically parents and children, who are less expensive to cover than other Medicaid beneficiaries. . . . Despite the growing enthusiasm for managed care in Medicaid, evidence is mixed on whether such programs actually save money or im-prove the quality of care" (p. 2154).

Medicaid, both as a national program and as an individual state program, is con-fronted by two distinct patient populations with differing needs for care: the large pop-ulation of children and nonelderly, nondisabled adults who account for about one-third of costs, and the much smaller group of disabled and elderly patients who account for most of the costs. Is there a way to improve primary care and preventive access for the former group while also developing more efficient and effective methods of providing the latter group with the care they need at a lower cost?

A growing number of analysts are suggesting that accountable care organ-izations (ACO), created under ACA to reduce costs while maintaining quality for Medi-care beneficiaries, might also have the same potential for the complex mix of Medicaid beneficiaries. Applying the ACO model to Medicaid will need to focus on improving primary care access, quality, and efficiency through the expansion of the PCMH model—a central need of both groups of beneficiaries.

The US Agency for Healthcare Research and Quality (2015b) supported a trial of just such an approach for Medicaid beneficiaries in Colorado. Beginning in 2011, the Colo-rado Accountable Care Collaborative established a statewide network of regional care collaborative organizations, or RCCOs. Each RCCO serves a specified geographic re-gion of the state and contracts with primary care providers within its region that have been designed to act as a PCMH. Medicaid patients with an established relationship with these providers are then included in the RCCO and assigned to receive care from that PCMH. Patients without an established provider are assigned to the RCCO and asked to select from among the participating primary care providers to receive their care. Payment for the care of patients in the RCCO is provided in several forms, including:

- fee-for-service payments to the PCMH for care provided;
- a separate, per-member-per-month capitated payment, shared by the RCCO and the PCMH, to support care coordination and management for high-risk patients; and
- a supplemental per-member-per-month payment, shared by the RCCO and the PCMH, if certain quality metrics are maintained.

By June 2013, 47 percent of all Colorado Medicaid beneficiaries were enrolled in the program and receiving care from a PCMH. During the first two years of the program, the state saved an estimated $6 million in Medicaid costs, based on a combination of enhanced access to coordinated care in the PCMH, fewer hospital admissions and fewer hospital readmissions, reduced use of the emergency room, and less use of high-cost imaging such as CAT scans and MRIs.

As described in the previous chapter, one of the central new federal agencies established by ACA has been the Center for Medicare & Medicaid Innovation (CMMI). As stated on its website, CMMI "supports the development and testing of innovative health care payment and service delivery models" (CMMI 2015f). One of the models being developed by CMMI that has direct relevance to Medicaid is the Medicaid Innovation Accelerator Program, whose goal is "to support states in accelerating new payment and service delivery reforms to improve health and improve care for Medicaid beneficiaries, and, through these improvements, reduce costs for the Medicaid program and, by extension, the health system more generally" (CMMI 2015e).

When Medicaid and Medicare were both created in 1965, the two programs had fundamentally different goals. While Medicare was intended to provide essentially universal coverage for the elderly, Medicaid was initially intended to provide limited coverage to only certain subsets of the poor. The expansion of Medicaid eligibility under ACA, despite initial reluctance on the part of some states following the Supreme Court's decision, shows every sign of shifting Medicaid to a form of universal coverage for all those who are poor or near poor. In reviewing the 50-year history of Medicaid, Sparer (2015) came to a similar conclusion, suggesting that as "Medicaid itself continues to evolve, and as it becomes more a part of the American mainstream, it moves further away from its public insurance roots and more toward a public-private hybrid program, one that is becoming the core health program for both the poor and low-wage workers more generally" (p. 1087). The next several years will provide valuable insight on how well the program will achieve this new goal.

8

The Uninsured

To gain access to most types of health care in this country, an individual or family needs to be covered by some sort of health insurance plan. The high cost of care, even relatively simple care, is often more than most people can afford to pay out of pocket. Fortunately, the vast majority of Americans are covered by some type of plan that will pay for their care when needed. In 2010, the year ACA was passed, 83.7 percent of Americans had some form of health insurance coverage.

The remaining 16.3 percent of Americans—50 million people—faced the prospect of illness or injury with no health insurance, however, and thus no way to pay for their health care. One in six Americans remained uninsured throughout the entire year and as a result was often unable to obtain needed care due to the cost of that care. An even higher percentage went without health insurance for at least part of the year. Compared to people with insurance, the uninsured seldom obtain the type of preventive health services that can substantially reduce rates of illness and death (Ayanian et al. 2000). Providing health care to these people has for years been one of the most difficult policy issues facing the United States.

THE CREATION AND EXPANSION OF HEALTH INSURANCE IN THE TWENTIETH CENTURY

Our focus on the issue of the uninsured developed relatively recently in US political history. For much of the twentieth century, being uninsured was the norm and was not thought to pose a serious national policy issue. Before the Great Depression of the 1930s, few Americans were covered by any type of health insurance plan. Most insurance companies shied away from providing health insurance because of the difficulties in predicting or controlling the cost of care. It was the national economic crisis of the 1930s that stimulated the first widespread interest in health insurance.

Many hospitals were facing severe financial difficulties during the Depression, due largely to patients' inability to pay their hospital bills. The survival of the US system of voluntary, nonprofit hospitals required some type of prepaid hospital insurance. If enough people were willing to pay a small amount each month to insure against the possible costs of a hospitalization, these funds could then be pooled to pay for the care of those who did become sick. Rather than relying on private insurance companies to offer this type of insurance, hospitals in most parts of the country banded together to form their own, nonprofit hospital insurance program. This was the birth of the national Blue Cross movement.

The Blue Cross insurance plans were principally intended to pay the costs of hospitalization. They did not pay for the cost of physician care. Shortly after the creation of the Blue Cross system, physicians in many areas of the country created a parallel system of nonprofit insurance for the cost of physician care: the Blue Shield program. The American Hospital Association (AHA) and the American Medical Association (AMA) worked together to assure that "the Blues" (as the combined Blue Cross / Blue Shield programs were often called) remained under the local control of hospital and physician associations and out of the hands of commercial insurers (a situation that changed dramatically in the 1990s, as discussed in chapter 9).

These new insurance plans had a potential problem that could threaten their financial stability: adverse selection. Because health insurance was a relatively new option for most Americans, there was a risk that only those individuals who were facing illness would choose to have coverage. The success of the programs depended on spreading the cost of care over as many people as possible. If only sick people signed up for the plans, the cost of care would be more than the premiums paid by patients could support.

The solution to this problem lay in focusing on large groups of relatively healthy people as the principal market for the new health insurance. The best way to enroll large numbers of healthy people was to offer the insurance through employee groups. The concept of health insurance as an employee benefit was established through the marketing of the Blues to employee groups.

By the beginning of World War II, the idea of health insurance had caught on. Seeing the initial success of the Blues in enrolling large numbers of subscribers, private, for-profit insurance companies began to follow suit and offer plans of their own. By 1940, more than 6 million people had enrolled in the Blues, with more than 3 million

---

CONCEPT 8.1

At the beginning of World War II in 1941, fewer than 10 million Americans were covered by health insurance. The vast majority of the population was uninsured, paying for needed health care out of pocket.

people covered by some type of private health insurance. The vast majority of Americans, however, were still uninsured and paid for health care out of pocket.

Chapter 5 describes the two major policy decisions enacted by the federal government that led over time to employer-provided health insurance becoming the norm.

1. The federal government exempted employer-paid fringe benefits from the national wage/price controls that were imposed during World War II.
2. The federal government decided that fringe benefits obtained through work would not be taxable as income to the worker.

These two policy decisions created powerful economic incentives for the expansion of employer-sponsored health plans. As labor unions bargained for improved wages and benefits for workers, one of the first benefits sought after was health insurance. By the 1960s, most large companies routinely offered health insurance to their full-time workers. Health insurance became the norm for most Americans.

The 1960s saw two major shifts in health care policy: (1) the expansion of health insurance to the poor and elderly through the Medicaid and Medicare programs and (2) the beginning of the rapid escalation in health care costs. By 1970, the cost of health care began to rise more rapidly than the national economy and continued to do so for the next forty years. In 1970, the average per capita cost of health care for all Americans was $297. By 1993, the year of the debate over President Bill Clinton's proposed health care reforms, this figure had increased by a factor of 10 to $2,937 per capita.* As the cost of health care rose relentlessly throughout the 1970s and 1980s, more and more people at the economic margins of American society found it difficult if not impossible to find or maintain health insurance for themselves and their families. By 1980, more than 31 million people lacked health insurance.

THE ISSUE OF THE UNINSURED FINDS THE AMERICAN MAINSTREAM: WOFFORD VERSUS THORNBURGH, 1991

Until 1991, there was relatively little emphasis in either the public policy arena or the national media on how many Americans did or did not have health insurance. This situation changed dramatically following the upset victory of Harris Wofford over Richard Thornburgh in the 1991 Pennsylvania election for US senator. Wofford had been appointed on an interim basis to fill an empty Senate seat. A special election had been called for November 5, 1991, to fill the seat on a permanent basis. Wofford, a Democrat, had been a cofounder of the Peace Corps and former state labor secretary, but he was relatively unknown in either Pennsylvania or national politics. His Republican opponent was Richard Thornburgh, who had been governor of Pennsylvania

---

*These data are from the federal government and are not adjusted for inflation.

from 1979 to 1987 and attorney general in the George H. W. Bush administration. Wofford had been given little chance of beating Thornburgh. At one point, he trailed Thornburgh by 40 points in preelection polls.

Wofford made a strategic decision that was to have far-reaching national implications. He began to focus his campaign on the plight of the uninsured and the need for national health insurance. This message struck a chord with Pennsylvanian voters, and Wofford rapidly gained ground on Thornburgh. On election day, Wofford defeated Thornburgh by a margin of 10 percent. By focusing the public spotlight on the uninsured, Wofford had not only beaten one of the strongest contenders in the Republican Party but also set the stage for Clinton's proposal for national health care reform and the changes that followed it, as discussed in chapter 5.

WHO ARE THE UNINSURED, AND WHY ARE THEY UNINSURED?

The successive victories by Harris Wofford and Bill Clinton placed the problem of the uninsured squarely before the American public. The defeat of the Clinton health reform proposals meant that the problem remained in front of us as we entered the 2008 election cycle. As shown in figure 8.1, the proportion of uninsured Americans has grown nearly continuously since the Wofford and Clinton elections.*

When Wofford campaigned in 1991 on the issue of national health insurance, 13 percent of Americans were uninsured. When the Clinton health reform proposals were defeated in 1994, 14 percent were uninsured. By 1998, the number had grown to 14.6 percent of people without insurance. Dipping in 2000 to 13.7 percent after years of economic expansion and strikingly low rates of unemployment, by 2001 the number of uninsured began to rise again, reaching 15.8 percent of the population in 2007, the year before the economy went into recession. As a consequence of the recession and the high rate of unemployment that went along with it, by 2010 the number of uninsured had jumped to 16.3 percent (US Census Bureau 2011).

At this point, I would like to note that the federal government actually has two different agencies that track the number of uninsured Americans. The aforementioned data are from the US Census Bureau, which publishes annual updates on the uninsured as part of its ongoing Current Population Survey (CPS). CPS surveys about 60,000 households that are representative of the overall US population and asks respondents if they have had health insurance at any time during the previous year. Those who answer "no," thus having been uninsured for an entire year, are considered uninsured.

---

*It should be noted that, in 2000, the Census Bureau changed the way it defined "uninsured," leading to an approximate 8 percent decrease in the number of uninsured calculated using the previous method. In reporting the number of uninsured in years before 2000, I have applied this adjustment factor, so that data before and after 1999 use the same measurement instrument.

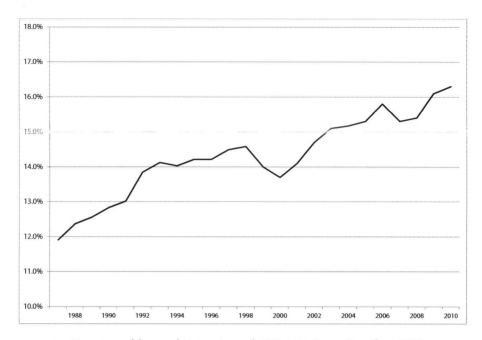

FIGURE 8.1. Percentage of the population uninsured, 1987–2010. *Source:* Data from US Census Bureau; data previous to 2000 adjusted for change in methodology.

Those who answered "yes" are not considered uninsured, even though they may have been uninsured at the time of the interview. By contrast, the National Center for Health Statistics (NCHS) of the US Department of Health and Human Services Centers for Disease Control and Prevention conducts a regular survey of approximately 35,000 representative households, asking a range of questions about the health status of household members. One of the questions for each household member is whether he or she is covered by health insurance at the time of the interview. Thus, anyone who lacks health insurance on the day of the interview is considered uninsured. Therefore, CPS, measuring lack of health insurance for an entire year, will typically report somewhat lower rates than the NCHS. NCHS has published a comparison of the methodologies of the two surveys and the results derived from them (US Centers for Disease Control and Prevention 2015a).

> **CONCEPT 8.2**
>
> The problem of the uninsured is not principally a problem affecting low-income families. In 2010, two-thirds of uninsured Americans were in families with annual household income above $25,000.

In addition to the 50 million people who fell into the category of "uninsured" in 2010, millions of others were without insurance for some period of time during the year but were not uninsured for the entire year. Many people would change jobs and be without coverage in the interim. Many college students went without health insurance coverage for short periods between graduation and beginning employment.

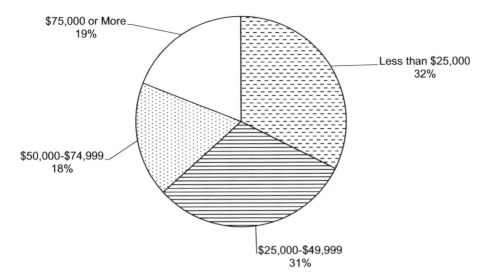

$75,000 or More
19%

Less than $25,000
32%

$50,000-$74,999
18%

$25,000-$49,999
31%

FIGURE 8.2. The uninsured, by household income, 2010. *Source:* Data from US Census Bureau.

People who were self-employed may have canceled their coverage for a period of time and then enrolled with a new insurance carrier. These are not the people we are talking about when we discuss the uninsured. The data in the following paragraphs apply only to those who are without health insurance for the full year.

Figure 8.2 shows the breakdown of the population of uninsured Americans in 2010 by household income. The first thing to note is that only 32 percent of the uninsured came from low-income families (families with income less than $25,000). Nearly half of the uninsured were from families with a household income between $25,000 and $75,000 per year.

Figure 8.3 looks at the uninsured by age. As would be expected, only 1 percent of the uninsured were elderly. Medicare has been effective in maintaining nearly universal coverage for elderly Americans. Forty percent of the uninsured were young adults between 18 and 34. Fifteen percent of the uninsured were children. This high rate of uninsured children persisted despite expansions in Medicaid eligibility for children and the creation of the Children's Health Insurance Program (CHIP).

CONCEPT 8.3

At the time the Affordable Care Act was passed by Congress, the uninsured were made up mostly of young Americans—in 2010, 15 percent were children and 40 percent were young adults.

By looking at figure 8.4, we see that the uninsured are not distributed equally among the principal ethnic groups in the United States. In 2010, about 65 percent of the US population were white (non-Hispanic), while only 47 percent of the uninsured were white (non-Hispanic). The overall population was about 13 percent black, while the uninsured were 16 percent black. The population was 17 percent Hispanic, while the uninsured were

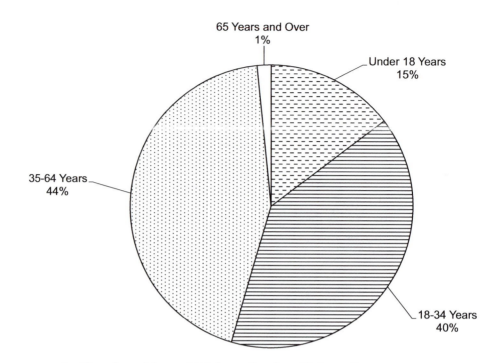

FIGURE 8.3. The uninsured, by age, 2010. *Source:* Data from US Census Bureau.

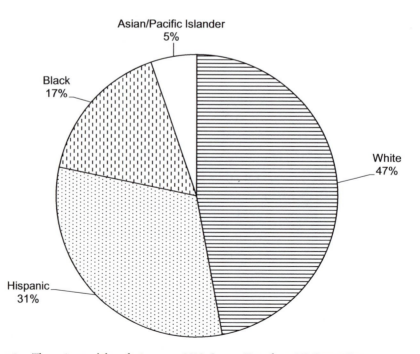

FIGURE 8.4. The uninsured, by ethnic group, 2010. *Source:* Data from US Census Bureau.

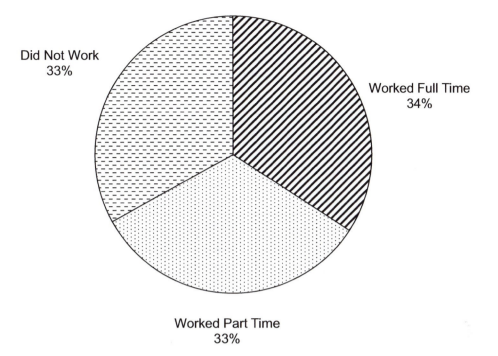

Did Not Work
33%

Worked Full Time
34%

Worked Part Time
33%

FIGURE 8.5. Uninsured adults, by work status, 2010. *Source:* Data from US Census Bureau.

31 percent Hispanic. Asian/Pacific Islanders made up about 5 percent of the population and 5 percent of the uninsured.

As shown in figure 8.5, the problem of the uninsured was principally a problem of working families. During 2010, only 33 percent of uninsured adults did not work. Thirty-four percent of uninsured workers were employed full time during the year, with the remaining 33 percent working part time.

CONCEPT 8.4

Minority ethnic groups are over-represented among the uninsured. This is especially true for Hispanics.

From the aforementioned data, it is possible to draw the following conclusions. When ACA was passed in 2010, those Americans who were uninsured were principally

- young (55% under 35 years of age);
- from middle-income, working families (34% of adults worked full time, 70% of families had incomes above $25,000 per year); and
- more likely to be from minority ethnic groups (31% Hispanic and 17% black).

The problem of the uninsured has not been primarily a problem of the poor and the unemployed. It has been a problem of middle-class, working families. How is it that, with most people obtaining health insurance through their work, so many working Americans remained without coverage before ACA? To answer this question, I will look in detail at the employment characteristics of the uninsured.

THE SOURCE OF THE UNINSURED: LOW-WAGE WORKERS AND SMALL EMPLOYERS

Not all workers have equal access to health insurance through their work. In addition, not all workers take advantage of the availability of health insurance at their work. The likelihood a worker will have coverage available and the likelihood the worker will accept coverage when offered seems to be closely associated with the worker's hourly wage. Figure 8.6 shows data from 2001 that illustrate this point. At that time, only 53.3 percent of workers who earned $7.00 per hour or less were offered the chance to participate in employer-sponsored health insurance. Either their employer did not sponsor a plan or the worker was not eligible for the employer's plan. For workers earning between $7.01 and $10.00 per hour, the figure rose to 72.2 percent. Ninety-two percent of workers earning more than $15.00 per hour had health insurance offered to them through their work.

Even if an employer offered health insurance coverage to workers, not all workers accepted this coverage. Typically, the employer will pay only part of the cost of coverage, with the employee responsible for paying the balance. It is possible to arrange to

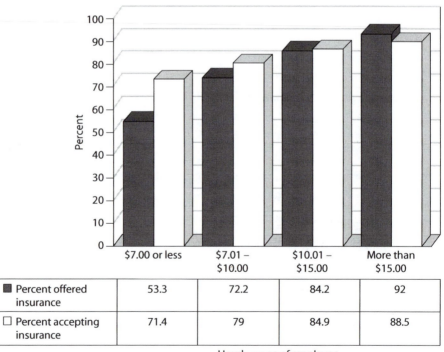

	$7.00 or less	$7.01 – $10.00	$10.01 – $15.00	More than $15.00
■ Percent offered insurance	53.3	72.2	84.2	92
□ Percent accepting insurance	71.4	79	84.9	88.5

Hourly wage of employee

FIGURE 8.6. The availability and acceptance of employer-sponsored health insurance for workers at different income levels, 2001. *Source:* Data from Kaiser Family Foundation.

have the employee's share of the insurance premium exempt from income tax. For lower-wage workers, however, the advantage of tax exemption holds less benefit, because these workers typically pay taxes at a lower rate (if at all). In addition, the impact of the reduction in take-home pay resulting from enrolling in the employer's health insurance plan will be greater for low-wage workers than for higher-wage workers. As a result, even when offered coverage through their work, low-wage workers choose to accept that coverage less often than their higher-wage counterparts. Of those earning $7.00 per hour or less in 2001 who were offered health insurance, only 71.4 percent accepted the offer and enrolled in the employer's health plan. The comparable number for higher-wage workers was 85 to 89 percent.

> **CONCEPT 8.5**
>
> Low-wage workers are offered employer-sponsored health insurance less often and accept enrollment less often than higher-wage workers. As a result of the combination of these two forces, the rate of health insurance coverage is substantially lower among low-wage workers than higher-wage workers, even though many employers make coverage available.

Data from 2012 showed that this pattern of lower acceptance of health insurance coverage offered by employers has persisted (ADP Research Institute 2013). Looking at annual income rather than hourly income, among full-time workers offered the option of health insurance,

- 37 percent of workers earning between $15,000 and $20,000 per year elected health coverage;
- 58 percent of workers earning between $20,000 and $25,000 per year elected coverage;
- 82 percent of workers earning between $40,000 and $45,000 per year elected coverage; and
- 81 percent of workers earning over $45,000 per year elected coverage.

The rate of health insurance coverage depends not only on the wage of the employee but also on the size of the firm in which the worker is employed. In 2010, only 44 percent of workers employed in firms with fewer than 25 employees were covered by their employer's health insurance. This compares to 60 percent of employees in firms with 25 to 199 employees and 63 percent of employees in firms with 200 or more employees (Kaiser Family Foundation and Health Research Educational Trust 2010).

There may well be substantial overlap between the effect of hourly wage and the effect of the size of the firm on the likelihood of coverage. Many small firms such as restaurants and independent retail stores rely on lower-wage workers to maintain their business. The cost of providing health insurance to these workers can be prohibitive.

> **CONCEPT 8.6**
>
> Workers in small firms (fewer than 25 employees) are substantially less likely to be covered by health insurance than workers in large firms (100 employees or more).

When Congress discussed requiring all employers to provide health insurance to their workers as part of the debate over the Clinton health reform proposals, small businesses spoke with a clear voice that such a mandate would have been a severe hardship for them.

Our system of employer-based health insurance has evolved over several decades since the federal government made the two policy decisions described previously. These decisions were intended to address specific issues of wage stabilization and taxation, however, and not to create national health policy. This employment-based system was neither consciously designed nor explicitly adopted. It simply developed as a result of market forces and the unintended consequences of federal tax and wage policies. While the system has worked well for most Americans, it has failed a growing segment of our population and has contributed substantially to the national policy dilemma of finding a way to extend coverage to the uninsured.

A number of people have argued that if we are going to have a system that provides health insurance through one's work, all employers should be required to provide that insurance. Employers provide other types of mandatory benefits—coverage for unemployment or on-the-job injuries, for example—so it would be straightforward to mandate that employers also provide health insurance. Opponents to this "employer mandate" approach have argued in response that it would place an unreasonable burden on employers, especially smaller businesses, to pay for health insurance for their workers. While a number of states have considered adopting a statewide employer mandate for health insurance, only one has actually adopted such a policy.

EXPANDING HEALTH INSURANCE COVERAGE IN HAWAII: THE EMPLOYER MANDATE

In 2010, only 7.7 percent of the population of the state of Hawaii was without health insurance coverage. Of all fifty states, only Massachusetts had fewer uninsured. By comparison, in 2010 California had 19.4 percent of its population uninsured and Texas had 24.6 percent (US Census Bureau 2011). Much of the credit for Hawaii's high rate of health insurance coverage for its population rests with the Prepaid Health Care Act (PPHCA), the country's only statewide employer-mandate system of health insurance.

In the 1970s, the number of uninsured in Hawaii was typical of the rest of the United States, with 12 percent of the population without hospital insurance and 17 percent without insurance for physician care (Lewin and Sybinsky 1993). Seeing the rising cost of health care as a threat to the local population and the local economy, the Hawaii state legislature enacted PPHCA in 1974. Virtually all employers were required to provide health insurance for employees working at least half-time. The cost of the insurance was to be paid by a payroll tax on employees (not to exceed 1.5% of wages), with the balance paid by the employer. With these funds, the employer would purchase a basic health insurance policy, covering at least a specified list of services, from one of the private health insurance providers in the state. The mandated coverage would be for the employee only, but employers and employees would have the option of covering other family members. (Most employers extended coverage to family members.)

The law was successful, with between 4 and 5 percent of the population remaining without insurance by the mid-1980s. A serious economic downturn in Hawaii following the Asian currency crisis of the early 1990s led to higher rates of unemployment in the state. For example, the unemployment rate in Hawaii was 2.6 percent in January 1991 and rose to 6.4 percent in January 1997. In the same period, the overall US unemployment rate fell from 6.4 to 5.3 percent (data from US Bureau of Labor Statistics website). Even with this rise in unemployment relative to the rest of the country, Hawaii had one of the lowest uninsured rates of all fifty states. Those who have remained without health insurance in Hawaii are part-time workers, the unemployed, and dependents of low-income workers.

Whenever an employer mandate to provide health insurance to workers is proposed, whether at the national or state level, the business community raises serious objections. The principal concern has been that such a mandate would place an unreasonable burden on businesses, especially small businesses. The concern is that adding the cost of health insurance to the other costs of doing business would drive some firms out of business and lead others to scale back the number of people they are willing to employ. The result is predicted to be higher unemployment and reduced business activity. Similar predictions were made when PPHCA was first proposed in 1974.

In Hawaii, these predictions did not prove to be accurate. A study by the federal government showed that PPHCA did not adversely affect businesses in Hawaii (Lewin and Sybinsky 1993). More than 90 percent of businesses in Hawaii employed fewer than fifty people. In a state with one of the highest proportions of small businesses in the country, the creation of an employer mandate for the provision of health insurance did not appreciably harm small business owners or employees.

One aspect of the PPHCA that was especially important, and which holds particular significance for consideration of the general policy issue of the employer mandate, was the experience with the premium supplementation fund. As part of PPHCA, employers that had eight or fewer employees and that were not able to afford the added costs of health insurance for workers were eligible to apply for state assistance in paying these premiums. In the first seventeen years of the program, only $85,000 was expended

> **CONCEPT 8.7**
>
> Requiring all employers to provide health insurance to their regular employees and their families has been demonstrated to reduce the number of uninsured substantially without imposing undue hardship on small businesses.

from this fund. Even the smallest businesses in Hawaii seem to have been able to comply with the employer mandate without undue hardship.

Hawaii's experience with an employer mandate for health insurance suggests that this method of extending health insurance to all workers and their families holds substantial promise. The year after PPHCA was enacted, however, the federal government passed the Employee Retirement Income Security Act (ERISA), which forbids other states from establishing new employer mandates. As a result, for many years the success of the Hawaii experiment was not duplicated elsewhere in the country.

EXPANDING HEALTH INSURANCE COVERAGE IN MASSACHUSETTS: THE INDIVIDUAL MANDATE

Largely as a consequence of the restrictions imposed on state governments by ERISA, no other state followed Hawaii's lead in attempting to reduce the number of uninsured through the imposition of an employer mandate. In 2006, however, Massachusetts addressed the issue of the rising number of uninsured through another mechanism: the individual mandate.

In 1997, Massachusetts was granted a Section 1115 Medicaid waiver by the federal government, which provided added federal funding to allow Massachusetts to expand access to care to the uninsured. The extra funds provided by the waiver—more than $300 million per year—were scheduled to expire in 2006. With the help of Senator Ted Kennedy, Massachusetts was able to negotiate an agreement with the federal government. If, by July 1, 2006, Massachusetts was able to enact a statewide program of near-universal coverage, the state could keep the extra federal funding to assist in paying for the expanded coverage. After a series of intense negotiations involving not only the governor and the legislature but private interests as well, in April 2006 the legislature approved and the governor signed the Massachusetts Health Care Reform Plan.

The central element of the law was a new requirement that, by July 1, 2007, all adults in Massachusetts must acquire health insurance. Those who did not meet this requirement would be assessed a penalty on their yearly tax return. In the first year of the program, the penalty for individual noncompliance was fairly small: $219. In subsequent years, the penalty was to increase to approximately half the price of the lowest-price health plan available, up to a maximum of $912 per year in 2008. In certain circumstances, individuals who could provide documentation that they could not afford to purchase coverage were exempted from this penalty.

In addition to establishing a mandate that individuals who can afford to must acquire health insurance, the new law gave employers with eleven or more employees a choice: either provide health insurance to employees or contribute what was referred to as a "fair share" contribution to the state (initially $295 per employee per year). The state would use these funds as part of a pool to provide subsidized health insurance to those unable to obtain coverage through their work. Thus, the state did not technically mandate that employers provide health insurance to their workers. Rather, it gave employers a choice of paying a new fee to the government or providing coverage to workers in lieu of the fee.

Some in Massachusetts were concerned that the state's imposition of an individual mandate and "fair share" obligation for employers would be seen as violating ERISA. Most analysts concurred, however, that the approach adopted by Massachusetts did not violate ERISA. During the early years of the plan, no serious legal challenge was brought against it based on ERISA violations.

Realizing that most of the uninsured were in low-income families or worked for employers who did not offer coverage, Massachusetts established two new programs to make coverage available to these groups. The first was referred to as Commonwealth Care. Under this plan, individuals and families with incomes below 300 percent of the federal poverty level (FPL) were eligible to enroll in one of a series of managed care plans that had previously contracted to provide care to those eligible for MassHealth, Massachusetts's Medicaid program. Those in Commonwealth Care would not technically be enrolled in Medicaid. Instead, they were provided a sliding-scale subsidy to enroll in the plan directly. For those with incomes below 150 percent of the FPL, the state provided a full subsidy to cover the price of health coverage in one of the plans. Those with incomes between 150 and 300 percent of the FPL paid an increasing share of the premium.

For those residents with incomes greater than 300 percent of the FPL but without health insurance coverage from their work, Massachusetts established the Commonwealth Health Connector. The Health Connector was modeled after the Health Insurance Purchasing Cooperative, described in chapter 5. Managed by a Connector Board, the Connector arranged for several insurance companies in the state to make their plans available for purchase by individuals or small businesses. Each plan offered through the Connector first had to be reviewed and approved by the Connector Board. Beginning in May 2007, the approved plans were available for purchase by the public. Thus, everyone in Massachusetts who lacked health insurance yet had an income above 300 percent of the FPL had a single place to go to review and select among available health insurance options, thereby satisfying the requirements of the state's individual mandate.

By January 2008, 6 months after the imposition of the individual mandate and the "fair share" requirement for employers, 316,000 formerly uninsured residents had acquired coverage. This number represented nearly half of the estimated 650,000 uninsured residents in 2006, the year before the law went into effect (The Commonwealth Fund 2008). More than half of these newly insured residents were enrolled in

Commonwealth Care. By 2009, 97.3 percent of Massachusetts residents were covered by some form of health insurance that met minimum state standards of coverage, giving Massachusetts by far the lowest rate of uninsured residents of any state (Weissman and Bigby 2009).

While the Massachusetts Health Care Reform Plan was largely successful in its principal goal of bringing near-universal health insurance coverage to residents of the state, there was another problem the plan was not able to address successfully: the rising cost of health care. While access to health insurance in Massachusetts expanded markedly between 2006 and 2009, the cost of health care continued to increase rapidly. To study the issue, Massachusetts created a Special Commission on the Health Care Payment System. In July 2009, the commission reported its findings (Massachusetts Department of Health and Human Services 2009). The commission's report underscored that per capita health care costs in Massachusetts, already among the highest in the country, would continue to grow substantially faster than per capita gross domestic product (GDP). With the ongoing obligation to subsidize the cost of health insurance for large numbers of state residents, the government of Massachusetts would face growing budgetary pressures. The impact on state revenues of the recession of 2008–09 only exacerbated those pressures.

Realizing that Massachusetts's commitment to near-universal coverage for its residents would be seriously threatened by continuing escalation in the cost of care, the Massachusetts legislature charged the Special Commission with recommending alternative means of constraining rising health care costs. In its report, the commission was explicit about what it saw as the root cause of rising health care costs and what it saw as the best means of constraining those costs.

> It is widely recognized that the current fee-for-service health care payment system is a primary contributor to the problem of escalating costs and pervasive problems of uneven quality. . . . To promote safe, timely, efficient, effective, equitable, patient-centered care, and thereby reduce growth and levels of per capita health care spending, the Special Commission recommends that global payments with adjustments to reward provision of accessible and high quality care become the predominant form of payment to providers in Massachusetts. (2009, pp. 4, 10)

As described by Robert Steinbrook in the *New England Journal of Medicine*, Massachusetts's Special Commission "proposed that Massachusetts effectively end fee-for-service medicine . . . and replace it with a system of global payments" (2009, p. 1026).

The commission recommended that the state encourage health care providers to create accountable care organizations (ACOs) that are "composed of hospitals, physicians and/or other clinician and non-clinician providers working as a team to manage both the provision and coordination of care for the full range of services that patients are expected to need" (Massachusetts Department of Health and Human Services 2009, p. 53). An ACO would then receive a risk-adjusted payment that would "prospectively compensate providers for all or most of the care that their patients may require over a contract period, such as a month or year" (p. 8). The commission was careful to distinguish its concept of global payments from the concept of capitation payment adopted in the 1990s as part of the managed care revolution (see chapter 5). To prevent some of the abuses that developed as part of the earlier capitation system, global payments would be coupled with a requirement of electronic health records that would permit ongoing monitoring of the quality of care provided and of patients' access to care.

The Massachusetts legislature has not yet followed through with the commission's recommendations, so Massachusetts continues to struggle to find a way to pay for its expansion of health insurance. Many aspects of ACA may relieve Massachusetts of some of its responsibility for subsidizing the acquisition of health insurance by lower-income residents.

There is an additional aspect of the impact of Massachusetts's health insurance reform that warrants acknowledgment. While overall access to care has been substantially increased by the expansion of health insurance coverage, a growing segment of Massachusetts residents found it difficult to find a physician who would accept them into their practice. Data from surveys of Massachusetts residents from 2008 and 2009 found growing numbers of people "who reported difficulties obtaining care because a provider was not accepting patients—either not accepting new patients, or not accepting patients with the respondent's type of insurance" (Long and Stockley 2010, p. 1238). As discussed in more detail in chapter 12, access to health insurance is not synonymous with access to health care. In order to provide access to care for those with newly acquired insurance coverage, Massachusetts is focusing continued attention on expanding the availability of primary care services in the state.

PREDICTING THE FUTURE NUMBERS OF UNINSURED PEOPLE

The debate over the passage of ACA took place in the context of what has come to be called the Great Recession. Beginning in the last quarter of 2007, the US economy experienced falling GDP for five of the next six quarters. Only in the last quarter of 2009—the precise time ACA was undergoing the final stages of passage—did the US economy begin to show recovery.

The Office of the Actuary at the federal Centers for Medicare and Medicaid Services reported that in 2009 national health care expenditures grew by 5.8 percent, to a total of $2.5 trillion (Sisko et al. 2010). This translated into 17.4 percent of GDP. While the rise to 17.4 percent of GDP was worrisome, it was not wholly unexpected.

In August 2010, the US Census Bureau reported that the proportion of the US population that was uninsured had grown from 15.4 percent in 2008 to 16.7 percent in 2009. While the two rates—the percentage of GDP going to health care and the percentage of the population that is uninsured—are reported by different federal agencies at different times of the year, it is useful to compare historical trends in these two indicators. Figure 8.7 combines data about the rising numbers of uninsured from figure 8.1 with data about rising health care costs for the same time period. These two percentages seem to follow nearly identical trajectories. Except for the period 1995–2000, when the number of uninsured remained high despite a temporary flattening in the health care costs curve associated with the shift to managed care, the two rates seem to follow similar patterns. It should not be surprising that they do, as the economic forces that affect one also affect the other. Health care costs as a percent of GDP will rise or fall based on changes in either the numerator (aggregate health care costs) or the denominator (GDP) of the fraction. When aggregate health care costs go up, many at the margins of the health insurance market lose coverage, independent of what is happening to GDP. Correspondingly, a falling GDP indicates a shrinking economy, with falling levels of employment and concomitant losses in employment-based insurance coverage. It makes sense that health insurance rates

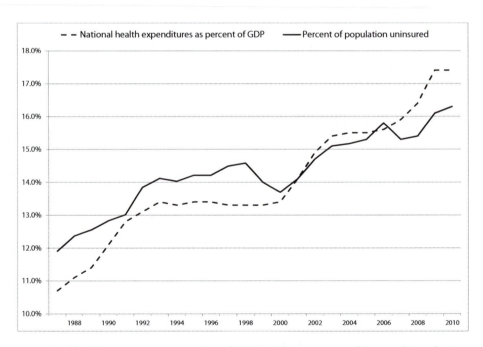

FIGURE 8.7. Health care costs as a percentage of GDP and the percentage of the population that is uninsured, 1987–2010. *Sources:* Data from US Centers for Medicare and Medicaid Services; US Census Bureau.

and health care costs should be closely related. (See Chernew, Cutler, and Keenan 2005, and Gilmer and Kronick 2005 for a more mathematical discussion of this fundamental principle of US health policy.)

Given the close association between the rise over time in the percentage of GDP going to health care and the increase in the percentage of the population that is uninsured, it was possible, using federal projections in the future rise in health care costs, to gain a rough idea of the proportion of the US population that would be without health insurance in 2019 if nothing were done. Using this method, it looked as though approximately 18.5 percent of the US population, or roughly 62 million Americans, would have been uninsured in 2019 had ACA not been passed.

As we have seen, the problem of the uninsured has historically been a problem principally among young, working families. With Medicare providing near-universal coverage for seniors and Medicaid and CHIP covering many of the poorest people in our country, relatively few of the uninsured have an income below the FPL. In a substantial majority of uninsured families, there is at least one adult who is working on a regular basis.

While we have adopted an employment-based system for providing health insurance for most Americans, that system tended to break down for low-wage workers, especially those working in small firms. Whereas most high-wage workers in larger firms have health insurance provided as a fringe benefit from work, small employers had found it economically unfeasible to extend that coverage to their lower-wage workers. As low-wage workers are disproportionately drawn from minority racial and ethnic groups, it is not surprising that these groups are disproportionately uninsured as well.

This was the situation confronting Congress and the American public at the end of 2009. Two of the states had taken action to increase the availability of health insurance to their residents: Hawaii through an employer mandate and Massachusetts through an individual mandate. There was clear evidence that the model adopted by Massachusetts was showing early success in reducing the number of uninsured within the state, although costs of the program continued to rise. Congress chose to act, passing ACA, which was signed into law by President Obama on March 23, 2010. Passage of ACA was and remains controversial. It is important for us at this point to ask, "How well has it worked?"

EXTENDING HEALTH INSURANCE TO THE UNINSURED UNDER THE AFFORDABLE CARE ACT

Throughout the development and the enactment of ACA, one of the principal goals its supporters had in mind was extending health insurance coverage to the uninsured. While the debate over how this expansion would be accomplished was often intense, most of those opposing the final version of ACA had earlier supported at least some form of expansion of coverage to reduce the number of uninsured. Accordingly, the core elements of ACA focus on this issue.

In order to reduce the number of uninsured Americans, ACA did the following.

1. As described in chapter 7, ACA extended Medicaid coverage to all citizens and permanent residents with incomes below 138 percent of the FPL. The federal government will pay 100 percent of the cost of this new coverage for the first few years, reduced to 90 percent starting in 2020. Under the Supreme Court decision, states have the option of participating or not participating in this expansion.

2. ACA requires that, beginning in 2014, all citizens and permanent residents with incomes at or above 138 percent of the FPL either obtain private health insurance coverage or pay a tax penalty not to exceed 2.5 percent of taxable income.

3. For those with incomes between 138 and 400 percent of the FPL who do not have access to affordable health insurance from their employer, ACA provides a tax credit to subsidize the purchase of private coverage. The credit will cap the amount an individual or family must pay for coverage, starting with a cap of 2 percent of income for those at 138 percent of the FPL and increasing to a cap of 9.5 percent of income for those at 400 percent of the FPL.

4. In order to assure that affordable, private health insurance coverage is available to all those who wish to purchase it, ACA established health benefit exchanges (HBEs) for each state, operated either by the state government or by the federal government on behalf of the state. These exchanges offer at least two options for health insurance coverage, one of which must be offered by a nonprofit insurer. Insurers will be able to offer different predefined levels of care for different premiums (known as bronze, silver, gold, and platinum). For those enrollees with incomes below 400 percent of the FPL, the plans must cap out-of-pocket expenses according to a predefined schedule.

5. Beginning in 2015, ACA requires employers with 100 or more full-time employees either to provide coverage for employees or to pay a penalty for each employee, as long as at least one employee acquires coverage from the state insurance exchange and qualifies for the premium tax credit. This mandate also applies to employers with 50–99 employees beginning in 2016. ACA exempts employers with fewer than 50 employees from this requirement while offering them tax incentives to provide coverage for their employees through newly established Small Business Health Options Program (SHOP) exchanges. ACA exempts larger employers from paying the penalty on the first 30 employees.

It should not be difficult to notice the similarity between the steps ACA takes to expand health insurance coverage and the steps the Massachusetts Health Care Reform Plan took to expand coverage. Both rely on an individual mandate coupled with penalties for employers not offering coverage, with subsidized coverage for those below certain incomes who purchase care privately and a publicly organized exchange for the acquisition of coverage. It was the intent of those developing ACA to use the Massachusetts plan as a model.

Some policies adopted by ACA differ from the Massachusetts plan. For example, ACA places a complex set of restrictions on the coverage of abortion under plans offered through the state exchanges. In addition, ACA relies on existing Medicaid programs for coverage for those with incomes below 138 percent of the FPL who previously were uninsured, while Massachusetts provided private coverage for those below 150 percent of the FPL without previous coverage. ACA also imposes additional restrictions on how insurers can set premiums.

Based on estimates developed by the Congressional Budget Office at the time of the enactment of ACA, there was general agreement that the steps outlined earlier would have extended health insurance coverage to an additional 32 million Americans by the time they are fully implemented in 2019. Approximately half of these newly insured were expected to be covered through the expansion of Medicaid, with the other half covered either through expansion of employer-provided coverage or through the newly established health insurance exchanges. These estimates changed, of course, with the Supreme Court decision exempting states from mandatory Medicaid expansion.

We must also recall that Massachusetts continued to experience regular increases in the cost of health care that make the expansion of coverage unsustainable without fundamental reform in the way providers are paid. While ACA addresses the issue of expanding coverage to the uninsured, there is little in ACA that will slow the continued rise in the cost of health care nationally in the foreseeable future. As described previously, the Office of the Actuary at the federal Centers for Medicare and Medicaid Services had estimated that, as a result of ACA, national health spending will grow from 17.3 percent of GDP in 2009 to 19.6 percent of GDP in 2019. Previous estimates that did not include the effects of ACA had projected a spending level of 19.3 percent of GDP in 2019. ACA was expected to have a relatively small impact on the long-term growth in health care spending, leaving the sustainability of the current health care system and its underlying financing structure still open to serious question. I discuss this issue in more depth in the final chapter of this book.

How has ACA actually impacted access to health insurance and overall health care spending? Figure 8.8 shows the change between 2010 and 2014 in the percentage of the population that is uninsured as well as the percentage of GDP that has gone to pay for health care. It should be clear that, at least for the uninsured rate, ACA has indeed had a profound and positive impact. By 2014, the percentage of the population that was uninsured had fallen to 10.4 percent.

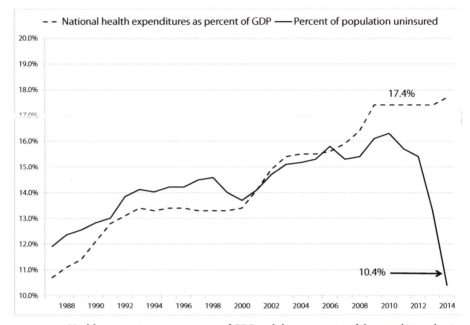

FIGURE 8.8. Health care costs as a percentage of GDP and the percentage of the population that is uninsured, 1987–2014. *Sources:* Data from US Centers for Medicare and Medicaid Services; US Census Bureau.

Immediately following enactment of ACA in 2010, the percentage of the population without health insurance began to decline. This is despite the fact that the major expansions of coverage, through the new exchanges and through the Medicaid expansion, did not take effect until 2014. In 2010, 16.3 percent of the population was uninsured. This number fell to 15.7 percent in 2011 and 13.3 percent in 2013. Even though the exchanges and the Medicaid expansion didn't take effect until 2014, there were some changes that took effect immediately upon enactment of ACA. One of the most important of these was the requirement that parents be allowed to keep children covered under their existing health insurance until age 26. Previously, children were typically dropped from their parents' coverage when they turned 18 or, for those going to college, when they graduated from college. In 2009, the year before the ACA inclusion of older children took effect, 9.2 million people between the ages of 19 and 25 were uninsured, constituting 31.4 percent of this age group. In 2011, this number had decreased by nearly 1 million young adults, and the uninsured rate among this group had fallen to 27.7 percent. By 2014, it had fallen further, to 17.1 percent.

Other changes established by ACA in 2010 included prohibiting insurance companies from excluding children from coverage because of preexisting health conditions, prohibiting insurers from including a lifetime limit on covered benefits, and requiring that preventive health procedures be covered for all patients without copayment. In the lead up to the full expansion of coverage in 2014, these changes also made it easier for many people to enroll in coverage they could afford.

Another important change established by ACA was a new prohibition of health insurance companies considering a subscriber's past medical history in either offering coverage or setting rates (other than smoking history) and of companies applying what had been referred to as "preexisting condition exclusions" to coverage, through which companies excluded from coverage payment for care for a health condition the subscriber has before enrolling in coverage. These changes took effect in the first ACA open enrollment period in 2013.

As described in chapter 5, the availability of multiple health insurance options through the new HBEs in addition to these new enrollment regulations resulted in 8 million new health plan enrollees in 2014, which grew to 11.7 enrollees in 2015. While not all of these enrollees followed through by paying their required premium, the substantial majority did. In February 2016, one week after the end of the open enrollment period, HHS secretary Burwell announced that the number of people enrolling through either healthcare.gov or state exchanges had grown to 12.7 million (Burwell 2016).

As described in chapter 7, the expansion of Medicaid eligibility, despite some of the states with the highest uninsured rates electing not to participate, resulted in a substantial increase in the number of beneficiaries covered by Medicaid—from 58.9 million in September 2013 (when open enrollment under ACA began) to 71.7 million in May 2015, an increase of 12.8 million new enrollees. Not all of these new enrollees were covered under the expanded eligibility established by ACA; a substantial number of them were eligible under the preexisting Medicaid standards but had not previously enrolled.

Perhaps not surprisingly, the decrease in the uninsured rate affected poor and low-income individuals more than higher income individuals. The rate for those making less than $25,000 per year fell from 26.9 percent in 2010 to 16.6 percent in 2014. For those making between $25,000 and $50,000, the rate went from 21.8 percent to 14.1 percent. By comparison, the rate for those making between $50,000 and $75,000 dropped from 15.4 percent to 10.7 percent, and the rate for those making more than $75,000 was essentially unchanged. Similarly, the decrease affected those in different age groups differently, with young adults (age 19–25) going from 29.7 percent to 17.1 percent and those aged 26–34 going from 28.4 percent to 18.2 percent, while the rate for adults aged 45–64 dropped from 16.3 percent to 11.0 percent. The uninsured rate for young adults began to drop even before the broader changes in insurance coverage became effective in 2014. Beginning in September 2010, those aged 19–25 were eligible to remain on their parents' health insurance, with the result that by the end of 2011, the uninsured rate among this group had already dropped to less than 25 percent (McMorrow et al. 2015a). By the end of 2014, an estimated 3 million young adults, many of whom would likely have been uninsured in the market prior to ACA, were covered under their parents' policies.

The drop in the uninsured rate also affected different racial/ethnic groups differently. Among Hispanics, the uninsured rate dropped from 30.7 percent in 2010 to 19.9 percent. By comparison, the rate for blacks dropped from 20.8 percent to 15.9 percent, for Asians from 18.1 percent to 9.3 percent, and for whites from 11.7 percent to 7.6 percent. These data reflect the uninsured rate among the entire population. Given the availability of health insurance under Medicaid and CHIP for children in poor and low-income working families (as discussed in the previous chapter), the uninsured rate for working-age adults, age 18–64, is typically higher. These rates also showed substantial declines following the rollout of ACA coverage options in 2014. Between the end of 2013 and the end of 2014, uninsured rates for Hispanics aged 18–64 fell from 40.1 percent to 31.8 percent, while the rate for black adults went from 25.5 percent to 17.2 percent and for white adults from 14.8 percent to 10.5 percent (McMorrow et al. 2015b).

The persistent higher rate for Hispanics can be attributed to a number of issues, of which immigration status is only one. As described by Doty et al. (2014), many Hispanics are impacted by language (those who speak only Spanish are 50% more likely to be uninsured than those who can speak English) and by a relative lack of knowledge and awareness of eligibility for enrollment and the enrollment process itself. The authors point out an additional important factor: "Twenty million Latinos live in these states that have not expanded Medicaid, including 14 million in Texas and Florida alone" (p. 1735). The drop in the uninsured rate among Hispanics has been largely confined to states that have expanded Medicaid.

California has been one of the states with the largest expansion in new access to health insurance and a corresponding decrease in the uninsured rate. An analysis done by Lucia et al. (2015) found that in the first year of open enrollment under ACA, 3 million Californians enrolled in Medicaid and an additional 1 million gained coverage through the state's HBE. These expansions of coverage were associated with reduced out-of-pocket spending among California residents with incomes less than 200 percent of the FPL (Golberstein et al. 2015).

Despite this new enrollment, more than 3 million Californians were still uninsured and expected to remain uninsured through 2019. Of these, approximately one-third were eligible either for Medicaid or for subsidies through the HBE. Approximately half of those in California who remain uninsured are not eligible for coverage due to their immigration status. California, however, has opened Medicaid enrollment eligibility to certain undocumented residents, using only state funds (Covered California 2015).

Schwartz and colleagues (2015) estimated that if Congress implements the proposed immigration exemptions for "Deferred Action for Parents of Americans and Lawful Permanent Residents (DAPA)" and "Deferred Action for Childhood Arrivals (DACA)," an estimated 1.1 million additional Californians may be able to gain health insurance coverage, including 609,000 DAPA parents and 485,000 children and young adults who either qualify as DACA or are already eligible as citizens or lawful residents but simply have not been enrolled by their undocumented parents out of concern over risking deportation. Again, coverage for those eligible for DAPA or DACA would be solely with state funds and thus not subject to federal approval.

SUMMARY

Largely as a result of ACA, the problem of the uninsured in this country has been reduced substantially and further reductions can be expected in the future. Historically, lack of health insurance has disproportionately affected low-wage workers and their families, young adults, blacks, and Hispanics. The impact on Hispanics has been from a combination several factors: the likelihood they work in relatively low-wage jobs, the likelihood they live in states that have not yet expanded Medicaid, problems of language access and understanding the health insurance enrollment process, and a substantial problem of immigration status. While the progress on expansion of coverage has been substantial, there continues to be the opportunity to extend eligibility for that expansion to additional millions of Americans, depending on state and federal policy decisions.

9

The Increasing Role of For-Profit Health Care

HISTORICAL CHANGES IN PERCEPTIONS ABOUT HMOS

As described in chapter 5, in the 1980s health maintenance organizations (HMOs) such as Kaiser Permanente and the Group Health Cooperative of Puget Sound were shown to be extremely successful in providing high-quality health care at a cost that was about one-third less than the traditional, fee-for-service model. They developed broad support among both the public and politicians. In the discussions surrounding the HMO Act of 1973, they enjoyed strong, bipartisan support, as evidenced by the following two quotes:

> The Health Maintenance Organization concept is a central feature of my national health strategy. . . . The HMO is a method . . . for providing health care that has won great respect. (President Richard Nixon 1972, p. 6)

> Health maintenance organizations have been proven to work. . . . The HMO concept will result in the creation of organized health care delivery systems. (Senator Ted Kennedy 1973, p. 15497)

Then, in 1997, actress Helen Hunt, playing a beleaguered waitress in the movie *As Good As It Gets*, learns that her HMO has been shortchanging her in the care they provided for her asthmatic son. She blurts out, "Fucking HMO bastard pieces of shit!"

The crowd in the movie theater I was in burst out in loud cheers. Apparently, I was not alone. As Ellen Goodman (1998) wrote in the *Boston Globe*, "At this outburst—with none of the expletives deleted—audiences all over America spontaneously burst

out in applause. It was one of those moments when you know the tide has turned. . . .
Managed-care companies are rapidly replacing tobacco companies as corporate
demons. . . . The HMOs are taking the place of the Russkies as the bad guys."

This single burst of cinematic obscenity captured the American mood and became
a cultural icon of the growing disgust with HMOs. Matthew Rees (1998), offering the
Canadian perspective, wrote in the *Ottawa Citizen* that "the story of how movie
audiences erupt in cheers when HMOs are berated by Helen Hunt in the film *As
Good As It Gets* has become the stuff of legend in Washington political circles."

What happened? How, in twenty-five years, did HMOs change from being widely
popular to being widely reviled? The answer lies in a broad change in the health care
market engendered by legislative changes adopted during the Reagan administration.

After passage of the HMO Act, HMOs became much more widespread, thanks to
federal protections and subsidies contained in the act. To be eligible for federal support, an HMO had to meet three basic requirements.

1. The HMO had to offer a specified list of benefits to all members.
2. The HMO had to charge all members the same monthly premium, regardless of
   their health status (referred to as "community rating").
3. The HMO had to be structured as a nonprofit organization.

For the first several years of the expansion of HMOs, nearly the entire industry met
these requirements, including the requirement that they operate on a nonprofit basis.
In 1981, nearly 90 percent of HMO patients were members of nonprofit plans.

Throughout most of the twentieth century, there was little room in our health care
delivery system for for-profit organizations. While a number of for-profit insurance
companies offered health insurance as one of their products, the predominant model
for health insurance was the Blue Cross / Blue Shield system, organized on a nonprofit
basis. Physicians often practiced as professional corporations, but few worked for
organizations that operated on a for-profit basis. Writing in 1951, Harvard sociologist
Talcott Parsons described the view of medical care that predominated at that time: "The
'ideology' of the profession lays great emphasis on the obligation of the physician to put
the 'welfare of the patient' above his personal interests, and regards 'commercialism' as
the most serious and insidious evil with which it has to contend. . . . The 'profit motive'
is supposed to be drastically excluded from the medical world. This attitude . . . is perhaps more pronounced in the medical case than in any single [profession] except
perhaps the clergy" (Parsons 1951, p. 435).

The 1980s brought a fundamental change to the American political landscape,
however. Ronald Reagan was elected president and a Republican majority was elected
to the Senate. Fundamental to President Reagan's free-market philosophy, legislation
was introduced to end the government's ability to regulate HMOs. By 1988, the end of

President Reagan's term in office, Congress had eliminated all federal funding for new HMOs and had relaxed considerably the criteria for HMOs to obtain federal certification, including the elimination of any requirement that HMOs operate on a nonprofit basis. As a harbinger of things to come, by 1989, nearly half of all HMOs operated on a for-profit basis. By 1998, 79 million people were enrolled in HMOs (American Association of Health Plans 1999); nearly two-thirds of this enrollment was in for-profit plans. For-profit enrollment has continued at this level. Preferred provider organizations (PPOs), the principal managed care alternative to HMOs, are organized predominantly as for-profit entities. In 2015, 52 percent of workers covered by an employment-based health insurance plan were enrolled in a PPO, while 14 percent were enrolled in an HMO (Kaiser Family Foundation and Health Research and Educational Trust 2015).

Many people were concerned that this shift to a for-profit orientation in the provision of health insurance created potential problems, including

- problems for the autonomy of physicians and other professionals (Would business managers end up telling physicians what they could and could not do?),
- problems for patients in obtaining needed care (Would for-profit corporations try to cut down on the level of care provided to increase profits?), and
- ethical problems for physicians revolving around conflict of interest (Would physicians have to choose between making money for the corporation and doing what is best for the patient?)

The debate for and against for-profit plans was echoed in two articles published in 1996 in the *New England Journal of Medicine*. Malik Hasan, representing a for-profit health plan, referred to nonprofit plans as "a byproduct of the past." His principal concern was that nonprofit plans lack the accountability inherent in a for-profit corporation and as a result develop inefficient operations that lead to higher costs. For-profit plans, on the other hand, lead to increased efficiency in the provision of health care and as a result "more affordable health care." "This direct accountability in the marketplace sets the standard for both nonprofit and investor-owned plans. . . . Nonprofit plans are organizationally less well suited to a competitive environment and are therefore less able, over the long haul, to ensure sufficient resources to meet patients' needs" (Hasan 1996, p. 1056).

Countering Hasan's view were Phillip Nudelman and Linda Andrews, representing the nonprofit Group Health Cooperative of Puget Sound. They argued that more important than the tax status of a health care organization were its purpose, values, and behavior. Nonprofit plans, they reasoned, would invest more of the health care dollar in care for covered patients, while for-profit plans would necessarily divert a substantial portion of the health care dollar to shareholder profit, thus reducing the amount and quality of the available care. "The need to show a profit focuses the for-profit plans on cost structure rather than the structure of care. . . . Group Health Cooperative and similar not-for-profit health plans have the inherent values that the patient rather than the profit is the most important part of the health equation" (Nudelman and Andrews 1996, p. 1059).

This debate has not let up. Supporters of for-profit and nonprofit approaches to health care argue as vehemently today as these authors did two decades ago. In the sections that follow, I consider the data about which side is more accurate. It was this debate, and the shift to a health care system built largely on a for-profit organizational structure, however, that led to the public view of HMOs reflected by the cheers that erupted in response to Helen Hunt's obscene comments.

THE EFFECTS OF FOR-PROFIT MANAGED CARE ON PUBLIC PERCEPTIONS OF THE QUALITY OF CARE

As discussed in chapter 3, one of the key policy issues in health care, and one that differs substantially between the United States and Canada, is striking the proper balance between the marginal cost of health care services and their marginal benefit. In the RAND health insurance experiment (described in chapter 5), the way that the HMO saved money compared to the fee-for-service system was by providing less hospital care that had a poor marginal benefit / marginal cost ratio. By doing a better job with this ratio, the HMO was able to eliminate unneeded hospital care and thus reduce costs.

The managers of the new for-profit HMOs realized that a great deal of inefficient care (i.e., care with low marginal benefit and high marginal cost) was being provided. To reduce costs while maintaining overall quality, they would need to establish mechanisms to control the use of care. In the 1990s, HMOs and other managed care organizations developed a variety of utilization-control mechanisms. Some of the more common mechanisms are described in the following sections.

Gatekeepers

A number of managed care organizations established a policy that patients must first see their primary care physician before being permitted to consult a specialist, have a test, or be admitted to the hospital. Patients could choose their primary care physician only from among those belonging to the medical group or plan they selected. Patients were referred to a specialist by the primary care physician; they were not free to select their own specialist. They usually could go to only the specialist chosen by the primary care physician. Thus, the primary care physician became the "gatekeeper" for other care the patient might need.

The gatekeeper approach was used in two general ways:

1. The primary care physician had no direct financial stake in whether a patient was referred to a specialist or for a test. The physician's only financial interest was in maintaining the overall economic health of the medical group.
2. The primary care physician received a fixed amount of money to provide all outpatient care and tests for each patient in his or her practice for a given period of time. Every time the physician referred a patient to a specialist or ordered a test, the money to pay for it came from this pool of money. Whatever was left in the pool was the physician's salary for that period of time. (While common during the early days of managed care, linking the gatekeeper function directly to the physician's income created an obvious ethical conflict and so this type of arrangement became much less common.)

Utilization Review

Many managed care organizations maintained a staff of physicians and nurses who reviewed the care provided by physicians. Before a physician was permitted to hospitalize a patient or order an expensive test such as an MRI, he or she had to obtain permission from the utilization review department. Failure to obtain this prior authorization for nonemergency treatments and procedures might lead to the managed care company refusing to pay for the service. Once a patient had been hospitalized, the utilization review staff followed the patient's progress and made sure the physician did not keep the patient in the hospital too long.

Physician Practice Profiles

Many managed care companies gathered statistics on how often each physician used expensive resources such as MRIs, drugs, hospitals, operations, and the like. The company then penalized physicians whose profile exceeded what the reviewers thought was appropriate. In a number of cases, managed care companies terminated the contract of physicians who continually exceeded expectations in the services they provided.

Financial Incentives

Managed care companies developed a variety of financial incentives intended to encourage physicians to reduce the amount of care they provided. These incentives included the following:

- *Holdbacks*
  Managed care companies that paid physicians on a fee-for-service basis (e.g., independent practice association [IPA] HMOs) would often hold back a portion of the payment due to the physician, typically 10 to 15 percent. This money was

held in a reserve account for each physician. If the medical group the physician belonged to provided more care, in aggregate, than the managed care company had budgeted, the money to cover the cost overruns came from the pool of physicians' held-back pay. Physicians received only their portion of the pool that was left over at the end of the year.

- *Direct bonus*

  Under many managed care contracts, each physician was eligible to receive a cash bonus at the end of the year, typically several thousand dollars. The amount of the bonus was determined by how well the physician had kept down costs during the year. Each physician's bonus was tied directly to the cost of the care that the physician had ordered during the year.

- *Indirect bonus*

  In many medical groups that treated patients on a capitation basis, any surplus funds left over at the end of the year were placed in a bonus pool. Each physician in the group received a share of the pool in the form of a yearly bonus. Contrary to the direct bonus, in which the amount is tied directly to the individual physician's treatment decisions, the indirect bonus is tied to the ability of the medical group as a whole to hold down costs. (A consensus appears to have developed that the indirect bonus provides a more ethical type of financial incentive to physicians. It gives each physician a stake in the financial health of the overall medical group without tying bonuses directly to the physicians' specific treatment decisions during the year.)

Education and Feedback

A number of medical groups that have assumed capitated risk for their patients have initiated structured programs of education and feedback to remind physicians which types of care are most appropriate and which types may be inappropriate. These programs do not directly involve any type of utilization control or financial incentive.

From the perspective of the health care manager in a for-profit plan, steps such as those I have described may seem reasonable and rational. The manager's job is to reduce inefficient care and to curb physicians' historic tendency to use care that has small marginal benefit—that is, to "manage" care. In the words of Malik Hasan, such utilization-control activities "are in the best interests of consumers, patients, physicians, and payers and are imperative for a healthy economy" (Hasan 1996, p. 1056).

Utilization-control mechanisms raised serious public concern about the quality of care provided under for-profit managed care—but "quality" had a different meaning for the general public than for health plan managers. Both physicians and patients often approach quality in health care as reflecting both the process of care and the outcomes from care. Care that does not meet expectations regarding process can easily be perceived as low-quality care, even if health outcomes are maintained and economic efficiency is increased. Take, for example, the treatment of ankle injuries. There is ample scientific evidence that certain specific types of ankle injuries have an extremely low likelihood of involving injury to the bone. Taking X-rays of these patients will add substantial cost with little or no change in the eventual healing of the injury. Nonetheless, many patients who seek treatment for an injured ankle believe that unless the physician orders an X-ray, the quality of care has been substandard.

This focus on process over outcomes in defining quality became increasingly common as more and more patients experienced managed care. News reports included numerous instances of patients being denied care that on the surface seemed appropriate. Whether it was CAT scans for headaches, MRIs for knee injuries, hospitalization, referral to a specialist, use of the latest antibiotic, or access to allergy testing (as was the case for Helen Hunt's son), many patients came away from their interaction with managed care systems believing that they had been denied appropriate care simply to save money. In the minds of many people (including the waitress played by Helen Hunt and the movie audiences who watched her), for-profit HMOs and other forms of for-profit managed care meant by definition low-quality care. Perhaps the public mood was best captured by a *New Yorker* cartoon that appeared in the 1990s. It showed Humpty Dumpty, having fallen off his wall, lying cracked on the ground. A passerby looks down and remarks, "He's in an H.M.O. Get some of the King's horses and a few of the King's men."

The rising public outcry over the limitations inherent in for-profit managed care led to increasing scrutiny of managed care organizations. Many employers and other large purchasers of care began to insist that managed care providers produce comprehensive data about the quality of the care they provide. The most prevalent data tool used to assess quality is the Healthcare Effectiveness Data and Information Set (HEDIS), a detailed reporting of adherence to certain process standards in care. (As with other monitoring tools, HEDIS does little to assess health outcomes.) In addition, the federal government and many state governments began to take steps to monitor and control the quality of care provided by HMOs and other managed care organizations. A growing list of actual or proposed legislation began to define what have come to be called "patients' rights" regarding health care, including a right to see a specialist, a right to have emergency room care paid for, and a right to appeal a denial of care. As a result of what came to be called the "managed care backlash," many, if not most, HMOs began in the late 1990s to reduce the stridency of their efforts at utilization control. As a result, costs began to rise, and the HMOs had little choice but to raise their rates to employers and individual subscribers. As shown in figure 5.9, in the late 1990s, when for-profit HMOs and other managed care plans began to relax their control mechanisms, the steep rise in the cost of health care resumed.

(It is especially ironic that both government and the public began to refer to "patients' rights" to care in the context of managed care. As discussed in chapter 2, the United States historically has failed to acknowledge a right to health care, a policy position that is unique among developed countries. As a society, we have historically acknowledged a right to expensive, often high-tech care for those with health insurance, while denying a right to basic care for those without health insurance.)

I should note that few of the more onerous methods of controlling the use of care were ever used by the large, nonprofit HMOs that formed the basis for federal policy in 1973. Kaiser Permanente, for example, included for many years an indirect bonus for physicians. The bonus pool was budgeted prospectively, however, and was always planned to be part of physician compensation. If the cost of care exceeded the amount budgeted, the bonus pool was used as a reserve cushion to make up the shortfall, and the remainder was distributed to physicians as part of their regular compensation. If, on the other hand, the cost of care was less than the amount budgeted, the surplus was not added to the bonus pool but rather was reinvested in the Kaiser Permanente system. Kaiser Permanente also relied heavily on physician education and feedback, and on gatekeeper systems that were not linked to physician compensation.

Outside of the Kaiser Permanente system, the conflict that developed between patients' expectations of care and the need of managed care organizations to constrain the amount of care provided in order to control costs often placed the physician directly in the middle. Physicians often found themselves in the role of wanting to provide a certain service or type of care but having the managed care company refusing to authorize or pay for care. Medical meetings and newsletters frequently bemoaned the added burden that had been placed on physicians by managed care. Physicians described spending hours on the phone with managed care reviewers (most of them with no medical training) debating the necessity of a certain type of care. Many physicians complained that clinical decision making had been taken out of their hands and placed in the hands of bureaucrats. (One orthopedic surgeon from a somewhat conservative medical community, whose son was in my health policy class at Stanford, shared his experiences with me by waving his hand under his chin and exclaiming, "I've had it up to here with HMOs!")

Many of these complaints and concerns about the effect of managed care on quality were in response to actions that were taken by the HMOs and that had substantial scientific support. When a physician asks for approval to undertake a procedure that has been shown to have little benefit in carefully controlled, scientific studies, it is both understandable and defensible to deny coverage for that care. This is precisely how HMOs and other managed care organizations save money.

CONCEPT 9.1

In the 1990s, the public came to perceive many of the reductions in care initiated by managed care companies in an effort to control costs as unwarranted reductions in quality.

(See, e.g., an article in the *New England Journal of Medicine* from 1994 titled "I Had a Tough Day Today, Hillary" by Dr. Stephen D. Boren, the assistant medical director of a large insurance company.) Nonetheless, the public response to denials of this type is often one of criticism and complaint about low-quality care.

PUBLICITY ABOUT THE "MEDICAL LOSS RATIO" AND PUBLIC REACTION TO IT

The insurance industry coined the term "loss ratio." For an insurance company, any claim that must be paid is viewed as a loss—that is, it decreases the company's profit for that year. The "loss ratio" is simply the percentage of premiums received from customers that are paid out in claims in a given period of time. The percentage obtained by subtracting the loss ratio from 100 percent measures the amount available to the company to cover administrative costs and provide a profit to shareholders. The lower the loss ratio, the more money is available as profit.

In the health insurance industry, analysts refer instead to the "medical loss ratio" (MLR). The MLR is the percentage of every dollar taken in as premiums that goes to pay for the provision of medical care. An MLR of 90 percent would mean that 90 percent of every premium dollar goes to pay for medical care, with the remaining 10 percent available to cover activities not involved directly in patient care such as marketing, administrative overhead, and shareholder profit. To many, MLR is an odd term, because it implies that health insurance companies consider any funds spent providing care to patients to be a loss and that they seek to keep this ratio as low as possible.

Historically, the MLR of nonprofit HMOs such as Kaiser Permanente has been in the range of 95 percent. The MLR for the Medicaid program is also typically about 95 percent and for Medicare about 98 percent. Nearly all of the money in these traditional programs goes to pay for care. In the world of for-profit managed care, MLRs have typically ranged from 70 to 85 percent. Any for-profit company that maintains an MLR above 80 to 85 percent is at a potentially serious competitive disadvantage. Their disadvantage, though, is not in competing for patients but rather in competing for stock market investment. In the face of rising cost pressures in health care, companies that are unable to maintain low MLRs have had difficulty giving shareholders an adequate return on their investment.

In the 1990s, newspapers began publishing the MLRs of various HMOs and other managed care plans. The MLR provided the public with a readily understandable measure of the extent to which for-profit health care organizations balanced providing care to patients with the need to make a profit. Negative perceptions of the for-profit motive, cou-

---

CONCEPT 9.2

Negative perceptions of the expansion of for-profit care and growing awareness of efforts to reduce the medical loss ratio compounded the public's negative reaction to managed care, creating the "managed care backlash."

pled with public awareness of the pressure to maintain a low MLR, added to public concern and compounded the negative public reaction to the managed care industry, contributing to the "managed care backlash."

Neither the public nor legislators seem to be able to distinguish between problems in quality that stem from the profit motive and perceived problems that stem from otherwise justifiable efforts to control unnecessary care. The negative reaction to the managed care industry was remarkably uniform and widespread, and seems to have lumped these two issues together. In this increasingly critical and competitive climate, investors began to lose interest in for-profit health care companies, sometimes with negative results for the companies. A number of large, for-profit managed care companies faced substantial financial losses starting in the late 1990s, leading to a series of mergers and acquisitions that resulted in considerable consolidation in the managed care industry. By 2001, the ten largest HMOs accounted for two-thirds of all HMO enrollment nationally. In 2009, a study by the AMA found that in twenty-four states, two managed care companies controlled 70 percent or more of the health insurance market within the state. In 54 percent of large metropolitan areas, a single health insurance company had a market share of 50 percent or more (American Medical Association 2010).

The pattern of mergers has continued, as reported in 2015 in the *New York Times*, in an article titled "Health Insurers Seeking Mergers Play Down Antitrust Concerns" (Pear 2015). As reported in the *Times*, the private managed care company Aetna announced plans to acquire its competitor Humana, at about the same time that two competing managed care companies, Anthem and Cigna, also announced plans to merge. If these mergers were completed, it was reported that the two merged companies that resulted would control nearly half of the commercial market for health insurance (Abelson 2015). As reported in the story, in testimony before the Senate Judiciary Committee, "Mark T. Bertolini, the chief executive of Aetna, and Joseph R. Swedish, the chief executive of Anthem, said the transactions would improve care and cut costs for consumers." The story also quotes Senator Richard Blumenthal, Democrat of Connecticut, who expressed serious reservations about further consolidation in the managed care market: "I am deeply concerned about these mergers because of the potential impact on competition and the concentration of power in fewer hands."

Responding to these proposed mergers, Cutler (2015b) suggested that "if these mergers go through, the 'big 5' health insurers will be down to the 'big 3'" (p. 1329). He notes that the insurers argue they need this type of consolidation in order to compete effectively with the growing number of vertically integrated physician/hospital systems. As described in chapter 4, there is an emerging pattern of these integrated delivery systems charging higher prices without corresponding reductions in the volume of care. Cutler argues that we need to be fully aware of the implications of these issues. "What we are witnessing is nothing less than a battle for control of medical care itself, driven by spiraling costs and the belief that we are not getting our money's worth in a sector representing close to 20% of the economy. Will it be a system overseen by physicians, by insurers, or by organizations that dispense with them both?" (p. 1330).

We should acknowledge, however, that concern about growing market consolidation is not confined to the for-profit sector. In 1994, two of the largest and most influential nonprofit hospitals in Massachusetts—Massachusetts General Hospital and Brigham and Women's Hospital—and the physician groups associated with them collaborated to form Partners HealthCare, described on its website as "a not-for-profit health care system that is committed to patient care, research, teaching, and service to the community" (Partners HealthCare 2015). By 2015, the organization had expanded to include fifteen hospitals, twenty outpatient health centers, and several specialty facilities. When Partners announced plans to add three additional clinical sites to its network, a county Superior Court ruled that the merger would have been anticompetitive and blocked it from occurring. Responding to the court's ruling, Herzlinger et al. (2015) commented that the proposed merger "could have squashed opportunities for innovation. . . . We believe it is not enough to stop dominant hospital systems from acquiring more power. Policies must encourage innovative entrants" (p. 1288).

THE QUALITY OF CARE IN FOR-PROFIT AND NONPROFIT MANAGED CARE PLANS

Much of the public debate about for-profit managed care plans centered on the issue of quality of care. The public perception was that for-profit plans offered lower-quality care as a result of efforts to maintain a low MLR. In response, supporters argued that for-profit plans were more responsive to competitive pressures in the market and were able to provide better care at a lower cost.

A series of studies was published in major journals, addressing this issue. I describe three of them, covering the following questions:

1. How do for-profit and nonprofit plans compare on the quality-of-care measures included in the HEDIS scale?
2. Do for-profit plans provide the same quality care to poor children on Medicaid as they do to children with private insurance?
3. Do for-profit plans respond to financial incentives by restricting access to higher-cost procedures?

Quality of Care on the HEDIS Scale

In 1991, a private consortium of large employers, health care corporations, and private foundations established the National Committee for Quality Assurance (NCQA).

The NCQA's job was to create a reliable measure of the quality of care that could be used to compare health plans and medical groups. The NCQA developed and disseminated the Health Plan Employer Data and Information Set, commonly referred to by its acronym, HEDIS. Subsequently renamed the Healthcare Effectiveness Data and Information Set, HEDIS does not measure health outcomes, such as death rates or complication rates. Rather, it measures how often health plans follow well-established guidelines for the prevention or treatment of certain conditions (National Committee for Quality Assurance 2015a). Examples of items included in HEDIS are rates of immunization for children, frequency of Pap smears and mammograms as cancer screening in women, and the extent that the recommended treatment schedule is followed for patients with diabetes. These quality measures all pertain to the process with which care is provided. While process measures such as these reflect the quality of health care, they measure only one aspect of quality and may need to be combined with other aspects (e.g., health outcomes, patient satisfaction) to give a full picture of quality. Nevertheless, HEDIS has come to be seen as an important means of comparing health plan quality. Accordingly, the NCQA gathers HEDIS scores from a variety of health plans and managed care organizations nationally.

In 1999, Himmelstein et al. published a major study that compared average HEDIS scores for 248 for-profit and 81 nonprofit HMOs. Combined, these 329 HMOs represented 56 percent of the total HMO enrollment in the country. Using data from 1996, they compared the plans on fourteen quality-of-care measures included in HEDIS. They found statistically significant differences in thirteen of the fourteen measures; in each case, for-profit HMOs scored lower than nonprofit HMOs.

Quality of Care for Poor Children in For-Profit Managed Care Organizations

Thompson et al. (2003) also used HEDIS indicators to compare the quality of care provided to poor children enrolled in one of eighty-one private, for-profit managed health plans. Each of these plans covered both poor children enrolled through a Medicaid managed care contract and nonpoor children covered by their parents' private health insurance. The question the authors asked was, "Do poor children receive the same quality of care as nonpoor children enrolled in the same plan?" They found that poor children, despite being in the same health plan, had lower HEDIS scores for the following indicators: immunization rates, frequency of visits for well children and adolescents, and frequency of prenatal care for mothers. They also found significantly lower rates of tonsillectomy and myringotomy (inserting tubes into the ear drums for chronic fluid in the middle ear) for the poor children, although subsequent research has questioned the effectiveness of these procedures. The authors noted that a few of the plans maintained the same quality for their poor and nonpoor children, and they acknowledged that socioeconomic forces affecting poor children (e.g., problems with transportation to scheduled visits) may be out of the health plan's control. Nevertheless, the authors were able to conclude that "most commercial plans do not deliver high-quality care on a number of performance indicators for children enrolled in Medicaid."

ACCESS TO HIGHER-COST PROCEDURES FOR MEDICARE BENEFICIARIES

Recall from chapter 6 that several million Medicare beneficiaries have voluntarily enrolled in managed care plans as an alternative to traditional Medicare. These plans receive a yearly capitation payment from Medicare and must provide all necessary care to enrolled patients. The question arises as to whether for-profit managed care plans will define "necessary" in a more restrictive way than nonprofit plans, especially when it comes to using high-cost procedures such as cardiac catheterization or the insertion of artificial knee or hip joints. Schneider, Zaslavsky, and Epstein (2004) compared the rates at which twelve high-cost procedures were used for enrolled Medicare beneficiaries. Using data from 1997 on more than 3.7 million beneficiaries enrolled in one of 254 health plans, they compared procedure rates in for-profit and nonprofit plans. They tested the common assertion that for-profit plans, in an effort to hold down costs, will be more restrictive in the access they provide to these procedures.

After taking into account factors such as patients' age, income, education, and geographic region, they found that the for-profit plans had higher utilization rates for two of the twelve procedures measured; for the remaining ten, there were no differences between the for-profit and the nonprofit plans. The authors concluded that "contrary to our expectations about the likely effects of financial incentives, the rates of use of high-cost operative procedures were not lower among beneficiaries enrolled in for-profit health plans than among those enrolled in not-for-profit health plans" (p. 143).

CONCEPT 9.3

There is evidence that for-profit managed care organizations provide lower-quality care than nonprofit organizations, although the evidence is not consistent across all studies.

THE MOVEMENT TOWARD FOR-PROFIT HOSPITAL OWNERSHIP

A move to for-profit ownership of hospitals has also taken place in the United States, in parallel with the movement to for-profit managed care, but it has not been nearly as extensive as in the case of managed care. Hospitals have traditionally been run on a nonprofit basis in the United States. After the enactment of Medicare and Medicaid, many investors saw the potential of operating hospitals as money-making businesses. Beginning in the 1970s, investor-owned, for-profit corporations began to purchase hospitals and other types of institutional care facilities. Using capital obtained through the sale of stock, corporations took over formerly nonprofit hospitals and began to run them on a for-profit basis. Firms such as American Medical International and National Medical Enterprises developed chains of hospitals throughout the country, all operated as for-profit entities.

This trend continued into the 1990s, supported by the stock market boom. In the 1990s, newer firms such as the Hospital Corporation of America (later Columbia HCA) rapidly expanded their network of for-profit hospitals by using sales of new stock in the booming stock market to acquire community hospitals that were struggling with the problems of high costs and low occupancy described in chapter 4. For-profit hospital chains, however, never developed the market penetration that for-profit HMOs did. In 1992, only 11 percent of community hospital beds were in for-profit hospitals; by 2003, that number was 14 percent (data from Kaiser Family Foundation website).

A number of eyebrows were raised in the medical community over the increasing role of for-profit corporations in hospital ownership and operation. In addition to the general concerns about for-profit care, cited previously, there were also concerns about

- the goals and policies that for-profit hospitals would adopt (Would for-profit hospitals ignore local community needs and exploit employees?), and
- the effects on medical research and education (Would for-profit hospitals benefit from publicly financed research and educational programs without contributing to them?).

In 1986, the Institute of Medicine, a branch of the federal National Academy of Sciences, looked into the effect of for-profit care in hospitals and issued a report (Gray 1986). The report found that, when compared to traditional nonprofit hospitals, for-profit hospitals

- are slightly *less* efficient in producing a given service or procedure,
- charge somewhat more for comparable services,
- provide less uncompensated care to low-income patients, and
- have been able to raise capital for expansion more easily than nonprofit hospitals (for-profit hospitals raise capital through issuing stock; nonprofit hospitals raise capital by borrowing it).

The report found no data available at that time to compare the quality of the care at for-profit and nonprofit hospitals. It did raise the question of whether for-profit hospitals "skim" the patient population (i.e., treat only those patients with good insurance who can pay for their care, thus leaving the unprofitable patients for the nonprofit hospitals).

The report identified some arguments in favor of for-profit hospitals:

- For-profit hospital systems had the potential to provide care more efficiently if managed well; financial incentives could be structured to support efficient care.
- Competition among for-profit and nonprofit hospitals would, in theory, weed out inefficient systems of care, thus reducing overall costs.

Another study comparing for-profit with nonprofit hospitals was published in 1999 (Silverman et al. 1999). Rather than looking at quality per se, the study looked at the effect of for-profit hospitals on the rate of increase in spending to provide hospital care to Medicare beneficiaries. Also, rather than comparing individual hospitals, the study compared spending among more than three thousand "hospital service areas," which reflect local markets for hospital services. The study compared Medicare's average per capita spending on hospital care in 1989 with spending in 1995. After controlling for a number of possibly confounding characteristics, the study found that the lowest increase in per capita spending for hospital care was in those markets that remained predominantly nonprofit over the six-year study period. The largest increase in spending was found in those regions that had converted (through corporate acquisition) from predominantly nonprofit to predominantly for-profit. Regions that had remained consistently for-profit saw increases in spending that were slightly lower than those of the regions that converted to for-profit status but substantially higher than those of the nonprofit regions. Coupled with the findings from the Institute of Medicine's study, these results suggest that, rather than reducing hospital costs, for-profit hospitals increase costs compared to nonprofit hospitals, without corresponding increases in quality or improvements in outcome. As stated by the authors of the 1999 study, "Our findings are consistent with the possibility that for-profit hospital ownership itself contributes to higher per capita costs for the Medicare populations served by these hospitals" (p. 425).

Joynt et al. (2014) evaluated changes in outcomes for 237 hospitals that switched from nonprofit to for-profit status between 2003 and 2010, comparing them to a matched set of 631 hospitals that maintained their nonprofit status. Consistent with the aforementioned data, they found that the hospitals that switched to for-profit had significant improvements in their financial performance, with no evidence of differences in their quality metrics. Part of the way these hospitals improved their financial performance was by increasing the amount they charge for care. Bai and Anderson (2015) looked at the 50 hospitals nationally that had the highest ratio of charges for care to the cost of actually providing that care. Forty-nine of the 50 hospitals with the

---

CONCEPT 9.4

The rise in for-profit ownership of hospitals in the United States has been associated with increases in hospital costs without evidence of concomitant increases in the quality of care or improvements in health outcomes.

highest charge-to-cost ratios were for-profit. Of these, 46 were owned by national or regional chains of for-profit hospitals, 25 of which were owned by a single for-profit system. Of interest, they also found that 20 of the 50 hospitals with the highest charge ratios (40%) were located in Florida.

Physicians and For-Profit Care

Until now, this chapter has addressed the implications of the increasing prevalence of for-profit medical care in hospitals, HMOs, and managed care organizations. Physicians have been some of the loudest critics of the intrusion of these for-profit entities into what had previously been a system of health care centered on nonprofit organizations. What, though, was the record of physicians themselves during the era of the expansion of for-profit care? Were they immune from the financial incentives and opportunities available in this new world of medical care?

Sociologist Talcott Parsons was quite explicit regarding his views of how physicians should behave in the context of the profit motive: "The medical man is expected to place the welfare of the patient above his own self-interest, financial or otherwise. . . . Thus the physician is both debarred from a variety of immediate opportunities for financial gain which are open to the businessman, and is positively enjoined to promote the welfare of his patients" (Parsons 1951, p. 472).

Parsons has been criticized for being overly idealistic in his view of how physicians are expected to behave. After all, the fee-for-service system of paying for medical care has built into it a financial incentive to provide more care than may be necessary. Recall also from chapter 5 that even in the Kaiser Permanente system, the health plan and hospitals are organized on a nonprofit basis, but the Permanente Medical Group, representing the physicians within the system, is a for-profit corporation. Nonetheless, Parsons echoes the common perception that physicians, as part of their privileged position in society, face higher ethical standards regarding financial self-interest than those outside the profession who are engaged in business.

In considering this issue, I will not look at physicians who have chosen to enter directly into businesses related to health care. A number of physicians have become entrepreneurs and have been involved in the creation or management of HMOs, physician practice management companies, or biotech firms. These business activities do not relate concurrently to the practice of medicine, and so they should be judged by the ethical standards of business rather than medicine. There are a number of contexts, however, in which practicing physicians have become involved in the ownership or management of for-profit enterprises that offer care to the physicians' own patients. These physicians are in the somewhat tenuous dual role of self-interested businessperson and (presumably) disinterested physician. I examine two such for-profit practice entities that have become quite common: kidney dialysis centers and specialty hospitals.

For-Profit Kidney Dialysis Centers

As described in chapter 6, the federal Medicare program covers patients who experience kidney failure, regardless of age. The treatment of kidney failure involves regular kidney dialysis, using a machine to do the work of cleansing the blood otherwise done by the kidneys. To survive, patients with kidney failure must undergo dialysis several times per week. Eventually, some of these patients will receive a kidney transplant, which, if successful, means that the patient no longer needs dialysis.

Patients with kidney failure come under the regular care of nephrologists—physicians specially trained in the treatment of kidney diseases. The nephrologist will refer the patient to a dialysis treatment center and will manage the patient's condition on an ongoing basis. Medicare will pay both for the care provided by the nephrologist and for the care provided by the dialysis center. Some dialysis centers are operated on a nonprofit basis by hospitals or other organizations, and some are operated on a for-profit basis with private ownership. This situation has created the opportunity for some nephrologists to become involved both in the care of the patient and in the ownership or management of the dialysis center. Some have questioned the ethics of such dual roles for physicians (see, e.g., Bennett 2004) and also have suggested that for-profit centers may not provide high-quality care for their patients. Two major studies have addressed this issue.

Garg et al. (1999) followed more than 3,500 kidney patients for between three and six years, comparing the results of care received in for-profit dialysis centers with that received in nonprofit centers. After adjusting for patients' socioeconomic, demographic, and clinical circumstances, they were able to conclude two things:

1. Patients treated at for-profit dialysis centers had a higher death rate than patients treated at nonprofit centers.
2. Patients treated at for-profit dialysis centers were referred less often than patients treated at nonprofit centers for kidney transplantation as an alternative to dialysis.

In an editorial accompanying this study, Norman Levinsky (1999) concluded that "the increased mortality among patients treated at for-profit facilities, reported by Garg et al., and the lower quality of care in such facilities, reported by other investigators, suggest that, faced with the same financial pressures, for-profit facilities respond differently from not-for-profit facilities—to the detriment of patient care" (p. 1692).

Devereaux et al. (2002) reviewed the available literature comparing death rates in for-profit and nonprofit dialysis centers. They were able to identify eight separate studies, using data spanning the period 1973–97 and involving more than 500,000 patients.

These authors concluded that "hemodialysis care in private not-for-profit centers is associated with a lower risk of mortality compared with care in private for-profit centers" (p. 2449).

Private, For-Profit Specialty Hospitals

As an editorial in the journal *Circulation* stated: "There is a suggestion in health care today that the nonprofit acute-care hospital has outlived its usefulness—that its days are numbered. Such hospitals are, in fact, anachronisms—a relic of another era. Their replacement? New, single-specialty, investor-owned hospitals or surgery centers, many of which are at least in part owned by physicians who can refer their own patients to these facilities" (Hupfeld 2004, p. 2379). These comments speak to a relatively new phenomenon in US health care. Historically, the general hospital was the source of most medical care that could not be provided in physicians' offices. As surgical equipment and patient monitoring became more advanced, a number of surgical procedures previously performed only in a hospital could safely be done in outpatient "surgicenters"—freestanding operating rooms and recovery rooms, often affiliated with local physicians' groups.

> **CONCEPT 9.5**
>
> Compared to treatment in nonprofit kidney dialysis centers, the treatment of patients with kidney failure in for-profit dialysis centers is associated with higher death rates and lower rates of referral for kidney transplantation. These for-profit centers also present potential ethical conflicts for physicians involved in their ownership or management.

In the early 1990s, as part of the general expansion of for-profit organizations, a number of investors—physicians among them—realized that certain aspects of hospital care were generally more profitable than others. While it might be relatively unprofitable to operate a labor and delivery ward or an emergency room, certain surgical procedures had relatively high rates of payment. For the general hospital, the low-profit centers and the high-profit centers balance each other out. What, though, if a hospital could focus on only those types of care with high reimbursement rates and simply not offer the less profitable types of care? These types of specialized hospitals had the potential of generating substantial profit for the owners.

Physicians in several areas of the country began to invest in these "specialty hospitals." Principal among them were orthopedic hospitals and cardiac care hospitals. Typically, physicians whose practice included the type of specialized care offered in the hospital would team up with private investors to build the specialty hospital. Physicians would maintain their position on the staff of the general hospital, but now they could choose to refer patients either to the general hospital (in which they had no financial interest) or to the specialty hospital (in which they maintained a financial interest). It should be apparent that such arrangements were disadvantageous from the perspective of the general hospital, and so general hospitals usually opposed them.

Specialty hospitals were advantageous to their physician owners in a number of ways. As licensed hospitals, they often received higher reimbursement rates from Medicare and other payers than surgicenters did for comparable care. In addition, the physician could select which patients to refer to the general hospital and which to refer to the specialty hospital, creating the opportunity to have the sicker (and thus more costly) patients treated in the general hospital and the less sick (and thus less costly) patients treated in the specialty hospital. A study by Horwitz (2005) confirmed that for-profit hospitals such as specialty hospitals are more likely than nonprofit or government hospitals to provide relatively profitable types of services.

Between 1997 and 2003, the number of specialty hospitals in the country went from 31 to 113. (During this same period, the number of surgicenters went from 2,462 to 3,735.) By 2003, 14 percent of general hospitals were operated on a for-profit basis, while more than 90 percent of specialty hospitals were operated on a for-profit basis (Iglehart 2005).

Cram, Rosenthal, and Vaughan-Sarrazin (2005) reported a study of nearly 70,000 patients who received cardiac revascularization surgery (unblocking clogged arteries to the heart) between 2000 and 2001 at either a general hospital or a cardiac specialty hospital. They were able to identify several differences between the two types of hospital:

- Specialty hospitals treated patients who tended to be less severely ill than patients in general hospitals.
- Specialty hospitals treated patients who tended to come from higher-income neighborhoods than patients in general hospitals.
- Specialty hospitals tended to have a higher volume of treatment than general hospitals. (It could not be determined from this study if the higher volume of treatment was because of a larger patient population served by the specialty hospitals or a higher rate of treatment within the same patient population compared with that served by general hospitals.)
- Specialty hospitals reported lower unadjusted mortality rates than general hospitals; however, after adjusting for patients' severity of illness and the procedural volume at the hospital, the mortality rates did not differ.

Concerns such as these led Congress in 2003 to clamp a moratorium on new specialty hospitals until the issue could be studied in more depth. After hearing the reports from these preliminary studies, the Centers for Medicare and Medicaid Services acted in June 2005 to extend that moratorium.

CONCEPT 9.6

The number of specialty hospitals in the United States increased from 31 in 1997 to 113 in 2003; more than 90 percent of these hospitals operated on a for-profit basis. Concerns about selective referral of patients and potential physician conflict of interest led Congress in 2003 to impose a moratorium on the opening of new specialty hospitals.

THE "NEW" TYPE OF MEDICAL PRACTICE:
THE PHYSICIAN CONCIERGE

In July 2005, an article appeared in the *New York Times* describing a physician who of-fered patients an exemplary level of service—longer appointments, no waiting, access to the doctor's cell phone number. Rather than reporting a resurgence in patient-centered medical care and the resurrection of Marcus Welby, M.D., this story was about a *new* type of medical practice that was taking root in many parts of the country—concierge medicine (Zipkin 2005). The physicians in these types of stories were entrepreneurs who believe that well-to-do patients will pay a cash premium for a superior level of service. Frustrated with the low reimbursement and high level of hassle offered by managed care companies, an increasing number of physicians are offering care only to patients willing to pay an enrollment fee, typically several thousand dollars per year, to be included in their practice. For this fee, the patient will be assured of in-creased personal service. The enrollment fee does not pay for that service itself, however—it simply provides the patient access to it. The patient must still pay the physician's full charge for treatment and must not expect the physician to accept the patient's health insurance. While the physician's staff will assist the patient in filing a claim for reimbursement from the insurance company, payment of the physician's charge is solely the patient's responsibility.

There are two opposing views of this new level of service provided by physicians. (A 2005 editorial by Anthony DeMaria, editor-in-chief of the *Journal of the American College of Cardiology*, describes these two sides very well.) Some argue that concierge medicine is the only way to guarantee the level of quality patients deserve. In a local newspaper story, a concierge doctor in my home community touted concierge prac-tice as creating freedom for her and her patients from time constraints and regula-tions imposed by HMOs. (She also drove a Jaguar convertible.)

Others point to the obvious inequity inherent to concierge practice, as shown in a cartoon from the *New Yorker* (figure 9.1). Only those patients who can afford the en-rollment fee and the physician's charges for care—often substantially higher than charges approved by insurance companies—will receive the level of care offered by the physician concierge. Those without that level of income or wealth must continue to cope with the time constraints and regulations cited by concierge physicians as the reason they got out of mainstream medicine.

THE RETAIL CLINIC: MEDICAL CARE AT A "BIG BOX" STORE

In about 2000, a new type of medical care resource began to become available—the retail clinic. These clinics are typically located within a "big box" retail store, such as a Wal-Mart or a large commercial pharmacy such as Walgreens or CVS. Typically

*"My fees are quite high, and yet you say you have little money.
I think I'm seeing a conflict of interest here."*

FIGURE 9.1. The downside of concierge medical practice. *Source:* © The New Yorker Collection 1989 Leo Cullum from cartoonbank.com. All rights reserved.

operated either by a for-profit enterprise that contracts with the larger store for clinic space or by the store itself, the clinics are typically available during the hours the store is open, usually including evenings and weekends. The clinic is usually staffed by a nurse practitioner and will provide care only for a specified list of conditions. About 90 percent of the care at these clinics is for ten common problems, such as upper respiratory infections, ear infections, urinary tract infections, or immunizations and other preventive care services (Mehrotra et al. 2010). Most of these clinics accept Medicare or other private insurance. When a patient presents to a retail clinic with a more serious problem, the nurse practitioner will refer the patient either to a physician's office or to an emergency room.

The concept behind retail clinics is making medical care for routine problems rapidly and conveniently available, at a lower price than usually charged by a physician's office. By 2008, there were nearly one thousand retail clinics in operation. A study of the care provided by these clinics for three common problems (ear infection, sore throat, or urinary tract infection) found the quality of the care provided by the clinics to be comparable to care provided in a physician's office, but at a lower cost (Mehrotra et al. 2009).

Based on the early success of these clinics, their corporate owners elected to invest extensively in their expansion. By 2015, there were more than 1,900 clinics in operation, with hundreds more in the planning stages. As described by Chang et al. (2015), "The industry is highly centralized; four operators—CVS, Walgreens, Kroger, and Target—account for more than 85% of the market" (p. 383). Chang goes on to advise that "a growing body of evidence suggests that retail clinics provide a quality of care that is equal to or higher than that of other ambulatory care sites. . . . The vast majority of retail-clinic users (90%) report being satisfied with their care" (p. 384). In an article published concurrently with the article by Chang et al., Iglehart (2015) acknowledged the data supporting the quality of care provided by retail clinics but cautions: "Nevertheless, primary care physician groups have raised concerns about both the care at these clinics and their potential for disrupting patients' continuity of care" (p. 301). It remains to be seen, especially in light of growing concerns about the availability of primary care services following ACA enactment, to what extent these clinics will become a central part of our health care delivery system.

THE AFFORDABLE CARE ACT AND FOR-PROFIT HEALTH CARE

In the thirty years leading up to the passage of ACA, health care in the United States underwent a substantial shift, from a system based primarily on provision of care in a nonprofit context to a system with a major role played by for-profit hospitals, clinics, HMOs, and managed care plans. Proponents of this shift argue that for-profit organizations are better able to react to the competitive environment of the health care market and are able to improve the efficiency and quality of care. Opponents argue that for-profit organizations reduce the quality of care by constraining access to care in an effort to maximize profits. There is evidence that these concerns may be justified.

Physicians have played a substantial role in the expansion of for-profit care. Whether in the creation of specialty hospitals, the expansion of specialized treatment centers, or the founding of concierge practices, a number of physicians have felt both comfortable and justified in combining the role of physician and entrepreneur.

Perceptions from the 1950s of the medical profession and the health care system always placing the interests of the patient first, immune from financial self-interest or the profit motive, have proven to be outdated in many cases. Instead, as described by Arnold Relman, former editor of the *New England Journal of Medicine*, health care in America has been "largely shaped by the entry and growth of innumerable private investor-owned businesses that sell health insurance and deliver medical care with a primary concern for the maximization of their income" (Relman 2007, p. 2668). Relman goes on to caution that "the continued privatization of health care and the continued prevalence and intrusion of market forces in the practice of medicine will not only bankrupt the health care system, but also will inevitably undermine the ethical foundations of medical practice and dissolve the moral precepts that have historically defined the medical profession" (p. 2669).

As health care in the United States enters an age of increasing scarcity of resources, and as our society reexamines its fundamental assumptions about the appropriate role and limits of health care, serious consideration has been given to defining the core ethical and legal principles governing the role of the profit motive in the provision of care. Rather than moving to exclude for-profit care, however, ACA incorporates many of the aspects of health care financing and delivery that have emerged out of the historical shift to a system with a larger role for for-profit organizations.

Consider, for example, the role of utilization review in managing care delivery. As described earlier, initial public reaction was overwhelmingly negative to the concept that someone would be following the testing and follow-up care recommended by physicians. Yet, as we learn more about the overutilization of certain tests and procedures by some physicians, it becomes essential to build in a system to monitor the value of care provided by physicians individually or collectively, whether from a comparative-effectiveness or cost-effectiveness perspective. The physician practice profiles and payment incentives originally introduced by for-profit managed care companies have evolved into the types of systems included in ACA for monitoring, measuring, and paying physicians based on the value of the care they provide rather than the volume of that care. These new systems are central to the development of accountable care organizations (ACO) and their emphasis on developing systems of paying for value. The funds saved in this way will be shared within the ACO while also reducing the overall cost of care without decreasing quality.

ACA has also built its system of state health benefit exchanges based on the concept of market competition. Each exchange is expected to have a minimum of one nonprofit health insurance provider competing directly with one or more for-profit providers. Consumers are able to compare competing plans directly, selecting the one that provides optimal value. In order to remain competitive, for-profit providers will need to keep their prices and the quality of the care they offer comparable to those offered by the nonprofit providers.

The increased role of for-profit hospital ownership is also taken into account in ACA, with continued tax advantages provided to nonprofit hospitals, which enables them to compete more effectively with their for-profit counterparts. Historically, for-profit hospitals have been taxed on their net earnings while nonprofit hospitals have not. Rosenbaum et al. (2015) reported that in 2011, the overall value of this tax exemption provided to nonprofit hospitals was estimated to be $24.6 billion.

Rather than paying taxes on their earnings, nonprofit hospitals have been under a legal obligation to use a defined fraction of their overall earnings to provide care without compensation to segments of the community identified as the "medically indigent" and therefore unable to afford to pay for care provided. Hospitals can also qualify for their tax exemption by investing portions of their income in "community health improvement" programs designed to improve overall health of the community they serve. Rosenbaum found that in 2011, nonprofit hospitals provided a range of community benefits valued at $62 billion. ACA continues the program of tax exemption, with the added expectation that nonprofit hospitals invest more extensively in community health improvement initiatives. As described by Rosenbaum et al. (2015), ACA now "require[s] that beginning in 2012, tax-exempt hospital facilities . . . undertake a triennial community health needs assessment developed with community and public health input and establish annual implementation strategies that identify the community health needs that will be addressed" (p. 1226).

One of the most important provisions in ACA that pertains to for-profit insurers is new federal regulation of the medical loss ratio (MLR). As described earlier, the MLR is the percentage of funds received by a managed care company in premiums that is paid out for the provision of health care to covered patients. Historically, it has been typical for managed care companies to maintain MLRs in the range of 75 to 85 percent. This would imply that 15 to 25 percent of the premium income received by the company would go for administrative costs unrelated to the provision of care and for shareholder profit. ACA divides for-profit insurers into two groups: those providing coverage in the market for large employee groups and those providing coverage for individuals and small employee groups. ACA established a minimum MLR of 80 percent for plans in the small group market and 85 percent for plans in the market for large groups. Beginning in 2011, any plan with an MLR that fell below this mandated level is required to provide a rebate to its enrollees to make up the difference.

Expenses that can be applied in calculating the MLR include direct payment for medical claims and funds spent on improving the quality of care provided. All other administrative expenses, such as marketing, administrative overhead, and corporate profit, are not included. Those insurance providers with a MLR lower than the permitted amount will have two choices: reduce administrative expenses or pay the mandated rebates, thus reducing corporate profit.

McCue and Hall (2015) have followed the impact of the MLR requirements since its establishment in 2011. In 2012, the first year insurers were required to make rebate payments, insurers made a total of $1.1 billion in payments. Building on this experience, by 2014, the annual rebates had been reduced to $325 million. The principal way insurers were able to reduce their rebate payments was by reducing administrative expenses. McCue and Hall estimate that over the first three years the MLR regulations were in effect (2011–2013), insurers collectively reduced their overhead expenses by more than $3 billion. Absent the regulations included in ACA, consumers would have been paying this amount through their premiums. Thus, by limiting the allowable MLR, consumers have received nearly $2 billion in direct rebates while also saving $3 billion in premium reductions over what they would have paid absent ACA.

In addition to regulating MLRs, ACA imposed a new fee that large health insurance companies were required to pay, beginning in 2014, based on the size of their market share. Nonprofit managed care or insurance plans pay a reduced fee. In 2014, these fees were expected to bring in approximately $8 billion in new revenue, rising to more than $14 billion in 2018.

ACA also requires health plans to report a range of new data and calls for health plans to be certified by the federal or state government in order to be eligible to participate in the health benefit exchanges established by ACA. As a response to public outcry over extraordinarily large increases in annual premiums reported by some insurers in the weeks leading up to its passage, ACA also established a process by which annual increases in health plan premiums are subject to federal or state review, with plans required to provide data justifying the increases.

One additional aspect of ACA is important to mention at this point. Under ACA, no new physician-owned hospitals are permitted, and existing physician-owned hospitals are not allowed to expand, except under strict conditions. It remains to be seen how and to what extent these new regulations will affect the future role of for-profit, physician-owned hospitals and similar care facilities in our health care system.

Pharmaceutical Policy and the Rising Cost of Prescription Drugs

The way we organize, pay for, and deliver pharmaceutical products to patients has become one of the central issues of US health policy. It is a core issue for Medicare, with the initiation in 2006 of the Medicare prescription drug benefit. It remains a contentious issue for Medicaid, as state governments make difficult decisions about trade-offs between rising costs and maintaining access to newer pharmaceutical products. Managed care organizations, both for-profit and nonprofit, struggle to stay within their budgets as a continuing stream of newer and very expensive products becomes available. In addition, discussions about pharmaceutical policy go directly to the heart of the debate over the role of for-profit corporations in US health care. Understanding the history, structure, and problems of the pharmaceutical sector of our health care system will increasingly be a fundamental part of the knowledge base required of physicians, health care administrators, and health policy makers.

THE ORIGINS OF THE PHARMACEUTICAL INDUSTRY

The modern pharmaceutical industry in the United States has its origins in the Pure Food and Drug Act, passed by Congress in 1906. Before that time, there was little regulation of the manufacturing or marketing of drugs and other remedies. There was, however, widespread popular concern about the safety of many of the remedies offered to doctors and patients—so-called patent medicines. As mandated by the act, the federal government established a mechanism to test pharmaceutical products through its Bureau of Chemistry. In close collaboration with the bureau, the American Medical Association (AMA) established its own Council on Pharmacy and Chemistry. At that time, the AMA had extensive influence with the editors and publishers of medical journals, which acted as the chief source of information about new drugs for practicing physicians. The AMA enforced a policy that permitted only those drugs that had been submitted for analysis and subsequently approved by the Council to be advertised to physicians in medical journals. As a key part of its policy, the AMA's Council would not approve any drug that was advertised by its manufacturer directly to the public. (This policy prohibiting the advertisement of prescription drugs directly to consumers was to have a continuing effect until it was altered by the federal government in 1997.)

Federal regulation of the pharmaceutical industry was strengthened in 1938, following a national scandal in which more than one hundred people died from taking a drug that was marketed for use in children and contained toxic materials. After Franklin Roosevelt signed the Food, Drug, and Cosmetic Act, the federal government required all new drugs coming to the market to be tested for safety before being made available for prescription by physicians. The act also strengthened the role of the Bureau of Chemistry, which had changed its name to the US Food and Drug Administration (FDA). The FDA was charged with conducting the premarket testing for drug safety required by the act.

The FDA's role was expanded again in 1962 by the Kefauver-Harris Amendments, passed by Congress following a series of widely publicized hearings conducted by Senator Estes Kefauver (D-Tennessee). Manufacturers of new pharmaceutical products were required by the new law to provide the FDA with scientific proof of a new product's safety *and efficacy*. Before 1962, there was no requirement for scientific evidence that a drug worked—only that it did not cause harm.

At the time of the Kefauver hearings in 1962, relatively few pharmaceutical products were on the market, compared to the vast pharmacopoeia available to physicians today. Penicillin had been discovered only twenty years earlier, and many of the drugs used now for the treatment of common conditions such as diabetes, high blood pressure, and heart disease had yet to be identified. To encourage the development of new pharmaceutical products, Congress provided extensive patent protection to the developer of a new drug. Once a pharmaceutical company identified a new drug and a patent was granted, no other company was allowed to manufacture or sell that drug for a period of seventeen years. (The period of patent protection was extended to twenty years in 1995.) This does not mean that a manufacturer will be able to sell the drug exclusively for that long, as the time required to obtain FDA approval (often several years) is part of this period. It was typical for a manufacturer who developed and received approval for a new drug, however, to be able

CONCEPT 10.1

The federal government requires manufacturers of new pharmaceutical products to provide evidence of their safety and efficacy. It also grants the manufacturer patent protection for successful new products that allows for substantial economic gain in return for the manufacturer's investment in developing the products.

to sell the drug for ten years or more without any competition from other manufacturers. This period of patent protection created a government-sanctioned monopoly on the sale of that drug. As one might imagine, holding a protected monopoly on an important new drug conveys a tremendous economic advantage to the manufacturer, in that the manufacturer is permitted to charge whatever the market will bear for that new drug. A company that is able to bring a new drug to market under patent protection stands to make a tremendous profit. The reasoning behind this protection is that the economic gains to be realized from successful new drugs will provide a powerful incentive for manufacturers to invest the years of work and millions of dollars required to obtain marketing approval.

THE RISING COST OF PRESCRIPTION DRUGS

Most of the new pharmaceutical products approved by the FDA are available only by prescription from a licensed physician or other health care provider. Some new products are available for sale "over the counter" (OTC)—directly to patients without a prescription—but these play a lesser role in pharmaceutical policy. At the time of the Kefauver hearings in the 1960s, the relatively small number of drugs available and their relatively modest cost meant that the cost of prescription drugs was not a major national policy concern. When Medicare was passed in 1965, Congress did not feel it was necessary to include coverage for prescription drugs in the program.

As the health care system began to experience rapidly increasing costs in the 1970s, the cost of prescription drugs also began to rise. Improved scientific and technical capabilities contributed to an increasing supply of new drugs coming to market. By 1980, prescription drugs accounted for 4.9 percent of all health care expenditures nationally (data from US Centers for Medicare and Medicaid Services website). By 1990, their share of national health expenditures had risen slightly to about 5.8 percent and remained there through 1995. Then, as shown in figure 10.1, the cost of prescription drugs began to grow rapidly. By 2003, they had risen to 10.0 percent of all health expenditures. Between 1993 and 2013, while overall national health expenditures increased 229 percent, *expenditures for prescription drugs increased 447 percent*. Most of the increase in the cost of prescription drugs occurred in the decade between 1993 and 2003. Between 2003 and 2013, the cost of prescription drugs either remained flat or declined slightly, accounting for 9.3 percent of national health expenditures in 2013. The federal government has predicted that through 2019, prescription drug costs will maintain a fairly constant share of overall health expenditures. However, the recent introduction of some highly effective yet *very expensive* new medications has raised questions about this projection. I discuss this issue later in this chapter in the section on new specialty drugs.

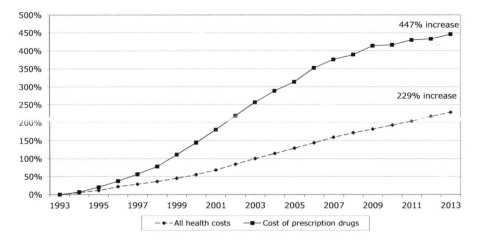

FIGURE 10.1. Increase in all health care costs and costs of prescription drugs, 1993–2013 (as a percentage of 1993 costs). *Source:* Data from US Centers for Medicare and Medicaid Services.

CONCEPT 10.2

Between 1993 and 2013, the overall cost of prescription drugs increased 447 percent, while the cost of health care in general increased 229 percent. The cost of prescription drugs is projected to remain at approximately 10 percent of national health expenditures through 2019.

The Kaiser Family Foundation (2004) analyzed federal data for the period 1997–2002 on the factors that contributed to the rapid increase in expenditures for prescription drugs during that time frame and concluded that

- 42 percent of the increase in expenditures was due to increases in the number of prescriptions issued,
- 25 percent of the increase was due to manufacturers' price increases for existing drugs, and
- 33 percent of the increase was due to shifting from a less expensive drug to a more expensive drug for the same illness.

It should not be surprising that this rapid increase in spending, much of it on newer drugs still under patent protection, was beneficial to pharmaceutical manufacturers. For every year in the period studied by the Kaiser Family Foundation, pharmaceutical manufacturers enjoyed the highest profit margin of any industry in the United States.

As might be expected, the increase in the cost of prescription drugs is not experienced equally by all population groups. For example, a federal study of outpatient prescription drug use found that, for those patients who filled at least one prescription in 2000, the average number of prescriptions filled by a person younger than 65 was 10.1, at an average cost per year of $485. For those 65 and older, the average number of prescriptions filled was 23.5, at an average cost of $1,102. If, instead of looking at the cost of the drugs irrespective of who paid for them, we look at how much the patient paid out of pocket, we find an average expenditure of $199 for those younger than 65 and of $623 for those 65 and over (Stagnitti 2004). This wide difference in out-of-pocket expenditures was due largely to the lack of coverage for prescription drugs under Medicare before 2006. The disparate impact on seniors of rising drug costs is discussed later in this chapter, as part of the discussion of the Medicare prescription drug benefit.

One way to make drugs more affordable might be to let patients who are given a prescription fill that prescription through a pharmacy in Canada. While the United States leaves the pricing of prescription drugs to the market, Canada has a federal policy of controlling drug prices. As a result, the price of prescription drugs is often substantially less in Canada. In many cases, the drugs in Canada are the same as those in the United States—same name, same manufacturer, sometimes even manufactured in the same plant. Canada has both a government review agency and drug review guidelines that are similar to those administered by the US FDA.

A growing number of people in the United States have become aware of the availability of cheaper prices in Canada for the same (or substantially similar) drugs in the United States. Because Canadian law permits pharmacists in Canada to fill a prescription written by a physician in the United States, it has become common for people in the United States to turn to Canadian pharmacies to fill their prescriptions. This has been done in person by crossing the border into Canada, by mail order, or over the Internet. Under the George W. Bush administration, however, the FDA declared this process to be illegal. The reason given was the threat to the patient's safety. Because the drugs have not been reviewed by the FDA, it was argued, their safety cannot be assured, and they therefore should be banned from the US market. Pharmaceutical manufacturers have voiced loud and enthusiastic support for this position. Other observers have questioned this reason for prohibiting drug reimportation from Canada, suggesting instead that the threat to pharmaceutical company profits is the real reason behind the ban. (See Zuger 2003b and Choudry and Detsky 2005 for a further discussion of these issues.)

THE CONTROVERSY SURROUNDING PRESCRIPTION DRUG COSTS AND PHARMACEUTICAL MANUFACTURERS

Dr. Marcia Angell is a former editor-in-chief of the *New England Journal of Medicine*, one of the most respected medical journals in the country. The journal has a history of publishing only the most significant and scientifically accurate articles. In her tenure as editor, Dr. Angell upheld this tradition.

Dr. Angell left her position at the journal, and in 2004 published a book titled *The Truth about Drug Companies: How They Deceive Us and What to Do About It*. In this book, she characterized the US pharmaceutical industry as "primarily a marketing machine to sell drugs of dubious benefit, [that] uses its wealth and power to co-opt every institution that might stand in its way, including the U.S. Congress, the Food and Drug Administration, academic medical centers, and the medical profession itself" (p. xviii).

By any standard, Dr. Angell's remarks offer a scathing indictment of the pharmaceutical industry. Yet Dr. Angell was not alone in her criticisms—a number of scholars and analysts have leveled harsh criticism at the pharmaceutical industry. The appropriate role of the pharmaceutical industry and the issue of controlling or reducing the price of drugs are hotly debated topics, in the press as well as in scholarly books and journals.

The debate over pharmaceutical policy seems to revolve around one fundamental issue: how valuable are the new drugs developed and marketed by pharmaceutical companies? The differing positions on this issue can be summarized as follows.

- *Position in support of pharmaceutical companies*
  One of the principal advances in medical care in recent years has been the availability of a wide array of new pharmaceutical products. From drugs for heart disease and cancer to vaccines, drugs for HIV, and drugs for Hepatitis C, medical care today has advanced substantially from where it was previously. The policies that support patent protection for new drugs have been crucial in providing the economic incentive to invest the vast sums required. Using data provided by ten large drug development companies, a study published in 2014 suggested that the average cost of developing a new drug and bringing it to market could be as high as $2.6 billion (Tufts Center for the Study of Drug Development 2014). If the government weakened that patent protection or adopted policies that reduce the price of drugs, pharmaceutical manufacturers could no longer afford to take the risk involved in developing new drugs, and our supply of new drugs would dry up in the future.

- *Position critical of pharmaceutical companies*
  The research done by pharmaceutical companies does not really result in new drugs. Most of their research is dedicated to finding a way to develop a drug that is similar in effect to a drug patented by a competing manufacturer but that is sufficiently different in chemical structure to qualify for a new patent under federal law. To boost the sales of their drug over a competing drug that does essentially the same thing, pharmaceutical companies spend billions of dollars for marketing and advertising. Many of these promotional activities—especially those targeting physicians—raise serious ethical concerns. In these times of health care scarcity, patients would be better served by selecting drugs based on value rather than on marketing glitz.

Resolving these competing claims is essential for any effort to establish a coherent national policy regarding pharmaceuticals. While there may be objectively derived data that speak to either side, it may not be possible to settle the argument based on data alone. For example, Keyhani and colleagues published a study in 2010 questioning the claim that higher prices and extended patent protection are necessary in the United States to maintain the incentive for pharmaceutical companies to develop new products through research. They found that the United States did not contribute disproportionately to innovation in the development of new types of drugs when compared to countries that had adopted price regulation for pharmaceuticals (Keyhani et al. 2010).

Avorn (2015) also questioned the high cost of drug development cited by drug developers as a justification for the high prices of new drugs. He first points out that 80 percent of potential new drug compounds are abandoned due to problems with safety or efficacy, with their costs added to the figure cited as necessary to bring one new drug to market. He also underscores the fact that, of the $2.6 billion figure cited earlier, the cost of raising the capital invested in drug development is estimated to be $1.2 billion. Thus, a large segment of the $2.6 billion figure is used in exploratory efforts that appear to have little chance of producing new products. He cites evidence that "more than half of the most transformative drugs developed in recent decades had their origins in publicly funded research at nonprofit, university-affiliated centers" (p. 1878), going on to suggest that "as risky as drug development is, the pharmaceutical and biotech industries remain among the most profitable sectors of the U.S. economy and actually spend only a small fraction of their revenues on truly innovative research."

The debate over pharmaceutical policy also involves issues of cultural values and institutional structure. As discussed in chapter 3, the US health care system reflects the values and institutions that are unique to the United States. One of the principal differences between the United States and Canada is the approach we adopt to balancing marginal cost and marginal benefit in the allocation of health care resources. A system that values principally the right of patients to have available the most advanced treatment, regardless of its cost/benefit ratio, will accept treatments that are very costly but only marginally better than the alternatives. A system that values balancing the needs of all individuals in society, however, will not always consider the more costly option as the best choice.

PHARMACEUTICAL RESEARCH AND THE ISSUE OF "ME-TOO" DRUGS

New pharmaceutical products fall into one of two general categories:

1. drugs that are in an entirely new class of therapeutic agent and
2. drugs that are within an established class of therapeutic agents but have certain characteristics that distinguish them from other drugs within that category.

The description in chapter 3 of successive new classes of drugs to treat high blood pressure provides an excellent example of this distinction. Historically, diuretics were a mainstay of the treatment for high blood pressure. Among the diuretics, there were several products produced by several manufacturers. Then, scientists discovered calcium channel blockers, a new class of drug for high blood pressure. Within several years of their discovery, several alternative calcium channel blockers were available for physicians to use, each from a different manufacturer. Then came ACE-inhibitors as the newest class of drug, and again within several years of their introduction, several manufacturers offered drugs within this class.

It should be apparent that the manufacturer able to bring to market the first alternative within a new class of drugs has a tremendous economic advantage over its competitors. It may also be apparent that, for competing manufacturers, the sooner they can get their own drug approved within a new class, the sooner they will be able to tap into the economic advantage and share in the profits realized from newer, advanced treatments. (It should not be surprising that, in most cases, newer drugs are substantially more expensive than older alternatives.) The problem, of course, is that the manufacturer of the first drug enjoys patent protection, and it is against the law for a competing manufacturer to produce the same drug without permission.

> **CONCEPT 10.3**
>
> Between 1990 and 2004, less than 10 percent of new drug applications approved by the US Food and Drug Administration were for new compounds that represent a significant improvement in therapy. Most new drugs are chemical modifications of existing drugs.

This is where the research process known as "molecular manipulation" begins. It becomes the job of the scientists at the competing manufacturers to take the new drug into the lab and analyze the details of its chemical structure. If a new drug can be produced that has a different chemical structure ("different" according to federal guidelines) but maintains the beneficial therapeutic effect of the original drug, the second manufacturer can apply for a new patent and, if approved, market the second drug within the new class of drugs. Thus, a substantial part of the research of scientists within pharmaceutical companies is involved with the production of new chemical compounds that are patentable and still clinically effective—"me-too" drugs.

As an excellent example of this phenomenon, let us look at a category of drugs called the macrolides. These are antibiotics that have a well-defined spectrum of effectiveness in fighting infection and provide an alternative for patients who need a penicillin-type antibiotic but who are allergic to penicillin. The original member of the macrolide category is erythromycin. This drug has been available for several decades, originally under a few patented forms (most of them me-too reformulations of the original compound), but for several years erythromycin has been available as an inexpensive generic formulation no longer under patent protection. In 1996, two pharmaceutical manufacturers received approval for new macrolide antibiotics, clarithromycin and azithromycin, each chemically related to erythromycin. According to a commonly used online pharmacy, the retail price in 2005 for treatment with each of these drugs was slightly less than $10 for erythromycin, $96 for clarithromycin, and $121 for azithromycin. The manufacturer of each of the newer macrolide antibiotics heavily promoted its drug as superior to the others, usually based on factors such as ease of administration and fewer unpleasant side effects. We need not settle here which alternative is best; rather, we should simply note the phenomenon.

How many new drugs represent new classes of treatment rather than me-too reformulations of existing drugs? When the FDA receives an application for approval of a new drug, its scientists study the drug and assign it to one of two categories (US Food and Drug Administration website):

1. those drugs appropriate for "priority review" because they constitute a "significant improvement compared to marketed products in the treatment, diagnosis, or prevention of a disease"; and
2. those drugs appropriate for "standard review" because they "appear to have therapeutic qualities similar to those of one or more already marketed drugs."

Beyond categorizing new drugs within this priority/standard framework, the FDA also determines whether a drug is a "new molecular entity" (NME) or a chemical derivative of an existing drug. Figure 10.2 shows the proportion of new drugs falling into these categories from among the 2,004 new drug applications that were approved by the FDA between 1990 and 2004, a period of rapid escalation in pharmaceutical costs. Of these new drugs, 23 percent were categorized as appropriate for priority review; about 4 in 10 of these "priority" drugs represented an NME. Thus, 9 percent of all new drug applications were for new compounds offering a significant improvement in therapy.

THE MARKETING OF NEW DRUGS TO PHYSICIANS

Once a pharmaceutical manufacturer receives approval for a new drug that represents a chemical modification of an existing drug, it becomes incumbent on the manufacturer's marketing department to convince physicians that the new drug is superior to the original drug. Only a prescription by a physician will make the drug available to a patient. The issue becomes one of providing the physician with information about the drug in a format that the physician will pay attention to. There are three principal ways pharmaceutical companies do this:

1. through advertisements in medical journals;
2. through educational meetings and conferences sponsored by the pharmaceutical company; and

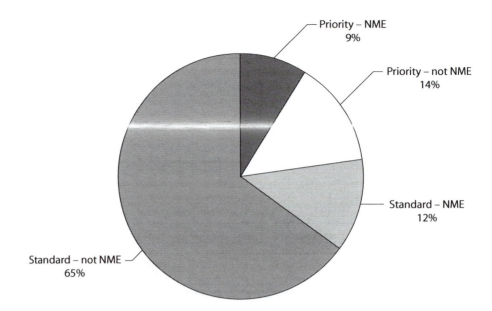

FIGURE 10.2. Types of new drugs approved by the US Food and Drug Administration, 1990–2004. NME = new medical entity. A total of 2,004 drugs were approved during this period. *Source:* Data from US Food and Drug Administration.

3. through direct marketing to the physician, using the mail and visits to the physician's office.

Marketing to Physicians through Medical Journal Advertisements

The link between pharmaceutical companies and medical journals was established more than one hundred years ago, and it continues today. Pick up one of the many journals intended for physicians and you will often see colorful, expertly created ads—many of them occupying several successive pages—encouraging physicians to recognize the therapeutic advantage of the advertised drug over its competitors. These ads are expensive to produce and expensive to run, yet they are a mainstay of pharmaceutical marketing. The problem is that many journals rely on the income from drug ads to offset the costs of production and circulation. A number of the journals are free to physicians, because the entire cost of the journal is covered by revenue from drug ads. (My physician colleagues refer to these journals as "throw-away" journals.) Critics question whether the editor of the journal can exercise independent, scientific judgment in evaluating material related to the drugs advertised in the journal.

A second criticism regarding journal advertising relates to the accuracy of the research on which the claims in the ad are based. While a great deal of important research concerning new drugs is done in academic centers under strict rules about scientific methods, a substantial share of the research reported in journal advertising is done by the pharmaceutical company itself, free of academic oversight. Frequently, pharmaceutical companies will ask community-based physicians to use a new drug on a trial basis with a few of their patients. These studies are usually done according to an approved scientific protocol and in a manner that provides patient protections. The drug company, however, typically pays the physician a substantial fee for enrolling patients in the trial. Critics have questioned the ethics and accuracy of this type of research, although manufacturers respond that they are following the same ethical and scientific standards as academic researchers.

Marketing to Physicians through Educational Meetings and Conferences

Most practicing physicians are required to participate in formal programs of continuing medical education (CME) to maintain their medical license. A substantial portion of CME takes place in meetings and conferences, often held in resort settings. While many of these meetings are organized by hospitals and medical schools with no direct financial interest in the drugs discussed, a substantial number of CME conferences are put on by for-profit companies referred to as medical education and communication companies (MECCs). About 90 percent of the revenues to MECCs come from pharmaceutical companies. The amount spent on CME by MECCs and other commercial sources went from $302 million in 1998 to $971 million in 2003 (Steinbrook 2005).

The educational content of these types of CME events is often provided by speakers who are paid consultants of pharmaceutical companies. These relationships have led many to criticize the objectivity of the educational content of CME meetings supported by pharmaceutical companies. The Accreditation Council for Continuing Medical Education is an independent national body that certifies CME events. It established new standards that took effect in 2005–06 to address the issue of possible conflict of interest in commercially sponsored CME events. These standards apply equally to CME provided by private companies and that provided by hospitals and medical schools. It will be important to follow the changes resulting from these standards to determine if CME events are principally marketing events or are more accurately seen as educational events.

Dr. Arnold Relman, like Dr. Marcia Angell a former editor-in-chief of the *New England Journal of Medicine*, published an article in 2003 in the *New York Times* titled "Your Doctor's Drug Problem," describing the relationship that has evolved between pharmaceutical companies that put on CME events for doctors and the doctors who attend them. He describes this relationship in the following way: "As for the doctors attending these industry-sponsored educational programs, they like the slick presentations. . . . They also like the low or nonexistent fees, the free food, and the numerous small gifts. . . . And naturally they are confident that their own independence is wholly unaffected by all of this. . . . But the companies providing the support wouldn't pour money into education unless they were confident of a return on their investment. And there is evidence that industry-sponsored programs increase the writing of prescriptions for the sponsor's products."

Marketing Directly to Physicians

From their first days in the profession, the young physicians I trained with were courted by the marketing representatives of pharmaceutical companies. When I was in medical school in the 1970s, we referred to these representatives as "detail men"—to "detail" was to provide physicians with the details about a new drug, and they were nearly all men. With substantial numbers of women now working as representatives of pharmaceutical companies, they are now more commonly referred to as "drug reps." Whether it is the 1970s or the 2010s, the issue is the same. Drug reps have tried to create a favorable impression with young physicians, and they did this to a substantial degree by providing them with gifts. When I was training, medical students routinely were offered gifts of textbooks, medical equipment such as stethoscopes or black doctor bags, or simply free meals. Dr. David Blumenthal (2004) described in some detail the types of financial inducements made available to physicians, both those in training and those in practice, by drug reps. It is not necessary to repeat the details of Dr. Blumenthal's analysis here. It is, however, sufficient to say that for many years, pharmaceutical companies provided a physician with a wide array of incentives in exchange for one commodity: access to the physician.

Most physicians receive regular contact from drug reps requesting the opportunity to meet with the physician to provide him or her with information about the new products available from that manufacturer. In addition to marketing brochures, the reps offer the physicians free starter-samples of the drug in question. These are packets containing a small supply of the drug being marketed—usually not enough for a full treatment—that the physician can give to patients free of charge. The physician is encouraged to try the drug, and if it proves effective, to use it with his or her patients. In all the marketing efforts, the drug rep emphasizes the benefit this drug has over its competitors—that is, its marginal benefit, as seen through the eyes of the pharmaceutical company's marketing department.

Manz et al. (2014) raised concerns about the many new forms pharmaceutical marketing to physicians is taking in the digital age. They pointed out that pharmaceutical companies spend an estimated 25 percent of their marketing budget on digital applications such as websites and social media. They are also placing online ads on some sites that assist physicians in maintaining patients' electronic health records, as well as issuing "eCoupons" that physicians can dispense to their patients in lieu of actual drug samples to help patients pay for a marketed drug. With the expansion of these digital approaches to marketing, Manz and colleagues raise the concern that "current policies are not designed to address the insidious nature of digital marketing tools that are seamlessly integrated into electronic resources used for patient care and are less easily recognized as marketing devices" (p. 1858).

OVERSIGHT OF PHYSICIANS' RELATIONSHIPS WITH THE PHARMACEUTICAL INDUSTRY

The recent awareness in the press and in the profession of potential problems in the ways pharmaceutical companies and physicians relate to each other has led to a number of changes in the standards governing professional conflict of interest. In an article published in 2004 in the *New England Journal of Medicine*, Studdert, Mello, and Brennan (2004a) summarized these changes. According to these authors, the changes were triggered by "a growing realization, inside and outside medical circles, of the troubling influence that pharmaceutical marketing can have on patient care" (p. 1891). In response, the Pharmaceutical Research and Manufacturers of America adopted its own standards for affiliated pharmaceutical companies to follow. The standards address in detail allowable conduct surrounding CME activities and other issues with economic relationships that may place the physician in a position of conflict of interest. The authors conclude that this new attention and oversight may reflect "the same kind of sea change in business practices and industry oversight that other segments of corporate America faced in the wake of Enron and other corporate scandals" (p. 1899).

The issue of the relationship between the medical profession and the pharmaceutical industry received added attention in 2009, with the publication of a report by the Institute of Medicine of the National Academies of Science titled *Conflict of Interest in Medical Research, Education, and Practice* (Institute of Medicine of the National Academies of Science 2009). The report concluded that "there is growing concern among lawmakers, government agencies, and the public that extensive conflicts of interest in medicine require stronger measures. Responsible and reasonable conflict of interest policies and procedures will reduce the risk of bias and the loss of trust while avoiding undue burdens or harms and without damaging constructive collaborations with industry" (p. 3).

In a similar vein, in 2008 the Association of American Medical Colleges issued a report on the funding of medical education by pharmaceutical companies (Association of American Medical Colleges 2008). Among the recommendations of the report was the following: "Academic

---

CONCEPT 10.4

Pharmaceutical manufacturers have invested substantial resources in marketing to physicians through ads in medical journals, continuing medical education events, visits to physicians' offices, and more recently digital media. Some of the practices of this marketing effort have raised questions about conflict of interest for physicians and have received increased regulatory scrutiny.

medical centers should establish and implement policies that prohibit the acceptance of any gifts from industry by physicians and other faculty, staff, students, and trainees of academic medical centers" (p. vii). The report explicitly included food, provided either on-site or off-site, as a form of a "gift" that faculty and medical students should be prohibited from accepting. The report went on to recommend that "academic medical centers should strongly discourage participation by their faculty in industry-sponsored speakers' bureaus" (p. viii), and that "academic medical centers should prohibit their physicians, trainees, and students from directly accepting travel funds from industry" (p. ix). It is interesting to note that the recommendations in the report were approved by all but three of the thirty-seven members of the task force. The three members who did not vote to approve the report each were CEOs of major pharmaceutical companies.

Kesselheim et al. (2013) cite data indicating that as of 2009, 71 percent of physicians nationally receive gifts of some type from pharmaceutical companies. Using data from the Massachusetts Department of Health and Human Services, which records pharmaceutical company payments of $50 or more to physicians in Massachusetts, the authors reported both the percentage of physicians within a specialty receiving payments and the amount of those payments. They found that 25 percent of physicians in the state received at least one payment between July 2009 and December 2011. The average payment per physician in 2011 was $4,944, with specialists such as orthopedic surgeons and certain medicine subspecialists averaging as much as $7,378 per year.

A NEW AREA FOR THE MARKETING OF PHARMACEUTICALS: DIRECT-TO-CONSUMERS

As described in the opening section of this chapter, in the early parts of the twentieth century the AMA prohibited manufacturers of prescription drugs from marketing their drugs directly to the public. Because only physicians and other practitioners had the necessary knowledge to select the most appropriate drug for a patient, it was seen as wholly inappropriate for manufacturers to target patients with their marketing efforts. Beginning in the 1980s, some manufacturers began to explore ways to include the general public in their marketing. They had some early success but also some problems related to unexpected side effects from the drugs they were marketing. At this point, the FDA stepped in and issued regulatory guidelines about the marketing of pharmaceutical products directly to consumers. In response to continually increasing marketing activity, in 1997 the FDA revisited the issue and published new guidelines that made it both easier and more attractive for manufacturers to sponsor direct-to-consumer ads, now commonly referred to as "DTC" ads.

In 1994, pharmaceutical manufacturers spent $266 million on DTC drug ads. By 1997, the year the new FDA guidelines were published, that amount had tripled, to $791 million. By 2000, it had tripled again, to $2.5 billion. Of this amount, $1.6 billion, or nearly two-thirds, was spent on television ads, with the remainder on print and other types of ads (Kreling et al. 2001). By 2007, the amount spent on DTC ads had grown to $4.9 billion.

Anyone in the United States who watched television during this time could not help but notice the extensive new presence of drug ads on television. A study done in the summer and fall of 2000 recorded 90 hours of network primetime television and 90 hours of network daytime television and found 319 ads for prescription drugs during the 180 hours of programming, for an average of 1.8 drug ads per hour (Lipton 2001).

This onslaught of DTC ads has been characterized in two ways. The manufacturers support them as providing valuable educational material to patients, encouraging them to discuss with their physicians new treatments that the patients may not have been aware of. Others criticize the ads as a purely profit-oriented attempt to get patients to request from their physicians the newest (and often most expensive) drug available.

A national survey of 643 physicians found that when patients came to them requesting a medication they had seen in a DTC ad, 39 percent prescribed the requested drug. The five most common conditions for which patients requested drugs seen in a DTC ad were impotence, anxiety, arthritis, menopausal symptoms, and allergies. Physicians who did prescribe the requested DTC drug were about evenly split on whether that drug was the best alternative for the patient: 46 percent said that the drug was the most effective one for their patient, while 48 percent said that there were other, equally effective drugs that they might have used. While 74 percent of the physicians agreed that the DTC ads had positive educational aspects for their patients, 79 percent also concurred that DTC ads encouraged patients to seek treatment that they did not need (Weissman et al. 2004).

To evaluate the economic effect of the increase in DTC ads, the Kaiser Family Foundation commissioned an economic analysis by several leading scholars at Harvard University and MIT (Rosenthal et al. 2003). These researchers looked at changes in spending from 1999 to 2000 for the twenty-five classes of drugs with the highest retail sales. Combined, the drugs in these classes accounted for 75 percent of all pharmaceutical sales and 60 percent of DTC advertising expenditures. They estimated that 12 percent of the increase in pharmaceutical spending nationally was due to DTC ads, and that manufacturers realized approximately $4.20 in increased sales for every $1 they spent on DTC ads. A 2010 review of research on the effects of DTC advertising concluded that "the limited body of evidence suggests that DTCA-prompted prescription requests increase both appropriate and inappropriate prescribing" (Frosch et al. 2010, p. 27).

The rapid expansion of the internet and associated online resources have created another venue for DTC activity. Wang and Kesselheim (2013) reported that of the approximately $4 billion spent in 2012 by pharmaceutical and device manufacturers on DTC ads, an estimated $1 billion was for online ads. Much of this spending went for sponsored links on online search engines. In 2015, I entered Google searches for "treatment of high blood pressure" and found three sponsored links at the top of the response page, each for a drug to treat high blood pressure and one offering me a coupon to "Save up to $50 on each of your next 6 prescriptions," so long as the prescription was for the advertised drug. In their analysis, Wang and Kesselheim raised the concern that "online DTCA has been criticized for using seemingly neutral third parties to present biased information about drugs without appropriate sponsorship disclosure" (p. 962).

> **CONCEPT 10.5**
>
> Since 1997, pharmaceutical manufacturers have marketed their products directly to consumers, principally using TV ads, and more recently, internet sites.

It seems clear that, from a policy perspective, there are two sides to DTC ads (Berndt 2005). In a number of cases, they have affected the doctor-patient relationship in a positive way, contributing to patients' education about various health conditions. Many of these conditions, however, while doubtless important, are not the types of conditions in which increased investment in new, expensive pharmaceutical products is likely to yield substantial marginal returns in health status. The impact of DTC ads has been considerable, explaining a large portion of the recent increase in pharmaceutical spending and yielding high profits for pharmaceutical manufacturers.

Two articles published concurrently in 2015 in the *New England Journal of Medicine* describe the increased scrutiny the FDA is beginning to focus on DTC ads. Greene and Watkins (2015) pointed out that, "aside from New Zealand, the United States is the only country with a strong pharmaceutical regulatory infrastructure that allows direct-to-consumer advertising (DTCA) of prescription drugs." They also note that "that may soon change, however, as the Food and Drug Administration (FDA) moves to enact new regulations regarding risk communication in DTCA" (p. 1087). Robertson (2015) reported that the FDA is in the process of revising regulations that pertain to DTC advertising to assure that, in whatever format they encounter DTC ads, consumers will receive warnings written in clear, readily understandable terms of the most significant risks associated with the advertised product. While these revisions will help consumers become more aware of these potential risks, Robertson raises the concern that "the FDA's guidance will do nothing to help consumers understand whether drugs really have substantial benefits" (p. 1087).

MARGINAL BENEFIT AS THE BASIS OF PHARMACEUTICAL MARKETING

In all three types of marketing to physicians, and especially in marketing directly to consumers, a pharmaceutical company emphasizes the marginal benefit of its drug over competitors in the same class of drugs or over those in different drug classes. Rarely does the marketing material address marginal cost, and almost never does it contain an unbiased evaluation of the marginal cost / marginal benefit relationship. This approach to marketing should not be surprising. It represents what has been proven over time to be the most successful way to increase sales and maximize profits of commodities distributed through the market. As health care in the United States has for more than a century been principally a market commodity, there seems to be little inconsistency in approaching pharmaceutical products in the same way.

While marketing based on perceived marginal benefit irrespective of added marginal cost seems wholly appropriate for consumer goods such as cars or sneakers, it raises disturbing issues when applied to pharmaceuticals and other core aspects of our increasingly troubled health care system. Our discussion in the previous chapters has identified this issue as central to many of the differences between health care in the United States and health care in Canada and other developed countries. In times of scarcity such as we are now confronting, when trade-offs are inevitable among cost, quality, and access and between the absolute good of an individual patient and the aggregate good of all patients, serious reform of our system of health care will of necessity include a reevaluation of our approach to this issue.

> **CONCEPT 10.6**
>
> The marketing of pharmaceutical products to physicians and to consumers emphasizes the marginal benefits of one product over another. Issues of marginal costs rarely are considered.

New drugs usually come under the influence of the "technologic imperative" and the "technologic benefit of the doubt," described in chapter 3. Because they are new, they are commonly perceived to be better. How much better they are (i.e., the magnitude of their marginal benefit) has typically been of substantially less importance. If we must allocate pharmaceutical resources under constrained budgets, however, it will mean that an extra dollar spent on a newer drug for one patient will mean one dollar less spent on providing drugs to another patient. As described in the following section, we have entered an era of budgetary constraints in selecting pharmaceutical products. This is true for private-sector managed care plans, and it is true for Medicaid and Medicare.

MANAGED CARE PLANS' EFFORTS TO CONTROL PHARMACEUTICAL COSTS

The rapid increases in pharmaceutical costs have had a substantial effect on private-sector managed care companies. Unless they are able to constrain increases in drug costs, managed care plans will have to raise their rates to employers and other purchasers by even more than they already have. Not surprisingly, they have focused on precisely the same issue as pharmaceutical manufacturers—marginal benefits—but from the opposite perspective. Managed care plans have not focused their efforts on getting physicians to write fewer prescriptions but rather on getting them to select the most cost-effective alternative within the class of medications needed to treat their patients. They have done this using a number of tools.

Tiered Formularies

A formulary is a published list of medications approved for the treatment of certain conditions. Typically, a formulary will first divide drugs by the disease or medical problem treated, then by the classes of drugs available to treat those problems, and lastly by the name of specific drugs within each class. Using either its own experts or private consultants, the managed care company will then assess the relative cost and effectiveness of each drug. When multiple drugs with comparable effects are available, the formulary will typically identify one or more of them as the preferred choice for a given condition. The preferred drug is often one that is available in generic form. These are usually referred to as the "first-tier" alternative. It will then identify other drugs that are alternatives to the preferred drugs, but for reasons of either cost or effectiveness have some disadvantage. These are the "second-tier" drugs. The managed care company may further subdivide these second-tier drugs into those it is willing to provide partial coverage for and those it will provide no coverage for. Drugs that receive either limited coverage or no coverage under the plan are often referred to as "third-tier" drugs. A study by the Kaiser Family Foundation (2004) found that 68 percent of workers who received their health insurance through their employer have at least three tiers of cost sharing in the drugs available to them.

Having defined the first-, second-, and third-tier drugs for each condition on the list, the managed care plan will leave it up to the physician and the patient to select the best option. While the plan will cover the cost of the first-tier drugs (less a small patient copayment, typically $10 to $20), it will usually cover second-tier drugs at a lower level, requiring a higher copayment from the patient, typically $25 to $35. If it covers third-tier drugs at all, the formulary will require the patient to make a much higher copayment, in the range of $50–$100 per prescription. Often, it will require the patient to pay the full cost of the third-tier option.

Some insurance plans have established a fourth tier of coverage. Instead of having the patient pay a fixed-dollar copayment for second- or third-tier drugs, fourth-tier plans have started asking the patient to pay a fixed percentage of the cost of a drug, typically in the range of 20–33 percent. The drugs in the fourth tier are typically high-priced drugs for which there are few lower-priced alternatives. As reported in the *New York Times* in 2008, this shift has meant that some patients, despite having prescription drug coverage, can still end up paying thousands of dollars a month out of pocket (Kolata 2008).

Pharmaceutical Benefit Managers

As one might imagine, the administrative work involved in creating and managing a drug formulary can be substantial. A number of private firms have been created to address this issue. These firms focus their business on managing the use of pharmaceuticals and frequently on providing mail-order options for filling prescriptions as well. Many large managed care companies have subcontracted their capitated pharmaceutical coverage to these pharmaceutical benefit managers (PBMs). Patients who have health coverage that includes a PBM can often reduce their out-of-pocket costs by obtaining their prescriptions by mail directly from the PBM. While patients may need to make a separate copayment for each thirty-day supply of medication obtained through a private pharmacy, they can typically get a ninety-day supply from the PBM's mail-order pharmacy for a single copayment. This also allows the PBM to obtain large quantities of medications from manufacturers at more competitive prices than some smaller pharmacies.

A study from 2003 (Huskamp et al.) looked at the effect of using a PBM to switch employees and their families in two large firms to a three-tier formulary. The switch to the three-tier plan resulted in lower overall costs and increased use of medications from lower tiers for three classes of medication. It also resulted in some patients discontinuing therapy, however, which raises important questions about the effects of increasing copayments on health care quality and access.

> **CONCEPT 10.7**
>
> Managed care companies have used a number of methods to constrain rising pharmaceutical costs, including tiered formularies and pharmaceutical benefit managers.

Educational Efforts and Financial Incentives for Prescribing Physicians

A study of several large health plans in California (Wallack et al. 2004) found that health plan managers were also increasing their efforts to educate their physicians about the relative cost and therapeutic advantages of alternative pharmaceutical products. Some of the plans also expanded financial incentives such as cash bonuses to encourage physicians to prescribe the least expensive available drug whenever appropriate.

STATES' EFFORTS TO LIMIT MEDICAID PHARMACEUTICAL COSTS

As described in chapter 7, Medicaid's overall costs have been going up sharply in recent years, leading a number of states to cut back on the benefits they provide under the program. Rising pharmaceutical costs have been a principal contributor to these problems. Recall that prescription drugs are not one of the benefits required by the federal government for states to participate in the original Medicaid program; it is one of the optional benefits states are permitted to include in their program for which they can receive partial federal reimbursement.

Between 1996 and 2000, Medicaid expenditures for outpatient prescription drugs nearly doubled, from $10.6 billion to $21.0 billion (Iglehart 2003). Faced with worsening budget problems, states had to rethink their provision of prescription drugs to their Medicaid beneficiaries. A number of states initiated various programs to reduce their pharmaceutical costs. These programs have included

- requiring physicians to obtain prior authorization from Medicaid administrators before certain pharmaceuticals are prescribed,
- requiring physicians to use the least expensive medication available within a class of medications,
- requiring patients to make a copayment for each prescription filled, and
- limiting the number of prescriptions patients may have filled each month.

Cunningham (2005) used an existing national survey that included 1,600 adults on Medicaid to assess the effect of these policy changes on patients' access to medications. Depending on the type of program limitation, between 56 and 79 percent of respondents reported encountering limits on their access to prescription drugs.

Another way states have attempted to reduce pharmaceutical costs has been to conduct their own evaluations of the relative costs and benefits of various drugs within a treatment class. If they are unable to find scientific support for using a newer, more expensive drug rather than an older, generic drug no longer under patent protection, states have often required the use of the generic option. In 2001, Oregon began an effort to gather scientific evidence about the comparable benefits of alternatives in several drug classes. Working with researchers at the state's Health and Science University, they identified several classes of medication and began an extensive review of the available scientific evidence. After reviewing fifteen different drug classes, the medical director for the project reported that, "to date, we found no evidence that one drug was more effective than others intended to treat the same illness" (quoted in Pear and Dao 2004).

Finding no evidence that one drug is better than another does not prove that the drugs are equivalent. In most cases, it was impossible for the reviewers to identify a clearly preferable option, because few controlled studies had been done comparing drugs with each other. Most published research compared drugs to a placebo, not with each other (Padrez et al. 2005). Nonetheless, the findings represented the best available information about drug effectiveness and permitted the Oregon Medicaid program to develop a list of preferred drugs within a drug class, based on a combination of scientific evidence and relative costs. Several other states have teamed with Oregon to create a Drug Effectiveness Review Project (DERP), and to expand this research to include twenty-five of the most commonly used classes of medications. In addition to making the reports of the scientific reviews available to the participating state Medicaid programs, DERP is also making them available to the public on its website. By 2015, Medicaid programs in thirteen states were participating in DERP.

MAKING PRESCRIPTION DRUGS MORE AFFORDABLE TO SENIORS: THE MEDICARE MODERNIZATION ACT

Until now, we have been looking at the efforts of managed care companies and state Medicaid programs to reduce pharmaceutical costs while maintaining the quality of available drugs. The federal Medicare program, described in chapter 6, has had to deal with a different problem: expanding coverage to include pharmaceuticals. Since its creation in 1965, Medicare had excluded outpatient prescription drugs as a covered benefit. (Congress did add prescription drug coverage to Medicare for a few months as part of the Catastrophic Coverage Act of 1988, but when seniors found out they were going to have to pay the cost of coverage themselves, they lobbied fiercely and effectively to have the act repealed.) As the price of pharmaceuticals rose steeply in the years following 1988, seniors felt the brunt of the change. By 2003, the average per capita cost of pharmaceuticals for Medicare beneficiaries was $2,318. As with Medicare expenditures in general, this spending was highly skewed, with 28 percent of seniors using less than $500 in pharmaceuticals, while 16 percent used more than $4,000 (Kaiser Family Foundation 2004).

In 1999, 62 percent of seniors had some form of pharmaceutical coverage, leaving 38 percent of seniors with no coverage. Coverage for the 62 percent was partitioned as employer-sponsored coverage (28%), private Medigap coverage (7%), Medicare HMO (15%), Medicaid (10%), and other public programs (2%). Despite this coverage, seniors face substantial out-of-pocket expenses for pharmaceuticals. In 2000, the average Medicare beneficiary spent $644 on outpatient drugs; by 2004, that figure had reached $1,147. Recalling from chapter 6 that in 2004 half of all elderly households in the United States had a total annual income under $24,500, it is easy to see that drug expenditures at this level can create a severe financial strain. Because of the cost of their medications, 30 percent of seniors with chronic medical problems such as heart failure, diabetes, or high blood pressure but without pharmaceutical coverage were found either to skip doses of medication or to fail to fill a prescription altogether (Kaiser Family Foundation 2004).

With the rising cost of prescription drugs having such a severe impact on seniors, President George W. Bush made a commitment when he was elected in 2000 to add coverage for prescription drugs to Medicare. While he was ultimately able to keep this commitment, finding a way to do so proved very difficult. The reason it was important to expand Medicare coverage, of course, was the rising cost of prescription drugs—but Medicare was already placing a severe strain on the federal budget, a strain projected only to get worse in coming years. President Bush needed to add prescription drug coverage in a way that was not perceived to increase the federal deficit unreasonably. That deficit had already ballooned in the early years of the Bush presidency as a result of the extensive tax cuts he had worked with Congress to pass. What he decided to do was to establish a budget cap for a prescription drug program, and then to leave it largely to Congress to design a program that stayed within that cap. He did indicate to Congress, though, that he could only support a program that provided prescription drug benefits through private carriers analogous to Medicare + Choice health plans. He did not want the federal government to become involved in the administration of the drug benefit in the same manner it administers the Part A hospital plan and Part B outpatient coverage.

The budget cap established by President Bush was $400 billion to cover the first ten years of the prescription drug plan. Congress spent several months debating the proposal and, in the end, passed the plan by a single vote—a vote obtained only at the last minute through the use of some heavy-duty arm twisting, in what John Iglehart referred to in the *New England Journal of Medicine* as "a pure power play" (see Iglehart 2004—an excellent account of the history and politics of the new law).

The Medicare Prescription Drug, Improvement, and Modernization Act, commonly referred to as the Medicare Modernization Act (MMA), was finally passed in November 2003. As the details of the plan became more widely known, it became clear that it was more than simply a new prescription drug plan. It also contained a provision to increase substantially the capitation rates paid to private Medicare + Choice health plans to attract more plans back into the program following their earlier exodus. The MMA also changed the way Part B premiums are calculated, expanded the role of health savings accounts for the general public, increased payments to many rural hospitals, reduced payments to home health agencies, and blocked scheduled cuts in Part B payments to physicians triggered by the sustainable growth rate (SGR) formula discussed in chapter 6.

Shortly after the MMA was approved by Congress and signed by President Bush, a controversy arose over the financial projections used during the congressional review process. As described, the MMA was passed in the House of Representatives by a single vote after contentious discussions in the House-Senate Conference Committee. The last votes in favor of the legislation came forward only after receiving assurance that the $400 billion cost of the program was accurate and would not be exceeded. Within a few months of final passage, news stories around the country reported that the chief actuary within Medicare had estimated the true ten-year cost to be closer to $530 billion. The stories also reported that the actuary's superiors within the executive branch had threatened to fire him if he made these estimates public. It is uncertain at best whether Congress would have passed the MMA had the financial projections from the Medicare actuary been shared with them.

To stay within the $400 billion target, congressional negotiators created a complex plan for covering prescription drugs for Medicare beneficiaries. The structure of the coverage is illustrated in figure 10.3.

There are four tiers of coverage under the MMA:

- Tier 1: The patient is responsible for the first $250 per year in pharmaceutical costs—this is referred to as the "deductible."
- Tier 2: For yearly pharmaceutical costs between $250 and $2,250, Medicare will pay 75 percent and the patient will pay 25 percent.
- Tier 3: Once a patient has incurred $2,250 in costs per year, the patient is responsible for 100 percent of additional costs, up to a total cost of $5,100.
- Tier 4: After a patient incurs $5,100 in costs per year, Medicare will pay 95 percent of all additional costs for that year.*

This coverage plan has come to be called the "doughnut hole" plan, in that it provides coverage initially, then has nothing, then resumes coverage after the patient has spent $3,600 out of pocket. The gap in coverage between $2,250 in total costs and $5,100 in total costs is the "doughnut hole." The reason given for this plan was the need to accommodate the $400 billion budget cap established by President Bush. Congressional negotiators agreed on the need for the 95 percent catastrophic coverage for those few beneficiaries with extremely high costs. They also agreed on $250 as an appropriate level for the deductible. Once the high and low ends of the coverage were established, they began adding 75 percent coverage until they used up the budgeted funds. This occurred at $2,250 of total drug costs, so that was where they began the "doughnut hole." (It is worth noting what happens when one expands coverage

---

*These figures were for the first year of the new pharmaceutical benefit. Each year they are adjusted for inflation.

FIGURE 10.3. The tiered structure of the pharmaceutical benefit under the Medicare Modernization Act.

for health care but does so under a defined budget cap—one finds that one "can't treat all of the people all of the time" and instead must allocate resources based on relative need. Congress, it seems, followed Barr's Law, which is described in chapter 13.)

Coverage under the MMA began on January 1, 2006. Consistent with the limitations President Bush established, all coverage under the MMA is provided by private, market-based companies. The enrollment period for coverage began on October 1, 2005. On that day, dozens of private companies offering pharmaceutical coverage began marketing their plans to Medicare beneficiaries. Because pharmaceutical coverage is optional rather than universal, it is up to the individual beneficiary to sign up with a plan. The large number of companies offering coverage and the intensity of their marketing efforts raised concerns that seniors would become confused, and they either would not sign up due to the confusion or may select a plan that did not best meet their needs. In Oregon, where seniors had twenty plans to choose from, the state Medicare coordinator was quoted in the *New York Times* as saying, "It's mind boggling. If you try to explain the whole program at one time, people will be shellshocked" (Pear 2005). In the same article, the director of the American Association of Retired Persons was quoted as saying, "The jury is out in terms of enrollment and public acceptance. Half of Medicare beneficiaries have no clue that the new program is on its way."

After this initial period of confusion, enrollment in the new prescription drug coverage progressed fairly smoothly. By the end of 2006, 22.5 million Medicare beneficiaries were enrolled in a drug plan—either a stand-alone plan (16.2 million) or a plan that was part of a Medicare Advantage (MA) plan (6.3 million). In 2012, approximately 90 percent of Medicare beneficiaries had some form of drug coverage, either through Medicare Part D or through private coverage, leaving about 5 million beneficiaries, or 10 percent of the Medicare population, without any drug coverage (Donohue 2014). By 2015, 39.3 million beneficiaries were enrolled in a plan, with 39 percent in a MA plan (Hoadley et al. 2015).

As is the case with Part B of Medicare, beneficiaries who choose to enroll in one of the available plans have to pay a monthly premium to cover 25 percent of the cost of the plan. The premium is in addition to any out-of-pocket costs incurred under the plan. Once beneficiaries have signed up with a plan, Medicare will reimburse the plan for 75 percent of its costs. For a plan to be eligible, it must meet minimum federal standards for things such as numbers of drugs available in a class and expected costs for program coverage.

By 2015, the typical Medicare beneficiary would have about 30 plans to choose from. Premiums for the plans have gone up somewhat, with the average stand-alone plan premium going from $26 per month in 2006 to $37 per month in 2015. Part D coverage under MA plans has been less expensive, going from about $12 per month to $18 per month in 2015. There has been concern, however, that these rates may be increasing in the future, as Medicare pays for the growing number of extremely expensive, new specialty pharmaceutical products for diseases such as cancer and hepatitis C (discussed in the next section of this chapter). Other concerns have been raised about the growing market concentration of Medicare Part D providers, especially in light of the proposed mergers of managed care providers discussed in chapter 9. As described by Hoadley et al. (2015), "Proposed acquisitions of Humana by Aetna and Cigna by Anthem, if approved, will increase market concentration and make the consolidated Aetna-Humana firm the largest sponsor of both types of plans. While consolidation could simplify the market by streamlining choices, it could also weaken competition and increase costs" (p. 1684).

There are provisions to make the plans and the drugs they cover more affordable to poor and low-income seniors. Those beneficiaries below 135 percent of the federal poverty level (FPL) will not pay either a premium or a deductible, and their coverage will continue after they have reached their "doughnut hole." They will be required to pay a $2 copayment for each prescription for a generic drug (those no longer under patent) and $5 for other prescriptions, with limits on yearly out-of-pocket expenditures. Those between 135 and 150 percent of the FPL will have slightly higher out-of-pocket costs, with small monthly premiums, a small deductible, and small required copayments. In 2015, 11.7 million Medicare beneficiaries benefited from these low-income subsidies, either through joint Medicare-Medicaid coverage or through the reduced pricing provisions.

It should be noted that Medicare now offers prescription drug coverage to a number of poor seniors who previously had drugs covered by Medicaid. Medicaid will no longer cover prescriptions for seniors, and states will be required to reimburse the federal government for the state's share of prescription drug costs under the MMA for poor seniors, using the usual federal-state matching formula.

Actuarial projections of the benefits of the MMA suggest that they will help most Medicare beneficiaries somewhat and a few beneficiaries quite a lot. Overall, the beneficiaries who qualify for the low-income support in the program were expected to have their out-of-pocket drug expenditures reduced by 83 percent. The beneficiaries projected to enroll in the program who do not qualify for low-income support were expected to see a reduction in their out-of-pocket expenditures of 28 percent. Altogether, 3.8 million beneficiaries were expected to reach the "doughnut hole" in coverage without qualifying for catastrophic coverage, thus paying for all extra prescriptions themselves (Mays et al. 2004).

Follow-up studies have largely confirmed these initial projections, although the savings in out-of-pocket costs have been somewhat lower than expected. A study published in 2008 found that, once enrollment in Part D plans had stabilized in mid-2006, average out-of-pocket costs decreased by 13.1 percent, with monthly drug utilization increasing by 5.9 percent (Yin et al. 2008). A second study found a "small but significant overall decrease" in the rate of Medicare patients not adhering to their prescribed drug regimen because of cost, although this decrease was not seen in the sickest beneficiaries (Madden et al. 2008). In 2007, 3.4 million beneficiaries had reached the "doughnut hole" in their coverage (Hoadley et al. 2008).

While seniors' access to affordable pharmaceuticals have increased, the extensive competition among Part D providers has not always brought seniors coverage that offers the best value for them. A study by Zhou and Zhang (2012) found that only about 5 percent of beneficiaries enrolled in Part D coverage actually choose the plan that provides the cheapest coverage for them, given the current medications they are taking. Hoadley et al. (2015) reported that relatively few enrollees switch plans during the annual open enrollment period, suggesting that "this low switching rate means that beneficiaries are not necessarily getting the best value for their dollars and that plan sponsors have little incentive to reduce premiums to retain or attract enrollees" (p. 1683).

The MMA represents the best efforts of the federal government to deal with the pressing problem of rising pharmaceutical expenditures for seniors, many of whom have been unable to get the medications they need because of their high cost. Medicare has relied completely on private, market-based companies to administer the plans in a manner originally intended to remain within the ten-year budget cap established for the program. (Whether that cap is the $400 billion used by Congress or the $530 billion projected by the executive branch is still under analysis and debate.) Preliminary data suggests that the plan has been successful in sticking to these caps (Hoadley 2012).

Medicare Part D represents a major effort to deal with the rapidly rising cost of pharmaceutical products confronting the entire health care system. The lessons learned from MMA may provide valuable guidance in addressing the broader questions of health care reform.

> **CONCEPT 10.8**
>
> The Medicare Modernization Act extended pharmaceutical coverage to Medicare beneficiaries, beginning in 2006. It includes four tiers of coverage, based on the amount of pharmaceuticals used during the year. It was estimated that it will reduce out-of-pocket expenditures for pharmaceuticals by 83 percent for low-income seniors and by 28 percent for other seniors.

NEW QUESTIONS OF PHARMACEUTICAL POLICY: SPECIALTY DRUGS AND PRICE MANIPULATION OF GENERICS TO INCREASE PROFITS

As described previously in the discussion of the development of "me-too" drugs, for several decades new pharmaceutical products were developed largely through manipulation of preexisting chemical compounds in the laboratory. The tremendous advancement in the biological sciences of genetic manipulation has created an entirely new pathway for the development of pharmaceutical products. One of the first of these was the development of recombinant DNA, in which the human gene that regulates the production of an enzyme or other substance is extracted from human DNA and inserted into (recombined with) the DNA of a bacteria or fungus, leading the microorganism to produce the human enzyme as part of its normal metabolism. The bacteria with this recombinant DNA is then grown in large quantities in the lab, and the human enzyme is extracted, purified, and administered to humans.

One of the first examples of this was the development of the compound tissue plasminogen activator (tPA). tPA is an enzyme that naturally occurs in the cells lining human blood vessels and acts to break down blood clots that might form in the vessel. Scientists at Genentech were able to produce tPA through recombinant methods and make it available for use in treating patients with heart attacks or strokes, caused by blood clots forming in the vessels to the heart or brain. Rapid administration of tPA in the emergency room could often reverse the heart attack or stroke after it had occurred. Another recombinant DNA product is the hormone erythropoietin, often referred to simply as EPO. EPO is produced naturally in the kidney and is essential for the production of new red blood cells in the bone marrow. Patients with kidney failure who are treated with kidney dialysis are unable to produce EPO, so they require regular blood transfusions to avoid becoming anemic. Amgen was able to use recombinant methods to produce EPO, which fundamentally changed the treatment of kidney failure by enabling patients to produce their own red blood cells, thus avoiding the need for transfusion.

It should not be surprising that Genentech and Amgen set extremely high prices for their new products. Both were essential to the treatment of potentially life-threatening conditions. Under federal regulations passed in the 1980s, hospital emergency rooms are required to treat patients with life-threatening conditions such as heart attacks or strokes regardless of the patient's insurance status or ability to pay. The extremely high cost of tPA was paid either by the patient's insurance or, for those lacking insurance, by the hospital itself. Medicare pays for the treatment of kidney failure, which includes the cost of EPO. These new compounds, developed through biotechnology, have advanced treatment substantially—while also adding substantially to the cost of care.

Since the 1980s, nearly 300 new products have been developed through biotechnology. In 2013, these products accounted for $175 billion in sales globally (Evens and Kaitin 2015). In addition to enzymes such as tPA and EPO, they include antibody proteins, referred to as monoclonal antibodies, bioengineered to attack cells with specific genetic mutations such as those that can cause cancer. Monoclonal antibody therapy can be extremely expensive, sometimes costing thousands of dollars for each treatment, and can add more than $100,000 to the cost of cancer care. New bioengineered drugs have also been developed to treat rheumatoid arthritis, an autoimmune disorder that can lead to severe degeneration of the joints, as well as cystic fibrosis, an inherited genetic disorder that can lead to permanent lung damage and premature death. A news report in 2015 indicated that a new bioengineered drug to treat certain types of cystic fibrosis was priced at $259,000 per patient per year (Pollack 2015c).

Another bioengineered therapy that has received extensive public attention has been the development of bioengineered products to treat, and in most cases cure, chronic hepatitis C infections. Before these therapies, hepatitis C was a chronic viral infection of the liver that over time could lead to liver failure or liver cancer. As described in a 2014 article in *The New Yorker*,

> Hepatitis C affects 3.2 million Americans. . . . Until now, the best treatments cured only about half of patients and often had debilitating side effects. But in December the F.D.A. approved the first in a new wave of hep-C drugs, Gilead's Sovaldi®. This is huge news. . . . Sovaldi® can cure ninety per cent of patients in three to six months, with only minor side effects. There's just one catch: a single dose of the drug costs a thousand dollars, which means that a full, twelve-week course of treatment comes to more than eighty grand. (Surowiecki 2014, p. 23)

By 2015, four drugs had been approved for the treatment of Hepatitis C. A second drug, Harvoni, is made by the same company as Sovaldi but is priced even higher, with a price of $95,000 for a twelve-week course of therapy. A *New York Times* (2015) editorial described the dilemma created by these new drugs. "The benefits of these new drugs are undeniable. They can essentially cure the infection in eight to 24 weeks. . . . Unfortunately, most state Medicaid programs, in an effort to control costs, have placed restrictions on making the drugs widely available. . . . The restrictions run counter to guidelines published by the Infectious Diseases Society of America and the American Association for the Study of Liver Diseases" (p. A24).

These new types of products developed through bioengineering have come to be called "specialty pharmaceuticals." Based on the growing market for these products, Hirsch et al. (2014) predicted that "specialty pharmaceuticals could account for 50 percent of drug spending by 2019" (p. 1714). They go on to caution that "many specialty pharmaceuticals are likely to improve both life expectancy and quality of life for patients. However, the financial implications of their increased use cannot be ignored" (p. 1715).

Congress has given the FDA clear instructions not only to support but in some cases to accelerate the review and approval of new specialty products (Darrow et al. 2014). Congress has not allowed the FDA to consider the cost implications of new products in its review. As a consequence, in the context of rapidly increasing costs of these products, Robinson and Howell (2014) argued that "the principal responsibility for appropriate use, therefore, lies outside the FDA's domain but within those of insurers, physicians, and patients themselves" (p. 1747).

Economist Uwe Reinhardt (2015) argued that the pricing of new specialty drugs underscores the need to consider cost-effectiveness as well as comparative effectiveness—something Congress has been unwilling to do up to this point. Referring to the use of the quality-adjusted life year (QALY) as the most common measure of cost-effectiveness in health care, Reinhardt identified the difficult questions society must face. "The health system's QALY supply curve confronts society with 2 vexing moral questions that physicians are not in a position to determine on their own. First, how much is society willing to pay for an additional QALY derived from a particular intervention? And second, should the maximum price to be paid per additional QALY be the same for everyone, or can it vary with the individual patient's ability to pay for it?" (p. 981).

Brennan and Shrank (2014) echoed Reinhardt's perspective: "The evidence documenting the effectiveness and tolerability of the newer . . . regimens, and the expected reductions in downstream costs associated with averted progression of disease, suggest that these newer expensive medications may represent a relatively good 'deal' by typical cost-effectiveness thresholds. . . . The simple math is that treatment of patients with HCV could add $200 to $300 per year to every insured American's health insurance premium for each of the next 5 years" (p. 593).

Another example of new specialty pharmaceuticals that offer the potential of measurable benefit for some population groups, but at an especially high cost for the entire system of care, is a new category of drug recently approved for the treatment of high cholesterol—a major risk factor for cardiovascular disease. This new category is referred to as PCSK9 inhibitors and has been shown to further lower blood cholesterol levels in especially high-risk patients based on family history of elevated cholesterol or documented atherosclerotic disease (clogging of the arteries as a result of high cholesterol). Statins, a group of drugs commonly used to treat high cholesterol and broadly available as less expensive generic drugs, have proved only partially effective in these high-risk patients. PCSK9 inhibitors can further lower blood cholesterol levels beyond the level attainable with statins.

As newly developed specialty pharmaceuticals, PCSK9 inhibitors are priced extremely high—in the range of $15,000 per patient per year. Compared to the use of drugs for Hepatitis C, which are used for a finite period of time and offer result in a cure, PCSK9 inhibitors will need to be used on an ongoing basis to maintain lowered cholesterol levels. Additionally, while they have been shown to reduce cholesterol levels in the blood, Schulman et al. (2015) pointed out that, in approving the use of alirocumab, one of the first of these drugs, "the FDA label clearly states that 'the effect of alirocumab on cardiovascular morbidity and mortality has not been determined'" (p. 1591). We are not even sure yet that these new drugs will actually lower death rates from cardiovascular disease. Given that 27 percent of adults in the United States between the ages of 40 and 64 have elevated cholesterol, which of these patients should receive these new drugs? Even if we limit access to PCSK9 inhibitors to the estimated 5 percent of those with high cholesterol who are at elevated risk for the reasons cited previously, the added cost to the health care system as a whole could be tremendous. Who will pay these added costs? How will these added costs impact Medicare when these new drugs are used in the Medicare population? Once again, the absence of a coordinated national policy on pharmaceutical pricing and access leaves us with the dilemma cited by Schulman et al.: "The health care market seems to have limited tools for restraining the pricing power of suppliers. This market is nearly unique in fostering demand that is seemingly impervious to price escalation" (p. 1592).

Our society and our health care system will have little choice but to find new ways to confront these issues in the context of new specialty pharmaceuticals. In the past, the pharmaceutical industry has been able to avoid issues of cost-effectiveness and social justice in the distribution of potentially lifesaving yet scarce products; however, this may be changing, as health economist James Robinson (2015) suggested: "The life sciences industry has won every battle but appears to be losing the war against the use of comparative clinical and cost-effectiveness research" (p. 205).

The development of specialty pharmaceuticals developed through biotechnology and recombinant methodologies has changed another aspect of the market for pharmaceuticals. When more traditional chemical compounds were granted a new patent, it was only a matter of time until a competing producer could offer the generic version of the same chemical compound after the patent had expired. One of the reasons for the rather modest increases in pharmaceutical costs between 2003 and 2013, discussed earlier, was the expiration of patents on a number of "blockbuster" drugs for which generic options became readily available, at a substantially reduced cost. By 2015, generic drugs comprised 80 percent of all prescriptions written (Falit et al. 2015).

The same will not be happening with specialty pharmaceuticals, which often represent both a complex production process and a complex molecular structure that cannot simply be replicated. Instead of producing generic equivalents of other drugs, manufacturers competing with the producers of specialty drugs will only be able to produce "biosimilars"—products produced through similar biotechnological processes and having similar molecular structure and pharmaceutical effect but not representing an exact replica of the original compound. As described by Chandra and Vanderpuye-Orgle (2015), "Biologics are manufactured using complex living systems, are made of very large and complex molecules, and cannot be copied identically. Therefore, a biosimilar is not automatically interchangeable with its reference product and cannot be marketed as generating the same results as the reference product" (p. 225).

Until the passage of ACA, the FDA did not have statutory authority to regulate biosimilars. Each new biosimilar product had to undergo the same FDA review and approval as a newly developed compound. As a consequence, "Cost savings for biologic drugs, however, are inherently limited because they are more complex and therefore harder to produce than small-molecule drugs" (Sarpatwari et al. 2015, p. 2381). These constraints have made investing in either new biologic products or biosimilar products more risky for manufacturers and developers. Those who are successful in this process, such as the new specialty products discussed previously, are able to gain substantial return on investment through charging unusually high prices for the new products. Berndt et al. (2015) suggested that the overall profitability of new biologic products may end up being no greater than traditional drugs.

A series of press reports released in 2015 raised another issue pertaining to the unusually high prices being charged for some pharmaceutical products. There are some diseases that have had established treatments available for years or even decades under generic formulations, yet the relatively small number of patients with the disease treated by the drug has led to a single manufacturer of the generic product. Rather than investing in the development of new drugs, some pharmaceutical entrepreneurs have instead purchased the rights to produce these generic products, and then taken advantage of being the only producer of the product to raise prices exorbitantly. As described by Alpern et al. (2014), "Manufacturers of generic drugs that legally obtain a market monopoly are free to unilaterally raise the prices of their products" (p. 1860).

Pyrimethamine is a drug essential to treating certain parasitic infections that has been available for over 60 years. Due to the relatively small number of patients needing the drug, it has had only one manufacturer in the United States. In September 2015, the *New York Times* reported that a start-up company formed by a former hedge fund manager had purchased the right to produce the drug. Once it had acquired the rights to the drug, it immediately raised the price from $13.50 per pill to $750 per pill (Pollack 2015b, p. B1).

This action was similar to the acquisition at about the same time of the rights to sell cycloserine, a drug used to treat cases of tuberculosis that proved to be resistant to traditional anti-TB drugs. Another entrepreneurial company purchased the rights to sell cycloserine from its former owner, a nonprofit entity that was the sole producer of the drug in the United States. At about the same time that the price increase for pyrimethamine was announced, this new company announced that it had raised the price for thirty pills of cycloserine from $500 to $10,800. Within days of the announcement of this price increase, the acquiring company backed off in the face of growing public outrage and returned the rights to produce the drug to its previous nonprofit owner (Pollack 2015a, p. B3). (It should be noted that the generic version of this drug produced by foreign manufacturers costs $20 for one hundred pills; however, these manufacturers are not permitted to sell in the United States.) The next day, *Fox News* reported that the company that had purchased pyrimethamine had also backed off in the face of criticisms over price gouging, indicating that it would reduce the price of the drug for which it had purchased the rights, though not saying what the new price would be (Long 2015).

The news coverage of these two drugs brought added attention to another company: Valeant Pharmaceuticals International. Valeant was created in 2010 when a Canadian company acquired a US company and relocated it to Canada. As reported in the *New York Times*, "Rather than developing drugs, though, Valeant acquires them. Since 2010, it has acquired companies with a total value of at least $36 billion" (Morgenson 2015, p. B1). Pollack and Tavernise (2015) described our current situation, in which "the United States, unlike most countries, does not control drug prices, and pharmaceutical manufacturers have relied heavily on steady and sometimes outsize price increases in this country to bolster their revenue and profits" (p. A1). Since its formation in 2010, Pollack and Tavernise reported that Valeant has acquired the rights to produce several generically available drugs used to treat specific conditions, then raised the price of these drugs substantially. These acquisitions and price increases included:

- isoproterenol, a drug to treat irregular heart rhythms: price of 25 0.2 ml ampules going from $4,489 in 2013 to $36,811 in 2015;
- cuprimine, a drug to treat Wilson's disease, an inherited genetic disorder of copper metabolism: 100 250mg capsules going from $888 in 2013 to $26,189 in 2015; and
- Glumetza (metformin), a drug to treat diabetes: 90 1,000mg capsules going from $896 in 2013 to $10,200 in 2015.

It should be noted that Pollack and Tavernise also reported that in the weeks following the controversy over the generic price increases just discussed, the price of Valeant's stock dropped by about 25 percent.

There is little disagreement in the United States over the need to continue the process of new drug development. There is rising disagreement as to whether this process should continue to take place in a market that permits pharmaceutical companies, once a drug's safety and efficacy have been established, to set the price for that drug at a point that maximizes corporate profits without consideration of cost/benefit comparisons and concerns about impacts on cost or access. These issues will need to be addressed as part of the ongoing discussion and debate about pharmaceutical policy in the context of overall health care reform.

THE AFFORDABLE CARE ACT AND PHARMACEUTICAL POLICY

For many Medicare beneficiaries, the principal impact of the Affordable Care Act (ACA) on pharmaceutical policy is on the "doughnut hole" gap in coverage under Medicare Part D plans. Effective in 2010, all beneficiaries who reached the "doughnut hole" gap in their coverage were eligible for a $250 rebate directly from Medicare. Beginning in 2011, any beneficiary reaching the gap and having a prescription for a brand-name drug (i.e., a drug not yet available in generic form) was eligible to receive a 50 percent discount on the price of the drug, provided by the drug's manufacturer.

Also beginning in 2011, there was a gradual increase in coverage provided in the gap. The amount the beneficiary who reaches the gap has to pay began to decline gradually from the original level of 100 percent of the cost of the drug to 25 percent of the cost in 2020. As a means of financing this increased level of coverage, ACA imposes a new fee on pharmaceutical manufacturers. These fees were expected to raise $2.8 billion in new revenue in 2012, rising to $4.1 billion in 2018, and then falling again to $2.8 billion in 2019 and beyond.

ACA made a fundamental change in national policy regarding the payments physicians receive from pharmaceutical companies through what has come to be called the

Physician Payment Sunshine Act (PPSA) (Santhakumar and Adashi 2015). As described earlier, these payments are quite common, can take many forms, and sometimes can be substantial. While not preventing these payments, ACA instead requires that pharmaceutical companies and device makers now make these payments public, through a federal "open payments" website (US Centers for Medicare and Medicaid Services 2015b). Beginning in 2014, these data were available online. Summary data for 2014 showed that companies made $2.56 billion in general payments to physicians and other providers while also contributing $3.23 billion to physicians as well as academic medical centers to support research. Analysts at the journal *Health Affairs* looked at the role of PPSA in the broader context of health reform, concluding that "the full effects of the PPSA will likely not be felt for several more years, as industry and physicians adapt to its requirements and the broader public responds to the information that becomes available" (*Health Affairs* 2014, p. 5).

ACA also took a step to fundamentally alter coverage of prescription drugs for those with health insurance by including prescription drugs as one of the ten "essential health benefits" all qualified insurance plans must now offer (Healthcare.gov 2013). The coverage of prescription drugs in the new health benefit exchanges is subject to the deductibles and copayments included with the various levels of coverage, leading some who gain coverage through the exchanges to have higher out-of-pocket drug costs than they would in more traditional plans still offered by many employers. Thorpe et al. (2015) compared coverage in patients with chronic medical conditions who selected a silver plan on a state exchange with coverage provided by a patient's employer and found that "out-of-pocket expenses for medications in a typical silver plan are twice as high as they are in the average employer-sponsored plan" (p. 1695), raising the question of whether these patients might hold off on filling prescribed medication due to cost. As part of the continued discussion of pharmaceutical policy under ACA, affordability for patients will remain a central issue, along with those pertaining to pharmaceutical pricing and payments to physicians.

Long-Term Care

Up to this point, this book has talked mostly about the system of acute care in the United States. Most of the money spent on health care and most of the attention given to recent changes in health policy have focused on the care we provide to people with specific conditions that need treatment from a physician or at a hospital.

What happens, though, when elderly or disabled people are not sick enough to require hospitalization but, due to chronic illness or general frailty, are not able to take care of themselves? These types of people are provided assistance through our system of long-term care. As the name implies, this type of care is ongoing and has less to do with the treatment of a specific disease until it is cured than with care for chronic conditions for which there is no cure.

There are many reasons why people need long-term care. Most often, an elderly person will simply have physical difficulty undertaking normal daily activities such as dressing, bathing, eating, and going to the toilet. (Activities such as these are referred to as activities of daily living, or ADLs.) Alternatively, a person may have a serious mental impairment such as Alzheimer's disease that necessitates continuous supervision. Some people may have both physical difficulty with ADLs and mental impairment.

Traditionally, the need for long-term care was met principally by the family. As people became frail and in need of assistance, younger family members often teamed together to provide care. Because the dynamics of the American family has changed over the years, however, more and more frail elderly patients need organized institutions or services to help them.

THE GROWING NEED FOR LONG-TERM CARE
AMONG FRAIL ELDERLY PEOPLE

Most people over 65 years old are able to care for themselves without any need for long-term care services. The problem of long-term care is mainly a problem of frail elderly individuals. It is very old people—those over 85—who typically need long-term care. Nearly half of all people in nursing homes and one-fourth of all people with long-term care needs living in the community are over 85. Of the 46.2 million people age 65 or over in the United States in 2014, about 13 percent were age 85 or older (data from US Census Bureau website). As figure 11.1 shows, the number of people over 85 is growing much more rapidly than the number of elderly overall.

In 2014, 6.2 million people in this country were 85 years old or older. By 2020, this number is projected to increase to 7.3 million. This number is expected to triple between 2014 and 2050 (AARP 2012). As a result of the baby boom generation moving into their elder years, those over 85 will grow from 13.3 percent of the elderly population in 2014 to 19.2 percent by 2040. Whatever problems our health care system has in providing and financing long-term care will be multiplied within a few decades. As stated in a 1998 report submitted to Congress by the US General Accounting Office: "Increased demand for long-term care, which will be driven in part by the aging baby boom generation, will contribute further to federal and state budget burdens" (p. 2).

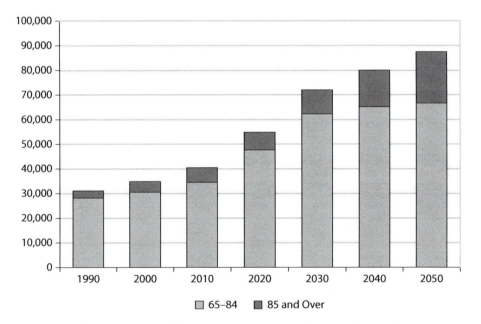

FIGURE 11.1. Projected growth (in thousands) in the elderly population of the United States, 1990–2050. *Source:* Data from US Census Bureau.

The report went on to say that the increasing needs of the baby boom generation for long-term care "will lead to a sharp growth in federal entitlement spending that, absent meaningful reforms, will represent an unsustainable burden on future generations" (p. 3).

NURSING HOME CARE

> **CONCEPT 11.1**
>
> The population group that is most in need of long-term care—those over 85 years old—is also the fastest-growing population group in the United States.

If an elderly or disabled person is in need of long-term care that, for whatever reason, cannot be provided in the home or other community setting, that person can receive care in a nursing home or other type of residential care facility. In 2013, there were 1.4 million people receiving care in nursing homes, of whom 42.8 percent were between age 65 and 84, and an additional 42.3 percent were age 85 or over (US Centers for Disease Control and Prevention 2015c). The average age of people in nursing homes is about 84. Sixty-eight percent are women. Three-fourths of these residents needed assistance with at least three ADLs. Seventy percent had severe memory loss (data from Kaiser Family Foundation 1999 and National Center for Health Statistics website).

Not all people in nursing homes, however, are there for chronic long-term care. Many people will spend time in a nursing home following an acute illness or injury, and then will return home after a short stay. As many as one in five elderly people will spend at least some time in a nursing home at some point. In 1999, the average length of stay for residents in nursing homes was about twenty-nine months; however, 68 percent of residents discharged from nursing homes had stays of less than three months. About 20 percent of nursing home residents stay there for two years or more.

Many people have the impression that Medicare pays for most of the nursing home care needed by elderly people, but this is usually not the case. Of the $357 billion spent nationally on all types of long-term care services, Medicare paid 21 percent, with most of that going for post–acute rehabilitation services including home care (Kaiser Family Foundation 2013). Medicare pays for about 12 percent of nursing home care. To qualify for Medicare payment, a patient must have an acute medical problem that requires skilled nursing care as part of the treatment program. Examples of skilled nursing care would be the administration of intravenous antibiotics or assistance with rehabilitation following surgery or an injury. In each case, a physician must certify that skilled care of this type is medically indicated. In most cases, the patient must have been in an acute care hospital just before entering the nursing home to qualify for Medicare payment. Even when a patient qualifies for skilled nursing care of this type, Medicare will pay the full cost only for the first 20 days. For skilled nursing care required beyond 20 days, in 2015 the patient was required to pay a copayment of $157.50 per day up to a maximum of 100 days of care. Any care required after

100 days is totally the responsibility of the patient, with no further coverage from Medicare.

Medicare distinguishes between *skilled nursing care* and *custodial nursing care*. Once a patient's medical condition has plateaued—that is, once he or she has attained the maximum level of healing or rehabilitation that can be expected in the short term— the patient no longer qualifies for Medicare's skilled nursing benefit. If the patient has to remain in the nursing home due to a need for assistance with ADLs, he or she is now considered to be receiving custodial care rather than skilled nursing care. Medicare does not pay for custodial care in nursing homes. Patients who need this type of care must find another way to pay for that care.

One of the advantages of Medicare Advantage (MA), Medicare's managed care option, has been a relaxation of Medicare policies pertaining to the use of skilled nursing facilities. A physician treating a patient covered by MA is allowed to treat a patient in a skilled nursing facility at his or her discretion. It is not necessary that a patient be in a hospital first. The cost of skilled nursing care comes out of the overall yearly capitation received by the MA plan, so there typically will be some type of control on the use of long-term care. The type of utilization control depends on the type of MA plan a patient selects, but it often involves a case manager—a nurse or social worker who supervises the overall process of care a frail elderly patient will receive. The patient still must require skilled nursing care to be eligible for nursing home payment under MA, however. If the patient needs ongoing custodial care, MA, like traditional Medicare, provides no coverage.

> **CONCEPT 11.2**
>
> Medicare pays very little of the cost of nursing home care. Patients who need long-term, custodial nursing home care are not eligible for Medicare payment.

What does the person do, then, who no longer requires skilled nursing care but still needs constant assistance with ADLs? Consider the case, for example, of an elderly widow who has been living alone in her own home but who has had a stroke and is partially paralyzed. Medicare will pay the costs of a short-term rehabilitation program, but after a few weeks the patient is no longer eligible for coverage. Returning home is not a realistic option, so the patient finds herself in a nursing home. The cost of that nursing home will typically be between $60,000 and $90,000 per year—often more. Who pays for the ongoing care this patient needs? There are three principal sources to pay for this care: out of pocket, Medicaid, and private insurance.

1. Payment out of pocket for nursing home care

Many patients find themselves with no way to pay for nursing home care other than to pay out of pocket. In 2013, patients and their families paid 19 percent of the overall cost of nursing home care from personal resources. About one in four patients pays for nursing home care out of pocket when she or he is admitted. At a cost of $80,000–$90,000 a year or more, it does not take long to exhaust the patient's resources. Few seniors have sufficient assets to be able to generate an income of $90,000 a year on an ongoing basis. Nonetheless, in many cases there is no alternative for the patient but to exhaust her personal assets in paying for care.

2. Medicaid payment for nursing home care

Unlike Medicare, the Medicaid program will pay the costs of ongoing, custodial care in nursing homes for poor seniors. Recall from chapter 7 that nearly 70 percent of Medicaid funds goes to pay for the care of elderly and disabled people who are also poor. Elderly, poor people who need long-term care in a nursing home or other type of custodial care facility are eligible to have Medicaid pay the full cost of their care. This is our country's final safety net to assure that no elderly or disabled person who needs custodial care will be denied that care because he or she is unable to pay for it. About 60 percent of nursing home residents nationwide are covered by Medicaid.

An irony of our system of paying for nursing home care is the extent to which it causes people who were not originally poor to become poor. As described previously, about one nursing home resident in four who needs ongoing custodial care will pay for that care out of pocket. For many of these people, it takes little time to completely exhaust one's life savings paying for nursing home care. Once a person, such as the elderly widow who is partially paralyzed, spends all (or nearly all) of her money paying for nursing home care, she then becomes eligible for Medicaid payment for any further care. She is allowed to keep up to $2,000 in a personal savings account, but otherwise she must sell all her assets and use all her funds before Medicaid will pay for her care. Of those patients who initially pay for their nursing home care out of pocket and end up staying in the nursing home for two to three years or more, half will become impoverished and become eligible for Medicaid payment for their care.

What happens in the case of an elderly couple who has been living in their own home for years and one spouse sustains an illness or injury that requires long-term, custodial care in a nursing home? The spouse in the nursing home requires ongoing care, yet the healthy spouse is still able to stay at home and live independently. Historically, both spouses were required to spend all their money, including exhausting their combined savings *and* selling their house, and use the proceeds to pay for the nursing home care of the ill spouse. It was necessary for both spouses to become impoverished for the care of the ill spouse to be covered by Medicaid. The spouse remaining in the couple's home faced a heart-wrenching choice:

> **CONCEPT 11.3**
>
> Medicaid will pay the cost of long-term, custodial nursing care for those seniors who need it. However, before becoming eligible for Medicaid payment, seniors must exhaust nearly all their own resources by paying for care out of pocket.

either spend all the money, lose the home, and become poor or divorce the spouse and sever legal responsibility for the cost of the nursing home care. For a number of years, the need to protect the financial independence of the healthy spouse was a major contributor to the divorce rate among elderly couples, many of whom had been married for decades.

Fortunately, Congress changed the rules on what has come to be called "Medicaid spend-down." Now, if a couple faces the need to have one spouse cared for in a nursing home, the other spouse is allowed to maintain assets sufficient to remain in the couple's home and live independently.

What if an elderly person—again, let's consider the partially paralyzed widow—has substantial personal assets and finds that she needs to be in a nursing home? Why not simply give all her money to her children, thus becoming poor and qualifying for Medicaid? When Congress changed the law to protect the remaining spouse from Medicaid spend-down, it also changed the law regarding giving away one's assets. There is now a "look-back" period, typically about three to five years, in which Medicaid can look to see if the patient gave away significant assets to children or other family members. If it is found that she did give away assets that she otherwise would have been required to spend before qualifying for Medicaid, the family members who received the gifts must first use those funds to pay for the needed nursing home care. Only after the gifted funds have been used will the patient qualify for Medicaid coverage for her long-term care needs.

3. Private long-term care insurance

A number of private insurance companies offer insurance specifically to cover the cost of long-term care. These types of policies are usually made available to large employee groups. Only those not currently in need of long-term care are eligible to obtain the policies. The cost of these policies can be prohibitive—more than $3,000 per year for someone who is 60 years old and substantially more for someone 65 years or older. As a result, few individuals can afford such coverage. About 7 percent of the elderly population is covered by private long-term care insurance, and about 7 percent of the cost of nursing home care is paid by these policies.

HOME HEALTH CARE

A substantial number of elderly or disabled people in this country need help with ADLs on an ongoing basis but are not so ill that they need to be in a nursing home. If they are provided with a limited amount of assistance, these people are capable of remaining in their home. Many of them qualify for in-home, long-term care under either Medicare or Medicaid.

Typically, people who qualify for home care assistance will have a nurse visit them on a regular basis, checking on their situation and assuring that their basic needs are met. These nurses can provide services such as monitoring the patient's medications, assessing the patient's nutrition, and evaluating ongoing home safety. In addition, some of these patients may be eligible to have the assistance of a home health aide. An aide of this type is not a nurse but rather someone trained specifically in providing assistance with ADLs. The aide will visit the patient on a regular basis and help with such activities as bathing and meal preparation. (See Levine, Boal, and Boling 2003 for further discussion of the clinical aspects of home health care.)

In 2013, Medicare spent $34.4 billion on home health care (data from US Centers for Medicare and Medicaid Services website). By comparison, in 2013 the Medicaid program, covering both elderly and nonelderly people in need of home health care, spent $29.1 billion.

The Medicare home health benefit was originally intended to be similar to the nursing home benefit: it would cover only a short period of care and only after hospitalization for an acute medical problem. In the 1980s, Congress modified the eligibility rules in two important ways:

1. They removed the requirement that the patient must be in the hospital before being eligible for home care services.
2. They removed the cap on the number of services an eligible patient may receive per year.

Now, any Medicare beneficiary who meets the following criteria is eligible for payment of home health services on an ongoing basis. If the patient meets these criteria, he or she is eligible to have Medicare pay for both the skilled care services and the custodial care services provided in the home. The criteria are that

- the patient is homebound;
- the patient is under the care of a physician, who periodically reviews the plan for home care services;
- the patient has an intermittent need for skilled care services from either a nurse or other care provider (e.g., physical therapist); and
- the patient's care is provided by a home health agency that is a certified provider of services under the Medicare program.

The costs associated with Medicare's home care program began to increase around 1980 when some of the initial program restrictions were relaxed. In 1989, there was a further loosening of eligibility requirements, and the costs of the program began to soar. In the nine years from 1980 to 1989, the cost of the program nearly tripled, from $662 million to $1.95 billion. A large part of the increase in the cost of the program was due to the increased frequency with which home care services were used over this time period. For most of the period from 1974 to 1989, those beneficiaries who qualified for Medicare home health services received about twenty-five visits per year. With the relaxation of eligibility requirements in the late 1980s, the average number of visits per home health care beneficiary jumped to nearly seventy-five per year.

The Medicare home health program was initially intended as a low-cost supplement to hospital care. In 1967, it accounted for less than 1 percent of all Medicare expenditures. Over the next thirty years, it became a major service program, accounting for nearly 5 percent of Medicare expenditures by 1997. In 2014, home health care accounted for 3 percent of overall Medicare expenditures.

As discussed in chapter 6, the cost of home health care originally came out of the Part A Medicare trust fund. As Part A costs rose and the trust fund was facing potential insolvency, Congress modified Medicare's home health program in 1997 as part of the Balanced Budget Act. It reallocated most of the costs of the program to Medicare Part B and instituted new limitations on the use of home health services. It also introduced a Prospective Payment System for home health care, under which Medicare would make a fixed, capitated payment to the home health agency for each sixty-day episode of care. The payment level was adjusted based on the level of the patient's care needs. These changes in eligibility and payment were initially successful in reducing costs, with a 12.9 percent decline in expenditures between 1997 and 1998.

> **CONCEPT 11.4**
>
> Medicare has become the principal source of payment for home health services for elderly and disabled people. Following a relaxation in eligibility guidelines in the 1980s, both the number of visits per homecare patient and overall program costs increased dramatically.

HOSPICE CARE

Consider the case of an elderly patient who discovers that he has cancer or some other terminal illness and is told by his doctor that he will most likely die within the next six months. Often this type of patient is not sick enough to be in the hospital, or alternatively, simply does not want to be in the hospital due to the futility of future attempts at treatment. It can be difficult for the family by itself to provide adequate care to a dying person, yet neither the patient nor the family wants placement in a nursing home. For this patient, a hospice may provide the best care available.

A hospice can be either a place for a person with a terminal disease to go for treatment or a team of professionals who assist the family to provide care to the terminally ill at home, or both. The hospice program focuses on relieving suffering rather than prolonging life. Hospice care involves a shift in the emphasis of care away from further attempts at cure to controlling the symptoms of the illness and providing emotional support during the dying process, often referred to as palliative care. Emotional support is offered both to the patient and to family members. Hospice care begins at the point that the inevitability of death is recognized and carries beyond the patient's death to help family members adjust to the loss.

The modern hospice movement, with an emphasis on symptom control and on dying as a process, began in England in the 1960s. The first modern hospice was named St. Christopher's and is described in the following quotation: "Several factors differentiate St. Christopher's from hospitals: allowing children to visit and play, personalized care, little patient-staff protocol, an informal social life, a continuum of care including home care, freedom to issue drugs and liquor as requested for symptom control, and follow-up with the family members after the patient's death" (Plumb and Ogle 1992, p. 812).

As it has developed in the United States over the past thirty years, a hospice program usually involves a health care team, often including a physician, a nurse, a social worker, a member of the clergy, trained home health aides, and community volunteers. The team will come to the patient's home and provide as much care as is feasible. Team members often will provide respite care for the family, relieving them for periods of time so they can take a break from the intense responsibilities of caring for a dying person. Some hospice programs will also have a care center, similar to that described for St. Christopher's. The patient who needs intensive assistance can stay in the facility, with family members visiting freely. Alternatively, the patient can split his or her time, spending part of the week in the hospice facility and part of the week at home with family members. As one might expect, hospice patients are three times as likely to die at home than in a hospital or nursing home when compared to patients who do not use hospice services.

Congress amended the Medicare program in 1982 to allow payment of hospice services for beneficiaries. To be eligible for hospice care, the beneficiary

- must be certified by a physician to have an incurable disease and be expected to live six months or less, and
- must agree to waive Medicare coverage for treatment of the illness provided outside the hospice program.

Thus, a hospice patient under Medicare agrees to forgo further surgery or other types of therapy that are not intended for palliation and symptom relief. In return, the beneficiary is eligible for a substantially wider range of services than is available under traditional Medicare, such as drugs required for symptom relief, respite care at an inpatient facility, and bereavement counseling for the family.

An important study from 2010 evaluated the effect of receiving palliative care, such as that provided by hospice services, for patients with metastatic lung cancer—a condition that carries with it a grave prognosis. The patients in the study were not actually enrolled in hospice programs. They thus maintained the option of aggressive care, even as they neared the end of their life. Nonetheless, those patients receiving palliative care were less likely to choose aggressive care (33% as compared to 54% for those not receiving palliative care). Despite reduced use of aggressive care, the palliative care patients actually survived longer than patients not receiving palliative care (11.6 months as compared to 8.9 months) and reported a significantly better quality of life (Temel et al. 2010). An editorial accompanying the report of the study concluded "that life-threatening illness, whether it can be cured or controlled, carries with it significant burdens of suffering for patients and their families and that this suffering can be effectively addressed by modern palliative care teams. Perhaps unsurprisingly, reducing patients' misery may help them live longer" (Kelley and Meier 2010, p. 782).

The number of Medicare beneficiaries choosing to use hospice programs increased substantially during the 1990s, from 143,000 in 1992 to nearly 488,000 in 2000. During this same time period, the number of hospice programs providing care grew from 1,208 in 1992 to 2,244 in 2001. By 2013, 1.3 million Medicare beneficiaries received hospice care from more than 3,900 hospice providers (data from US Centers for Medicare and Medicaid Services website). Of all Medicare beneficiaries who died in 2013, 47 percent had received hospice care.

Nursing homes make up a growing percentage of hospice providers. As described previously, hospice care can be provided either in a patient's home or in a nursing facility. Recall also that nursing home patients requiring custodial care are not eligible for Medicare payment. Patients receiving long-term, custodial care in a nursing home are likely to experience an ongoing decline in overall health. At some point, the patient may face a life expectancy of six months or less, thus making them eligible for hospice care given at the same facility. By enrolling in hospice care, the cost of the nursing home is paid by Medicare as part of the hospice benefit. In a study comparing patients who died in a nursing home while in hospice with those who were not in hospice at the time of death, Gozalo et al. (2015) found that the hospice patients had a higher quality of life in the period preceding death, at an average increased cost of $6,761 per patient, leading the authors to raise "the policy concern that profit motives may be driving selective enrollment of nursing home residents without cancer, who have longer hospice lengths of stay" (p. 1829).

As the use of hospice programs and facilities expanded, the type of patient using hospice care changed somewhat. In 1992, 76 percent of all hospice patients were eligible for services because of a diagnosis of cancer. In 2008, this number had decreased to 31 percent and has remained relatively stable since that time. An increasing number of patients with diseases other than cancer, such as heart disease, lung disease, stroke, and Alzheimer's disease, are entering hospice programs. Despite this relative decline, nearly half of all Medicare patients who died of cancer were enrolled in a hospice program at the time of their death.

Although Medicare beneficiaries are eligible for a full six months of hospice care, the actual length of time in a hospice program before death is usually considerably shorter.

In 1992, the median length of hospice service was twenty-six days. In 2000, the median had decreased to seventeen days and remained at that level in 2013 (Medicare Payment Advisory Commission 2015b). This means that half of all hospice patients in 2013 received fewer than three weeks of service. Teno et al. (2013) found that in 2009, 28 percent of people who died while under hospice care had been enrolled in hospice for three days or less, with 40 percent of these decedents having been cared for in a hospital ICU immediately before transfer to hospice. These data suggest that it is often difficult for physicians, patients, and family members to face the inevitability of death that confronts many patients, and to begin to plan for death in advance of the final stages of illness.

There is another aspect of these data that has important policy implications. Looking instead at the average length of stay in hospice, we find that it has risen somewhat, from 48 days in 2000 to 88 days in 2013. As mentioned earlier, a growing number of Medicare beneficiaries receive hospice care for diseases other than cancer. One of the largest groups of these noncancer patients are those with Alzheimer's disease and other forms of dementia or similar neurological problems. While the median length of stay in hospice in 2013 was 18 days for patients with cancer, the median stay for those with neurological disorders such as dementia was 31 days. There is a subset of these noncancer patients with substantially longer lengths of stay than the six-month prognosis required for hospice admission. At the 75th percentile of length of stay, patients with neurological problems stayed 167 days, as compared to 57 days for cancer patients. At the 90th percentile, cancer patients stayed 129 days (slightly more than four months), while patients with dementia stayed 443 days—well over a year (Medicare Payment Advisory Commission 2015b).

There is an additional policy issue pertaining to the Medicare hospice program that we should be aware of. As described in chapter 9, beginning in the 1990s there has been a growing number of for-profit organizations providing care in hospitals and specialty care centers such as kidney dialysis centers. The same is true for hospice providers. In 2000, 30 percent of hospice providers operated on a for-profit basis. By 2013, that number had grown to 59 percent. Many of these for-profit agencies were part of companies operating large chains of providers. By 2011, 45 percent of hospice patients were cared for by a provider that was part of a large chain, with about three-quarters of these chains operating on a for-profit basis (Stevenson et al. 2015). While Medicare reimburses for-profit providers the same amount per patient per day, for-profit

> **CONCEPT 11.5**
>
> Hospice care has become an increasingly important source of care for people with terminal illness. Hospice care involves treating symptoms rather than prolonging life, as well as providing emotional support for the dying person and his or her family. When hospice was first created, most hospice patients had cancer. An increasing share of hospice patients are under care for dementia and other neurological conditions, and often have lengths of stay considerably longer than 6 months.

providers spend substantially less than nonprofit providers providing patient care. In 2012, the median expenditure of for-profit providers was $127 per patient per day, while the median daily expenditure of nonprofit providers was $155 (Medicare Payment Advisory Commission 2015b).

One of the factors that may have contributed to this difference in per-patient expenditures are the polices adopted by the hospice provider that limit the type of patient they will accept into care. For example, a hospice is allowed under Medicare policies not to accept patients who need intensive treatments such as chemotherapy or parenteral nutrition. The cost of caring for these types of patients can be quite high, while the Medicare daily reimbursement is the same as other patients. In a study comparing for-profit and nonprofit hospice providers, Carlson et al. (2012) found that "for-profit hospices, which represent more than half of all hospices, have the most restrictive enrollment policies" (p. 2696).

Responding to the rapid growth of the cost to Medicare of providing the hospice benefit, Stevenson (2012) raised an important policy issue: "Beyond the scrutiny that inevitably accompanies increased government spending, policymakers have paid particular attention to the emergence of a robust for-profit hospice sector and increased use by nursing home residents, raising questions about the extent to which some agencies are aggressively targeting more profitable patients" (p. 1684). If patients with dementia and other similar problems have substantially longer stays in hospice and cost less to care for than patients with cancer, it would make sense for a profit-oriented company to try selectively to enroll these lower-cost patients.

LIFE-CARE COMMUNITIES AS AN ALTERNATIVE TO LONG-TERM CARE

The options for long-term care have expanded recently by the addition of a relatively new type of senior care facility—the life-care community. A life-care community offers a permanent place for seniors to live, in which their needs for assistance with living will be taken care of no matter how long they need them. Whatever level of services a resident needs will be provided for one fixed cost.

In a life-care community, different levels of care typically are available:

1. Independent living

The life-care community provides individual apartments or condominiums for those residents capable of living alone. Residents in this level of care are fully independent, providing their own meals, and do not rely on assistance for any activities of daily living. They may, however, obtain meals from a central dining facility when desired, have assistance with transportation, and have someone always available for assistance in case of an emergency.

2. Assisted living

Some residents are not fully capable of living independently but are not frail enough to require constant assistance. Typically, the life-care facility provides these residents with an apartment in a central facility that has staff immediately available. These residents can make the apartment their own home. They usually require little if any help with ADLs, although they may eat in a central dining room and may have assistance managing their medications and bathing. The apartments usually have call buttons and other surveillance devices, so if a resident ever needs assistance, it is immediately available. These facilities are staffed around the clock, usually with aides rather than nurses.

3. Custodial care

Some residents in life-care communities have an illness or injury that necessitates round-the-clock assistance with ADLs or medical needs. This is the level of care that is usually provided in a nursing home. The life-care facility has a fully staffed nursing center available for these residents. They may need this level of care for only a short period of time, after which they can move back to their own home or apartment, or they may need this care for the rest of their life, in which case they will remain in the nursing center.

The unique aspect of life-care communities is that all these services are available for one fixed fee. The fee usually includes both a cash buy-in when the resident first enters the community and a monthly maintenance fee. In return for the buy-in and the monthly fee, residents are guaranteed whatever level of care they need for the rest of their life. The only requirements are that the residents demonstrate sufficient income to assure lifetime payment of the maintenance fees, and that they enter the community at level 1 (i.e., they are healthy enough initially to live independently).

Life-care communities offer an attractive alternative to many seniors who face the prospect of growing old alone at home and possibly ending their life in a nursing home. For a life-care community to work, however, seniors must plan for their remaining years when they are still relatively healthy. If they wait until they need extensive assistance, they are no longer eligible to enter these communities.

As one might imagine, it can often be very expensive to enter a life-care community, making them realistic alternatives for only the wealthiest seniors. A number of religious and other nonprofit institutions have established life-care communities, however, making them available to people without a large number of assets.

FUTURE POLICY ISSUES IN LONG-TERM CARE

A number of policy questions remain to be answered regarding the future of long-term care in the United States. As difficult as the problems of the health care system are in general, the problems confronting our long-term care system are often even more vexing and are complicated by the relative lack of attention long-term care receives in the public health policy arena.

How Will We Provide Long-Term Care for the Growing Number of Frail Elderly People?

As discussed earlier, the number of people in this country over 85, the population most in need of long-term care services, is expected to triple by 2050, growing to 19 percent of the population. Many of these people will need nursing home care. How will we build the nursing home facilities to meet the growing future need?

An alternative to building more nursing home beds is to develop more community-based services. In many cases, a well-designed program of home health services can allow patients in need of substantial assistance to remain in the home with their families. For those without families to help them, smaller, community-based residential facilities that provide more of a homelike atmosphere can be an attractive alternative to traditional nursing homes.

The journal *Health Affairs* (2015) published a policy brief addressing the shift to community-based care rather than institutional care for Medicaid beneficiaries needing long-term services and supports (LTSS) (*Health Affairs* 2015). The authors describe how in 2013, "the majority of Medicaid LTSS spending was for the first time focused on home and community-based settings instead of institutional care, and the Centers for Medicare and Medicaid Services (CMS) projects that community-based spending will reach 63 percent of all Medicaid LTSS spending by 2020" (p. 1). Robinson et al. (2015) reported on a "Money Follows the Person" demonstration project in Connecticut that between 2008 and 2014 transitioned 2,262 residents of nursing homes and other institutional care facilities to community-based facilities. The patients had an average age of 63 years, with 9 percent age 85 or older and 11 percent younger than 45. Among the community-based facilities into which these residents moved were the home of the patient or a family member (21%), a leased apartment (71%), or an assisted living facility or other type of residential care home (8%). The authors found that, despite having a relatively high level of disability as measured by needing help with ADLs, "the wide range of outcomes measured tell a consistent story of improved quality of life, which led to higher rates of global life satisfaction for people who remained in the community" (p. 1634). The one outcome that worsened in the community setting was the frequency of falls experienced by the study subjects, going from 20 percent per year before transition to 26 percent per year after transition to the community-based care setting. As described in the section discussing its impact on long-term care policy, ACA includes changes in policies and funding intended to increase the role of community-based care settings for those in need of LTSS.

How Will We Pay for Long-Term Care in the Future?

More challenging than simply building the facilities needed for care is the question of how we will pay for that care. Few will argue that the current system of financing long-term care is optimal. Many question whether the impoverishment of elderly, middle-class nursing home residents is a wise choice. Is the best option to ask people to pay for nursing home care out of pocket? Similarly, is the way we split responsibility between Medicaid and Medicare wise, with Medicaid paying for nursing home care and Medicare paying for home health care?

Long-term care can be seen as a broad social need that must be addressed through broad social policy. A system of social insurance, similar to the Medicare system of paying for acute care, could potentially meet the financing needs for long-term care. To do so, however, the system will need to be broadly financed by all taxpayers, not just those who need care. The American taxpayer has been especially reluctant in recent years to take on new social programs. Yet, a substantial portion of the financing burden of long-term care falls on middle-class families and individuals. Will the American taxpayer be willing to invest in long-term care now so that needed care is available in the coming decades?

How Will We Maintain the Quality of the Long-Term Care System?

For years there has been concern over the quality of long-term care services, especially care in nursing homes. As many as one nursing home in four has been found to have ongoing problems with quality (Feder, Komisar, and Niefeld 2000). Issues such as the appropriate level of staffing, the use of physical and chemical restraints, and the quality of the nursing services provided have led to continued federal and state oversight.

One of the issues contributing to these problems has been the relatively low level of Medicaid payment for nursing home care. As with acute medical care, Medicaid pays providers substantially less than private sources pay. With the large number of Medicaid beneficiaries in nursing homes, it has often been difficult for providers both to meet quality requirements and to maintain financial viability. The trade-off between cost and quality will remain an important issue in long-term care.

Who Will Provide Medical Care for Frail Elderly People?

Good-quality long-term care requires the continuous participation and oversight of medical personnel. A number of physicians, however, are either unwilling or unable to provide active supervision of long-term care. Recent years have seen a reduction in interest in primary care among physicians. If the growing needs of the elderly are to be met, interest in primary care will have to expand and will need to include additional emphasis on geriatric care. This can be done either by including more involvement in geriatric care in the training of general internists and family physicians or by increasing the number of physicians who focus their practice on geriatric care. As an alternative, nurse practitioners and other types of mid-level health care practitioners can assume a greater role in monitoring and supervising long-term care.

What Are the Ethical Issues Surrounding Care of Frail Elderly People?

In recent years, increased attention has focused on important ethical aspects of long-term care. The increasing role of advanced directives, such as living wills and durable power of attorney, has provided the opportunity for many elderly people to consider the appropriate level of care they wish to receive in the event that they become seriously ill. Issues of the autonomy and privacy of nursing home residents, especially those with cognitive impairment, are only beginning to be examined. The question of physician-assisted suicide has begun to receive increased attention as an option for patients facing inevitable death combined with intractable suffering. A number of states, including California in 2015, have legalized physician-assisted suicide for terminally ill patients under strict guidelines. Future policy discussions will need to include consideration of these and other ethical issues that surround long-term care.

THE AFFORDABLE CARE ACT AND LONG-TERM CARE

ACA makes a number of changes to payment policies for long-term care services, although none of them will fundamentally change the system. Under ACA, the CMS is authorized to change the formula it uses to calculate payments to providers of home health services and to hospice providers. The Prospective Payment System for home health care services, created by the Balanced Budget Act of 1997, is updated under ACA to reflect more recent cost and utilization data. The updated payments were expected to reduce Medicare home health expenditures by $25 billion over a period of ten years. Rosati et al. (2014) evaluated the potential impact of these payment changes on patients who receive home health services. In their analysis, they raise the concern that "these payment reductions could create financial disincentives for home health care agencies to serve patients with complex clinical conditions and limited social and economic resources. . . . Left unchecked, the financial disincentives within the current payment system could lead to reduced access for these less profitable groups of patients" (p. 952).

ACA also authorizes CMS to revise the payment system to hospice providers. The Medicare Payment Advisory Commission (MedPAC) recommended payment changes that would "make long stays less profitable by adjusting payments to reimburse providers at higher rates at the resource-intensive beginning and end of a hospice episode but at lower rates in between" (Stevenson 2012, p. 1685). MedPAC also recommended ending the exclusion of hospice services from the care provided by MA plans, a policy that has been in effect since the creation of the hospice benefit in the 1980s. If a MA beneficiary needs hospice care, Medicare payment reverts to fee-for-service under Part A and Part B, with the MA plan responsible only for Part D pharmaceutical coverage. Under the proposed changes, the full hospice care benefit would be included in the services provided by MA plans. Payment for these hospice services would be included in the reimbursement the plans already receive from Medicare. As described by Stevenson and Huskamp (2014), "plans currently have a strong incentive to encourage patients with terminal conditions to enroll in hospice, thereby ending the plans' clinical and financial responsibilities for the care of such patients" (p. 1493). Accordingly, the authors recommended increased monitoring of the adequacy of the hospice network maintained by the plans and the quality of the hospice care provided.

One issue that was left out of ACA was that of improving the quality of end-of-life counseling of patients with terminal or potentially terminal illnesses. A report by the Institute of Medicine recommended that physicians and other caregivers increase both the quality and availability of the counseling support they provide patients in these circumstances. The IOM panel recommended that "conversations about patients' end-of-life options, goals, and preferences should become a priority and be reimbursed by Medicare, Medicaid, and private insurers" (Graham 2014, p. 1845). While this added Medicare benefit was openly discussed in the months leading up to passage of ACA, critics of ACA focused on these conversations with physicians and other professionals as constituting "death panels," effectively removing them from consideration as part of ACA. The IOM report, made by a nonpartisan panel convened under the auspices of the National Academy of Sciences, has brought the issue back for consideration, in a context that (hopefully) removes the political labeling previously associated with it.

I should also mention one additional change in long-term care policy included in ACA, even though that change has since been dropped from further consideration. ACA created a new program of voluntary long-term care insurance, referred to as the Community Living Assistance Services and Supports (CLASS) Act. As initially described on the White House website (2015), "the Act provides Americans with a new option to finance long-term services and care in the event of a disability. . . . The benefit is flexible: it could be used for a range of community support services, from respite care to home care." CLASS only supports community-based services and not institutionally based services such as nursing homes. I should also note that the White House description of the plan states explicitly the conditions placed on CLASS by ACA: "No taxpayer funds will be used to pay benefits under this provision. . . . Safeguards will be put in place to ensure its premiums are enough to cover its costs."

In preparation to enact CLASS, the US Department of Health and Human Services (HHS) (2011) issued a report on an extensive series of simulations and feasibility studies it had conducted. The final paragraph of the report acknowledged "substantial uncertainty" about the fiscal solvency of the program, concluding that "we cannot with any confidence predict that the CLASS program would be able to honor its commitments to individuals who had already enrolled" (p. 46). Accordingly, Sherry Glied, the assistant secretary for planning and evaluation of HHS reported to a congressional committee that, based on HHS's inability to "identify a benefit plan that was actuarially solvent over the next 75 years and consistent with the other statutory requirements," HHS "would not go forward with implementing the CLASS program." It appears that private long-term care insurance may not be a fiscally viable way to approach our society's growing need for long-term care services.

THE CONNECTION BETWEEN HOSPITAL CARE AND SKILLED NURSING CARE UNDER THE AFFORDABLE CARE ACT

As described previously, Medicare will pay for the first twenty days of skilled nursing care as long as the care program is part of a rehabilitation plan and as long as the patient first was treated for at least three days in the hospital. This three-day requirement is waived for skilled nursing care under MA plans. ACA has brought up a number of potential policy changes intended to break down this separation of payment approaches for hospital care and rehabilitative care. As described in chapter 6, ACA created a series of trials involving various forms of accountable care organizations (ACO).

ACOs are expected to shift over time from fee-for-service reimbursement to alternative payment methods based either on bundled payment per episode of care or risk-adjusted capitation payment. A central component of ACOs is creating a collaborative, shared-risk association between hospitals, physicians, and rehabilitative care providers such as skilled nursing facilities. MedPAC has recommended that these changes in payment policies also include dropping the three-day hospital stay requirement (Lipsitz 2013).

In 2015, CMS proposed a new, mandatory bundled payment policy for two categories of joint surgery: hip replacement and knee replacement. Referred to as the Comprehensive Care for Joint Replacement (CCJR) program, it would require all hospitals in 75 different metropolitan areas of the country (a total of about 750 hospitals) to accept bundled payments for these surgeries for a five-year period beginning in 2016. As described by Mechanic (2015), a single bundled payment would cover "hospitalizations, professional fees, and all clinically related Medicare Part A and Part B services for 90 days after discharge, including skilled nursing facility care, home care, and hospital readmissions" (p. 1291). By breaking down the barriers between hospital care and skilled nursing, rehabilitative care, this payment system would necessitate close collaboration and care coordination among physicians, hospitals, and skilled nursing facilities to optimize both patient outcomes as well as income. This type of innovative approach to payment is part of the move to innovative payment and delivery systems created by ACA, as discussed in chapter 13.

In the past, policy issues pertaining to long-term care have tended to receive less attention than those pertaining to health care more generally. As the baby boom generation ages—especially as they move into their eighties—long-term care will increasingly become more of a central policy concern. Increasingly, providing nursing and other support services in a person's home or community will become a core component of the long-term care system. Finding ways to pay for the expected increase in the need for long-term care services will be one of the key policy challenges facing our country in coming years. Additional policy issues involve maintaining the quality of long-term care services and ensuring adequate personnel to provide these services.

12

Factors Other Than Health Insurance That Impede Access to Health Care

As discussed in chapter 8, the growing number of Americans with no health insurance has for years been a major national problem. The principal focus of the Affordable Care Act (ACA) is to reduce the number of Americans without health insurance. It is important, however, to note that simply having health insurance does not always assure full access to care. As complex as the issue of universal health insurance is, the issue of universal access is even more so.

A number of barriers to gaining access to high-quality care have little to do with whether a person has health insurance. These barriers generally stem from forces within the organizational environment of the health care delivery system or within the broader social system itself. In this chapter, I examine a number of these forces and describe how they create barriers to full access to health care.

TYPE OF HEALTH INSURANCE COVERAGE AND ACCESS TO CARE FOR URGENT PROBLEMS

Certain types of urgent medical problems, once diagnosed, have a well-defined treatment. Acute appendicitis is one such problem. While it is not always easy to diagnosis appendicitis, once diagnosed the treatment is clear: appendectomy (the surgical removal of the appendix). In addition, it is well known that delays in the diagnosis and treatment of appendicitis will increase the chances of developing a potentially serious complication: rupture of the appendix.

A study reported by Braveman et al. in 1994 asked, "Will the type of insurance a patient has affect the chances of developing a ruptured appendix for those patients with acute appendicitis?" Appendicitis was studied because

- it is an illnesses that is apparently not affected by social or lifestyle factors, and thus it can be expected to occur with approximately equal frequency in different socioeconomic groups; and
- once diagnosed, it is promptly treated in almost all cases, regardless of insurance status.

The key variable in whether a patient will have his or her appendix removed before it ruptures is how easily the patient is able to obtain access to care. The study looked at this question in four groups, three of which had health insurance coverage:

1. patients with traditional fee-for-service insurance,
2. patients with insurance through a health maintenance organization (HMO),
3. patients on Medicaid, and
4. patients with no health insurance.

The study had two important findings:

1. Patients with either Medicaid or no insurance had approximately a 50 percent greater risk of developing a ruptured appendix than patients with HMO coverage.
2. Patients with fee-for-service insurance were at a 20 percent greater risk of developing a ruptured appendix than those with HMO coverage.

For patients with Medicaid, it appears that the barriers to obtaining care for acute appendicitis are similar to the barriers faced by patients with no insurance at all. Lacking a regular source of care, both populations often have to rely on the emergency room of large, often crowded hospitals to obtain care for urgent problems. The study by Tang and colleagues (2010), described in chapter 7, confirmed the pressure on emergency rooms from patients covered by Medicaid, but nonetheless still having to rely on busy hospital emergency rooms to obtain access to care, even routine care. Between 1999 and 2007, the rate at which Medicaid patients sought care from emergency rooms increased by 37 percent. In many areas of the country, for those on Medicaid simply having health insurance does little to assure prompt access to health care.

It is interesting, though, that in the Braveman study the patients with traditional, fee-for-service insurance also faced an increased chance of developing a ruptured appendix when compared to HMO patients. Though the difference between fee-for-service and HMO patients was smaller than that between Medicaid patients and HMO patients, it was nonetheless substantial. Why would patients with full insurance have problems obtaining prompt diagnosis and treatment for acute appendicitis? Although the study did not definitively answer this question, there are two possible explanations:

1. Patients with fee-for-service insurance do not automatically have a physician available to them as part of their insurance. They still have to seek out a physician on their own. Patients with full insurance but no established physician can face delays in obtaining care and may end up finding care in the emergency room. By comparison, patients with HMO insurance are given a list of providers from which to choose, and they are often required to select a primary care physician at the time of their enrollment. Having a previously identified provider can facilitate obtaining care in an urgent situation.

2. Fee-for-service insurance often involves deductibles and copayments that the patient must pay. These out-of-pocket expenses are typically higher for fee-for-service patients than for patients with HMO coverage and, as a result, may lead to patients delaying necessary care.

In the following sections, I will look more closely at the way out-of-pocket expenses for health care can affect access to care and the effect of Medicaid coverage on access to care.

CONCEPT 12.1

For patients with health insurance coverage, the type of insurance may affect the accessibility of care, with potential adverse health consequences.

THE EFFECT OF OUT-OF-POCKET EXPENSES ON THE RATE AT WHICH PATIENTS ACCESS CARE

As described in chapter 5, the RAND health insurance experiment, conducted in the 1970s and 1980s, looked closely at the question of how the amount a patient has to pay out of pocket to obtain care will affect the frequency with which the patient seeks care. This study demonstrated an association between the amount a patient must pay and the frequency with which the patient will obtain care (Newhouse et al. 1981). The study looked at people who were randomly assigned to one of four different insurance plans, each with a different level of payment required from the patient. The percentage of the cost that the patient must pay is called the "coinsurance rate." In plans 2–4, the patient had a yearly cap of $1,000 in out-of-pocket expenditures. After that amount, all additional care was 100 percent covered. Table 5.4 showed the results of this study, comparing the frequency with which the patient visited the doctor and the overall cost of care for different coinsurance rates.

The study documented that the amount of coinsurance a patient faces will affect both the frequency with which the patient visits the doctor and the overall cost of care (including both doctor care and hospital care) for that patient. Patients with free care visited the doctor 23 percent more often than those with 25 percent coinsurance and 69 percent more often than patients with 50 percent coinsurance.

The researchers looked at the types of outpatient visits and hospitalizations the different groups made, using a panel of experts to categorize the care received (or forgone) as necessary or unnecessary. They found that those with higher coinsurance had fewer visits and hospitalizations characterized as "necessary" as well as those characterized as "unnecessary." From this study, I was able to conclude that when a patient is responsible for paying for part of the cost of care, he or she is less likely to use that care. This association applies to necessary care as well as to unnecessary care.

Based on the conclusion from the RAND health insurance experiment that people who are required to pay a substantial share of their initial health care costs end up using less health care, the George W. Bush administration adopted a policy of encouraging more individuals and families to shift to health insurance policies that included high deductibles, that is, that required patients to pay out-of-pocket all health care costs up to a certain limit. The intent of this new policy was to encourage more employees to shift out of HMOs or other plans that had higher coverage and lower deductibles (and thus, it was believed, contributed to the rising cost of health care), and to enroll instead in a high-deductible health plan (HDHP). As reported in chapter 5, by 2009, approximately 8 percent of employees who receive their health insurance through their work had opted for the HDHP/HSA option. That number has grown steadily, reaching 24 percent of all employees who obtained health insurance through their work in 2015. A major reason for this growth has been the relatively low cost of these plans, both to the employer and to the employee. The average annual premium for a HDHP was $5,567 for single coverage and $15,970 for family coverage, as compared to HMO premiums of $6,212 for single coverage and $17,248 for family coverage, and PPO premiums of $6,575 for single coverage and $18, 469 for family coverage. In 2015, the average deductible under these plans was $2,099 for single coverage and $4,345 for family coverage (Kaiser Family Foundation and Health Research and Educational Trust 2015).

Haviland et al. (2012) estimated the potential impact on the cost of health care if HDHPs continue to increase their share of the employment-based health insurance market, concluding that if HDHPs were to grow to 50 percent of the market for employment-based health care, health care costs for this population would be reduced by $57 billion (2010 dollars). Part of this savings would be achieved through reduced use of inpatient care, outpatient care, and prescription drugs. The authors also raised the concern that patients covered by HDHPs are also likely to reduce the use of important preventive services such as cancer screening for cervical, breast, and colon cancer, as well as ongoing monitoring of diseases such as diabetes, high cholesterol, or kidney disease.

Recall from chapter 5 that the original RAND study that documented the impact of high cost sharing on consumer spending also documented that, in their response to that cost sharing, those with higher out-of-pocket costs had fewer visits and hospitalizations characterized as "necessary" as well as those characterized as "unnecessary." The RAND Corporation, developers of the original RAND study, revisited this issue in 2012, examining how consumer-driven health plans (CDHP) such as HDHP impacted the care patients sought. They confirmed that those employees and families that switched to CDHPs had fewer visits with specialists, filled fewer prescriptions with brand-name (as compared to generic) drugs, and had fewer hospitalizations. They also found recent data confirming the findings of Haviland et al., that patients also reduced their use of valuable preventive health services such as cancer screening and chronic disease management. Based on these data, the RAND analysis concludes: "If high-deductible plans stimulate more prudent purchasing over time, they could be an important part of the answer to rising health care costs. If, however, patients skimp on highly valuable services that can prevent more costly problems later, the savings may be short-lived" (Rand Corporation 2012, p. 3).

THE EFFECT OF MEDICAID COVERAGE ON ACCESS TO PRIMARY CARE

In chapter 7, we learned that people with Medicaid insurance may have problems accessing care. Due to low reimbursement rates, only a limited number of physicians are willing to accept new Medicaid patients in their practice. In the Braveman et al. (1994) study discussed previously, we also learned that Medicaid patients had difficulty accessing care for acute appendicitis, leading to a rate of ruptured appendix that is 50 percent greater than the rate in HMO patients.

Another 1994 study took a detailed look at the experience Medicaid patients face in trying to obtain medical care for common problems (Medicaid Access Study Group 1994). Researchers called a wide variety of private doctors' offices, hospital-based clinics, and community clinics in several locales. The callers posed as a Medicaid patient and asked to obtain care for a common, relatively minor type of complaint (low back pain, bladder infection, sore throat). They asked if they could be seen for this problem, and if so, how quickly. The researchers let a few weeks go by, and then they called back many of these same offices and clinics, this time posing as someone with full private insurance. They asked for an appointment for the same problem as the Medicaid caller. They recorded how many of the physicians or clinics were willing to see them, and how soon they could be seen. The results are shown in table 12.1.

Since 1994, when this study was done, a majority of Medicaid patients have been enrolled in managed care plans, reducing somewhat this barrier to access. A more recent study, conducted in a manner similar to the 1994 study, however, suggests that

TABLE 12.1. Percentage of offices and clinics that offered appointments for callers during the study of Medicaid access to care

Medicaid recipients	
Appointment available at any time	44
Appointment available within two days	35
Patients with private insurance	
Appointment available within two days	60

Source: Data from Medicaid Access Study Group 1994.

the problem of access to care for Medicaid recipients persists. Asplin et al. (2005) trained graduate students to call clinics and doctors' offices, stating that they had recently been discharged from an emergency room and had been told by the ER doctor that they had a potentially serious medical problem that required medical attention within one week. The problems included pneumonia, severe high blood pressure, and possible ectopic pregnancy. The callers asked for an appointment to see a doctor within this recommended time frame. On a randomized basis, the callers would state that they had private health insurance, Medicaid, or no health insurance. The trained callers would then wait two weeks and call back the same clinic or office, this time stating that they had the opposite type of insurance (e.g., if they had previously stated they had Medicaid or were uninsured, they would state on the second call that they had full private insurance).

For medical problems that had potentially serious consequences if not treated promptly, patients with private insurance were able to get an appointment for follow-up care within one week 64 percent of the time, whereas patients with Medicaid were able to get such an appointment 34 percent of the time. Callers who stated they were uninsured and could afford to pay only $20 on the day of the visit were able to get an appointment 25 percent of the time; uninsured callers who stated they would bring full payment in cash on the day of the visit were able to get an appointment 63 percent of the time.

In the period between passage of ACA and the expansion of Medicaid under ACA scheduled for 2014, Rhodes et al. (2014) used a similar methodology to assess the availability of new-patient primary care appointments in more than seven thousand primary care practices located in one of ten states. Trained research staff called a primary care office requesting a new primary care appointment, either for a general checkup or because of a very high blood pressure reading identified at a pharmacy or health fair. Of the more than eleven thousand calls made in the study, 47 percent indicated they had private insurance, 39 percent indicated they had Medicaid, and 14 percent indicated they had no insurance. All the practices that received calls from Medicaid patients were listed as having contracted with a Medicaid managed care plan to accept Medicaid patients.

The study found that 85 percent of callers with private insurance and 58 percent of Medicaid patients were able to make an appointment to be seen. Of the uninsured patients, 79 percent were able to make an appointment, *so long as they agreed to pay cash at the time of the visit*. Of those without insurance indicating that they could not pay cash, 15 percent were able to get an appointment. Responding to these results, Bindman and Coffman (2014) raised a policy that has added implications in the context of the Medicaid expansion under ACA: "The combination of the low participation rate and the low numbers of Medicaid patients in the practices that do participate suggests that there is a real shortage of physicians available to care for Medicaid beneficiaries, resulting in inadequate access to care" (p. 870). It is important to appreciate that, even in the era of managed care, having Medicaid insurance still does not guarantee access to care. Any state or national policy proposal—for example, ACA—that seeks to extend health insurance coverage to those currently uninsured by expanding the Medicaid program will have to cope with this problem of access.

RACIAL BARRIERS TO ACCESS TO CARE

Throughout much of the twentieth century, the United States maintained a health care system that, in many parts of the country, divided access to care along racial lines: the race of the patient as well as the race of the physician. There were separate hospitals for black patients and white patients. Even those physicians and clinics that agreed to treat both groups of patients often maintained separate waiting rooms for black and white patients. Separate medical schools were created to train black physicians. With the official sanctioning of national and local medical societies, fully qualified black physicians were prevented from joining the medical staff of white hospitals.

In the 1960s, as part of the civil rights movement and following landmark civil rights legislation, the federal government took action against this segregated system of care. Hospitals that maintained segregated treatment and medical staff policies were ineligible to obtain federal payment through the Medicare and Medicaid programs. Over the period of a few years, the segregated system of care was largely dismantled. Black patients and black doctors finally obtained access to previously all-white institutions.

The hope was that by desegregating the health care system our country could attain a level of care that, while still depending on a patient's ability to pay, otherwise treated all patients equally. Unfortunately, we have seen a continuing litany of evidence that we have not yet met this goal. One of the first studies that pointed to continuing racial barriers in access to care looked at the way in which patients receive care for heart attacks in the federal Veterans Affairs (VA) health system.

The VA health system operates a series of hospitals throughout the United States. Many of these hospitals are affiliated with academic medical centers. Eligibility for care depends on a patient having served in the US armed forces and meeting certain income requirements. Once deemed eligible, any veteran may receive free medical care.

A study looked closely at the experience of male patients, all eligible for VA care, who came to a VA hospital in the years 1988–90 with a heart attack (Peterson et al. 1994). At that time, it was common practice at most hospitals, including VA hospitals, to consider all patients with an acute heart attack for a procedure called cardiac revascularization. Because a heart attack is caused by a blocked artery in the heart, using a surgical procedure to reopen the blocked artery can improve the patient's outcome. There are two principal types of revascularization procedure:

1. angioplasty, in which a thin balloon is inserted into the blocked vessel, and by inflating the balloon, the vessel is reopened; or
2. coronary artery bypass graft surgery (referred to as CABG), in which a section of blood vessel is taken from the patient's leg and is surgically implanted into the blocked vessel in a way that bypasses the blockage.

Before either procedure is done, the patient undergoes cardiac catheterization, in which dye is injected directly into the arteries of the heart and X-rays are taken, showing the exact location and size of the blockage. The VA study examined whether black patients and white patients, all coming to a VA hospital with a heart attack, received different levels of treatment. After controlling for individual characteristics of the patients (age, other illness, etc.), the study came to the following conclusions:

- Blacks were 33 percent less likely than whites to undergo cardiac catheterization.
- Blacks were 42 percent less likely than whites to undergo angioplasty.
- Blacks were 54 percent less likely than whites to undergo CABG surgery.
- Blacks were 54 percent less likely than whites to undergo any type of revascularization procedure.

The study then went on to look at the likelihood a patient would survive his heart attack, examining whether the demonstrated differences in access to revascularization procedures were associated with differences in survival. It came to some interesting conclusions:

- In the first thirty days after the heart attack, survival among black patients was significantly *higher* than among white patients.
- At one year and two years after the heart attack, there was no difference in survival among whites and blacks.

> **CONCEPT 12.2**
>
> Among male patients who came to a VA hospital for treatment of a heart attack, blacks were significantly less likely than whites to receive aggressive care involving revascularization. While the lower rate of revascularization did not affect long-term survival, it did result in a lower quality of life for black patients.

• When one looked at the quality of life for patients who did survive the heart attack, surviving black patients had more chest pain and a lower overall quality of life than white patients.

Since the VA heart study was published, a number of additional studies have been reported about racial differences in access to care. These papers paint a disturbing picture of continuing racial differences in access. Among the findings are the following:

•   Black patients with heart disease and other serious health problems received less aggressive and lower-quality care, even after taking into account the type of insurance the patient has (Kahn et al. 1994; Ayanian et al. 1999b).
•   Black patients with early-stage lung cancer (a stage at which patients have a higher chance of cure if treated appropriately) were treated less aggressively, with lower rates of surgery than comparable white patients (Bach et al. 1999).
•   Black patients with kidney failure who were receiving regular kidney dialysis (thus being automatically eligible for Medicare insurance coverage) were referred less often than white patients for consideration of kidney transplantation (Ayanian et al. 1999a).
•   Despite a higher incidence among the black population of a form of bone marrow cancer called multiple myeloma, blacks with the disease received bone marrow transplantation less often than whites, even though the evidence shows that this treatment substantially prolongs survival (Boyce 2000).
•   Both black patients (Todd et al. 2000) and Hispanic patients (Todd et al. 1993) who received emergency treatment for broken bones received less pain medication while in the emergency room than white patients with similarly broken bones.

The question arises as to whether other racial and ethnic minorities face the same disadvantages as blacks in obtaining full and equal access to care. Fewer studies have been done looking at Hispanics, Native Americans, Asians, and other groups, so we do not fully know the answer to this question. Future research will need to be done to understand whether racially based differences in access to care also exist for other ethnic groups.

Decades after the federally mandated integration of health care facilities in this country, the issue of racial disparities in our medical care system persists. Why do black patients receive less access to medical care than white patients, even after taking into account economic differences and differences in insurance coverage? The Institute of Medicine of the National Academy of Sciences—one of the most respected and prestigious scientific groups in the country—attempted to answer this question. They convened a national panel of experts from a variety of disciplines, and they asked this panel to review the scientific evidence pertaining to racial disparities in access to medical care that are not based on economic or insurance differences. The panel reviewed several

> **CONCEPT 12.3**
>
> For a variety of serious medical conditions and in a variety of settings and geographic locations, black patients receive less aggressive and lower-quality medical care than white patients with the same disease, even after taking into account the type of insurance the patient has.

hundred published research reports and, in its published report in 2003 (Smedley et al. 2003), concluded that three basic factors contribute to these ongoing disparities:

1. factors pertaining to the patient's approach to medical care, including issues such as personal preferences, mistrust of the system, and refusal of recommended treatment;
2. factors pertaining to the health care system, such as language barriers, cultural barriers, or a lack of coordination of care; and
3. factors pertaining to the physician, such as the application of racial stereotypes and the effects of racial bias, either conscious or unconscious.

The Institute of Medicine report generated quite a controversy. Could it be that physicians in this country are biased in the way they approach patients from differing racial groups? Some were incensed at the accusation that physicians in the United States continued to exhibit racial bias, pointing instead to decades of efforts to strip bias from the health care system. Others responded that bias continues to pervade US health care, only in ways that are less obvious than historical forms of explicit racial discrimination.

The question of racial bias raises important ethical issues yet often triggers powerful emotional responses. This dilemma is not unique to medical care. Whether in housing, employment, education, or health care, the history of racial discrimination in the United States evokes memories of reprehensible behavior on the part of individuals and governments, often involving hatred and open hostility toward blacks and other minorities. The available evidence suggests, however, that intentional, explicit racism of this type is probably not the most likely explanation of the widespread racial differences we continue to see in treatment and outcomes. Approaching racial bias as a single, uniform phenomenon inappropriately simplifies what is a complex, multifaceted set of psychological mechanisms.

Racial bias can exist and exert its effects on many levels and in many ways, even in people who would honestly be horrified to have racist beliefs attributed to them.

Hatred and overt bigotry represent only one type of bias, although this form of bias is what most people think of when the issue is discussed. We can identify other mechanisms that do not involve conscious racism but that nonetheless can lead to differences in the treatment of members of differing racial groups.

Statistical Bias

Statistical bias involves an individual making a seemingly rational decision based on data about differences in behavior among racial groups. The example of the inner-city taxi driver illustrates statistical bias. In deciding whether to pick up a potential customer, is it justifiable to consider the race of the customer? Though the likelihood of robbery with any customer is exceedingly small, in many inner-city contexts the incidence of robbery is higher among black taxi customers than among white customers. Can we blame the driver who passes a black man hailing the cab and picks up a white man instead?

In choosing to pick up the white customer, the cab driver is assigning a stereo-typed group characteristic to an individual perceived to be a member of that group. In this case, the perceived group is all blacks living in the area where the driver works; the pertinent group characteristic is the probability the customer will attempt to rob the driver. The driver has no information pertaining specifically to the potential customer other than racial appearance. Nonetheless, an argument can be made that, in the absence of other information, it is "rational" to assign the group characteristic to the individual.

A decision of this type, purportedly based on principles of rationality, can lead to unequal outcomes for racial groups. The unequal outcomes do not necessarily invalidate the decision. In some contexts, for certain public purposes, however, we can preclude the application of statistical inference based on racial groupings. In New York City, for example, cab drivers are enjoined from racial differentiation among customers based on the overriding public need to have transportation by cab equally available to all.

In the medical care setting, statistical bias can exist in many ways. For example, many physicians will consider the potential for patient compliance in deciding whether to recommend certain types of procedures. Kidney specialists, for example, may believe that black patients are more likely than white patients to have difficulty in following the stringent medication schedule required to prevent rejection after a kidney transplant, and they may in response hesitate in referring those patients for transplantation. In attributing the likelihood of noncompliance to a patient based on racial grouping, the kidney specialist creates the same fundamental situation as the cab driver. The public value of treating people as individuals in matters as crucial as the availability of organ transplantation (or cardiac revascularization, or cancer treatment) overrides the validity of assigning clinical characteristics to individual patients based on group inference.

Unconscious Bias

There is considerable empirical evidence that even self-described color-blind individuals can manifest racially discriminatory attitudes of which they are unaware (Dovidio and Gaertner 1998). While these people openly endorse fair and equal treatment of all racial groups and disavow overt racism, they harbor some type of negative feelings or association toward blacks or other minorities. When interacting with someone of a different race, they may feel discomfort on an unconscious level. They may express this discomfort in subtle ways that can have the effect of disadvantaging minority groups. Despite their biased actions, people acting on this unconscious level are not racists, but rather they are acting based on cultural preferences learned long ago. (See Calman 2000 for a description of how this type of bias affected one patient in particular.)

A study in the medical literature concluded that physicians, without necessarily being conscious of personal bias, react differently to patients of different races (Van Ryn and Burke 2000). The study's authors evaluated the care given to 618 patients who had recently undergone cardiac catheterization, the procedure to test for blocked arteries in the heart. Of the patients in the study, 265 were black and 353 were white. All had recently completed a visit to their physician to discuss the results of their test. The researchers first surveyed the patients about their personal circumstances and about their perceptions of the visit with the physician. They then surveyed the physicians about their perceptions of the patients they had just seen. In comparing them to their white patients, the physicians responded that they perceived their black patients to be

- less likely to comply with medical advice,
- less likely to participate in cardiac rehabilitation,
- less likely to want a physically active lifestyle, and
- more likely to abuse drugs.

The physicians also responded that, compared to their white patients, their black patients appeared less intelligent and less well educated—even when the patients' levels of education and income were the same. Studies such as this one led the Institute of Medicine researchers to conclude that "bias, stereotyping, prejudice, and clinical uncertainty on the part of healthcare providers may contribute to racial and ethnic disparities in healthcare. . . . Stereotyping and biases may be conscious or unconscious, even among the well intentioned" (Smedley et al. 2003, p. 178).

> **CONCEPT 12.4**
>
> Based on stereotypes and subtle, often unconscious bias, physicians may treat patients from certain minority ethnic groups differently from comparable white patients. While this bias may not necessarily constitute racism in the classical sense, it nonetheless can result in lower-quality care for black and other minority patients.

Another study looked at the attitudes of first- and second-year medical students toward patients seen on a video. It demonstrated that these students adopted a more aggressive approach to diagnosing a white, male patient with heart disease than a black, female patient, even though each was an actor reading the same script (Rathore et al. 2000). The unconscious bias that may lead to racially based differences in treatment appears to exist even before physicians receive their clinical training.

A series of articles was published in 2005, looking at changes over time in patterns of racial disparities in care. Each examined a different aspect of historical disparities. The authors found that

- for the period 1992–2001, there was "no evidence, either nationally or locally, that efforts to eliminate racial disparities in the use of high-cost surgical procedures were successful" (Jha et al. 2005a, p. 683);
- for the period 1994–2002, racial differences in access to therapy for clogged arteries in the heart (referred to as "reperfusion therapy") did not narrow (Vaccarino et al. 2005, p. 671); and
- for the period 1997–2003, "racial disparities declined for most, but not all, HEDIS [Health Plan Employer Data and Information Set] measures we studied" (Trivedi et al. 2005, p. 692).

While the last study did find some reduction in racial disparities, the other two studies carried the disturbing message that, in the words of an accompanying editorial, "disparities between white patients and black patients have not substantially improved during the past decade or so" (Lurie 2005, p. 727).

One positive outcome that was recently reported has been a substantial reduction in disparities in access to kidney transplantation. Sood et al. (2015) reported on their analysis of data from a national organ transplantation registry on the incidence of kidney transplantation among black and white patients with end-stage renal disease. Between 1998 and 2010, the rate of kidney transplantation among black patients went from 98 per 1,000 to 128 per 1,000, equaling in 2010 the rate among white patients. The authors attribute this apparent elimination in black/white differences in transplantation rates to a combination of increased awareness of the existence of disparities among professionals, improved communication between doctor and patient, and changes in national policies regarding tissue matching between donor and recipient.

In 2007, Blendon and colleagues reported results of a national survey administered to more than four thousand randomly selected adults, representing fourteen different racial or ethnic groups. They found that two groups in particular reported continuing problems in accessing high-quality care. African Americans born in the United States and Native Americans were significantly more likely than other racial or ethnic groups (including African Americans born in Africa or the Caribbean) to report that they had received poor quality medical care because of their race or ethnicity. The same two groups were also more likely than other groups to report having experienced racial discrimination when they tried to obtain medical care.

The US Agency for Healthcare Research and Quality (AHRQ) is charged by Congress with monitoring on an ongoing basis racial and ethnic disparities in access to and quality of health care. In their report for 2009, AHRQ found that "disparities related to race, ethnicity, and socioeconomic status still pervade the American health care system. Although varying in magnitude by condition and population, disparities are observed in almost all aspects of health care" (US Agency for Healthcare Research and Quality 2009). The report went on to consider the extent to which differences in socioeconomic status, and associated differences in access to health insurance, might explain these continuing disparities. After using multivariate analysis to control for these factors, the report concluded that "uninsurance did not explain all differences in care related to race, ethnicity, and socioeconomic status, suggesting that mitigating uninsurance would greatly reduce but not completely eliminate disparities in care."

In 2015, AHRQ issued its report of racial and ethnic disparities in health care as assessed in 2014 (US Agency for Healthcare Research and Quality 2015a). It found that "disparities in quality of care remained prevalent and few disparities were eliminated" (p. 3). In a more detailed analysis of regional disparities in the quality of care, it reported that "overall quality and racial/ethnic disparities varied widely across states, and often not in the same direction. Southern states tended to have poorer quality but smaller disparities while Middle Atlantic and West North Central states tended to have higher quality but larger disparities." Especially in the context of regional differences in the approach states have taken to support ACA and expand eligibility for Medicaid, it appears that disparities need to be measured both at the national level and at the state or regional level.

LIVING CONDITIONS AND ACCESS TO CARE

It is well recognized that certain types of economic and living conditions can affect the health of individuals and social groups. Can living conditions also affect the way in which patients access care? This question can be answered, at least in part, by considering two separate studies looking at poor children with asthma.

The first study looked at differences in the way black children and white children with asthma use health services (Lozano et al. 1995). The study considered only children who were covered by Medicaid. All children in the study lived in the same city, had the same insurance coverage, and had access to the same hospitals and clinics. It found that black children went to the doctor's office less frequently yet had higher use of the emergency room and the hospital. Something other than insurance led to black children with asthma being sicker than their white counterparts and to the parents of black children relying more on the emergency room for care than the doctor's office.

The second study (Rosenstreich et al. 1997) was ingenious. The researchers thought that there might be something in poor children's home environment, especially in the child's bedroom, that could cause an allergic reaction in some children, triggering an asthma attack. They took a group of poor children with asthma and tested them for allergy to the following three typical components of house dust:

- cat dander,
- dust mites, and
- cockroach droppings or body parts.

The researchers then went into the bedroom of each of the children in the study and vacuumed up all the dust they could find. They took the dust to the laboratory and analyzed it for these same three components. The study found that those children who were both allergic to cockroaches and had cockroaches in their bedroom were significantly sicker from their asthma than other children. Neither children with bedroom cockroaches but no allergy to cockroaches nor children who were allergic to cockroaches but had no cockroaches in their bedroom had as much problem with their asthma as those children with both conditions. The combination of cat or dust mite allergy and cat dander or dust mites in the bedroom did not seem to affect children nearly as much.

It appears that cockroaches in the home may have a lot to do with the pattern asthma takes in poor children. While there were no data about the presence or absence of cockroaches in the bedrooms of the children in the first study, one has to wonder whether the differences in the pattern of illness and medical care for poor black and white children with asthma may have to do, at least in part, with differences in the living conditions of black and white families within the same city.

OTHER FACTORS THAT MAY AFFECT ACCESS TO CARE
Location

Regardless of their type of insurance, many patients in rural areas simply are not as close to health care facilities and thus face greater problems with access compared to patients in urban areas. The growing difficulty of rural hospitals to survive financially may lead to increased differences in access to care for urban and rural populations. Similarly, the relative scarcity of health care services and facilities in many inner-city areas and other low-income neighborhoods makes access difficult even for those with insurance. Problems with transportation, arranging child care, and taking take time off work to seek care may all contribute to geographic differences in access to care.

Culture

Language frequently presents a barrier to obtaining care. Patients who do not have facility in speaking English may find it difficult to find a source of care. Realizing just how serious a barrier to access language could be, in 2000 the US Department of Health and Human Services (HHS) published its National Standards on Culturally and Linguistically Appropriate Services in Health Care, referred to as the CLAS standards (US Department of Health and Human Services website). All health care providers who receive federal funds are required to adhere to four of the standards that pertain to language access. These four are shown in table 12.2.

Despite these efforts to improve language access, a study by Blendon and colleagues described earlier found persistent problems in communication between patients and physicians or other providers of care. The authors found that about 20 percent of Mexican, Puerto Rican, and Central/South Americans as well as Vietnamese Americans "felt that they received poor care because of their inability to speak English" (2007, p. 1446).

TABLE 12.2. National standards on culturally and linguistically appropriate services in health care

Standard 5	Offer language assistance to individuals who have limited English proficiency and/or other communication needs, at no cost to them, to facilitate timely access to all health care and services.
Standard 6	Inform all individuals of the availability of language assistance services clearly and in their preferred language, verbally and in writing.
Standard 7	Ensure the competence of individuals providing language assistance, recognizing that the use of untrained individuals and/or minors as interpreters should be avoided.
Standard 8	Provide easy-to-understand print and multimedia materials and signage in the languages commonly used by the populations in the service area.

Source: US Department of Health and Human Services, http://minorityhealth.hhs.gov/omh/browse.aspx?lvl=2&lvlid=53.

In addition to language barriers, cultural belief systems about the nature of illness may delay obtaining care. The book *The Spirit Catches You and You Fall Down* (Fadiman 1997) tells the story of an immigrant family from Asia whose child had a seizure disorder. The strikingly different perceptions about the nature of seizure disorders and how the disorder should be treated led to a serious schism between the family and the health care system, with unfortunate results.

Concerns about language and cultural barriers to health care access have led medical educators and government officials alike to call for better training of physicians and other health care providers in what has come to be called "cultural competence." A joint committee sponsored by the American Medical Association (AMA) and the Association of American Medical Colleges published a standard describing the level of cultural competence expected of physicians and students in US medical schools: "The faculty and students must demonstrate an understanding of the manner in which people of diverse cultures and belief systems perceive health and illness and respond to various symptoms, diseases, and treatments. Medical students should learn to recognize and appropriately address gender and cultural biases in health care delivery, while considering first the health of the patient" (Association of American Medical Colleges 2005, p. 1).

ORGANIZATIONAL COMPLEXITY OF HEALTH CARE AS A BARRIER TO CARE

Our system of health care has moved from one based on fee-for-service care provided mostly by independent physicians in relatively small offices and groups to one in which care is provided, often on a capitation basis, by complex systems of care increasingly involving large groups of physicians. In many cases, physicians have shifted from being independent health care professionals to being employees of large systems of care. Unfortunately, these changes have sometimes contributed to a sense of breakdown in the relationship between the physician and the patient. Nowhere is this truer than at the primary care level.

Maintaining high quality in the delivery of primary care depends on maintaining a strong relationship between the doctor and the patient. From a variety of research, it has been possible to identify factors that create a satisfying doctor-patient relationship from the perspective of the patient.

- *Humanistic behavior by physicians*
  Patients need to have a sense that the doctor cares about them as a person and will take the time to listen to and understand their concerns.
- *Caring interpersonal interaction with other employees*
  Patients need to be treated in a sensitive and courteous manner by the other employees who work with the doctor.

- *Continuity of care*
  Patients need to develop an ongoing relationship with a physician they can count on seeing over a period of time.

- *Accessibility of care*
  Patients need to be able to arrange to see their physician in a timely manner when the need arises and to be able to get through to the doctor's office easily by phone or e-mail.

- *Physician satisfaction with work conditions*
  To be fully satisfied with their relationship with their physician, patients need to have a sense that their physician is also satisfied in the work he or she does. There appears to be a strong correlation between patient satisfaction with the quality of their relationship with their physician and physician satisfaction with work conditions.

When you ask patients to describe what constitutes high quality in primary care, they will usually describe the factors just listed. The technical competence of the physician seems to be less important than the humanistic competence, at least at the level of primary care. Thus, patient satisfaction has emerged as a principal measure of primary care quality. While health care regulators and health care managers who measure quality may look at the technical competence of the physician and the extent to which the physician follows standard procedures, patients tend to look more at the strength of their personal relationship with their doctor.

Unfortunately, throughout the history of HMOs and other types of managed care delivery systems, reductions in the cost of care have often been at the expense of the quality of primary care as measured by patient satisfaction. Recall from chapter 5 that, in both the RAND health insurance experiment (table 5.2) and the Medical Outcomes Study (table 5.3), HMOs score significantly lower than traditional fee-for-service systems on issues of the interpersonal nature of care, access to care, and continuity of care. As managed care delivery systems have become the rule rather than the exception, problems in patient satisfaction similar to those identified in these research studies have become more widespread. Looking at the changes in US health care that have accompanied the managed care revolution, one group of authors concluded, "Our patients want high-quality service and do not believe they receive it" (Kenagy et al. 1999, p. 661).

Why would a change in the way health care is organized and financed lead to a decrease in the quality of the relationship between the patient and the physician? To answer this question, we need to understand some general principles of organizations theory (Barr 1995). Two characteristics of managed care are especially pertinent in this regard: (1) the increasing size of medical practice groups that typically comes with a shift to managed care and (2) the strengthening of management controls over certain aspects of medical practice.

In general, as an organization such as a medical practice group increases in size, it tends to become more complex internally. This complexity involves increasing task specialization, with individual workers performing a narrower range of duties. For example, while in a smaller medical practice one person may answer the phones, greet patients, and make appointments, in a larger group each task is done by a separate person. Task specialization often leads to increasingly complex paths of communication and to a more complex process for the customer (in this case, the patient) to interact with the organization.

Added to the increased organizational complexity associated with increased organizational size is the effect on the medical care process of strengthened management systems. The capitation method of payment for health care requires that someone manage the provision of care to stay within the established budget. No individual practitioner has a sufficiently broad perspective to keep track of how available resources are being spent and how the demand for care is being met. Managed care as it is often constructed requires a set of managers and management tools that are sufficiently removed from the care process to maintain direction and control of organizational activities.

A problem arises out of the potential conflict such a management structure creates when the purpose of the organization is to provide a human service such as health care. As with other human services, health care, particularly at the primary care level, is based on high-quality interaction between the provider and the patient. While cognizant of the need for strong provider-patient interaction, managers of a human service organization nonetheless tend to emphasize efficiency in the work of the organization. Efficiency in this context is often measured in units of production per unit of time (e.g., patients seen per hour). It is difficult to provide high-quality human service while under pressure to be efficient.

This type of role conflict, however, often extends beyond the physician to encompass all types of employees who interact directly with patients. In general, these workers want to be able to provide good service to patients, having chosen a service occupation over other alternatives. They, too, often face pressure to work more quickly and efficiently, based on management's need to maintain the efficiency of overall organizational processes. This situation has the potential to lead to what is described as role conflict: the conflict faced by a worker caught between the patient's desire for good service and management's emphasis on efficient work. Role conflict often leads to decreased worker satisfaction and a tendency to become less sensitive to the needs of patients.

The sum of these effects, associated with the larger organizations that are increasingly typical of managed care, is the potential for a less satisfactory experience for patients. In the managed care setting, patients often encounter systems that tend to be more complex and impersonal than the smaller types of medical groups that predominated under the historical fee-for-service system. It is these characteristics of primary care in a managed care

> **CONCEPT 12.5**
>
> The large organizational systems that are typical of managed care tend to be more complex and more impersonal, and to have problems with patient satisfaction with care.

setting that have resulted in the spread of "concierge medicine," described in chapter 9. The problems in patient satisfaction associated with large, complex managed care systems such as those studied in the RAND health insurance experiment and the Medical Outcomes Study may have been caused by these types of characteristics associated with large organizational systems.

In my own research, I have looked at the extent to which factors within the organizational environment of a large primary care delivery system can affect patients' perceptions of the quality of their direct interaction with the physician (Barr et al. 2000). Using a survey questionnaire that has been widely used in medical practice, we asked 291 patients who visited a primary care physician the following questions about their visit.

In terms of your satisfaction, how would you rate each of the following?

- the time spent with the doctor you saw,
- the explanation of what was done for you,
- the technical skills of the doctor you saw, and
- the personal manner of the doctor you saw.

Each question was answered on a 5-point scale, ranging from excellent to poor. We also asked patients to rate the quality of their interaction with the nurses and receptionists they encountered during their visit, using the same 5-point scale. When we analyzed the data, we found that 20 percent of the variation in the way patients rated their satisfaction with their direct interaction with the physician could be explained by two main factors:

1. how courteously they were treated by the nurses and receptionists, and
2. how long they had to wait at the doctor's office to see the doctor.

> **CONCEPT 12.6**
>
> Factors external to the doctor-patient interaction can exert a strong influence on patients' perceptions of the quality of the care they receive from their doctor.

Chang and colleagues published a study confirming that patients' perceptions of the quality of care they receive from their physician are powerfully affected by the quality of the communication between doctor and patient (Chang et al. 2006). In a study of 245 elderly patients receiving care from a managed care organization, using the same measure of patient satisfaction we used in our research, the authors measured patients' reported satisfaction with:

1. the technical quality of the care they received from their doctor,
2. the quality of their communication with their doctor, and
3. the overall quality of the care they received.

They found that patients' perceptions of the quality of the doctor-patient communication was significantly associated with their overall rating of the quality of care, while patients' perceptions of the technical quality of the physician's care were not associated with overall satisfaction with care.

CONCEPT 12.7

"Unfortunately, the track record of American health care, especially in recent times, does not support the belief that coverage is equivalent to access" (Friedman 1994, p. 1535).

SUMMARY OF THE BARRIERS TO HEALTH CARE ACCESS LEADING UP TO ACA

This chapter has identified a variety of factors that have impeded access to medical care. These factors have little to do with whether a patient does or does not have health insurance. Issues as divergent as geographic location, cultural norms, racial bias, and organizational complexity can get in the way of patients having full access to medical care.

Barriers in access to care can be as simple as how much the patient is expected to pay for care. Some insurance policies require patients to pay a substantial part of the cost of visits to a doctor. Research has shown that, in the face of these "copayments," patients will sometimes avoid needed care.

The Medicaid program offers another example of impeded access to care for those with insurance. In many states, the Medicaid program pays physicians an amount that is substantially lower than their usual fee, with the result that many doctors refuse to treat Medicaid patients. Without an available source of primary care, many Medicaid patients often have no choice but to go to hospital emergency rooms to obtain treatment for problems that would be more appropriately treated in a medical office or clinic.

Racial and ethnic factors also impair access to care, even for those with insurance. When language barriers exist or when providers have difficulty understanding or accepting a patient's cultural beliefs, access to care is often reduced. In addition, numerous research studies and government advisory reports have identified lingering racial bias on the part of physicians and other providers. While this bias is most likely unintended and often unconscious, it nonetheless creates one of the most important challenges to the medical profession and the health care system.

Finally, a growing emphasis on the provision of care by large health care organizations has created an added barrier to access. These organizations, by their very nature, are often more complex and less personal than smaller types of health care organization. Because access to care is one of the key components of quality of care, any discussion of new policies for the organization, financing, and delivery of care should include this important principle.

THE AFFORDABLE CARE ACT AND ACCESS TO HEALTH CARE

As described in chapter 8, one of the largest changes ACA has effected is an expansion of health insurance to nearly 25 million people through a combination of the availability of affordable insurance on state insurance exchanges and expansion of Medicaid eligibility in those states that have elected to do so. As described previously, however, patients on Medicaid historically have had difficulty finding a physician or other source of regular care. Adding 13 million new enrollees to Medicaid confronts the issue of identifying providers willing to accept these new enrollees as regular patients. As described by Pitts and colleagues (2010), "Today's primary care physicians are hard pressed to meet existing levels of demand, much less the pent-up needs of the estimated thirty-two million Americans who will soon acquire health insurance" (p. 1626).

Poor access to high-quality primary care has a range of impacts on both the quality as well as the cost of care provided through Medicaid. Given the high costs associated with providing care to Medicaid beneficiaries with chronic health conditions, as described in chapter 7, ongoing barriers to access can be expected to lead to increased costs for hospital care that might otherwise have been prevented had high-quality primary care been available. Mukamel et al. (2015) evaluated factors that are associated with these "ambulatory care-sensitive" (ACS) hospital admissions, which they define as "admission . . . for conditions that could have been prevented had the patient received high-quality primary care" (p. 931). Examples of conditions that make patients at risk for ACS admission include diabetes, asthma, congestive heart failure, and hypertension. The authors found that for the period 2003–09, the frequency of ACS hospital admissions increased among black patients in the six states studied, while they declined for white patients in these same states. While the authors did not have data on insurance coverage of the patients studied, the higher rates of Medicaid coverage among blacks as compared to whites led the authors to suggest that expansion of Medicaid under ACA may not be effective in reducing ACS hospital admissions unless there is concurrent expansion of the availability of high-quality primary care to black patients and those on Medicaid.

Oronce et al. (2015) looked at both minority racial status and Medicaid insurance in association with potentially preventable rehospitalization of patients in California undergoing hip replacement surgery. They looked specifically at rehospitalization within the first thirty days following surgery, a situation that often represents an ACS admission. They found that the risk of rehospitalization was higher for black patients and for patients on Medicaid. In discussing these results, the authors concluded that "Medicaid patients experienced the highest readmission rate in our study and were 86% more likely to be readmitted compared with those with private insurance" (p. 928). They identified improved access to both primary care and care by an orthopedist as a central factor that might prevent rehospitalization.

ACA has a number of new and expanded programs to address the issue of access to care for the newly insured. A first step ACA took in this regard was to provide for an increase in reimbursement for a two-year period, 2013–14, for primary care physicians who treat Medicaid patients. (In this context, "primary care" means care provided by a physician in family medicine, general internal medicine, or general pediatrics.) Effective January 1, 2013, these physicians were paid at 100 percent of the rate paid by the Medicare program, with the incremental cost of the increased reimbursement paid by the federal government. The hope was that by equalizing the payment rate for Medicare patients and Medicaid patients, those primary care physicians who include Medicare patients in their practice will also be willing to include Medicaid patients. The hope also was that, after this initial two-year period, the states would opt to incorporate this new reimbursement rate into their own Medicaid program—something that few states have elected to do.

Realizing that simply paying physicians more to treat Medicaid patients will not assure access to care, ACA also invests heavily in the expansion of nonprofit community health centers. Often referred to as federally qualified health centers (FQHCs), these clinics receive extra federal funding to treat Medicaid patients. In the study by Rhodes et al. (2014) cited earlier, in which trained surveyors called primary care offices to see how available appointments were to patients with different types of insurance, the sample included 544 calls made to FQHCs. The researchers found that surveyors indicating that they were covered by Medicaid were able to make a new primary care appointment 80 percent of the time when calling a FQHC, as compared to a 56 percent success rate when calling a non-FQHC provider.

ACA expands funding for FQHCs, allowing them to hire additional personnel. In an effort to expand the number of physicians selecting a primary care specialty, ACA allocates additional funding to allow primary care residency programs to expand their training sites to include FQHCs and other community-based resources. ACA also expands support for the National Health Service Corps, the federal program that provides medical students with either scholarship support during medical school or educational loan repayment after medical school in return for spending a period of years in primary care practice in a FQHC.

ACA also provides additional support for FQHCs to strengthen their organizational capacity to act as the "patient-centered medical home" (PCMH) for their patients by developing a team-based approach to the management of chronic disease. Through expansion of electronic health records and the strengthening of connections with referral sources of specialty care, organizations adopting the PCMH model are expected to be able to increase the comprehensiveness of care, the continuity of care, and ultimately the quality of care for their patients (American Academy of Family Physicians, American Academy of Pediatrics, American College of Physicians, and American Osteopathic Association 2007). The study by Rhodes et al. (2014) also compared appointment availability at private practice groups that had met the requirements for certification as a PCMH (Aysola et al. 2015). Of the more than seven thousand offices they contacted seeking a new primary care appointment, 397 had received PCMH certification. In this part of the study, they compared the availability of appointments in PCMH practices as compared to non-PCMH practices. The PCMH practices were somewhat more available for a new appointment (80 percent as compared to 76 percent for non-PCMH), and they were more available for after-hour appointments, either in the evening or on weekends.

Rather than looking at the availability of appointments, Rosenthal et al. (2015) evaluated the quality of care available in a group of seven primary care practices in the Rochester, New York, area that had received PCMH certification. Using the quality metrics contained in the Healthcare Effectiveness Data and Information Set (HEDIS), a national quality monitoring resource, they compared the quality of care provided by these seven practices with that provided by a comparison group of non-PCMH practices. Compared to the non-PCMH practices, the PCMH practices had lower rates of imaging tests and of potentially preventable visits to the emergency room, higher rates of primary care visits and laboratory tests, and improved preventive care services. While the PCMH practices did have significant improvements in these areas, they also had extra costs associated with qualifying as a PCMH, with the net result that their overall cost of care was not reduced.

ACA has a number of provisions that would support the expansion of the PCMH model, including funds specifically targeting the PCMH certification among FQHCs. Many of the new payment models being developed by the new Center for Medicare and Medicaid Innovation created by ACA focus on including extra support for PCMH practices. However, the extent to which the PCMH delivery model will be able to substantially reduce access barriers experienced by those on Medicaid and by racial and ethnic minority groups remains to be determined.

While ACA does not address directly the issue of disparities in access to care based on a patient's race or ethnicity, it does impose on providers the responsibility for collecting data on the race, ethnicity, primary language, disability status, and similar demographic characteristics of the patients cared for. The federal government will then be able to analyze this data in order to monitor racial and ethnic disparities in either access to care or quality of care.

Key Policy Issues Affecting the Direction of Health Care Reform

Three principles, each addressed earlier in this book, largely defined the problems facing policy makers, health care managers, health care providers, and patients in the years leading up to the passage of the Affordable Care Act (ACA):

1. The cost of health care was higher in the United States than anywhere else in the world. After a period of relative stability in the 1990s, these costs were once again on the rise.

2. The American public had largely come to expect the highest-quality care available, regardless of the cost. Recent data had highlighted shortcomings in the quality of health care in the United States. Attempts to hold down the cost of care by constraining the availability of care had been met with resistance on many fronts.

3. The United States is the only industrialized country that does not guarantee access to health care for all its citizens. An increasing segment of the US population was living without even basic health insurance, with negative consequences for access to care, quality of care, and health outcomes.

Each of these issues was pressing in its own right. The conundrum of US health care was that all three existed simultaneously and that attempting to remedy one would inevitably affect the others.

The problem of US health care can be represented by an equilateral triangle. As illustrated in figure 13.1, each point of the triangle represents one of these fundamental policy issues: cost, quality, or access. Imagine that the triangle is made of cardboard and that it is situated horizontally. It is possible to find a single point of balance

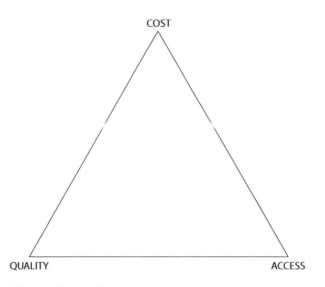

COST

QUALITY   ACCESS

FIGURE 13.1. The dilemma of US health care.

for this cardboard triangle. Once you find this point, it is possible to balance the tri-angle on the tip of your finger. So long as you leave the triangle alone, it will remain balanced. Now try to move one of the points of the triangle either up or down. Mov-ing any one point in this manner will inevitably cause the other points to move.

The same is true for our health care system. As soon as we try to address one of the fundamental problems facing the system, we find that our proposed solution will affect the other parts of the system, often adversely. Consider the following:

- If we try to control the cost of care, we either will reduce the quality of the care by making fewer services available or will further decrease access to care.
- If we increase access by expanding insurance coverage to those who are cur-rently uninsured, we will further increase the overall cost of care. Attempts to improve access while also reducing cost will often be perceived as impairing quality.
- Attempts to improve the quality of care by introducing new treatments, tech-nologies, or medications will add to the cost of the health care system, with the risk of driving more people into the ranks of the uninsured.

For several decades in the mid-twentieth century, the US health care system was like the triangle, perched on its balance point, albeit somewhat unsteadily. While serious problems remained in our system, we had achieved a rough equilibrium between the competing needs of cost, quality, and access. The extension of health insurance to the elderly and the poor through the federal Medicare and Medicaid programs of the 1960s

FIGURE 13.2. Health care costs too much: So, how can you reduce costs?
Source: Based on Fuchs 1993a.

coincided with the beginnings of the explosion in medical technology. Attempts in the 1990s to hold down the cost of care through the expansion of managed care led to the perception that quality was being impaired in ways that were unacceptable. Each point of our triangle had the forces of social and political change tugging at it. As a result, our health care system was thrown out of balance and was wobbling precariously.

How were we to gain control of our health care system in a way that adequately addresses and balances competing problems and needs? This was the dilemma of US health care at the time ACA was enacted.

Victor Fuchs, one of the founders of the discipline of health economics, described our dilemma accurately and succinctly: "No pain, no gain" (Fuchs 1993b). He pointed out that the issue of health care costs can be seen as simple arithmetic, represented by the equation illustrated in figure 13.2.

To calculate overall health care costs, one simply has to multiply the following three numbers:

1. The number of services provided to patients
This includes the number of office visits, the number of hospitalizations, the number of operations and other procedures, the number of tests, and the number of medications.

2. The number of resources used in producing each service
Here is where the issue of technology enters in so clearly. Does the doctor's office include all types of new, high-tech apparatus? Does the hospital include all the latest monitoring and diagnostic equipment? Will an operation incorporate laser scalpels and robotics? Will we rely on newer, high-priced medications over less expensive standbys?

3. The price of the various resources used in providing services
How much will we pay doctors for their care? How much will we pay hospitals? Will we allow the producers of medical equipment and pharmaceutical products to charge whatever price the market will bear?

It is a simple fact of arithmetic that, to reduce the cost of health care, we will have to reduce at least one of the numbers appearing on the right side of the equation. The problem is, whenever we reduce one of these numbers, someone feels pain. When someone feels pain, he or she generally complains.

- If you try to reduce the number of services provided to patients, patients will perceive the reduction as a decrease in quality. Recent history has shown that, in response to constraints in the 1990s on the availability of services inherent to many types of managed care organizations, patients turned both to legislators and to the courts to prevent the reduction in their perceived access to the care they wanted.

- If you try to reduce the intensity of the resources used in providing services, patients, providers, and producers alike will oppose the reductions. Patients often view the latest, high-tech treatment as the only acceptable alternative. Physicians frequently oppose constraints on the use of technology in providing service. Producers such as pharmaceutical companies and device manufacturers are often adamantly opposed to formal limitations on the way physicians use medications or devices.

- There have been numerous attempts to reduce the cost of care by reducing the amount we pay for specific services. Most recently, attempts at cost control have often been through limitations in the amount physicians and hospitals are paid for providing care. Both managed care organizations in the private market for care and government programs such as Medicare and Medicaid have reduced or restricted the amount they are willing to pay health care providers. These reductions have begun to have serious effects on many of these providers. In addition, a number of physician groups have responded to further reductions in reimbursement by refusing to see patients covered by these insurance plans.

A powerful social force acting against health care reform is the tremendous heterogeneity of American society. Often, gains by one segment of society are perceived as losses by another segment, and thus they are resisted. As the aforementioned equation illustrates, however, our need both to expand health care access and to contain costs will necessitate some form of limitation on the amount of health care we make available. Unfortunately, for those who currently have few limits on the amount of care available, any imposition of new limits will be seen as an unwarranted rationing of care. The very concept of rationing in health care seems somehow to be fundamentally un-American. Accordingly, in creating as part of ACA the Medicare Independent Payment Advisory Board and charging it with restraining Medicare spending in the future, Congress nonetheless mandated that any proposals for reducing future Medicare spending "shall not include any recommendation to ration health care" (ACA Section 2403).

RATIONING HEALTH CARE: IS IT INEVITABLE? CAN IT BE ACCEPTABLE?

To understand the concept of rationing as it applies to health care, I will look first at the rationing of consumer goods that took place during World War II, and then at experiences the United States has had with explicit, federally sanctioned health care rationing: the rationing of flu shots and the rationing of health care to the poor as part of the Oregon Health Plan, discussed in chapter 7.

Rationing Consumer Goods during World War II

During World War II, certain foods and industrial raw materials were in scarce supply. These scarce resources were not enough both to supply the war effort and to meet the needs of the civilian population. Under government direction, these scarce resources were allocated on a prioritized basis. The military often had first priority. Those in the civilian population who were most in need came next (babies got milk; ambulances got tires). Finally, those resources still available were allocated on an even basis to those remaining. The system of rationing of scarce consumer goods was widely perceived to be both generally fair and in support of a crucial national goal. As such, the rationing received wide support.

> **CONCEPT 13.1**
>
> Rationing involves the prioritized allocation of scarce resources.

Rationing Flu Shots

Each year, the federal government collaborates with private manufacturers to identify the strains of influenza most likely to strike the American public during the coming flu season. Flu shots have proven to be effective in reducing serious illness and death from the flu, especially in vulnerable populations such as frail elderly people. In 2004, the United States projected that 100 million doses of flu vaccine would be needed to provide adequate protection to the public. Unfortunately, one of the principal manufacturers of flu vaccine discovered serious problems with possible bacterial contamination of its vaccine, and the manufacturer was unable to supply the approximately 50 million doses that providers in the United States had ordered. It was too late in the season for other manufacturers to produce more vaccine. The country suddenly faced the prospect of going through a flu season with only half the number of flu shots it needed.

The shortage of flu shots received broad coverage in the press. A public consensus rapidly developed around how the available doses of vaccine would be distributed: to those who needed it most (DesRoches et al. 2005). Few argued that flu shots should go to those willing to pay the most. For a commodity as necessary to the public's health

TABLE 13.1. Priority groups established by the federal government for influenza vaccination at times of vaccine shortage

Priority group	
1A	Persons aged > 65 years with comorbid conditions Residents of long-term care facilities
1B	Persons aged 2–64 years with comorbid conditions Persons aged > 65 years without comorbid conditions Children aged 6–23 months Pregnant women
1C	Health care personnel Household contacts and out-of-home caregivers of children aged < 6 months
2	Household contacts of children and adults at increased risk for influenza-related complications Healthy persons aged 50–64 years
3	Persons aged 2–49 years without high-risk conditions

Source: US Centers for Disease Control and Prevention 2005.

as flu vaccine, it would be unethical to distribute that commodity on the basis of ability to pay rather than the basis of relative need. After extensive consultation, the federal government published the list shown in table 13.1 that prioritized population subgroups by relative need.

The supply of flu vaccine in the United States remained both stable and adequate until a new flu strain showed up unexpectedly: H1N1 flu. In April 2009, two boys in California, one 10 years old and one 8 years old, were diagnosed with a new strain of the influenza virus that had never been identified before. Based on its unique genetic markings, the virus was named Influenza H1N1. As the two boys lived 150 miles apart and had never met, the federal Centers for Disease Control and Prevention (CDC) became quite concerned about the early signs of a more widespread outbreak of the new flu strain (Centers for Disease Control and Prevention 2010). Within two weeks of the initial identification of the new flu strain in these two boys, the CDC had identified the H1N1 virus in blood samples from several patients in Mexico who had become ill with influenza. Concerned that a new and potentially dangerous strain of the flu was spreading rapidly in North America, the CDC notified the World Health Organization (WHO), and on April 25 the director-general of WHO declared the 2009 H1N1 outbreak a "Public Health Emergency of International Concern." By June 2009, the WHO had relabeled the H1N1 outbreak as a "Global Pandemic."

The CDC immediately began working with vaccine manufacturers to produce enough vaccine to vaccinate a majority of Americans. It was clear, though, that it would take months to produce sufficient vaccine for all those who needed it. Accordingly, the CDC developed a prioritized list of those most at risk for serious outcomes from H1N1. This listing included pregnant women; household contacts and caregivers for children younger than 6 months of age; health care and emergency medical services personnel; children from 6 months through 18 years of age; young adults 19 through 24 years of age; and persons aged 25 through 64 years who had health conditions associated with higher risk of medical complications from influenza (Centers for Disease Control and Prevention 2009). By October, the H1N1 vaccine began to become available and was administered on a prioritized basis to those in these high-risk groups. Those at lesser risk were able to receive the vaccine only after the high-risk groups had been vaccinated. Supplies were carefully rationed, based upon relative need. There was widespread public support for this approach. The concept of making the vaccine preferentially available to those in a low-risk group who nonetheless were willing to pay a high price for it was never seriously considered.

Our experience with the 2004 vaccine shortage and the sudden need for H1N1 vaccine underscores a fundamental ethical principle, one the federal government and the American public have agreed on (at least in the case of flu vaccine). In a situation of scarcity of a crucially important health care resource, the scarce resource should be allocated on a prioritized basis based on relative need rather than ability to pay.

Rationing Health Care for Poor People as Part of the Oregon Health Plan

The reasons behind and structure of the original Oregon Health Plan (OHP) are described in chapter 7. In allocating health care services for poor adults in Oregon, the broadly representative Oregon Health Services Commission applied the same ethical principle as that used in distributing scarce flu shots. Figure 13.3 illustrates again the fundamental concept behind the plan.

> **CONCEPT 13.2**
>
> In the case of the 2004 shortage of flu vaccine and the 2009 shortage of H1N1 flu vaccine, the federal government and the American public agreed on the following fundamental ethical principle: in a situation of scarcity of a crucially important health care resource, that resource should be allocated on the basis of need rather than ability to pay.

Oregon decided that it was better both for its low-income adults and for the state overall to reallocate some health care funds. By explicitly withholding some services from previous Medicaid beneficiaries, the funds thus saved were redirected to provide broader coverage (albeit limited in number of services) to all those under the federal poverty level (FPL). Health services were rationed so that more could benefit from basic coverage. The rationing was based on the relative need for services.

When Oregon first proposed rationing health care in this manner, a number of sources voiced opposition. Rationing of health care, it was argued, was simply not acceptable. It somehow ran contrary to fundamental American principles to ration something so important.

How should we respond to such arguments? How should we view plans for rationing health care in general? The OHP involved the prioritized allocation of a scarce

Medicaid Population

FIGURE 13.3. The Oregon Health Plan: Rationing health care based on need.

resource: health care for the poor. It allocated that resource on the basis of need. Those services that provided the highest benefit were provided to all. Those services that provided the lowest benefit were provided to none. Some people had to forgo services that had a low level of expected benefit so that all people could receive those services with a high level of expected benefit. It appears that the OHP was fully consistent with the ethical principle identified earlier in our discussion of flu vaccines.

It is important to appreciate, however, that the OHP did not create rationing where rationing did not previously exist. It simply shifted public policy from one form of rationing to another form. To understand this, let us look again at the situation that existed in Oregon before the establishment of the OHP, as illustrated in figure 13.4.

Even before the establishment of the OHP, the Oregon state government approached health care for poor adults as a scarce commodity. It prioritized the allocation of Medicaid coverage; it did so based on the income of the poor adult. Only the poorest Oregonians—those with an income below 60 percent of the FPL—were covered. So that the poorest could receive full coverage, those among the poor with an income above this level received no coverage at all.

Before the OHP, Oregon rationed health care to poor people based on income. After the plan was established, Oregon rationed care to the poor based on relative need. It simply switched from one form of rationing to another.

The previous rationing of care was done implicitly, without a formal public decision to do so. The new rationing was done explicitly, after a thorough process of public discussion and debate.

FIGURE 13.4. Before the Oregon Health Plan: Rationing health care based on income.

The previous discussion is about how health care was made available to poor people in Oregon. If, instead, we look at how health care has been made available to people throughout this country, we find a comparable situation. Figure 13.5 illustrates the distribution of health care in the United States at the time of the passage of ACA, in a format similar to the one used to look at health care in Oregon. The horizontal axis again lists all the services poten-

> **CONCEPT 13.3**
>
> The Oregon Health Plan did not create rationing where none previously existed. It instead shifted state policy from rationing health care based on income to rationing care based on need.

tially available to people, from the most necessary to the least necessary. (There is, of course, no mechanism to establish such a list for the United States as a whole. For the purposes of discussion, I use the ranking of services created for the OHP as if it were to apply to the entire country.) In this case, the vertical axis is not the percentage of the poverty line a person falls into but rather the income percentile at which a person is located. A person who earns the median income would be at 50 percent. Low-income people are at low percentiles and high-income people are at high percentiles.

Given the complexity of our insurance system and the inequity between the very poor who were covered by Medicaid and the somewhat poor who were mostly without health insurance, the diagonal line representing the division between those who are covered and those who are not is not actually straight. A truly accurate line would be somewhat zigzagged at the bottom income percentiles. The principle, though, is the same: health care in the United States has been distributed largely along income

U.S. Population

FIGURE 13.5. The way we ration health care in the United States.

CONCEPT 13.4

The health care system in the United States involves rationing health care according to income. In contrast to the Oregon Health Plan, this rationing is implicit, with no explicit decision to ration care ever having been agreed to.

lines. The lower your income, the less care you have available to you. In the United States, as in Oregon before the OHP, we have for many years rationed health care according to income. We have done so, however, implicitly, never having engaged in a public debate about whether we should ration health care and on what basis we should do so.

In the case of Oregon, why didn't the state government simply provide enough money to cover all its poor residents with comprehensive health insurance? In the case of the US health care system, why doesn't the federal government simply adopt a program of full, comprehensive health care, providing all services to all people? The answer in both cases is fairly simple. Oregon could not afford to provide all care to all poor people in the state. Similarly, the US government cannot afford to pay for health care for all American people without limitation. Health care has become so expensive that it simply is not feasible for government, whether state or federal, to assure full access to all services for all people. This inevitable conclusion leads us to the central conundrum of US health care, which my students refer to as "Barr's Law." I offer it with apologies to Abraham Lincoln.

You can treat some of the people all of the time, or you can treat all of the people some of the time, but you can't treat all of the people all of the time.

This is the conundrum for politicians. Their constituents will not accept the rationing of their medical treatment. People do not want to be told that good health has a price. On the other hand, neither the politicians nor their constituents want to pay the higher taxes or higher insurance premiums required for unlimited health care.

To date, the United States has been unable to find a solution to this conundrum. Some would say that the problem is not one of being unable to find a solution but rather of being unwilling. As a consequence, we have failed to arrive at a consensus about a uniform national policy concerning access to health insurance. As the cost of providing high-tech, high-quality care has gone up, it has historically been our national policy largely to look the other way as more and more people found themselves without health insurance. There have been incremental attempts to address the issue of the uninsured, but until the passage of ACA, we were unable to agree on a consistent national policy approach. The continuing controversy over the full implementation of ACA suggests that we still may not have been able to reach such a consensus.

> **CONCEPT 13.5**
>
> You can treat some of the people all of the time, or you can treat all of the people some of the time, but you can't treat all of the people all of the time (Barr's Law).

Even as ACA is fully implemented, finding a solution to the three-pointed dilemma of US health care will still be extremely difficult. If we are ever to constrain costs, assure increased access while also maintaining quality, we are going to need to lessen our expectations somewhat about what type of health care we should receive. As a society, we are going to need collectively to agree that in some cases, for some people, we will need to forgo certain care that might still hold out the possibility of some benefit.

Recall from our discussion of marginal cost and marginal benefit in chapter 3 that we often make decisions in health care that we would not make for other types of goods or services. Victor Fuchs has underscored our differing perceptions of economic efficiency and medical efficiency. In economic theory, allocation of marginal resources that result in marginal benefits that are of lesser value constitutes what Fuchs refers to as "economic waste." By contrast, Fuchs suggests that, as a society, we have come to view "medical waste" only in the case of an "intervention that has no possible benefit for the patient or in which the potential risk to the patient is greater than potential benefit" (Fuchs 2009, p. 2481). For many people, as long as a procedure has any measureable marginal benefit, any effort to prevent access to that procedure constitutes unwarranted rationing. An illustration of this principle is provided by the public reaction to updated recommendations issued in 2009 regarding mammography screening.

NEW RECOMMENDATIONS FOR MAMMOGRAPHY SCREENING: RATIONING OR RATIONAL?

The US Preventive Services Task Force (USPSTF) is an independent advisory body made up of medical experts with a range of backgrounds and charged with the task of reviewing scientific evidence regarding preventive health services. In November 2009, USPSTF published the results of its review of the best available scientific evidence regarding mammography screening for breast cancer in women (Nelson et al. 2009; US Preventive Services Task Force 2009). In 2002, USPSTF had issued a recommendation that all women age 40 or over get mammography screening every one to two years. Based on more recent research, USPSTF changed its recommendation to suggest that only women between ages 50 and 74 get routine screening, and that they do so every two years. The report then recommended that women aged 40 to 49 years not be routinely screened; instead, women in this age group should consult with their doctor to discuss the pros and cons of screening, and make an individual decision based a woman's individual risk profile and preferences.

As soon as the new guidelines were issued, there was a loud public outcry from many quarters regarding the recommendation that women aged 40 to 49 not be routinely screened. As summarized in a story in the *New York Times* by Kevin Sack, "the science of medicine bumped up against the foundations of American medical consumerism: that more is better, that saving a life is worth any sacrifice, and that health care is a birthright" (Sack 2009, p. A1).

The USPSTF did conclude that routine, annual screening for women aged 40 to 49 would save lives. In order to save one woman's life through early detection of breast cancer, however, 1,900 women would need to get mammograms every year for 10 years. It was not the cost of these 19,000 mammograms that gave the task force pause; it was the toll these extra screening examinations would take on the women undergoing them (Mandelblatt et al. 2009). The task force found that for every 1,000 screening mammograms there would be an average of 99 false positive results—examinations that identified suspicious lesions that, after further testing and, for many of the women after surgical biopsy of the breast, turned out not to be cancer. Thus, for any individual woman, the risk was substantially higher that she would experience the stress and the anxiety of a false positive result and the additional procedures necessary to confirm that the lesion was not actually cancer. As stated in an editorial published concurrently with the USPSTF recommendations, the results of scientific studies "provide consistent results and suggest that the number of additional breast cancer deaths averted by starting screening mammography at age 40 is small and the earlier screening involves important harms" (Kerlikowske 2009, p. 750).

With the USPSTF's explicit acknowledgment that following the new guidelines would result in more women dying (albeit few women), did the updated recommendations constitute a recommendation that we ration care? One commentator writing in the *New England Journal of Medicine* suggested that they did. In a commentary titled "Screening Mammography and the 'R' Word," Truog (2009) concluded that "critics of the Task Force recommendations and of health care reform in general are offering a false choice. The choice is not about health care rationing and some undefined alternative, since there is no alternative. Rather, the choice concerns what principles we will use to ration health care. . . . If the debate about health care reform is to progress with clarity, transparency, and honesty, we must lose our fear of the 'R' word and discuss how, not whether, we should ration health care" (p. 2502).

In commenting on what they referred to as the "Mammography Wars," Quanstrum and Hayward (2010) emphasized an important principle underlying the USPSTF recommendations. "Behind the panel's conclusions regarding mammography lurks an unwelcome reality that our profession has often failed to acknowledge. Every medical intervention—no matter how beneficial for some patients—will provide continuously diminishing returns as the threshold for intervention is lowered. Mammography is just one case in point" (p. 1076).

In 2014, the International Agency for Research on Cancer (IARC) convened a group of experts from sixteen countries "to assess the cancer-preventive and adverse effects of different methods of screening for breast cancer" (Lauby-Secretan et al. 2015, p. 2353). After reviewing extensive clinical and research data, the IARC group issued guidelines that reiterate the USPSTF guidelines—that women with average risk of breast cancer initiate mammography screening at age 50.

Largely in response to the 2009 USPSTF recommendations, the American Cancer Society (ACS) initiated a reassessment of its own recommendations regarding mammography screening. As described on its website (2015), ACS "is a nationwide, community-based voluntary health organization dedicated to eliminating cancer as a major health problem." In 2003, a year after USPSTF had issued its original recommendation that women get yearly mammograms starting at age 40, ACS had issued its own recommendation, largely coincident with that of USPSTF, that "women at average risk should begin annual mammography at age 40" (Smith et al. 2003, p. 142). In 2015, ACS issued revised guidelines for mammography screening, recommending "that women with an average risk of breast cancer should undergo regular screening mammography starting at age 45 years" (Oeffinger et al. 2015, p. 1599). While USPSTF recommends screening every two years starting at age 50, ACS recommends screening every year from age 45–54 and screening every two years at age 55 and older. In issuing these recommendations, the authors explained that "the ACS recommendations are made in the context of maximizing reductions in breast cancer mortality and reducing years of life lost while minimizing the associated harms among the population of women in the United States" (p. 1611). Thus, ACS and USPSTF largely agree on balancing reductions in breast cancer mortality with potential harms from screening of low-risk women, while they differ somewhat in how that balance should be achieved.

As a society, we commonly elect to receive (and have come to expect) many types of care that have a small marginal benefit relative to marginal cost—either the cost in dollars or the cost in added risk or discomfort. Because the marginal benefit of that care is small, this also implies that forgoing that care would lead to only a small decrement in our health. Once we as a society come to appreciate that health care is truly a scarce commodity, one for which resources are limited, it will become easier for us to accept the form of health care rationing that will be necessary if we are to solve our dilemma. If health care is seen as a zero-sum commodity, it will mean that any extra care provided to one person will necessarily lead to a reduction in care for someone else. (This clearly was the case in the flu vaccine shortages discussed earlier.) If we are able to accept this conclusion as a principle of our social policy, we will be able to develop mechanisms that ensure that we attain a rough level of justice in health care, under which no one is denied care so that someone else may receive care of lesser benefit.

Consistent with our comparison in chapter 3 of the US and Canadian health care systems, a system of fully equal access for all is probably not compatible with our national emphasis on the needs of the individual over the needs of the group. Whatever system we adopt will doubtless need to include the option for those with enough money to be able to purchase whatever level of care they wish. If there is a level of care that has small marginal benefit but large marginal cost, and if there are adequate resources to provide that care, if an individual still wants to purchase it with his or her own money, our system need not prevent that. Rather than adopting the one-class system found in Canada, we will probably need to adopt a form of the two-class system found in Great Britain, where those wishing to buy care outside the National Health Service are free to do so.

Whatever system we adopt, it will need to incorporate some limits on care, and it will need to be seen as fair. Without widely held perceptions of fairness, few will be willing to forgo care so that someone else may be treated instead. Changes in our system of care occurring over the last two decades, however, may have made this goal of fairness substantially more difficult to attain.

PROFIT AS A COMPETITOR TO COST, QUALITY, AND ACCESS

As discussed in chapter 9, US health care has undergone a major change over the past twenty to thirty years. Once organized largely on a nonprofit basis, our health care system now includes an increasing number of for-profit corporations: for-profit HMOs and other insurers, for-profit hospitals, and for-profit medical care providers. This shift to for-profit health care has added a fourth factor to our national health care dilemma: the need to maintain shareholder profits. This new health care dilemma is illustrated in figure 13.6.

Once represented by the triangle of cost, quality, and access, we now have a system stretched among four points: cost, quality, access, and profit. At nearly every level, the issue of profit plays some role in deciding who will receive what care. For-profit hospitals have to factor in the need to maintain shareholder return in decisions about which patients to admit, what equipment to buy, and how to measure quality. For-profit insurers must factor shareholder profit into their decisions about how much of the premiums they receive from employers is available to be paid as payments to physicians and other providers, and about what types of services and medications will be included under the coverage they offer.

As difficult as it may be to somehow find a new equilibrium between cost, quality, and access, the added presence of the profit motive makes finding a comprehensive solution to the problems of US health care even more difficult to attain.

To understand why this is, consider a patient in the position of having to forgo care so that someone else can receive care of greater marginal benefit. If we are able to create a system of care in which the medical needs of all patients are fairly balanced, patients can have some assurance that by giving up certain care, some other patient will benefit directly, and the marginal benefit for that patient is greater than the marginal decrement of forgoing care. It may be possible to move to this type of system so long as this assurance can be maintained.

FIGURE 13.6. The new dilemma of US health care.

In the new, four-cornered American system of care, this assurance cannot be maintained. In a system in which profit competes with quality and access for scarce health care dollars, it is impossible to be certain that money saved by forgoing care of small marginal benefit but large marginal cost will go to providing care to other patients who need it more. It may well be the case that money saved in this way would also go to provide added profit to shareholders. It is simply not reasonable to expect any patient at any level of income to willingly forgo care, regardless of the cost/benefit profile of that care, if the money saved by doing so will end up going to corporate profit.

I once had as a patient a professor of economics. That professor was upset because his for-profit health insurance company had established a medication formulary, with payment available only for those specific drugs on the list. A medication the professor had previously taken was excluded from the list, and in its place was another, less expensive medication that was equally effective in treating the professor's problem. The second medication, however, had some unpleasant (but not dangerous) side effects. I suggested to the professor that a rational economic argument could be made to have only the less expensive medication covered. The marginal benefit of the more expensive drug (fewer side effects) did not justify its substantial marginal cost over the less expensive yet equally effective alternative. The professor, however, contended that issues of marginal cost and marginal benefit were not appropriate when it was his health that was involved. The insurance company had no right, he argued, to withhold the more expensive drug simply to make a profit.

I could offer little in response. Were I in his situation, I would probably feel the same way. The presence of the profit motive throughout our health care system makes it unreasonable to expect either individual patients or society as a whole to be willing to move toward an accommodation of the competing needs of cost, quality, and access. So long as we have a system that includes a major role for for-profit corporations, we will be unlikely to find a national health policy that can guarantee access to basic, high-quality health care to all people at a cost our society can afford.

PHYSICIAN, HEAL THYSELF: PHYSICIANS AND THE PROFIT MOTIVE

Physicians, both individually and collectively, are not strangers to the profit motive. A review of the history of medical practice throughout much of the twentieth century (Starr 1982) revealed that medical practice in this country was historically based on the profit motive: profit for the individual physician. Individual physicians practicing medicine under the fee-for-service system of payment were acting as for-profit entrepreneurs. A physician was not only allowed but also encouraged to do everything he could for the patient, so long as he did not harm the patient directly. The more the physician did, the more the physician was paid. For decades, there were essentially no limits on how much income a physician could earn, and no one was looking over the physician's shoulder to ask how necessary or appropriate the care being provided was. At that time, however, the incentive to make more profit by providing more care coincided closely with the patient's desire to receive all possible care.

As it turns out, the appropriateness of much of the care provided in the fee-for-service system was questionable. It appears that in many instances physicians were offering if not actually encouraging unnecessary tests and procedures, with a resulting increase in their income. This history of mixing the economic self-interest of the physician with the medical needs of the patient led Dr. George Lundberg, at that time editor of *JAMA*, to offer the following warning: "*Caveat aeger*—let the patient beware" (Lundberg 1995). Dr. Lundberg suggested that few physicians are in medicine just for the money (those he labels "money grubbers") and few exhibit pure altruism (those he labels "altruistic missionaries"). Most physicians are somewhere in between and include at least some level of economic self-interest in their medical decisions. Each physician strikes his or her own balance between the needs of the patient and economic self-interest.

Dr. Lundberg suggested that physicians are approximately evenly distributed across a wide spectrum in the way they balance these competing needs. According to Dr. Lundberg's model, this distribution of physicians approximates the shape of the bell-shaped curve, which statisticians refer to as the "standard normal distribution." This curve is illustrated in figure 13.7.

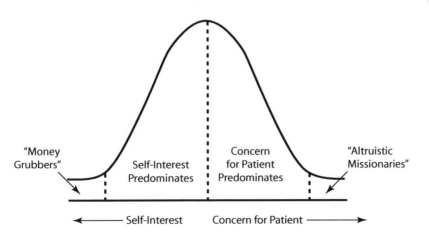

FIGURE 13.7. The distribution of physicians in the United States along a scale of self-interest versus concern for the patient. *Source:* Adapted from Lundberg 1995.

Students of statistics will recall that the standard normal distribution has certain characteristics. The mean, median, and mode of the curve are all the same. Ninety-five percent of all points under the curve will lie within two standard deviations of the mean.

If Dr. Lundberg's model is correct (and I suspect it is), this would suggest that the medical profession in the United States is about equally divided between those situated to the left of the median and those situated to the right of the median. This would mean that, while most physicians attain some type of balance between their own economic needs and the needs of their patients, half of all physicians are more self-interested than they are interested in the benefit of their patients. While few physicians are in it just for the money (those in the left tail of the curve), few physicians are purely altruistic in their approach to care (those in the right tail of the curve). All the rest of us are situated somewhere between the missionaries and the money grubbers.

This conclusion presents an ethical dilemma for physicians. What steps should we take to assure that neither physicians' self-interest nor the financial interests of for-profit corporations take precedence over the genuine medical need of patients? In discussing this dilemma, Leon Eisenberg suggested that medicine as a profession needs to strengthen and reinforce the culture of professionalism, and in doing so strengthen the commitment of physicians to the needs of their patients. To those of us in the role of teachers and mentors, he suggested: "It can only promote cynicism among our students if we preach humanism and ignore the realities of the contemporary scene. . . . The words 'physician' and 'patient' are embedded in a proud ethical tradition. Have we always lived up to the ideal we profess? It is obvious that the answer is no. . . . No physician could proclaim that the business of medicine is business without losing the respect of her peers. Physicians ought to be advocates for their patients. The best always have been" (1995, p. 333).

I suggest that it is up to the US health care professionals, including physicians, nurses, public health analysts, and others, to lead the way toward a system and an ethic that addresses this issue of economic interests and the needs of the patient. Our professional practice should embrace simultaneously the tremendous advances medicine has made in the past fifty years and a genuine commitment to justice in the allocation of health care resources. Part of this concept of justice in health care must be a clear commitment that the needs of the patient come before the financial needs either of individual physicians or of health care corporations.

Many of you who are reading this book will be faced with these issues and these challenges. I suggest that each of you currently working or planning to work either as a physician or in some other capacity in the health care system consider fully the issues raised here. Many forces in society are pushing individual professionals toward the left side of the diagram. These forces include the high cost of a professional education, the need to put children through college, and simply the desire to live comfortably. The forces strengthening the right side of the diagram are the ethical tradition of medicine and a commitment to service on behalf of the patient. Every health care professional needs to be aware of this choice.

I propose that each of you in the health professions, from time to time throughout your career, ask the following three questions:

1. In my current professional work, where on this diagram am I situated?
2. Where on this diagram do I want to be situated?
3. Am I willing to do what is necessary to move from where I am now to where I want to be?

SUMMARY

In chapter 2 of this book, I identified the three problems that lie at the center of US health policy: (1) constraining the cost of care, (2) maintaining and improving the quality of care, and (3) increasing access to care. As we have gone through this book, we have learned that these are not three separate problems. Instead, they are the three faces of a single problem. Policies that address only one of these issues will inevitably affect the other two.

To be successful in restructuring the US system of health care, we will need to deal with all three problems simultaneously. Despite our technological sophistication and the substantial resources we invest in our health care system, we are confronted by the reality of "Barr's Law": we cannot provide all imaginable care to all of the people all of the time. We can optimize our system of health care only if we establish and maintain a policy of making care available according to a system of prioritization and only if that system has popular support.

Accepting the inevitability of limits on the amount of care we can provide and the need for prioritizing the care we do provide implies the need to ration health care. Often considered to be antithetical to the core values of American society, a closer examination reveals that approaching health care as a market commodity, available preferentially to those with the economic means to pay for it, is in itself a form of rationing. The challenge facing the American public as well as the American medical profession is finding a way to distribute our scarce health care resources that optimizes outcomes and reduces the role of providers' economic self-interest.

How the Affordable Care Act Addresses Issues of Cost, Quality, and Access

Throughout the initial debate over ACA, one of the central aspects under scrutiny was its impact on the cost of health care and on the federal deficit. The Congressional Budget Office thoroughly evaluated the final legislation and concluded that the combination of increased federal spending and increased revenues under ACA would result in a net reduction in the federal deficit of $124 billion over ten years. While ACA was expected to result in a net reduction in federal outlays for health care, it was also expected to result in a net increase in overall health care expenditures. Following its initial passage, the actuary at the federal Centers for Medicare and Medicaid Services concluded that as a result of ACA, overall national expenditures for health care would rise faster than they would have had ACA not been adopted. By 2019, national health expenditures under the provisions of ACA were predicted to rise to 19.6 percent of GDP, as compared to 19.3 percent had ACA not been enacted.

In its plans to reduce federal (as compared to national) health care spending, ACA focused largely on reducing costs in Medicare. As described in chapter 6, ACA established a new mechanism for addressing the specific issue of the rising cost of the Medicare program through creation of a new Independent Payment Advisory Board (IPAB). ACA delegated to IPAB principal responsibility for monitoring the rate at which Medicare's spending increases over time. If Medicare spending rises faster than new targets established under ACA, IPAB was given the responsibility of coming up with a plan to rein in spending to meet the target amount. ACA tied the hands of IPAB somewhat, however, by requiring that steps taken by the board "shall not include any recommendation to ration health care, raise revenues [i.e., taxes] or Medicare beneficiary premiums . . . or otherwise restrict benefits or modify eligibility criteria" (ACA Section 3403). As also described in chapter 6, as a consequence of continuing and intense political differences between Congress and the White House, IPAB has never come to fruition. By 2015, President Obama still had not appointed any members of IPAB.

In the absence of IPAB, it has largely been up to the new Center for Medicare and Medicaid Innovation (CMMI) to develop the means to reduce the growth in Medicare spending over time. Established in 2011, CMMI moved rapidly to initiate a series of pilot programs evaluating the effectiveness of accountable care organizations (ACOs) and other forms of innovative payment reform for Medicare providers. ACOs can adopt one of two basic options for payment reform. In the basic model, the ACO agrees to accept responsibility for the care of a defined group of Medicare beneficiaries and receives as a bonus payment a share of any cost savings it is able to generate. As an alternative, ACOs can elect either the Shared Savings Model or the Pioneer Model, in both of which the ACO also accepts responsibility for a defined group of Medicare beneficiaries and is eligible for a larger share of the cost savings generated in return for accepting partial risk for any cost increases over a target amount. These shared-risk models have proven more effective in reducing costs for a defined group of patients, typically in the range of 1–4 percent per year. While not large, if aggregated over time these savings could contribute to reduced growth in Medicare spending if more widely adopted.

A second alternative payment approach adopted on a trial basis for Medicare has been the bundled payment model, in which all providers involved in a specific episode of care for a patient will share in a fixed payment amount. This approach has recently been adopted by Medicare in several regions of the country for surgical replacement of knee or hip joints in Medicare beneficiaries. They are intended to cover payment for hospital care, physician services, and rehabilitative services, and will provide a strong incentive for these providers to work collaboratively to reduce costs while maintaining quality.

In 2015, HHS Secretary Sylvia M. Burwell announced the goal of shifting 50 percent of all Medicare expenditures to these and other similar alternative models as a means of constraining Medicare spending over time. As these alternative models become more widespread among those providing care to Medicare beneficiaries, the expectation is that private payers will also begin to adopt them. While growth in Medicare spending has not become flat, it has been reduced by a combination of these alternative payment models and the overall slowing of health care spending in the period 2010–14. However, as described in chapter 6, in 2015 the Medicare Boards of Trustees predicted that Medicare spending, which represented 3.5 percent of GDP in 2014, will increase to 5.4 percent of GDP by 2035, with even greater increases predicted for the future. Similarly, while overall national health care expenditures remained largely flat over the period 2009–13 at 17.4 percent of GDP, CMS has predicted that level will continue to rise, reaching 18.0 percent in 2015 and 19.6 percent in 2024—a level largely in line with initial projections (Keehan et al. 2015). Thus, ACA has addressed the issue of rising health care costs but has not solved it.

ACA addressed the issue of access to care through its expansion of health insurance through a combination of expansion of Medicaid eligibility and the creation of tax-subsidized health insurance coverage available to individuals and families with income between 100 percent and 400 percent of the FPL. While it was originally estimated that 32 million people who otherwise would have been uninsured would gain coverage under ACA, that prediction has been reduced somewhat as a consequence of the Supreme Court decision to make Medicaid expansion optional to the states. As reported in chapter 8, at the end of the second open enrollment period under ACA in 2015, an estimated 22.8 million people had gained insurance coverage—10 million through the state exchanges and 12.8 million newly enrolled in Medicaid. While not all of these enrollees had been uninsured previously, the expansion of coverage under ACA was principally responsible for reducing the uninsured rate nationally from 16.3 percent of the population in 2010 to 10.4 percent in 2014. In addition, an estimated 3 million young adults (younger than 26 years) have gained insurance coverage by being eligible for continued coverage under their parents' health insurance. If, as many people expect, those states that have not expanded Medicaid are able to negotiate alternative approaches to expansion under the federal waiver program, the national uninsured rate can be expected to fall further in the future.

Sommers et al. (2015) reported results from a national poll of more than 500,000 adults, measuring changes between 2013 (before ACA expansion took effect) and 2015 in their reported insurance coverage, access to care, and self-reported health status. They reported improvements across all three metrics, with the largest improvements seen in black, Hispanic, and other minority populations. We must, of course, temper this assessment with the realization that expansion of health insurance coverage through Medicaid is not the same thing as expansion in access to care. As described previously, patients covered under Medicaid often have difficulty finding a provider—especially a primary care provider—who is willing to accept Medicaid and who has available and timely appointments for his or her patients on Medicaid. Fortunately, ACA includes extensive investment in the expansion of the PCMH model of care and in the expansion of FQHCs nationally. These well-respected models of primary care delivery, especially when combined, hold real potential for expanding access to care for those on Medicaid, especially those newly eligible. Were Congress to extend the two-year experiment in increased payment to primary care providers under Medicaid to match the payment under Medicare, there is reason to believe that access to care will expand for Medicaid recipients to the same extent as access to insurance.

When it was enacted, a principal goal of ACA was to make health care more accessible through expansion of coverage. To date, it has been largely successful in attaining this goal, yet continued monitoring and assessment of increases in on-the-ground access to care are warranted.

The third issue addressed by ACA is the quality of care available both to those newly covered under ACA insurance expansion and those previously covered. As with the issue of cost containment, ACA principally addresses the issue of quality of care through its modifications to Medicare policies. As described in chapter 6, under ACA reforms, Medicare has adopted a range of new programs that shift payment for care from a system based strictly on the volume of care provided to one that pays instead for value. The concept of value in the context of health care incorporates both what is done for a patient and how well it is done. Recall that under the RBRVS system, each service provided to a Medicare beneficiary by a physician was measured in resource-based relative value units, or RVUs. A physician visit qualifying for 1.5 RVUs was paid at a level that was 50 percent higher than a visit qualifying for 1.0 RVU. A surgical procedure qualifying for 10 RVUs was reimbursed at a level that was ten times greater than the visit qualifying for 1.0 RVU. In many physician practice groups, the more RVUs one generates, the more one takes home in salary or other forms of pay. The issue of the value added for a higher RVU-level service was rarely discussed.

Under ACA, Medicare is shifting payments for both hospitals and physicians. As described in chapter 6, in 2013, CMS began to adjust the amount they pay a hospital annually based on two metrics: the quality of the care received in the hospital based on the value-based purchasing measures and the frequency with which Medicare patients treated in the hospital are subsequently readmitted to the hospital within thirty days of discharge. By 2017, up to 6 percent of a hospital's Medicare revenues could be at risk based on poor performance on these and other similar quality measures.

In addition to the integration of quality into the payment for hospitals, Medicare has also adopted policies to integrate quality metrics in combination with volume metrics in paying physicians. Again, as described in chapter 6, when in 2015 Congress abandoned the sustainable growth rate (SGR) formula for limiting aggregate payments to physicians and other providers under Medicare Part B, it replaced SGR with a new merit-based incentive payment system (MIPS) that links future increases in payment rates to physicians with an individual physician's performance based on a composite measure of quality. MIPS is an extension of the Physician Quality Reporting System, established under ACA in 2011, under which payments to physicians can be adjusted up or down based on the quality of the care provided.

A third way Medicare has integrated quality of care into its payments for care is in the metrics used to assess the care provided by ACOs. In determining whether an ACO qualifies for a bonus payment, Medicare will use a metric that combines the volume of care provided with the quality of that care. As described by CMMI (2015a), "When an ACO succeeds in both delivering high-quality care and spending health care dollars more wisely, it will share in the savings it achieves for the Medicare program." Physicians, hospitals, and other providers participating in ACOs will need to monitor the quality of the care they provide as well as the volume of care, so as to insure that reductions in care volume focus on low-value services while maintaining those services with documented quality. Medicare applies the same principle in its supplementary payment program for primary care provided by PCMHs. To qualify for the supplemental payment, the providers must continue to be certified as a PCMH based on recognized national standards.

The Affordable Care Act and the Health Care Triangle

At the beginning of this chapter, we discussed the dilemma facing health care in the United States as a triangle, shown in figure 13.1, with the apices of cost, quality, and access. How has ACA done in trying to get that triangle back in balance? On the 5-year anniversary of the signing of ACA, Blumenthal et al. (2015) addressed this question. Looking both at the changes enacted in the first five years following enactment as well as the changes expected in the future, the authors concluded:

In the final analysis, the law will be judged on its cumulative effects on three critical dimensions of our health care system: adequacy of access to care, as measured by the proportion of Americans who lack meaningful protection against the cost of illness and the ability of Americans to get the care they need; the cost of care, as measured by the rate of increase in health care spending and the proportion of our national wealth devoted to health care services; and the quality of care experienced by Americans, as measured by national indicators of quality, such as those reported in the Agency for Healthcare Research and Quality annual report on quality. (p. 2451)

ACA is simultaneously addressing the three issues represented by the triangle, albeit with a somewhat different emphasis and priority, as illustrated in figure 13.8. The top apex of the triangle, representing the top priority issue addressed by ACA, is an expansion of access to care, principally through the expansion of health insurance coverage in the state exchanges, Medicaid, and insurance for young adults. The bottom apices are represented by policy changes that affect both the cost of care and the quality of care available in the United States.

Health economist David Cutler (2015a) suggested that "the single most important issue in health care is eliminating unnecessary medical spending" (p. 337). The principal cost issue ACA focuses on is the cost of Medicare, and future federal spending on

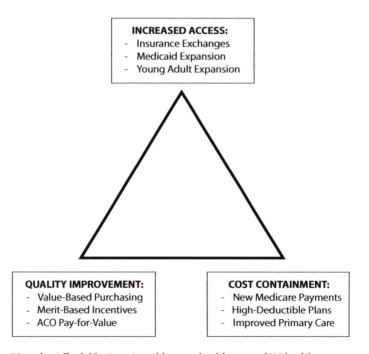

FIGURE 13.8. How the Affordable Care Act addresses the dilemma of US health care.

health care. The new approaches to paying providers for care provided to Medicare beneficiaries are expected to keep growth in Medicare costs more closely aligned with growth in GDP overall. While it is hoped that shifting to improved forms of primary care delivery, especially in providing care management for those with chronic and complex medical conditions, will reduce the rate of hospitalization and associated spending, these outcomes are not assured. Similarly, by including substantial patient responsibility through high deductibles and copayments for care provided through the state insurance exchanges, it is hoped that long-term spending patterns in the private sector will also be reduced. We should recall, however, that at the time it was passed, the projected net impact of ACA on national health care costs will be to *increase* overall health spending, from an initially projected 19.3 percent of GDP in 2019 to 19.6 percent.

ACA has made substantial improvements in the role quality assessment and improvement will play in US health care, especially in the Medicare system. In a number of areas, Medicare has shifted its focus from paying for the volume of care provided to paying instead for the value of the care provided. The concept of value includes providing care shown to be effective while reducing care shown to be less effective, as well as approaching the volume of care as appropriate for the condition or conditions being treated. ACOs as well as new payment systems such as MIPS and bundled payment will contribute to this new emphasis on value over volume. Hopefully, physicians individually and collectively will contribute to this shift. As suggested by Milstein (2015): "It seems likely that greater value improvement would occur if health care professional organizations more actively appealed to their members' ethical obligation to avoid wasteful use of health care resources or if improvement incentives targeted individual physicians more directly" (p. 1).

At the beginning of this chapter, we described the US health care system in the period leading up to passage of ACA as a triangle of competing cost/quality/access issues that had been "thrown out of balance and was wobbling precariously." It appears that ACA is having at least initial success in its efforts to stabilize each of these issues, and in doing so create greater stability and balance in our health care system. ACA has addressed the access and quality of care more so than the issue of national health care costs. However, as Blumenthal et al. (2015) suggested in their review of the impact of ACA after its first five years, "The provisions in the ACA regarding delivery-system reform have reinforced the impression that Americans are determined to bring health care costs under control and that providers would be well advised to help guide that process" (p. 2456). Blumenthal's apparent optimism about eventual cost stabilization seems reasonable. Close attention to the eventual balance ACA is able to attain among the issues of cost, quality, and access will let us know if Blumenthal's optimism was warranted.

14

Epilogue/Prologue to Health Care Reform in America

From the discussion in the previous chapters, it should be apparent that our former system of health care in the United States was not sustainable in the long term. There simply were too many areas of potential financial instability to expect our system to survive without fundamental reform. While enactment of the Affordable Care Act (ACA) will substantially reduce the number of Americans who are uninsured, it may or may not change the underlying cost structure of American health care. At some point in the future, we may either run out of the money or lose the political will to maintain our current system of care.

As a society, we have never openly and explicitly confronted the fundamental questions of social norms and public policy on which a system of health care is founded. We identified these questions as part of the discussion in chapter 3 of the fundamental differences between the US and Canadian systems of health care. We were able to identify four questions, the answers to which have formed the core of our social policy regarding health care:

1. Should we acknowledge a right to a basic level of health care for all Americans?
2. Should we establish explicit caps on the national health care budget?
3. Should the federal government take principal responsibility for the organization and financing of the health care system?
4. Should we establish a uniform standard of care for all people?

We know what the system looks like if we answer "no" to all four questions. We have the system that was in place before the passage of ACA, with all its inherent problems. We have never explicitly established "no" as our answer to these questions in a national forum—our system simply evolved to these answers over a period of decades and through a series of incremental decisions, many of them dealing with health care only peripherally. (The decision to rely on an employment-based system, as described in chapter 5, is an example of a decision not directly pertaining to health policy yet having profound effects on the structure of our system.)

If we were instead to answer "yes" to all four questions, as Canada has done, we would have a Canadian-style system. This option for reform has been before the American public since 1989, when Himmelstein and Woolhandler first suggested it as an alternative to Enthoven's proposal for managed competition, discussed in chapter 5. This "single-payer" (SP) proposal, as a Canadian-style approach has come to be called, was published in 2003 in revised form by Physicians for a National Health Program (Physicians' Working Group 2003).

The SP system would establish a right to comprehensive health care and would use a budgeting and payment system modeled on the Canadian system. As in Canada, it would rely on tax revenues to pay for care, and it would sever the historical link between employment and health insurance. By relying on global budgets for hospitals and other capital equipment such as MRI scanners, it would create a fixed level of available care, relying on physicians to select those patients needing care the most. In doing so, it can be reasonably expected to result in waiting lists—queues—for certain types of tests or procedures, as is the case in Canada.

The Canadian system of care is based on and consistent with the fundamental organization of Canadian society. To successfully import an SP system based on the Canadian model requires that the United States shift the basic organizing principles underlying our social structure. Our outlook and our cultural norms would have to coincide with those of Canada. This change simply does not seem feasible. For this reason, a pure SP approach has garnered only narrow support, despite having been in the public forum for more than two decades.

How does ACA answer these four questions? It would seem that ACA offers two qualified "yes" answers and two "no" answers. As for a right to health care, perhaps President Barack Obama stated it most clearly. Upon signing ACA, Obama spoke to the American public regarding the implications of what he had just done: "We have now just enshrined the core principle that everybody should have some basic security when it comes to their health care" (Obama 2010).

Is a "core principle" the same as a "right"? Not exactly. ACA does not intend to cover everyone living in the United States by right. Rather, it proposes to offer most Americans the opportunity to purchase affordable health insurance if it is not otherwise available to them either through their work or as part of a government program. Those who work for firms with fewer than fifty employees may still face the prospect of being uninsured, as such small employers are exempt from the requirements of

ACA. Individuals who provide evidence that they cannot afford even the subsidized premiums available through the newly established health exchanges will likewise be exempted from the requirement to maintain coverage. Finally, those immigrants who live in our country and participate in our society, yet who are undocumented, will not have access to health insurance through ACA.

The second "yes" ACA applies to the series of four questions pertains to the appropriate role of government in organizing and financing the delivery system. For much of the twentieth century, the federal government played a relatively small role in how health care was organized and financed. That began to change in 1965, with the establishment of the Medicare and Medicaid programs. The federal government became further involved with enactment of the HMO Act of 1973 and with the various reforms of the manner in which Medicare pays doctors and hospitals. Even before ACA, the federal government had developed a major role in determining how health care in America would be delivered.

With passage of ACA, more than half of all health care expenditures will be from public sources, either federal, state, or local. As it is responsible for a majority of health expenditures, it should not be surprising that government is asserting substantial influence over the organization and financing of care. Several aspects of ACA will increase that influence. As the federal government invests increasingly in comparative effectiveness research (CER), both the medical profession and the public will gain increased understanding of which of the available alternative treatments seems optimal. Similarly, as ACA develops and enforces standards for private health insurance options, the market for these plans will come under tighter government scrutiny.

It is not clear if the increased government influence that will come as a consequence of ACA will constitute "principal responsibility" for the organization and financing of health care delivery. The private market will still play a substantially larger role in the United States than in Canada. It is clear, however, that the era of limited government involvement in health care in the United States is over.

While ACA provides a qualified "yes" in response to two of the four core questions of health policy listed previously, it also leaves our response to the remaining two questions as "no." At no time during the debate leading up to enactment of ACA was there serious consideration of adopting a single, uniform standard of health care for all people in the United States. Such a uniform standard continues to be both the norm and the law in Canada, with some growing exceptions, as discussed in chapter 3. The idea that those with more wealth can purchase a different level of care than those without wealth continues to be anathema to most Canadians.

Quite the contrary, the concept that those with more wealth might be prevented by law from purchasing a different level of care than those without wealth remains anathema to many people in the United States (at least to those with the financial resources to purchase the higher level of care). President Obama committed to assuring all Americans "some basic security when it comes to their health care." This standard is consistent with the standard articulated by the Universal Declaration of Human Rights, as discussed in chapter 2. That declaration asserts that all people have a right to a level of health care that is "adequate for the health and well-being of himself and of his family." The principle established both by the declaration and by President Obama's statement is that there is a basic level of health care that all people should have access to, and that level will be measured by its adequacy to maintain well-being. Nothing in this assurance, however, suggests that those with greater resources should be prevented from acquiring, with their own resources, a higher level of care.

In a similar vein, ACA is largely silent on the issue of establishing explicit caps on the national budget for health care—either a cap on federal expenditures or a cap on aggregate national expenditures. There are systems of care in the United States that function under a fixed global budget—and do so quite successfully. The Kaiser Permanente system, discussed in chapter 5, has done so for several decades. The federal Veterans Affairs (VA) Health System also provides high-quality care to millions of veterans under a global budget, although recent discussions regarding long waiting lists for care have focused attention on areas in need of improvement. ACA, however, does not extend this model to the health care system more generally, thus leaving us potentially open to the continued adverse impacts of rising health care costs.

LONG-TERM IMPLICATIONS OF HEALTH CARE COSTS AFTER THE AFFORDABLE CARE ACT

The enactment of ACA did mark a major milestone in the history of health policy in the United States. It was the first time we came even close to acknowledging and supporting a right to a basic level of health care for all Americans. By 2019, somewhere between 20 and 30 million people who previously were uninsured will benefit from health insurance coverage. Access to health insurance, however, is only part of the story, and part of the problem.

As discussed in previous chapters, we can evaluate our health care system from at least three perspectives: access, cost, and quality. No one of these dimensions alone defines the success of our system. We must simultaneously evaluate that success from those three perspectives. ACA will substantially improve access to health insurance, and we hope access to health care (although, as discussed in chapter 12, providing people with health insurance does not guarantee that there will be a provider willing to accept that insurance). As projected by the Office of the Actuary of the Centers for Medicare and Medicaid Services, however, ACA will not reduce the continuing escalation in the cost of our health care system, measured as a percentage of gross domestic product (GDP). In fact, ACA is predicted to *increase* the percentage of GDP going to health care, albeit by a small amount.

For more than two decades, we have seen a strikingly consistent rise in national health care expenditures measured as a percentage of GDP. Between 1987 and 2009, that percentage increased from 10.5 to 17.3 percent. For reasons related both to the impact of ACA and the lingering effects of the recession of 2007–09, spending stabilized at 17.4 percent of GDP for the period 2010–14. New estimates from CMS, however, predict that this level will begin to rise again, reaching 19.6 percent by 2024 or before. At some point, this rate of increase will become unsustainable. At some point, the health care system will put such a drain on the rest of the US economy that overall economic stability will be threatened. Whether that point will be at 19.6 percent of GDP or some level higher than that—or whether we have already reached that point—remains unclear.

In an Op-Ed published in 2010 in the *New York Times*, Peter Orszag, director of the White House Office of Management and Budget under President Obama, suggested that we may already have topped out in our ability to fund the health care system (Orszag 2010). He cited data that, in order to pay the continually rising costs of the Medicaid program, many states had substantially reduced funding to public higher education, including flagship public universities such as the University of California, Berkeley. Consequently, the ability of these universities to attract and retain top faculty and to maintain academic programs had been seriously compromised. Orszag also argued that constraining health care costs is "central to raising workers' take-home pay, because increasing costs for health care are holding down wages" (p. WK10).

Our central problem is that we have no mechanism, either political or economic, to define a national cap in health care spending. There have been proposals to establish mechanisms to cap national health care spending, but they have never received the political support necessary for passage. In 2005, Ezekiel Emanuel, a medical ethicist at the National Institutes of Health and subsequently a health policy advisor to President Obama, and Victor Fuchs, a health economist at Stanford University, proposed a health care system that would have established near universal coverage under a national cap in spending by relying on health care vouchers (Emanuel and Fuchs 2005). They proposed to fund their system with a new value-added tax (VAT) dedicated solely to paying for health insurance. That health care tax would have been separate and distinct from general income tax revenues and thus would not have added to the federal deficit. National spending for health care would have been capped at the amount collected under the VAT. While individuals would have been free to spend additional funds over and above the basic coverage, they believed that relying on a fixed source of funding under the VAT would have stabilized the share of GDP going to health care.

The health reform proposals under President Bill Clinton would also have created a mechanism to cap national health expenditures through the establishment of a national board with the power to cap premiums charged by health insurance companies participating in the health insurance exchanges the Clinton proposal would have created. The specter of bureaucrats arbitrarily capping health insurance premiums and in so doing denying Americans necessary medical care was one of the images used by opponents of the Clinton proposal to defeat it.

As early as 1970, Senator Ted Kennedy had proposed a national plan that would have provided universal coverage while also capping national health expenditures. He proposed a nationally regulated system that combined capitated payments to non-profit managed care plans (or for-profit plans, if the patient prefers), combined with the option for direct hospital and physician payment under regional global budgets. Kennedy's proposal, titled the Health Security Act of 1970, called for a system of universal coverage in which consumers could either enroll in a capitated plan or select care from physicians not affiliated with a plan. If they chose the unaffiliated option, it would be up to the physicians as a group to establish local or regional policies to stay within the regional budget for care.

It is interesting to note the striking similarity between the plan Senator Kennedy proposed in 1970 and the recommendations issued in 2009 by the Massachusetts Special Commission on the Health Care Payment System (discussed in chapter 8). The commission recommended that, in order to sustain the state's new health plan, Massachusetts would need to shift away from an open-ended, fee-for-service system of paying for care to a global payment system of care, relying on accountable care organizations (ACOs) to administer and provide care under the fixed budget inherent to such capitated systems. Responding to this recommendation, in 2012 the Massachusetts legislature enacted legislation that sets an annual target for all health care spending within the state. While the legislation does not establish the legal means to enforce that target, the hope is that the state's Health Policy Commission can "encourage, cajole, and, if needed, shame [providers] into doing their part to control costs" (Steinbrook 2012, p. 1216). Steinbrook goes on to say, however, that "there will be no way to know if this plan for Massachusetts is working until it has been in effect for at least several years. Until then, skepticism about the amount of projected savings is appropriate" (p. 1216).

ACA has essentially avoided the issues being addressed by the Massachusetts Special Commission. Absent a mechanism to cap expenditures nationally, either through global payments, vouchers, or similar approaches, it is understandable that health care costs may continue to escalate. What movement there is will be in the upward direction. Discussions about "bending the curve" of health care costs, a regular part of the debate over ACA before it was enacted, may need to take place again.

GOVERNMENT OR MARKET: WHICH IS BETTER
TO GUIDE SPENDING ON HEALTH CARE?

In chapters 5 and 6, we saw that capitation systems of health care are able to eliminate certain types of inefficiencies within a given institutional context, but on their own, they seem powerless to change the surrounding context. Constraining the rapid escalation of technology, minimizing local variations in patterns of care, and coping with defensive medicine have proven to be no less a problem for well-run managed care plans than they were for their fee-for-service predecessors. Would a system that relies on market-based capitated care, such as that recommended by the Massachusetts commission, be able to achieve alone the balancing of costs and outcomes required for ACA or any other universal health care reform to succeed?

If the inefficiencies embedded in the health care system were all based on market factors, then market mechanisms alone might hold promise of success. As I have discussed throughout this book, however, the institutions in the United States that have led to increasing costs and resultant limited access for many stem from a range of social, political, and professional forces. Improving the market for health care can overcome problems created by the market, but it cannot change all of society. In the words of Victor Fuchs: "The market is a powerful and flexible instrument for allocating most goods and services, but it cannot create an equitable, universal system of insurance, cannot harness technologic change in medicine, and cannot cope with the potentially unlimited demand for health care by the elderly" (1993c, p. 1679).

Changing only market structures will not be sufficient to change the institutional structure of US health care. Any additional movement toward a more optimal balancing of costs, quality, and access beyond what markets alone can achieve requires a shift in the surrounding social, political, and professional institutional context. Few forces affect all segments of society and are sufficiently powerful to alter the broad range of existing health care institutions so as to guide the system toward needed improvements. To be effective, such a force would have to exert its influence concurrently in the market for health care, in the system of professional knowledge and norms that govern the medical profession, in the political system, and in the expectations of society at large. Only by acting across all levels of our social and professional system can we change the beliefs of both patients and providers to redefine what constitutes appropriate care in a way that attains a more appropriate balance of cost, quality, and access.

The federal government is one of the few forces in our society with the potential to act across this broad range of institutions to shift the direction of health care. Historically in this country, as in Canada, it has been the federal government that has acted to shift our core health care institutions. Several of the most important changes in US health care have been initiated by the federal government. Medicare and Medicaid are clear examples of the power of the federal government to change the direction of health care. The HMO Act of 1973, while not achieving all its intended goals, nonetheless replaced a historic hostility to health maintenance organizations (HMOs) with widespread acceptance and general success (at least initially). The prospective payment system (PPS) and the resource-based relative value scale (RBRVS) schedule of physician payment fundamentally altered how we pay for government-sponsored health care and have affected payment patterns in the broader market for health insurance. By guiding the market for health care while not controlling it, the US federal government has shown that it has the ability to alter in a constructive way inefficient institutions that structure health care.

In order for us finally to constrain the ongoing increase in the cost of our health care system—in order to "bend the curve" of health care costs—I believe it will be necessary for the federal government to assume a considerably larger role in the market for health care, even larger than that called for in ACA, while stopping short of the monopsony control. The central element currently missing from that role is a mechanism to define and enforce a national cap on health care spending.

It seems inevitable that the American public and the American Congress will be discussing and debating this issue again. Not to do so could simply perpetuate the escalation of health care costs that is already starting to put both our economy and our system of care in jeopardy. When we do confront the cost issue, we will have to do so in the context of maintaining health care quality. If we continue to define "quality" in terms of getting the newest, most high-tech (and most expensive) care available, however, we are going to have trouble. As described by Daniel Callahan, achieving a new balance of cost and quality that will sustain the increased access provided by ACA "will require nothing less than changes in medical and professional values, patients' demands and expectations, industry profit seeking, research aims and aspirations, and the culture of American medicine, much of which has been dedicated to unlimited progress and technological innovation, cost be damned" (Callahan 2009, p. e10[2]).

What Callahan seems to be saying is that we as a society will have to make a fundamental choice. We will either have to reduce the expansion in access to care created by ACA or we will have to accept that unlimited access to the most advanced technology without consideration of comparative costs or comparative effectiveness is no longer a viable basis for our system of care. In other words, "We can treat some of the people all of the time, or we can treat all of the people some of the time, but we can't treat all of the people all of the time."

Debates about the "R" word, about whether such a system would invoke health care rationing, are essentially vacuous. We must come to grips with the reality that health care resources are not unlimited, and that under the condition of scarcity created by limits on key resources, a system of prioritized allocation of those resources is essential. The key question we have yet to answer is whether the allocation of our inevitably scarce health care resources will be based on concepts of justice and relative need rather than on wealth and relative income.

SUMMARY

Solving the conundrum of balancing health care cost, quality, and access in the face of powerful economic forces will, of necessity, invoke an examination of core American values. Is health care a right? Are health care resources limited? What role should the government play? Should we establish a uniform level of care for all people?

Answering these questions explicitly provides a means to identify future options for stabilizing and securing our system of health care. We have historically shied away from open public debate on these issues. Finding a path to the next steps in health care reform may require that we address these issues head on, relying on the democratic process to balance the interests of all.

APPENDIX

Summary of the Changes Contained in the
Affordable Care Act

HOW THE AFFORDABLE CARE ACT ADDRESSES THE ISSUES
OF HEALTH CARE COST, QUALITY, AND ACCESS

- In 2014, health insurance became available to those who previously were uninsured. This expansion of coverage took place through a combination of reform of the private market for health insurance and a major expansion of the existing federal-state Medicaid program.
- These expansions have the potential to extend health insurance coverage to 90–95 percent of all Americans. Those remaining uninsured will typically be those working for small companies not required under the new law to provide health insurance to their workers and those residents who are undocumented.
- The Affordable Care Act (ACA) addresses the issue of cost containment in two main ways: (1) changes to the Medicare program and (2) new sources of tax revenues.
- ACA addresses the issue of maintaining the quality of health care in two principal ways. The first is through an expansion of primary care services through a restructuring of the way primary care is delivered. The second is through a major expansion of comparative effectiveness research (CER).
- CER will bring a major new focus to the issue of comparing the clinical outcomes of alternative ways of approaching the diagnosis and treatment of illness. CER, if successful, will shift the definition of "quality" in medical care from one that focuses on whether a treatment is newer or more high-tech, to one focusing on how well the treatment actually works in the context of alternative approaches to care.

PROVISIONS IN THE AFFORDABLE CARE ACT TO ADDRESS THE
APPROPRIATE USES OF MEDICAL TECHNOLOGY AND OTHER
HIGH-COST MEDICAL CARE

- In order to expand the reach and impact of CER, ACA established a national Patient-Centered Outcomes Research Institute (PCORI). PCORI is structured as an independent, nonprofit organization. It has a nationally representative board of governors, a series of national advisory panels, and a staff of experienced researchers. With funding provided by ACA, PCORI will either carry out or arrange to have carried out a series of research studies that compare existing alternatives for diagnosis or treatment.

- ACA is explicit in requiring that CER provide recommendations for the optimal approach to care, but not create mandates as to how specific conditions should be approached. Similarly, CER results are not to be used to determine insurance coverage or payment for differing approaches to care. Thus CER, at least as carried out under ACA, is not intended to be cost-effectiveness research, in that it will not make recommendations as to which of the available alternatives provides the optimal balancing of costs and benefits.

- ACA leaves unanswered the question of when, if ever, it is appropriate to deny a patient care that has some small yet well documented marginal benefit, but an extremely high marginal cost.

PROVISIONS IN THE AFFORDABLE CARE ACT TO EXPAND PRIMARY CARE DELIVERY

- ACA shifts funding for graduate medical education (GME) away from programs that train specialists and redirects it to programs that train primary care physicians. It also provides for new types of primary care training programs that are based in community settings rather than the traditional hospital setting. These "teaching health centers" represent collaborations between academic training centers and nonprofit, federally certified community clinics.

- ACA provides for increased payment for primary care services. Beginning in 2011, the federal Medicare program provided a 10 percent increase in payment to primary care physicians who treat Medicare beneficiaries. For the period 2013–2014, primary care physicians who treated Medicaid patients saw their payment rate, historically substantially lower than Medicare rates, raised to the same rate as that paid by Medicare. In 2015, when the federal government ended funding for this increase, some states maintained the higher rates with state support, while most states reverted to the previous payment rates.

- ACA provides increased federal funding for the National Health Service Corps and other programs that provide repayment of educational loans for primary care physicians who practice in areas of the country, typically rural areas and inner cities, which have documented medical manpower shortages.

- ACA provides substantially increased support for a new model of organizing primary care: the patient-centered medical home (PCMH). The PCMH involves a team of providers, including physicians, allied professionals such as nurse practitioners or physician's assistants, as well as support personnel with a range of professional skills. This team approach will be supported by an electronic health record system that will enable providers' access to the records of a patient's care and facilitate ongoing quality assessments of the care provided to patients.

- By expanding the training of primary care physicians, increasing the payment for primary care services, and supporting high-quality PCMHs, ACA will expand access to primary care for those expected to obtain new health insurance coverage.

THE AFFORDABLE CARE ACT AND THE MARKET
FOR HEALTH INSURANCE

- In order to expand health insurance coverage to those who previously were uninsured, ACA requires every employer with more than fifty employees to offer health insurance coverage to their workers or else pay a tax to the federal government.

- ACA mandates that all US citizens and permanent residents obtain health insurance coverage. If workers are unable to obtain affordable coverage through their employer, they will be guaranteed the option of obtaining coverage through a newly created entity: the health benefit exchange (HBE).

- The HBE is an organization that was to be created by each state with the purpose of making competing health insurance plans available to those individuals and families who do not obtain coverage through their work. In states that were unable or unwilling to create an exchange by 2014, the federal government was authorized to establish and operate an exchange on behalf of those states. This federal exchange has come to be known as Healthcare.gov.

- The purpose of the HBE is to match those seeking health insurance coverage with companies offering coverage. In order to have their plans made available through the HBE, health insurance companies will have to obtain certification from the operator of the exchange that the plan meets certain requirements having to do with level of benefits, and that the company offering the plan has met licensure and regulatory requirements.

- Each exchange must arrange for at least two qualifying plans to be available. Qualified plans will offer one of four predefined level of benefits, referred to as bronze, silver, gold, and platinum. Other than variations in price based on the subscriber's age, family composition, tobacco use, and geographic area of residence, each plan must be available at the same price to all subscribers without regard to the subscriber's past medical history.

- Beginning in 2014, individuals who do not receive affordable coverage through their work were eligible to contact the HBE, get information about competing plans and their comparative prices for a given level of coverage, and select a plan for himself or herself and their family. In addition, small businesses with up to fifty employees are eligible to obtain coverage for their employees through a version of the HBE referred to as the Small Business Health Options Program ("SHOP exchange"), with employees selecting from among the competing plans.

- For individuals and families earning between 100 and 400 percent of the federal poverty level (FPL), there will be a cap on the premium paid by the subscriber, with the balance paid through a federal subsidy. The cap ranges from 2 percent of income for those earning 100 percent of the FPL to 9.5 percent of income for those earning 400 percent of the FPL.

CHANGES IN MEDICARE UNDER THE AFFORDABLE CARE ACT

- ACA revised the formula under which Medicare Advantage (MA) plans are paid. Beginning in 2011, the rates paid to plans participating in MA were gradually reduced, with the expectation that by 2014 they will be more nearly equivalent to the average cost of providing care for beneficiaries under traditional Medicare. Payments are also risk-adjusted based on an enrollee's current and previous health status, so as to avoid favorable selection among MA enrollees. ACA also sets explicit quality targets for the care provided by plans under MA, paying a bonus to those plans that meet or exceed the target.
- ACA makes changes to the Medicare prescription drug benefit, described in more detail below.
- Beginning in 2011, Medicare beneficiaries have had no copayment or deductible charged for certain types of preventive health services that have been recommended by the US Preventive Services Task Force. In addition, beneficiaries may receive a yearly general preventive health examination and consultation without charge.
- ACA included a mechanism for addressing the issue of the rising cost of Medicare over time. This issue was to be the responsibility of a newly established Independent Payment Advisory Board (IPAB), to be made up of fifteen members appointed by the President and confirmed by the Senate. It was to be the explicit responsibility of IPAB to monitor the rate at which Medicare's per beneficiary spending increases over time. ACA sets a target rate of growth for Medicare spending, tied initially to the growth in the consumer price index and subsequently to the overall growth in GDP. Beginning in 2014, if it turns out that projected per beneficiary spending would exceed the target amount, IPAB was charged with the responsibility of coming up with a plan to rein in spending to meet the target amount. The Secretary of Health and Human Services must then carry out the IPAB's plan to control spending, unless Congress overrides the plan with one of its own.
- In granting IPAB responsibility for enforcing the limits on Medicare spending growth, Congress has limited IPAB's effectiveness. Section 3403.d.2.A.ii of ACA

specifically states that any proposal from IPAB "shall not include any recommendation to ration health care, raise revenues [i.e., taxes] or Medicare beneficiary premiums . . . or increase Medicare beneficiary cost sharing (including deductibles, coinsurance, and copayments), or otherwise restrict benefits or modify eligibility criteria." ACA does not define what is meant by "rationing" care under Medicare.

- Due to continued political disagreement between Congress and the Obama Administration, as of 2015 the President had not nominated IPAB members, with the result that the agency had not been established.

- ACA provides new funding for demonstration projects intended to identify new ways to reduce costs while maintaining quality. ACA creates a new Center for Medicare and Medicaid Innovations (CMMI) to study these new arrangements for care.

- One focus of CMMI is on encouraging groups of physicians and hospitals to come together to form accountable care organizations (ACOs). An ACO would take full responsibility for the care of a group of Medicare beneficiaries, planning, coordinating, and providing their care. If the ACO is able to reduce the cost of caring for its patients as compared to Medicare's average per beneficiary cost, the ACO would receive a share of the cost savings as an incentive payment.

- Through demonstration projects, ACA extends the prospective payment system (PPS), used previously to pay for hospital care, to encompass physician care, hospital care, outpatient services such as laboratory or X-ray, and rehabilitative services.

- ACA changes the formula by which the Part A Medicare payroll tax is calculated, increasing the tax rate from 1.45 to 2.35 percent for high-income taxpayers. It also creates some new taxes to be imposed on pharmaceutical companies, medical device companies, and certain health insurance companies.

- ACA increased Medicare Part B premiums for high-income beneficiaries.

- ACA reduces certain payments to hospitals. Among these are payments previously made to hospitals that provide a disproportionate amount of care to the poor and the uninsured.

- ACA changes the way yearly updates in payment rates to providers will be calculated. ACA assumes that, over time, providers of services under Medicare will be able to improve their efficiency and productivity, and thus their cost of providing service. Based on these assumed efficiency enhancements, Medicare's increases in payment to providers will be about 1.1 percent less each year than they would have been without the expected changes in provider efficiency.

- The Medicare trustees estimated that, as a result of ACA, the predicted exhaustion of the Part A trust fund will be postponed, from 2017 (before ACA) to 2029.

- Under ACA, annual increases in the cost of Part B are expected to fall from historical growth rates that were 4.2 percent greater than the growth in GDP, to rates approximately equal to the growth in GDP.

THE AFFORDABLE CARE ACT AND ITS IMPACT ON
MEDICAID AND CHIP

- Beginning in 2014, ACA fundamentally changed the structure of Medicaid by making benefits available to *all* people who are poor, regardless of health status or family status. In addition, under ACA Medicaid will provide coverage to all those with incomes below 138 percent of the FPL. It was originally estimated that approximately 16 million uninsured individuals would obtain coverage through Medicaid as a result of ACA. Following the Supreme Court decision that made Medicaid expansion optional for the states, the expected number of new Medicaid beneficiaries is expected to be less than this number.

- In 2012 the US Supreme Court ruled on a suit brought by several states challenging this mandatory expansion of Medicaid. The Court overturned the requirement that each state expand Medicaid eligibility, making the expansion optional for each state.

- ACA makes Medicaid analogous to Medicare, in that it will provide the same level of benefits to all those in poverty. Both Medicare and Medicaid are intended to provide universal coverage to eligible populations.

- ACA defines a new level of federal support for those who become newly eligible for benefits under ACA. When the expanded Medicaid coverage became available in 2014, the federal government paid 100 percent of the cost of the care provided to newly eligible enrollees. Over a period of six years the federal reimbursement rate for these enrollees will gradually drop to 90 percent, with the states ultimately responsible for 10 percent of the cost of their care. For those who were previously eligible for Medicaid at the time ACA was enacted, the federal government has maintained the previous reimbursement rates. Thus after 2014, states opting to expand Medicaid will receive a substantially higher federal reimbursement rate for those who became newly eligible for Medicaid than they will receive for the traditional Medicaid coverage groups.

- This split level of reimbursement, especially in light of the financial strains many states have been experiencing, may create a new area of disagreement and political tension. Many of the states may argue that the federal government should provide a 90 percent reimbursement rate for *all* Medicaid enrollees, not just new enrollees.

- ACA extended the authorization of the Children's Health Insurance Program (CHIP) through 2019, and provided funding through 2015. In 2015, Congress extended that funding through 2017.

- If a family with a child eligible for CHIP is unable to enroll the child because the state in which they live has reached its enrollment cap, the family would become eligible for a federal tax credit that would allow the family to enroll the child in coverage through the newly established HBEs.

THE AFFORDABLE CARE ACT AND FOR-PROFIT HEALTH CARE

- The medical loss ratio (MLR) is the percentage of funds received by a health insurance company in premiums that is paid out for the provision of health care to covered patients. ACA divides insurers into two groups: (1) those providing coverage in the market for large employee groups and (2) those providing coverage for individuals and small employee groups. ACA established a minimum MLR of 80 percent for plans in the small group market and 85 percent for plans in the market for large groups. Any plan with a MLR that falls below this mandated level is now required to provide a rebate to its enrollees covering the difference.

- ACA imposed a new fee that large health insurance companies are required to pay, beginning in 2014, based on the size of their market share. Nonprofit managed care or insurance plans will pay a reduced fee. In 2014, these fees were expected to bring in approximately $8 billion in new revenue, rising to more than $14 billion in 2018.

- ACA established a series of regulations on how health plans are administered. Under ACA, companies are prohibited from considering preexisting conditions to deny coverage to an applicant. Similarly, all applicants must be charged the same premium regardless of preexisting conditions, with a few important exceptions. Different rates may be charged based on a patient's age, family composition, tobacco use, participation in a health promotion program, and geographic region of residence. Similarly, caps on the amount an insurance plan will pay for care, either per year or for a patient's lifetime, will be prohibited.

- ACA requires health plans to report a range of new data, and requires health plans to be certified by the federal or state government in order to be eligible to participate in the health insurance exchanges established by ACA. ACA also established a process by which annual increases in health plan premiums are subject to review, with plans required to provide data justifying the increases.

- Under ACA, new physician-owned hospitals are not permitted, and existing physician-owned hospitals are not permitted to expand, except under strict conditions.

THE AFFORDABLE CARE ACT AND PHARMACEUTICAL POLICY

- The principal impact of ACA on pharmaceutical policy is on the "doughnut hole" gap in coverage under Medicare Part D plans. Effective in 2010, all beneficiaries who reached the "doughnut hole" gap in their coverage were eligible for a $250 rebate directly from Medicare. Beginning in 2011, any beneficiary reaching the gap and having a prescription for a brand name drug (i.e., a drug not yet available in generic form) received a 50 percent discount in the price of the drug, provided by the drug's manufacturer. Also beginning in 2011, there has been a gradual increase in coverage provided in the gap. The amount the beneficiary who reaches the gap will have to pay will gradually decline from the original level of 100 percent of the cost of the drug, to 25 percent of the cost in 2020.

- ACA imposes a new fee on pharmaceutical manufacturers. These fees are expected to raise $2.8 billion in new revenue in 2012, rising to $4.1 billion in 2018, and then falling again to $2.8 billion in 2019 and beyond.

THE AFFORDABLE CARE ACT AND LONG-TERM CARE

- ACA authorized the establishment of a "community living and assistance services and supports" (CLASS) program to offer a new type of long-term care insurance to those who wish to purchase it. The benefits of the program were intended to be used to purchase support services that would allow individuals in need of assistance to maintain a residence in the community. However, subsequent analysis by the Department of Health and Human Services determined that the program was not financially viable, and it was never established.
- ACA established a series of new reporting requirements for skilled nursing facilities, covering issues such as ownership, accountability, expenditures, and quality data. This information is posted to a website so Medicare enrollees can review it in order to compare facilities.

COVERING THE UNINSURED UNDER THE AFFORDABLE CARE ACT

- ACA extends Medicaid coverage to all citizens and permanent residents with incomes below 138 percent of the FPL who live in states opting to participate in the Medicaid expansion.
- ACA requires that, beginning in 2014, all citizens and permanent residents with incomes at or above 138 percent of the FPL either obtain private health insurance coverage or pay a tax penalty not to exceed 2.5 percent of taxable income.
- For those with incomes between 100 and 400 percent of the FPL who do not receive health insurance from their employer, ACA provides a tax credit to subsidize the purchase of private coverage. This credit caps the amount an individual or family must pay for coverage, starting with a cap of 2 percent of income for those

at 100 percent of the FPL and increasing to a cap of 9.5 percent of income for those at 400 percent of the FPL.

- ACA requires that an HBE be established for each state, either by the state itself or by the federal government on behalf of the state. Each exchange offers at least two options for health insurance coverage. Insurers will be able to offer different pre-defined levels of care for different premiums. For those enrollees with incomes below 400 percent of the FPL, the plans must cap out-of-pocket expenses according to a predefined schedule.

- ACA requires employers with more than fifty employees either to provide coverage for employees or to pay a penalty for each employee without coverage from work who instead acquires coverage from the state insurance exchange. ACA exempts employers with fifty or fewer employees from this requirement and also exempts larger employers from paying the penalty on the first thirty employees who obtain coverage from an exchange.

- ACA places restrictions on the coverage of abortion under plans offered through the state exchanges.

- There is general agreement that the steps outlined above will extend health insurance coverage to an additional 25–30 million Americans by the time it is fully implemented in 2019. Approximately half of these newly insured will be covered through the expansion of Medicaid, with the other half covered either through expansion of employer-provided coverage or through the newly established health insurance exchanges.

THE AFFORDABLE CARE ACT AND ACCESS TO HEALTH CARE

- ACA invests in the expansions of nonprofit community health centers. Often referred to as federally qualified health centers (FQHCs), these clinics receive extra federal funding to treat Medicaid patients and uninsured patients. ACA expands this funding, allowing FQHCs to hire additional personnel.

- ACA allocates additional funding to allow primary care residency programs to expand their training sites to include FQHCs and other community-based resources.

- ACA expands support for the National Health Service Corps, the federal program that provides medical students with either scholarship support during medical school or educational loan repayment after medical school in return for spending a period of years in primary care practice in a rural or urban community that has a documented shortage of health manpower.

- ACA provides additional support for FQHCs to strengthen their organizational capacity to act as the "patient-centered medical home" (PCMH) for their patients by developing a team-based approach to the management of chronic disease, expanding the use of electronic health records, and strengthening connections with referral sources of specialty care.

- ACA requires providers to collect data on the race, ethnicity, primary language, disability status, and similar demographic characteristics of the patients cared for. The federal government will then analyze these data to monitor racial and ethnic disparities in access to care.

LONG-TERM IMPLICATIONS OF HEALTH CARE COSTS AFTER THE AFFORDABLE CARE ACT

- The Congressional Budget Office has projected that ACA will result in a net reduction in the federal deficit of $124 billion over ten years.
- ACA is expected to result in a net increase in overall health care expenditures nationally. The actuary at the federal Centers for Medicare and Medicaid Services concluded that, as a result of ACA, overall national expenditures for health care will rise faster than they would have had ACA not been adopted. By 2019, national health expenditures under the provisions of ACA are predicted to rise to 19.6 percent of GDP, as compared to 19.3 percent had ACA not been enacted.

WEB RESOURCES TO LEARN MORE ABOUT THE AFFORDABLE CARE ACT

US Department of Health & Human Services, HealthCare.Gov—Understanding the Affordable Care Act, http://www.hhs.gov/healthcare/about-the-law/.

The Commonwealth Fund—Health Reform Resource Center, http://www.common wealthfund.org/interactives-and-data/health-reform-resource-center.

Kaiser Family Foundation—Health Reform, http://kff.org/health-reform/fact-sheet/summary-of-the-affordable-care-act/.

REFERENCES

Aaron HJ. 2014. Here to stay—Beyond the rough launch of the ACA. *New England Journal of Medicine* 370:2257–59.

Aaron HJ. 2015. Three cheers for logrolling—The demise of the SGR. *New England Journal of Medicine* 372:1977–79.

AARP. 2012. Across the states: Profiles of long-term services and supports. http://www.aarp .org/content/dam/aarp/research/public_policy_institute/ltc/2012/across-the-states -2012-full-report-AARP-ppi-ltc.pdf.

Abell I. 1938. Address to the special session of the House of Delegates of the American Medical Association. *JAMA* 111:1192–94.

Abelson R. 2015. Bigger may be better for health insurers, but doubts remain for consumers. *New York Times*, August 3.

ADP Research Institute. 2013. Planning for health care reform: How income impacts employee health benefits participation, http://www.adp.com/tools-and-resources/adp -research-institute/research-and-trends/research-item-detail.aspx?id=%7BAAF343EB -A0FE-4EF7-A24F-0416B0FDB6B6%7D.

Agency for Healthcare Research and Quality. 2009. National Healthcare Disparities Report, 2009, www.ahrq.gov/qual/nhdr09/Key.htm.

Agency for Healthcare Research and Quality. 2014. 2014 National Healthcare Quality & Disparities Report, http://www.ahrq.gov/research/findings/nhqrdr/nhqdr14/.

Aiken LH, Clarke SP, Sloane DM, Sochalski J, and Silber JH. 2002. Hospital nurse staffing and patient mortality, nurse burnout, and job dissatisfaction. *JAMA* 288:1987–93.

Alexander GC, and Stafford RS. 2009. Does comparative effectiveness have a comparative edge? *JAMA* 301:2488–90.

Allen H, Baicker K, Finkelstein A, et al. 2010. What the Oregon Health Study can tell us about expanding Medicaid. *Health Affairs* 29(8):1498–1506.

ALLHAT Collaborative Research Group. 2002. Major outcomes in high-risk hypertensive patients randomized to angiotensin-converting enzyme inhibitor or calcium channel blocker vs diuretic. *JAMA* 288:2981–97.

Alpern JD, Stauffer WM, and Kesselheim AS. 2014. High-cost generic drugs: Implications for patients and policymakers. *New England Journal of Medicine* 371:1859–62.

Altman D, and Blumenthal D. 2015. How primary-care physicians are handling the influx of newly insured. *The Wall Street Journal*, September 18. http://blogs.wsj.com/washwire /2015/09/18/how-primary-care-physicians-are-handling-the-influx-of-newly-insured /tab/print/.

American Academy of Family Physicians, American Academy of Pediatrics, American College of Physicians, and American Osteopathic Association. 2007. Joint principles of the patient-centered medical home, March, www.medicalhomeinfo.org/downloads /pdfs/JointStatement.pdf.

American Association of Family Physicians. 2013. FPs at top of recruitment list for seventh straight year, http://www.aafp.org/news/practice-professional-issues/20130916 recruitingstudy.html.

American Academy of Nurse Practitioners. n.d. About nurse practitioners, www.aanp.org /AANPCMS2/AboutAANP/About+NPs.htm.

American Academy of Nurse Practitioners. 2015. NP Facts, http://www.aanp.org/images/documents/about-nps/npfacts.pdf.

American Academy of Physician Assistants. 2013. AAPA Annual Survey Report, https://www.aapa.org/WorkArea/DownloadAsset.aspx?id=2902.

American Association of Health Plans. 1999. Enrollment, Growth, Accreditation, www.aahp.org/.

American Medical Association. 1932. The committee on the costs of medical care (editorial). *JAMA* 99:1950.

American Medical Association. 1934a. Minutes of the eighty-fifth annual session. *JAMA* 102:2200.

American Medical Association. 1934b. Proceedings of the House of Delegates from June 12, 1934. *JAMA* 102:2199–2201.

American Medical Association. 1935. Minutes of the special session of the House of Delegates of the American Medical Association. *JAMA* 104:747–53.

American Medical Association. 1938. Minutes of the special session of the House of Delegates of the American Medical Association. *JAMA* 111:1191–1217.

American Medical Association. 1948. Report of the council on medical services. *JAMA* 138:683–86.

American Medical Association. 1965. AMA urges defeat of Medicare. *JAMA* 192:15–17.

American Medical Association. 2010. AMA study shows competition disappearing in the health insurance industry. *American Medical Association News*, February 23.

Anderson GF, Hussey PS, Frogner BK, and Waters HR. 2005. Health spending in the United States and the rest of the industrialized world. *Health Affairs* 24(4):903–14.

Andriole GL, Crawford ED, Grubb RL, et al. 2009. Mortality results from a randomized prostate-cancer screening trial. *New England Journal of Medicine* 60:1310–19.

Angell M. 2004. *The truth about drug companies: How they deceive us and what to do about it*. New York: Random House.

Annas GJ, Ruger TW, and Ruger JP. 2014. Money, sex, and religion—The Supreme Court's ACA sequel. *New England Journal of Medicine* 371:862–66.

Arrow K. 1963. Uncertainty and the welfare economics of medical care. *American Economic Review* 53:941–69.

Asplin BR, Rhodes KV, Levy H, et al. 2005. Insurance status and access to urgent ambulatory care follow-up appointments. *JAMA* 294:1248–54.

Association of American Medical Colleges. 2005. Cultural Competence Education for Medical Students. www.aamc.org/meded/tacct/culturalcomped.pdf.

Association of American Medical Colleges. 2008. *Industry funding of medical education: Report of an AAMC task force*.

Association of American Medical Colleges. 2014. Diversity in the physician workforce: Facts & figures 2014, http://aamcdiversityfactsandfigures.org/section-ii-current-status-of-us-physician-workforce/#fig10.

Association of American Medical Colleges. 2015. The complexities of physician supply and demand: Projections from 2013 to 2025, https://www.aamc.org/download/426248/data/thecomplexitiesofphysiciansupplyanddemandprojectionsfrom2013to2.pdf.

Auerbach DI, Buerhaus PI, and Staiger DO. 2015. Will the RN workforce weather the retirement of the baby boomers? *Medical Care* 53(10):850–56.

Avorn J. 2015. The $2.6 billion pill: Methodologic and policy considerations. *New England Journal of Medicine* 372:1877–79.

Ayanian JZ, Clark SJ, and Tipirneni R. 2014. Launching the Healthy Michigan Plan—The first 100 days. *New England Journal of Medicine* 371:1573–75.

Ayanian JZ, Cleary PD, Weissman JS, and Epstein AM. 1999a. The effect of patients' preferences on racial differences in access to renal transplantation. *New England Journal of Medicine* 341:1661–69.

Ayanian JZ, Weissman JS, Chasen-Taber S, and Epstein AM. 1999b. Quality of care by race and gender for congestive heart failure. *Medical Care* 37:1260–69.

Ayanian JZ, Weissman JS, Schneider EC, et al. 2000. Unmet health needs of uninsured adults in the United States. *JAMA* 284:2061–69.

Aysola J, Rhodes KV, and Polsky D. 2015. Patient-centered medical homes and access to services for new primary care patients. *Medical Care* 53(10):857–62.

Bach PB, Cramer LD, Warren JL, and Begg CB. 1999. Racial differences in the treatment of early-stage lung cancer. *New England Journal of Medicine* 341:1198–1205.

Bai G, and Anderson GF. 2015. Extreme markup: The fifty US hospitals with the highest charge-to-cost ratios. *Health Affairs* 34:922–28.

Baicker K, Taubman SL, Allen HL, et al. 2013. The Oregon Experiment—Effects of Medicaid on clinical outcomes. *New England Journal of Medicine* 368:1713–22.

Baker LC, Bundorf MK, and Kessler DP. 2014. Vertical integration: Hospital ownership of physician practices is associated with higher prices and spending. *Health Affairs* 33(5):756–63.

Baker RB, Caplan AL, Emanuel LL, and Latham SR, eds. 1999. *The American medical ethics revolution: How the AMA's code of ethics has transformed physicians' relationships to patients, professionals, and society.* Baltimore: Johns Hopkins University Press.

Baker RB, Washington HA, Olkanmi O, et al. 2008. African American physicians and organized medicine, 1846–1968. *JAMA* 300:306–13.

Ball RM. 1995. What Medicare's architects had in mind. *Health Affairs* 14(4):62–72.

Bardy GH, Lee KL, Mark DB, et al. 2005. Amiodarone on an implantable cardioverter-defibrillator for congestive heart failure. *New England Journal of Medicine* 352:225–37.

Barnett ML, Hsu J, and McWilliams JM. 2015. Patient characteristics and differences in hospital readmission rates. *JAMA Internal Medicine* 175(11):1803–12.

Baron RJ. 2010. What's keeping us so busy in primary care? A snapshot from one office. *New England Journal of Medicine* 362:1632–36.

Barr DA. 1995. The effect of organizational structure on primary care outcomes under managed care. *Annals of Internal Medicine* 122:353–59.

Barr DA, Vergun P, and Barley SA. 2000. Problems in using patient satisfaction data to assess the quality of care of primary care physicians. *Journal of Clinical Outcomes Management* 7(9):1–6.

Barry MJ. 2008. Screening for prostate cancer—the controversy that refused to die. *New England Journal of Medicine* 360:1351–54.

Bennett WM. 2004. Ethical conflicts for physicians treating ESRD patients. *Seminars in Dialysis* 17(1):1–3.

Berndt ER. 2005. To inform or persuade? Direct-to-consumer advertising of prescription drugs. *New England Journal of Medicine* 352:325–28.

Berndt ER, Nass D, Kleinrock M, Aitken M. 2015. Decline in economic returns from new drugs raises questions about sustaining innovations. *Health Affairs* 34:245–52.

Bevan AD. 1907. Chairman's address—Third annual conference of the Council on Medical Education of the American Medical Association. *JAMA* 48:1701–3.

Bindman AB. 2015. The other physician payment problem. *JAMA* 313(21): 2112–13.

Bindman AB, and Coffman JM. 2014. Calling all doctors: What type of insurance do you accept? *JAMA Internal Medicine* 174(6): 869–70.

Blavin F, Shartzer A, Long SK, and Holahan J. 2015. An early look at changes in employer-sponsored insurance under the Affordable Care Act. *Health Affairs* 34(1):170–77.

Blendon RJ, Altman DE, Benson JM, et al. 2008a. Voters and health care reform in the 2008 presidential election. *New England Journal of Medicine* 359:2050–61.

Blendon RJ, Altman DE, Dean C, et al. 2008b. Health care reform in the 2008 presidential primaries. *New England Journal of Medicine* 358:414–22.

Blendon RJ, Buhr T, Cassify EF, et al. 2007. Disparities in health: Perspectives of a multi-ethnic, multi-racial America. *Health Affairs* 26(5):1437–47.

Blumenthal D. 2004. Doctors and drug companies. *New England Journal of Medicine* 351:1885–90.

Blumenthal D, Davis K, and Guterman S. 2015. Medicare at 50—Moving forward. *New England Journal of Medicine* 372:671–77.

Blumenthal D, Stremikis K, and Cutler D. 2013. Health care spending—A giant slain or sleeping? *New England Journal of Medicine* 369:2551–57.

Boards of Trustees of the Federal Hospital Insurance and Federal Supplementary Medical Insurance Trust Funds. 2015. 2015 Annual Report, https://www.cms.gov/Research-Statistics-Data-and-Systems/Statistics-Trends-and-Reports/ReportsTrustFunds/Downloads/TR2015.pdf.

Boozary AS, Manchin J III, and Wicker RF. 2015. The Medicare Hospital Readmissions Reduction Program—Time for reform. *JAMA* 314(4):347–48.

Boren SD. 1994. "I had a tough day today, Hillary." *New England Journal of Medicine* 330:500–502.

Bovbjerg RR. 2010. Will the Patient Protection and Affordable Care Act address the problems associated with medical malpractice? Urban Institute, http://www.rwjf.org/en/library/research/2010/08/will-the-patient-protection-and-affordable-care-act-address-the-.html.

Bovbjerg RR, and Berenson RA. 2012. The value of clinical practice guidelines as malpractice "safe harbors." Urban Institute, http://www.rwjf.org/en/library/research/2012/04/the-value-of-clinical-practice-guidelines-as-malpractice--safe-h.html.

Bowman JG. 1918. Standard of efficiency. *Bulletin of the American College of Surgeons* III, no. 3:1.

Boyce EA. 2000. Access to Bone Marrow Transplants for Multiple Myeloma Patients: The Role of Race. Undergraduate thesis, Program in Human Biology, Stanford University.

Braveman P, Schaaf VM, Egerter S, Bennett T, and Schecter W. 1994. Insurance-related differences in the risk of ruptured appendix. *New England Journal of Medicine* 331:444–49.

Brennan TA, Leape LL, Laird NM, et al. 1991. Incidence of adverse events and negligence in hospitalized patients: Results of the Harvard Medical Practice Study I. *New England Journal of Medicine* 324:370–76.

Brennan TA, and Shrank W. 2014. New expensive treatments for Hepatitis C infection. *JAMA* 312(6):593–94.

Brennan TA, Sox CM, and Burstin HR. 1996. Relation between negligent adverse events and the outcomes of medical-malpractice litigation. *New England Journal of Medicine* 335:1963–67.

Brenner DJ. 2010. Medical imaging in the 21st century—getting the best bang for the rad. *New England Journal of Medicine* 362:943–45.

Brook RH, Keeler EB, Lohr KN, et al. 2006. The health insurance experiment—A classic RAND Study speaks to the current health care reform debate. RAND Corporation, http://www.rand.org/pubs/research_briefs/RB9174.html.

Buerhaus PI. 2008. Current and future state of the US nursing workforce. *JAMA* 300:2422–24.

Brotherton SE, and Etzel SI. 2014. Graduate medical education, 2013–2014. *JAMA* 312(22): 2427–45.

Burke GL, Sprafk a JM, and Folsom AR. 1991. Trends in serum cholesterol levels from 1980 to 1987. *New England Journal of Medicine* 324:941–46.

Burns LR, and Pauly MV. 2012. Accountable care organizations may have difficulty avoiding the failures of integrated delivery networks of the 1990s. *Health Affairs* 31:2407–2416.

Burwell SM. 2015. Setting value-based payment goals—HHS efforts to improve US health care. *New England Journal of Medicine* 372:897–99.

Burwell SM. 2016. Success by the numbers: 2016 open enrollment, http://www.hhs.gov/node /4355.

Callahan D. 2009. Cost control—time to get serious. *New England Journal of Medicine* 361:e10.

Calman NS. 2000. Out of the shadow. *Health Affairs* 19(1):170–74.

Canadian Journal of Cardiology. 2005. Vol. 21:Supplement A contains a series of papers reporting on the guidelines for the use of ICDs and the policy considerations surrounding their use.

Carlson MDA, Barry CL, Emily J. Cherlin EJ, et al. 2012. Hospices' enrollment policies may contribute to underuse of hospice care in the United States. *Health Affairs* 31:2690–98.

Casalino LP. 2015. Pioneer accountable care organizations—Traversing rough country. *JAMA* 313(21):2126–27.

Cassel CK, and Kronick R. 2015. Learning from the past to measure the future. *JAMA* 314(9): 875–76.

Center for Medicare & Medicaid Innovation. 2015a. Accountable Care Organizations (ACOs): General Information, http://innovation.cms.gov/initiatives/ACO/; ACO Investment Model, http://innovation.cms.gov/initiatives/ACO-Investment-Model/.

Center for Medicare & Medicaid Innovation. 2015b. Bundled payments. http://innovation .cms.gov/initiatives/Bundled-Payments/.

Center for Medicare & Medicaid Innovation. 2015c. Comprehensive Care for Joint Replacement Model, http://innovation.cms.gov/initiatives/ccjr/.

Center for Medicare & Medicaid Innovation. 2015d. Comprehensive Primary Care Initiative, http://innovation.cms.gov/initiatives/Comprehensive-Primary-Care-Initiative/.

Center for Medicare & Medicaid Innovation. 2015e. Medicaid Innovation Accelerator Program. http://innovation.cms.gov/initiatives/MIAP/.

Center for Medicare & Medicaid Innovation. 2015f. The CMS Innovation Center. http:// innovation.cms.gov/.

Chandra A, and Vanderpuye-Orgle J. 2015. Competition in the age of biosimilars. *JAMA* 314(3):225–26.

Chang JE, Brundage SC, and Chokshi DA, 2015. Convenient ambulatory care—Promise, pitfalls, and policy. *New England Journal of Medicine* 373:382–88.

Chang JT, Hays RD, Shekelle PG, et al. 2006. Patients' global ratings of their health care are not associated with the technical quality of their care. *Annals of Internal Medicine* 144:665–72.

Chief Actuary of the Centers for Medicare & Medicaid Services. 2015. IPAB determination, July 22, 2015, https://www.cms.gov/Research-Statistics-Data-and-Systems/Research /ActuarialStudies/IPAB-Determination.html.

Chernew M, Cutler DM, and Keenan PS. 2005. Increasing health insurance costs and the decline in insurance coverage. *Health Services Research* 40:1021–39.

Chernew ME, Baicker K, and Hsu J. 2010. The specter of financial Armageddon—health care and federal debt in the United States. *New England Journal of Medicine* 362:1166–68.

Choudry NK, and Detsky AS. 2005. A perspective on US drug reimportation. *JAMA* 293: 358–62.

Cleary BL, McBride AB, McClure ML, and Reinhard SC. 2009. Expanding the capacity of nursing education. *Health Affairs* 28(4):w634–w645.

Clough JD, Richman BD, and Glickman SW. 2015. Outlook for alternative payment models in fee-for-service Medicare. *JAMA* 314(4): 341–42.

Colby SL, and Ortman JM. 2015. Projections of the size and composition of the US population: 2014 to 2060. US Census Bureau, http://www.census.gov/content/dam/Census/library/publications/2015/demo/p25-1143.pdf.

Cole ES, Walker D, Mora A, and Diana ML. 2014. Identifying hospitals that may be at most financial risk from medicaid disproportionate-share hospital payment cuts. *Health Affairs* 33:2025–33.

Colla CH, Lewis VA, Shortell SM, and Fisher ES. 2014. First national survey of ACOs finds that physicians are playing strong leadership and ownership roles. *Health Affairs* 33: 964–71.

Commonwealth Fund. 2008. Massachusetts health care reform—on secondary anniversary of passage, what progress has been made? States in Action, April/May, www.commonwealth fund.org/Publications/Newsletters/States-in-Action.aspx.

Commonwealth Fund. 2015a. Experiences and attitudes of primary care providers under the first year of ACA coverage expansion, http://www.commonwealthfund.org/publications/issue-briefs/2015/jun/primary-care-providers-first-year-aca.

Commonwealth Fund. 2015b. How strong is the primary care safety net? Assessing the ability of federally qualified health centers to serve as patient-centered medical homes, http://www.commonwealthfund.org/~/media/files/publications/issue-brief/2015/sep/1836_ryan_how_strong_is_primary_care_safety_net_fqhc_ib_v2.pdf.

Congressional Budget Office. 2006. The sustainable growth rate formula for setting Medicare's physician payment rates, September, www.cbo.gov/ft pdocs/75xx/doc7542/09-07-SGR-brief.pdf.

Congressional Budget Office. 2014. Payments of penalties for being uninsured under the Affordable Care Act: 2014 update, https://www.cbo.gov/sites/default/files/113th-congress-2013-2014/reports/45397-IndividualMandate.pdf.

Congressional Budget Office. 2015. Insurance coverage provisions of the Affordable Care Act—CBO's March 2015 baseline, https://www.cbo.gov/publication/43900.

Conway PH, and Clancy C. 2009. Comparative-effectiveness research—Implications of the Federal Coordinating Council's report. *New England Journal of Medicine* 361:328–30.

Council on Medical Education. 1905. Report of Council on Medical Education to House of Delegates of the AMA. *JAMA* 40:269–70.

Covered California. 2015. Eligibility and immigration, http://www.coveredca.com/individuals-and-families/getting-covered/immigrants/.

Cram P, Rosenthal GE, and Vaughan-Sarrazin MS. 2005. Cardiac revascularization in specialty and general hospitals. *New England Journal of Medicine* 352(14):1454–62.

Cubanski J, Swoope C, Boccuti C, et al. 2015. A primer on Medicare—Key facts about the Medicare program and the people it covers. Kaiser Family Foundation, http://kff.org/medicare/report/a-primer-on-medicare-key-facts-about-the-medicare-program-and-the-people-it-covers/.

Cunningham PJ. 2005. Medicaid cost containment and access to prescription drugs. *Health Affairs* 24:780–89.

Cunningham PJ. 2015. Many Medicaid beneficiaries receive care consistent with attributes of patient-centered medical homes. *Health Affairs* 34:1105–12.

Cunningham PJ, Hadley J, and Reschovsky J. 2002. The effects of SCHIP on children's health insurance coverage: Early evidence from the community tracking study. *Medical Care Research and Review* 59:359–83.

Cutler DM. 2015a. From the Affordable Care Act to affordable care. *JAMA* 314(4): 337–38.

Cutler DM. 2015b. Insurers again at odds with hospitals and physicians. *JAMA* 314(13): 1329–30.

Danelski AE, Altman DE, Eldred J, et al. 1995. The California single-payer debate: The defeat of Proposition 186. Kaiser Family Foundation, http://kff.org/health-costs/report/the-california-single-payer-debate-the-defeat/.

Darrow JJ, Avorn J, and Kesselheim AS. 2014. New FDA breakthrough-drug category: Implications for patients. *New England Journal of Medicine* 370:1252–58.

David PA. 1985. Clio and the economics of QWERTY. *AEA Papers and Proceedings* 75:332.

Davies AR, Ware JE, Brook RH, et al. 1986. Consumer acceptance of prepaid and fee-for-service medical care: Results from a randomized controlled trial. *Health Services Research* 21:429–49.

Davis RM. 2008. Achieving racial harmony for the benefit of patients and communities: Contrition, reconciliation, and collaboration. *JAMA* 300:323–25.

De Alteriis M, and Fanning T. 1991. A public health model of Medicaid emergency room use. *Health Care Financing Review* 12(3):15–20.

DeLeire T, Joynt K, and McDonald R. 2014. Impact of insurance expansion on hospital uncompensated care costs in 2014. ASP issue brief, Department of Health and Human Services, Office of the Assistant Secretary for Planning and Evaluation, http://aspe.hhs.gov/sites/default/files/pdf/77061/ib_UncompensatedCare.pdf.

DeMaria AN. 2005. Concierge medicine: For better or for worse? *Journal of the American College of Cardiology* 46:377–78.

DesRoches CM, Blendon RJ, and Benson JM. 2005. Americans' responses to the 2004 influenza vaccine shortage. *Health Affairs* 24(3):822–31.

Devereaux PJ, Schunemann HJ, Ravindran N, et al. 2002. Comparison of mortality between private for-profit and private not-for-profit hemodialysis centers: A systematic review and meta-analysis. *JAMA* 288:2449–57.

Deville C, Hwang W-T, Burgos R, et al. 2015. Diversity in graduate medical education in the United States by race, ethnicity, and sex, 2012. *JAMA Internal Medicine*. Published online. Doi: 10.1001.

DeVoe JE, Marino M, Angier H, et al. 2015. Effect of expanding medicaid for parents on children's health insurance coverage—Lessons from the Oregon Experiment. *JAMA Pediatrics* 169(1):e143145.

DiJulio B, Firth J, and Brodie M. 2015. Kaiser health tracking poll: August 2015. http://kff.org/health-costs/poll-finding/kaiser-health-tracking-poll-august-2015/.

DiMaggio PJ. 1988. Interest and agency in institutional theory. Pp. 3–21 in Zucker L., ed., *Institutional Patterns and Organizations*. Cambridge, Mass.: Ballinger.

Docteur E, and Berenson RA. 2009. How does the quality of US health care compare internationally? The Urban Institute, August, www.urban.org/publications/411947.html.

Donohue JM. 2014. The impact and evolution of Medicare Part D. *New England Journal of Medicine* 371:693–95.

Dorn S, McGrath M, and Holahan J. 2014. What is the result of states not expanding Medicaid? The Urban Institute, http://www.urban.org/sites/default/files/alfresco /publication-pdfs/413192-What-is-the-Result-of-States-Not-Expanding-Medicaid-.PDF.

Doty MM, Blumenthal D, Collins SR. 2014. The Affordable Care Act and health insurance for Latinos. *JAMA* 312(17):1735–36.

Dovidio J, and Gaertner S. 1998. On the nature of contemporary prejudice: The causes, consequences, and challenges of aversive racism. In Eberhardt J, and Fiske S, eds., *Confronting racism: The problem and the response.* Thousand Oaks, Calif.: Sage Publications.

Dummit L, Marrufo G, Marshall J, et al. 2015. CMS Bundled Payments for Care Improvement (BPCI) Initiative models 2–4: Year 1 evaluation & monitoring annual report. The Lewin Group, http://innovation.cms.gov/Files/reports/BPCI-EvalRpt1.pdf.

Dranove D, Garthwaite C, and Ody C. 2015. The economic downturn and its lingering effects reduced Medicare spending growth by $4 billion in 2009–12. *Health Affairs* 34: 1368–75.

Duffin J. 2011. The impact of single-payer health care on physician income in Canada, 1850–2005. *American Journal of Public Health* 101(7):1198–1208.

Eisenberg L. 1995. Medicine: Molecular, monetary, or more than both? *JAMA* 274:331–34.

Emanuel EJ, and Fuchs VR. 2005. Health care vouchers: A proposal for universal coverage. *New England Journal of Medicine* 352:1255–60.

Enthoven A. 1980. *Health Plan: The Only Practical Solution to the Soaring Cost of Medical Care.* Reading, Mass.: Addison-Wesley.

Enthoven AE, and Kronick R. 1989. A consumer-choice health plan for the 1990s. *New England Journal of Medicine* 320:29–37 (Part 1); 94–101 (Part 2).

Enthoven AE, and Kronick R. 1991. Universal health insurance through incentives reform. *JAMA* 265:2532–36.

Entman SS, Glass CA, Hickson GB, et al. 1994. The relation between malpractice claims history and subsequent obstetrical quality. *JAMA* 272:1588–91.

Epstein AM, Jha AK, Orav JE, et al. 2014. Analysis of early accountable care organizations defines patient, structural, cost, and quality-of-care characteristics. *Health Affairs* 33:95–102.

Evans CS, Smith S, Kobayashi L, and Chang DC. 2015. The effect of community health center (CHC) density on preventable hospital admissions in Medicaid and uninsured patients. *Journal of Health Care for the Poor and Underserved* 26(3):839–51.

Evens R, and Kaitin K. 2015. The evolution of biotechnology and its impact on health care. *Health Affairs* 34:210–19.

Fadiman A. 1997. *The spirit catches you and you fall down.* New York: Farrar, Straus and Giroux.

Falit BP, Singh SC, and Brennan TA. 2015. Biosimilar competition in the United States: Statutory incentives, payers, and pharmacy benefit managers. *Health Affairs* 34: 294–301.

Feder J. 2013. Bundle with care—Rethinking Medicare incentives for post-acute care services. *New England Journal of Medicine* 369:400–401.

Feder J, Komisar HL, and Niefeld M. 2000. Long-term care in the United States: An overview. *Health Affairs* 19(3):40–56.

Federal Register. 2013. Vol. 78, No. 127, http://www.gpo.gov/fdsys/pkg/FR-2013-07-02/pdf /2013-15866.pdf.

Finkelstein A, Taubman S, Wright B, et al. 2012. The Oregon Health Insurance Experiment: Evidence from the first year. *The Quarterly Journal of Economics* 127(3):1057–1106.

Fishbein M. 1948. Health and Social Security. *JAMA* 138:1254–56.

Flexner A. 1910. *Medical education in the United States and Canada.* New York: Carnegie Foundation for the Advancement of Teaching.

Fox AM, and Blanchet NJ. 2015. The little state that couldn't could? The politics of "single-payer" health coverage in Vermont. *Journal of Health Politics, Policy, and Law* 40(3): 447–85.

Freidson E. 1970. *Profession of Medicine: A Study of the Sociology of Applied Knowledge.* New York: Dodd, Mead.

Friedberg MW, Rosenthal MB, Werner RM, et al. 2015. Effects of a medical home and shared savings intervention on quality and utilization of care. *JAMA Internal Medicine* 175 (8):1362–68.

Friedberg MW, Schneider EC, Rosenthal MB, et al. 2014. Association between participation in a multipayer medical home intervention and changes in quality, utilization, and costs of care. *JAMA* 311(8):815–25.

Friedman AB, Saloner B, and Hsia RY. 2015. No place to call home—Policies to reduce ED use in Medicaid. *New England Journal of Medicine* 372:2382–85.

Friedman E. 1994. Money isn't everything: Nonfinancial barriers to access. *JAMA* 271: 1535–38.

Frosch DL, Grande D, Tam DM, and Kravitz RL. 2010. A decade of controversy: Balancing policy with evidence in the regulation of prescription drug advertising. *American Journal of Public Health* 100:24–32.

Fuchs VR. 1983. *Who Shall Live?* New York: Basic Books.

Fuchs VR. 1986. *The Health Economy.* Cambridge, Mass.: Harvard University Press.

Fuchs VR. 1993a. The "competition revolution" of the 1980s. Chapter 11 in Fuchs VR, *The Future of Health Policy.* Cambridge, Mass.: Harvard University Press.

Fuchs VR. 1993b. Cost containment: No pain, no gain. Chapter 10 in Fuchs VR, *The Future of Health Policy.* Cambridge, Mass.: Harvard University Press.

Fuchs VR. 1993c. Dear President Clinton. *JAMA* 269:1678–79.

Fuchs VR. 1993d. *The Future of Health Policy.* Cambridge, Mass.: Harvard University Press.

Fuchs VR. 2009. Eliminating "waste" in health care. *JAMA* 302:2481–82.

Fuchs VR. 2010. Health care is different—that's why expenditures matter. *JAMA* 303:1859–60.

Fuchs VR. 2014. Critiquing US health care. *JAMA* 312(20):2095–96.

Furman B. 1948. Truman gets report urging big 10-year health program. *New York Times,* September 3.

Galewitz P. 2013. ACA's "woodworking" effect playing out as 91,000 people eligible for Medicaid learn they can get coverage. *Kaiser Health News.* November 14, 2013, http://khn.org/news/acas-woodworking-effect-playing-out-as-91000-people-eligible-for-medicaid-learn-they-can-get-coverage/.

Garfield S, Cutting C, Feldman R, Taller SL, and Collen MF. 1987. Total health care project: Final report. Oakland, Calif.: Permanente Medical Group.

Garfield SR. 1974. The Permanente Medical Group—historical remarks. Presented to the Executive Committee on April 24.

Garg PP, Frick KD, Diener-West M, and Powe NR. 1999. Effect of the ownership of dialysis facilities on patients' survival and referral for transplantation. *New England Journal of Medicine* 341:1653–60.

Gawande A. 2009. The cost conundrum—what a Texas town can teach us about health care. *The New Yorker,* June 1, www.newyorker.com/reporting/2009/06/01/090601fa_fact_gawande?currentPage=1.

Gilman M, Adams EK, Hockenberry JM, et al. 2015. Safety-net hospitals more likely than other hospitals to fare poorly under Medicare's value-based purchasing. *Health Affairs* 34:398–405.

Gilmer T, and Kronick R. 2005. It's the premiums, stupid: Projections of the uninsured through 2013. *Health Affairs* (web exclusive) W5:143–51. http://content.healthaff airs .org/cgi/con tent/abstract/hlthaff.w5.143v1.

Golberstein E, Gonzales G, and Sommers BD. 2015. California's early ACA expansion increased coverage and reduced out-of-pocket spending for the state's low-income population. *Health Affairs* 34:1688–94.

Goodman E. 1998. The HMO horror show. *Boston Globe*, March 29.

Gostin LO. 2014. The ACA's contraceptive mandate—Religious freedom, women's health, and corporate personhood. *JAMA* 312(8):785–86.

Gozalo P, Plotzke M, Mor V, et al. 2015. Changes in Medicare costs with the growth of hospice care in nursing homes. *New England Journal of Medicine* 372:1823–31.

Graham J. 2014. IOM report calls for transformation of end-of-life care. *JAMA* 312(18): 1845–47.

Grassley C. 2009. Health care reform—A Republican view. *New England Journal of Medicine* 361:2397–99.

Gray B. 1986. *For-profit enterprise in health care*. Washington, D.C.: National Academies Press.

Greene JA, and Watkins ES. 2015. The vernacular of risk: Rethinking direct-to-consumer advertising of pharmaceuticals. *New England Journal of Medicine* 373:1087–89.

Guyer J, Shine N, Musumeci MB, and Rudowitz R. 2015. A look at the private option in Arkansas. Kaiser Family Foundation, http://kff.org/medicaid/issue-brief/a-look-at-the -private-option-in-arkansas/.

Hall, MA. 2015. *King v. Burwell*—ACA Armageddon averted. *New England Journal of Medicine* 373:497–99.

Hamel L, Norton M, Levitt L, et al. 2015. Survey of non-group health insurance enrollees, wave 2. Kaiser Family Foundation, http://kff.org/health-reform/poll-finding/survey-of -non-group-health-insurance-enrollees-wave-2/.

Hamilton WH. 1932. Statement. Pp. 189–200 in *Medical Care for the American People: The Final Report of the Committee on the Cost of Medical Care, Adopted October 31, 1932*. Chicago: University of Chicago Press.

Hartman M, Martin AB, Benson J, et al. 2013. National health spending in 2011: Overall growth remains low, but some payers and services show signs of acceleration. *Health Affairs* 32(1):87–99.

Hartman M, Martin AB, Lassman D, et al. 2015. National health spending in 2013: Growth slows, remains in step with the overall economy. *Health Affairs* 34(1):150–60.

Hasan MM. 1996. Let's end the nonprofit charade. *New England Journal of Medicine* 334: 1055–57.

Haviland AM, Marquis MS, McDevitt RD, and Sood N. 2012. Growth of consumer-directed health plans to one-half of all employer-sponsored insurance could save $57 billion annually. *Health Affairs* 31(5):1009–15.

Health Affairs. 2008. The imaging boom. *Health Affairs* 27(6):1466.

Health Affairs. 2014. The Physician Payments Sunshine Act: New regulations require medical product manufacturers to publicly report payments made to physicians and teaching hospitals. Health Policy Brief, http://healthaffairs.org/healthpolicybriefs/brief_pdfs /healthpolicybrief_127.pdf.

Health Affairs. 2015. Medicaid primary care parity: Health policy briefs, May 11, http://www
.healthaffairs.org/healthpolicybriefs/brief.php?brief_id=137.

Health Canada. 2009. Canada Health Act annual report 2008–2009, www.hc-sc.gc.ca/hcs-sss
/pubs/cha-lcs/2009-cha-lcs-ar-ra/index-eng.php#intro.

HealthCare.gov. 2013. 10 health care benefits covered in the health insurance marketplace.
https://www.healthcare.gov/blog/10-health-care-benefits-covered-in-the-health-insur
ance-marketplace/.

Herrin J, St Andre J, Kenward K, et al. 2015. Community factors and hospital readmission
rates. *Health Services Research* 50(1):20–39.

Herszenhorn DM. 2009. An invitation to protestors. *New York Times*, November 5.

Herszenhorn DM. 2010. Budget reconciliation. *New York Times*, March 3.

Herzlinger RE, Richman BD, and Schulman KA. 2015. Market-based solutions to antitrust
threats—The rejection of the partners settlement. *New England Journal of Medicine*
372:1287–89.

Hibbard JH, Stockard J, and Tusler M. 2005. Hospital performance reports: Impact on
quality, market share, and reputation. *Health Affairs* 24(4):1150–60.

Hickson GB, Clayton EW, Entman SS, et al. 1994. Obstetricians' prior malpractice experience and patients' satisfaction with care. *JAMA* 272:1583–87.

Hillman BJ, and Goldsmith JC. 2010. The uncritical use of high-tech medical imaging. *New
England Journal of Medicine*, June 23, www.nejm.org.

Himmelstein DU, and Woolhandler S. 1989. A national health program for the United States:
A physicians' proposal. *New England Journal of Medicine* 320:102–8.

Himmelstein DU, Woolhandler S, Hellander I, and Wolfe SM. 1999. Quality of care in
investor-owned vs not-for-profit HMOs. *JAMA* 282:159–63.

Hing E, Decker SL, and Jamoom E. 2015. Acceptance of new patients with public and private
insurance by office-based physicians: United States, 2013. *NCHS Data Brief*, no. 195
March 2015, http://www.cdc.gov/nchs/data/databriefs/db195.pdf.

Hirsch BR, Balu S, and Schulman KA. 2014. The impact of specialty pharmaceuticals as
drivers of health care costs. *Health Affairs* 33:1714–20.

Hoadley J. 2012. Medicare Part D spending trends: Understanding key drivers and the role of
competition. Henry J. Kaiser Family Foundation. http://kaiserfamilyfoundation.files
.wordpress.com/2013/01/8308.pdf.

Hoadley JF, Cubanski J, and Neuman P. 2015. Medicare's Part D drug benefit at 10 years:
Firmly established but still evolving. *Health Affairs* 34:1682–87.

Hoadley J, Hargrave E, Cubanski J, and Neuman T. 2008. The Medicare Part D coverage gap:
Costs and consequences in 2007. Kaiser Family Foundation, www.kff.org/medicare
/7811.cfm.

Hobby Lobby Facebook page. https://www.facebook.com/HobbyLobby/info?tab=page
_info.

Horwitz JR. 2005. Making profits and providing care: Comparing nonprofit, for- profit, and
government hospitals. *Health Affairs* 24(3):790–801.

Howlett K, Paperny AM, and Walton D. 2009. Private-clinic patients jump the line for flu
shot. *The Globe and Mail*, November 2.

Hu J, Gonsahn MD, and Nerenz DR. 2014. Socioeconomic status and readmissions: Evidence
from an urban teaching hospital. *Health Affairs* 33:778–85.

Hulse C. 2010. Another long march in the name of change. *New York Times,* March 21.

Hupfeld S. 2004. Evolution of the American hospital system: Subspecialization and physician
ownership. *Circulation* 109(20):2379–80.

Hurley RE, and Somers SA. 2003. Medicaid and managed care: A lasting relationship? *Health Affairs* 22:77–88.

Huskamp HA, Deverka PA, Epstein AM, Epstein RS, McGuigan KA, and Frank RG. 2003. The effect of incentive- based formularies on prescription-drug utilization and spending. *New England Journal of Medicine* 349(23):2224–32.

Iglehart JK. 1993a. The American health care system: Community hospitals. *New England Journal of Medicine* 329:372–76.

Iglehart JK. 1993b. The American health care system: Medicaid. *New England Journal of Medicine* 328:896–900.

Iglehart JK. 2000. Revisiting the Canadian health care system. *New England Journal of Medicine* 342:2007–12.

Iglehart JK. 2002. Medicare's declining payments to physicians. *New England Journal of Medicine* 346:1924–30.

Iglehart JK. 2003. The dilemma of Medicaid. *New England Journal of Medicine* 348:2140–48.

Iglehart JK. 2004. The new Medicare prescription-drug benefit: A pure power play. *New England Journal of Medicine* 350:826–33.

Iglehart JK. 2005. The emergence of physician-owned specialty hospitals. *New England Journal of Medicine* 352:78–84.

Iglehart JK. 2007. The fate of SCHIP—surrogate marker for health care ideology? *New England Journal of Medicine* 357:2104–77.

Iglehart JK. 2009a. Building momentum as Democrats forge health care reform. *New England Journal of Medicine* 360:2385–87.

Iglehart JK. 2009b. Expanding coverage for children—the Democrats' power and SCHIP reauthorization. *New England Journal of Medicine* 360:855–57.

Iglehart JK. 2009c. Prioritizing comparative effectiveness research—IOM recommendations. *New England Journal of Medicine* 361:325–28.

Iglehart JK. 2010a. The Democrats' last ditch—reconciliation or bust. *New England Journal of Medicine* 362:e39.

Iglehart JK. 2010b. Historic passage—reform at last. *New England Journal of Medicine* 362: e48, posted March 24, 2010, http://content.nejm.org/cgi/content/full/362/14/e48.

Iglehart JK. 2015. The expansion of retail clinics—Corporate titans vs. organized medicine. *New England Journal of Medicine* 373:301–3.

Iglehart JK, and Sommers BD. 2015. Medicaid at 50—From Welfare program to nation's largest health insurer. *New England Journal of Medicine* 372:2152–59.

Ignagni K. 2009. Health insurers at the table—industry proposals for regulation and reform. *New England Journal of Medicine* 361:1133–34.

Institute of Medicine of the National Academies of Science. 2009. Conflict of interest in medical research, education, and practice. April, httm://iom.edu/Reports/2009 /Conflict-of-Interest-in-Medical-Research-Education-and-Practice.aspx.

Institute of Medicine of the National Academies of Science. 2011a. Clinical preventive services for women—Closing the gaps, http://iom.nationalacademies.org/~/media /Files/Report%20Files/2011/Clinical-Preventive-Services-for-Women-Closing-the -Gaps/preventiveservicesforwomenreportbrief_updated2.pdf.

Institute of Medicine of the National Academy of Sciences. 2011b. Committee on the Robert Wood Johnson Foundation Initiative on the Future of Nursing. The Future of Nursing—Leading Change, Advancing Health, http://www.thefutureofnursing.org /sites/default/files/Future%20of%20Nursing%20Report_0.pdf.

Institute of Medicine of the National Academies of Sciences, Engineering, and Medicine, 2014. Graduate medical education that meets the nation's health needs—Report brief. http://iom .nationalacademies.org/~/media/Files/Report%20Files/2014/GME/GME-RB.pdf.

Interdepartmental Committee to Coordinate Health and Welfare Activities. 1938. *JAMA* 111: 432–54.

Jacob JA. 2015. Medicare at 50: Reflections from former CMS administrator Donald M. Berwick. *JAMA* 314(4):324–26.

Jacobs LR. 2008. All over again? Public opinion and health care. *New England Journal of Medicine* 358:1881–83.

Jacobson G, Damico A, Neuman T, and Gold M. 2015. Medicare Advantage 2015 spotlight: Enrollment market update. Kaiser Family Foundation, http://kff.org/medicare/issue -brief/medicare-advantage-2015-spotlight-enrollment-market-update/.

Jeffe DB, Whelan AJ, and Andriole DA. 2010. Primary care specialty choices of United States medical graduates, 1997–2006. *Academic Medicine* 85:947–58.

Jha AK. 2015. Readmissions penalty at year 3: How are we doing? Ounce of Evidence. Blog of Ashish Jha, https://blogs.sph.harvard.edu/ashish-jha/.

Jha AK, Fisher ES, Li Z, Orav EJ, and Epstein AM. 2005a. Racial trends in the use of major procedures among the elderly. *New England Journal of Medicine* 353:683–91.

Jha AK, Li Z, Orav EJ, and Epstein AM. 2005b. Care in US hospitals: The Hospital Quality Alliance program. *New England Journal of Medicine* 353:265–74.

Johnson H, and Broder DS. 1996. *The System.* Boston: Little, Brown.

Joynt KE, Orav EJ, and Jha AK. 2014. Association between hospital conversions to for-profit status and clinical and economic outcomes. *JAMA* 312(16):1644–52.

Kahn CN, Ault T, Potetz L, et al. 2015. Assessing Medicare's hospital pay-for-performance programs and whether they are achieving their goals. *Health Affairs* 34:1281–88.

Kahn KL, Pearson ML, Harrison ER, et al. 1994. Health care for black and poor hospitalized Medicare patients. *JAMA* 271:1169–74.

Kaiser Family Foundation. n.d.-a. Medicaid/CHIP data, www.kff.org/Medicaid/index .cfm.

Kaiser Family Foundation. n.d.-b. Tracking Medicare health and prescription drug plans, www.kff.org/medicare/advantagetrackingreport_current.cfm.

Kaiser Family Foundation. 1999. Long-term care: Medicaid's role and challenges. Publication No. 2172. www.kff.org/medicaid/2172-index.cfm.

Kaiser Family Foundation. 2004. Prescription drug trends. Fact Sheet No. 3057. www.kff.org /rxdrugs/3057.cfm.

Kaiser Family Foundation. 2005. Medicaid: A primer. Publication No. 7334. www.kff.org /medicaid/7334.cfm.

Kaiser Family Foundation. 2009. Health coverage of children: The role of Medicaid and CHIP, October, www.kff.org/uninsured/7698.cfm.

Kaiser Family Foundation. 2010. Kaiser health tracking poll, April, www.kff.org/kaiserpolls /upload/8067-F.pdf.

Kaiser Family Foundation. 2012. A guide to the Supreme Court's Affordable Care Act decision, https://kaiserfamilyfoundation.files.wordpress.com/2013/01/8332.pdf.

Kaiser Family Foundation. 2013. A short look at long-term care for seniors. *JAMA* 310(8):786–87.

Kaiser Family Foundation. 2014. 2014 Employer Health Benefits Survey, http://kff.org/health -costs/report/2014-employer-health-benefits-survey/, accessed 9/3/15.

Kaiser Family Foundation. 2015a. Medicaid expansion in Pennsylvania: Transition from waiver to traditional coverage. http://kff.org/medicaid/fact-sheet/medicaid-expansion -in-pennsylvania/.

Kaiser Family Foundation. 2015b. The role of Medicare Advantage, http://kff.org/slideshow /the-role-of-medicare-advantage/.

Kaiser Family Foundation. 2015c. State-by-state effects of a ruling for the challengers in *King v. Burwell*, http://kff.org/interactive/king-v-burwell-effects/.

Kaiser Family Foundation. 2015d. Status of state action on the Medicaid expansion decision, http://kff.org/medicaid/state-indicator/state-activity-around-expanding-medicaid -under-the-affordable-care-act/.

Kaiser Family Foundation and Health Research and Educational Trust. 2009. Employer Health Benefits 2009 Annual Survey, http://ehbs.kff.org/.

Kaiser Family Foundation and Health Research and Educational Trust. 2010. Employer Health Benefits 2010 Annual Survey, http://ehbs.kff.org/.

Kaiser Family Foundation and Health Research and Educational Trust. 2015. 2015 Employer Health Benefits Survey, http://kff.org/health-costs/report/2015-employer-health -benefits-survey/.

Kaiser Family Foundation State Health Facts. Medicaid spending per enrollee (full or partial benefit). http://kff.org/medicaid/state-indicator/medicaid-spending-per-enrollee/#.

Katz SJ, Cardiff K, Pascali M, Barer ML, and Evans RG. 2002. Phantoms in the snow: Canadians' use of health care services in the United States. *Health Affairs* 21(3):20–31.

Keehan SP, Cuckler GA, Sisko AM, et al. 2015. National health expenditure projections, 2014–24: Spending growth faster than recent trends. *Health Affairs* 34(8):1407–17.

Kelley AS, and Meier DE. 2010. Palliative care—a shifting paradigm. *New England Journal of Medicine* 363:781–82.

Kenagy JW, Berwick DM, and Shore MF. 1999. Service quality in health care. *JAMA* 281: 661–65.

Kennedy E. 1973. Senate speech regarding the Health Maintenance Organizations Act of 1973, May 14. *Congressional Record-Senate* 15497.

Kerlikowske K. 2009. Evidence-based breast cancer prevention: The importance of individual risk. *Annals of Internal Medicine* 151:750–52.

Kesselheim AS, Robertson CT, Siri K, et al. 2013. Distributions of industry payments to Massachusetts physicians. *New England Journal of Medicine* 368:2049–52.

Keyhani S, Wang S, Hebert P, Carpenter D, and Anderson G. 2010. US pharmaceutical innovation in an international context. *American Journal of Public Health* 100: 1075–80.

Kingdon JW. 1984. *Agendas, Alternatives, and Public Policies.* Boston: Little, Brown.

Kirby JB, Machlin SR, and Cohen JW. 2003. Has the increase in HMO enrollment within the Medicaid population changed the pattern of health service use and expenditures? *Medical Care* 41(7 Suppl.):III-24–III-34.

Ko DT, Tu JV, Samadashvili Z, et al. 2010. Temporal trends in the use of percutaneous coronary intervention and coronary artery bypass surgery in New York State and Ontario. *Circulation* 121:2635–44.

Ko DT, Tu JV, Austin PC, et al. 2013. Prevalence and extent of obstructive coronary artery disease among patients undergoing elective coronary catheterization in New York State and Ontario. *JAMA* 310(2):163–69.

Kohn LT, Corrigan JM, and Donaldson MS, eds. 1999. *To Err Is Human: Building a Safer Health System.* Washington, D.C.: National Academies Press.

Kolata G. 1993. How demand surged for unapproved prostate test. *New York Times,* September 29.

Kolata G. 2008. Co-payments go way up for drugs with high prices. *New York Times,* April 14, p. 1.

Krahn MD, Mahoney JE, Eckman MH, et al. 1994. Screening for prostate cancer: A decision analytic view. *JAMA* 272:773–80.

Krasner SD. 1983. *International Regimes.* Ithaca, N.Y.: Cornell University Press.

Krauss C. 2005. Canadian court chips away at national health care. *New York Times,* June 9.

Kreling DH, Mott DA, Wiederholt JB, Lundy J, and Levitt L. 2001. Prescription drug trends: A chartbook update. Publication No. 3112. The Kaiser Family Foundation. www.kff .org/rxdrugs/3112-index.cfm.

Krugman P. 2014. The Medicare miracle. *New York Times,* opinion pages, August 31.

Krumholz HM, Nuti SV, Downing NS, et al. 2015. Mortality, hospitalizations, and expenditures for the Medicare population aged 65 years or older, 1999–2013. *JAMA* 314(4): 355–65.

Larson EB, and Reid R. 2010. The patient-centered medical home movement. *JAMA* 303: 1644–45.

Lauby-Secretan B, Scoccianti C, Loomis D, et al. 2015. Breast-cancer screening: Viewpoint of the IARC Working Group. *New England Journal of Medicine* 372:2353–58.

Lee TH. 2012. Care redesign—A path forward for providers. *New England Journal of Medicine* 367:466–72.

Leff B, and Finucane TE. 2008. Gizmo idolatry. *JAMA* 299:1830–32.

Lepore J. 2012. The lie factory—How politics became a business. *The New Yorker,* September 24, p. 50.

Lett D. 2008. Private health clinics remain unregulated in most of Canada. *Canadian Medical Association Journal* 178:986–87.

Levine SA, Boal J, and Boling PA. 2003. Home care. *JAMA* 290:1203–7.

Levinsky N. 1999. Quality and equity in dialysis and renal transplantation. *New England Journal of Medicine* 341:1691–93.

Levinson W. 1994. Physician-patient communication, a key to malpractice prevention. *JAMA* 272:1619–20.

Lewin JC, and Sybinsky PA. 1993. Hawaii's employer mandate and its contribution to universal access. *JAMA* 269:2538–43.

Lewis S. 1924. *Arrowsmith.* New York: Penguin-Putnam. Reprinted 1998.

Lewis VA, McClurg AB, Smith J, et al. 2013. Attributing patients to accountable care organizations: Performance year approach aligns stakeholders' interests. *Health Affairs* 32:587–95.

Liebhaber A, and Grossman JM. 2007. Physicians moving to mid-sized, single-specialty practices, August, www.hschange.org/CONTENT/941/.

Lindenauer PK, Rothberg MB, Pekow PS, et al. 2007. Outcomes of care by hospitalists, general internists, and family physicians. *New England Journal of Medicine* 357: 2589–2600.

Lipset SM. 1990. *Continental Divide.* New York: Routledge, Chapman, and Hall.

Lipsitz LA. 2013. The 3-night hospital stay and Medicare coverage for skilled nursing care. *JAMA* 310(14):1441–42.

Lipton S. 2001. Comparison of Direct-to-Consumer Prescription Drug Advertising on Hispanic versus Mainstream Broadcast Media. Undergraduate thesis, Program in Human Biology, Stanford University.

Localio AR, Lawthers AG, Brennan TA, et al. 1991. Relation between malpractice claims and adverse events due to negligence. Results of the Harvard Medical Practice Study III. *New England Journal of Medicine* 325:245–51.

Long H. 2015. "Hated" CEO lowering price of $750 AIDS drug Daraprim. CNN. http://money.cnn.com/2015/09/22/investing/daraprim-aids-drug-price/index.html.

Long SK, and Stockley K. 2010. Sustaining health reform in a recession: An update on Massachusetts as of fall 2009. *Health Affairs* 29(6):1234–41.

Lozano P, Connell FA, and Koepsell TD. 1995. Use of health services by African-American children with asthma on Medicaid. *JAMA* 274:469–73.

Lucia L, Dietz M, Jacobs K, et al. 2015. Which Californians will lack health insurance under the Affordable Care Act? UCLA Center for Health Policy Research, http://healthpolicy.ucla.edu/publications/search/pages/detail.aspx?PubID=1363.

Lundberg GD. 1995. The failure of organized health system reform: Now what? (Caveat aeger—let the patient beware). *JAMA* 273:1539–41.

Lurie N. 2005. Health disparities: Less talk, more action. *New England Journal of Medicine* 353:727–29.

Mackey J. 2009. The whole foods alternative to ObamaCare—eight things we can do to improve health care without adding to the deficit. *Wall Street Journal,* August 11, Opinion page.

Madden JM, Graves AJ, Zhang F, et al. 2008. Cost-related medication nonadherence and spending on basic needs following implementation of Medicare Part D. *JAMA* 299: 1922–28.

Mandelblatt JS, Cronin KA, Bailey S, et al. 2009. Effects of mammography screening under different screening schedules: Model estimates of potential benefits and harms. *Annals of Internal Medicine* 151:738–47.

Mann C, and Artiga S. 2004. The impact of recent changes in health care coverage for low-income people: A first look at the research following changes in Oregon's Medicaid program. Report #7100. Prepared for the Kaiser Commission on Medicaid and the Uninsured. www.kff.org/medicaid/7100a.cfm.

Mann C, and Artiga S. 2006. New developments in Medicaid coverage: Who bears financial risk and responsibility. Kaiser Family Foundation, June, www.kff.org/Medicaid/upload/7507.pdf.

Manning WG, Leibowitz A, Goldberg GA, et al. 1984. A controlled trial of the effect of a prepaid group practice on use of services. *New England Journal of Medicine* 310: 1505–10.

Manz C, Ross JS, and Grande D. 2014. Marketing to physicians in a digital world. *New England Journal of Medicine* 371:1857–59.

Mariner WK, Glantz JH, and Annas GJ. 2012. Reframing Federalism: The Affordable Care Act (and broccoli) in the Supreme Court. *New England Journal of Medicine* 367: 1154–58.

Marleau D. 1995. Letter RE: Canada Health Act, January 6, 1995, in Health Canada (2009), p. 229.

Marmot MG, and Theorell T. 1988. Social class and cardiovascular disease: The contribution of work. *International Journal of Health Services* 18:659–74.

Marron DB. 2006. Medicare's physician payment rates and the sustainable growth rate. Testimony before the Subcommittee on Health, Committee on Energy and Commerce, US House of Representatives. July 25. www.cbo.gov/ft pdocs/74xx/doc7425/07-25-SGR.pdf.

Massachusetts Department of Health and Human Services. 2009. Recommendations Special Commission on the health care payment system, July 16, p. 1, www.mass.gov/?pageID

= eohhs2subtopic&L=4&L0=JP,e&L1=Government&L2=Special+Commissions+and
+ Initiatives&L3=Special+Commission+on+the+Health+Care+Payment+System&sid
= Eeohhs2.

Maule WF. 1994. Screening for colorectal cancer by nurse endoscopists. *New England Journal of Medicine* 330:183–87.

Mays J, Brenner M, Neuman T, Cubanski J, and Claxton G. 2004. Estimates of Medicare beneficiaries' out-of-pocket drug spending in 2006—modeling the impact of the MMA. Publication No. 7201. Actuarial Research Corporation and the Kaiser Family Foundation. www.kff org/medicare/7201.cfm.

McClellan M. 2015. Accountable care organizations and evidence-based payment reform. *JAMA* 313(21):2128–30.

McClellan MB, and Tunis SR. 2005. Medicare coverage of ICDs. *New England Journal of Medicine* 352:222–24.

McCue MJ, and Hall MA. 2015. The federal medical loss ratio rule: Implications for consumers in year 3. The Commonwealth Fund, http://www.commonwealthfund.org/publications/issue-briefs/2015/mar/medical-loss-ratio-year-three.

McDonough JE. 2015. The demise of Vermont's single-payer plan. *New England Journal of Medicine* 372(17):1584–85.

McGinnis JM, Williams-Russo P, and Knickman JR. 2002. The case for more active policy attention to health promotion. *Health Affairs* 21(2):78–93.

McMorrow S, Kenney GM, Long SK, and Anderson N. 2015a. Uninsurance among young adults continues to decline, particularly in Medicaid expansion states. *Health Affairs* 34:616–20.

McMorrow S, Long SK, Kenney GM, and Anderson N. 2015b. Uninsurance disparities have narrowed for black and hispanic adults under the Affordable Care Act. *Health Affairs* 34:1774–78.

McNaughton-Collins M. 2009. Perspective roundtable: Screening for prostate cancer. *New England Journal of Medicine* 360:e18, http://content.nejm.org/cgi/reprint/360/13/e18.pdf.

McWilliams JM, Hsu J, and Newhouse JP. 2012. New risk-adjustment system was associated with reduced favorable selection in Medicare Advantage. *Health Affairs* 31:2630–40.

Mechanic R. 2014. Post-acute care—The next frontier for controlling Medicare spending. *New England Journal of Medicine* 370:692–94.

Mechanic R. 2015. Mandatory Medicare bundled payment: Is it ready for prime time? *New England Journal of Medicine* 373:1291–93.

Medicaid Access Study Group. 1994. Access of Medicaid recipients to outpatient care. *New England Journal of Medicine* 330:1426–30.

Medicaid.gov. 2015. Medicaid and CHIP Enrollment Data, http://www.medicaid.gov/medicaid-chip-program-information/program-information/medicaid-and-chip-enrollment-data/medicaid-enrollment-data-collected-through-mbes.html.

Medicare Boards of Trustees. 2015. 2015 annual report, https://www.cms.gov/Research-Statistics-Data-and-Systems/Statistics-Trends-and-Reports/ReportsTrustFunds/Downloads/TR2015.pdf.

Medicare Payment Advisory Commission. 2009. Report to the Congress: Medicare payment policy, March, www.medpac.gov/docuoment_TOC.cfm?id=563.

Medicare Payment Advisory Commission. 2015a. June 2015 data book, http://www.medpac.gov/-documents-/data-book.

Medicare Payment Advisory Commission. 2015b. Report to the Congress: Medicare Payment Policy, March 13, 2015. http://www.medpac.gov/documents/reports/mar2015 _entirereport_revised.pdf?sfvrsn=0.

Mehrotra A, Adams JL, Armstrong K, et al. 2010. Health care on aisle 7—the growing phenomenon of retail clinics. RAND Health, www.rand.org/publs/research_briefs /RB9491–1/.

Mehrotra A, Liu H, Adams JL, et al. 2009. Comparing costs and quality of care at retail clinics with that of other medical settings for 3 common illnesses. *Annals of Internal Medicine* 151:321–28.

Meilicke CA, and Storch JL, eds. 1980. *Perspectives on Canadian Health Services Policy: History and Emerging Trends.* Ann Arbor, Mich.: Health Administration Press.

Mello MM, Studdert DM, and Kachalia A. 2014. The medical liability climate and prospects for reform. *JAMA* 312(20):2146–55.

Meltzer DO, and Ruhnke GW. 2014. Redesigning care for patients at increased hospitalization risk: The Comprehensive Care Physician Model. *Health Affairs* 33:770–77.

Mennig PA, Quan R, Chiuzan C, and Glied S. 2015. Considering whether medicaid is worth the cost: Revisiting the Oregon Health Study. *American Journal of Public Health* 105(5):866–71.

Miller DC, Gust C, Dimick JB, et al. 2011. Large variations in Medicare payments for surgery highlight savings potential from bundled payment programs. *Health Affairs* 30: 2107–15.

Miller RS, Dunn MR, Richter TH, and Whitcomb ME. 1998. Employment-seeking experiences of resident physicians completing training during 1996. *JAMA* 280:777–83.

Milstein A. 2015. Precision health care efficiency via accountable care organizations. *JAMA Internal Medicine.* Published online September 21, 2015. Doi: 10.1001.

Mirel LB, and Carper K. 2014. Trends in health care expenditures for the elderly, age 65 and over: 2001, 2006, and 2011. US Agency for Healthcare Research and Quality, Medical Expenditure Panel Survey Statistical Brief #429, http://meps.ahrq.gov/mepsweb/data _stats/Pub_ProdResults_Details.jsp?pt=Statistical+Brief&opt=2&id=1129.

Mitka M. 2010. Recession helped put brakes on growth in US health care spending for 2008. *New England Journal of Medicine* 303:715.

Morgenson G. 2015. Valeant's high-price drug strategy: Fair game. *New York Times*, October 2, 2015.

Moses H, Matheson DHM, Dorsey ER, et al. 2013. The anatomy of health care in the United States. *JAMA* 310(18):1947–64.

Mukamel DB, Ladd H, Li Y, et al. 2015. Have racial disparities in ambulatory care sensitive admissions abated over time? *Medical Care* 53(11):931–39.

Mulcahy AW, Wynn B, Burgette L, and Mehrotra A. 2015. Medicare's step back from global payments—Unbundling postoperative care. *New England Journal of Medicine* 372: 1385–87.

Nash IS, and Pasternak RC. 1995. Physician, educate thyself. *JAMA* 273:1533–34.

National Committee for Quality Assurance. 2015a. HEDIS® & performance measurement, http://www.ncqa.org/HEDISQualityMeasurement.aspx.

National Committee for Quality Assurance. 2015b. PCMH recognition program redesign and online feedback, http://www.ncqa.org/Newsroom/Statements/PCMHIdeas.aspx.

National Research Council and Institute of Medicine. 2013. US health in international perspective: Shorter lives, poorer health—Report brief. http://iom.nationalacademies .org/Reports/2013/US-Health-in-International-Perspective-Shorter-Lives-Poorer -Health/Report-Brief010913.aspx.

Nelson HD, Tyne K, Naik A, et al. 2009. Screening for breast cancer: An update for the US Preventive Services Task Force. *Annals of Internal Medicine* 151:727–37.

Neprash HT, Chernew ME, and Hicks AL. 2015. Association of financial integration between physicians and hospitals with commercial health care prices. *JAMA Internal Medicine*. Published online October 19, 2015. Doi: 10.1001.

Newhouse JP, and Garber AM. 2013. Geographic variation in Medicare services. *New England Journal of Medicine* 368:1465–68.

Newhouse JP, Manning WG, Morris CN, et al. 1981. Some interim results from a controlled trial of cost sharing in health insurance. *New England Journal of Medicine* 305:1501–7.

New York Times. 2015. House votes repealing or defunding the Affordable Care Act, http://politics.nytimes.com/congress/votes/house/aca-repeal-defund.

Nixon R. 1972. Message from the President of the United States relative to his health care program. House of Representatives Document No. 92-261, March 2.

North DC. 1986. *Institutions, Institutional Change and Economic Performance.* New York: Cambridge University Press.

Nudelman PM, and Andrews LM. 1996. The "value added" of not-for-profit health plans. *New England Journal of Medicine* 334:1057–59.

Nyweide DJ, Lee W, Cuerdon TT, et al. 2015. Association of pioneer accountable care organizations vs traditional Medicare fee for service with spending, utilization, and patient experience. *JAMA* 313(21):2152–61.

Obama B. 2009a. Remarks to a joint session of Congress on health care, September 9, www.whitehouse.gov/the_press_office/remarks-by-the-president-to-a-joint-session-of-congress-on-health-care/.

Obama B. 2009b. Why we need health care reform. *New York Times,* August 16.

Obama B. 2010. Remarks at the health care bill signing. *New York Times,* March 23.

Oberg CN, and Polich CL. 1988. Medicaid: Entering the third decade. *Health Affairs* 7(4): 83–96.

Oberlander J, and Jones DK. 2015. The children's cliff—Extending CHIP. *New England Journal of Medicine* 372:1979–81.

Oberlander J, and Laugesen MJ. 2015. Leap of faith—Medicare's new physician payment system. *New England Journal of Medicine* 373:1185–87.

Oeffinger KC, Fontham ETH, Etzioni R, et al. 2015. Breast cancer screening for women at average risk: 2015 guideline update from the American Cancer Society. *JAMA* 314 (15):1599–1614.

Oliver T. 2004. Policy entrepreneurship in the social transformation of American medicine: The rise of managed care and managed competition. *Journal of Health Politics, Policy and Law* 29:701–33.

Oronce CI, Shao H, and Shi L. 2015. Disparities in 30-day readmissions after total hip arthroplasty. *Medical Care* 53(11):924–30.

Orszag, Peter. 2010. A health care plan for colleges. *New York Times,* September 19, Op-Ed Page.

Padrez R, Carino T, Blum J, and Mendelson D. 2005. The use of Oregon's evidence-based reviews for Medicaid pharmacy policies: Experiences in four states. Publication no. 7319. The Health Strategies Consultancy LLC, published by the Kaiser Family Foundation. www.kff.org/medicaid/7319.cfm.

Paradise J. 2015. Medicaid moving forward. Kaiser Family Foundation. http://kff.org/health-reform/issue-brief/medicaid-moving-forward/.

Parsons T. 1951. *The social system.* New York: Free Press.

Parsons T. 1975. The sick role and the role of the physician revisited. *Milbank Memorial Fund Quarterly* 53:257.

Partners HealthCare. 2015. About Partners HealthCare, http://www.partners.org/About/Default.aspx.

Patel MR, Peterson ED, Dai D, et al. 2010. Low diagnostic yield of coronary angiography. *New England Journal of Medicine* 362:886–95.

The Patient Protection and Affordable Care Act. 2010. http://www.gpo.gov/fdsys/pkg/PLAW-111publ148/pdf/PLAW-111publ148.pdf.

Pear R. 2000. Forty states forfeit health care funds for poor children. *New York Times,* September 24.

Pear R. 2005. Drug plans in Medicare start effort on marketing. *New York Times,* October 1.

Pear R. 2015. Health insurers seeking mergers play down antitrust concerns. *New York Times,* September 22.

Pear R, and Dao J. 2004. States' tactics aim to reduce drug spending. *New York Times,* November 21.

Peckham C. 2015. Medscape Physician Compensation Report 2015, http://www.medscape.com/features/slideshow/compensation/2015/public/overview#page=1.

Peikes D, Zutshi A, Genevro J, et al. 2012. Early evidence on the patient-centered medical home. US Agency for Healthcare Research and Quality, https://pcmh.ahrq.gov/sites/default/files/attachments/Early%20Evidence%20on%20the%20PCMH%202%2028%2012.pdf.

Peterson ED, Wright SM, Daley J, and Thibault GE. 1994. Racial variation in cardiac procedure use and survival following acute myocardial infarction in the Department of Veterans Affairs. *JAMA* 271:1175–80.

Pham HH, Cohen M, and Conway PH. 2014. The Pioneer Accountable Care Organization Model—Improving quality and lowering costs. *JAMA* 312(16):1635–36.

Pham HH, Grossman JM, Cohen G, and Bodenheimer T. 2008. Hospitalists and care transitions: The divorce of inpatient and outpatient care. *Health Affairs* 27(5):1315–27.

Pham HH, Pilotte J, Rajkumar R, et al. 2015. Medicare's vision for delivery-system reform—The role of ACOs. *New England Journal of Medicine* 373:987–90.

Phillips C. 1949. Bitter debate begins over health program. *New York Times,* February 27.

Physicians' Working Group for Single-Payer National Health Insurance. 2003. Proposal of the Physicians' Working Group for single-payer national health insurance. *JAMA* 290:798–805.

Picard A. 2006. Public wants Medicare changed, poll finds. *The Globe and Mail,* June 8.

Pilote L, Saynina O, Lavoie F, and McClellan M. 2003. Cardiac procedure use and outcomes in elderly patients with acute myocardial infarction in the United States and Quebec, Canada, 1988 to 1994. *Med Care* 41(7):813–22.

Pitts SR, Carrier ER, Rich EC, and Kellerman AL. 2010. Where Americans get acute care: Increasingly, it's not at their doctor's office. *Health Affairs* 29(9):1620–29.

Plumb JD, and Ogle KS. 1992. Hospice care. *Primary Care; Clinics in Office Practice* 19(4):807–20.

Pollack A. 2008. The minimal impact of a big hypertensive study. *New York Times,* November 28.

Pollack A. 2015a. Big price increase for tuberculosis drug is rescinded. *New York Times,* September 21, 2015.

Pollack A. 2015b. Drug goes from $13.50 a tablet to $750, overnight. *New York Times,* September 20, 2015.

Pollack A. 2015c. Orkambi, a new cystic fibrosis drug, wins F.D.A. approval. *New York Times,* July 2, 2015.

Pollack A, and Tavernise S. 2015. Valeant's drug price strategy enriches it, but infuriates patients and lawmakers. *New York Times*, October 4, 2015.

Polsky D, Richards M, Basseyn S, et al. 2015. Appointment availability after increases in Medicaid payments for primary care. *New England Journal of Medicine* 372:537–45.

Quanstrum KH, and Hayward RA. 2010. Lessons from the mammography wars. *New England Journal of Medicine* 363:1076–79.

Rajaram R, Chung JW, Kinnier CV, et al. 2015. Hospital characteristics associated with penalties in the Centers for Medicare & Medicaid Services hospital-acquired condition reduction program. *JAMA* 314(4):375–83.

Rand Corporation. 2012. Skin in the game: How consumer-directed plans affect the cost and use of health care. http://www.rand.org/content/dam/rand/pubs/research_briefs/2012 /RAND_RB9672.pdf.

Rathore SS, Lenert LA, Weinfurt KP, et al. 2000. The effect of patient sex and race on medical students' ratings of quality of life. *American Journal of Medicine* 108:561–66.

Rees M. 1998. Will Helen Hunt save US health care? *Ottawa Citizen*, July 2.

Reid RO, Deb P, Howell BL, and Shrank WH. 2013. Association between Medicare Advantage Plan star ratings and enrollment. *JAMA* 309(3):267–74.

Reinhardt U. 2015. Probing our moral values in health care: The pricing of specialty drugs. *JAMA* 314(10):981–82.

Reinhardt UE, and Relman AS. 1986. Debating for-profit health care and the ethics of physicians. *Health Affairs* 5(2):5–31.

Religious Freedom Restoration Act of 1993. http://www.gpo.gov/fdsys/pkg/STATUTE-107 /pdf/STATUTE-107-Pg1488.pdf.

Relman AS. 2003. Your doctor's drug problem. *New York Times*, November 18. http://www .nytimes.com/2003/11/18/opinion/your-doctor-s-drug-problem.html.

Relman AS. 2007. Medical professionalism in a commercialized health care market. *JAMA* 298: 2668–70.

Reschovsky JD, and Rich E. 2015. Hospital acquisition of physician groups—On the road to value-based or higher-priced care? *JAMA Internal Medicine*. Published online October 19, 2015. Doi: 10.1001.

Rhodes KV, Kenney GM, Friedman AB, et al. 2014. Primary care access for new patients on the eve of health care reform. *JAMA Internal Medicine* 174(6):861–69.

Robertson CT. 2015. New DTCA guidance: Enough to empower consumers? *New England Journal of Medicine* 373:1085–87.

Robinson JC. 2015. Biomedical innovation in the era of health care spending constraints. *Health Affairs* 34:203–209.

Robinson JC, Porter M, Shugrue N, et al. 2015. Connecticut's "money follows the person" yields positive results for transitioning people out of institutions. *Health Affairs* 34:1628–36.

Robinson JC, and Howell S. 2014. Specialty pharmaceuticals: Policy initiatives to improve assessment, pricing, prescription, and use. *Health Affairs* 33:1745–50.

Romanow RJ. 2002. Building on values: The future of health care in Canada. Final Report of the Commission on the Future of Health Care in Canada. www.hc-sc.gc.ca/english /care/romanow/index1.html.

Romanow RJ. 2005. Now's the time to stand up for Medicare. *The Globe and Mail*, June 10.

Rosati RJ, Russell D, Peng T, et al. 2014. Medicare home health payment reform may jeopardize access for clinically complex and socially vulnerable patients. *Health Affairs* 33:946–56.

Rosenbaum L, and Lamas DL. 2012. Cents and sensitivity—Teaching physicians to think about costs. *New England Journal of Medicine* 367:99–101.

Rosenbaum S, Kindig DA, Bao J, et al. 2015. The value of the nonprofit hospital tax exemption was $24.6 billion in 2011. *Health Affairs* 34:1225–33.

Rosenstreich DL, Eggleston P, Kattan M, et al. 1997. The role of cockroach allergy and exposure to cockroach allergen in causing morbidity among inner-city children with asthma. *New England Journal of Medicine* 336:1356–63.

Rosenthal MB, Alidina S, and Friedberg MW. 2015. A difference-in-difference analysis of changes in quality, utilization and cost following the Colorado multi-payer patient-centered medical home pilot. *Journal of General Internal Medicine*. Published online October 8, 2015. Doi: 10.1007.

Rosenthal MB, Berndt ER, Donohue JM, Epstein AM, and Frank RG. 2003. Demand effects of recent changes in prescription drug promotion. Publication No. 6085. Kaiser Family Foundation. www.kff.org/rxdrugs/6085-index.cfm.

Rosenthal R. 2015. Medical costs rise as retirees winter in Florida. *New York Times*, February 1, p. A1.

Ross JS. 2002. The committee on the cost of medical care and the history of health insurance in the United States. *Einstein Quarterly Journal of Biology and Medicine* 19:129–34.

Royal Commission on Health Services. 1964. *Report*. Ottawa: Queen's Printers.

Ruger JP, Ruger TW, and Annas GJ. 2015. The elusive right to health care under US law. *New England Journal of Medicine* 372:2558–63.

Sack K. 2009. Screening debate reveals culture clash in medicine. *New York Times*, November 20.

Sade RM. 1971. Medical care as a right: A refutation. *New England Journal of Medicine* 285: 1288–92.

Safran D, Tarlov AR, and Rogers WH. 1994. Primary care performance in fee-for-service and prepaid health systems. *JAMA* 271:1579–86.

Sage WM. 2014. Medical malpractice reform—When is it about money? Why is it about time? *JAMA* 312(20):2103–105.

Salkever DS, Skinner EA, Steinwachs DM, and Katz H. 1982. Episode-based efficiency comparisons for physicians and nurse practitioners. *Medical Care* 20(2):143–53.

Santhakumar S, and Adashi EY. 2015. The Physician Payment Sunshine Act: Testing the value of transparency. *JAMA* 313(1):23–24.

Sarpatwari A, Avorn J, and Kesselheim AS. 2015. Progress and hurdles for follow-on biologics. *New England Journal of Medicine* 372:2380–82.

Scheffler RM. 2015. Accountable care organizations: Integrated care meets market power. *Journal of Health Politics, Policy and Law* 40(4):637–43.

Schneider EC, Zaslavsky AM, and Epstein AM. 2004. Use of high-cost operative procedures by Medicare beneficiaries enrolled in for-profit and not-for-profit health plans. *New England Journal of Medicine* 350:143–50.

Schröder FH, Hugosson J. Roobol MJ, et al. 2009. Screening and prostate-cancer mortality in a randomized European study. *New England Journal of Medicine* 360:1320–28.

Schroeder SA. 2007. We can do better—Improving the health of the American people. *New England Journal of Medicine* 357(12):1221–28.

Schulman KA, Balu S, and Reed SD. 2015. Specialty pharmaceuticals for hyperlipidemia: Impact on insurance premiums. *New England Journal of Medicine* 373:1591–93.

Schwartz AL, Chernew ME, Landon BE, and McWilliams JM. 2015. Changes in low-value services in year 1 of the Medicare Pioneer Accountable Care Organization Program. *JAMA Internal Medicine*. Published online September 21, 2015. Doi: 10.1001/jamainternmed.2015.4525.

Schwartz S, Testa KG, and Jose K. 2015. Immigration relief for parents and youth = Whole family health coverage in California. Georgetown University, Center for Children and Families, http://ccf.georgetown.edu/wp-content/uploads/2015/07/DAPA-and-DACA-California-final.pdf.

Schwenk TL. 2014. The patient-centered medical home—One size does not fit all. *JAMA* 311(8):802–3.

Scott WR. 1987. The adolescence of institutional theory. *Administrative Science Quarterly* 32: 493–511.

Seabury SA, Helland E, and Jena AB. 2014. Medical malpractice reform: Noneconomic damages caps reduced payments 15 percent, with varied effects by specialty. *Health Affairs* 33(11):2048–56.

Sebelius, K. 2010. A message from Health and Human Services Secretary Kathleen Sebelius, February 4, www.insurekidsnow.gov/chip/report.html.

Shi L, Lebrun-Harris LA, Daly CA, et al. 2013. Reducing disparities in access to primary care and patient satisfaction with care: The role of health centers. *Journal of Health Care for the Poor and Underserved* 24(1):56–66.

Shin P, Sharac J, and Rosenbaum S. 2015. Community health centers and Medicaid at 50: An enduring relationship essential for health system transformation. *Health Affairs* 34: 1096–1104.

Shortell SM, Colla CH, Lewis VA, et al. 2015. Accountable care organizations: The national landscape. *Journal of Health Politics, Policy and Law* 40(4):645–66.

Silverman EM, Skinner JS, and Fisher ES. 1999. The association between for-profit hospital ownership and increased Medicare spending. *New England Journal of Medicine* 341: 420–26.

Simpson J. 2005. The new face of medicare. *The Globe and Mail*, June 10.

Sisko AM, Truffer CJ, Keehan SP, et al. 2010. National health spending projections: The estimated impact of reform through 2019. *Health Affairs.* 10.377/hlthaff.2010.0788, published online September 9.

Skocpol T. 1997. *Boomerang: Health Care Reform and the Turn against Government.* New York: W. W. Norton.

Sloss EM, Keeler EB, Brook RH, et al. 1987. Effect of a health maintenance organization on physiologic health. *Annals of Internal Medicine* 106:130–38.

Smart DR. 2010. *Physician Characteristics and Distribution in the US.* Chicago: American Medical Association.

Smedley BD, Sith AY, and Nelson AR, eds. 2003. *Unequal Treatment: Confronting Racial and Ethnic Disparities in Health Care.* Washington, D.C.: National Academies Press.

Smillie JG. 1991. *Can Physicians Manage the Quality and Costs of Health Care? The Story of the Permanente Medical Group.* New York: McGraw-Hill.

Smith DB. 1999. *Health care divided: Race and healing a nation.* Ann Arbor: University of Michigan Press.

Smith JC, and Medalia C. 2015. Health insurance coverage in the United States: 2014–current population reports. US Census Bureau, http://www.census.gov/content/dam/Census/library/publications/2015/demo/p60-253.pdf.

Smith RA, Saslow D, Sawyer KA, et al. 2003. American Cancer Society guidelines for breast cancer screening: Update 2003. *CA: A Cancer Journal for Clinicians* 53(3):141–69.

Smith V, Snyder L, and Rudowitz R. 2014. CHIP enrollment snapshot: December 2013. Kaiser Family Foundation, https://kaiserfamilyfoundation.files.wordpress.com/2014/06/7642-09-chip-enrollment-snapshot_december-2013.pdf.

Sommers BD, Gunja MZ, Finegold K, and Musco T. 2015. Changes in self-reported insurance coverage, access to care, and health under the Affordable Care Act. *JAMA* 314(4):366–74.

Soni A. 2015. Trends in the five most costly conditions among the US civilian noninstitutionalized population, 2002 and 2012. US Agency for Healthcare Research and Quality, Medical Expenditure Panel Survey Statistical Brief #470, http://meps.ahrq.gov /mepsweb/data_files/publications/st470/stat470.shtml.

Sood A, Abdullah NM, Abdollah F, et al. 2015. Rates of kidney transplantation from living and deceased donors for blacks and whites in the United States, 1998 to 2011. *JAMA Internal Medicine* 175(10):1716–18.

Sox HC, and Greenfield S. 2009. Comparative effectiveness research: A report from the Institute of Medicine. *Annals of Internal Medicine* 151(3):203–205.

Sparer MS. 2015. Medicaid at 50: Remarkable growth fueled by unexpected politics. *Health Affairs* 34:1084–91.

Stagnitti MM. 2004. Statistical Brief #21: Trends in outpatient prescription drug utilization and expenditures, 1997–2000. Agency for Health Care Research and Quality. www .meps.ahrq.gov/papers/st21/stat21.htm.

Staiger DO, Auerbach D, and Buerhaus PI. 2012. Registered nurse labor supply and the recession—Are we in a bubble? *New England Journal of Medicine* 366:1463–65.

Stange KC, Nutting PA, Miller WL, et al. 2010. Defining and measuring the patient-centered medical home. *Journal of General Internal Medicine* 25:601–21.

Starr M, Dominiak L, and Aizcorbe A. 2014. Decomposing growth in spending finds annual cost of treatment contributed most to spending growth, 1980–2006. *Health Affairs* 33(5):823–31.

Starr P. 1982. *The social transformation of American medicine.* New York: Basic Books.

Steinbrook R. 2005. Commercial support and continuing medical education. *New England Journal of Medicine* 352:534–35.

Steinbrook R. 2009. The end of fee-for-service medicine? Proposal for payment reform in Massachusetts. *New England Journal of Medicine* 361:1036–38.

Steinbrook R. 2012. Controlling health care costs in Massachusetts with a global spending target. *JAMA* 308(12):1215–16.

Steinbrook R. 2015. The repeal of Medicare's sustainable growth rate for physician payment. *JAMA* 313(20):2025–26.

Steinhauer J. 2000. Many not eligible in state program to insure children. *New York Times,* September 30.

Stevenson DG. 2012. Growing pains for the Medicare hospice benefit. *New England Journal of Medicine* 367:1683–85.

Stevenson DG, Dalton JB, Grabowski DC, and Huskamp HA. 2015. Nearly half of all Medicare hospice enrollees received care from agencies owned by regional or national chains. *Health Affairs* 34:30–38.

Stevenson DG, and Huskamp HA. 2014. Integrating care at the end of life: Should Medicare Advantage include hospice? *JAMA* 311(15):1493–94.

Studdert DM, Mello MM, and Brennan TA. 2004a. Financial conflicts of interest in physicians' relationships with the pharmaceutical industry: Self-regulation in the shadow of federal prosecution. *New England Journal of Medicine* 351:1891–1900.

Studdert DM, Mello MM, and Brennan TA. 2004b. Medical malpractice. *New England Journal of Medicine* 350:283–92.

Supreme Court of the United States. 2012. *National Federation of Independent Business v. Sebelius.* June 28, 2012, http://www.supremecourt.gov/opinions/11pdf/11-393c3a2.pdf.

Supreme Court of the United States. 2014. *Burwell, et al. v. Hobby Lobby Stores, Inc., et al.*, http://www.supremecourt.gov/opinions/13pdf/13-354_olp1.pdf.

Supreme Court of the United States. 2015. *King, et al., v. Burwell, et al.*, http://www.supremecourt.gov/opinions/14pdf/14-114_qol1.pdf.

Surowiecki J. 2014. Biotech's hard bargain. *The New Yorker*, April 28, 2014, p. 23.

Tang N, Stein J, Hsia RY, Maselli JH, and Gonzales R. 2010. Trends and characteristics of US emergency department visits, 1997–2007. *JAMA* 304:664–70.

Taubman SL, Allen HL, Wright BJ, et al. 2012. Medicaid increases emergency-department use: Evidence from Oregon's health insurance experiment. *Science* 343(6168):263–68.

Taylor EF, Anglin G, Dale S, et al. 2015. Evaluation of the Comprehensive Primary Care Initiative: First annual report. Mathematica Policy Research, http://innovation.cms.gov/Files/reports/CPCI-EvalRpt1.pdf.

Taylor MG. 1987. *Health insurance and Canadian public policy*, 2nd ed. Montreal: McGill-Queens University Press.

Temel JS, Greer JA, Muzikansky A, et al. 2010. Early palliative care for patients with metastatic non-small-cell lung cancer. *New England Journal of Medicine* 363:733–42.

Teno JM, Gozalo PL, Bynum JPW, et al. 2013. Change in end-of-life care for Medicare beneficiaries: Site of death, place of care, and health care transitions in 2000, 2005, and 2009. 2013. *JAMA* 309(5):470–77.

Thompson JW, Ryan KW, Pinidiya SD, and Bost JE. 2003. Quality of care for children in commercial and Medicaid managed care. *JAMA* 290:1486–93.

Thorpe KE, Allen L, and Joski P. 2015. Out-of-pocket prescription costs under a typical silver plan are twice as high as they are in the average employer plan. *Health Affairs* 34:1695–1703.

Thorpe KE, Florence CS, and Joski P. 2004. Which medical conditions account for the rise in health care spending? *Health Affairs* (Web Exclusive) W4:437–45. http://content.healthaffairs.org/cgi/content/abstract/hlthaff.w4.437.

Todd KH, Deaton C, D'Adamo AP, and Goe L. 2000. Ethnicity and analgesic practice. *Annals of Emergency Medicine* 35:11–16.

Todd KH, Samaroo N, and Hoffman JR. 1993. Ethnicity as a risk factor for inadequate emergency department analgesia. *JAMA* 269:1537–39.

Trivedi AN, Zaslavsky AM, Schneider EC, and Ayanian JZ. 2005. Trends in the quality of care and racial disparities in Medicare managed care. *New England Journal of Medicine* 353:692–700.

Truffer CJ, Keehan S, Smith S, et al. 2010. Health spending projections through 2019: The recession's impact continues. *Health Affairs* 29(3):522–29.

Truog, RD. 2009. Screening mammography and the "R" word. *New England Journal of Medicine* 361:2501–503.

Tsai TC, Joynt KE, Wild RC, et al. 2015. Medicare's Bundled Payment Initiative: Most hospitals are focused on a few high-volume conditions. *Health Affairs* 34:371–80.

United Nations General Assembly. 1948. The Universal Declaration of Human Rights. Resolution 217 A (III). www.un.org/Overview/rights.html.

US Agency for Healthcare Research and Quality. 2015a. 2014 National Healthcare Quality and Disparities Report. http://www.ahrq.gov/sites/default/files/wysiwyg/research/findings/nhqrdr/nhqdr14/2014nhqdr.pdf.

US Agency for Healthcare Research and Quality. 2015b. State-financed, primary care-led, accountable care collaborative provides comprehensive, coordinated care to Medicaid beneficiaries, reducing admissions, use of imaging services, and costs.

https://innovations.ahrq.gov/profiles/state-financed-primary-care-led-accountable-care-collaborative-provides-comprehensive.

US Bureau of Labor Statistics. 2015. Registered nurses—Job outlook, http://www.bls.gov/ooh/healthcare/registered-nurses.htm#tab-6.

US Census Bureau. 2005. Income, poverty, and health insurance coverage in the United States, 2004. Publication No. P60-229. www.census.gov/hhes/www/hlthins/hlthin04.html.

US Census Bureau. 2010. Income, poverty, and health insurance coverage in the United States: 2009. September, www.census.gov/hhes/www/hlthins/hlthins.html.

US Census Bureau. 2011. Income, poverty, and health insurance coverage in the United States: 2010. http://www.census.gov/prod/2011pubs/p60-239.pdf.

US Centers for Disease Control and Prevention. 2005. Tiered use of inactivated influenza vaccine in the event of a vaccine shortage. *MMWR (Morbidity and Mortality Weekly Report)* 54(30):749–50.

US Centers for Disease Control and Prevention. 2009. H1N1 vaccination recommendations, www.cdc.gov/h1n1flu/vaccination/acip.htm.

US Centers for Disease Control and Prevention. 2010. The 2009 H1N1 pandemic: Summary highlights, April 2009–April 2010, www.cdc.gov/h1n1flu/cdresponse.htm.

US Centers for Disease Control and Prevention. 2015a. Health insurance coverage: Early release of estimates from the National Health Interview Survey, January–March 2015. http://www.cdc.gov/nchs/data/nhis/earlyrelease/insur201508.pdf.

US Centers for Disease Control and Prevention. 2015b. National Center for Health Statistics. Comparison of the prevalence of uninsured persons from the National Health Interview Survey and the current population survey, 2014 and 2015, http://www.cdc.gov/nchs/data/nhis/health_insurance/NCHS_CPS_Comparison092015.pdf.

US Centers for Disease Control and Prevention. 2015c. National Center for Health Statistics. Fast Stats—Nursing Home Care. http://www.cdc.gov/nchs/fastats/nursing-home-care.htm.

US Centers for Medicare and Medicaid Services. 2015a. March 31, 2015, effectuated enrollment snapshot. https://www.cms.gov/Newsroom/MediaReleaseDatabase/Fact-sheets/2015-Fact-sheets-items/2015-06-02.html.

US Centers for Medicare and Medicaid Services. 2015b. Open Payments. https://openpaymentsdata.cms.gov/.

US Congress, Office of Technology Assessment. 1986. *Nurse Practitioners, Physician Assistants, and Certified Nurse-Midwives: A Policy Analysis.* Washington, D.C.: US Government Printing Office.

US Department of Health and Human Services. 2011. *A report on the actuarial, marketing, and legal analyses of the CLASS program.* http://aspe.hhs.gov/sites/default/files/pdf/76321/index.pdf.

US Department of Health and Human Services. 2014a. The future of the nursing workforce: National- and state-level projections, 2012–2025. http://bhpr.hrsa.gov/healthworkforce/supplydemand/nursing/workforceprojections/nursingprojections.pdf.

US Department of Health and Human Services. 2014b. Health insurance marketplace: Summary enrollment report for the initial annual open enrollment period. Office of the Assistant Secretary for Planning and Evaluation, http://aspe.hhs.gov/sites/default/files/pdf/76876/ib_2014Apr_enrollment.pdf.

US Department of Health and Human Services. 2015a. Health insurance marketplaces 2015 open enrollment period: March enrollment report. Office of the Assistant Secretary for

Planning and Evaluation, http://aspe.hhs.gov/sites/default/files/pdf/83656/ib_2015mar _enrollment.pdf.

US Department of Health and Human Services. 2015b. Medicare spending growth since 2009. http://aspe.hhs.gov/pdf-document/medicare-spending-growth-2009.

US General Accounting Office. 1998. Long-term care: Baby boom generation presents financing challenges. Report No. GAO/T-HEHS-98-107. www.gao.gov/.

US General Accounting Office. 2014. Demographics and service usage of certain high-expenditure beneficiaries. GAO-14-176, http://www.gao.gov/products/GAO-14-176.

US Health Resources and Services Administration. 2013. Projecting the supply and demand for primary care practitioners through 2020, http://bhpr.hrsa.gov/healthworkforce /supplydemand/usworkforce/primarycare/.

US Health Resources and Services Administration. 2014. 2014 Health Center data, http:// bphc.hrsa.gov/uds/datacenter.aspx.

US Preventive Services Task Force. 2009. Screening for breast cancer: US Preventive Services Task Force recommendation statement. *Annals of Internal Medicine* 151:716–26.

US Preventive Services Task Force. 2012. Final recommendation statement—prostate cancer: Screening, May 2012, http://www.uspreventiveservicestaskforce.org/Page/Document /RecommendationStatementFinal/prostate-cancer-screening.

Vaccarino V, Rathore SS, Wenger NK, et al. 2005. Sex and racial differences in the management of acute myocardial infarction, 1994 through 2002. *New England Journal of Medicine* 353:671–82.

Van Ryn M, and Burke J. 2000. The effect of patient race and socioeconomic status on physicians' perceptions of patients. *Social Science and Medicine* 50:813–28.

van Walraven C. 2015. The utility of unplanned early hospital readmissions as a health care quality indicator. *JAMA Internal Medicine* 175(11):1812–14.

Vladeck BC. 2010. Fixing Medicare's physician payment system. *New England Journal of Medicine* 362:1955–57.

Wachter RM, and Goldman L. 1996. The emerging role of "hospitalists" in the American health care system. *New England Journal of Medicine* 335:514–17.

Wallack SS, Weinberg DB, and Thomas CP. 2004. Health plans' strategies to control prescription drug spending. *Health Affairs* 23:141–48.

Wang B, and Kesselheim AS. 2013. The role of direct-to-consumer pharmaceutical advertising in patient consumerism. *Virtual Mentor: American Medical Association Journal of Ethics* 15(11):960–65.

Wehrwein AC. 1965. A.M.A. opens bid to kill Medicare. *New York Times,* January 27.

Weinstein MC, and Skinner JA. 2010. Comparative effectiveness and health care spending—implications for reform. *New England Journal of Medicine* 364:460–65.

Weissman JS, and Bigby JA. 2009. Massachusetts health care reform—near-universal coverage at what cost? *New England Journal of Medicine* 361:2012–15.

Weissman JS, Blumenthal D, Silk AJ, et al. 2004. Physicians report on patient encounters involving direct-to-consumer advertising. *Health Affairs* (Web Exclusive) W4:219–33. http://content.healthaff airs.org/cgi/content/abstract/hlthaff.w4.219v1.

Wennberg JE. 1993. Future directions for small area variations. *Medical Care* 31:YS75–YS80.

Wennberg JE, Barnes BA, and Zubkoff M. 1982. Professional uncertainty and the problem of supplier-induced demand. *Social Science and Medicine* 16:811–24.

Wennberg JE, and Cooper MM, eds. 1998. *The Dartmouth Atlas of Health Care, 1998.* Chicago: American Hospital Publishing.

Wennberg JE, and Gittelsohn A. 1973. Small area variations in health care delivery. *Science* 182: 1102–8.

Whitcomb ME, and Cohen JJ. 2004. The future of primary care medicine. *New England Journal of Medicine* 351:710–12.

Wijeysundera HC, Machado M, Farahatin F, et al. 2010. Association of temporal trends in risk factors and treatment uptake with coronary heart disease mortality, 1994–2005. *JAMA* 303:1841–47.

Williams SC, Schmaltz SP, Morton DJ, Koss RG, and Loeb JM. 2005. Quality of care in US hospitals as reflected by standardized measures, 2002–2004. *New England Journal of Medicine* 353:255–64.

World Health Organization. 2000. Health systems: Improving performance. The World Health Report 2000. www.who.int/whr/en/.

Yin W, Basu A, Zhang JX, et al. 2008. The effect of Medicare Part D prescription benefit on drug utilization and expenditures. *Annals of Internal Medicine* 148:169–77.

Zarabozo C, and Harrison S. 2009. Payment policy and the growth of Medicare Advantage. *Health Affairs* 28(1):w55–w67.

Zhou C, and Zhang Y. 2012. The vast majority of Medicare Part D beneficiaries still don't choose the cheapest plans that meet their medication needs. *Health Affairs* 31:2259–65.

Zipkin A. 2005. The concierge doctor is available (at a price). *New York Times,* July 31.

Zuger A. 2003a. In an age of specialists, one doctor is primary. *New York Times,* January 7.

Zuger A. 2003b. Rx: Canadian drugs. *New England Journal of Medicine* 349:2188–90.

INDEX

AAMC, 83

Aaron, Henry, 148

access to care: barriers to, xvi, 330–54; culturally appropriate care, 345–46; Medicaid coverage, 331, 334–36; organizational complexity, 346–50; out-of-pocket costs, 332–34; racial barriers, 336–39

accountable care organizations, xiv, 179–84, 226–27; pioneer model, 182; shared savings program, 181

activities of daily living (ADLs), 311

adverse selection, 164

Affordable Care Act: access to primary care, 107–08, 351–53; addressing the balance of cost, quality, and access, 373–79; changes in private market for health insurance, 146–48; changes to Medicaid, 216–24; changes to Medicare, 178–95; contraceptive services, 17; coverage gap, 218; efforts in Congress to repeal, 18; employer mandate, 146; health benefit exchanges, 15, 146; impact on for-profit health care, 273–76; impact on health care spending, 39; impact on health insurance enrollment, 148–49, 245–50; impact on long-term care, 326–29; impact on pharmaceutical policy, 309–10; impact on quality of health care, 41; impact on uninsured rate, 39–40; individual mandate, 146; legal challenges, 13; limits on comparative effective research, 79; long-term impact on health care costs, 383–85; main policy goals, 11; mechanisms to reduce inappropriate use of technology, 78; outcomes of, 1;

passage in Congress, xi, xiv, 1–6, 13; patient-centered medical home, 108; political debate preceding, x; Republican opposition in Congress, 1; signing by Obama, 5

Agency for Health Care Research and Quality (AHRQ), US, 30

American College of Surgeons, 19–20

American Medical Association, xiv; authority over organization of health care, 22; control of number of physicians, 84; Council on Pharmacy and Chemistry, 277; definition of code of medical ethics for physicians, 84; gender segregation in, 86; health care reform as "socialized medicine," 8, 11; historical association with drug manufacturers, 84; history of, 83; opposition to Canadian Medicare, 47; opposition to capitated service plans, 119–20, 130; opposition to health care reform, 7–9; opposition to Medicare, 9, 151–52; racial segregation in, 84

American Nursing Association, 87

America's Health Insurance Plans, 3

Angell, Marcia, 281–82

As Good As It Gets (film), 252–53

Association of American Medical Colleges (AAMC), 83

Bachman, Michele, 6

balance billing, 48

Balanced Budget Act of 1997, 160, 166–72

Barr's Law, 365

Baucus, Max, 3

Berwick, Donald, 178

Bill of Rights, US, 43

Blackburn, Marsha, 6

Blendon, Robert, 2

Blue Cross system, 100, 113, 229

Bowman, John, 19

British North America Act, 43

bundled payment, 106, 188–90

Burwell, Sylvia M., 184, 188

Burwell v. Hobby Lobby, 16

Bush, George W., 145, 173, 215, 298

California Public Employees Retirement System, 137

Canadian Charter of Rights and Freedoms, 43

Canadian health care system, xiv; history of, 44–49

Canadian Medical Association, 45, 55

Canadian Medicare system: development of private clinics, 54–55; global budget for physicians' services, 53; increasing costs, 48–49; Ontario physicians' strike, 48; organizing principles, 49–50; passage of, 46; physicians' incomes, 53; Quebec physicians' strike, 47; queueing for care, 50–51

Canadian Supreme Court, decision about private clinics in Quebec, 55

capitation payment for health care, 118–20

Carnegie Foundation for the Advancement of Teaching, 83

Center for Medicare and Medicaid Innovation (CMMI), 179–81

Centers for Medicare and Medicaid Services, 69

Children's Health Insurance Program (CHIP), xv, 212–16

churning in health care, 53

Clinton, Bill, 1, 118

Clinton health care reform proposals, x, 3, 10, 135–37

CMMI, 179–81
COBRA benefits, 5
coinsurance rate, 144
Commission on the Future of Health Care in Canada, 51
Committee on the Costs of Medical Care (1927–1932), 7, 11, 42
Commonwealth Health Connector, 241
comparative effectiveness research, xvi, 41, 78; limits on, in ACA, 79; to reduce inappropriate use of technology, 78
concierge practice, 271
Consolidated Omnibus Budget Reconciliation Act, 5
Constitution, US, basis for ACA, 14
costs of health care. See health care costs
Council on Medical Education, 83

Dartmouth Atlas of Health Care, 29
Declaration of Independence, 43
declining marginal returns, 60–62
Deferred Action for Childhood Arrivals (DACA), 251
Deferred Action for Parents and Lawful Permanent Residents (DAPA), 251
Department of Health and Human Services, US, xiii
diagnosis related group (DRG) system. See prospective payment system
DSH. See hospitals: disproportionate share

Emergency Medical Treatment and Active Labor Act (EMTALA), 20
employer mandate, 238–40
employer provided health insurance, 230; employment characteristics, 236–37; indemnity model, 116; origins, 113; self-insured plans, 117; tax incentives of, 114–15
Enthoven, Alain, 131

evidence-based medicine, 29
Ewing, Oscar, 8

favorable selection, 164
Federal Employees Health Benefits Plan, 137–38
federally qualified health centers (FQHC), 223–24; expansion under ACA, 110–11
fee-for-service delivery system, xiv, 23, 52, 56, 118, 126
fiscal intermediaries, 46, 153–54
Fishbein, Morris, 9
Flexner Report, 22, 56, 83
Food, Drug, and Cosmetic Act, 278
Food and Drug Administration, 278
for-profit health care, xvi, 252–76; hospitals, xvi; mergers and acquisitions, 261–62; physician ownership, 267–70; quality of care, 262–64; retail clinics, 271–73; specialty hospitals, 269–70
FQHC, 110–11, 223–24
Fuchs, Victor, 24, 36–37, 64, 67, 140, 357

Garfield, Sidney, 119–21
Gawande, Atul, 97
gender segregation in medical profession, 86, 107
Grand Coulee Dam construction project, 120
Grassley, Charles, 3
Group Health Cooperative of Puget Sound, 119

Hamilton, Walton H., 42
Harry and Louise ads, 136, 147
Hawaii Prepaid Health Care Act, 238–40
health benefit exchange, 3, 249; 2014–15 enrollment, 39
health care, as a right, 11
health care costs, xi, xiv, 2, 24–28, 38, 230; causes of increasing, 27; comparison with Canada, 49–50, 67–68; impact of indemnity insurance on, 116; impact on government finances, 25–27; increase following enactment of Medicare, 10; long-term

impact of ACA, 383–85; projections of future costs, 25, 40; sources of expenditure, 25
HealthCare.gov: creation of, 15; initial difficulties in enrollment, 2013, 148
health care rationing, xvi, 41, 207–10, 359–68
health care system: history, 56–57; organizing principles, 57
Health Employer Data and Information Set (HEDIS), 263
health insurance: expansion of, 228–30; experience rating in, 116; indemnity model, 118; private, 81; public, types of, 81
health insurance exchange, 3, 39, 249
Health Insurance Plan of New York, 119
health insurance purchasing cooperative (HIPC), 132–33; examples of, 137–38
health maintenance organizations, xiv–xv; effect of cultural institutions on, 139–40; group model, 125; incentives to reduce cost of care, 126; IPA model, 125; as part of Clinton reform proposals, 118; shift to for-profit, 252–55; staff model, 126
Health Maintenance Organizations Act of 1973, 124, 129–30
health policy, definition, xii–xiv
health savings accounts (HSAs), 145
health status, individual, 36–37; national, 32–38
heart disease, differences in treatment between US and Canada, 68–72, 78
HEDIS, 263
Hepatitis C treatment, 304–06
high-deductible health plan (HDHP), 145, 333–34
Hill-Burton program for hospital construction, 101
HIPCs, 132–33, 137–38
history of arguments for and against health care reform, 12

HMO Act, 124; requirements for federal certification, 129–130
HMOs. *See* health maintenance organizations
Hobby Lobby, 17
hospitalist physicians, 100–01
hospitals: acquisition of physician practice groups, 105; administrative system, 101; community, xiv; and disproportionate share, 219; for-profit ownership, 264–67; history of, 100; impact of declining occupancy rates, 104; role in establishing Blue Cross system, 100
HSAs, 145

Ignagni, Karen, 3
individual mandate, 13–15, 240–41
infant mortality rates, 32–33, 36
institutional norms, xiv
institutions, cultural: affecting health care, 42, 58–59; defining characteristics, 59; differences between US and Canada, 43, 59; impact on malpractice law, 73–75; that inhibit market efficiency in health care, 138; origins, 59
insurance model, traditional, 112–13
Interdepartmental Committee to Coordinate Health and Welfare Activities (1938), 8
International Medical Graduates, training of, 98–99

Johnson, Lyndon, 1, 9, 56
Joint Commission on the Accreditation of Healthcare Organizations (JCAHO), 30

Kaiser, Henry J., 119–21
Kaiser Permanente health care system, xv, 119–22, 180, 259
Kefauver, Estes, 278
Kennedy, Ted, 4; attempts at health care reform, 10, 124
Kerr-Mills Program, 196–97, 224
key policy issues: balancing of cost, quality, and access, 355–59; core social policy

questions, 380–83; health care rationing, 359–68, 387–88; physicians and profit motive, 370–73; role of for-profit care, 368–70; role of government vs. private market, 386–88
King v. Burwell, 16
Kronick, Richard, 131
Krugman, Paul, 178

legal challenges to Affordable Care Act, 13
Lévesque, René, 47
Lewis, Sinclair, 82
life expectancy, 33–34
long-term care, xvi, 311–29; custodial, 314; future policy issues, 323–26; growing need for, 312–13; home health care, 316–18; hospice, 318–22; life care communities, 322–23; under Medicaid, 315–16; under Medicare Advantage, 314; nursing homes, 313–16

Mackey, John, 19
malpractice law, 73–76
mammography screening, 366–68
managed care: and backlash, 143, 258–61; as distinct from managed competition, 134; expansion of, 137–38; impact of national shift on cost of care, 140–41; pharmaceutical coverage, 294–95; shift to for-profit, 255–58
managed competition, 130–35; factors impeding success of, 142–43
market-based health care, xiii, 19, 21
market failure, theory of, 96
Massachusetts Health Care Reform Plan, 3, 240–43, 246–47
McAllen, Texas, cost of care in, 97
McCain, John, 2
Medicaid, xiii, 196–227; access to primary care, 223–24; eligibility, 199–201; enactment in 1965, 1; expansion under ACA, 39, 217–18, 222–23, 249; funding of,

197–98; increases in cost of drugs, 296–97; managed care coverage, 204–06, 225; non-expansion states, 220–22; passage in Congress, 9–12, 196–97; physician payment under, 203–04, 223–24; rising costs, 201–04, 211–12, 225; services provided, 198–99; skewed nature of covered population, 202–03, 225; waivers, 205–07
medical licensure laws, xiii
medical loss ratio, 260
Medical Outcomes Study, 128–29
medical profession: agents of reason vs. agents of power, 22–24; authority over organization of health care, 21; history of, xv
medical savings accounts (MSAs), 168–69
Medicap insurance, 156–57
Medicare, xiii, 150–95; accountable care organizations, 179–84; administrative efficiency, 176–77; bundled payment system, 106, 188–90; changes under ACA, 178–95; comprehensive care for joint replacement, 190; comprehensive primary care initiative, 188; "doughnut hole" in drug coverage, 299–300; end-stage renal disease, 157–58; fiscal intermediaries, 153–54; graduate medical education support, 98, 177; home health care, 153, 169–70; hospice care, 153; hospital readmission reduction program, 185–87; impact on reducing racial segregation in hospitals, 86; Independent Payment Advisory Board (IPAB), 192–93; managed care option, 161–68, 171–72; medical savings accounts, 168–69; Medicare Advantage, 173–74; Medicare+Choice, 167–68; Merit-based Incentive Payment System, 175–76; Part A, 152–54; Part B, 154–56; passage in Congress, 1, 9–10,

Medicare (*cont.*)
12, 151–52; pay for performance, 184; prescription drug
coverage (Part D), 277,
297–303; prospective payment
system, 99; resource-based
relative value scale, 160; rising
costs, 158–60, 172–73; skewed
nature of covered population,
161; skilled nursing care, 153,
314; spending, 40; structure,
152; Sustainable Growth Rate,
174–76; trust fund, 153–54,
160; value-based purchasing
program, 185–86
Medicare Modernization Act,
145, 173, 191, 298–99
Merit-based Incentive Payment
System (MIPS), 175–76
MMA, 145, 173, 191, 298–99
monopsony, 45
MSAs, 168–69

National Committee on Quality
Assurance, 109
*National Federation of Indepen-
dent Business v. Sebelius,* 13,
15, 217–18
National Healthcare Quality
Report, 30
National Health Service Corps,
108
National Medical Association,
84–85
Nixon, Richard, 10
North, Douglass, 58, 138
nurse practitioners, 93–94
nursing profession: history of,
xv, 86–87; models of training,
87; potential shortage in,
87–88; shortage of trained
faculty, 88

Obama, Barack: budget proposal
of 2009, 3; election of, 2; goals
for health care reform, 38;
role in passage of ACA, 4–5;
signing of ACA, 5–6, 19
Oregon Health Insurance
Experiment, 210
Oregon Health Plan, xvi,
207–10, 361–65
Organization for Economic
Co-operation and Develop-
ment (OECD) countries,

health care expenditures,
25–26
outpatient surgical centers, 103

Pacific Business Group on
Health, 137
Parsons, Talcott, 267
patient-centered medical home,
108–10
Patient-Centered Outcomes
Research Institute (PCORI),
79
Patient Protection and Affordable Care Act. *See* Affordable
Care Act
PCORI, 79
Pearson, Lester, 46
peer-review organizations
(PROs), 103
pharmaceutical policy, xvi,
277–310; direct-to-consumer
marketing, 290–92; drug
reimportation, 281; impact of
specialty drugs, 303–09;
increases in cost of drugs,
279–81, 307–09; marketing to
physicians, 282–88; "me-too"
drugs, 283–86, 303; patent
protection for new drugs, 278;
pharmaceutical benefit
managers, 295; physician
conflicts of interest, 289–90;
use of formularies, 294; value
of new drugs, 282
Pharmaceutical Research and
Manufacturers of America,
289
physician assistants, 94
physicians: average income, 82;
factors affecting occupational
status, 82; number of, 82;
role in rising health care
costs, 82
point-of-service plan, 128
political polarization: over
Clinton health reform
proposals, 136; regarding the
ACA, xiv, 1–6, 10
preferred provider organizations
(PPOs), 127–28
Preventive Services Task Force,
US, 65
primary care, definition of, 89
primary care physicians,
90–93

professional standards review
organizations (PSRO), 102
prospective payment system
(PPS), 102–03
prostate specific antigen (PSA)
test, 64–65
public opinion, 2, 10, 41, 149
Pure Food and Drug Act, 277

QALY, 305
quality, ix–x, 28–30, 38; change
in definition, 41; provided by
hospitals, 29–30; provided by
physicians, 29
quality-adjusted life year
(QALY), 305
quaternary care, 89, 106

racial bias in care, 339–42
racial/ethnic diversity in
medical profession, 107
racial segregation in hospitals,
86
Rand Health Insurance
Experiment, 122–23, 126, 255;
impact of coinsurance on cost
and quality of care, 143–45
rationing of health care. *See*
health care rationing
RBRVS, 160
reconciliation process in
Congress, 5
Reinhardt, Uwe, 21, 305
relative value units, 160
Religious Freedom Restoration
Act of 1993, 17
Relman, Arnold, 287
resource-based relative value
scale, 160
Reuther, Walter, 124
right to health care, 1, 19–20
Roberts, John, Supreme Court
opinion by, 14, 16
role of government, 1, 6–7
Romanow, Roy, 52, 55
Roosevelt, Franklin, 56, 278;
attempts at health care
reform, 7, 11
Roosevelt, Theodore, attempts
at health care reform, 6
RVU, 160

safety-net hospitals, 186
Saskatchewan Hospital Services
Plan, 44

Saskatchewan Medical Association physicians' strike, 45
secondary care, 89, 95–97
service plans, as form of health insurance, 118–19
SGR, 174–76
single-payer system, proposals for, 77
small area variations in health care costs, 29
Small Business Health Options Program (SHOP), 147
socialized medicine, 47; AMA opposition to, 56; definition of, by the AMA, 9; in UK, 21
Social Security Act, initial proposal to include health care reform, 7
South Africa, health care rights, 21
specialist physicians, average income, 95–98
specialty hospitals, 104–05

State Children's Health Insurance Program (S-CHIP). *See* Children's Health Insurance Program
Sustainable Growth Rate (SGR), 174–76

technological benefit of the doubt, 64
technological imperative, xv, 64, 139
tertiary care, 106; definition of, 89
triple option plans, 128
Trudeau, Pierre, 47
Truman, Harry, x, 10, 56; attempts at health care reform, 8, 151

uninsured rate, xv, 31–32, 38, 228–51; changes 1987–2010, 232; changes 2010–2015, 39; demographic characteristics, 233–35; future predictions, 243–47; principal causes of uninsured workers, 31–32; ways of measuring, 231–32
United Auto Workers, attempts at health care reform, 124
United Nations, 21
Universal Declaration of Human Rights, 21

Vladeck, Bruce, 1

Watergate scandal, x, 10
Wennberg, John, 28, 97
Whitehall Study, 36
Wilson, Woodrow, 7
Wofford, Harris, 230–31
women's health care, 16
World Health Organization (WHO) national health care quality ratings, 35

Zuger, Abigail, 92